Handbook of Child Behavior Therapy In the Psychiatric Setting

WILEY SERIES ON PERSONALITY PROCESSES

IRVING B. WEINER, *Editor*
University of South Florida

Handbook of Child Behavior Therapy In the Psychiatric Setting

Edited by

ROBERT T. AMMERMAN
Western Pennsylvania School for Blind Children

MICHEL HERSEN
Nova Southeastern University

A Wiley-Interscience Publication
John Wiley & Sons, Inc.
New York • Chichester • Brisbane • Toronto • Singapore

Library of Congress Cataloging-in-Publication Data:

Handbook of child behavior therapy in the psychiatric setting / edited
    by Robert T. Ammerman, Michel Hersen.
        p. cm. — (Wiley series on personality processes)
      "Wiley-interscience."
      Includes indexes.
      ISBN 0-471-57844-4 (cloth : alk. paper)
      1. Behavior therapy for children. I. Ammerman, Robert T.
    II. Hersen, Michel. III. Series.
      [DNLM: 1. Behavior therapy—In infancy & childhood.
    2. Behavior therapy—methods.   3. Mental disorders—In infancy &
    childhood.   4. Mental disorders—Therapy. WS 350.6 H2356 1995]
    RJ505.B4H35 1995
    618.92'89142—dc20
    DNLM/DLC
    for Library of Congress   93-50916

Printed in the United States of America

10 9 8 7 6 5 4 3 2 1

To my college era mentors, Jeffrey D. Cartwright-Smith, Michael G. Wessells, Robert E. Bowman, and Elisabeth A. Murray

RTA

To the memory of my mother, Betty Hersen

MH

Contributors

Robert T. Ammerman, Ph.D.
Supervisor, Research and Clinical
    Psychology
Western Pennsylvania School for Blind
    Children
Pittsburgh, Pennsylvania

Debora Bell-Dolan, Ph.D.
Assistant Professor of Clinical
    Psychology
University of Missouri—Columbia
Columbia, Missouri

Susanne Blix, M.D.
Director, Section of Child and
    Adolescent Psychiatry
Indiana University School of Medicine
Indianapolis, Indiana

Ronald T. Brown, Ph.D.
Associate Professor of Psychiatry and
    Behavioral Science and Pediatrics
Emory University School of Medicine
Atlanta, Georgia

John V. Campo, M.D.
Assistant Professor of Psychiatry
Medical College of Pennsylvania
Allegheny General Hospital
Pittsburgh, Pennsylvania

Michelle Delaune, B.A.
Doctoral Candidate
Department of Educational Psychology
The University of Texas at Austin
Austin, Texas

Ronald S. Drabman, Ph.D.
Professor of Psychiatry

University of Mississippi Medical Center
Jackson, Mississippi

Michael Ferrari, Ph.D.
Associate Professor
Departments of Individual and Family
    Studies and Psychology
University of Delaware
Newark, Delaware

John P. Foreyt, Ph.D.
Professor of Medicine
Baylor College of Medicine
Houston, Texas

Greta Francis, Ph.D.
Assistant Professor of Psychiatry and
    Human Behavior
Brown University School of Medicine
East Providence, Rhode Island

Paul J. Frick, Ph.D.
Assistant Professor of Psychology
University of Alabama
Tuscaloosa, Alabama

David M. Garner, Ph.D.
Center for Cognitive Therapy
University of Pennsylvania
Philadelphia, Pennsylvania

G. Ken Goodrick, Ph.D.
Assistant Professor of Medicine
Baylor College of Medicine
Houston, Texas

Benjamin L. Handen, Ph.D.
Associate Professor of Psychiatry

Western Psychiatric Institute and Clinic
Pittsburgh, Pennsylvania

Michel Hersen, Ph.D.
Professor of Psychology
Center for Psychological Studies
Nova Southeastern University
Ft. Lauderdale, FL

Arthur C. Houts, Ph.D.
Professor of Psychology
Memphis State University
Memphis, Tennessee

Betsy Hoza, Ph.D.
Assistant Professor of Psychiatry
Western Psychiatric Institute and Clinic
Pittsburgh, Pennsylvania

Cynthia R. Johnson, Ph.D.
Assistant Professor of Psychiatry
Western Psychiatric Institute and Clinic
Pittsburgh, Pennsylvania

Jon D. Kassel, M.S.
Doctoral Candidate
Department of Psychology
University of Pittsburgh
Pittsburgh, Pennsylvania

Joan Kaufman, Ph.D.
Assistant Professor of Psychiatry
Western Psychiatric Institute and Clinic
Pittsburgh, Pennsylvania

Wallace A. Kennedy, Ph.D.
Private Practice
Tallahassee, Florida

Lyndee Knox, M.S.
Doctoral Candidate
Department of Educational Psychology
The University of Texas at Austin
Austin, Texas

Frank H. Kobe, Ph.D.
Clinical Instructor in Pediatrics

The Ohio State University
Columbus, Ohio

Catherine Koverola, Ph.D.
Assistant Professor of Psychology
University of Manitoba
Winnipeg, Manitoba
Canada

Gina E. Laite, M.D.
Assistant Professor of Psychiatry
Indiana University School of Medicine
Indianapolis, Indiana

Anthony P. Mannarino, Ph.D.
Associate Professor of Psychiatry
Allegheny General Hospital
Department of Psychiatry
Pittsburgh, Pennsylvania

Irwin J. Mansdorf, Ph.D.
Director
Behavioral Stress Center
Elmhurst, New York

D. Richard Martini, M.D.
Director, Medical Psychology and
    Psychiatry Consultation Services
Children's Memorial Hospital
Chicago, Illinois

Michael W. Mellon, Ph.D.
Assistant Professor of Pediatrics
University of Arkansas for Medical
    Sciences
Arkansas Children's Hospital
Little Rock, Arkansas

James A. Mulick, Ph.D.
Professor of Psychology
Department of Pediatrics
The Ohio State University
Columbus, Ohio

Katharine P. Newcomb, M.S.
Department of Clinical and Health
    Psychology

University of Florida
Gainesville, Florida

Bridget S. O'Brien
Graduate Research Assistant
University of Alabama
Tuscaloosa, Alabama

William E. Pelham, Jr., Ph.D.
Associate Professor of Psychiatry
Director, Attention Deficit Disorder
    Program
Western Psychiatric Institute and Clinic
Pittsburgh, Pennsylvania

Theodore A. Petti, M.D., M.P.H.
Arthur B. Richter Professor of Child
    Psychiatry
Indiana University School of Medicine
Indianapolis, Indiana

Christine Shafer, M.D.
Associate Professor of Psychiatry
Michigan State University
East Lansing, Michigan

Kevin D. Stark, Ph.D.
Interim Director of the School
    Psychology Program
Associate Professor of Educational
    Psychology

The University of Texas at Austin
Austin, Texas

Susan Swearer, M.S.
Doctoral Candidate
Department of Educational Psychology
The University of Texas at Austin
Austin, Texas

Kenneth J. Tarnowski, Ph.D.
Associate Professor of Psychology
University of South Florida
Fort Meyers, Florida

Gary Vallano, M.D.
Medical Director, Attention Deficit
    Disorder Program
Western Psychiatric Institute and Clinic
Pittsburgh, Pennsylvania

Eric F. Wagner, Ph.D.
Post-Doctoral Fellow
Center for Alcohol and Addiction Studies
Brown University
Providence, Rhode Island

Jason Winter, M.S.
Doctoral Candidate
Department of Educational Psychology
The University of Texas at Austin
Austin, Texas

Series Preface

This series of books is addressed to behavioral scientists interested in the nature of human personality. Its scope should prove pertinent to personality theorists and researchers, as well as to clinicians concerned with applying an understanding of personality processes to the amelioration of emotional difficulties in living. To this end, the series provides a scholarly integration of theoretical formulations, empirical data, and practical recommendations.

Six major aspects of studying and learning about human personality can be designated: personality theory, personality structure and dynamics, personality development, personality assessment, personality change, and personality adjustment. In exploring these aspects of personality, the books in the series discuss a number of distinct but related subject areas: the nature and implications of various theories of personality; personality characteristics that account for consistencies and variations in human behavior; the emergence of personality processes in children and adolescents; the use of interviewing and testing procedures to evaluate individual differences in personality; efforts to modify personality styles through psychotherapy, counseling, behavior therapy, and other methods of influence; and patterns of abnormal personality functioning that impair individual competence.

IRVING B. WEINER

University of South Florida
Tampa, Florida

Preface

Child behavior therapy has made considerable headway in recent years. It is one of the few types of clinical approaches to childhood disorders that has been subjected to empirical scrutiny. Meta-analyses of treatment-outcome research support behavioral interventions as the strategy of choice for a variety of disorders, particularly those involving disturbances in conduct. In the past decade, more traditional behavioral strategies have incorporated newly developed cognitive techniques, thereby adding to the overall utility of the behavioral strategies. Moreover, childhood disorders that, until recently, had been all but ignored in the empirical literature are now being addressed by behavior therapists. Illustrative are obsessive-compulsive disorder and separation anxiety disorder.

The efficacy and relatively short-term, directive nature of behavior therapy make it especially well suited for the psychiatric setting. In both outpatient clinics and hospitals, there is much value to using behavioral approaches. From the perspective of behavior therapists, the inpatient psychiatric setting offers numerous opportunities for observational assessment and control over environmental consequences. However, psychiatric settings also provide unique challenges to the behavior therapist. An integrated, team approach to treatment is essential in such settings. Moreover, pharmacotherapy is widely used, so that behavioral interventions are often carried out in combination with psychotropic drugs. Finally, the short-term nature of most inpatient hospitalizations may constrain full evaluation of behavioral interventions.

The chapters in this book cover the practice of behavior therapy in psychiatric settings. Specifically, the book is divided into three parts. Part 1 considers assessment. Chapter 1 provides an overview of behavioral assessment in both inpatient and outpatient settings. Chapters 2 through 5 examine issues that impact on the behavioral assessment process, including psychiatric diagnosis, medical complications, child maltreatment, and developmental processes. Part 2 covers general treatment issues: combined use of behavior therapy and pharmacotherapy in chapter 6 and of unit management and behavioral programming in chapter 7. The bulk of the book is found in Part 3, chapters 8 through 22, in which each childhood disorder is examined. To insure parallel structure across chapters in Part 3, uniform headings were followed: description of the problem, prototypic assessment, actual assessment, prototypic treatment, actual treatment, and summary. The distinction between prototypic and actual assessment and treatment allows for consideration of potential pitfalls and impediments that are encountered by clinicians in psychiatric settings.

A number of individuals assisted us in bringing this book to fruition, and we acknowledge their help and support. We are especially grateful to the contributors of this book for sharing with us their insights and expertise. We also thank our editor, Herb Reich, for his encouragement throughout the publication process. A number of our support staff provided us with considerable help; we extend our gratitude to Burt Bolton, Gretchen Deitrick, Angela Dodson, Ann Huber, Melodi Janosko, Jennifer McKelvey, Mary Newell, Kathy Novak, Nancy Simpson, and Mary Trefelner.

ROBERT T. AMMERMAN
MICHEL HERSEN

Pittsburgh, Pennsylvania
Fort Lauderdale, Florida

Contents

PART 1

General Assessment Considerations

CHAPTER 1

Child Behavioral Assessment in the Psychiatric Setting

KATHARINE P. NEWCOMB AND RONALD S. DRABMAN

INTRODUCTION

Over half of all patient visits to medical facilities concern problems that are primarily psychological in origin (Wright, Schaefer, & Solomons, 1979) and approximately 80% of all children who manifest a psychological disorder present with active behavior problems (Thomas, Chess, & Birch, 1968). It is widely recognized that problems relating to antisocial conduct characterize the majority of children referred to psychologists for diagnosis and treatment (Reid, Patterson, Baldwin, & Dishion, 1988). There is increasing evidence that these disorders, if left untreated, are associated with impaired functioning in later life (Quay, 1986).

Adequate treatment for children with behavioral and psychiatric disturbances requires systematic assessment of the biological and environmental variables underlying their difficulties. In addition to descriptive functions, assessment of relevant variables can help to identify target behaviors and can serve as baseline, outcome, and follow-up measures of treatment (Ciminero & Drabman, 1977).

The role of assessment in our clinical work with children has been strongly influenced by Public Law 94-142, which mandated that special education services for physical and behavioral disabilities of children take place in the least restrictive environment available to meet their needs. We believe that children and families needing psychological or psychiatric treatment should be served by the least restrictive and least intrusive interventions available to meet their needs. In an attempt to deliver services in this manner, we place special emphasis on thorough assessment and analysis of relevant variables before attempting interventions involving the home, school, or hospital environment or before recommending or seeking pharmacological treatments. Our basic model is summarized in Figure 1.1, with the degree of restrictiveness increasing as the model is read from left to right.

This model reflects our assumption that skillful assessment, by identifying the relevant factors underlying children's behavioral difficulties, will minimize or even eliminate the need for expensive and time-consuming treatment. In addition, we believe that when drug therapy is a necessary component of a child's treatment plan, smaller amounts may suffice if the other steps are pursued first (Pelham, 1977). Finally, we believe that assessment leading to a parsimonious approach to treatment is particularly useful when dealing with children whose problems are severe enough to warrant intensive, and possibly prolonged, multidisciplinary care in a psychiatric setting.

Least Restrictive Treatment Model

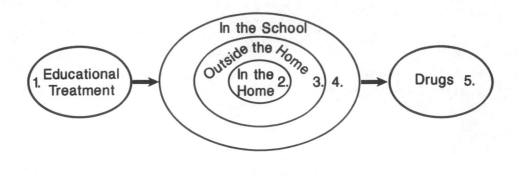

Behavioral Treatment

Figure 1.1. Least restrictive treatment model.

In this chapter, we will review general issues in the assessment of children and features of child behavioral assessment as it is currently conceptualized. Next, we will describe applications and unique features of carrying out child behavioral assessments in psychiatric settings. Finally, we consider a special case of child behavioral assessment, the psychoeducational evaluation. We will describe a set of procedures we use to evaluate children who have been referred by parents, teachers, physicians, or other members of the treatment team when it is suspected that problems in learning contribute significantly to poor psychological adjustment, behavior problems, or psychiatric symptoms.

GENERAL ISSUES IN THE ASSESSMENT OF CHILDREN

In the provision of clinical services to children, several practical problems may be encountered by practitioners, regardless of their orientation (Ciminero & Drabman, 1977). First, children are typically referred for treatment by an adult for whom the child's behavior is problematic, such as a parent, a teacher, or a nurse. If the child does not share this view of the situation, disagreements may arise about the need for treatment, and there will be little motivation to participate. Second, child behavioral assessments are conducted within a developmental framework, and information as to what is normative behavior may conflict with a parent's view of what is acceptable behavior or with behavioral norms on a particular unit. Third, the analysis of a child's behavioral difficulties generally requires assessing the behavior of other relevant persons in the child's environment (e.g., nurses, teachers, and other ward staff, as well as parents), and this may be uncomfortable for a referring adult who believes that the problem lies solely with the child. Communicating with the child's parents, or members of a health-care team, about their own behavior requires considerable tact and skillful interviewing. It is important to establish rapport as early as possible so that, throughout the process, psychiatric staff and parents feel comfortable providing accurate information and receiving honest feedback.

From a behavioral perspective, we view a child's responses as a sample of his or her behavioral repertoire in a specific stimulus situation. Given that a good assessment requires adequate sampling of the relevant settings and stimuli, one issue that must be addressed is the variability of children's behaviors across settings. The situational specificity of children's behaviors (problematic and otherwise) underscores the need for multimodal assessment and multiple informants (Achenbach, 1978) and has led to the recommendation that behaviors to be targeted for treatment should be observed, when it is feasible, in the setting where the problem behavior is reported (Reed & Edelbrock, 1983). This may be a labor-intensive process, and such efforts may not be readily accepted by all participants (e.g., parents and school or hospital administrators) to whom they may seem costly, time-consuming, and, at times, intrusive.

FEATURES OF CHILD BEHAVIORAL ASSESSMENT

Mash and Terdal (1988) have described child and family behavioral assessment as a set of deliberate problem-solving strategies for understanding both disturbed and nondisturbed children and their social systems, including their families and peer groups. Behavioral assessment involves an ongoing process of hypothesis testing regarding the nature of the problem, its causes, likely outcomes in the absence of specific intervention, and the anticipated effects of treatment. According to these authors, common features of behavioral assessment as it is currently practiced may include (a) a conceptualization of personality and abnormal behavior that considers thoughts, feelings, and behaviors in specific situations, rather than as manifestations of global underlying traits or dispositions; (b) a view of behaviors, cognitions, and affects as direct samples of the domains of interest, rather than as signs of some underlying or remote causes; (c) an emphasis on the importance of situational influences on behavior and the need to assess them in formulating effective treatments; (d) an emphasis on contemporary controlling variables, in addition to the role of historical and more distal-setting events; (e) a recognition of the changes over time that often characterize child and family behavior; (f) a reliance on a multimethod approach that involves the flexible use of different informants and a variety of procedures, including observations, interviews, and questionnaires; (g) the utilization of empirically validated assessment procedures; and (h) the use of a relatively low level of inference in interpreting assessment findings.

BEHAVIORAL ASSESSMENT IN PSYCHIATRIC SETTINGS

One of the challenges of conducting behavioral assessments in psychiatric settings is determining the content and timing of the assessment within the consultation or treatment encounter. This determination will inevitably be influenced by the assessor's conceptual model of health and illness (Russo, Hamada, & Marques, 1988).

The biopsychosocial model of health and illness (Schwartz, 1982) represents a systems-based model that argues that assessment and treatment of illness should encompass consideration of the interactions of biological, social, and psychological factors. This model demands a multilevel, interactive approach to evaluating the problems of children and organizes clinical data in a manner that acknowledges the interactive, multilevel nature of illness and behavioral disturbance. The model, with its emphasis on interdisciplinary collaboration and integration of variables at numerous conceptual levels, has particular utility in the treatment of children's disorders that clearly result from the interaction of biological, behavioral, and environmental factors (e.g., ADHD, childhood anxiety disorders, eating disorders).

For the behaviorally oriented clinician, assessment and treatment are complementary and interactive processes (Mash, 1989). The following are guidelines for behavioral assessments and treatment in psychiatric settings, adapted from guidelines for contextually based assessments in pediatric health care settings (Russo et al., 1988).

1. What is the referral/assessment question?
   a. Is the request reasonable?
   b. Does this request take into account multiple factors that may influence psychiatric treatment?
2. What other areas appear to require intervention?
   a. Family issues
   b. Stress
   c. Behavior problems
3. What factors require assessment to provide an adequate formulation?
   a. Physical status: medical issues, drug effects
   b. Developmental factors
   c. Family functioning
   d. Stress issues
   e. Care routines, environmental issues
   f. Other factors, as relevant
4. What methods will be used over the course of assessment and treatment?
   a. Interview
   b. History
   c. Ratings
   d. Behavior recordings
   e. Physical data
5. What are the goals of treatment?
   a. What is a satisfactory outcome?
   b. Do goals fit with medical care?
6. What are the methods of treatment?
   a. Are interventions defined specifically?
   b. Who will conduct treatment?
   c. How will assessment and treatment be linked?
7. How will communication between health-care-team members occur?
8. Is the treatment ethical, appropriate, and defendable?
   a. Who is the "patient"?
   b. Does treatment serve the long-term best interests of the child?
9. Under what circumstances should treatment be curtailed or reevaluated?
   a. Specify failure criteria.
   b. Monitor psychiatric parameters as a basis for decision.

10. How will treatment be maintained or generalized?
    a. Is there a plan for parent training or home care?
    b. What will be necessary to assist the child over the course of long-term psychiatric illness?
    c. What future problems may arise that should trigger a response by the care team?
    d. Who will follow the case to identify these issues?

Sources of Information in Child Behavioral Assessment

Professionals working with children increasingly recognize the importance of children's perceptions of themselves and others and gather this information through use of interviews, self-report measures (La Greca, 1990), and self-monitoring. Interviews with children can be valuable in terms of both content and process. Although reports of children will naturally have age-related effects, accuracy and reliability of young children's reports may be enhanced by phrasing questions in developmentally appropriate terms and by minimizing verbal demands. More specifically, the validity of self-report data is influenced by whether the report is written or verbal, by the form of the questions asked, by the actual contents of the questions, and by situational factors (Kratochwill & Roseby, 1988). At this time, the most widely used self-report instruments assess internal states, such as fear, anxiety, or depression, and self-perceptions; but measures are also available for assessing children's interpersonal, behavioral, and affective functioning (La Greca).

Parents' descriptions of children's behaviors are an important source of information about patterns of behavior because of their familiarity with the child. However, parents' reports of child-behavior problems are subject to both positive and negative biases that may be related to their own functioning, as well as to contextual factors. In spite of these potential sources of bias, parents will continue to play a crucial role in determining whether and how a child is evaluated.

Therapists, psychiatric nurses, and teachers in psychiatric settings may also supply information that is useful in the diagnostic process and ongoing assessment of children's behavior. Treatment-team members, like academic teachers, see the child daily, often for long periods of time, and within complex social situations (Funderburk & Eyberg, 1988). Teachers are typically very familiar with children of a given age and are generally able to assess a child relative to appropriate standards of normal development (Conners, 1969).

Agreement between descriptions and/or ratings of children's behaviors by different observers appears to be a function of not only the type of behavior being rated, but also of the extremity of the behavior (Ledingham, Younger, Schwartzman, & Bergeron, 1982). Agreement between parents is highly variable and seems to be strongly affected by the method used to gather information; but it can be improved by wording questions more specifically. Agreement between parents and teachers is often lower than agreement between parents. This is thought to be a function of the different situations in which parents and teachers observe children and their differing degrees of familiarity with a child, rather than of unreliable reporting (Shelton & Barkley, 1990b). In addition, low correlations between teacher and parent ratings for nonreferred children may suggest that teachers report more variability in normal behavior than parents do, perhaps because their extensive experience with many children of a given age provides a wider basis for comparison (Funderburk & Eyberg, 1988).

Methods Used in Child Behavioral Assessment

Behavioral assessment is a process of sampling behavior. Assessment methods can be ordered along the dimension of directness of assessment: from direct observation in the natural setting, to direct observation in analogue settings, to self-monitoring, self-report, and informant report (Cone, 1978). Directness is determined by the extent to which the method measures the behavior of interest as it naturally occurs in the environment. As one moves toward the indirect pole of the continuum, one gets further away from assessing behavior as it actually occurs, and the distance increases the inferences needed to describe behavior in the natural setting.

A psychological test, which is also a sample of behavior, is a method by which some attribute or behavior is scaled to assign numerical values to observable events so as to separate people as widely as possible on the dimension of interest (Nunnally, 1978). In our clinic, we regard psychological tests as one of many tools we may use to sample and assess relevant behaviors. Thus, in addition to direct observation in the naturalistic setting and analogue assessments of one or more interactants, we rely on interviews, checklists and rating scales completed by parents, teachers, physicians and nurses, self-report measures, and measures of IQ and achievement to increase our understanding of a child's behavior.

Although some of these tests are considered tools of traditional assessment, it is chiefly the assumptions underlying the data they yield and how the data will be used in treatment that distinguishes behavioral from traditional assessment (Ciminero & Drabman, 1977). As with assessment in general, each source of information must be evaluated in terms of reliability, validity, and utility. Our goal is to maximize the true variance among responses and minimize error variance due to informant bias or differences due to method.

Direct Observational Assessment

Direct observation of a child's performance in the natural environment, when it is feasible, can be a very useful way to gain information relative to treatment. Typically, an observer records behavior as it occurs, a process that should require minimal inference on the observer's part. The clinician must choose the target response or responses, the dimension(s) of interest (e.g., frequency, duration, or response quality), and the actual recording procedures. These include real-time recording (actual occurrence of the behavior in an uninterrupted time flow), event or duration recording (recording behavior during a discrete trial), and interval recording (the clinician observes, records, and scores an interval if the behavior of interest occurs throughout the interval or at any time during the interval) (Kratochwill & Roseby, 1988).

A significant benefit of naturalistic observation, of which there are many methods, is identifying environmental factors that may maintain behaviors. Observations should be made with trained observers whose level of agreement is periodically checked to ensure consistent coding of behavior. The accuracy of this type of measurement depends largely upon the training and performance of the observers. Therefore, careful monitoring of the data for observer effects (e.g., reactivity, bias, or drift) is necessary.

Analogue Observational Assessment

In the psychiatric setting, an alternative to direct observation in the naturalistic setting is analogue assessment within the unit. Analogue assessment encompasses procedures in which the child responds to stimuli that simulate those found in his or her natural environment (Kratochwill & Roseby, 1988) and may range from informal observations of a child to observations using systematic codes and trained observers. Behavioral coding systems are currently available for assessing children's behavioral manifestations of anxiety, depression, noncompliance, classroom behavior, dental and other fears, interactions with family members, mealtime behaviors, activity level, obsessive-compulsive behaviors, pain behaviors, social skills, and assertiveness (Hersen & Bellack, 1988; La Greca, 1990).

An advantage of analogue assessment is that, by scheduling and structuring the assessment situation, a clinician gains more control over variables, such as noise and interruptions, that can contaminate the assessment process. Such structured assessments may allow monitoring of variables that are difficult to monitor in natural settings. Analogue assessment, like direct observations in the naturalistic setting, requires special considerations to ensure consistency among raters. However, this form of observation may be more feasible than observations conducted in the natural setting.

Self-Monitoring and Self-Assessment

Self-monitoring requires that a child be aware of and systematically record the response that is the focus of assessment. With some children, self-monitoring has been employed for assessment, as well as treatment of various psychological problems, by using record booklets, checklist forms, counters, timers, and meters. Self-monitoring may be a cost-efficient method and, depending upon the child's capabilities, can be the method of choice for assessing private or low-frequency activities. Self-monitoring can minimize the obtrusive and sometimes reactive effects of direct observations; however, a number of variables are known to influence the accuracy and reactivity of this type of data collection (Kratochwill & Roseby, 1988).

The accuracy of self-monitoring is affected by training in the way to self-monitor, use of systematic methods, use of devices, timing of recording, response competition, response effort, reinforcement, awareness of accuracy assessment, selection of target behaviors, and characteristics of the child. Variables affecting the reactivity of self-monitoring include the child's motivation to change behavior; the valence, nature, and number of target behaviors; timing; schedule of self-monitoring; use of devices; and the child's goals and whether he or she receives feedback about self-monitoring activities.

Rating Scales and the Use of Direct Observations

Complex observational measures, while yielding important information, are not always available for use in behavioral assessment in clinical settings because of the problems alluded to earlier as well as constraints in the amount of time available for training reliable observers. In such cases, behavioral rating scales may be used as an efficient means to supplement interview data, provided they are valid measures of the problems of interest. Rating scales filled out by children's caregivers have earned an important place in the complete assessment of children with a variety of problem behaviors (La Greca, 1990).

When using rating scales, it should be remembered that these measures are indirect samples of performance that are usually obtained retrospectively and that the relation of the ratings obtained with the measure to actual occurrences of the target behavior in the natural setting may not be high. Additionally, ratings on such a measure may reflect "perceptions" that do not reliably relate to the actual occurrences of the behavior (Kratochwill & Roseby, 1988).

Some of these problems may be minimized by combining information from interviews and rating scales with data from direct observations; however, complete agreement across methods cannot be expected (Achenbach, McConaughy, & Howell, 1987). Although the knowledge gained from each of these methods overlaps, each also contributes unique sources of information. Rating scales permit the collection of data on behaviors that occur infrequently (which might be missed by in vivo measures) and filter out situational variation, thereby measuring the most stable and enduring characteristics of the child (Barkley, 1988). On the other hand, systematic behavioral observations by properly trained observers permit the precise description of moment-by-moment child behavior at a level different from that of more global reports of others (Reid, Patterson, Baldwin, & Dishion, 1988).

Specific Applications of Behavioral Assessment in Psychiatric Settings

Clinicians conducting behavioral assessments in psychiatric settings will encounter children with a wide variety of presenting problems and psychiatric symptoms. Inpatient behavioral assessments require an open and flexible approach when dealing with the problems of children in acute distress. These children present with problems ranging from transient behavior change with an identifiable antecedent (e.g., crying and food refusal in a young patient who has never been separated from parents before) to problem behaviors with a lengthy and complicated history (e.g., addictive disorders, conduct disorders), to behaviors that may be life-threatening (e.g., suicide attempts and medical noncompliance). Behavioral assessment may also be of a highly structured, ongoing nature, as in the use of behavioral coding systems and token economies or point systems to document treatment gains.

Psychiatric settings are typically diagnostically focused (e.g., DSM-IV; American Psychiatric Association, 1993), and the combined use of rating scales and direct observations has valuable contributions to make to the diagnostic process when behavioral manifestations are part of diagnostic criteria. This is particularly true in the diagnosis of disruptive behavior disorders, which have a high degree of overlap and share diagnostic criteria such as restlessness and poor concentration with other disorders, notably anxiety and dysthymia. Approximately 65% of children meeting the criteria for attention-deficit hyperactivity disorder (ADHD) will also meet the diagnosis of oppositional defiant disorder (ODD), and approximately 20% to 30% of ADHD children will meet the criteria for conduct disorder (CD) (Barkley, 1990). Adequate assessment of the behavioral referents of the diagnostic criteria is important, because, although these disorders overlap significantly in their clinical presentations, they may be distinct in etiology, developmental course and outcome, and types of treatments to which they respond (Edelbrock, 1989).

A serious impediment to diagnostic clarity is the well-documented variability across settings of the behaviors of conduct-problem children. Many aggressive boys fail to show aggressive behavior in the clinician's office or reception room (Patterson, 1964), and hyperactive children do not always act hyperactive in a doctor's office or in the presence of strangers, in spite of parents' reports of high levels of disruptive behavior at home and at school (Loney, 1980). In fact, observations of conduct-problem children interacting with their families in a clinic setting may not be significantly correlated with observations of the same children interacting with family members at home (Zangwill & Kniskern, 1982).

A second diagnostic issue in psychiatric settings is obtaining unbiased data for clinical decision making. Of necessity, clinicians often rely heavily on parents' reports of child behavior; however, parent-report data are subject to both positive and negative biases. Depression and extreme environmental stressors have been shown to affect mothers' perceptions of children and parental monitoring skills (Patterson, 1982; Wahler & Dumas, 1989), and a variety of factors may affect memory and recall. For these reasons, behavioral assessments most often rely on data from multiple informants (Achenbach, 1978), and some forms of bias in the diagnostic process may be minimized by combining information from interviews with data from empirically validated behavioral rating scales and direct observations of adult-child or peer interactions.

We believe that the methods for objectively assessing the frequency, duration, or quality of children's responding also have great promise in evaluation of the effects of medicines on behavior. This is well illustrated in behavioral studies of children with ADHD undergoing medication trials. These studies have documented that stimulant medications have positive effects on the ability of children with ADHD to sustain attention to assigned tasks and to reduce task-irrelevant restlessness and motor activity (Barkley, 1977); treatment with these medications has been found to significantly improve the quality of the interactions of these children and their parents, teachers, and peers (DuPaul & Barkley, 1990) and is associated with reductions in aggressive behavior (Whalen et al., 1989). Studies based on systematic observation have helped document dose-related effects and the nature of long- and short-term side effects (DuPaul & Barkley, 1990).

Another obvious application of behavioral assessment in inpatient settings is behavior management. Functional analysis of factors maintaining behavior has proved useful in the treatment of children with primary psychiatric disturbance (e.g., Fremouw, de Perczel, & Ellis, 1990), as well as with children who develop behavioral difficulties or psychiatric symptoms, such as depression, as a consequence of chronic illness or of their hospitalization experiences (Eyberg, 1985; Roberts, 1986; Wright, Shaefer, & Solomons, 1979).

In its simplest form, analysis of the functions of behavior (i.e., to obtain reward, to avoid or escape an aversive event, or to regulate one's level of stimulation) is a type of direct observational assessment that involves observing and recording in sequence events that occur closest in time to the onset and to the ending of target behaviors. These data are then used to generate hypotheses about the possible function(s) or purpose(s) of the child's behavior. The goal is not to alter the function of the behavior, but rather to teach the child an alternate response that represents a more efficient or more adaptive way to get this need met, or to alter the environment in such a way as to make the problem behavior unnecessary or inefficient (Horner, 1992).

Understanding a child's behavior at the functional level can be very helpful in planning and assessing interventions because two children who present with the same response topography (e.g., fighting during social-skills group) may actually have very different motivations and, therefore, may benefit from different interventions. A functional analysis of in-group behavior may reveal that for one child, picking fights during group functions predictably gets him removed from an activity that he does not enjoy, whereas similar behavior in the second child maximizes attention she receives from other group members and group leaders, which she finds pleasurable. For the therapist or psychiatric nurse planning how to respond to fighting during group sessions, it may be useful to know that "leaving the group for misbehavior" may actually be reinforcing for the first child but may function as an effective deterrent to fighting for the second child. On a practical level, analysis of patterns in behavior may help explain daily occurrences in psychiatric units that are the direct result of demands placed upon the child in a highly structured treatment setting and may help in treatment planning.

In psychiatric settings where staff members will frequently encounter children or adolescents whose behavioral problems interfere with or are the focus of treatment, it is hard to overstate the value of assessing empirically what actually is reinforcing or punishing to a particular child. Repeated and systematic observations of behavior may make a child's needs and preferences obvious to staff members and may reveal information that a child may not be able to communicate verbally but may nevertheless act upon. Observations of unstructured play activities and interactions, for example, can provide valuable information in the assessment of suicidal thoughts and behaviors. Repetition of certain themes and intensity of demonstrated affect have been shown to distinguish suicidal from nonsuicidal children (Pfeffer, 1986).

A form of treatment that has widespread use in psychiatric settings is token economies, or point systems. These are unitwide systems of behavioral contingency management in which positive and negative consequences of specific behaviors are clearly spelled out, sometimes in contractual form, so that each child in the unit knows what to expect and how to earn privileges. A number of behaviors are monitored simultaneously by some or all members of the treatment team. This type of assessment requires time and planning, is extremely difficult to carry out in less-structured and -controlled settings, and depends upon the coordinated efforts of trained observers, including psychiatric nurses, therapists, and other staff members. The comprehensiveness of this type of assessment makes it attractive for monitoring treatment effects, for program evaluation, and for programmatic research on clinical interventions with children.

Unique Features of Conducting Behavioral Assessments in Psychiatric Settings

Psychiatric settings are often highly structured learning environments in which definitions of acceptable and unacceptable behaviors are made clear, criteria for earning privileges are behaviorally defined, and daily activity schedules are posted for each child and for the unit as a whole. However, the very characteristics of an inpatient environment that may make it therapeutic for a child (structure and predictability) and that may provide a relatively controlled setting for assessing behavior increase the need for careful transition planning to avoid loss of treatment gains as the child moves back into a less structured setting. At a minimum, involvement of the child's family or caregivers in treatment and strategic use of passes and home visits are recommended, and may be discussed on a contractual basis at the time of admission.

The highly structured nature of psychiatric settings may also limit the generalizability of findings. When assessing children's behavior in psychiatric settings where inpatient stays are brief and both physical surroundings and staff are likely to be novel stimuli to a child, great care must be taken to address the timing and validity of assessment procedures and to reduce the obtrusiveness of the measurement process whenever possible. As with assessment in general, each source of information used in behavioral assessment must be evaluated in terms of reliability and validity, as well as utility.

A number of observational measures have been developed specifically for use in psychiatric settings, such as the Observational Record of Inpatient Behavior (Rosen et al., 1980), the Time-Sample Behavioral Checklist (Power, Paul, Licht, & Engel, 1982), the Staff-Resident Interaction Chronograph (Licht, Paul, Power, & Engel, 1980), and the Staff Behavior Observation procedure (Delamater, Conners, & Wells, 1984). The first three measures have been used in adult psychiatric facilities, but the fourth measure was specifically developed to study staff training procedures in child psychiatric inpatient settings.

Psychoeducational Assessment

Work with children in inpatient settings often begins with an accurate assessment of a child's mental and behavioral status and ability to comprehend what he or she is asked to do. In psychiatric settings, it is helpful to those responsible for treatment and discharge planning to be able to distinguish children with a clearly psychiatric presentation and possible psychoeducational complications from those whose presenting problem is primarily psychoeducational, with secondary psychiatric or behavioral complications. We will now present procedures we use for this type of assessment, the goal of which is to identify the relevant cognitive processing variables for a particular child and to offer recommendations that address the child's psychological and educational problems proactively.

Assessing Relevant Variables

The goal of behavior analysis has been described as "the creation of competent environments that make problem behaviors inefficient" (Horner, 1992), and behavior therapy is characterized by the pragmatic search for effective treatments. As a result, principles guiding behavioral interventions with children and their families have become increasingly heterogeneous and may draw from theories of learning, developmental psychology, social psychology, cognitive psychology, and the neurosciences (Mash, 1989).

The biopsychosocial model (Schwartz, 1982; Shelton & Barkley, 1990a) is a useful tool for organizing information about children, both as individuals expressing unique genetic influences and as members of complex social systems. In this model, levels of functioning are compared to a series of concentric circles, with the innermost circle representing the biological level of functioning and surrounding circles representing the successive levels of cognitive and neuropsychological functioning, behavioral-environmental interactions, social-familial functioning, and, finally, the socioeconomic or sociopolitical level, as represented by the outermost circle. Impairments in functioning at any level may affect a child's functioning at adjacent levels, and effects may be bidirectional.

Using this model to organize data from several sources, we assess variables at each of the levels of functioning in an attempt to identify the relevant variables for a particular child. Results of our psychoeducational assessment are then used to make recommendations that address the child's problems at whatever levels they exist.

Initially, we seek an adequate description of the behaviors of interest (e.g., frequency, rate, duration, latency, form, intensity, and variability), and we use this information to determine whether there actually is a problem. This may be followed by assessment of biological factors, including information from the physical examination to rule out organic problems. We seek detailed information concerning the child's developmental history and early illnesses and integrate this with information about the genetic characteristics of the child's first-degree relatives, the child's sleep habits, eating habits, and handedness.

We assess a variety of environmental influences, including characteristics of the child's family and the relationships among its members. Particular emphasis is placed on sibling relationships and how they have affected each child's development (Dunn, 1992). We also assess the child's relationships with teachers.

In the biopsychosocial model, the first level of a child's functioning includes his or her physical integrity, especially the neurological integrity of the central nervous system, which is the final common pathway for all behavior. Therefore, an important goal of our assessment is to obtain valid estimates of the child's intellectual and perceptual functioning, as well as academic achievement. This information suggests how the child may be expected to perform relative to other children and allows us to consider his or her placement and whether the school is making developmentally appropriate demands on the child. Additionally, we carefully assess reading skills because reading is the most critical component of the educational process. Monitoring potential reading problems when the chances of remediation are greatest may make a valuable contribution toward prevention of reading disabilities and the emotional problems that can be associated with them (Berninger, Thalberg, DeBruyn, & Smith, 1987).

Subtest scores on the IQ and achievement testing are further analyzed. Using the child's mean scores as a standard of comparison, we conduct a detailed analysis of the child's relative strengths and weaknesses by subtest scores and by relative loadings on factors (Kaufman, 1979). The main factors that we obtain from our assessment include verbal comprehension, perceptual organization, freedom from distractibility, processing speed, long- and short-term memory, auditory processing, visual processing, comprehension-knowledge, and fluid reasoning. Weightings on these factor scores, or processing variables, may suggest how a particular child can best use information in learning situations and may lead to recommendations for changes in curriculum, program design, or presentation of tasks.

The Format of Psychoeducational Assessment

The first step is meeting with the child's parent or parents privately. Following an interview that begins with open-ended questions to elicit a description of the problems, the Child Behavior Checklist (CBCL) (Achenbach & Edelbrock, 1983) is administered orally to the primary caregiver. While this procedure departs from its usual use as a paper-and-pencil parent report measure, we find there are several advantages, including increases in the amount and accuracy of the data obtained. In this verbal format, parents often volunteer information that we might not have otherwise requested, and item content is clarified when parents elaborate on answers; for example, a parent may simply endorse the item "prefers playing with younger children" only to reveal in a later comment that there are no age-appropriate children available with whom their child can play.

Next, we orally administer a Learning Styles Questionnaire that was developed in our clinic and contains 50 items representing behavioral referents of the processing variables from the Wechsler Intelligence Scale for Children-Third Edition (WISC-III) (Wechsler, 1991) and the Woodcock-Johnson Psychoeducational Battery-Revised (WJ-R) (Woodcock & Mather, 1989). Items are worded in simple language. The purpose of administering this questionnaire is to get corroborating information about the child's performance on the factor scores or processing variables. The questionnaire also assesses parents' feelings about their child's behavior and whether any first-degree biological relatives have had behavioral, emotional, educational, or addictive problems. Finally, we ask the parents to provide a detailed year-by-year medical, developmental, and social history of their child.

The second step of our assessment involves the extensive testing of the child by using a battery of standardized intellectual and achievement tests, as well as measures of reading, memory, and perceptual capabilities. As part of testing, we interview the child's teachers. This is done for several reasons. First, the interview serves as a reliability check on our impressions of the child's behavior during testing. Since we are in contact with the child for only a short period and under highly novel conditions, teacher interviews help us make a more accurate assessment of variables such as motivation and attention span. The second reason for the interview is to gather more information about the child's academic strengths and weaknesses, which we can compare with our testing results. Additionally, we will question the teacher concerning the rate at which the child is progressing and those areas in which he or she does best. Finally, the teacher interview, in combination with the history and questionnaire data obtained from parents, provides information on whether or not the child presents with a motivation/discipline problem at home or at school, has difficulty with peer relationships, or perhaps has a personality conflict with a particular teacher.

The third step of our assessment is an information interview with the child. If the child is old enough, the Youth Report Form of the CBCL and/or the Tennessee Self-Concept Scale may be administered orally, with many of the same advantages as previously noted for an oral presentation of items to their parents. Finally, the child is asked to draw a picture of his or her family "doing something together" and of themselves. For each of the family members in turn, including himself or herself, the child is then asked to name "the three things you like best about this person" and "the three things you'd like to change about this person." Finally, when the child is comfortable with the interviewer, his or her view of the presenting problem is sought.

From a review of the information gathered in the first three steps of the assessment, we then determine if additional testing (e.g., anxiety or other self-report measures) is necessary. Also, a determination is made as to more formal observations beyond those obtained during interviews. Generally, we use role-playing procedures and/or direct observations in order to clarify conflicting information or to have families demonstrate processes that they cannot adequately describe.

Specific Measures Used in Psychoeducational Assessment

Child Behavior Checklist—Parent Report Form (CBCL).

The CBCL is an inventory that is widely used for the assessment of social competencies and behavior problems of children 4 to 16 years of age, with norms for ages 2 to 16 years (Achenbach & Edelbrock, 1983). There are 113 behavior-problem items and 20 social-competence items. In addition to the specific factors, such as schizoid, depressed, and hyperactive, the scale also yields scores on two broad-band factors, internalization and externalization.

Wechsler Intelligence Scale for Children-Third Edition (WISC-III).

The WISC-III is an individually administered instrument for assessing intellectual abilities of children aged 6 years 0 months to 16 years 11 months. We use all subtests of the battery. This test retains the essential features of the WISC-R but incorporates several improvements designed to make the testing experience more interesting for children. Along with updated test materials (including color plates), content, and administration procedures, the manual includes updated norms. The WISC-III consists of 13 subtests and, like the WISC-R, yields estimates of intellectual abilities, the verbal IQ, the performance IQ, and the full scale IQ. With the inclusion of the extra subtest (Symbol Search), four factors (Verbal

Comprehension, Perceptual Organization, Freedom from Distractibility, and Processing Speed) can be found (Wechsler, 1991).

Woodcock-Johnson Psychoeducational Battery-Revised (WJ-R).

The WJ-R is a wide-range set of individually administered tests for measuring intellectual development, school aptitude, and achievement in people from ages 2 years to 95 years old (Woodcock & Johnson, 1989). We use all subtests in the battery. The Tests of Cognitive Ability, in addition to measuring broad cognitive abilities, yield scores on the seven cognitive factors, which are auditory processing, visual processing, comprehension-knowledge, fluid reasoning, long-term retrieval, short-term memory, and processing speed. The Tests of Achievement measure accomplishments in reading, mathematics, written language, knowledge, and skills. Analysis of WJ-R scores can be useful in detecting discrepancies between aptitude and achievement and in detecting specific deficits in cognitive abilities (e.g., language processing) or in achievement (Woodcock & Mather, 1989).

Wide Range Assessment of Memory and Learning (WRAML).

It has been observed that children with memory deficiencies often exhibit uneven levels of achievement and develop problems with motivation that may be the result of performing well conceptually but experiencing failure and frustration when faced with schoolwork that involves memorization (Sheslow & Adams, 1990). For this reason, we also administer all subtests of the Wide Range Assessment of Memory and Learning, or WRAML, which can be used to evaluate the ability to actively learn and memorize a variety of information of children aged 5 to 17. There are three verbal, three visual, and three learning subtests, yielding a verbal memory index, a visual memory index, and a learning index, and a combined (nine subtest) general memory index.

The Gray Oral Reading Test-Third Edition (GORT-3).

The GORT-3 is designed to measure, in terms of rate, accuracy, and comprehension, oral reading skills of children aged 7 to 18 years 11 months (Wiederholt & Bryant, 1992). After reading a passage orally, the child is required to answer multiple-choice content questions that are read to him or her by the examiner. It is interesting to compare oral reading and comprehension on the WJ-R.

Developmental Test of Visual-Motor Integration (VMI).

The VMI is a pencil-and-paper task in which a child is asked to copy figures from a set of 24 geometric forms that are arranged in order of increasing complexity. This copying task can be used with children aged 2 to 15 years (Beery, 1967).

Interpretation of Test Results

In the search for the child's strengths and weaknesses, information from all of these tests is combined. Additionally, the main factors that we obtain from our assessment (verbal comprehension, perceptual organization, freedom from distractibility, processing speed, long- and short-term memory, auditory processing, visual processing, comprehension-knowledge, and fluid reasoning) from the WISC-III and the WJ-R are treated as processing variables that are interpreted within the context of an empirically based processing model of reading and spelling, which is described more fully in the following sections.

Summary of Basic Research in Reading

In the 1970s and 1980s, converging lines of research with both skilled and poor readers have added much to the practical knowledge of reading skills. Three main areas of research have emerged: studies of linguistic awareness, or "phonological processing;" studies of word recognition, or "orthographic processing;" and studies of reading comprehension (Perfetti, 1991).

Briefly, it is known that phonological processes are important in all aspects of reading, that phonological processing skill is strongly related to the initial ease of reading acquisition, and that the lack of ability to segment and/or blend sounds is implicated in most cases of severe reading difficulty for adults and children (Stanovich, 1991). Further, it appears that the processes and sources of knowledge underlying language comprehension become fully functional in reading only after the reader is able to achieve a degree of fluency in word recognition, or orthographic processing (Vellutino, 1991). Thus, the component processes of reading are complexly related and interdependent in their development and functioning (see comprehensive review by Adams, 1990).

Comparisons between normally skilled readers and disabled readers show that normal readers tend to have a more integrated development of phonetic and orthographic-coding processes than do disabled readers (Olson, Wise, Conners, & Rack, 1990). Studies of twin probands show that variance in phonological coding is significantly heritable in about 10% of the population, but variance in orthographic coding, or word recognition, is less heritable (Olson et al.). Data suggest that environmental factors (the degree of exposure to print in the home, reading instruction in the school) are most important in determining a subject's knowledge of the specific orthographic pattern for words. Reading generally improves with exposure to print, even in children with severe phonological deficits. Thus, Olson and his colleagues have concluded that "genetically based deficits in phonological coding may constrain the speed or ease of reading development, but environmental factors such as improved reading instruction and greater reading experience can sometimes compensate for genetic constraints."

A Model for Reading and Spelling

Components of the Reading Model

The first feature of this model is processing speed, or speed of mental operations, which is represented by an arrow in the right margin of Figure 1.2. Processing speed is considered to be an underlying variable in all the operations that occur in this model. In practical terms, for a child with slow processing speed, tasks will take longer, which makes them seem harder. This variable is measured by tests that load on both the WISC-III and WJ-R processing-speed factors.

Next, reading requires transformation of abstract visual codes to recognition, phonological (sound), and semantic (meaning) codes. These three functional or coding operations are represented in the reading model as orthographic comparison, phonetic processing, and comprehension and are depicted with large rectangles.

Orthographic comparison functions, possibly through neural networks, in the recognition of visually presented material and relates to reading. It is thought of as a list, or lexicon, of all the words the reader can recognize. The lexicon is not conceptualized as being available in a yes/no fashion, but, depending on the reader's previous exposure to the word, words may vary from easily available to not yet available; that is, words in the

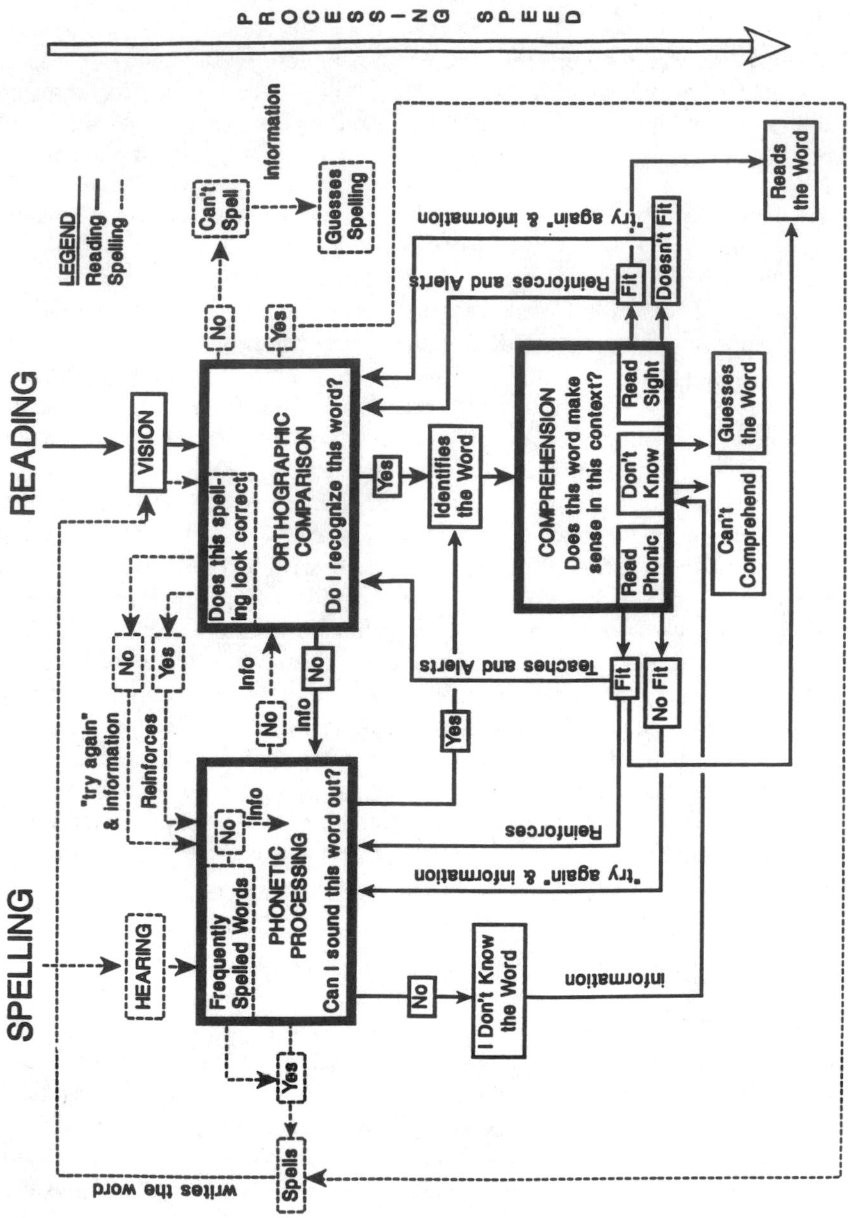

Figure 1.2. A model for reading and spelling.

lexicon may range from easily accessible ones, such as *the*, to difficult to access or emerging words. This lexicon is viewed as being organized into smaller lists so that it is possible, with a search strategy, to save time by searching a piece of the lexicon instead of the entire list. This processing variable is difficult to directly measure, but tests loading on the visual-processing factor give some indication of this ability. Additionally, children who score higher on word identification than their phonetic ability suggests they will score may have a strength in this area.

Phonetic processing depends on segmentation skills and is conceptualized in this model as the ability to sound out words that are read and to phonetically spell words that are heard. Phonological-processing skills are more genetically influenced than the other two operations (Olson et al., 1990). This processing variable is measured by the WJ-R test Word Attack and cognitive tests, which load on the auditory-processing factor.

The third operation or function is *comprehension processing*, a collection of abilities such as vocabulary, memory abilities, knowledge of syntax (i.e., the probability of words in a sequence that is unique to each language or dialect), reasoning abilities, fund of knowledge, and use of contextual clues. These are drawn upon to process and integrate information from the other two operations. Poor readers may use context and redundancies in the language to their advantage in guessing; they may miss a particular word but are still able to grasp the meaning of a passage. It is believed that reading to a child, by increasing his or her exposure to the language, can increase the child's ability to predict what is likely to come next in a sentence. This processing variable is measured by WISC-III verbal comprehension factor and by the comprehension-knowledge and fluid reasoning factors of the WJ-R. Also, one can evaluate how well a child uses comprehension to aid memory by looking at the discrepancies between subtests that measure basic memory and those in which reasoning can be used to aid memory.

These three operations function in a stepwise and collaborative manner, sharing information and providing corrective feedback. It is important to understand that the model is seen as "intelligent"; when a processor is unable to perform its task, it provides whatever information it can to the next level so that each processor can be efficient.

How does the model work for reading and spelling? First, with visual input, the orthographic processor performs its initial operation "Do I recognize this word?" (e.g., *Jack*). If *yes* (the word is identified), the information is sent to the comprehension processor, where it is again evaluated: "Does this word make sense in this context?" If *yes*, the word is read and a message is sent back to the orthographic processor to be alerted that the next word is likely to be *and* or a verb. If *no* (the word does not make sense, e.g., Jack and Jim *desk*), the comprehension processor provides whatever information it can and the message is sent "try again." If the orthographic processor still cannot identify the word, it passes whatever information it has (e.g., has *ing*) to the phonetic processor, which performs its initial operation, namely, "Can I sound this word out?" If *yes*, it sends this information to the comprehension processor, which again asks "Does this word make sense in this context?" If *yes*, it teaches and alerts the lexicon and reinforces the phonetic processor. If *no*, the comprehension processor provides information and prompts the phonetic processor to "try again"; and if the word still cannot be sounded out, the comprehension processor may then either register *Don't know* or may guess at the word. It is believed that the more advanced the comprehension processor is (e.g., the greater the reader's exposure to oral or printed language), the better chance one has to produce a correct response.

Recommendations from the Reading Model

In addition to recommendations for changes in curriculum, program design, or presentation of tasks that may arise from interpretation of factors and strengths and weaknesses on subtests, the reading model allows more specific recommendations. Basic reading research suggests that phonological skills, which are likely to be poor in approximately 10% of beginning readers, are important in reading success. Data suggest, and the model predicts, that genetically based deficits in phonological coding may constrain the speed or ease of reading development but may sometimes be compensated for by environmental factors such as improved reading instruction and greater reading and language experiences in the home (Olson et al., 1990). These factors can strengthen the other processors, which are less influenced by inheritance.

Thus, for example, with children who have phonological processing deficits, it is recommended that the parents attempt to build the comprehension processor by supplementing the child's reading experiences. They can do this by reading to the child until the child reaches an age at which he or she will no longer allow it. When parents read, they should explain any word or concept that the child does not understand. This practice increases the listener's vocabulary and sensitivity to the way in which language works. By listening, the child learns to be better able to predict language and to make use of its redundancies to improve reading comprehension. Parents should also read ahead in their child's textbooks and make flashcards for words that the child does not know. The child uses a sight-word approach with these flashcards. This builds the lexicon and increases orthographic abilities. When the child successfully reads these words at school, success reinforces his effort. Over time, these procedures expose the child to increasingly complex sight words and oral language and may prevent the onset of the Matthew effects, whereby, over a period of time, the rich get richer in reading and the poor get poorer in reading (Stanovich, 1986).

Components of the Spelling Model

The way in which individuals spell is also addressed by the model. Reading and spelling are seen as having a reciprocal but complementary relationship. The command "Spell *word*," is presumed to enter the system through the auditory channel. As indicated in the model by dashed lines, this command goes directly to the phonetic processor. Part of the phonetic processor is conceptualized to act as a relatively short-term memory store for frequently spelled words. Words that one spells often are kept here. However, this storage capacity is conceptualized as being limited. These words must be frequently used and, thus, reinforced, or they will be lost. If the word that one is trying to spell is contained in this part of the processor, then it is spelled. When one writes the word, visual input goes to the orthographic processor, and the processor asks the question "Does this spelling look correct?" If it looks correct, reinforcement is provided to the phonetic processor. If it does not look correct, a "try again" message is sent to the phonetic processor along with information from the orthographic processor. On the other hand, if the word is not in the frequently spelled list, then the phonetic processor attempts to sound it out. If it can sound out the word, then the word is spelled and the checking process begins. If the phonetic processor cannot sound the word out, it sends that message along with information to the orthographic processor. The orthographic processor checks to see if this word is accessible enough that it can be spelled. The model suggests that this is not a particularly frequent event. Most words in the orthographic processor are seen as being only clear enough to be recognized but not clear enough that their exact spelling can be recalled. It would take too much memory for most words to be at a level in which each letter could be sequentially accessed. However, if the orthographic processor does recall the spelling, then one spells the word. If the word is written, it is again checked by the orthographic processor. If the orthographic processor cannot spell the word, then one guesses the spelling, taking advantage of whatever information the phonetic and orthographic processors have been able to provide.

Recommendations from the Spelling Model

Kearney and Drabman (1993) have shown that children with learning disabilities can be taught to improve their spelling scores through the use of the 3-5-10-15 technique. Within the model, this is viewed as putting the words that will be on the spelling test into the Frequently Spelled Words portion of the phonetic processor. Improved grades on spelling tests tend to increase the student's level of self-confidence while decreasing parent-child tension. Although the spelling grades of children who use this technique improve, parents must be made aware that their child may well misspell the same word a few days later. According to the model, this is because words that are not frequently reinforced do not stay in the processor. (Soon after the spelling test, the child begins to put next week's words into the processor.) Since the phonetic processor has a strong genetic component, alternate ways of helping these children spell on a daily basis must be sought. Currently, we advocate the use of portable spelling checkers. These are about the size of a hand-held calculator, so they can be easily carried. A child types a word in the way they think it should be spelled and, like the spell checking function in word processing software, the machine provides the correct spelling.

SUMMARY

As behaviorally oriented clinicians, we view a child's response as a sample of his or her behavioral repertoire given a specific stimulus situation. Therefore, we collect measures from various response channels and from different informants using a combination of methods to ensure representativeness of the data. Although there may be considerable overlap in some of the methods shared by behavioral assessment and traditional assessment (e.g., measures of IQ and achievement, interviews, self-report measures), behavioral assessment can be distinguished from traditional assessment most reliably by the assumptions underlying the data collected and by the way(s) the data will be used in treatment (Ciminero & Drabman, 1977). In our view, assessment is only worthwhile when data generated by the assessment procedures can lead directly to interventions.

In this chapter, we have reviewed current features and practices in child behavioral assessment and offered guidelines for comprehensive behavioral assessment in psychiatric settings. We have described specific applications and noted unique features of conducting behavior assessment in psychiatric settings. Behavioral assessments most often rely on data from multiple informants (Achenbach, 1978). Some forms of bias in the diagnostic process may be minimized by combining information from interviews with data from empirically validated behavioral rating scales and direct observations of adult-child or peer interactions. In inpatient behavioral assessment, it is particularly important to assess both the naturalistic context of behavior (the context that presumably gave rise to psychiatric symptoms) and the current context (the psychiatric unit) in which the child's functioning is being evaluated and altered so that issues of generalization may be addressed.

Finally, we have described procedures and instruments we use for a specialized form of assessment we call "educational treatment." The goal of this assessment is to identify the relevant cognitive processing variables for a particular child and offer recommendations that address the child's psychological and educational problems proactively. It is hoped that, in many cases, a comprehensive behavioral assessment will lead to interventions involving the educational process and may minimize the costs of treatment in clinical settings.

REFERENCES

Achenbach, T. M. (1978). The Child Behavior Profile: I. Boys aged 6–11. *Journal of Consulting and Clinical Psychology, 46*, 478–488.

Achenbach, T. M., & Edelbrock, C. S. (1983). *Manual for the Child Behavior Checklist and Revised Child Behavior Profile.* Burlington, VT: University of Vermont, Department of Psychiatry.

Achenbach, T. M., McConaughy, S. H., & Howell, C. T. (1987). Child/adolescent behavioral and emotional problems: Implications of cross-informant correlations for situational specificity. *Psychological Bulletin, 101*, 213–232.

Adams, M. J. (1990). *Beginning to read: Learning and thinking about print.* Cambridge, MA: MIT Press.

American Psychiatric Association. (1993). *DSM-IV draft criteria.* Washington, DC: Author.

Barkley, R. A. (1977). A review of stimulant drug research with hyperactive children. *Journal of Child Psychology and Psychiatry, 18*, 137–165.

Barkley, R. A. (1988). Child behavior rating scales and checklists. In M. Rutter, H. Tuma, & I. Lamm (Eds.), *Diagnosis and assessment of child and adolescent psychopathology* (pp. 113–155). New York: Guilford Press.

Barkley, R. A. (1990). *Differential diagnosis. In Attention-deficit hyperactivity disorder: A handbook for diagnosis and treatment* (pp. 169–208). New York: Guilford Press.

Beery, K. E. (1967). *Developmental test of visual-motor integration: Administration and scoring manual.* Chicago: Follett.

Berninger, V. W., Thalberg, S. P., DeBruyn, I., & Smith, R. (1987). Preventing reading disabilities by assessing and remediating phonetic skills. *School Psychology Review, 16*, 554–565.

Ciminero, A. R., & Drabman, R. S. (1977). Current developments in the behavioral assessment of children. In B. B. Lahey & A. E. Kazdin (Eds.), *Advances in clinical child psychology: Vol. 1* (pp. 47–82). New York: Plenum Press.

Cone, J. D. (1978). The Behavioral Assessment Grid (BAG): A conceptual framework and a taxonomy. *Behavior Therapy, 9*, 882–888.

Conners, C. K. (1969). A teacher rating scale for use in drug studies with children. *American Journal of Psychiatry, 126*, 884–888.

Conners, C. K. (1970). Symptom patterns in hyperactive, neurotic, and normal children. *Child Development, 41*, 667–682.

Delamater, A. M., Conners, C. K., & Wells, K. C. (1984). A comparison of staff training procedures: Behavioral applications in the child psychiatric inpatient setting. *Behavior Modification, 8*, 39–58.

Dunn, J. (1992). Siblings and development. *Current Directions in Psychological Science, 1*, 6–8.

DuPaul, G., & Barkley, R. (1990). Medication therapy. In R. A. Barkley (Ed.), *Attention-deficit hyperactivity disorder: A handbook for diagnosis and treatment* (pp. 573–612). New York: Guilford Press.

Edelbrock, C. S. (1989). Childhood conduct problems: Developmental considerations and a proposed taxonomy. Unpublished manuscript, cited in R. A. Barkley (Ed.), *Attention-deficit hyperactivity disorder: A handbook for diagnosis and treatment* (pp. 164–167). New York: Guilford Press.

Eyberg, S. M. (1985). Behavioral assessment: Advancing methodology in pediatric psychology. *Journal of Pediatric Psychology, 10,* 123–139.

Fremouw, W., de Perczel, M., & Ellis, T. (1990). *Suicide risk assessment and response guidelines.* New York: Pergamon Press.

Funderburk, B. W., & Eyberg, S. M. (1988). Psychometric characteristics of the Sutter-Eyberg School Behavior Inventory: A school behavior rating scale for use with preschool children. *Behavioral Assessment, 11,* 297–313.

Goyette, C., Conners, K., & Ulrich, R. (1978). Normative data on Revised Conners Parent and Teacher Rating Scales. *Journal of Abnormal Child Psychology, 6,* 221–236.

Hersen, M., & Bellack, A. (1988). *Dictionary of behavioral assessment techniques.* New York: Pergamon Press.

Horner, R. H. (1992, September). The effects of predictability on the problem behavior of students with severe intellectual disabilities. In W. Sailor (Chair), *Social and educational issues. Symposium conducted at the 5th annual NIDRR Research and Training Center Conference on Nonaversive Behavior Management.* Nashville, TN.

Kaufman, A. S. (1979). *Intelligent testing with the WISC-R.* New York: Wiley.

Kearney, C. A., & Drabman, R. S. (1993). The write-say method for improving spelling accuracy in children with learning disabilities. *Journal of Learning Disabilities, 26,* 52–56.

Kratochwill, T. R., & Roseby, V. (1988). Psychoeducational assessment. In P. Karoly (Ed.), *Handbook of child health assessment: Biopsychosocial perspectives* (pp. 173–226). New York: Wiley.

La Greca, A. M. (1990). *Through the eyes of the child: Obtaining self-reports from children and adolescents.* Boston: Allyn and Bacon.

Ledingham, J., Younger, A., Schwartzman, A., & Bergeron, G. (1982). Agreement among teacher, peer, and self-ratings of children's aggression, withdrawal, and likability. *Journal of Abnormal Child Psychology, 10,* 363–372.

Licht, M., Paul, G., Power, C., & Engel, K. (1980). The comparative effectiveness of two modes of observer training on the Staff Resident Interaction Chronograph. *Journal of Behavioral Assessment, 2,* 175–205.

Loney, J. (1980). Child hyperactivity. In R. H. Woody (Ed.), *Encyclopedia of clinical assessment* (Vol. 1, pp. 265–285). San Francisco: Jossey-Bass.

Mash, E. J. (1989). Treatment of child and family disturbance. In E. J. Mash & R. A. Barkley (Eds.), *Treatment of childhood disorders* (pp. 3–36). New York: Guilford Press.

Mash, E. J., & Terdal, L. G. (1988). Behavioral assessment of child and family disturbance. In E. J. Mash & L. G. Terdal (Eds.), *Behavioral assessment of childhood disorders* (2nd ed.) (pp. 37–65). New York: Guilford Press.

Nunnally, J. C. (1978). An overview of psychological measurement. In B. B. Wolman (Ed.), *Clinical diagnosis of mental disorders* (pp. 97–146). New York: Wiley.

Olson, R., Wise, B., Conners, F., & Rack, J. (1990). Organization, heritability, and remediation of component word recognition and language skills in disabled readers. In T. H. Carr & B. A. Levy (Eds.), *Reading and its development: Component skill approaches* (pp. 261–322). San Diego: Harcourt Brace Jovanovich.

Patterson, G. R. (1964). An empirical approach to the classification of children. *Journal of Clinical Psychology, 20,* 326–337.

Patterson, G. R. (1982). *Coercive family process*. Eugene, OR: Castalia.

Pelham, W. E. (1977). Withdrawal of a stimulant drug and concurrent behavioral intervention in the treatment of a hyperactive child. *Behavior Therapy, 8*, 473–479.

Perfetti, C. A. (1991). The psychology, pedagogy, and politics of reading. *Current Directions in Psychological Science, 2*, 70–76.

Pfeffer, C. R. (1986). *The suicidal child.* New York: Guilford Press.

Power, C., Paul, G., Licht, M., & Engel, K. (1982). Evaluation of self-contained training procedures for the Time-Sample Behavioral Checklist. *Journal of Behavioral Assessment, 4*, 223–261.

Quay, H. C. (1986). Conduct disorders. In H. C. Quay & J. S. Werry (Eds.), *Psychopathological disorders of childhood* (3rd ed.) (pp. 35–72). New York: Wiley.

Reed, M., & Edelbrock, C. S. (1983). Reliability and validity of the Direct Observation Form of the Child Behavior Checklist. *Journal of Abnormal Child Psychology, 11*, 521–530.

Reid, J., Patterson, G., Baldwin, B., & Dishion, T. (1988). *Assessment and diagnosis in child psychopathology*. New York: Guilford Press.

Roberts, M. C. (1986). *Pediatric psychology: Psychological interventions and strategies for pediatric problems*. New York: Pergamon Press.

Rosen, A., Tureff, S., Daruna, J., Johnson, P., Lyons, J., & Davis, J. (1980). Pharmacotherapy of schizophrenia and affective disorders: Behavioral correlates of diagnostic and demographic variables. *Journal of Abnormal Psychology, 89*, 378–389.

Russo, D., Hamada, R., & Marques, D. (1988). Linking assessment and treatment in pediatric health psychology. In P. Karoly (Ed.), *Handbook of child health assessment: Biopsychosocial perspectives* (pp. 30–50). New York: Wiley.

Schwartz, G. E. (1982). Testing the biopsychosocial model: The ultimate challenge facing behavioral medicine? *Journal of Consulting and Clinical Psychology, 50*, 1040–1053.

Shelton, T., & Barkley, R. A. (1990a). Clinical, developmental, and biopsychosocial considerations. In R. A. Barkley (Ed.), *Attention-deficit/hyperactivity disorder: A handbook for diagnosis and treatment* (pp. 209–231). New York: Guilford Press.

Shelton, T., & Barkley, R. A. (1990b). Behavior rating scales. In R. A. Barkley (Ed.), *Attention-deficit/hyperactivity disorder:* A handbook for diagnosis and treatment (pp. 278–326). New York: Guilford Press.

Sheslow, D., & Adams, W. (1990). *Wide Range Assessment of Memory and Learning Administrative Manual*. Wilmington, DE: Jastak Associates.

Stanovich, K. E. (1986). Matthew effects in reading: Some consequences of individual differences in the acquisition of literacy. *Reading Research Quarterly, 21*, 360–407.

Stanovich, K. E. (1991). Cognitive science meets beginning reading. *Current Directions in Psychological Science, 2*, 70, 81–83.

Thomas, A., Chess, S., & Birch, H. G. (1968). *Temperament and behavior disorders in children*. New York: New York University Press.

Vellutino, F. R. (1991). Has basic research in reading increased our understanding of reading and how to teach reading? *Current Directions in Psychological Science, 2*, 70, 81–83.

Wahler, R. G., & Dumas, J. E. (1989). Attentional problems in dysfunctional mother-child interactions: An interbehavioral model. *Psychological Bulletin, 105*, 116–130.

Wechsler, D. (1991). *Wechsler Intelligence Scales for Children-Third Edition*. The Psychological Corporation. San Antonio, TX: Harcourt Brace Jovanovich.

Whalen, C. K., Henker, B., Burmester, D., Hinshaw, S., Huber, A., & Laski, K. (1989). Does stimulant medication improve the peer status of hyperactive children? *Journal of Consulting and Clinical Psychology, 57*, 5435–5449.

Wiederholt, J. L., & Bryant, B. R. (1992). *Gray Oral Reading Tests-Third Edition: Examiner's Manual*. Austin, TX: Pro-Ed.

Woodcock, R. W., & Johnson, M. B. (1989). *Woodcock-Johnson Psycho-Educational Battery-Revised*. Allen, TX: DLM Teaching Resources.

Woodcock, R. W., & Mather, N. (1989). *Woodcock-Johnson Tests of Cognitive Ability-Standard and Supplemental Batteries: Examiner's Manual*. Allen, TX: DLM Teaching Resources.

Wright, L., Schaefer, A. B., & Solomons, G. (1979). *Encyclopedia of pediatric psychology*. Baltimore: University Park Press.

Zangwill, W., & Kniskern, J. (1982). Comparison of problem families in the clinic and at home. *Behavior Therapy, 13*, 145–152.

CHAPTER 2

Psychiatric Assessment and Diagnosis

THEODORE A. PETTI, GINA E. LAITE, AND SUSANNE BLIX

INTRODUCTION

Assessment and diagnosis are critical components of psychiatric practice. This chapter will provide an overview of the major features of both. Two diagnostic systems, categorical and dimensional, will be considered. The process of assessment and the various standardized instruments available for assessment and diagnosis will be discussed. The reader is expected to develop a greater understanding of the rationale behind the diagnostic process and accompanying assessment and of how they may be of value to the behaviorally oriented child clinician.

Psychiatric assessment provides clinicians with hypotheses or diagnoses to guide further assessment and treatment. These hypotheses involve several layers of categorization: psychiatric diagnosis of the symptom complex; biological or organic factors; psychodynamic formulation including developmental, familial and other psychosocial contributors, personality or temperament dimensions, defenses, and conflicts; and behavioral or learning-theory-oriented considerations. The child psychiatrist employs the diagnostic process to set a course of action that can be changed such that new insight leads to modified hypotheses. Data obtained through assessment provide the distinguishing features of a case (Achenbach, 1988) and the basis for such a process. Assignment of a diagnosis from a classification system represents a major point in this process.

Classifications employed by psychiatrists generally fall within the rubric of categorical, dimensional, or "ideographic" systems. Categorical systems are characterized by viewing disorders as dichotomous: present or absent. These models assume that similarities within a given diagnosis outweigh differences and, as such, assist with understanding key features (e.g., course, pathophysiology, and treatment). Dimensional models reduce clinical phenomena to various dimensions along a continuum from normal to severe pathology upon which a child's symptoms can be placed. "Ideographic classifications," on the other hand, attempt to explain the totality of the child's pathology and overall functioning based on formal classification schema that are often driven by particular schools of thought such as psychoanalytic or learning theory based (Volkmar, 1991). Categorical (nosological/Kraepelian) classification is the official system of child and adolescent psychiatry. Categorical models are considered to be "public," in that they provide a useful framework for communication in day-to-day practice by clinicians with differing theoretical orientations. They are organized within generally accepted principles and are expected to be modified as the result of advances in scientific understanding (Schwab-Stone, Towbin, & Tarnoff, 1991). A similar argument has been made for the public nature of dimensional or multivariate models (Achenbach, 1980).

Considerable misunderstanding occurs when the classification system is viewed as synonymous with the medical model. Oversimplification of the properties of a medical model, such as equating it with authority over patient care or physical abnormality, results in many behavior therapists becoming hesitant about learning more about it and leery of its employment. *Medical model* is defined as "the formulation of diagnoses to serve as hypotheses to be tested either through response of the patient to specific interventions or to observing longitudinally the patient's clinical course." It does *not* require the presence of biological abnormality, discontinuity between health and disorder or between disorders, or homogeneity of symptoms within a diagnostic category (Spitzer & Williams, 1980). Dimensional or ideographic approaches can serve the purpose of a medical model as equally well as the categorical.

Considering implications of psychiatric diagnosis for child behavior therapy, Kazdin (1983) notes the inability of behavior therapy as currently practiced to delineate the population being treated, even if the target behavior has been well specified and evaluated. Critical aspects of the child's presentation (e.g., severity, specificity of the symptom complex, chronicity, living situation) are not generally available in the behavioral literature. Yet, these factors are often included in a description of psychiatric diagnosis. Kazdin views psychiatric diagnoses as one means to provide a system for describing behavioral disorders and for understanding similarities and differences in populations under consideration. He suggests that alternative diagnostic approaches to categorical systems can be developed, as in those based on factor and cluster analyses.

Hersen and Last (1989) summarize reasons for behavioral assessors to integrate psychiatric-diagnosis processes into their clinical practice. Psychiatric diagnosis can (a) provide a fuller rendition of the complexity of a clinical problem or issue under consideration, (b) improve summary communication concerning dimensions of a patient beyond that offered by specific target selection and complementary guide for treatment, (c) allow more effective communication with other professionals, and (d) support the development of reliability and validity of psychiatric diagnoses and provide an opportunity to engage in development of structured and semistructured interview schedules. In addition, classification schemes theoretically can be employed to identify the most appropriate treatment strategies, assist in defining the legal status of the patient, and aid in the reimbursement process from third-party payers (Hersen & Last).

HISTORICAL PERSPECTIVE

Some means of classification has existed throughout the history of psychiatry (Sprock & Blashfield, 1983; Wiens & Matarazzo, 1983). Classification of childhood disorders is a much newer phenomenon. The Group for the Advancement of Psychiatry (GAP) categorical classification (1966) was the first major system applied to child and adolescent psychiatric disorders. Although it has been asserted that the *Diagnostic and Statistical Manual of Mental Disorders* (DSM-I) (American Psychiatric Association, 1952) had no special categories for child or adolescent psychopathology, a careful reading indicates that attention was given to disorders currently of concern to clinicians working with juveniles. These include schizophrenic reaction, childhood type; psychotic reactions manifesting primarily autism occurring before puberty; and adjustment reaction of infancy, of childhood, and of adolescence. The reactions were viewed as superficially resembling personality or psychoneurotic disorders and required differentiation from more serious disorders. There was reluctance to classify children with serious or chronic diagnoses.

Other DSM-I subcategories reflect current nomenclature: habit disturbance, "such as repetitive, simple activities;" conduct disturbance under which symptomatic manifestations, (e.g., truancy, use of alcohol, cruelty) were to be listed and could occur in home, school or community; and neurotic traits manifested "primarily as physical or emotional symptoms" (e.g., tics of nonorganic nature, phobias, overactivity, and somnambulism).

DSM-II (American Psychiatric Association, 1968) represented a marked advance in nosologic efforts. Specific categories of childhood disorders were derived from correlational studies of a large data set (Jenkins, 1971), which became the general rubric of Behavior Disorders of Childhood and Adolescence. Some categories are still in use, although with different names and more clearly defined criteria, such as overanxious, runaway, withdrawing, hyperkinetic, unsocialized aggressive, and group delinquent reactions. The category *schizophrenia, childhood type* remained. A section entitled "Special Symptoms" includes categories associated with specific childhood dysfunctions, with the symptom representing the criteria: speech disturbance, specific learning disturbance, tic, feeding disturbance, enuresis, and encopresis.

DSM-III and DSM-III-R (American Psychiatric Association, 1980, 1987) continued the evolution of categorical classification, with greater numbers of categories, explicit criteria and rules for each category, exclusionary criteria, and movement towards a polythetic approach. The polythetic approach of DSM-III-R and DSM-IV (American Psychiatric Association, 1993) permits the diagnosis after certain cutoff criteria are met. It expands underlying constructs by increasing the variety of ways a particular diagnosis can be made—the presence of a certain number of symptoms out of a list of commonly associated criteria became the basis of the diagnosis. This more flexible approach with broadened categories became the basis of the diagnosis, and has allowed greater ease in diagnosis and assures better reliability among clinicians. The monothetic approach of DSM-III requires that all of the criteria of particular diagnoses be met. It has been considered too rigid, with reliability depending on the least reliable of the criteria.

The advances of DSM-III in better reflecting contemporary research and improved structural consistency (Sprock & Blashfield, 1983) continue in the revised versions. The section "Disorders Usually First Evident in Infancy, Childhood or Adolescence" comprises the bulk of disorders generally diagnosed in child psychiatry. However, criteria from the remaining sections are employed to make the other diagnoses in juveniles, such as major depressive disorder (MDD), phobic disorders, obsessive-compulsive disorder (OCD), borderline personality disorder (BPD), and schizophrenia. Many of the improvements have been retained or further refined in currently available draft versions of DSM-IV. Introductory and contextual statements from DSM-III have been reinstated. Field trials played a major role in determining the required criteria. In addition, the childhood disorders are expected to be more compatible with those in the next draft of the International Classification of Disorders-10 (ICD-10).

DSM-IV remains a system of discrete disorders, even with significant overlap, as contrasted with the more global approach of the ICD-9 (WHO, 1977) (Shaffer, 1993). Caron and Rutter (1991) discuss many such issues, noting those related to comorbid diagnosis (i.e., the co-occurrence of two or more disorders considered independent of each other) have not been adequately addressed by either of the major classificatory systems. Impairment has been built into each diagnostic entity as necessary for meeting criteria, and significant modifications in criteria for the disruptive disorders have been introduced. Most criteria have been rewritten and simplified, but examples have been omitted (Shaffer, 1993). Several disorders arising in childhood or adolescence have been incorporated into such adult disorders as social phobia and generalized anxiety disorders.

With regard to assessment, prior to the availability of advances in classification systems, standardized testing, scientific knowledge of the intricate functioning of the brain, and medical understanding of psychiatric and neurological disorders, a discursive approach to the psychiatric interview was accepted practice early in the 20th century (Costello, 1991). The indirect approach became even more passive with the ascendancy of psychoanalysis. This particular psychodynamic approach remains the most widely taught and employed in child psychiatry. Greenspan (Greenspan & Greenspan, 1991) represents an eloquent proponent of this approach. An equally psychodynamic and more direct model of psychiatric interviewing has been advocated by Simmons (1987). Moreover, structured, criteria-based interviewing has increasingly become incorporated into parts of psychiatric interviews. A later section describes many currently available scales for this purpose. Direct observation beyond the mental status exam is beginning to be employed more frequently in research studies but has not become common practice. Diagnosis of disorders seen with infants is the exception.

DIAGNOSIS AND CLASSIFICATION

The diagnostic process requires a classificatory system within which to operate. Cantwell (1988) suggests that the diagnostic process is expected to address several critical questions:

1. Do the symptoms experienced by the child result in problems sufficient in severity and duration to result in disability or distress?

2. If disability exists, does it meet criteria for an established psychiatric disorder?

3. To what extent do the etiologic factors related to intrapsychic, biological, sociocultural, and family exist and function to maintain the disorder?

4. What facilitates the child's developing normally and to what extent do the competencies of the child and family operate?

5. If intervention is necessary, which types will likely be effective?

Garber (1984) depicts the lack of a reliable and well-defined system for classifying childhood disorders as a major obstacle to research on psychopathology of childhood. She and others (Peterson, Burbach, & Chaney, 1989) have decried the "adultomorphic classification" of current categorical schemes. The continuously changing nature of symptom presentation for the same child over time, the fluidity of normality, and the developmental thrust towards greater differentiation in children are in marked contrast to characteristic psychopathology in adults. Moreover, the child's dependence on the environment to varying degrees over the school-age years makes the context of the psychopathology's presentation quite unique as compared with that of teens or adults. Most classificatory systems fail to consider context and demands across various settings (Garber). This includes those which are behaviorally oriented (Kazdin, 1983).

Classification Systems

Categorical

It is generally agreed that there is no absolutely correct way to classify child psychiatric disorders (Achenbach, 1988; Cantwell, 1988; Rapoport, 1989; Rutter & Tuma, 1988; Volkmar, 1991). Most "official" diagnostic schema tend to be categorical (Volkmar). Psychiatric disorders are currently represented as deviant behavior resulting in dysfunction within an individual. Two formal categorical schemes of classifying childhood disorders guide most psychiatrists: the DSM-III-R and the ICD-9. Both attempt to adequately cover the range of psychopathology while still being parsimonious. DSM-III-R is intended to be useful for both clinical and research purposes.

Psychiatrists agree that categorical labels provide only a fraction of the critical information required to plan interventions and that the labels vary with the individual child, environment, and other related factors. Predictive and construct validity remain to be demonstrated (Volkmar, 1991). The DSM (III, III-R and IV) has become a theory-free system. As such, the clinician must turn to the ideographic systems for determination of etiology and formulation of the case.

From the behavioral perspective, Kazdin (1983) describes major advances in the DSM-III system, particularly around specification of criteria to facilitate achieving reliable diagnosis, and suggests that the clinician's task is to clarify the presence or absence of symptoms and then to apply the rules of classification. He notes obstacles and considerations in applying the DSM-III classification for diagnosis of childhood disorders (e.g., inadequate weight given to developmental stages and to the environment, which are not considered critical in adult disorders, and the greater difficulty children have reporting symptoms). Kazdin provides a guide to "diagnostic levels of understanding" to clarify concepts and terms and suggests that most behavioral clinicians fail to appreciate the value of distinguishing different levels of problems in child behavior therapy. He contrasts this to the medical view that distinguishes between diagnostic conceptual levels of understanding from symptom (an overt behavior, affect, percept, or cognition) to syndrome (constellation of symptoms), disorder (constellation of symptoms independent of other conditions) and disease, in which a known etiology or pathophysiology is known.

The reader is encouraged to consider several references that deal with the historical and conceptual issues more extensively. Schwab-Stone, Towbin, and Tarnoff (1991) provide a useful historical perspective and overview of rules to use DSM-III-R and ICD-10 and identify differences between them regarding operational definition or specificity of diagnoses. Cantwell (1988) considers the diagnostic process and the manner in which clinicians make diagnoses. He also considers the validity and the reliability of DSM-III diagnoses. A number of these and similar issues are detailed in Rutter, Tuma, and Lann (1988). Criticism of the categorical schemes includes the loss of information and the seemingly arbitrary nature of cut-off points (Achenbach, 1980; Rutter & Tuma, 1988). Rapoport and Ismond (1990) also provide a useful guide in the use of DSM-III-R with children and adolescents.

Dimensional

Achenbach (1980) argues that describing childhood psychopathology in terms of syndromes or a profile of scores on age-relevant or developmentally relevant dimensions would be the classificatory system of choice. He succinctly summarizes the methods by which this system, aided by computer technology, has provided a framework and instruments for developing dimensional models. Factor analysis (deriving factors or dimensions of items with high correlation between them) and cluster analysis (grouping items into mutually exclusive clusters) are among the multivariate methods available to yield syndromes for diagnosis.

Criticism of this system includes the cumbersome nature of applying dozens of dimensions to an individual rather than a few main categories and an inability to assume that consistency of meaning throughout the distribution of the variables exists (Rutter & Tuma, 1988). It also makes communication for clinical and research purposes difficult.

Ideographic

Given the broad scope of problem areas with which many child patients present, clinicians generally target a limited number of difficulties for treatment, difficulties that only partially relate to categorical or even dimensional diagnosis (Volkmar, 1991). An ideographic approach is useful in implementing certain types of therapies, such as psychodynamic or family therapies, but problematic beyond individual cases. Cone (1987), to the contrary, discusses the value of an ideographic behavior assessment approach to the development of an assessment science.

A major limitation of the ideographic approach is the difficulty in communicating information to other clinicians and third-party payers in a readily understandable fashion. The same holds for conveying research results in assessment and treatment of childhood disorders (Volkmar, 1991).

Assessment

Considerable commonality exists between traditional psychiatric assessment and behavioral assessment; both rely on the interview and establishment of a positive relationship for elicitation of the presenting problem (Wiens & Matarazzo, 1983). The classification model the clinician employs sets the approach to assessment and diagnosis. Even within that framework, an overriding issue may be the type of medical model guiding that endeavor. Psychiatrists employ differing types of models and concepts to assessment and diagnosis.

Engel (1980) describes the clinical application of a biopsychosocial model in which most psychiatric physicians attempt to organize their knowledge and approach to patients. An alternative medical model is the biomedical, which represents a classic factor-analytic application of scientific methodology. This latter model has been criticized for failing to perceive the patient as a person and for its inability to account for the individual's psychological and social nature by reducing psychopathology to physicochemical terms. The biopsychosocial model acknowledges the complementary roles and expectations of the doctor and patient. The model employed directly affects the nature of the data collection, the diagnostic formulation, and treatment.

Lewis (1991) provides a comprehensive, succinct overview of a biopsychosocially oriented psychiatric assessment of infants and children. He concentrates on the clinical interview predominantly as the arena for eliciting the mental status exam across the age spectrum. He suggests that advantages in employing the traditional psychiatric clinical interview include the opportunity to follow up on clinical clues and to utilize skills in defining critical issues. Disadvantages include questions of reliability of information gained, gathering of sufficient data to support or refute categorical and dimensional diagnoses, levels of disagreement among clinicians, and possible obscuring of relevant data derived from other sources.

Extensive training and experience are believed to be required to achieve the requisite level of skills for effective interviewing. Special techniques and foci are required for differing levels of age and cognitive levels of functioning (Lewis, 1991; Lewis & Volkmar, 1990; Simmons, 1987). Reports of parents or adult informants are essential to assess younger children, particularly regarding more externalizing symptoms (e.g., stealing, lying, aggressive or disruptive behaviors).

In psychodynamic assessment, the mission of the diagnostic interview is to elicit the maximum information about the child (Greenspan & Greenspan, 1991). The interviewer is expected to create a setting for that purpose. The unstructured interview is meant to allow "children to tell the stories in their own way," to put their own structure on the situation. The general principles for unstructured interviews are outlined as follows: The clinician (a) should tolerate the patient's and his or her own discomfort in order to allow the psychopathology to completely emerge and (b) should observe in all relevant developmental areas. In the Greenspan developmental approach, these areas include physical functioning (neurological, sensory, motor-integrative), pattern of relationships, affects, anxieties and fears, and thematic expression.

The Greenspan interview is divided into three phases. The opening phase focuses on the child's communicating his or her understanding of being there, views of the clinician, and understanding of the situation. "The job of the diagnostician is to make sense of what may seem like a series of disjointed themes . . . by observing the evolution of play, words, affect, gestures, and relatedness to you throughout the interview" (Greenspan & Greenspan, 1991, p. 158). In the closing phase, the clinician queries the child in a more structured fashion about issues of concern and observes the child's handling of separation. However, Greenspan views any structure imposed by the clinician early in the interview as a form of structured interview.

Several workers have commented on the lack of superiority of any single taxonomy of childhood disorders. Achenbach (1988) summarizes reasons for employing multiple methods for assessment of childhood psychopathology:

1. No single classification system can identify the child's disorder when specific etiologies are unknown.

2. Multiple aspects of the child's functioning along social-emotional, cognitive, biological, and academic developmental dimensions across multiple contexts from home and school to clinic and community must be considered for treatment planning.

3. Multiple methods must be employed for assessment because no single method is considered totally accurate or comprehensive.

Regardless of the model employed, the following are critical to the process: data gathering, including the reviewing of prior psychiatric and other medical evaluations, psychometric assessment, and academic records; rating scales completed by the child, parents, teachers, and other reporters; clinical interviews, which can vary greatly in approach and format; standardized assessments, including psychoeducational, developmental, neuropsychological, and projective testing; and special studies, which might include electroencephalogram (EEG), cardiogram, (ECG), neuroimaging, and endocrine or other metabolic, medical laboratory measures as needed.

THE ASSESSMENT AND DIAGNOSTIC PROCESS

The assessment and diagnostic process described here is not meant to be totally comprehensive, but to outline common features in evaluating a child from the psychiatric perspective. It is an amalgam of the approaches of Lewis (Lewis, 1991; Lewis & Volkmar, 1990) and Simmons (1987) blended with the experience of the authors.

Initial Contact

An initial contact form is often used to provide basic information about the patient, presenting problems, and related data. This would include the patient's name, the date of the initial contact, birth date of the child and age, identity of the informant, names of parents and phone numbers where each can be reached, the address of the parents and that of the child if it is different than the parents, the referral source, the patient's physician, the patient's legal status, and dates of prior health and mental health contacts. Prior to the session, parents may request directions as to what to tell the child about the evaluation. They are encouraged to share their concerns with the child in a loving and caring way.

Beginning the Evaluation and Conducting the Interview

Efforts are made to ensure that both parents (or primary caretakers) are present for the first meeting. Some clinicians prefer to interview the parents without the child about reasons for referral. Others prefer to interview the family as a unit, with everyone's view of the problem and possible solutions elicited. This begins to lay the groundwork for working together in understanding and eventual resolution of any problems.

Explaining the evaluation process helps to allay anxiety and to provide assurances about opportunities for individual time with the clinician regarding confidential matters. Confidentiality is assured unless there is potential danger to someone or the evaluation involves an outside party (e.g., a judge).

In the authors' experience, 2 to 3 hours for the diagnostic process suffice in laying groundwork for understanding the child and family, discussing the possible causes of the problem, and determining requirements for further evaluation or deciding upon treatment modalities. The manner in which family members relate prior to entering the office and behavior in the office toward the interviewer and toward one another are of interest. Assessment of family dynamics may provide understanding of the roles of each family member in the development and maintenance of the problem and is useful in conceptualizing treatment.

At the initial session, everyone's understanding of reasons for the evaluation is elicited. The affect accompanying the response, the tone of voice, reactions and attitude of the people in the room, evidence of scapegoating, and other dynamics in relations between family members are noted. During this initial part of the evaluation, clarification is obtained concerning questions raised from the initial contact form, self-report surveys, records, and other sources of information obtained prior to the session. This could include a listing of all family members, their ages, years of schooling, types of employment and means of support, and legal status. Clarifying who is responsible for authorizing treatment is critical.

Understanding the parents' expectations of the evaluation and their agenda helps clarify problems with reliability and validity of elicited material; for example, parents seeking confirmation or refutation of a previous evaluation or diagnosis will present the clinical picture differently than those expecting the interviewer to fix all the problems immediately. Likewise, parents allowing evaluation only because it is demanded by the school, court, or Child Protective Services require a different approach.

Course of Symptoms

The course of symptoms delineates the specific problem for which the family has been referred. Delineating this from other aspects of the child's life may be difficult. Comorbidity, the presence of another independent disorder, is not unusual in childhood disorders. Therefore, it is important to note precisely why the referral was made at this time and to consider both the more acute difficulties and any persistent problems, such as if a child or adolescent is reacting to a physical illness or a learning disability.

The following are considered and recorded as clearly and concisely as possible:

Major concerns of each parent and the child.

Onset and chronological progression of symptoms.

Related areas of difficulty.

Precipitating or exacerbating events/stresses.

Level of current functioning, with areas of impairment and strengths.

Impact of symptoms on others.

Generalization of symptoms across settings.

Treatments/interventions instituted and results.

The clinician at this point has begun to develop a set of hypotheses or diagnoses, which often dictates the type of data and observations to be sought.

Background Information

The clinician will then work to clarify further aspects of an individual's history in light of the diagnoses being considered. These aspects include the following:

Developmental History

Depending on the nature of the presenting complaint, the developmental history may include data concerning:

1. Characteristics of the pregnancy (e.g., planned or unplanned, gestational duration, prenatal care, complications at birth, APCAR score) (Green, 1992).

2. Achievement of developmental milestone (e.g., walking without support, first words and phrases, response to adults, extent of eye contact with the parent, and toilet training) (Lewis, 1991; Lewis & Volkmar, 1990).

3. Details of any regressive periods and associated circumstances (e.g., moving to a

new home or school, new baby, deaths or losses in the family) can assist in understanding the possible precipitating events and factors maintaining a particular symptom or symptom complex.

4. The presence and timing of particular habits, fears, or other difficulties and the extent to which they were age appropriate. (The parents' understanding of the degree to which difficulties are age appropriate is another key area for inquiry.)

Past Medical History

Because diagnosis of many of the major psychiatric disorders in children requires that an organic or biological disorder is not a cause, inquiry is made concerning the following:

1. All prior illnesses, surgeries, allergies, accidents, medications, and emotional problems.

2. Biological functions (e.g., appetite, sleep, bladder and bowel control, sexual development).

3. Immunization status to provide an estimate of concern and care that the family has for their children.

4. Results of most recent physical exam. If none reported within the last year or since problem onset, a physical exam should be done.

5. Inquiry about alcohol, smoking, or street drug use (by both child and family members). This is critical when interviewing the older child with recent change in behavior and functioning, particularly with a history of prior episodes of depression or conduct disorder symptoms.

Strayhorn (1987) offers compelling reasons for including the medical assessment in the overall evaluation of a child with behavioral problems. Likewise, Woodbury, DeMaso, and Goldman (1992) report the presence of organic illness in more than 25% of children presenting with conversion symptoms. Again, the type and nature of the presenting problems and clinical picture dictate the extent to which the psychiatrist or other clinician manages the border between hyper- and hypovigilance concerning medical problems. Ruling out an organic illness and its contribution to the psychiatric presentation is never complete. The medical differentiation of psychiatric disorders is often demanding due to the complex presentation and complexity of the diagnoses that can be considered. Beyond mandates specified for as criteria in a number of psychiatric disorders in DSM III–IV, general guidelines to initiate exploration of organic contributions to the symptom complex (Strayhorn, 1987) include:

1. Presence of physical complaints or symptoms.
2. Degree of functional impairment. The greater the impairment in functioning, the more likely an organic contribution.
3. Loss of prior intellectual ability or memory.
4. Little other explanation for the clinical picture.

School History

A child's response to school situations, particularly entering or changing schools, affects the differential diagnosis in many disorders. The need to repeat a grade or requiring special assistance or special classes helps in delineating subtle developmental disabilities or disruptive disorders. The number of prior schools the child has attended helps estimate the degree of family stability and psychosocial stress.

History of Other Evaluations

A history of many prior evaluations raises possibilities of doctor shopping, noncompliance with recommendations, denial of problems, personality clashes, or multiple family moves. It can shape the approach to intervention. Permission is requested to contact the clinicians and obtain summaries from each.

Social History

Exploration of the social history places the child's problems into a developmental/social context and allows the psychiatrist to begin to formulate a conceptualization for diagnosis and treatment planning. Elicitation of the following data is crucial to understanding the etiology and maintenance of many childhood disorders and to estimating the degree to which change of the situation is desired and feasible:

1. Significant events (e.g., separations, losses, illnesses, deaths, accidents, moves).

2. Family constellation (e.g., current and past composition and "blending,") extent of socialization (e.g., eating meals or viewing TV together or separately, the person designated as "in charge" versus who is actually in charge), and rules for the home.

3. Disciplinary practices and consequences for breaking rules. Extent to which parents are either over- or undercontrolling, work together or apart in setting rules and consequences.

4. Nature of life for the patient and family outside of home and school (e. g., involvement in church or community, type and safety of the neighborhood and relations with neighbors, expectations for the child, extent of the family's activities together, and the child's social life outside the family). Delineating nature and number of friends and the degree of comfort of other family members with the relationships.

5. Living and sleeping arrangements.

Family History

A comprehensive family history may provide clues to pertinent classes of diseases or disorders. Each side of the family tree is explored for psychiatric disorders that have occurred in biological relatives. Medical diseases are investigated.

Mental Status Exam

The mental status exam provides a cross-sectional view of the child's current level of functioning for diagnosis and against which treatment and progress can be measured. Appearance, affect and mood, speech, language, thought processes, thought content (including fears, worries, compulsions, hallucinations, delusions, illusions, suicidal or homicidal ideation), cognitive functioning and orientation, and degree of dangerousness comprise the major components. The interview is meant to provide impressions of the child, including clinical inferences about levels of functioning, and establishing a therapeutic relationship; obtaining specific information is an ancillary objective. Limitations include low reliability for children and low agreement with data obtained from parents (Achenbach, 1988).

Lewis (1991, p. 452) describes the following critical areas and elaborates on each as to its role in the diagnostic and assessment process:

1. Physical appearance
2. Separation
3. Manner of relating
4. Orientation to time, place, and person
5. Central nervous system functioning
6. Reading and writing
7. Speech and language
8. Intelligence
9. Memory
10. Quality of thinking and perception
11. Fantasies, feelings, and inferred conflicts
12. Affects
13. Object relations
14. Drive behavior
15. Defense organization
16. Positive attributes

Observations and responses of the child, from the time seen with the parent(s) to the end of the interview, provide data for the mental status exam. The child's relatedness to family members and the interviewer is extremely important. Reading, writing, and drawing provide insight into general cognitive and motor functioning. Dysfunction in appropriate use of vocabulary, in comprehension of language and basic arithmetic, and in measures of memory can be due to anxiety, depression, psychotic processes, or to an organic etiology, and further testing is sometimes required for diagnosis.

Inquiry about three wishes the child would like to have provides insight into the child's fantasy life as well as into areas of major concern. Allowing the child to elaborate about each allows a fleshing out of possible underlying dynamics and areas of concern for therapy and future interventions.

Hallucinations and delusions are sometimes difficult to differentiate in children. Their presence compels the psychiatrist to consider an organic process (e.g., an overdose of medication/drugs, poisoning, infection epilepsy, or brain tumor) or a psychotic process (e.g., schizophrenic disorder or psychotic depression), although the differential must include intrusive thoughts as in a number of other nonpsychotic disorders (e.g., flashbacks of a posttraumatic stress disorder, perceptual illusion, dissociative phenomenon, or an overly active fantasy life). The presence of thought blocking also suggests a psychotic versus a dissociative process.

Having the child draw a person (Goodenough, 1926; Harris, 1963; Koppitz, 1968) or a kinetic family drawing (Burns, 1982) permits an estimate of mental age related to motor development and family interactions, respectively. Requesting a story also allows entrance into the child's fantasy life and a window into concerns and worries.

Parent Evaluation

Insight into the family situation follows from the overall assessment. Multiple approaches are available for more formal assessment. These vary from observations of the parents interacting with each other and with the children to and including interviewing each parent alone at some point (Simmons, 1987). The parents' personal histories, including sketches of their upbringing, family life, peer relationships, history of abuse or other trauma, losses, and coping mechanisms, assume importance in many but not all cases. Dynamics in the parents' families of origin may be critical in planning for treatment and comprehending problems encountered in implementing interventions.

An understanding of a parent's own mental or emotional state (e.g., depressed, angry, schizophrenic, delusional, or guilt ridden) provides pathways for developing further hypotheses. The extent to which parents perceive and show sensitivity to the child's needs and the "goodness of fit" between the parent and child (Turecki & Tonner, 1985) are critical components in clarifying the diagnosis and developing treatment strategies.

Psychological Assessment

Standardized data across a number of domains, from intellectual, educational, language, neuropsychological, adaptive, and personality dimensions, may be required. Requested testing or questions often relate to cognitive capacity, defense mechanisms, dynamics, or other issues not readily elicited in the traditional psychiatric assessment interview or with currently available structured or semistructured interviews. This aspect has been widely described (see Gittleman, 1980; Hynd, 1988; Keogh & Margolis, 1991; Racusin & Moss, 1991) and is beyond the scope of this review.

Prior Evaluations and School-Related Information

Summaries from prior evaluations and courses of treatment can be major contributors to the diagnostic process. Evaluations from the school (e.g., information from the school counselor or teacher by phone or through questionnaires, and records of grades and test results) assist to determine particular areas of weakness or strength. The school's view of the situation may be totally different from that of the family. School personnel should be asked to comment on their knowledge of parental involvement with the child, the child's interactions with peers, strengths, weaknesses, or areas to work for change. The use of standardized teacher report instruments as described later under Standardized Forms is encouraged.

Direct Observations

Reid, Patterson, Baldwin, and Dishion (1988) summarize many of the limitations associated with the standard psychiatric interview. They provide a succinct overview of the role of observational assessment in the diagnostic process. The characteristics of this component include use of specific, preset, and finite categories observed over specified time periods and at specified settings. Observations by teachers, parents, or staff are considered the most economical method to conduct observational assessment. This method allows monitoring on accuracy and reliability of collected data. Bias on the part of the observer can invalidate the data. Observations by independent, trained observers allow precise descriptions of the behavior in question and to "better distinctions and classifications in child disorders" (Reid et al., p. 159–160). Many types of methods to support this approach can be employed. Examples include pencil-and-paper checklists (including optic scannable sheets), audio recording, clocks, counters and digital keyboards, and event recorders.

ASSESSMENT INSTRUMENTS

While the clinical interview remains the mainstay of the diagnostic process, there is increasing use of semistructured and structured interviews and standardized report forms to further refine diagnostic certainty, particularly in research endeavors. As diagnostic criteria have become more explicit and taxonomies more differentiated, a more standardized approach to assessment of symptoms has evolved (Edelbrock & Costello, 1988).

Structured and Semistructured Interviews

Structured interviews for adults were developed in the 1960s and 1970s in response to a need for a standardized approach to interview content, techniques, and recording format (Young, O'Brien, Gutterman, & Cohen, 1987). There has been subsequent emphasis on developing and refining diagnostic schedules for children and adolescents. Due to a variety of factors that interact simultaneously (interview structure, informant variables, and interviewer variables), the clinical interview may produce erroneous or incomplete information. Edelbrock and Costello (1988) list the following advantages of structured interviewing over such standard methods as direct observation, paper-and-pencil questionnaires, and psychological testing: establishing rapport and maintaining interest; clarifying misunderstandings; documenting the context and chronicity of the disorder; resolving ambiguity; and eliciting child self-report data.

The information gathered in the typical clinical interview is influenced by such considerations as a lack of specificity or unwarranted assumptions in many questions and the wording or structure of the questions (Petti, Kane, & Lipton, 1973). The informant may not understand the question, may feel the need to give socially desirable answers, may have varying perceptions of the situation and purpose, or may feel stressed by the questioning. Interviewers may record incorrectly, may have their own preferences or biases, or may have variable understanding of the questions asked (Young et al., 1987). Semistructured interviews provide general and flexible interviewer guidelines and coding directions. They require greater degrees of training and prior clinical experience because the interviewer must make inferences during the course of the interview. Highly structured interviews specify exact wording and coding of each item, require less training and clinical experience, and leave little opportunity for inference by the interviewer (Edelbrock & Costello, 1988).

Structured interviews within the assessment process allow for a more comprehensive coverage of areas that might not ordinarily be considered in a clinical interview. In addition, they allow diagnostic homogeneity in approach to research and/or epidemiological populations. However, they may only cover limited diagnostic categories or consider many more categories than are applicable to the individual child, making for a lengthy interview process (Costello, 1991).

Several structured or semistructured psychiatric interviews are currently available for use in clinical or research settings with children. Edelbrock and Costello (1988) provide a comprehensive review of a number of such scales, systematically considering item content, response scaling, administration time, degree of structure, informant, age range, interviewer experience, training, alternate forms, information yield, psychometric properties (reliability and validity), and applications. Multiple questions about the reliability and validity of structured interviews and standardized instruments have been raised. These include inaccurate reporting by the child and/or parent informant for a number of reasons, including distortions or lapses in memory, cognitive and language abilities, extent of psychopathology, primary or secondary gain to be derived from someone being labeled *disturbed*, different awareness of affect/thought/behavior, and differing manifestations of the disorder across settings. Such threats to reliability and validity need to be addressed when standardized assessments are employed.

Each representative instrument described in the following paragraphs has undergone multiple revisions, is based on extensive empirical experience, generates DSM-III or DSM-III-R diagnoses, and uses parent and child informants. All have good test-retest reliability (repeat identical interview elicits same information from child or parent) or inter-rater reliability (different raters obtain the same information from the same interview stimuli). All have face validity (experts judge that the interview gives authentic diagnostic information, covering the criteria adequately) and content validity (interview assesses the intended range of diagnoses appropriately and accurately, as indicated by a match of questions or ratings to the specified criteria) (Orvaschel, 1985; Young et al., 1987).

Highly structured scales are the Diagnostic Interview for Children and Adolescents (DICA; Herjanic & Reich, 1982; Reich, Herjanic, Welner, & Gandhy, 1982; Welner, Reich, Herjanic, Jung, & Amado, 1987) and the Diagnostic Interview Schedule for Children (DISC; Cohen, Velez, Kohn, Schwab-Stone, & Johnson, 1987; Costello, Edelbrock, & Costello, 1985; Schwab-Stone et al., 1993). Semistructured instruments include the Kiddie Schedule for Affective Disorders and Schizophrenia (K-SADS; Ambrosini, Metz, Prabucki, & Lee, 1989; Chambers, et al., 1985; Orvaschel, Puig-Antich, Chambers, Tabrizi, & Johnson, 1982), the Child Assessment Schedule (CAS; Hodges, 1987; Hodges, Saunders, Kashani, Hamlett, & Thompson, 1990), and the Interview Schedule for Children (ISC; Kovacs, 1985a). Each interview was developed with different purposes in mind. Therefore, instruments are selected based on the diagnostic needs of the clinician or investigator and not upon the inherent superiority of one instrument over another.

The K-SADS and ISC are arranged with items grouped together as they relate to a certain diagnosis. The CAS, DICA, and DISC have questions ordered according to domains of activity in a child's life (family, friends, school) with questions regarding emotional and behavioral difficulties grouped in the most pertinent domain. All use a branching format; additional items such as onset and duration are inquired about only if a symptom is present. Therefore, children with numerous symptoms and problem behaviors require more interviewing time (Gutterman, O'Brien, & Young, 1987).

Edelbrock considered the impact of developmental maturity on the reliability of symptom scores over time (two interviews over a 1–3 week period) and found that reliability of scores increases with age. In general, the lower limit for structured interviews is 6 to 8 years of age and the upper limit is 16 to 18 years (Edelbrock, Costello, Dulcan, Kalas, & Conover, 1985).

The DICA is a highly structured interview modeled after the Diagnostic Interview Schedule and is useful in clinical and epidemiological research. It requires little exercise of clinical judgment by the interviewer and can be administered by trained lay observers or clinicians (Orvaschel, 1985). The interviewer may need to use judgment on how to follow up on certain items. It has been revised multiple times and currently generates DSM-III-R and ICD-9 diagnoses as well as summary scores that group symptoms. It is designed for use with children ages 6 to 16 and with parents (DICA-C[child] and DICA-P[parent], respectively); the interviews take 60 to 90 minutes each. The questions are organized by syndrome in a skip structure with items coded *present* or *absent*. The questions are phrased in the present tense for children. The instrument yields a wide range of information on symptom onset, duration, and severity as well as associated impairment (Costello, 1991). Rules for combining data from the different sources provide guidelines as to priority scoring when discrepancies arise (Reich & Earls, 1987).

The DICA was found to have good inter-interviewer agreement and good agreement between DICA-C and chart diagnoses. Parent-child agreement based on the DICA-C and DICA-P showed a good to moderate agreement for most DSM-III categories (Welner et al., 1987).

The DISC was developed primarily for epidemiological studies. It is the most highly structured instrument with predetermined wording of questions, order of presentation, and method of recording (Costello, 1991). It may be administered by lay or clinician raters. Training to administer the tests takes 2 to 3 days to complete. There are parent and child versions. The child version takes 45 to 60 minutes to administer; the parent version with more items takes 60 to 70 minutes. The interview covers the past year. Symptom items are coded 0 (*no* or *never*), 1 (*somewhat, sometimes*, or *a little*) or 2 (*yes, often*, or *a lot*). Computerized diagnoses are available (Costello, 1991; Dulcan, 1993).

Parent-child agreement between symptom scores for the DISC is fair (Edelbrock, Costello, & Dulcan, 1986). Agreement is highest for disruptive disorders and lowest for depressive and anxiety symptoms. Test-retest reliability at 7 to 14 days is good for parent reports (Edelbrock, Costello, & Duncan, 1986). It was greater for children aged 14 to 18 than for children aged 6 to 9 (Edelbrock, Costello, Duncan, Kalas, & Conover, 1985).

The K-SADS was developed by Puig-Antich and associates (Chambers et al., 1985). It was designed primarily to diagnose affective disorders. There are two versions available—one covers current episodes and the other covers current and past episodes. This instrument was designed to be administered by experienced interviewers. It allows for the interviewer to adapt questions to the respondent and also to make further probes as deemed necessary (Costello, 1991). There is no requirement regarding the order of questions; the interviewer can choose appropriate probes for each symptom (Gutterman et al., 1987).

The structure of the K-SADS follows a clinical format. The instrument was designed to be administered to the parent first. The first part of the interview elicits all presenting problems and symptoms. History of present illness and current symptoms are established by the first part of the interview. The second part of the interview elicits treatment history and includes questions in approximately 200 areas of symptomatology relevant to diagnosis. The third section includes observational items rated by the interviewer and a rating of the Global Assessment of Functioning (Children's Version). Diagnoses are arrived at by summary of the clinician's ratings. Computerized diagnoses are not available (Costello, 1991).

The CAS was developed by Hodges and associates (see Hodges, 1987) to cover ages 6 to 12. There is a form available for parents. Each section takes approximately 45 to 60 minutes to administer. It covers most childhood psychiatric diagnoses and generates DSM-III diagnoses. Specific interview training is required, but the interviewers need not be child mental health clinicians (Costello, 1991). The CAS is structured to include three parts. The first includes 75 items grouped by topic (not syndrome) covering the preceding 6 months. The child is asked questions about several content areas, including school, friends, activities and hobbies, family, fears, worries, self-image, mood, somatic concerns, anger expression, and questions aimed at eliciting thought disorder symptoms. The second part records onset and duration of symptoms. In the third part, the interviewer rates observational items. It is possible to substitute the CAS for the typical interview done with children in the evaluation process because it was developed from a traditional clinical interview (Costello, 1991; Hodges, McKnew, Burbach, & Roebuck, 1987). Adequate concordance was demonstrated between the CAS and the K-SADS in an outpatient setting for the parent interview and in combinations of the parent and child interviews for DSM-III diagnoses of conduct disorder, affective disorders, and attention deficit disorder (Hodges et al., 1987).

The ISC may be used with children 8 and up. It must be administered by clinically skilled individuals and requires extensive specific interview training. The ISC begins with an unstructured section to establish rapport and elicit current problems. The mother or care giver is interviewed first and then the child. The parent interview requires 90 to 120 minutes; the child interview requires 45 to 60 minutes. Forty-three symptoms are recorded and rated on a scale from 0 to 8. The interviewer then rates 12 observational items and dictates a clinical summary (Costello, 1991).

Standardized Forms

The psychiatric assessment of a child or adolescent usually depends heavily on information obtained from multiple sources including family members, caretakers, and teachers, as well as reports from the subject. Many rating scales and assessment instruments have been developed to assist in this process; some of the more frequently used will be considered. The majority of these are easily administered in the clinical, home, or community setting and provide the clinician with valuable additional information about the individual and family being assessed.

Dimensional Measures

Perhaps one of the most widely used, and certainly one of the more extensively researched, rating forms is the set of three profiles developed by Achenbach that includes the Child Behavior Checklist/4–18 (CBCL/4–18), the Youth Self Report (YSR), and the Teacher Report Form (TRF). As children's behavior is often different in the various settings of their lives (e.g., home vs. school), it is essential to coordinate observations across contexts. Achenbach's rating forms provide a systematic method of gathering this information.

The CBCL/4–18 (blue form) is completed by parents or parenting figures and provides descriptions of the competencies and behavioral/emotional problems of children ages 4 to 18 years (Achenbach, 1991). Informants must have at least a fifth-grade reading level. The form is available in 32 languages and takes about 15 minutes to complete. Sports, hobbies, clubs, chores, friendships, academic performance, and physical assets over the preceding 6 months comprise areas of competence. Problem items covering a considerable range of psychopathology are numbered 1 to 113 and include some open-ended items for reporting problems not already covered in the list. The sample has been formed on outpatient-clinic and community populations. A reanalysis may be required if an attempt is being made to use this dimensional approach with psychiatrically hospitalized populations (Nurcombe et al., 1989). A modification of the CBCL has been developed for use with hospitalized children (Kolko, 1988). This is important because few standardized and validated measures to evaluate hospitalized children exist (Kazdin & Bass, 1988).

The YSR (gold form) is administered to youth ages 11 to 18. Norms are not available for children younger than 11 years; the form assumes a mental age of at least 10 years, requires fifth grade reading skills, and takes about 15 minutes to complete. The TRF (green form) is filled out by the child's teacher and gives descriptions of academic functioning, emotional/behavioral problems, and adaptive functioning as seen in the school setting. Scoring norms are available for children ages 5 to 18. Eighty-nine items have counterparts on all three instruments (Achenbach, 1991).

Hand- or computer-scoring profiles are available for each form. The profiles generate scores in two major areas: (a) competence (CBCL and YSR) or adaptive functioning (TRF) and (b) core syndrome scales. There are eight core syndrome scales generated; these are grouped according to internalizing factors (withdrawn, somatic complaints, anxious/depressed), externalizing factors (delinquent behavior, aggressive behavior) and three additional scales, thought problems, social problems, and attention problems. These last three scales did not demonstrate high loadings on the internalizing or externalizing factors. T scores are generated for the internalizing and externalizing factors; a T score of 70 or greater is considered clinically significant (Achenbach, 1991).

Adaptive Functioning

Many instruments to assess adaptive functioning are available. Each has its own set of properties and reporters, ranging from teachers, parents, and counselors to treatment staff and probation officers. These scales provide one means to approximate a global level of functioning for Axis V of the DSM III, III-R, and IV classification system. An extensive review has been compiled by Orvaschel and Walsh (1984). These scales attempt to depict the interpersonal and intrapersonal life of the child, comprising peer relations, self-concept, and school, family, and leisure functioning. They include rating scales and checklists, interview schedules, direct observation, and peer-nomination inventories. The most widely currently used scales are the Global Assessment of Functioning (GAF) Scale (American Psychiatric Association, 1987) and the Children's Global Assessment Scale (CGAS; Shaffer et al., 1983). Both provide a measure of the highest level of functioning over a given time span. The CGAS rates only the lowest level of functioning over a time span. The decile of 100–91 represent superior functioning in all areas; that of 50–41 represents severe impairment of functioning in an area or moderate degree of interference in most social areas; 10–1 represents the need for constant supervision.

Both scales rely heavily on the clinical picture and represent more of a severity measure of psychopathology than of adaptive functioning. The Social Adjustment Inventory for Children and Adolescents (SAICA; John, Gammon, Prusoff, & Warner, 1987) is a semistructured interview that measures social functioning in school, spare-time activities, peer relations, and home life. It is meant to address developmentally relevant behaviors in each of the major areas. The Health-Sickness Rating Scale for Children (MSRS-C) (Liebowitz, Rembar, Kernberg, Frankel, & Kruger, 1988) is a global rating scale that seems anchored to the level of functioning and extent of intervention required.

Family Assessment

Collection of family-related information by instruments with normative values can be a helpful adjunct to the assessment process. Several family-assessment instruments and methods are available for the study of childhood psychopathology and may be applicable to clinical practice. The three organizing dimensions suggested by Jacob and Tennenbaum (1988) are the family unit, the source of information, and the major constructs being measured. The last one includes affect (as related to satisfaction, support, and nurturance in the relationship), control ("processes by which parents attempt to control and shape behavior . . . during early childhood and adolescence"), communication (patterns correlated with psychopathology, family problem solving), and systems properties (features typifying relationships within the family and extrafamilial relations influencing family functioning). Instruments have generally been either questionnaires or direct-observation measures.

The Family Environment Scale (FES) (Moos & Moos, 1981) was developed and piloted in the late 1970s to provide a meaningful assessment of family climate. It consists of 10 subscales that measure social-environmental characteristics of all types of families and is available in three forms. The scale considers three sets of dimensions: relationship, personal growth, and system maintenance. Each of these dimensions is measured by various subscales. The relationship dimensions are measured by the Cohesion, Expressiveness, and Conflict subscales. These subscales evaluate the degree of help and support family members provide each other, the degree of permission to express feelings openly, and the amount of conflict that is openly expressed. The personal growth dimensions are measured by the Independence, Achievement Orientation, Intellectual-Cultural Orientation, Active-Recreational Orientation, and Moral-Religious Emphasis subscales. Each of these subscales measures the degree to which these areas are promoted within the family. The system maintenance dimensions are assessed via the Organization and Control subscales. These assess the importance families place on clear organization and structure, rules, and procedure to run family life (Moos & Moos, 1981).

More comprehensive discussion and reviews of family-assessment methodologies are available (see Jacob & Tennenbaum, 1988). None of the measures adequately discriminate between the variables believed critical to family functioning and their relationship to childhood disorders (Achenbach, 1988; Jacob & Tennenbaum, 1988).

Symptoms Complexes

Childhood rating scales have been developed for a broad array of symptom complexes, including the disruptive behavior disorders, anxiety disorders, affective disorders, eating disorders, and autistic symptoms. A special issue of *Psychopharmacology Bulletin* (Rapoport, Conners, & Reatig, 1985) provides an extensive description of such instruments available for research and clinical use with children.

Affective symptoms may be assessed in a number of ways with a large selection of reliable instruments (Petti, 1985). The widely used Children's Depression Inventory (CDI; Kovacs, 1985b) is a self-report instrument for school-age children and adolescents, written at a first-grade reading level. It covers a range of depressive symptoms, including mood, sleep, appetite, interpersonal interactions, and activity level, as well as how the child perceives his school functioning. Each of the 27 items has three alternatives; the child is asked to select the one that best describes how they have felt over the last 2 weeks. The person administering the instrument may read the items aloud while the child reads along and marks answers on their copy. Item choices reflect least to greatest severity; for example, the alternatives for the first item read as follows: "I am sad once in awhile, I am sad many times, or I am sad all the time." The total score can range from 0 to 54; any score above 19 is considered clinically significant, while scores above 11 merit further attention

(Kovacs, 1985b). The CDI is best used as a severity rating instrument in conjunction with other assessment procedures and not as a diagnostic tool. It has value as an index of change during treatment (Kovacs, 1985b). Other rating scales for depression are both self-support and interview based (Kazdin & Petti, 1982; Petti, 1985). Rating scales for mania and manic behavior are also available (Fristad, Weller, & Weller, 1992).

Barkley (1988, 1990) reviews a number of child behavior checklists and rating scales considering their underlying assumptions, advantages, and issues related to their use; for example, a variety of symptoms may be assessed by parents and teachers via the Conners Parent Rating Scale (revised and abbreviated versions of this scale are in wide use) and the Conners Teacher Rating Scale (also available in revised and abbreviated forms). These scales have been extensively researched with regard to reliability and validity. The Conners Parent and Teacher Rating Scales both contain items pertaining to conduct problems, hyperactivity, and inattention and are widely used to document baseline symptomatology and response to treatment (particularly medication trials) in children who present with these symptoms. The Parent Rating Scale also contains items pertaining to aggression, anxiety, somatic complaints, fears/phobias, obsessive-compulsive symptoms, and school adjustment as perceived by the parent. The age range for use of the revised scales is 3 to 17 years (Conners & Barkley, 1985).

Children's Play

Many assessment instruments based on the evaluation of children's play have been developed. Most are primarily research tools but may also have practical clinical value. The reader is referred to *Play Diagnosis and Assessment* (Schaefer, Gitlin, & Sandgrund, 1991) for a comprehensive review of the subject. The Kiddie Formal Thought Disorder Rating Scale (K-FTDS) and Story Game were developed (Caplan & Sherman, 1991) in response to a need for assessing formal thought disorder in children within developmental guidelines and norms. DSM-III criteria for formal thought disorder (illogical thinking, loose associations, incoherence, and poverty of content of speech) were operationalized. A Story Game was developed to obtain speech samples for measuring formal thought disorder using the K-FTDS. The story game requires 20 to 25 minutes to administer. The K-FTDS can be used in differentiating children with schizotypal personality disorder or childhood schizophrenia (Caplan & Sherman).

Psychobiological Measures

Psychobiological approaches to support or refute diagnostic formulations are experiencing a resurgence of attention. This arena may prove of great utility as the taxonomic system becomes more specific. Interesting correlations between certain biological markers and specific psychiatric disorders have been reported (Botteron, Figier, Wetzel, Hudziak, & VanEerdewegh, 1992; Galvin, Shekhar, Simon, Stilwell, & Ten Eyck, 1991; Puig-Antich, et al., 1984; Rogeness, Javors, & Pliszka, 1992). At this time, their use is limited (Ryan & Dahl, 1993).

FORMULATION

The formulation represents the integration of the assessment process—a pulling together of the material into a brief, concise paragraph. Generally included are the child's age, grade, intellectual level, a description of the problem, and biological substrates known or suspected (i.e., preexisting conditions). Stressors, exacerbations, coping mechanisms or adaptive behaviors, and positive attributes of both child and parents are listed. The role of family and factors that can be changed or are expected to remain unchanged are described. The requisites for change to occur and potential interventions to assist in change are designated.

SUMMARY AND FUTURE DIRECTIONS

Assessment and diagnosis of child psychiatric disorders have been rapidly developing over the past decade. Advances in taxonomy as related to diagnoses with adults have contributed significantly to this progress. As criteria have been made more explicit, standardized assessment instruments with good reliability have been developed. There has been increasing emphasis on obtaining data with multiple methods (Achenbach, 1988) and from multiple sources and on both differentiating and evaluating the sources of variance in that process (Reich & Earls, 1987). These advances can be expected to accelerate. The role of development on the presentation and assessment of psychopathology in children will be subject to increasing examination. Instruments depicting functioning from infancy through school age will be developed in this process (Peterson, Burbach, & Chaney, 1989).

The future will also witness greater integration of the various approaches to classification, with the multivariate approach deeply embedded in the more traditional categorical schema. This synthesis should allow improved treatment planning and less reliance on ideographic conceptualizations. However, consideration of etiology and forces maintaining the disordered behavior, affect, and cognitions will remain critical for understanding prognosis and response to treatment. There is a need to resolve the blurring of overlap between populations with and without a psychiatric disorder (Zarin & Earls, 1993) and of diagnostic classification distinctions between disorders that are single and complex (i.e. ICD-9) and multiple independent disorder diagnoses with similar symptom complexes (i.e. DSM-III and IV) (Rutter & Tuma, 1988). Advances in outcome research and epidemiology should lead the way. The shifts of focus toward a disease-based model of childhood disorders that have allowed for greater specificity of diagnosis and exploration of biopsychosocial predictors (Costello & Benjamin, 1989) will be enhanced as psychosocial and risk factors are identified.

Active efforts are underway to identify patterns of risk and possible causal mechanisms, including the interaction of genes at the molecular level with the internal and external environment of the child at high risk for developing major psychiatric disorders (NIMH Molecular Genetics of Psychiatric Disorders Initiative Child Study Group, 1993). This parsimonious approach to refining efforts at classification holds great hope for the future. Until the predictive validity of psychiatric disorders is established, clinicians and researchers alike must avoid taking arbitrary stands about a "true" system of diagnosis (Rapoport, 1989) and must continue to proceed in as scientific a manner as possible. Rules for managing the accompanying diagnostic uncertainty in clinical and research practice must be made explicit (Zarin & Earls, 1993). This may be especially true in reporting psychiatric research into childhood disorders when structured interviews have been employed (Zarin & Earls).

Increased emphasis on direct behavioral assessment will assist in the overall process, as will the more active delineation of related cognitions and physiological aspects (Cone,

1987). The complementary benefit to behavioral therapists who employ psychiatric diagnosis and report diagnostic information will be more effective integration of learning theory into the clinical work of psychiatry and greater acceptance of the efficacy of behavioral therapies (Kazdin, 1983). The practice of behavioral therapists can also be expected to become more efficacious as a number of dimensions beyond the observable target behavior presented for treatment are considered in the diagnostic process.

Efforts will also be made to address problems associated with the DSM system attempting to be all inclusive, that is to sorting out the multiple roles that a categorical approach must fulfill and to finding consensus around defining the value of particular classification schema for differing purposes in different settings. Means must be developed to address the problematic nature of illnesses with varied presentations of symptoms over time (Hornstein & Putnam, 1992; Rettew, Swedo, Leonard, Lenane, & Rapoport, 1992). Considerable effort should be expended in developing reliable and valid instruments for assessment and diagnosis (Costello, 1989), incorporating the best of the traditional unstructured approach with the more standardized instruments. Reliability of current methods of data collection raises a number of questions. Inherent biases in the system, particularly with the traditional interview, will require critical appraisal.

Social functioning and adaptation to the environment are pivotal components of a meaningful diagnosis. The use of multi-axial scales will highlight their importance. As with shortcomings in currently available measures of social functioning in adults, similar problems arise in assessing children. Separating social and occupational functioning from measures of symptoms and psychological functioning has been suggested for adults (Goldman, Skodol, & Lave, 1992) and is being piloted in children (Petti, 1991). Reliable scales and instruments for this purpose are likely to be more readily available. Some may be in an interview or self-report format, while others will be based in systematic observation and behavioral assessment. Strayhorn (1988) has suggested that a skills axis be considered in psychiatric assessment to guide the content and direction of psychotherapy and learning-based interventions.

Advances in integrating systematically obtained observational data may fill in for the perceived loss of "clinical penetration" occasioned by depending on highly structured interviews and questionnaires (Rutter & Tuma, 1988). They may also assist in moving away from the overly tight relationship between the instruments and the classification system to which they serve and in advancing to a more rational system of classification. Reliance on the parent or child report in whatever format greatly limits the reliability of the diagnosis. Both parents and children selectively recall or report data and rarely provide an accurate portrayal of the total clinical picture; both have been demonstrated to be biased in their reporting, depending on many variables that interact and may correlate with the clinical picture.

More specific and useful systems of classification will be developed as the multiple sources of information employed in making a diagnosis are integrated. As occurred with pneumonia, cancers, or heart disease, careful observations and data collection through clinical studies and case reports have allowed us to separate a number of "borderline" disorders from each other (Petti & Vela, 1990). Similar success can be expected in delineating other childhood anxiety disorders, affective disorders (Kovacs, Feinberg, Crouse-Novak, Paulauskas, & Finkelstein, 1984), or disruptive disorders (Keller et al., 1992) into more definitive groups. Better understanding of the longitudinal course of the disorders and associated comorbidity should follow. The development of effective assessment instruments has a mutually enhancing relationship with reliable and valid systems of classification. The relative value of information and its sources in any given case should be more easily assessed. Clinicians and researchers will need training in synthesizing and integrating information from the assessment instruments and from the diagnostic systems they employ to provide the best clinical care available.

REFERENCES

Achenbach, T. M. (1980). DSM-III in light of empirical research on the classification of child psychopathology. *Journal of the American Academy of Child Psychiatry, 19*, 395–412.

Achenbach, T. M. (1988). Integrating assessment and taxonomy. In M. Rutter, A. H. Tuma, & I. S. Lann (Eds.), *Assessment and diagnosis in child psychopathology* (pp. 300–343). New York: Guilford Press.

Achenbach, T. M. (1991). *Integrative guide for the 1991 CBCL/4–18, YSR and TRF profiles.* Burlington, VT: University of Vermont, Department of Psychiatry.

Ambrosini, P. J., Metz, C., Prabucki, K., & Lee, J. (1989). Videotape reliability of the third revised edition of the K-SADS. *Journal of the American Academy of Child and Adolescent Psychiatry, 28*, 723–728.

American Psychiatric Association. (1952). *Diagnostic and statistical manual of mental disorders (DSM-I).* Washington, DC: Author.

American Psychiatric Association. (1968). *Diagnostic and statistical manual of mental disorders (2nd ed.) (DSM-II).* Washington, DC: Author.

American Psychiatric Association. (1980). *Diagnostic and statistical manual of mental disorders (3rd ed.) (DSM-III).* Washington, DC: Author.

American Psychiatric Association. (1987). *Diagnostic and statistical manual of mental disorders (3rd ed., rev.) (DSM-III-R).* Washington, DC: Author.

American Psychiatric Association. (1993). *DSM-IV draft criteria.* Washington, DC: Author.

Barkley, R. A. (1988). Child behavior rating scales and checklists. In M. Rutter, A. H. Tuma, & I. S. Lann (Eds.), *Assessment and diagnosis in child psychopathology* (pp. 113–147). New York: Guilford Press.

Barkley, R. A. (1990). *Attention-deficit/hyperactivity disorder: A handbook for diagnosis and treatment.* New York: Guilford Press.

Botterson, K. N., Figier, G. S., Wetzel, M. W., Hudziak, J., & VanEerdewegh, M. V. (1992). MRI abnormalities in adolescent bipolar affective disorder. *Journal of the American Academy of Child and Adolescent Psychiatry, 31*, 258–261.

Burns, R. C. (1982). *Self-growth in families.* New York: Brunner/Mazel.

Cantwell, D. P. (1988). DSM-III studies. In M. Rutter, A. H. Tuma, & I. S. Lann (Eds.), *Assessment and diagnosis in child psychopathology* (pp. 3–35). New York: Guilford Press.

Caplan, R., & Sherman, T. (1991). Kiddie formal thought disorder rating scale and story game. In C. Shaefer et al. (Eds.), *Play diagnosis and assessment* (pp. 169–192). New York: Wiley.

Caron, C., & Rutter, M. (1991). Comorbidity in child psychopathology: Concepts, issues and research strategies. *Journal of Child Psychology and Psychiatry and Allied Disciplines, 32*, 1063–1080.

Chambers, W. J., Puig-Antich, J., Hirsch, M., Paez, P., Ambrosini, P. J., Tabrizi, M. A., & Davies, M. (1985). The assessment of affective disorders in children and adolescents by semi-structured interview: Test-retest reliability of the schedule for affective disorders and schizophrenia for school-age children, present episode version. *Archives of General Psychiatry, 42*, 696–702.

Cohen, P., Velez, N., Kohn, M., Schwab-Stone, M., & Johnson, J. (1987). Child psychiatric diagnosis by computer algorithm: Theoretical issues and empirical tests. *Journal of the American Academy of Child and Adolescent Psychiatry, 26*, 631–638.

Cone, J. (1987). Behavioral assessment with children and adolescents. In M. Hersen & V. Van Hasselt (Eds.), *Behavior therapy with children and adolescents—a clinical approach* (pp. 29–49). New York: Wiley.

Conners, C. K., & Barkley, R. A. (1985). Rating scales and checklists for child psychopharmacology. *Psychopharmacology Bulletin, 21*, 809–815.

Costello, A. (1989). Reliability in diagnostic interviewing. In C. Last & M. Hersen (Eds.), *Handbook of child psychiatric diagnosis* (pp. 28–39). New York: Wiley.

Costello, A. (1991). Structured interviewing in child and adolescent psychiatry. In M. Lewis (Ed.), *Child and adolescent psychiatry: A comprehensive textbook* (pp. 447–463). Baltimore: Williams & Wilkins.

Costello, E., & Benjamin, R. (1989). Epidemiology and child diagnosis. In C. G. Last & M. Herson (Eds.), *Handbook of child psychiatric diagnosis* (pp. 497–516). New York: Wiley.

Costello, E. J., Edelbrock, C. S., & Costello, A. J. (1985). Validity of the NIMH diagnostic interview schedule for children: A comparison between psychiatric and pediatric referrals. *Journal of Abnormal and Child Psychology, 3*, 579–595.

Dulcan, M. K. (1993, March). *Research inteviews for psychiatric diagnosis in children and adolescents.* Paper presented at the meeting of the Society of Professors of Child and Adolescent Psychiatry, San Juan, Puerto Rico.

Edelbrock, C., & Costello, A. J. (1988). Structured psychiatric interviews for children. M. Rutter, A. H. Tuma, & I. S. Lann (Eds.), *Assessment and diagnosis in child psychopathology* (pp. 87–109). New York: Guilford Press.

Edelbrock, C., Costello, A., & Dulcan, M. (1986). Parent-child agreement on child psychiatric symptoms assessed via structured interview. *Journal of Child Psychology and Psychiatry, 27*, 181–190.

Edelbrock, C., Costello, A. J., Dulcan, M. K., Kalas, R., & Conover, N. C. (1985). Age differences in the reliability of the psychiatric interview of the child. *Child Development, 56*, 265–275.

Engel, G. L. (1980). The clinical application of the biopsychosocial model. *The American Journal of Psychiatry, 137*, 535–544.

Fristad, M. A., Weller, E. B., & Weller, R. A. (1992). The mania rating scale: Can it be used on children? A preliminary report. *Journal of the American Academy of Child and Adolescent Psychiatry, 31*, 252–257.

Galvin, M. R., Shekhar, A., Simon, J., Stilwell, B. M., & Ten Eyck, R. (1991). Low dopamine beta hydroxylase: A biological sequela of abuse and neglect? *Psychiatry Research, 39*, 1–11.

Garber, J. (1984). Classification of childhood psychopathology: A developmental perspective. *Child Development, 55*, 30–48.

Gittleman, R. (1980). The role of psychological tests for differential diagnosis in child psychiatry. *Journal of the American Academy of Child Psychiatry, 19*, 395–412.

Goldman, H., Skodol, A., & Lave, T. (1992). Revising Axis V for DSM-IV: A review of measures of social functioning. *American Journal of Psychiatry, 149*, 1148–1156.

Goodenough, F. L. (1926). *Measurement of intelligence by drawings.* New York: World Book.

Green, M. (1992). *Pediatric diagnosis: Interpretation of symptoms and signs in infants, children, and adolescents.* Philadelphia: Saunders.

Greenspan, S. I., & Greenspan, N. T. (1991). *The clinical interview of the child (2nd ed.).* Washington, DC: American Psychiatric Press.

Group for the Advancement of Psychiatry. (1966). *Psychological disorders in childhood: Theoretical considerations and a proposed classification* (Report No. 62). New York: Author.

Gutterman, E., O'Brien, J., & Young, G. (1987). Structured diagnostic interviews for children and adolescents: Current status and future directions. *Journal of the American Academy of Child and Adolescent Psychiatry, 26*, 621–630.

Harris, D. B. (1963). *Children's drawings as measures of intellectual maturity.* New York: Harcourt, Brace & World.

Herjanic, B., & Reich, W. (1982). Development of a structured psychiatric interview for children: Agreement between child and parent on individual symptoms. *Journal of Abnormal Child Psychology, 10*, 307–324.

Hersen, M., & Last, C. G. (1989). Psychiatric diagnosis and behavioral assessment in children. In C. G. Last & M. Hersen (Eds.), *Handbook of child psychiatric diagnosis* (pp. 517–528). New York: Wiley.

Hodges, K. (1987). Assessing children with a clinical research interview: The child assessment schedule. In R. J. Prinz (Ed.), *Advances in behavioral assessment of children and families, 3*, (pp. 203–233). Greenwich, CT: JAI Press.

Hodges, K., McKnew, D., Burbach, D., & Roebuck, L. (1987). Diagnostic concordance between the Child Assessment Schedule (CAS) and the Schedule for Affective Disorders and Schizophrenia for School-Age Children (K-SADS) in an outpatient sample using lay interviewers. *Journal of the American Academy of Child and Adolescent Psychiatry, 26*, 654–661.

Hodges, K., Saunders, W. B., Kashani, J., Hamlett, K., & Thompson, R. J. (1990). Internal consistency of DSM-III diagnoses using the symptom scales of the Child Assessment Schedule. *Journal of the American Academy of Child and Adolescent Psychiatry, 29*, 635–641.

Hornstein, N. L., & Putnam, F. W. (1992). Clinical phenomenology of child and adolescent dissociative disorders. *Journal of the American Academy of Child and Adolescent Psychiatry, 31*, 1077–1085.

Hynd, G. (1988). *Neuropsychological assessment in clinical child psychology.* Newbury Park, CA: Sage.

Jacob, T., & Tennenbaum, D. L. (1988). Family assessment methods. In M. Ruter, A. H. Tuma, & I. S. Lann (Eds.), *Assessment and diagnosis in child psychopathology* (pp. 196–225). New York: Guilford Press.

Jenkins, R. L. (1971). The runaway reaction. *The American Journal of Psychiatry, 128*, 168–173.

John, K., Gammon, G. D., Prusoff, B. A., & Warner, V. (1987). The Social Adjustment Inventory for Children and Adolescents (SAICA): Testing of a new semistructured interview. *Journal of the American Academy of Child and Adolescent Psychiatry, 26*, 898–911.

Kazdin, A. E. (1983). Psychiatric diagnosis, dimensions of dysfunction, and child behavior therapy. *Behavior Therapy, 14*, 73–99.

Kazdin, A. E., & Bass, D. (1988). Parent, teacher, and hospital staff evaluations of severely disturbed children. *American Journal of Orthopsychiatry, 58*, 512–523.

Kazdin, A. E., & Petti, T. A. (1982). Self-report and interview measures of childhood and adolescent depression. *Journal of Clinical Psychology and Psychiatry, 23*, 437–457.

Keller, M. B., Lavori, P. W., Beardslee, W. R., Wunder, J., Schwartz, C. E., Roth, J., & Biederman, J. (1992). The disruptive behavioral disorder in children and adolescents: Comorbidity and clinical course. *Journal of the American Academy of Child and Adolescent Psychiatry, 31*, 204–209.

Keogh, B., & Margolis, J. (1991). Psychoeducational assessment in schools. In M. Lewis (Ed.), *Child and adolescent psychiatry: A comprehensive textbook* (pp. 492–496). Baltimore: Williams & Wilkins.

Kolko, D. J. (1988). Daily ratings on a child psychiatric unit: Psychometric evaluation of the Child Behavior Rating form. *Journal of the American Academy of Child and Adolescent Psychiatry, 27*, 126–132.

Koppitz, E. (1968). *Psychological evaluation of children's human figure drawings.* New York: Grune & Stratton.

Kovacs, M. (1985a). The Interview Schedule for Children (ISC). *Psychopharmacology Bulletin, 21,* 991–994.

Kovacs, M. (1985b). CDI (The Children's Depression Inventory). *Psychopharmacology Bulletin, 21,* 995–998.

Kovacs, M., Feinberg, T., Crouse-Novak, M. A., Paulauskas, S. L., & Finkelstein, R. (1984). Depressive disorders in childhood: A longitudinal prospective study of characteristics and recovery. *Archives of General Psychiatry, 41,* 229–237.

Lewis, M. (1991). Psychiatric assessment of infants, children, and adolescents. In M. Lewis (Ed.), *Child & adolescent psychiatry: A comprehensive textbook* (pp. 447–463). Baltimore: Williams & Wilkins.

Lewis, M., & Volkmar, F. (1990). *Clinical aspects of child and adolescent development.* Philadelphia: Lea & Febiger.

Liebowitz, J., Rembar, J., Kernberg, P., Frankel, A., & Kruger, R. A. (1988). Judging mental health-sickness in children: Development of a rating scale. *Journal of the American Academy of Child and Adolescent Psychiatry, 27,* 193–199.

Moos, R., & Moos, B. (1981). *Family environment scale manual.* Palo Alto, CA: Consulting Psychologists Press.

NIMH Molecular Genetics of Psychiatric Disorders Initiative Child Study Group (1993, May). *Child and adolescent offspring study of bipolar affective disorder: Preliminary results from the NIMH molecular genetics of psychiatric disorders initiative.* Paper presented at the annual meeting of the Society of Biological Psychiatry, San Francisco, CA.

Nurcombe, B., Seifer, R., Scioli, A., Tramontana, M. G., Grapentine, W. L., & Beauchesne, H. C. (1989). Is major depressive disorder in adolescence a distinct diagnostic entity? *Journal of the American Academy of Child and Adolescent Psychiatry, 28,* 333–342.

Orvaschel, H. (1985). Psychiatric interviews suitable for use in research with children and adolescents. *Psychopharmacology Bulletin, 24,* 737–745.

Orvaschel, H., Puig-Antich, J., Chambers, W. J., Tabrizi, M. A., & Johnson, R. (1982). Retrospective assessments of child psychopathology with the Kiddie-SADS-E. *Journal of the American Academy of Child Psychiatry, 21,* 392–397.

Orvaschel, H., & Walsh, G. (1984). *The assessment of adaptive functioning in children: A review of existing measures suitable for epidemiological and clinical services research* (DHHS Publication No. ADM 84–1343). Washington, DC: U. S. Government Printing Office.

Peterson, L., Burbach, D., & Chaney, J. (1989). Developmental issues. In C. G. Last & M. Hersen (Eds.), *Handbook of child psychiatric diagnosis* (pp. 463–481). New York: Wiley.

Petti, T. A. (1985). Scales of potential use in the psychopharmacologic treatment of depressed children and adolescents. *Psychopharmacology Bulletin, 21,* 951–977.

Petti, T. A. (1991). *Component global assessment of functioning scale for children and adolescents.* Unpublished manuscript.

Petti, T. A., Kane, F. J., Jr., & Lipton, M. A. (1973). Problems in teaching psychopharmacology. *Psychosomatic, 14,* 326–330.

Petti, T. A., and Vela (1990). Borderline disorders of childhood: An overview. *Journal of the American Academy of Child and Adolescent Psychiatry, 29,* 327–337.

Puig-Antich, J., Novacenko, H., Davies, M., Tabrizi, M. A., Ambrosini, P., Goetz, R., Bianca, J., Goetz, D., & Sachar, E. J. (1984). Growth hormone secretion in prepubertal children with major depression. III. Response to insulin-induced hypoglycemia after recovery from a depressive episode and in a drug-free state. *Archives of General Psychiatry, 41,* 471–475.

Racusin, G., & Moss, N. (1991). Psychological assessment of children and adolescents. In M. Lewis

(Ed.), *Child and adolescent psychiatry: A comprehensive textbook* (pp. 415–421). Baltimore: Williams & Wilkins.

Rapoport, J. L. (1989). Future directions in child psychiatric diagnosis. In C. G. Last & M. Hersen (Eds.), *Handbook of child psychiatric diagnosis* (pp. 531–537). New York: Wiley.

Rapoport, J. L, Conners, C. K., & Reatig, N. (Eds.) (1985). Rating scales and assessment instruments for use in pediatric psychopharmacology research. *Psychopharmacology Bulletin, 21*, DHHS(ADM) 713–1125.

Rapoport, J. L, & Ismond, D. (1990). *DSM-III-R training guide for diagnosis of childhood disorders.* New York: Brunner/Mazel.

Reich, W., & Earls, F. (1987). Rules for making psychiatric diagnosis in children on the basis of multiple sources of information: Preliminary strategies. *Journal of Abnormal Child Psychology, 13*, 601–616.

Reich, W., Herjanic, B., Welner, Z., & Gandhy, P. R. (1982). Development of a structured psychiatric interview for children: Agreement of diagnosis comparing child and parent interviews. *Journal of Abnormal Child Psychology, 10*, 325–336.

Reid, J., Patterson, G., Baldwin, D., & Dishion, T. (1988). Observation in the assessment of childhood disorders. In M. Rutter, A. H. Tuma, & I. S. Lann (Eds.), *Assessment and diagnosis in child psychopathology* (pp. 156–195). New York: Guilford Press.

Rettew, D., Swedo, S., Leonard, H., Lenane, M., & Rapoport, J. (1992). Obsessions and compulsions across time in 79 children and adolescents with obsessive-compulsive disorder. *Journal of the American Academy of Child and Adolescent Psychiatry, 31*, 1050–1056.

Rogeness, G. A., Javors, M. A., & Pliszka, S. R. (1992). Neurochemistry and child and adolescent psychiatry. *Journal of the American Academy of Child and Adolescent Psychiatry, 31*, 765–781.

Rutter, M., & Tuma, A. H. (1988). Diagnosis and classification: Some outstanding issues. In M. Rutter, A. H. Tuma, & I. S. Lann (Eds.), *Assessment and diagnosis in child psychopathology* (pp. 437–452). New York: Guilford Press.

Rutter, M., & Tuma, A. H., & Lann, I. S. (Eds.) (1988). *Assessment and diagnosis in child psychopathology.* New York: Guilford Press.

Ryan, N. D. & Dahl, R. E. (1993). The biology of depression in children and adolescents. In D. Kupfer & J. J. Mann (Eds.), *The biology of depressive disorders.* New York: Plenum Press.

Schaefer, C., Gitlin, K., & Sandgrund, A. (Eds.). (1991). *Play diagnosis and assessment.* New York: Wiley.

Schwab-Stone, M., Towbin, K., & Tarnoff, G. (1991). Systems of classification: ICD-10, DSM-III-R, and DSM-IV. In M. Lewis (Ed.), *Child and adolescent psychiatry: A comprehensive textbook* (pp. 422–434). Baltimore: Williams & Wilkins.

Schwab-Stone, M., Fisher, P., Cohen, P., Piacentini, J., Davies, M., Conners, C. K., & Regier, D. (1993). The Diagnostic Interview Schedule for Children—Revised version (DISC-R):I. Preparation, field testing, interrater reliability, and acceptability. *Journal of the American Academy of Child and Adolescent Psychiatry, 32*, 643–650.

Shaffer, D. (1993, March). *The DSM-IV classification.* Paper presented at the meeting of the Society of Professors of Child and Adolescent Psychiatry, San Juan, Puerto Rico.

Shaffer, D., Gould, M. S., Brasic, J., Ambrosini, P., Fisher, P., Bird, H., & Aluwahlia, S. (1983). A Children's Global Assessment Scale (CGAS). *Archives of General Psychiatry, 40*, 1228–1231.

Simmons, J. E. (1987). *Psychiatric examination of children.* Philadelphia: Lea & Febiger.

Spitzer, R., & Williams, J. B. W. (1980). Classification in psychiatry. In: H. Kaplan, A. Freedman, B. Sadock (Eds.), *The comprehensive textbook of psychiatry* (3rd ed.). Baltimore: Williams & Wilkins.

Sprock, J., & Blashfield, R. K. (1983). Classification and nosology. In M. Hersen, A. E. Kazdin, &

A. S. Bellack (Eds.), *The clinical psychology handbook* (pp. 289–307). New York: Pergamon Press.

Strayhorn, J. M. (1987). Medical assessment of children with behavioral problems. In M. Hersen & V. Hasselt (Eds.), *Behavior therapy with children and adolescents: A clinical approach* (pp. 50–74). New York: Wiley.

Strayhorn J. M. (1988). *The competent child.* New York: Guilford Press.

Turecki, S., & Tonner, L. (1985). *The difficult child.* New York: Bantam Books.

Volkmar, F. (1991). Classification in child and adolescent psychiatry: Principles and issues. In M. Lewis (Eds.), *Child and adolescent psychiatry: A comprehensive textbook.* (pp. 415–421). Baltimore: Williams & Wilkins.

Welner, Z., Reich, W., Herjanic, B., Jung, K., & Amado, H. (1987). Reliability, validity and parent-child agreement studies of the Diagnostic Interview for Children and Adolescents (DICA). *Journal of the American Academy of Child and Adolescent Psychiatry, 26,* 649–653.

Wiens, A. N., & Matarazzo, J. D. (1983). Diagnostic interviewing. In M. Hersen, A. E. Kazdin, & A. S. Bellack (Eds.), *The clinical psychology handbook* (pp. 309–465). New York: Pergamon Press.

Woodbury, M. M., DeMaso, D. R., & Goldman, S. J. (1992). An integrated medical and psychiatric approach to conversion symptoms in a four-year-old. *Journal of the American Academy of Child and Adolescent Psychiatry, 31,* 1095–1097.

World Health Organization. (1977). *Manual of the international statistical classification of diseases, injuries and causes of death* (9th ed.). Geneva: Author.

World Health Organization (1988). Tenth revision of the international classification of diseases. (Draft). Geneva: Author.

Young, G., O'Brien, J., Gutterman, E., & Cohen, P. (1987). Structured diagnostic interviews for children and adolescents. *Journal of the American Academy of Child and Adolescent Psychiatry, 26,* 613–620.

Zarin, D. A., & Earls, R. (1993). Diagnostic decision making in psychiatry. *American Journal of Psychiatry, 150,* 197–206.

CHAPTER 3

Medical Issues and Complications

D. RICHARD MARTINI

INTRODUCTION

The presence of a medical disorder in conjunction with a psychiatric problem is thought to occur infrequently, and it is this belief that leads mental health professionals to avoid careful consideration of physical disorders in their differential diagnosis. The results may be particularly costly when patients are subjected to extensive psychiatric interventions for a problem that has a medical etiology and when appropriate pediatric care is, therefore, neglected. Psychiatric problems and physical illness may also occur together. Children and adolescents with a history of chronic illness are twice as likely to suffer one or more psychiatric disorders when compared to healthy controls (Cadman, Boyle, Satzmari, & Offord, 1987). Presence of disability along with medical illness increases the likelihood of a variety of mental-health-related disorders, including neurosis, attention-deficit/hyperactivity disorder (ADHD), and poor school performance. Serious chronic illness, particularly when it involves the central nervous system (CNS), poses a greater risk for behavioral or emotional disorders (Wieland, Pless, & Roghmann, 1992). Earlier studies have consistently demonstrated the role of CNS insult in the development of psychological disorder (Breslau, 1985; Pless & Roghmann, 1971). In addition, a greater number of chronic medical conditions increases the risk of disorder, including depressed mood, antisocial behavior, hyperactivity, peer conflicts, and social withdrawal (Newacheck, McManus, & Harriette, 1991). Children and adolescents are at greater risk for psychiatric disorder when the illness involves functional rather than cosmetic impairments. The role of illness severity has not been clearly defined, although it remains an important consideration. Parental response to illness is a fundamental determinant of childhood adjustment. Parents who rate their child's illness as moderately severe as opposed to mild are considered less well adjusted (Perrin, MacLean, & Perrin, 1989). The nature of the child's emotional response may be determined by a number of variables, including severity of illness, nature of the disease, the extent of disability, frequency of medical interventions, the visibility of the illness, and the nature of the child's environment. The last item includes family psychiatric history, socioeconomic status, intelligence of the parent, and availability of social supports (Pless & Pinkerton, 1975).

There are three primary relationships between physical illness and psychiatric disorder. In the first instance, patients may not have psychiatric disorders but may instead present with symptoms that are caused by the medical condition. Resolution of the medical problem completely alleviates the psychiatric symptoms. The second situation is characterized by a medical disorder that either precipitates psychiatric symptoms in a patient who is predisposed to mental disorder or aggravates a preexisting psychiatric condition. These patients may either completely recover with treatment of the medical illness or may require additional treatment of the psychiatric condition. The third category includes cases in which the physical illness and psychiatric disorder are not related but coexist. In these instances, the patient's medical problems may be attributed to psychological factors alone.

Among state hospital psychiatric inpatients evaluated by Hall, Gardner, Stickney, LeCann, and Popkin (1980), 46% had undiagnosed physical disorders that were either directly related to the psychiatric illness or were complicating the psychiatric presentation; and 43% of psychiatric patients seen in an outpatient setting have medical illness (Strain & Fullop, 1990). Reasons for missing the diagnosis include illness-related, patient-related, and physician-related factors. The medical illness may have masqueraded as a psychiatric disorder, may have presented initially with psychiatric symptoms, or may have produced an organic brain syndrome that left the patient unable to provide accurate information. Psychiatric patients may also be unpleasant to work with or be in contact with, and physicians may actively avoid them. An unfortunate result of this tendency is the lack of a thorough physical exam and missed medical diagnoses. Decisions by clinicians, however, are probably the most common cause of misdiagnosis. Diagnostic assessments are incomplete due to inadequate medical histories, cursory physical examinations, and/or insufficient laboratory testing. Physicians are also guided by false assumptions about psychiatric versus physical disorders. Among these assumptions are that all physical disorders should have cognitive impairment or that the psychiatric consequences of a medical disorder are limited to one or two diagnoses. Hyperthyroidism, for example, may product symptoms of both anxiety and depression, and corticosteroids may lead to symptoms of mania, depression, or psychosis.

The psychiatrist contributes to the inaccuracy in diagnosis by relying on medical specialists to determine the role of physical disorders in the psychiatric presentation. Psychiatrists should not lean too heavily on consultants for opinions on their patients but should assume responsibility for the overall quality of care. Difficulties in diagnosis are not limited to psychiatric physicians. Koranyi (1979), in a study of adult referrals for psychiatric treatment, noted that the rate of undiagnosed physical disorders was 32% in patients referred from medical physicians, 48% among those referred from psychiatrists, and 83% among patients referred from social workers and mental health clinics. Cases with an organic etiology usually present with rapid onset of symptoms, a history of drug and alcohol abuse, and a history of exposure to toxins. At times, it may be difficult to distinguish factors related to the disease from those related to medications chosen to treat the problem. Patients who present with visual, tactile, or olfactory hallucinations are frequently suffering from organic disease. Neurologic signs that are consistent with physical disease include inability to sustain attention, fluctuating levels of consciousness, disorientation, and deficits in recent or remote memory.

Medical disorders are present in the most obvious cases when the patient's level of functioning is grossly impaired and onset is progressive and dramatic. Changes may be more subtle, however, particularly when the illness is in its early stages and fluctuations in mental status are present. Absence of mental status changes does not rule out a physical condition. Pediatric illness should also be suspected when the child has a variety of physical complaints accompanying changes in behavior. Emotional sequelae may also be an early presentation of medical illness. Children who experience a sudden personality change with no clear environmental precipitant should be evaluated for presence of a medical disorder. Mental health professionals should be constantly exploring the possibility of medical illness as a contributing factor to a child's psychiatric presentation, even as the child is seen in ongoing treatment.

Laboratory screening tests are necessary as an initial step in considering medical conditions in the assessment of the psychiatric patient. The battery should include the following: a complete blood count with differential; chemistry panel with electrolytes, fasting blood glucose, and hepatic, renal, and parathyroid functions; thyroid functions, including a T_4, T_3 uptake, free-thyroxine index, free T_4, T_3 RIA, and TSH; B_{12}/folate; and urinalysis. Evaluation of symptoms of anxiety, depression, mental retardation, dementia, restlessness, mental status change, and psychosis that are consistent with thyroid dysfunction should be accompanied by characteristic physiologic signs (Zametkin, Andreason, & Kruesi, 1991). Blood levels of all medications taken by the patient should be drawn. Additional testing should reflect findings on physical examination, the patient's medical history, and the differential diagnosis. Patients suffering from symptoms of anxiety should be evaluated for presence of pheochromocytoma, particularly when the psychiatric symptoms are accompanied by autonomic dysfunction. The primary laboratory studies include 24-hour urine collection for homovanillic acid, vanillylmandelic acid, and metanephrines.

Sleep-deprived EEG evaluations are usually more productive than routine assessments and should be considered in all psychiatric patients, particularly in those with a history of violence. Routine EEGs are ordered in psychiatric assessments when presence of motor seizures, absence seizures, complex partial seizures, temporal lobe epilepsy, or dyscontrol syndromes are considered in the differential diagnosis (Zametkin et al.). CT scans may accompany assessments of psychotic states because of the possibility of a frontal lobe tumor. Brain imaging has been used with increasing frequency in the diagnosis of adult psychiatric disorders. There are few studies, however, that have demonstrated a practical relevance to child psychiatry (Campbell et al., 1982; Gillberg & Svendsen, 1983; Nasrallah et al., 1986). Indications for CT scan or MRI remain clinical and focused on neurologic findings that include degenerative neurologic signs, craniofacial malformations, or suspected or inherited syndromes.

The prospect of genetic illness is an important factor in the development of psychiatric illness in children and is supported by studies that have demonstrated an association between chromosomal variants and psychopathology, increased prevalence of disorder in adopted-away children of affected parents, a higher concordance among monozygotic twins when compared to dizygotic offspring, and a higher risk in families with affected individuals. Karyotyping is the most common genetic test performed in child and adolescent psychiatry. The disorders that are most commonly considered are Turner's Syndrome (45 XO), Klinefelter's syndrome (47 XXY), and Fragile X syndrome, all with neuropsychological deficits. Dyslexia occurs more frequently in Klinefelter's syndrome.

Coexistence of medical illness and psychiatric disorder presents several diagnostic challenges. Patients may require specialized criteria and diagnostic instruments in order to account for integration of medical and psychiatric symptoms. Patients with medical illness experience altered pharmacokinetics and end-organ response. There are few studies in adults or children that examine treatment outcomes for psychiatric disorders in patients with physical illness. Structured standardized instruments that diagnose psychiatric disorders describe a number of somatic symptoms among those required for diagnosis. Presence of medical illness may artificially increase the prevalence of psychiatric disorder. Even instruments like the Children's Depression Inventory that base diagnosis on cognitions may be affected by the presence of organic brain syndromes.

Patients suffering from depressive disorders, including major depression, dysthymia, adjustment disorder with depressed mood, and organic mood disorder, may be suffering from grief reactions secondary to medical illness, an adjustment disorder secondary to disease or disability, or a variety of organic encephalopathies. The role of adjustment disorders is particularly important because of a belief that depression experienced by medically ill patients may be less severe than other secondary depressions, as in cases of substance abuse or other psychiatric diagnoses, for example. Studies in adults have noted less severe symptoms of melancholia, suicidality, and low self-esteem among depressed medically ill patients (Bukberg, Penman, & Holland, 1984; Clark, Cavanaugh, & Gibbons, 1983; Noyes & Kathol, 1986). In addition, the literature suggests that recovery of these patients may be more rapid and their response to tricyclic antidepressants (TCA) more impressive at lower doses than in other cases of secondary depressions (Popkin, Callies, & Colon, 1988; Winokur, Black, & Nasrallah, 1988). In cases of adjustment disorder, elimination of the stressor relieves the patient of the psychiatric distress. With recurrent or permanent medical illness, adjustment disorders should be treated with standard somatic therapies. Rifkin, Reardon, & Siris (1985) demonstrated that with TCA use, depression in adult patients resolved without significant change in the patient's medical course.

Medical disorders may complicate the psychiatric presentation of the young patient. Each of the following pediatric diagnoses carries risk for psychiatric symptoms either in the characteristics of its presentation or in the nature of its treatment. The disorders are grouped according to general classification.

TOXIC EFFECTS

Lead Toxicity

Lead toxicity leads to increased irritability, decreased appetite, and decreased interest in play. Sources of lead are variable and include lead-based paint, soil, and fumes from leaded gasoline (Chisolm, 1983; Graef, 1983; Rutter, 1983). Behavioral changes have been noted in children exposed to lead without evidence of toxicity and are correlated with increased distractibility in school, disorganization, impulsivity, inability to follow directions, and lower school performance (Needleman et al., 1979). Screening for high lead levels includes free erythrocyte protoporphyrin levels and blood lead levels. Consideration should be given to routinely performing these tests when contemplating psychiatric treatment.

Diagnosis of lead toxicity should also follow consideration of the patient's clinical history. Children who have a history of pica (i.e., the eating of nonfood substances) are at risk for lead toxicity, particularly when they are living in poor urban neighborhoods where the prevalence of lead-based paint is higher. Homes that were painted before the 1950s usually have higher levels of lead-based paint. The clinician should also be more suspicious of lead toxicity when the home provides little supervision for the child. Occasionally, the child may ingest large quantities of lead when he or she has a habit of eating soil. These children may present with abdominal pain, loss of appetite, vomiting, constipation, and anemia. Mental status changes may also result and include confusion, staggering, persistent vomiting, seizures, and coma. Such symptoms require hospitalization and aggressive treatment.

Drugs

Exposure to recreational drugs is more common in adolescents than in children but should be considered in even the youngest patients who presents with mental status change. The history of drug ingestion may be based on reports from the patient or from observers or may be suspected by the clinician based on reports of family circumstances; for example, children may be living in a home with parents who have a history of drug or alcohol abuse and have these substances available.

Use of prescription and over-the-counter medications may produce psychiatric symptoms. Theophylline is a common treatment for asthma but frequently produces symptoms of irritability, insomnia, restlessness, and tremor. Children treated with theophylline are often given the diagnosis of ADHD. Another medication that is used in the treatment of asthma, as well as rheumatoid arthritis, inflammatory bowel disease, autoimmune disorder, and post-transplant recovery, is corticosteroids. Patients may experience emotional lability, depression, mania, and psychosis when these drugs are used. The most prominent symptoms seem to appear when dosage of the drug is either being increased or decreased (Judd, Burrows, & Norman, 1983). Antihistamines, prescribed for allergies and colds, may cause excitation, sedation, and inattention.

Among the medications prescribed for seizure disorder, phenobarbital has the highest risk for psychiatric complications. Symptoms may mimic attention-deficit disorder and include inattention, restlessness, hyperactivity, and impulsivity. In addition, use of phenobarbital poses increased risk for affective disorders, including symptoms of self-destructive behavior.

Hypoglycemia that results from an excessive dose of insulin is characterized by behavior change. Symptoms include irritability, confusion, and personality change. The patient may lose consciousness and the condition may become fatal if the dose is exceedingly large. The presentation may either be acute and characterized by episodes of extreme anxiety or subacute with the progressive development of aggressive and socially withdrawn behaviors (Lishman, 1988).

Children may be treated with antihypertensive medications as a consequence of several medical conditions, including both renal and cardiac disease. Occasionally, CNS side effects of the drugs may produce psychiatric symptoms, particularly with use of beta-blockers. Patients may suffer from mood disorders and cognitive impairment on these medications, although the choice of a hydrophilic beta-blocker that does not penetrate the blood brain barrier may be less problematic. Atenolol is one such medication (*Choice*, 1986).

NEUROPSYCHIATRIC CONDITIONS

Meningitis

Bacterial and viral meningitis may initially present with symptoms of increased irritability, personality change, and lethargy before the physical symptoms of fever, headache, and stiff neck become more prominent. Meningitis that develops as a consequence of a tuberculous infection is more insidious and may first appear with the psychological symptoms of decreased interest, irritability, inattention, lethargy, apathy, and declining school performance. Occasionally, these are the most prominent signs of infection, and the patient will not develop the more characteristic symptoms of headache and stiff neck. Brain abscesses may develop over several weeks as a consequence of infection. The initial symptom of this disorder may be irritability, followed by more typical neurologic signs such as weakness, numbness, trouble with eye movements, vision changes, seizures, loss of coordination, and loss of consciousness.

Tumors

Central nervous system (CNS) tumors, although not common in children, are particularly lethal. The symptom presentation is most often dependent upon the location and size of the tumor. In children, CNS tumors are often slow growing in areas that do not produce dramatic changes in neurologic functioning. Children may initially present with irritability, decreased concentration, and poor school performance. Recurrent headaches are a frequent sign of intracranial lesions and should be carefully examined because they do not occur often in children. Occasionally, location of the tumor may be identified by the nature of the behavioral change. Changes in patterns of sleep and appetite may indicate frontal lobe tumors; auditory and olfactory hallucinations are noted with lesions of the temporal lobe; and visual hallucinations are associated with tumors of the occipital lobe (Menkes, 1990).

Wilson's Disease

Wilson's disease is transmitted by an autosomal recessive gene and is characterized by a defect in the metabolism of copper. The problem is located in the liver and leads to accumulation of copper in the liver, kidneys, corneas, and brain. In 10% to 20% of Wilson's disease patients, the initial symptoms are psychiatric and include irritability, impulsivity, personality change, lability, and a variety of nonspecific psychological effects (Sternlieb & Scheinberg, 1964). These symptoms may progress to mania, neuroses, psychosis, schizophrenia, and antisocial behavior. Psychiatric symptoms are among the most common symptoms noted in Wilson's disease patients.

ENDOCRINE DISORDERS

Thyroid Dysfunction

A patient's level of energy is dependent to a large degree upon thyroid function. *Hyperthyroidism* is characterized by increased heart rate, hyperactive reflexes, weight loss with increased consumption, increased activity, diarrhea, diaphoresis, and racing thoughts. The activity level and irritability that accompany hyperthyroidism mimic ADHD. The clinician should be aware of the physical signs that accompany hyperthyroidism, including goiter, bulging of the eyes, tachycardia, and weight loss. The increased activity level may be accompanied by anxiety and deteriorating school performance.

Hypothyroidism has a very different presentation and is characterized by lower levels of energy, decreased heart rate, hyporeflexia, weight gain, decreased activity, and slowed thinking. These signs may be mistaken for depression. Among endocrine disorders in adults, hypothyroidism most commonly presents with psychiatric symptoms (Stoudemire & Levenson, 1990). The physical signs include constipation, hypothermia, slow rate of growth, sallow complexion, coarse hair, and an enlarged thyroid gland. The diagnosis is based on laboratory screening using thyroid function tests, and is treated with thyroid replacement therapy. Occasionally, psychiatric symptoms will persist after the successful initiation of thyroid replacement and will require psychopharmacologic intervention.

Diabetes

Children with diabetes or with diabetic complications may initially present with psychiatric symptoms. Poor diabetic control may be characterized by personality change that may proceed to anxiety, irritability, confusion, and psychotic behavior before the patient suffers changes in the level of consciousness in response to diabetic ketoacidosis. Symptoms of delirium may also accompany hyperglycemia. Patients with these symptoms as well as the typical symptoms of new-onset diabetes, like polydipsia, polyuria, and polyphagia with little weight gain, should be screened for the disease using fasting blood sugars and a glucose tolerance test (Kohrman, Netzloff, & Weil, 1987).

Other Disorders

Other endocrine disorders may be confused with psychiatric illness. Cushing's disease and Addison's disease, affecting secretion from the adrenal cortex, may produce symptoms of mood disorder. As noted previously, pheochromocytoma producing hypersecretion of adrenalin or noradrenalin can understandably change behavior and produce transient anxiety along with physiologic symptoms of palpitations, sweating, dizziness, tachycardia, and hypertension (Lishman, 1988).

SEIZURE DISORDER

The adult literature demonstrates a significantly higher rate of psychopathology among epileptics when compared to the general population. There is an increased rate of depression and anxiety among these patients (Betts, 1981). In addition, an "epileptic personality" (Bear & Fedio, 1977; Bear, Levin, Blumer, Chetham, & Ryder, 1982) (symptoms including rage, emotional lability, viscosity, religious and sexual changes) and a "schizophrenic-like" psychosis (Flor-Henry, 1983; Perez, Trimble, Murray, & Reider, 1985) are commonly observed in adults with temporal lobe epilepsy (TLE). Unfortunately, there are far fewer studies of psychopathology in children with epilepsy, and the rates of disorder are variable. From the information available, it appears that anywhere from 20% to 60% of epileptic children have some form of psychopathology (Cavazzuti, 1980; Hinton & Knights, 1969; Rutter, Graham, & Yule, 1970), including a much higher rate of cognitive disorders (mental retardation, learning disabilities) (Gerbert, 1980; Lewis & Smith, 1983) and behavior disorders (hyperactivity, rage/aggression, conduct disturbance) than the general population (Cavazzuti, Herzberg & Fenwick, 1988; Hinton & Knights, 1969; Holdsworth & Whitmore, 1974; Ounstead, 1955; Rutter et al., 1970).

The correlation between childhood epilepsy and specific psychiatric syndromes is not yet clear. This has largely been the result of limitations in the assessment process and the lack of appropriate diagnostic instruments. There is no literature to date documenting rate and types of psychiatric disorder prior to or at the onset of a seizure disorder. Virtually all of the information to date on psychiatric disorder associated with epilepsy comes from cross-sectional or retrospective studies of patients who have had a seizure disorder for a variable period of time. As a result, proper interpretation of the results must take into account the role of multiple potential confounding factors. These factors include the following:

1. *Duration of seizure disorder and age of onset of epilepsy.* Studies indicate that an earlier age of onset and a longer duration of epilepsy are associated with an increased risk of psychiatric morbidity (Hoare, 1984a; Rutter et al., 1970).

2. *Seizure frequency.* The literature supports both higher and lower rates of emotional disorder with increasing seizure frequency (Hodgman, McAnarney, & Myers, 1979; Rutter et al., 1970).

3. *Anticonvulsant medication.* Numerous studies have demonstrated behavioral and cognitive side effects of anticonvulsants (Herranz, Armijo, & Arteaga, 1988; Stores, 1975; Trimble & Cull, 1988). In particular, the older classes of drugs, such as phenobarbital and Dilantin, appear to have a higher rate of side effects than newer drugs such as Tegretol and Valproic Acid.

4. *Family psychiatric history.* High rates of psychiatric disorders exist in families of epileptic children (Hoare, 1984b; Rutter et al., 1970). However, the nature of this relationship is unclear.

5. *The psychological impact of having epilepsy and demographic factors.* Although not formally studied, the role of adjustment to the disability and the limitations that result from chronic epilepsy likely contribute to the development of psychopathology in children and adolescents. These factors are less relevant in newly diagnosed patients. Demographic variables, however, including socioeconomic status (SES), race, sex, and age, may be important determinants in the development of psychiatric disorder. This includes higher rates of disruptive disorders such as ADHD and conduct disorder among males, nonwhites, and lower SES children (Barkley, 1981; Robins, 1981).

Relationship Between Epilepsy and Specific Psychiatric Disorders

Despite several independent reports describing the association of explosive hyperkinetic behavior with epilepsy, controversy exists over the validity of this notion (Hermann, Black, & Chhabria, 1981; Herzberg & Fenwick, 1988; Hoare, 1984a; Ounsted, 1955; Stores, 1975). Lindsay (1972) reported that 26 out of 100 children with TLE suffered from hyperkinetic syndrome; 36 had catastrophic rage. However, the study was biased by an overrepresentation of males (2:1) in addition to the presence of a known brain insult and low IQ in 88% of the hyperactive explosive group. It is difficult to draw a conclusion from this study about the role of epilepsy in the development of these symptoms. The work by Stores (1978) also included an overrepresentation of males. Although epileptics were rated more hyperactive than their same-sex nonepileptic classmates by their teachers, minimal differences were found on several tests of vigilance and attentiveness. Each of these studies was also confounded by inclusion of children taking phenobarbital, an anticonvulsant known to cause hyperactivity.

At this time, evidence supporting the correlation of childhood epilepsy to other psychiatric disorders, such as depression, anxiety, or psychosis, remains very speculative and requires further clarification. Brent, Crumrine, Varma, Allan, and Allman (1987) have demonstrated an increased rate of depression among epileptic children while taking phenobarbital. Also, it has been reported that the rate of suicidal behavior is markedly elevated among epileptic youth (Brent, 1986; Hawton, Fagg, & Marsock, 1980). The etiology of the depressive disorders in these cases is not clear, however, and may be due to a combination of factors, including impact of chronic illness, neuropsychological deficits secondary to recurrent seizures, family stress, and the effects of anticonvulsant medications rather than an inherent predisposition of psychiatric illness. According to

Brent (1986), the suicide attempts by epileptic patients tend to be premeditated and followed by persistent suicidal ideation, not the impulsive acts that characterize behavior typical of an organic brain disorder.

A psychotic disorder in children with epilepsy is considered to be rare before puberty and may manifest in a minority of brain-damaged and mentally retarded patients (Corbett & Trimble, 1983; Lindsay, 1972). However, there has been no systematic study of psychosis in epileptic children.

Panic attacks are also included in the differential for seizure disorder (Weilberg, Bear, & Sachs, 1985). The diagnosis has been made in adults when the patient does not respond to treatment with anticonvulsant medication. Occasionally, patients will be treated with a combination of anticonvulsant and antianxiety medications (Silver, Hales, & Yudofsky, 1990).

SENSORY DEFICITS

Children may develop psychiatric disorder as a consequence of sensory loss. Youngsters have been identified as hyperactive or inattentive with complaints that the child cannot focus or maintain interest in academics. The problem may be due to varying degrees of hearing loss. Unfortunately when these behavioral symptoms persist and the etiology is not discovered, the child's presentation may be complicated by development of oppositional disorder, aggression, conduct disorder, or recurrent somatic complaints. Detection of hearing loss may involve reviewing the patient's medical history for presence of recurrent ear infections, a maternal history of rubella or cytomegalo virus (CMV) during pregnancy, treatment of the child with aminoglycoside antibiotics, or a family history of hearing loss. Children may also experience problems with attention and behavioral control in the classroom when their vision is poor. They may not be able to see the chalkboard or read the classroom materials. Progression of behavioral symptoms parallels those that accompany hearing loss and are a byproduct of continued frustration in the child.

SLEEP APNEA

Sleep apnea results when the patient periodically stops breathing during sleep. The etiology may be central and may involve an inability of the brain to signal the muscles to breathe or may be secondary to an obstruction that closes the throat. The patient wakes up frequently during the night in order to begin breathing again. The syndrome produces daytime sleepiness, irritability, sleep-continuity disorders, and personality change. Snoring may be the most characteristic sign of obstructive apnea. The diagnosis is most appropriate made in a sleep laboratory where the individual's sleep may be monitored throughout the night.

GASTROINTESTINAL DISORDERS

Recurrent Abdominal Pain

Psychological factors are thought to be major contributors to presentation in children and adolescents with recurrent abdominal pain (RAP) (Craig & Brown, 1984). These patients have generally been described as neurotic with a history of emotional disorders. Wasserman, Whitington, and Rivara (1988) examined a group of children between the ages of 6 and 16 who experienced abdominal pain of such severity to interfere with activities for at least 3 months. An evaluation was performed that included questionnaires and semistructured interviews for the child and the parent. Data were also collected from teachers. Patients with RAP were compared with a matched control group without disorder from the subjects' classrooms and pediatricians' offices. Children with RAP had higher scores on the internalizing scale of the Child Behavior Checklist and were generally described as more fearful, inhibited, and overcontrolled. RAP occurred concomitantly with the development of psychiatric disorder in 50% of the patients. In one-third of the patients, RAP occurred in the context of an adjustment disorder and usually accompanied the following stressors: death or separation from a loved one, psychiatric hospitalization of a family member, and family turmoil. The study's finding of the prevalence of anxiety disorders is consistent with the adult literature, which has found that RAP patients have levels of anxiety consistent with those of psychiatric inpatients (Hodges, Kline, Barbero, & Woodruff, 1985).

Inflammatory Bowel Disease

Inflammatory bowel disease (IBD) has been associated with psychiatric disorder, particularly depression and anxiety, in several studies (Gerbert, 1980; Helzer, Stillings, Charmmas, Norland, & Alpers, 1982; Tarter, Switala, Carra, Edwards, & Van Thiel, 1987). Burke et al. (1989) noted a significant rate of dysthymia and atypical depression in childhood IBD as well. These results are consistent with earlier work that demonstrated a tendency for pediatric patients with ulcerative colitis and Crohn's disease to be anxious, fearful, withdrawn, and depressed (Raymer, Weininger, & Hamilton, 1984; Wood et al., 1987).

Hepatic Diseases

Hepatic diseases present with behavior changes consistent with mood disorder, including lethargy, apathy, mania, and symptoms of anxiety and obsessive-compulsive disorder. Patients may also present with psychosis and delirium (Lishman, 1988). The course can wax and wane and is frequently attributed to changes in personality.

CONNECTIVE TISSUE DISEASE

Systemic lupus erythematosus (SLE) is often cited as a connective tissue disease that causes psychiatric disorders. In addition, the treatment of SLE usually involves use of steroids, medications that frequently produce emotional and behavioral side effects. Differentiating the psychiatric effects of the illness from those of the drugs can be challenging. Lupus can cause CNS vasculitis, hemorrhage, and meningitis. The progressive and multisystem nature of the illness may cause delirium (Stoudemire & Levenson, 1991). High doses of corticosteroids (40 mg or greater) may produce a variety of psychiatric reactions, including confusion, paranoia, hallucinations, mania, depression, and catatonia (Lewis & Smith, 1983). In addition, symptoms may also develop as the steroid medication is withdrawn (Judd et al., 1983).

AIDS

The number of AIDS cases in the pediatric population is rapidly increasing, and the psychiatric impact of the disorder should be considered in the process of evaluating at-risk patients. The most common early manifestations of AIDS in children are loss of developmental milestones and failure to thrive (Belfer & Munir, 1991). Neuropsychiatric effects of the disorder are noteworthy and include cognitive deterioration, psychosis, mania, obsessive-compulsive disorder, and depression. Young men with AIDS are considered a significant suicide risk. Presenile dementia occasionally seen in patients is called the AIDS dementia complex and is characterized by poor concentration, motor slowing, and memory loss (Navia, Jordan, & Price, 1986). Depressive symptoms in children and adolescents may have both a psychological and physiological etiology. In addition to the neuropsychiatric complications, AIDS produces a variety of metabolic and endocrinologic problems that contribute to the development of mood disorders. The pain, isolation, and family stress that accompany such a devastating illness may also precipitate depression in patients (Spiegel & Mayers, 1991). AIDS should be suspected in populations considered high risk. These include drug-using adolescents, hemophiliacs, runaways, gay and bisexual youth, sexually active patients with histories of unprotected sex, prostitutes, and patients with a history of sexual abuse and/or antisocial behaviors (Stiffman & Earls, 1990).

PREMENSTRUAL SYNDROME

The emotional impact of a premenstrual syndrome (PMS) has been discussed frequently in the literature and is being considered as a diagnostic entity. Patients complain of headaches, bloating, and fatigue that are complicated by accompanying symptoms of depression, irritability, anger, anxiety, substance abuse, and eating disorder (Stotland & Smith, 1991). The diagnosis is made when the development of the psychiatric symptoms can be clearly related to a specific phase of the menstrual cycle. No biochemical or physiologic markers exist for the disorder. Although the symptoms are consistent with a diagnosis of atypical depression, no association between PMS and depressive disorders has been identified based on studies of the longitudinal course of the syndrome (Rubinow & Schmidt, 1987).

HEAD TRAUMA

Each year in the United States, an estimated 375,000 children and adolescents sustain a closed-head injury; of those, approximately 100,000 result in hospitalization. The percentages by injury severity, as determined from the Glasgow Coma Scale, is as follows: 88% with mild brain injury, 7% with moderate brain injury, and 5% with severe brain injury (Kraus, Fife, & Conroy, 1987). Problems created by head trauma of even a mild degree are lasting and affect performance in cognitive, emotional, and social domains. Head trauma in children and adolescents occurs in a variety of situations, with the circumstances determined by the age of the patient. Under the age of 2, most are the result of accidents in the home. Early to middle childhood is marked by falls, usually from stairs and playground equipment. In later childhood and adolescence, head trauma usually involves traffic accidents where the victim is the driver, a passenger, or a pedestrian (Rutter, Chadwick, & Shaffer, 1983).

Rutter et al. (1983) note that 50% of children with preexisting psychiatric disorder have behavioral problems after significant head injury. At least as interesting was the high percentage (25%) of children with behavioral sequelae to head injury without premorbid psychiatric problems. The physiologic consequences of injury play an important role in posttraumatic adjustment. The most significant sequelae of injury is the presence of posttraumatic seizure disorder. Seizures generally indicate structural damage to the brain, and this is reflected in the lack of behavioral change in these patients despite seizure control.

Location of brain injury has not been directly related to the character of the psychiatric disorder in children. The nature of the injuries is most commonly diffuse with a resulting syndrome that includes deficits in social perception, judgment, and interaction. The problems in comparing adult to pediatric brain trauma include the belief that children have "greater brain plasticity" that results in less specific neurological deficits and a greater degree of recovery following injury. In addition, it has been difficult to compare the extent of deficit in a child who has not yet acquired cognitive and motor skills to an adult whose skill level may be quite sophisticated.

Psychiatric disorders following a mild head trauma have not been consistently identified. In a study by Brown, Chadwick, Shaffer, Rutter, and Traub (1981), children with severe injury had a much higher rate of new psychiatric illness in the follow-up period. The sample of mild-head-injured children had a higher baseline level of psychiatric disorder than the control group, while the severe-head-injured population had a premorbid level that was comparable to controls. There was no difference in the development of new psychiatric disorder when comparing the mild-head-injured population to the control group. The authors assumed that preexisting psychiatric disorders precipitated the mild head trauma.

The argument that behavior problems in children and adolescents with mild head trauma are premorbid conditions is not universally accepted. Bassett and Slater (1990) studied the neuropsychological functioning of 29 adolescents with mild to moderate trauma. These patients did not have premorbid histories of school failure or delinquency, nor were their head traumas more likely to be the by-product of drunk or reckless driving than those of more severe head trauma victims. A study by Fletcher, Ewing-Cobbs, Miner, Levin, and Eisenburg (1990) found little psychopathology in mildly injured children and did not demonstrate a tendency for mild- and moderate-head-injured children to have a higher incidence of behavioral disorders either at baseline or for up to 3 months after the trauma.

SOMATOFORM DISORDERS

The definition of *somatization* as described by the American Psychiatric Association (APA) is as follows: a case of somatoform disorder includes "one or more physical complaints" (e.g., fatigue, loss of appetite, gastrointestinal or urinary complaints), and either "appropriate evaluation uncovers no organic pathology or pathophysiologic mechanism (e.g., physical disorder or the effect of injury . . .) to account for the physical complaints" or "when there is related organic pathology, the physical complaints or resulting social or occupational impairment is grossly in excess of what would be expected from the physical findings" (APA, 1993).

Accompanying signs of distress are usually the hallmark of organic disease. Children and adolescents with physical illness usually have deteriorating school performance, visual loss, fatigue, posture abnormalities, and a variety of symptoms that suggest a medical disorder. Psychogenic disorders, on the other hand, usually have a rapid onset, a family history of similar presentations, a clear discrepancy between the physical findings and the patient's complaint, and some conscious or unconscious motivation for the maintenance of these symptoms. In the adult literature, 26% of patients presenting to a general medical clinic have evidence of a somatoform disorder. In the pediatric population, the rate may be as high as 50% (Kellner, 1991).

Presence of a somatoform disorder is dependent upon a thorough and appropriate medical evaluation. Yet, the extent of such an assessment is subjective and may be limited by practical and financial constraints. Physical disease and somatoform disorder can certainly coexist, and the presence of a diagnosed medical problem does not forego the need to treat the psychiatric component. The majority of pediatric conversion disorder patients seen by the psychiatric service have neurologic problems. These include pseudoseizures and syncope, motor dysfunction, sensory disturbances, headaches, dizziness, sleep difficulties, eating disorders, vomiting, hiccups, psychogenic cough, and tremors. Patients may be suffering from a medical disorder in the neurologic group, and the most commonly missed diagnoses are spinal cord tumors, epileptic seizures, and neurodegenerative diseases (Editorial, 1991).

Depression and somatic complaints certainly occur together, but the relationship between the two is not clear. When treated in a psychiatric setting, depression and somatic complaints do not necessarily improve together. Somatic complaints may hide a developing depressive disorder. Anxiety disorders and, more specifically, panic have been noted in the somatic population. Panic symptoms were more likely to focus on cardiac complaints (chest pain, tachycardia, and irregular heart beat), gastrointestinal complaints (epigastric distress), and neurologic complaints (headache, dizziness, vertigo, syncope, and parasthesias) (Kellner, 1991).

Children may express emotional distress through somatic complaints based on experience or learning. Few studies in adults or children have been able to clearly demonstrate this, however. The character of the home environment has been a determining factor. Socioeconomic class, level of education, and culture are all determining factors and may also influence the level of physiologic arousal in the patient. Generally, patients from lower socioeconomic class, with less education, and of the Hispanic community are at greater risk. An additional factor is the degree of attention that the individual pays to particular physical symptoms. With repetition, the threshold for sensing distress is likely to fall. This behavior, as well, can be modeled in the home (Kellner, 1991).

Theories about somatization have focused on the development of symptoms as a result of repressed anger developed through life experiences. Studies in this population do not support this view. Repression may be important because of the psychological stress that is created with the accompanying development of physical disorder and somatic complaints. In studies that have compared patients who practice self-disclosure with those who do not, self-disclosure results in improved immune function and more positive reports on health indexes (Pennebaker, 1989).

Secondary gain may be a factor in symptom development. Patients that are prone to neurotic disorders are more likely to develop somatic complaints in the face of financial gain or litigation (Bishop & Torch, 1979). In general, however, the literature on the effect of litigation has been inconsistent. There is no definitive proof that legal action aggravates symptoms or prolongs the duration. Furthermore, completion of litigation does not affect outcome in somatization cases. The design of such studies is problematic and contributes to the lack of conclusive data. Concomitant psychiatric disorder seems to be more important in the development of somatization disorder than any of the dynamics described.

SUMMARY

The treatment of the psychiatrically ill child or adolescent requires a thorough consideration of medical as well as psychological factors. The careful and diligent planning that goes into case management may be ineffective if the clinician has forgotten to consider the impact of organic disease. Few situations are as discouraging as those in which the patient has been treated with a variety of psychosocial interventions only for the therapist to later discover that a medical disorder was at the core of the problem. The child or adolescent may also have missed appropriate pediatric care, perhaps at some risk, as a consequence. Physicians may delay appropriate treatment for young patients because of a failure to recognize the role psychiatric symptoms play in the early presentation of medical illness. Treatment of physical disorders may be complicated by presence of psychiatric symptoms, and psychiatric symptoms occasionally lead physicians to order unwarranted medical tests and procedures when mental health treatment would have been more appropriate. These circumstances can be prevented with some fundamental knowledge of the interrelationship between organic and functional illness and with ready access to medical consultation.

REFERENCES

American Psychiatric Association (1993). *DSM-IV draft criteria.* Washington, DC: Author.

Barkley, R. (1981). *Hyperactive children: A handbook for diagnosis and treatment.* New York: Guilford Press.

Bassett, S. S., & Slater, E. J. (1990). Neuropsychological function in adolescents sustaining mild closed head injury. *Journal of Pediatric Psychology, 15,* 225–236.

Bear, D., & Fedio, P. (1977). Quantitative analysis of interictal behavior in temporal lobe epilepsy. *Archives of Neurology, 34,* 454–467.

Bear, D., Levin, K., Blumer, D., Chetham, D., & Ryder, J. (1982). Interictal behavior in hospitalized temporal lobe epileptics—Relationship to idiopathic psychiatric syndromes. *Journal of Neurology, Neurosurgery, and Psychiatry, 45,* 481–488.

Belfer, M. L., & Munir, K. (1991). Acquired immunodeficiency syndrome. In J. M. Wiener (Ed.), *Textbook of child and adolescent psychiatry,* (1st ed.) (pp. 495–506). Washington, DC: American Psychiatry Press.

Betts, T. (1981). Depression, anxiety and epilepsy. In E. Reynolds & M. Trimble (Eds.) *Epilepsy and psychiatry* (pp. 60–71). London: Churchill Livingstone.

Bishop, E. R., & Torch, E. M. (1979). Dividing hysteria: A preliminary investigation of conversion disorder and psycholgia. *Journal of Nervous and Mental Disease, 167,* 348–356.

Brent, D. (1986). Over-representation of epileptics in a consecutive series of suicide attempters seen at a children's hospital, 1978–1983. *Journal of the American Academy of Child and Adolescent Psychiatry, 25,* 242–246.

Brent, D., Crumrine, P., Varma, R., Allan, M., & Allman, C. (1987). Phenobarbital treatment and major depressive disorder in children with epilepsy. *Pediatrics, 80*, 909–917.

Breslau, N. (1985). Psychiatric disorder in children with physical disabilities. *Journal of the American Academy of Child and Adolescent Psychiatry, 24*, 87–94.

Brown, G., Chadwick, O., Shaffer, D., Rutter, M., & Traub, M. (1981). A prospective study of children with head injuries: III. Psychiatric sequelae. *Psychological Medicine, 11*, 63–78.

Bukberg, J., Penman, D., & Holland, J. C. (1984). Depression in hospitalized cancer patients. *Psychosomatic Medicine, 46*, 199–212.

Burke, P. M., Meyer, V., Kocoshis, S. A., Orenstein, D. M., Chandra, R., Nord, D. J., Sauer, J., & Cohen, E. (1989). Depression and anxiety in pediatric inflammatory bowel disease. *Journal of the American Academy of Child and Adolescent Psychiatry, 28*, 948–951.

Cadman, D., Boyle, M., Satzmari, P., & Offord, D. R. (1987). Chronic illness, disability, and mental and social well-being: Findings of the Ontario Child Health Study. *Pediatrics, 79*, 805–813.

Campbell, M., Rosenbloom, S., Perry, R., George, A. E., Kricheff, I. I., Anderson, L., Small, A. M., & Jennings, S. J. (1982). Computerized axial tomography in young autistic children. *American Journal of Psychiatry, 139*, 510–512.

Cavazzuti, G. (1980). Epidemiology of different types of epilepsy in school age children of Modena, Italy. *Epilepsia, 21*, 57–62.

Chisholm, J. J. (1983). Increased lead absorption and lead poisoning. In R. E. Behrman, V. C. Vaughan, & W. E. Nelson (Eds.), *Nelson textbook of pediatrics* (12th ed.). Philadelphia: W. B. Saunders.

Choice of a beta blocker. (1986). Medical letter.

Clark, D. C., Cavanaugh, S. V., & Gibbons, R. D. (1983). The core symptoms of depression in medical and psychiatric patients. *Journal of Nervous and Mental Disease, 171*, 705–713.

Corbett, J., & Trimble, M. (1983). Epilepsy and anticonvulsant medication. In M. Rutter (Ed.), *Developmental neuropsychiatry* (pp. 112–129). New York: Guilford Press.

Craig, T. K. J., & Brown, G. W. (1984). Goal frustration and life events in the aetiology of painful gastrointestinal disorder. *Journal of Psychosomatic Research, 28*, 411–421.

Editorial. (1991). Neurological conversion disorders in childhood. *Lancet, 337*, 889–890.

Fletcher, J. M., Ewing-Cobbs, L., Miner, M. E., Levin, H. S., & Eisenberg, H. M. (1990). Behavioral changes after closed head injury in children. *Journal of Consulting and Clinical Psychology, 58*, 93–98.

Flor-Henry, P. (1983). Determinants of psychosis in epilepsy: Laterality and forced normalization. *Biological Psychiatry, 18*, 1045–1057.

Gerbert, B. (1980). Psychological aspects of Crohn's disease. *Journal of Behavioral Medicine, 3*, 41–58.

Gillberg, C., & Svendsen, P. (1983). Childhood psychosis and computed tomographic brain scan findings. *Journal of Autism and Developmental Disorders, 13*, 19–31.

Graef, J. W. (1983). Environmental toxins. In M. D. Levine, W. B. Carey, A. C. Crocker, & R. T. Gross (Eds.), *Developmental behavioral pediatrics*. Philadelphia: W. B. Saunders.

Hall, R. C. W., Gardner, E. R., Stickney, S. K., LeCann, A. F., & Popkin, M. K. (1980). Physical illness manifesting as a psychiatric disease: II. Analysis of a state hospital inpatient population. *Archives of General Psychiatry, 37*, 989–995.

Hawton, K., Fagg, T., & Marsack, P. (1980). Association between epilepsy and attempted suicide. *Journal of Neurology, Neurosurgery, and Psychiatry, 43*, 168–170.

Helzer, J. E., Stillings, W. A., Chammas, S., Norland, C. C., & Alpers, D. H. (1982). A controlled study of the association between ulcerative colitis and psychiatric diagnosis. *Digestive Diseases and Sciences, 27*, 513–518.

Hermann, B., Black, R., & Chhabria, S. (1981). Behavior problems and social competence in children with epilepsy. *Epilepsia, 22*, 703–710.

Herranz, J., Armijo, J., & Arteaga, T. (1988). Clinical side-effects of phenobarbital, primidone, phenytoin, carbamazepine and valproate during monotherapy in children. *Epilepsia, 29*, 794–804.

Herzberg, J., & Fenwick, P. (1988). The etiology of aggression in temporal lobe epilepsy. *British Journal of Psychiatry, 1153*, 50.

Hinton, G., & Knights, R. (1969). Neurological and psychological characteristics of 100 children with seizures. In B. Richard (Ed.), *Proceedings of the first congress for the International Association for the Scientific Study of Mental Deficiency* (pp. 351–356). London: Michael Jackson Publishing.

Hoare, P. (1984a). The development of psychiatric disorders in school children with epilepsy. *Developmental Medicine and Child Neurology, 26*, 3–13.

Hoare, P. (1984b). Psychiatric disturbance in the families of epileptic children. *Developmental Medicine and Child Neurology, 26*, 14–19.

Hodges, K., Kline, J. J., Barbero, G., & Woodruff, C. (1985). Anxiety in children with recurrent abdominal pain and their parents. *Psychosomatics, 26*, 859–866.

Hodgman, C., McAnarney, R., & Myers, G. (1979). Emotional complications of adolescent grand mal epilepsy. *Journal of Pediatrics, 95*, 309–312.

Holdsworth, L., & Whitmore, K. (1974). A study of children with epilepsy attending normal schools. I: Their seizure patterns, progress and behavior in school. *Developmental Medicine and Child Neurology, 16*, 746–758.

Judd, F. K., Burrows, G. D., & Norman, T. R. (1983). Psychosis after withdrawal of steroid therapy. *Medical Journal of Australia, 2*, 350–351.

Kellner, R. (1991). *Psychosomatic syndromes and somatic symptoms.* Washington, DC: American Psychiatry Press.

Kohrman, A. F., Netzloff, M. L., & Weil, W. B. (1987). Diabetes mellitus. In A. M. Rudolph (Ed.), *Pediatrics* (p. 274). Norwalk, CT: Appleton and Lange.

Koranyi, E. K. (1979). Morbidity and rate of undiagnosed physical illness in a psychiatric clinic population. *Archives of General Psychiatry, 36*, 414–449.

Kraus, J. F., Fife, D., & Conroy, C. (1987). Pediatric brain injuries: The nature, clinical course, and early outcomes in a defined United States population. *Pediatrics, 79*, 501–507.

Lewis, D. A., & Smith, R. E. (1983). Steroid induced psychiatric syndrome. A report of 14 cases and a review of the literature. *Journal of Affective Disorders, 5*, 319–332.

Lindsay, J. (1972). The difficult epileptic child. *British Medical Journal, 3*, 283–285.

Lishman, W. A. (1988). *Organic psychiatry: The psychological consequences of cerebral disorder* (2nd ed.). Oxford: Blackwell Scientific Publications.

Menkes, J. H. (1990). Tumors of the nervous system. In J. H. Menkes (Ed.), *Textbook of child neurology* (4th ed.) (pp. 526–582). Philadelphia: Lea & Febiger.

Nasrallah, H., Loney, J., Olson, L., McCalley-Whitters, M., Kramer, J., & Jacoby, C. (1986). Cortical atrophy in young adults with a history of hyperactivity in childhood. *Psychiatry Research, 17*, 241–246.

Navia, B. A., Jordan, B. D., & Price, R. W. (1986). The AIDS dementia complex. I. Clinical features. *Annals of Neurology, 19*, 517–524.

Needleman, H. L., Gunnae, C., Leviton, A., Reed, R., Peresie, H., Maher, C., & Barrett, P. (1979). Deficits in psychologic and classroom performance of children with elevated dentine lead levels. *New England Journal of Medicine, 300*, 689–695.

Newacheck, P. W., McManus, M. A., & Harriette, B. F. (1991). Prevalence and impact of chronic illness among adolescents. *American Journal of Diseases in Children, 145*, 1367–1373.

Noyes, R., & Kathol, R. G. (1986). Depression and cancer. *Psychiatric Development*, *2*, 77–100.

Ounsted, C. (1955). The hyperkinetic syndrome in epileptic children. *Lancet*, *2*, 303–311.

Pennebaker, J. W. (1989). Confession, inhibition, and disease. *Advances in Experimental Social Psychology*, *22*, 211–244.

Perez, M., Trimble, M., Murray, N., & Reider, I. (1985). Epileptic psychoses: An evaluation of PSE profiles. *British Journal of Psychiatry*, *146*, 155–163.

Perrin, J. M., MacLean, W. E., & Perrin, E. C. (1989). Parental perceptions of health status and psychologic adjustment of children with asthma. *Pediatrics*, *83*, 26–30.

Pless, I. B., & Pinkerton, P. (1975). *Chronic childhood disorder: Promoting patterns of adjustment.* London: Henry Kimpton.

Pless, I. B., & Roghmann, K. J. (1971). Chronic illness and its consequences: Observations based on three epidemiologic surveys. *Journal of Pediatrics*, *79*, 351–359.

Popkin, M. K., Callies, A. L., & Colon, E. A. (1988, June). *The treatment and outcome of adjustment disorder in medically ill patients.* Paper presented at The Treatment of Mental Disorders in General Health Care Settings: A Research Conference, Pittsburgh, PA.

Raymer, J., Weininger, O., & Hamilton, J. R. (1984). Psychological problems in children with abdominal pain. *Lancet*, *1*, 439–440.

Rifkin, A., Reardon, G., Siris, S., Karagji, B., Kim, Y., Hackstaff, L., & Endicott, N. (1985). Trimipramine in physical illness with depression. *Journal of Clinical Psychiatry*, *46*, 4–8.

Robins, L. (1981). Epidemiological approaches to natural history research. *Journal of the American Academy of Child Psychiatry*, *20*, 556–580.

Rubinow, D. R., & Schmidt, P. J. (1987). Mood disorders and the menstrual cycle. *Journal of Reproductive Medicine*, *32*, 389–394.

Rutter, M. (1983). Low level lead exposure: Sources, effects and implications. In M. Rutter & R. Russell Jones (Eds.), *Lead versus health.* New York: Wiley.

Rutter, M., Chadwick, O., & Shaffer, D. (1983). Head injury. In M. Rutter (Ed.), *Developmental neuropsychiatry* (pp. 83–111). New York: Guilford Press.

Rutter, M., Graham, P., & Yule, W. (1970). A neuropsychiatric study in childhood. In *Clinics in developmental medicine Nos. 35/36.* London: Heinemann/Spastics International Medical Publications.

Silver, J. M., Hales, R. E., & Yudofsky, S. C. (1990). Psychiatric consultation to neurology. In A. Tasman, S. M. Goldfinger, & C. A. Kaufmann (Eds.), *American psychiatric press review of psychiatry* (Vol. 9, pp. 433–465). Washington, DC: American Psychiatric Press.

Spiegel, L., & Mayers, A. (1991). Psychosocial aspects of AIDS in children and adolescents. *Pediatric Clinics of North America*, *38*, 153–167.

Sternlieb, I., & Scheinberg, I. H. (1964). Penicillamine therapy for hepatolenticular degeneration. *Journal of the American Medical Association*, *189*, 748–754.

Stiffman, A. R., & Earls, F. (1990). Behavioral risks of human immunodeficiency virus infection in adolescent medical patients. *Pediatrics*, *85*, 303–310.

Stores, G. (1975). Behavioral effects on anti-epileptic drugs. *Developmental Medicine and Child Neurology*, *17*, 647–658.

Stores, G. (1978). School children with epilepsy at risk for learning and behavioral problems. *Developmental Medicine and Child Neurology*, *20*, 502–508.

Stotland, M. L., & Smith, T. E. (1990). Psychiatric consultation to obstetrics and gynecology: Systems and syndromes. In A. Tasman, S. M. Goldfinger, & C. A. Kaufman (Eds.), *American Psychiatric Press Review of Psychiatry* (*Vol. 9*, pp. 537–563). Washington, DC: American Psychiatric Press.

Stoudemire, G. A., & Levenson, J. L. (1990). Psychiatric consultation to internal medicine. In A.

Tasman, S. M. Goldfinger, C. A. Kaufman (Eds.), *American Psychiatric Press Review of Psychiatry* (*Vol. 9*, pp. 466–490). Washington, DC: American Psychiatric Press.

Strain, J. J., & Fullop, G. (1990). Mood disorders and medical illness. In A. Tasman, S. M. Goldfinger, & C. A. Kaufman (Eds.), *American Psychiatric Press Review of Psychiatry* (*Vol. 9*, pp. 537–563). Washington, DC: American Psychiatric Press.

Tarter, R. E., Switala, J., Carra, J., Edwards, K. L., & Van Thiel, D. H. (1987). Inflammatory bowel disease: Psychiatric status of patients before and after disease onset. *International Journal of Psychiatry in Medicine, 17*, 173–181.

Trimble, M., & Cull, C. (1988). Children of school age: the influence of anti-epileptic drugs on behavior and intellect. *Epilepsia, 29* (Suppl. 3), S15–S19.

Wasserman, A. L., Whitington, P. F., & Rivara, F. P. (1988). Psychogenic basis for abdominal pain in children and adolescents. *Journal of the American Academy of Child and Adolescent Psychiatry, 27*, 179–184.

Weilberg, J. B., Bear, D. M., & Sachs, G. (1985). Psychotic syndromes in epilepsy. *American Journal of Psychiatry, 142*, 1053–1056.

Weiland, S. K., Pless, I. B., & Roghmann, K. J. (1992). Chronic illness and mental health problems in pediatric practice: Results from a survey of primary care providers. *Pediatrics, 89*, 445–449.

Winokur, G., Black, D. W., & Nasrallah, A. (1988). Depression secondary to other psychiatric disorders and medical illnesses. *American Journal of Psychiatry, 145*, 233–237.

Wood, B., Watkins, J. B., Boyle, J. T., Nogueira, J., Zimand, E., & Carroll, L. (1987). Psychological functioning in children with Crohn's disease and ulcerative colitis: Implications for models of psychobiological interaction. *Journal of the American Academy of Child and Adolescent Psychiatry, 26*, 774–781.

Zametkin, A. J., Andreason, P., Kruesi, M. J. P. (1991). Laboratory and diagnostic testing. In M. Weiner (Ed.), *Textbook of child and adolescent psychiatry* (pp. 121–127). Washington, DC: American Psychiatric Press.

CHAPTER 4

Evaluation of Child Maltreatment

JOAN KAUFMAN AND ANTHONY P. MANNARINO

INTRODUCTION

For those clinicians who are about to turn to the next chapter because they do not treat maltreated children, we begin with a cautionary note. Never assume your patients do not have a history of abuse just because they or their parents fail to spontaneously report it. In a recent study conducted in an outpatient clinic at a major urban university center (Lanktree, Briere, & Zaidi, 1991), rates of abuse detected with and without direct inquiry were compared. Without direct inquiry, the rate of abuse in the clinic population was estimated at 6.9%. With direct inquiry, the rate rose to 31.4%, a 4.5-fold increase in the estimated number of children with a history of abuse. Utilization of multiple information-gathering techniques may also be necessary to obtain information about children's abuse history. Given the opportunity to report abuse in two independent formats, a standard psychiatric intake interview and a confidential self-report survey, children have been found to be twice as likely to report abuse utilizing the self-report measure (Dill, Chu, Grob, & Eisen, 1991). These studies and others highlight that it is important to make multiple inquiries and to use multiple informants in assessing children's abuse history (Kaufman, Jones, Stieglitz, Vitulano, & Mannarino, in press; McGee, Wolfe, Yuen, & Camochan, 1991).

There are two fundamental tenets to remember when working with maltreated children:

1. The treatment of maltreated children requires working as part of a larger multidisciplinary team consisting of child protective services workers, law enforcement agents, and others.

2. Assessing the treatment needs of maltreated children requires moving beyond clinical symptomatology and abuse-related issues to other family and environmental factors.

In some samples of maltreated children (Kaufman et al., in press), problems of parental substance abuse and/or spousal violence have been documented in over 90% of cases. Unless these issues are addressed by the clinician, or some other provider working with the child's family, individual treatment efforts with the child will be seriously compromised.

Child abuse cases usually involve four phases of intervention:

1. The investigation
2. A child protection assessment
3. Crisis intervention
4. Planned treatment

Mental health professionals may be asked to intervene at any one of these phases, and it is important for the clinician to be cognizant of the fact that progression through these phases is often not strictly linear. A clinician may become involved with a case after the first three phases of intervention have transpired; yet information gathered during the process of treatment may necessitate another formal investigation, reassessment of the child's protection needs, and additional crisis intervention (Sgroi, Blick, & Porter, 1982a).

In this chapter, each of the phases of intervention will be discussed, with the greatest emphasis given to the planned treatment section. The salience of the two fundamental tenets stated above, working as part of a multidisciplinary team and examining individual and environmental factors when assessing the treatment needs of maltreated children—will be highlighted throughout this chapter. Prior to beginning the discussion of each of the intervention phases, confidentiality issues pertinent to working with abuse cases will be discussed because these issues are relevant to all four phases of intervention.

CONFIDENTIALITY ISSUES

In the 1950s and 1960s, laws were passed by each of the 50 states in the United States requiring professionals to report suspected cases of child abuse and neglect (Solnit, 1980). These laws have precedence over therapeutic boundaries and legally mandate professionals to share with authorities information that suggests that a given child is currently or is at risk of being abused. Clinicians should be familiar with the guidelines for reporting in the state in which they practice because the statutes for reporting vary somewhat from state to state.

Mental health professionals should discuss the legal limits of confidentiality with new clients at their first appointment (MacNair, 1992). Issues of confidentiality should be discussed with parents and children alike, with the limits of confidentiality explained to children using developmentally appropriate language (e.g., "All that we talk about here will be kept between you and me . . . unless it is an issue of safety . . . and I am worried you are going to hurt yourself or that you are going to get hurt some other way. When things come up that make me worry that you may not be safe, I will need to talk to your mom and your protective service worker about my worries so we can come up with a plan to make sure you stay safe. If I had some specific worries about your safety, I would always try to talk to you first, before talking to your mom and/or protective service worker").

When information that necessitates reporting is revealed in the process of therapeutic or investigative encounters, the need to report must be addressed in an open and candid manner. The parent and/or child should be reminded of the clinician's legal responsibility to report the concerns. If the family is already actively involved with protective services, parents should be given the opportunity to report these issues with their worker first because it will be viewed favorably by their worker for them to acknowledge the problem. Having the parents report the problem to protective services first will also minimize any negative consequences to the family-clinician relationship that may result from reporting. Clinicians are still officially mandated to inform the worker of the problem, however, even if parents do report the problem to their worker.

Issues of confidentiality and reporting are even more complicated in cases of nonvoluntary clients who are mandated to receive treatment by protective service workers. In these cases, it is recommended that the involuntary nature of the relationship be acknowledged from the start, together with the client's desire to have the professional out of his or her life (Jones, 1990). Clear treatment goals should be established toward this aim, and the professional's power and authority should be openly addressed (e.g., the professional's ability to make recommendations that affect child-placement decisions). While the limits of confidentiality and the inherent power structure of the relationship may seemingly threaten the establishment of a therapeutic alliance, this need not be the case if the professional is willing to prove himself or herself useful to the client; for example, by facilitating the provision of concrete resources and functioning as an advocate with other agencies for the client, a productive working relationship can be established with nonvoluntary clients, despite legal limitations to confidentiality (Jones, 1990; Oxley, 1981).

There are many liability concerns that clinicians have in working with child abuse cases (DeKraai & Sales, 1991). Some clinicians have taken issue with reporting laws over the limitations they place on clinical judgment (Ansell & Ross, 1988). For further discussion of these and other confidentiality issues relevant to working with maltreated children, the reader is referred to Kalichman (1990) and MacNair (1992).

THE INVESTIGATION

The purpose of an investigation in child maltreatment cases is to determine if the alleged abuse actually occurred. Child protection and law enforcement agencies have a statutory responsibility to determine the validity of abuse allegations, and they often call upon mental health professionals to conduct interviews and provide expert testimony to facilitate the investigation process.

In cases of physical abuse, validation of allegations rests almost exclusively on availability of physical evidence, with investigative interviews playing a small part in the determination of whether or not abuse occurred. When children present at the clinic with physical injuries believed to be due to abuse, it is important to contact protective services and to obtain an emergency medical evaluation as soon as possible. Without a physician's documented report of physical injuries, abuse allegations cannot be indicated and prosecution against the perpetrator cannot be pursued in most states. Discussion of the medical criteria used to validate cases of physical abuse is beyond the scope of this chapter, but the interested reader is referred to "AMA Diagnostic and Treatment Guidelines Concerning Child Abuse and Neglect" published by the American Medical Association Council on Scientific Affairs (1986).

In contrast to the situation in cases of physical abuse, physical evidence is much less paramount in validating sexual abuse cases because corroborating physical evidence to support sexual abuse allegations is relatively rare (Muram, 1989). Allegations are validated by information obtained through investigative interviews and a survey of behavioral indicators. The greatest emphasis is given to information obtained from investigative interviews, however, as most behavioral indicators (e.g., anxiety, bedwetting), with the possible exception of hypersexuality (Friedrich, Beilke, & Urquiza, 1987; Mannarino, Cohen, & Gregor, 1989), are not specific to sexual abuse (Sgroi, Porter, & Blick, 1982b).

Investigative interviewing, like standard psychiatric clinical interviewing, requires utilizing techniques to establish rapport and accommodating to the child's age and developmental level. In cases of both intra- and extrafamilial abuse, it is best to interview the child alone. If the alleged perpetrator is one of the parents, reasons for not interviewing the child in the presence of that parent are likely self-evident; but it is also preferable not to interview the child in the presence of the nonabusive parent as well. If the nonabusive parent is hostile toward the alleged perpetrator, the child may feel obliged to make false accusations; and if the nonabusive parent does not believe the abuse allegations, the child may feel compelled to deny that abuse occurred in order to please his or her parent.

Most children know why they are coming for an appointment when they present themselves to the clinician for an investigative interview. They will often appear physically distressed at the beginning of the interaction. It is helpful to acknowledge the purpose of the interview at the onset ("Do you know why you are here today? That's right, we will need to talk about what happened to you"). The child's discomfort should also be acknowledged and reassurances should be made that the clinician is an adult who knows how to talk to children about these types of things ("You look kind of frightened. A lot of children feel scared to talk about these kinds of things, but most children that I have talked to about these types of things in the past found it wasn't as bad as they thought"). The clinician should let the child know that he or she will have an opportunity to pace the interview and that the clinician would like to get to know other things about the child (e.g., information about school, friends, hobbies) before talking about what allegedly happened.

Prior to proceeding to any direct inquiry about the alleged abuse, the interviewer should learn the names the child uses to describe his or her sexual anatomy (e.g., "private parts") because this knowledge is essential to understanding accounts of alleged abuse. The information can be obtained via a discussion about bath time, doctor's office visit, and displays of affection (e.g., "Who helps you when you take a bath? Does ——— help you wash your private parts, or do you wash them all by yourself? Kids have different names for their private parts. What do you call yours?"). When inquiring about the alleged abuse, it is imperative that the interviewer use the anatomical terms the child has identified (e.g., "pee-pee," "bum").

Questions about inappropriate touching should not be suggestive or leading, they should be open ended (e.g., "Has anyone ever touched you in your private parts? Tell me what happened"). As much detail as possible should be elicited about the alleged abuse incident. A full description of the room where the abuse occurred can be inquired about first. It allows the child to start describing nonthreatening aspects of such abuse. Information about the other people who were at the site of the abuse, and their location relative to the child, can then be acquired. The approximate time of day that the abuse occurred can then be obtained by asking if it was light or dark out when the abuse occurred or by comparing the time of day the abuse occurred to other standard reference points like mealtime or bedtime.

Allowing the child to describe the less threatening contextual features of alleged abuse often eases discussion of the more distressing details about what actually occurred. Having information about contextual features also adds to the validity of the allegations, providing objective data that can be corroborated by collateral sources. It is important that the interviewer be nonjudgmental and supportive. The interviewer should also resist the temptation to ease the child's discomfort by filling in details for the child. In order for the report to be valid, the *child* must provide the details of the alleged abuse.

Play materials may be used to facilitate the investigative interview. Some children who have a hard time directly describing the incident are able to draw what happened and then tell what happened indirectly using their picture to facilitate the telling. Use of regular or anatomically correct dolls can also facilitate the investigative interview (Powell, 1991).

For further discussion on conducting investigative interviews with maltreated children and their parents, the reader is referred to the work of the American Academy of Child and Adolescent Psychiatry (1988); the American Professional Society on the Abuse of Children (1990); Gwynn (1988); Mannarino and Cohen (in press); Sgroi et al. (1982b); Sgroi (1988); and Weissman (1991).

Investigative interviews conducted by mental health professionals are sometimes performed in collaboration with law enforcement or protective service agency personnel. At other times, the results of solo investigative interviews are compiled in reports for these agencies, with court appearances to present findings also being necessary. An investigation report is not complete without review of the sexual abuse medical examination findings and, in many cases, completion of collateral interviews. The mental health professional who completes an investigative interview needs to work in close cooperation with other agencies involved with the case. In accepting responsibility to conduct the interview, the mental health professional also is accepting the responsibility of being a member of a larger multidisciplinary team, be it a formal or an informal commitment.

CHILD PROTECTION ASSESSMENT

The purpose of a child protection assessment is to determine if the child will be safe if he or she is maintained in his or her current living situation. State child protection agencies have statutory responsibility for determining likelihood of future abuse, safety of children's current placements, and need for removal. They are the only ones with the legal mandate to authorize a child's change in placement. Information obtained from mental health professionals in the process of conducting investigative interviews, crisis intervention, and/or planned treatment, however, is often essential in making child placement decisions.

In the state of Connecticut, for example, to ensure consistent implementation of child protection laws throughout the state and to help workers resolve difficult cases, the State Protective Services Department and the Yale University Child Study Center worked cooperatively to develop guidelines for protective service workers to use in considering the removal of children for whom placement was indicated (State of Connecticut, Department of Children and Youth Services, 1981). In many states, the responsibility for making placement decisions rests on the judgments of the individual worker and supervisor. The primary assumption of the Connecticut guidelines is that every child deserves to feel secure in his or her home environment. Security is believed to involve aspects of both physical and emotional well-being, which are believed to be best served by a permanent and enduring relationship with a primary caretaker. Consistent with this assumption, the aim of long-term placement planning is to provide continuity of care for children (Goldstein, Freud, & Solnit, 1973, 1979; State of Connecticut, Department of Children and Youth Services, 1981).

According to the Connecticut guidelines, situations that warrant consideration of removal include nonaccidental serious physical injury, sexual assault, abandonment, and life-threatening behavior toward the child (e.g., dropping baby from window) attacking child with weapon). Injuries indicated in the guidelines to be serious enough to warrant removal consist of, but are not limited to, significant burns, wounds from stabbing or shooting, severe lacerations, damaged internal organs, and broken bones.

Beyond severity of abuse, additional factors to consider when making placement decisions are (a) chronicity, (b) proximity of the perpetrator, (c) availability of sufficient services to alleviate the risk of future abuse, (d) availability of a functioning adult ally (an adult who believes the child's accusations of abuse and is willing to protect the child from future abuse), (e) spousal violence, (f) parental alcohol/substance abuse, (g) other factors that may compromise the ability of a functioning adult ally to protect the child or the ability of a perpetrator to control his or her own behavior, (h) the parents' willingness to engage in treatment, and (i) the child's response to the situation. These factors are briefly discussed in the following paragraphs.

Milder forms of abuse may warrant a child's removal from the home if the abuse has been chronic, and if there is evidence that the child's physical and emotional well-being is compromised. In contrast, more severe forms of abuse may not necessitate a child's removal from the home if the perpetrator does not have ongoing access to the child, if the factors that caused the abuse were identified and steps taken to prevent reabuse, or if sufficient services are available to support the family and prevent reabuse (e.g., family preservation services). The likelihood of the success of steps taken to prevent reabuse depend greatly on the presence of a functioning adult ally (Sgroi, 1982). In the absence of a functioning ally, risk of reabuse is often quite high.

There are many reasons that a parent may not believe a child's accusations about abuse, even in the face of convincing physical evidence (e.g., anal scarring), and, thus, not be able to act as a functioning adult ally. Parents with a history of abuse themselves may have difficulty accepting their child's allegations because it forces them to confront traumatic memories of their own victimization. Information about parents' experiences of victimization should always be surveyed when working with maltreated children, especially when the parent is having difficulty supporting the child.

Spousal violence can also compromise a parent's ability to believe a child's allegations of abuse because the parent may be fearful that accepting such allegations will result in life-threatening personal consequences. It can also compromise the parent's ability to prevent reabuse because a parent who is also abused may be physically unable to protect the child—or psychologically unable to do what is required. Alcohol and substance abuse can also impair judgment and complicate a parent's ability to protect the child, as can factors such as parental psychiatric illness or physical disability. When the perpetrator has some of these other problems (e. g., alcohol/substance abuse, psychiatric illness) as well, the likelihood of reabuse is further enhanced.

Parents who are willing to participate in treatment and acknowledge their problems, be they utilization of excessive punishment, spousal violence, or substance abuse, are at lower risk of reabusing their children. Rates of reabuse of children among families receiving intervention services, however, have been documented to be as high as 47% in some studies (Cohn & Daro, 1987). Participation in treatment, therefore, is no guarantee against future abuse; so risk factors for reabuse must be continually monitored.

Multiple indicators should be sought to determine the child's ongoing safety, including utilization of observational data and material from direct interviews with the child. Parents may deny ongoing parent-child conflict or difficulty using appropriate disciplinary techniques, but observation of the dyad may provide strong evidence that these issues remain problematic. Information from direct evaluation of the child's perceived safety and accounts of the home situation may also contradict information provided by parents, and this information needs to be weighed heavily in making child protection decisions.

The child's safety inevitably will need to be reevaluated at different times during the course of treatment. Revelation of new incidents of abuse, parental substance abuse, spousal violence, or affiliation with a new paramour may lead to reconsideration of previous child placement decisions. As details about these and other things that affect the child's safety in his or her current placement are uncovered, it is imperative that the clinician report this information to the family's child protection worker, giving parents the opportunity to raise issues with their workers first. The reader can refer to Pecora (1991), Wald and Woolverton (1990), and Waterhouse and Carnie (1992) for further discussion on child protection issues.

As stated previously, information relevant for making child protection decisions may be obtained by mental health professionals at any one of the four phases of intervention. Once this information is obtained, it must be shared with protective services, who ultimately have the responsibility of making placement decisions. The nature of past abusive acts, as well as multiple family and environmental factors, must be considered in determining the likelihood of a child's risk for future abuse.

CRISIS INTERVENTION

The primary purpose of crisis intervention in child abuse cases is to meet the acute needs of children and families that arise after the disclosure or revelation of the abuse. Although it is officially the responsibility of the state protective services agencies to provide case management and crisis intervention services to maltreated children and their families, due to workers' large caseloads and limited state resources (Legislative Program Review and Investigations Committee, 1990), it is often necessary for mental health and other professionals working with the family to play an active role in crisis intervention efforts.

If the result of the child protection assessment indicates the need for placement, the initial phase of crisis intervention is designed to smooth the child's transition to out-of-home placement and to handle any problems that arise with this move. If the perpetrator, rather than the child, is removed from the home, a different set of issues usually needs to be addressed during this phase of intervention. Even when there are no changes in the family constellation, revelation of abuse may lead to an acute crisis that warrants intensive intervention.

If the child/victim is removed from the home, it may result in the development of acute psychiatric symptomatology. Symptoms may require (a) close monitoring from mental health professionals to assure the safety of the child, and (b) close work with foster parents so they are prepared to effectively address the child's mental health needs. All too many times, out-of-home placements fail because foster parents are not properly equipped to deal with intense acting-out behavior or other psychiatric symptoms in traumatized children (Henrey, Cossett, Auletta, & Egan, 1991; Twigg, 1991).

In addition to dealing with the child's response to removal, it is necessary to deal with the parents' response. Guidelines for visitation need to be established by protective services, with mental health professionals often given the responsibility of evaluating appropriateness of the guidelines and of working through problems that interfere with adherence to the guidelines. Much effort is also often required to help parents begin to work on the issues that need to be resolved prior to a child's return back to the home.

If the perpetrator is the main wage earner, removal of the perpetrator from the home may leave a family with few financial resources. Applications may have to be filed for rent assistance, food stamps, welfare, emergency placement in shelters, and the provision of other concrete needs. In cases involving spousal violence, it also may be necessary to file for a restraining order to protect the nonabusive parent and the remaining family members.

Without attention to these basic, life-sustaining needs, it will be impossible to address any of the therapeutic needs of the child and his or her family.

Removal of a perpetrator may raise other issues that will likely need to be addressed. The remaining parent may have ambivalent feelings about giving up the relationship with the abusive spouse, and the child may have intense feelings of guilt for "breaking up" his or her parents' marriage. Acute clinical symptomatology may have to be targeted for treatment at this phase of intervention in these cases as well.

In cases where there are no changes in the family constellation, crisis intervention may still be required. Revelations of abuse can elicit intense feelings of hopelessness, rage, and guilt. Crisis intervention efforts usually focus on processing the abuse and on coping with acute clinical symptomatology that emerged in response to trauma or to the revelation of the abuse.

As stated before, protective service workers' large caseloads are often prohibitive. Consequently, it is often necessary for mental health professionals working with abuse cases to step outside traditional roles and facilitate the provision of concrete material aid for maltreated children and their families. One service provider, however, is rarely able to provide the full range of services required, so it is necessary that professionals from different agencies work in close collaboration. For further discussion on providing crisis intervention services to maltreating families, the reader may refer to the work of Adnopoz, Nagler, and Sinanaglu (1987); Pecora, Fraser, and Haapala (1992); and Sgroi (1982).

PLANNED INTERVENTION

The purpose of the planned intervention phase of treatment is to address continuing problems that require ongoing care. In the case of the mental health professional, this usually involves treatment of specific psychiatric symptomatology. Although the mental health professional is ultimately responsible for quality of care provided, it is usually necessary to work collaboratively with protective services and other agencies to maximize treatment effectiveness.

The discussion up to this point has highlighted some of the complex issues that need to be considered when working with child abuse cases. The number of factors that must be evaluated in the process of treatment planning may appear unwieldy. However, the ecological model that has been proposed by Belsky (1980) to explain the etiology of abuse provides a valuable heuristic for organizing the factors that need to be considered when designing and implementing interventions with maltreated children (Kaufman & Zigler, 1992).

The Ecological Model of the Etiology of Child Abuse

Belsky (1980), in extending the work of Garbarino (1977), proposed the most comprehensive model of the etiology of child abuse that exists to date. He integrated Bronfenbrenner's (1979, 1977) conceptualization of the contexts in which development occurs with Tinbergen's (1951) analysis of ontogenetic development. Belsky organized the factors associated with the etiology of abuse into a framework comprised of four ecological levels: ontogenetic, microsystem, exosystem, and macrosystem. On the ontogenetic level, Belsky considered characteristics of parents who mistreat their children, such as history of abuse or poor impulse control. On the microsystem level, he discussed aspects of the family environment that increase the likelihood of abuse, such as having a poor marital relationship or significant family stressors. On the exosystem level, he included work and social factors, such as unemployment and lack of supports. On the macrosystem level, he depicted cultural determinants of abuse, such as society's acceptance of corporal punishment as a legitimate form of discipline. Table 4.1 includes examples of risk factors for abuse that have been organized using this ecological framework.

This ecological model is also helpful in conceptualizing the factors that affect the adaptation of maltreated children and in identifying foci for intervention efforts. Child attributes are considered on the ontogenetic level; parental and family characteristics are included on the microsystem level; economic and social factors are considered on the exosystem level; and cultural issues are included on the macrosystem level. Pertinent factors to be considered in designing planned interventions with maltreated children at each of these ecological levels are outlined in Table 4.2.

ONTOGENETIC FACTORS

Clinical Symptomatology

There are some clinicians who treat a history of sexual or physical abuse as an Axis I diagnosis (see DSM-IV; American Psychiatric Association, 1993). Knowing that a child has a history of abuse provides only the most rudimentary information necessary for planning interventions. Maltreated children represent a very heterogenous group, with very varied clinical pictures (Aber & Cicchetti, 1984). In planning interventions with maltreated children, it is important to conduct a comprehensive psychiatric assessment to identify the unique clinical needs of the child. Axis I diagnoses, such as major depression, conduct disorder, and enuresis, should be treated using accepted clinical approaches as part of a larger more comprehensive intervention plan that addresses the many other needs of the maltreated child and his or her family. There has been a tendency for clinicians working with abused children to believe that their psychiatric symptomatology will clear up with provision of a stable home environment. While it is necessary to address family problems that may maintain and exacerbate children's clinical symptomatology, there is preliminary evidence to suggest that focusing on these factors alone is not sufficient to produce changes in the clinical picture of maltreated children. While the merit of utilizing active psychopharmacological, cognitive, and/or behavioral treatments aimed at reducing Axis I symptomatology in maltreated children has not been empirically investigated, clinical experience suggests that these treatment approaches provide an important adjunct to intervention efforts.

In recent years, there has been considerable interest in diagnosing posttraumatic stress disorder (PTSD) and dissociative disorders in children. Prevalence of these disorders in maltreated children is currently unknown, but clinical experience suggests that they occur with moderate frequency among maltreated children presenting for treatment in psychiatric settings. Assessment of PTSD and dissociative phenomenon, therefore, should always be included as part of the initial psychiatric evaluation of maltreated children. While it is beyond the scope of this chapter to discuss the diagnosis and treatment of these disorders,

TABLE 4.1. Ecological Model: Risk Factors for Child Abuse

Ontogenetic factors	Microsystem factors	Exosystem factors	Macrosystem factors
History of Abuse	Marital discord	Unemployment	Cultural acceptance of corporal punishment
Poor impulse control	Single parenthood	Social isolation	View of children as possessions
Psychiatric or substance abuse problems	Family stressors (e.g., premature or unhealthy child)	Inadequate community resources	

TABLE 4.2. Ecological Model: Foci for Intervention Efforts with Maltreated Children

Ontogenetic factors	Microsystem factors	Exosystem factors	Macrosystem factors
Clinical symptomatology	Parental support	Limited economic resources	Priority given the development of services for children
Personal meaning of abuse events	Parental psychiatric or substance abuse disorders	Social service/Legal system factors	View of children as possessions
Issues of trust	Spousal violence	Access to community resources	Cultural acceptance of violence

the reader is referred to the work of Eth and Pynoos (1985), Lyons (1987/1988), Putnam (1991), and Terr (1985, 1991) for further consideration of the topic.

Personal Meaning of Abuse Events

A full understanding of a child's adaptation to trauma must take into account the unique meaning of the event for the child (McCann & Pearlman, 1990). Individual interventions must target misperceptions children have about their abuse experiences. How children make sense of the abuse and its aftermath can greatly affect their sense of self and influence their responsiveness to other psychotherapeutic interventions. Typical misattributions made by abused children are discussed in the following paragraphs.

1. *I was abused because I am bad and I deserve the mistreatment.* Children need to be told that they did not deserve what happened to them, even if misbehavior precipitated the abuse. Children need to be helped to understand that they were abused not because they were bad, but because their parents have a problem controlling their behavior. All children act bad sometimes, and it is the responsibility of adults to stay in control, even when children do things that make them angry.

2. *It is my fault that I was abused. . . I should have been able to stop it.* Since introduction of child sexual abuse prevention programs designed to teach children to say *No!* (e.g., Conte, Rosen, Saperstein, & Shermack, 1983; Downer, 1984; Plummer, 1984), there has been an increase in the number of children reporting guilty feelings because they were unable to prevent their sexual abuse. Because adults have the ability to outwit or physically overpower children and an estimated 84% of all sexual advances by adults involve some form of manipulation, threat, and/or use of aggression (Gomes-Schwartz, 1984), assertiveness training for children seems to be a futile endeavor (Kaufman & Zigler, 1992). Misperceptions regarding the child's ability to have prevented the abuse need to be dispelled, and children need to be given positive reinforcement for disclosing the abuse and for the strategies they used to cope with the abuse.

3. *I am dirty and different than other children.* Sexually abused children often report that they feel that they are dirty, different from other children, and irrevocably "damaged" by their abuse (Gil, 1991; Porter, Blick, & Sgroi, 1982). Group therapy for sexually abused children is a powerful means to overcome the feeling that they are alone and different from all other children. Meeting other children who have been through similar experiences and seeing that they do not look different can help to dispel the misperception that they are irrevocably damaged and the corresponding thoughts that can lead to isolation (Sgroi, 1988).

The list of misperceptions is not exhaustive, but it represents some of the most common misperceptions held by maltreated children. The reader is referred to the work of Herzberger, Potts, and Dillon (1983) and Porter et al. (1982) for further information about children's perceptions of their abuse experiences. Understanding how children make sense of their abuse, resulting changes in placement, and their feelings toward the perpetrator is an important component of the therapeutic process in working with maltreated children.

Issues of Trust

Maltreated children have been found to have significant problems with issues of trust (Aber & Cicchetti, 1984). Attachment theory provides a valuable aid for understanding the problems that chronically abused children have with issues of trust and for suggesting methods to affect these problems. According to attachment theorists, individuals construct internal working models (e.g., schemata) of relationships that are based on one's past experiences (Bowlby 1973, 1980; Bretherton, 1985). Individuals are believed to internalize both sides of the relationship (Sroufe & Fleeson, 1986), with maltreated children tending not only to develop an internal working model of the other as rejecting, but also a corresponding one of the self as unworthy of love.

These internal working models of relationships are believed to operate outside of consciousness once formed. They provide rules to appraise experiences, guide behavior, and shape expectations (Bretherton, 1985). Consistent with theoretical expectations, maltreated children have been found to infer hostile intent to events that others interpret as benign (J. Price, personal communication, October 1992). They also tend to expect to be rejected and to act in a manner consistent with this belief (Redl, 1972). In addition, because they view themselves as bad and unlikable, they often ignore and disregard evidence to the contrary. All these processes significantly impair maltreated children's capacity to trust others and to establish positive supportive relationships with others.

In childhood, it is believed that internal working models of relationships can only be altered by concrete changes in the environment and in the child's experiences. If children are maintained in a chronically abusive environment, therapeutic interventions aimed at affecting a child's perceptions about self and other will inevitably fail. Following onset of formal operations, working models of relationships can be altered through insight-oriented psychotherapeutic interventions, as formal operations permit the individual to think about thoughts and step outside a given relationship and evaluate it objectively (Main, Kaplan, & Cassidy, 1985). Even with onset of formal operations, however, it is necessary for individuals to have positive experiences in other relationships to reinforce the development of new internal models. Issues relevant to working with maltreated children around these issues are discussed further by McCann and Pearlman (1990).

MICROSYSTEM FACTORS

Parental Support

Within samples of adults with a history of childhood abuse, the availability of one supportive parent while growing up has consistently been documented as a protective factor in studies examining the intergenerational transmission of abuse (Egeland & Jacobvitz, 1984; Hunter & Kilstrom, 1979; Kaufman & Zigler, 1987, 1989). In studies examining the sequelae of abuse, the importance of the availability of a functioning adult ally has also been demonstrated, with children with at least one supportive parental figure found to have significantly less clinical symptomatology than children without parental support (Gomez-Schwartz, Salt, et al., 1984).

The nonabusive parent who fails to believe founded allegations of abuse needs to be gently confronted in an individual session with the professional (Sgroi, 1988). Such a parent needs not only to be told that the professional believes the child's accusations, but also to be given concrete reasons, in a matter-of-fact manner, why the allegations are highly plausible to the professional. The parent's rationale for not believing that the abuse occurred should be explored, together with issues that may be interfering with the nonabusive parent's capacity to support the child, such as childhood history of abuse and current spousal violence. The first session is likely to be insufficient to alter the parent's denial. The parent should be given an open invitation to meet with the professional at any time in the future, with nonjudgmental outreach efforts made episodically (see also Sgroi [1989] for additional discussion of clinical approaches to facilitate parents' capacity to support their children and become a functioning adult ally).

Parental Psychiatric or Substance Abuse Disorders

Substance abuse has been described as the dominant characteristic of parents in child protection service caseloads (National Committee for the Prevention of Child Abuse, 1989). These problems are often seen in conjunction with other mental health problems, with some studies estimating that as many as 76% of all parents receiving protective services have a mental health and/or substance abuse problem (Taylor et al., 1991). Lower compliance with court-ordered treatment recommendations, greater incidence of reabuse, and higher rates of permanent out-of-home placement have been documented in cases where substance abuse and/or mental illness is present (Famularo, Kinscherff, Bunshaff, Spivak, & Fenton, 1989).

Just as standard accepted clinical practice should be used to treat children's Axis I diagnoses, standard accepted clinical practice should be used to treat parent's Axis I and substance abuse disorders. These treatments should be implemented as part of a larger more comprehensive intervention plan that also addresses the many other needs of the maltreated child and his or her family. If these issues are not addressed, they will seriously jeopardize the stability of the child's placement and compromise his or her progress in individual treatment.

Spousal Violence

Just as strong links have been demonstrated between child maltreatment and parental psychiatric/substance abuse disorders, strong links have also been demonstrated between child maltreatment and spousal violence (Rosenbaum & O'Leary, 1991). Some studies have estimated that the rate of spousal violence in families receiving protective services is as high as 50% (Kaufman et al., in press). Because investigations examining the impact of witnessing spousal violence have consistently documented its adverse effects on child development (Rosenberg, 1987), the need to provide services, or to coordinate the delivery of services to address this problem, cannot be sufficiently underscored.

Some professionals are reluctant to frankly talk with clients about the negative consequences of remaining in an abusive spousal relationship and prefer that clients come to this realization on their own. In the opinion of the authors, failure to speak directly with clients about the negative impact of remaining in the abusive relationship amounts to colluding with the client and facilitating defenses of denial. As with problems of parental Axis I or substance abuse disorders, problems of spousal violence should likewise be targeted for treatment as part of a larger more comprehensive intervention plan (Fleming, 1979; NiCarthy, 1986; Walker, 1984). If this issue is not addressed, it will likewise compromise the child's safety and interfere with the child's responsiveness to other forms of therapeutic interventions.

EXOSYSTEM FACTORS

Limited Economic Resources

Poverty has consistently been shown to increase the likelihood of child maltreatment (Pelton, 1978; Trickett, Aber, Carlson, & Cicchetti, 1991). Although most poor people do not maltreat their children and poverty per se does not cause abuse and neglect, the correlates of poverty (e.g., stress, substance abuse, and inadequate resources for food and medical treatment) do increase the likelihood of abuse (Kaufman & Zigler, 1992). Given the association between poverty and maltreatment, as discussed in the crisis intervention section, it is often necessary to facilitate the provision of material resources to stabilize a maltreated child's family. Applications may have to be filed for rent assistance, food stamps, welfare, emergency placement in shelters, and other concrete needs. Without having these basic, life-sustaining needs taken care of, it will be impossible to address any of the higher level therapeutic needs of the child and his or her family.

Social Service/Legal System Factors

There are many delays in the social/legal system that hold up permanency planning in child abuse cases, and these delays have been identified as a significant stressor for maltreated children (Goodman et al., 1992). The mean length of time that elapses from the first official report of child abuse to that child's final placement is 4.9 years (Jellinek et al., 1991). Cases on average take 2.7 years from the time of the first official report of mistreatment to arraignment for a Care and Protection petition. Once in court, the average case requires 1.4 years from arraignment to deposition in Juvenile Court. Cases not dismissed from Juvenile Court usually go on to Probate Court, where on average they require an additional 1.6 years to reach final placement determination (Jellinek et al., 1991). Throughout this process, children are often aware of the uncertainty regarding the permanency of their current placement, and this awareness has devastating effects on children's socioemotional development.

Testifying in court has also been associated with adverse sequelae for maltreated children, with the need to testify multiple times associated with marked increases in clinical symptomatology (Goodman et al., 1992). When a child is going to need to testify in court, the mental health professional should expect to see an exacerbation of symptoms. For additional discussion of methods to help maltreated children cope with the legal system, the reader is referred to Goodman, Jones, et al. (1988); Goodman, Taub, et al. (1992); and Hennessey (1989).

Inadequate Community Resources

Clinical experience suggests that children maximally benefit from specialized mental health services when the delivery of these and other community services are coordinated and conducted in close collaboration (Cicchetti & Toth, 1987; Daro, 1988). Crisis hotlines (Johnston, 1976), respite child care facilities (Cohn, 1981), family preservation programs (Adnopoz et al., 1987), and foster and adoptive homes (Rosenstein, 1978) represent some of the different types of community programs used specifically to prevent and treat child abuse. Access to other community resources, such as low-income housing, health care, day care, and emergency shelters, is also often necessary for successful intervention in child maltreatment cases. Adequate knowledge of available community resources and the methods required to access care is essential when working with child abuse cases.

MACROSYSTEM FACTORS

While the individual treatment of an abused child never requires macrosystem level interventions, it often makes one desire macrosystem level changes. Few communities have adequate resources to truly effectively help maltreated children and their families. In a society where children are viewed as objects and services on their behalf have not been a national priority, mental health and other professionals are limited in their capacity to affect change in the lives of maltreated children. As Zigler (1976) has said, controlling child abuse in America will be an effort doomed to failure unless the nation commits to providing the resources necessary to tackle the problem and also examines society's value system that condones violence. For information on child advocacy approaches to the problem of child abuse, the interested reader is referred to Gerbner, Ross, and Zigler (1980); and Zigler, Kagan, and Klugman (1983).

SUMMARY

Complete treatment of the many topics covered in this chapter would have required several volumes. The purpose of addressing these varied issues, however, was not to discuss them exhaustively, but to highlight the many different factors mental health professionals need to consider when working with maltreated children. Whenever possible, references were provided to additional resources that cover in further detail the topics highlighted in this chapter.

The two fundamental tenets to remember are that the treatment of maltreated children requires working as part of a larger multidisciplinary team consisting of child protective services workers, law enforcement agents, and others; and that assessing the treatment needs of maltreated children requires moving beyond clinical symptomatology and abuse related issues to other family and environmental factors. The ecological model outlined in this chapter provides a valuable heuristic for conceptualizing foci for intervention efforts in maltreatment cases. Thorough consideration of ontogenetic, microsystem, and exosystem factors when evaluating the treatment needs of maltreated children will maximize the chances for successful intervention. All aspects of treatment may not be provided by the mental health professional, but cognizance of the issues that require attention and a willingness to work collaboratively with other providers will greatly facilitate mental health professionals' individual treatment efforts.

REFERENCES

Aber, J. L., & Cicchetti, D. (1984). Socioemotional development in maltreated children: An empirical and theoretical analysis. In H. Fitzgerald, B. Lester, & M. Yogman (Eds.), *Theory and research in behavioral pediatrics, Vol. II*. New York: Plenum Press.

Adnopoz, J., Nagler, S., & Sinanaglu, P. (1987). *The family support service: Serving families in crisis*. Unpublished Manuscript. New Haven: Yale University.

American Professional Society on the Abuse of Children. (1990). *Guidelines for psychosocial evaluation of suspected sexual abuse in young children.* Chicago: Author.

American Academy of Child and Adolescent Psychiatry. (1988). Perspectives: Guidelines for the clinical evaluation of child and adolescent sexual abuse. *Journal of the Academy of Child and Adolescent Psychiatry, 27,* 655–657.

American Medical Association Council on Scientific Affairs. (1986). AMA diagnostic and treatment guidelines concerning child abuse and neglect. *Connecticut Medicine, 50,* 122–128.

American Psychiatric Association. (1993). *DSM-IV draft criteria.* Washington, DC: Author.

Ansell, C. & Ross, H. (1988). When laws and values conflict: A dilemma for psychologists: Reply. *American Psychologist, 45,* 399.

Belsky, J. (1980). Child maltreatment: An ecological integration. *American Psychologist, 35,* 320–335.

Bowlby, J. (1973). *Attachment and Loss: Vol. 2: Separation.* New York: Basic Books.

Bowlby, J. (1980). *Attachment and Loss: Vol. 3: Separation.* New York: Basic Books.

Bretherton, I. (1985). Attachment theory: Retrospect and prospect. In I. Bretherton & E. Waters (Eds.), *Growing points of attachment theory and research. Monographs of the Society for Research in Child Development, 50,* (1–2, Serial No. 209) 3–35.

Bronfenbrenner, U. (1977). Toward an experimental ecology of human development. *American Psychologist, 32,* 513–531.

Bronfenbrenner, U. (1979). *The ecology of human development.* Cambridge, MA: Harvard University Press.

Cicchetti, D., & Toth, S. (1987). The application of a transactional risk model to intervention with multi-risk families. *Zero-to-Three, 7,* 1–8.

Cohn, A. (1981). *An approach to preventing child abuse.* Chicago: National Committee for Prevention of Child Abuse.

Cohn, A. H., & Daro, D. (1987). Is treatment too late: What ten years of evaluative research tell us. *Child Abuse and Neglect, 11,* 433–442.

Conte, J., Rosen, C., Saperstein, L., & Shermack, R. (1983, November). *An evaluation of a program to prevent the sexual victimization of young children.* Paper presented at the meeting of the National Association of Social Workers Professional Symposium, Washington, D C.

Daro, D. (1988). *Confronting child abuse: Research for effective program design.* N.Y. Free Press.

DeKraai, M. B., & Sales, B. D. (1991). Liability in child therapy and research. Special section: Clinical child psychology: Perspectives on child and adolescent therapy. *Journal of Consulting and Clinical Psychology, 59*(6), 853–860.

Dill, D., Chu, J., Grob, M., & Eisen, S. (1991). The reliability of abuse history reports: A comparison of two inquiry formats. *Comprehensive Psychiatry, 32,* 166–169.

Downer, A. (1984). *Evaluation of talking about touching.* Seattle, WA: Committee for Children.

Egeland, B., & Jacobvitz, D. (1984). *Intergenerational continuity of parental abuse: Causes and consequences.* Paper presented at the Conference on Biosocial Perspectives in Abuse and Neglect, York, ME.

Eth, S., & Pynoos, R. S. (Eds.). *Post-traumatic stress disorder in children.* Washington, DC: American Psychiatric Press.

Famularo, R., Kinscherff, R., Bunshaff, D., Spivak, G., & Fenton, D. (1989). Parental compliance to court-ordered treatment interventions in cases of child maltreatment. *Child Abuse and Neglect, 13,* 507–514.

Fleming, J. B. (1979). *Stopping the abuse.* New York: Anchor Books.

Friedrich, W., Beilke, R., & Urquiza, A. (1987). Children from sexually abusive families: A behavioral comparison. *Journal of Interpersonal Violence, 2,* 391–402.

Garbarino, J. (1977). The human ecology of child maltreatment: A conceptual model for research. *Journal of Marriage and the Family, 39*, 721–736.

Gerbner, G., Ross, C, & Zigler, E. (1980). *Child abuse: An agenda for action.* New York: Oxford University Press.

Gil, E. (1991). *The healing power of play: Working with abused children.* New York: Guilford Press.

Goldstein, J., Freud, A., & Solnit, A. (1973). *Beyond the best interest of the child.* New York: Free Press.

Goldstein, J., Freud, A., & Solnit, A. (1979). *Before the best interest of the child.* New York: Free Press.

Gomes-Schwartz, B. (1984). Nature of sexual abuse. In B. Gomes-Schwartz (Ed.), *Sexually exploited children: Service and research project* (draft final report). Washington, DC: U. S. Department of Justice, Office of Juvenile Justice and Delinquency Prevention.

Gomes-Schwartz, B., Salt, P., Myer, M., Coleman, L., Horowitz, J., & Sauzier, M. (1984). Characteristics of mothers of sexual abuse victims. In B. Gomes-Schwartz (Ed.), *Sexually exploited children: Service and research project* (draft final report). Washington, DC: U. S. Department of Justice, Office of Juvenile Justice and Delinquency Prevention.

Goodman, G., Jones, D., Pyle, E., & Prado-Estrada, L. (1988). The emotional effects of criminal court testimony on child sexual assault victims: A preliminary report. *Issues in Criminology and Legal Psychology, 13*, 46–54.

Goodman, G., Taub, E. P., Jones, D., England, P., Port, L., Rud, L., & Prado, L. (1992). Testifying in criminal court: Emotional effects on child sexual assault victims. With commentaries by John E. B. Myers and Gary B. Melton. *Monographs of the Society for Research in Child Development, 57*(5, Serial No. 229).

Gwynn, P. (1988). Investigating child abuse: The Bexley project. *Issues in Criminological and Legal Psychology, 13*, 62–66.

Hennessey, E. (1989). The family, the courts, and mental health professionals. *American Psychologist, 44*, 1223–1224.

Henrey, D., Cossett, D., Auletta, T., & Egan, E. (1991). Needed services for parents of sexually abused children. *Child and Adolescent Social Work Journal, 8*, 127–140.

Herzberger, S., Potts, D., & Dillon, M. (1983). Abusive and nonabusive parental treatment from the child's perspective. *Journal of Consulting and Clinical Psychology, 49*, 81–90.

Hunter, R., & Kilstrom, N. (1979). Breaking the cycle in abusive families. *American Journal of Psychiatry, 136*, 1320–1322.

Jellinek, M. S., Murphy, J. M., Poitrast, F., Quinn, D., Bishop, S. J., & Goshko, M. (1991). Serious child mistreatment in Massachusetts: The course of 206 children through the courts. *Child Abuse and Neglect, 16*, 179–185.

Johnston, C. (1976). *The art of the crisis line: A training manual for volunteers in child abuse prevention.* Oakland, CA: Parent-Stress Service.

Jones, M. (1990). Working with the unmotivated client. In S. Stith, M. B. Williams, & K. Rosen (Eds.), *Violence hits home: Comprehensive treatment approaches to domestic violence.* New York: Springer.

Kalichman, S. C. (1990). Reporting laws, confidentiality, and clinical judgment: Reply to Ansell and Ross. *American Psychologist, 45*, 1273.

Kaufman, J., Jones, B., Stieglitz, E., Vitulano, L., & Mannarino, A. P. (in press). The use of multiple informants to assess children's maltreatment experiences. *Journal of Family Violence.*

Kaufman, J., & Zigler, E. (1987). Do abused children become abusive parents? *American Journal of Orthopsychiatry, 57*, 186–192. Reprinted in S. Chess & A. Thomas (Eds.), *Annual progress in child psychiatry and child development* (pp. 591–600). New York: Brunner Mazel Publishers, 1988.

Kaufman, J., & Zigler, E. (1989). The intergenerational transmission of child abuse. In D. Cicchetti & V. Carlson (Eds.), *The handbook of child maltreatment* (pp. 129–150). Cambridge, MA: Cambridge University Press.

Kaufman, J., & Zigler, E. (1992). The prevention of child maltreatment: Programming, research, and policy. In D. Willis, E. Holden, & M. Rosenberg (Eds.), *Child abuse prevention* (pp. 269–295). New York: Wiley.

Lanktree, C., Briere, J., & Zaidi, L. (1991). Incidence and impact of sexual abuse in a child outpatient sample: The role of direct inquiry. *Child Abuse and Neglect, 15,* 447–453.

Legislative Program Review and Investigations Committee. (1990). *Department of children and youth services: Child abuse and neglect. Findings and recommendations.* Hartford, CT: State of Connecticut.

Lyons, J. (1988). Posttraumatic stress disorder in children and adolescents: A review of the literature. In S. Chess & A. Thomas (Eds.), *Annual progress in child psychiatry and child development.* New York: Brunner-Mazel. pp. 451–467. (Reprinted from *Developmental and Behavioral Pediatrics,* 1987, *8,* 349–356).

MacNair, R. R. (1992). Ethical dilemma of child abuse reporting: Implications for mental health. *Journal of Mental Health Counseling, 14,* 127–136.

Main, M., Kaplan, N., & Cassidy, J. (1985). Security in infancy, childhood, and adulthood: A move to the level of representation. In I. Bretherton & E. Waters (Eds.), *Growing points of attachment theory and research.* pp. 66–104. *Monographs of the Society for Research in Child Development, 50* (1–2, Serial No. 209).

Mannarino, A., & Cohen, J. Sexually and physically abused children. In M. Hersen & S. M. Turner (Eds.), *Diagnostic interviewing.* (2nd ed.). New York: Plenum Press.

Mannarino, A., Cohen, J., & Gregor, M. (1989). Emotional and behavioral difficulties in sexually abused girls. *Journal of Interpersonal Violence, 4,* 437–451.

McCann, L., & Pearlman, L. (1990). Constructionst self-development theory as a framework for assessing and treating victims of family violence. In S. Stith, M. B. Williams, & K. Rosen (Eds.), *Violence hits home: Comprehensive treatment approaches to domestic violence* (pp. 305–329). New York: Springer.

McGee, R., Wolfe, D., Yuen, S., & Camochan, J. (1991). *The measurement of child maltreatment: A comparison of approaches.* Poster presented at the Biennial Meeting of the Society for Research in Child Development, Seattle, WA.

Muram, D. (1989). Child sexual abuse: Relationship between sexual acts and genital findings. *Child Abuse and Neglect, 13,* 211–216.

National Committee for the Prevention of Child Abuse (NCPCA). (1989, April). NCPCA memorandum. Chicago: Author.

NiCarthy, G. (1986). *Getting free: A handbook for women in abusive relationships.* Seattle, WA: Seal Press.

Oxley, G. B. (1981). Promoting competence in involuntary clients. In A. N. Maluccio (Eds.), *Promoting competence in clients: A new/old approach to social work practice.* New York: Free Press.

Pecora, P. J. (1991). Investigating allegations of child maltreatment: The strengths and limitations of current risk assessment systems. *Child and Youth Services, 15,* 73–92.

Pecora, P. J., Fraser, M. W., & Haapala, D. A. (1992). Intensive home-based family preservation services: An update from the FIT project. *Child Welfare, 71,* 177–188.

Pelton, L. (1978). Child abuse and neglect: The myth of classlessness. *American Journal of Orthopsychiatry, 48,* 608–617.

Plummer, C., (1984, April). *Research prevention: What school programs teach children.* Paper presented at the Third National Conference on Sexual Victimization of Children, Washington, DC.

Porter, F. S., Blick, L. C., & Sgroi, S. (1982). Treatment of the sexually abused child. In S. Sgroi (Ed.), *Handbook of clinical intervention in child sexual abuse,* pp. 109–145. Lexington, MA: Health.

Powell, M. B. (1991). Investigating and reporting child sexual abuse: Review and recommendations for clinical practice. *Australian Psychologist, 26,* 77–83.

Putnam, F. W. (1991). Dissociative phenomena. In A. Tasman (Ed.), *Annual Review of Psychiatry* (pp. 159–174). Washington, DC: American Psychiatric Press.

Redl, F. (1972). *When we deal with children.* New York: Free Press.

Rosenbaum, A., & O'Leary, K. (1981). Marital violence: Characteristics of abusive couples. *Journal of Consulting and Clinical Psychology, 49,* 63–71.

Rosenberg, M. S. (1987). Children of battered women: The effects of witnessing violence on their social problem-solving abilities. *The Behavior Therapist, 10,* 85–89.

Rosenstein, P. (1978). Family outreach: A program for the prevention of child abuse and neglect. *Child Welfare, 57,* 515–525.

Sgroi, S. M. (1982). An approach to case management. In S. M. Sgroi, *Handbook of clinical intervention in child sexual abuse* (pp. 81–108). Lexington, MA: Health.

Sgroi, S. M. (1988). *Vulnerable populations.* Lexington, MA: Lexington Books.

Sgroi, S., Blick, L. C., & Porter, F. S. (1982a). A conceptual framework for child sexual abuse. In S. M. Sgroi, *Handbook of clinical intervention in child sexual abuse* (pp. 9–37). Lexington, MA: Heath.

Sgroi, S., Porter, F. S., & Blick, L. C. (1982b). Validation of child sexual abuse. In S. M. Sgroi, *Handbook of clinical intervention in child sexual abuse* (pp. 39–79). Lexington, MA: Heath.

Shay, S. (1980). Community council for child abuse prevention. In R. Helfer & C. H. Kempe (Eds.), *The battered child* (pp. 105–121). Chicago: University of Chicago Press.

Solnit, A. (1980). Too much reporting, too little service: Roots and prevention of child abuse. In G. Gerbner, C. Ross, & E. Zigler (Eds.), *Child abuse: An agenda for action.* New York: Oxford University Press.

Sroufe, L. A., & Fleeson, J. (1986). Attachment and the construction of relationships. In W. Hartup & Z. Rubin (Eds.), *Relationship and development.* New York: Cambridge University Press.

State of Connecticut, Department of Children and Youth Services (1981). *Standards for the removal and return of children by the Department of Children and Youth Services, Bulletin #30.* Hartford, CT: Division of Protective and Children's Services.

Taylor, C. G., Norman, D. K., Murphy, J. M., Jellinck, M., Quinn, D., Poitrast, F. G., & Goshko, M. (1991). Diagnosed intellectual and emotional impairment among parents who seriously mistreat their children: Prevalence type and outcome in a court sample. *Child Abuse and Neglect, 15,* 389–401.

Terr, L. (1985). Remembered images in psychic trauma. *Psychoanalytic Study of the Child, 40,* 493–533.

Terr, L. (1991). Childhood traumas: An outline and overview. *American Journal of Psychiatry, 148,* 10–20.

Tinbergen, N. (1951). *The study of instinct.* London: Oxford University Press.

Trickett, P. K., Aber, J. L., Carlson, V., & Cicchetti, D. (1991). Relationship of socioeconomic status to the etiology and developmental sequelae of physical child abuse. *Developmental Psychology, 27,* 148–158.

Twigg, R. (1991). The next step in foster care. *Child and Youth Care, 6,* 79–85.

Wald, M. S., & Woolverton, M. (1990). Risk assessment: The emperor's new clothes? *Child Welfare, 69*, 483–511.

Walker, L. (1984). *The battered woman syndrome.* New York: Springer.

Waterhouse, L., & Carnie, J. (1992). Assessing child protection risk. *British Journal of Social Work, 22*, 47–60.

Weissman, H. N. (1991). Forensic psychological examination of the child witness in cases of alleged sexual abuse. *American Journal of Orthopsychiatry, 61*, 48–58.

Zigler, E. (1976). Controlling child abuse in America: An effort doomed to failure.

In D. Adamovics (Eds.), *Proceedings of the First National Conference on Child Abuse and Neglect.* Washington, DC: Department of Health, Education and Welfare.

Zigler, E., Kagan, S. L., & Klugman, E. (1983). *Children, families, and government: Perspectives on American social policy.* Cambridge, MA: Cambridge University Press.

CHAPTER 5

Developmental Issues

MICHAEL FERRARI

INTRODUCTION

How many clinicians can honestly state that part of their assessment and treatment planning for a child includes a systematic comparison of that child's behavior to what should be expected developmentally? Few can probably answer this question in the affirmative, and some may not believe that it is even important.

As surprising as it may seem, there has been relatively little consistent communication between practitioners and researchers of child behavior therapy and those from developmental psychology. Though, in practice, it would seem that acquiring a thorough knowledge of child developmental principles and learning of the wealth of normative descriptive data would be standard parts of the child behavior therapist's training, only recently have there been efforts to integrate the findings of behavior therapy and developmental psychology (Ferrari, 1990; Harris & Ferrari, 1983; Hersen & Van Hasselt, 1987). This virtual lack of data-base integration from these two disciplines, which are indeed compatible, has been quite unfortunate: Many clinicians have been left not knowing what to expect developmentally, and, conversely, many developmentalists have been unaware of the clinical relevance of what it is they study (Johnson & Goldman, 1990; Pelligrini, Galinski, Hart, & Kendall, 1993).

This chapter concentrates on what developmental guidelines can be reasonably employed in child behavior assessment and discusses how those guidelines may have treatment implications. Also considered are the two questions of what aspects of development the child behavior therapist *should* be concerned with and what developmental markers might bear the greatest influence on the likelihood of a successful treatment outcome. As a caveat, this chapter is not intended to be exhaustive. The enormity of the developmental and clinical literatures precludes such a review. Rather, the ways in which a knowledge of development informs the practice of child behavior therapy will be addressed, and examples from several areas will be presented to illustrate the importance of integrating developmental psychology and child behavior therapy.

DEVELOPMENTAL FACTORS

Few today would likely argue that developmental considerations have *no* role in the modern clinical practice of child behavior therapy (Johnson & Goldman, 1990). In contrast, many published accounts of the past did not afford developmental variables much concern or view them as potentially important in the functional analysis of behavior problems (cf. Mischel, 1979). Nonetheless, while developmental concerns are receiving more attention, the fact is that there are still few firm answers to the two important questions raised earlier and a surprisingly small data base to which to turn to address those questions (Crnic & Harris, 1990; Kimball, Nelson, & Politano, 1993).

Ideally, it might be argued that child behavior therapy, by the very nature of whom this field serves, should derive a substantial portion of its data base from the empirical work and theoretical models of child development (Ferrari, 1990; Politano, 1993). However, a survey of the treatment literature does not readily convince the reader that behavior therapy is developmentally sensitive or that findings from developmental research are being regularly translated in meaningful ways. And yet, if for no other reason than that children have lived for a shorter period of time than adults, thus having shorter learning histories and a more limited range of experiences, the assessments and treatments of children should be geared to their stage of development.

Indeed, developmentalists have repeatedly had to remind behaviorists that developmental considerations are far too rarely employed in the treatment of children (Benner, 1992; Politano, 1993). This is so, even in the face of considerable research literature (cf. Flavell, Mumme, Green, & Flavell, 1992) that suggests that it is *not only* the quantitative differences in age and time that make children different from adults, it is rather the progressive, potentiated unfolding of forces from the environment and the developmental neurobiology of the child that must also be reconciled.

Developmental factors, as currently perceived, relate directly to the broad range of aspects concerned with the expression of the changing biological, cognitive, social, and affective lives of children. By understanding developmental issues and how they can shape the assessment and treatment of children in the psychiatric setting, clinicians can be better informed about which treatment to use and, thus, better ensure the generalization of treatment effects.

THE NORMAL CHILD

What constitutes *normality* in children? *Is* there a normal child? Are there numerous examples of abnormal ones? Scarr (1982) noted that "development is a probabilistic result of indeterminate combinations of genes and environments . . . genetically guided but variable and probabilistic because influential events in the life of every person can be neither predicted nor explained by general laws" (p. 852). This statement helps to make developmental processes clear for what they are: interactive, complex, multilinear, and plastic (Hetherington, Lerner, & Perlmutter, 1988).

Knowledge of child development assists in postulating a typical course of ontogeny but stops short of defining the normal child. As such, it is necessary to exercise caution in the application of the concept of normality in understanding behavior. While it is useful to know what is typical, it is essential to recognize that being typical may still not be normal nor particularly functional for a set of environmental circumstances.

From the outset, clinicians must learn not to generalize the concept of normality to populations in which that concept is less relevant (e.g., for sociocultural reasons) (Kimball et al., 1993). In dealing with children in the psychiatric setting, clinicians have to concern themselves with the relative heterogeniety of psychiatric disorder across developmental time (Achenbach, 1982; Ferrari & Matthews, 1983; Harris & Ferrari, 1988). Faced with knowing not only the factors of normative development that might affect formulation of assessment and treatment hypotheses, clinicians must also allow for the possibility that development in certain psychiatric disorders does not abide by the same set of rules with which they are so accustomed (Erickson, 1992).

This crucial issue is perhaps no more clearly observed than in the pervasive developmental disorders where research has shown various consequences of juxtaposed developmental events. It is known that the relative prognostic value of the IQ score and the sophistication of early communicative speech in children (i.e., before age 6) is remarkably more important for predicting the likelihood of autistic children leading reasonably independent lives in adulthood (Gillberg & Steffenburg, 1987) than for youngsters with conduct disorders or with an attention deficit. Thus, while knowledge of developmental information is important, one must also be informed about when it should be applied.

DEFINING A DEVELOPMENTAL APPROACH

What makes for a developmental approach and how does one go about applying appropriate developmental considerations? How significant a role can developmental theories play in daily clinical practice? What are age-gradings for normal behavior, and how can considerations regarding this concept of normality realistically affect approach to child patients?

Normal Behavior

It has never been easy to say with certainty what constitutes normal behavior in childhood. Indeed, it may even be more difficult to determine whether a child requires professional help for behavior that can be considered *not normal* than it is to make that same decision about an adult. Shaped by sociocultural factors and contextual variables, social norms for children change rapidly (Kimball et al., 1993). In addition, unlike adults who seek help, children rarely initiate treatment. They are instead referred for treatment by their parents, by teachers, or by other concerned professionals that may themselves not know what constitutes a normal range of child behavior.

Questions of normal behavior can manifest in a variety of ways in the clinical setting; for example, it would be inappropriate to show parents who complained about overactivity in their children how to get their children to be less active when their activity levels were already within normal limits for age (Harris & Ferrari, 1983). Instead, parents should be reassured about their children's activity levels and helped to adjust their expectations.

Obviously, the first task for the clinician questioning the "normality of behavior" is to determine how appropriate the child's behavior is given their age and the situation. Unless there is a better set of norms for children than parents, the clinician may not be able to test the veracity of claims and, instead, may respond out of personal biases. It is, therefore, important for the behavioral clinician to be able to recognize what constitutes behavior within a normal range and to be able to act on this information accordingly (i.e., urging the parents to seek treatment or reassuring them about their child's behavior).

Consider the example of aggressive behavior in children. Acts of aggression may take many different forms: intentional property destruction, behavior designed to cause injury to another, a threatening verbal gesture, theft, or, the one thought of most often, a physical attack. Ross (1981) has aptly pointed out that of itself, aggression is probably the most easily recognized behavioral excess in the psychiatric setting and the one with the single most important contemporaneous and long-term implications.

The identification of reliable developmental differences in aggressive behavior is important for the clinician who not only is required to formulate a plan of treatment, but also must determine when it is appropriate either to intervene with the child or perhaps to facilitate a greater understanding in an anxious teacher of the normal expressions of aggressive behavior. More centrally, this translates into the problem not only of determining the amount of aggressive behavior that is normal by age, but also of distinguishing between aggressive behavior that merits clinical attention and aggressive behavior that developmentally can be considered normative.

A number of studies have described how developmental norms for a variety of different behaviors (e.g., MacFarlane, Allen, & Honzik, 1954) and numerous norm-based child assessment procedures (see Achenbach & Edelbrock, 1983; Ireton, 1990) can aid the clinician in determining the normality of given behaviors, such as aggression, in children of different ages. While such data are useful, they are, of course, limited in scope and can potentially be misleading. First, it can be seen that there is an abundance of data in some areas and little to none in others. Guidelines for motor development (Culbertson & Gyurke, 1990) and language milestones (Van Kleeck & Schuele, 1987) are readily available. However, normative guidelines are generally lacking in areas such as affective development and social competencies.

In addition, the clinician should be cautious because many of the developmental surveys and inventories that provide normative information are based on parent report rather than direct observation of child behavior. Parents and children often have substantially different views of their life events. Moreover, a number of studies have exposed the tendencies of parents to distort their child's behavior or even factual information about their child (Lapouse & Monk, 1959). Thus, relying solely on normative data that derives from parent report could be a potentially great limiting factor, even though research shows that clinicians often rely heavily on parental expectations in formulating treatment goals (McCoy, 1976).

The Spectrum of Developmental Factors

Each time clinicians do an assessment of a child, they consider simultaneously a broad range of factors. They listen to the perspective of others (attempting to resist the trait-based information often received). They gather information about the child's history, antecedent conditions, and the effect of the behaviors on those around them. They also look for the presence of associated behaviors and relate their presence or absence to understanding of the linkages between known behavior disorders and diagnostic nosologies. Other factors that *should* concern clinicians include attention to the developing systems of the child (e.g., linguistic, cognitive, motor) as well as the developmental and demographic dimensions of the child's family (Carter & McGolderick, 1989; Janosik & Green, 1992).

Knowing what is typical behavior for children of different ages is a rudimentary but nonetheless essential first step to a developmental approach. Consider as an example the behavioral disruptions of a 7-year-old, second-grade boy who frequently gets out of his seat, seems excessively fidgety and distractible, and is progressing poorly with his school studies. In observing this youngster's behavior and questioning the parents and teacher, many developmental variables and other antecedent conditions are noted that could give rise to considering attention-deficit/hyperactivity disorder (ADHD) as part of a differential diagnosis for this child. But instead of attending solely to this conceptualization, suppose that attention was turned to other developmental events.

In this same scenario, suppose that the clinician was to observe that this youngster's fine motor skills were poorly developed, that he was small for his chronological age, and that he has frequently received peer reinforcement for socially disruptive behavior in the classroom. On psychometric assessment, it was further learned that his general cognitive capacities were below average for age, that gross and fine motor skills were also immature for chronological age, and that he was a low-birth-weight baby born at 35 weeks gestation. With this added information, the basic diagnostic formulation may have to be broadened.

An informed reading of the literature would tell this clinician that several of the noted factors have been considered in research as "risk factors" for ADHD (e.g., Campbell, 1990; Hartsough & Lambert, 1985). And yet it is not difficult to perceive how this child's developmental immaturities could have set the stage for inattentive, disruptive behaviors that are primarily motivated by task avoidance and attention seeking. Focusing treatment on the problems associated with ADHD (while arguably it might have actually proven helpful to this youngster) would have missed developmentally relevant considerations.

The Meaning of Behavior

Beyond knowing what is normal for age, the developmental approach requires the clinician to balance the value of age-based descriptive information with what a behavior is intended to mean; that is, simply knowing if the amount of behavior or its topography can be expected given a child's age is probably not enough to constitute a useful developmental assessment. It is essential that the clinician know how a behavior's intended purpose (or message) might be interpreted by others and how these interpretations might differ at various points in the developmental continuum.

Consider another example of aggressive behavior: the adolescent who firmly punches a peer in the shoulder. This behavior is likely to be interpreted very differently (particularly in the psychiatric setting) than if it had been exchanged between two different 5-year-olds even under similar conditions. In the case of aggressive behavior, it is useful for the clinician to know that developmental data suggest that the frequency of aggressive behavior appears to peak in early childhood and decline thereafter (Maccoby, 1980). However, how one defines an aggressive act can greatly influence the interpretation of this developmental trend. For this reason, developmental psychologists have long divided the spectrum of aggressive behavior into categories such as instrumental aggression and hostile aggression (Sears, Maccoby, & Levin, 1957). In the preschool years, true intentional hostile aggressive behavior is not frequent because aggression tends to be more instrumental in nature (Dawes, 1934; Flake-Hobson, Robinson, & Skeen, 1983). However, later in childhood, a relatively greater percentage of aggressive acts are hostile rather than instrumental (Hartup, 1974). By adolescence, aggressive actions may even have more of an affiliative purpose and/or be related to peer-group membership, adolescent egocentrism, and sensation seeking (cf. Arnett, 1992).

Theoretical Perspectives

The application of a developmental approach also requires acknowledgement of the role of theoretical perspectives. In developmental psychology, it is probably fair to say that Piagetian ideas continue to be one of the most frequently employed of the theoretical models in research. And, indeed, there are large bodies of empirical work that have shown the great utility of this model (e.g., Flavell & Markman, 1985). From this framework, the clinician will find it useful to know that the young child is more likely to rely on the consequences of a behavior to judge a person's actions, while the older child also considers the person's intention. It may be helpful to know that younger children (before age 10) are likely to confuse social dimensions with intellectual ones in their interpretations of others (good is smart; bad is dumb) (Heller & Berndt, 1981) and, hence, can behave differently from older children simply due to the way they have interpreted the observably "same" message.

The Piagetian approach has also given rise to many useful understandings about the development of various concepts in children; for instance, 3-year-olds (versus 5-year-olds) have more generous estimates of other's beliefs, thus making it more unlikely for them to attribute deviant beliefs to others than for older children (Flavell et al., 1992).

Despite these findings, it is useful to ask how helpful a specific theory might be in daily practice. In the case of the Piagetian model, some investigators have recently reported on the limitations in the applied use of this approach in the clinical setting. Fletcher and Johnson (1982), in a study of adolescents' understandings of a personal illness, argued that the concept of formal operational thinking was too limited and had no explanatory power in many clinical settings. Gochman (1985) contended that Lewinian developmental principles (Lewin, 1935) may be just as useful as Piagetian in explaining developmental trends in children's understandings.

Certainly, it can be seen that it would be important for the practicing clinician to be aware of the wide variety of theoretical perspectives and related research findings. However, the empirical literature is stocked with published research studies that have been difficult to replicate. Given this state of affairs, the clinician would be encouraged to avoid a strict allegiance to any one particular theory or conceptual model.

Risks of Overinterpretation

The clinician who wishes to apply a developmental approach must be cautioned against its overapplication. First, even the most extensively detailed knowledge of the developmental literature cannot (of itself) effectively prepare the clinician for the broad range of treatment applications in the psychiatric setting. In addition, supervised experience by practitioners and researchers who manifest a clear ability to interpret normative data in clinical context is essential for practice.

Second, the clinician would do well to recognize that while knowing a great deal about children may help in assessing their behavior and formulating meaningful treatment protocols, abstractions from the developmental data base to specific youngsters sometimes lack clarity of expectation. The comprehensive behavioral assessment should not be given short shrift by those that are privy to developmental factors. Clinicians should be wary of the limitations of the developmental approach, as well as of its strengths.

MEASURABLE DEVELOPMENTAL VARIABLES

By itself, a child's chronological age can be quite instructive in guiding clinicians' behavior in the clinical context (cf. Maddux, Roberts, Sledden, & Wright, 1986). However, clinicians should not use chronological age in isolation to explain development lest they be persuaded to believe that a child behaves a certain way just *because* he or she is 12 years old. This concern not withstanding, recognizing the relationship between age and development is crucial for the clinician who structures child assessments and effectively narrowing hypotheses about behavior.

Obviously, there are many aspects of age that extend beyond that of the amount of time passed since birth (chronological age). The clinician would do well to consider these also as potential contributors to the assessment and treatment process.

Mental Age

One such concept is that of a child's mental age, which may be one of the most important of the age-based developmental concepts. Typically defined as the normative age at which a child is functioning "mentally," *mental age* might be useful to the degree that this construct can provide an appropriate framework from which to base understanding of a child's behavior and also potential to behave. Meaningful assessments and interventions for populations of children with mental retardation, cerebral palsy, or autism as well as those with "borderline intellectual functioning" can be validly geared to normative estimates of behavior based upon mental rather than chronological age (Ferrari, 1990; Mans, Cichetti, & Sroufe, 1978). In fact, mental-age considerations might be most important in the hospital and psychiatric setting where behavioral regression is likely to be a common occurrence (Brown, 1979).

Biophysical Age

Like mental age, biophysiological markers of a child's age can also be of importance in assessment and treatment. In cases of psychosocial dwarfism, failure to thrive, and child neglect (Drotar, 1986) or for children with chromosomal abnormalities (Batshaw & Perret, 1992) or suffering from serious chronic illnesses requiring taxing treatments (i.e., chemotherapy and radiation), knowing a child's bone age or dental age can provide useful biophysical information that may help in determining a child's "true age," predicting a child's eventual height, assessing the degree of departure from statistical normality, or evaluating the effect of the child's environment or a treatment on his or her behavior.

Similarly, it can be important in instances such as eating disorder (Harris & Phelps, 1987) or child depression (Kolko, 1987) for the clinician to know the age of symptom onset or when an illness was first treated in order to informatively determine the sensitive and critical developmental areas that may have been most affected (Ferrari, 1986).

Puberty and Maturation

Maturational markers of development can also be helpful. There is now a substantial body of research that has identified a differential risk pattern to early-maturing versus late-maturing children and adolescents (cf. Escalona, 1987; Neinstein & Kaufman, 1991). Largely stemming from the early work in the Berkley Growth Study (Jones & Bayley, 1950), clinicians have learned through research that, at least for boys, interpersonal relationships and personality can be greatly affected by their maturational rate; for example, late-maturing boys are more likely to be perceived by others as insecure, awkward, and inappropriate in their social behaviors, despite extensive attempts to achieve social acceptance (Mussen, Conger, Kagan, & Huston, 1984). In contrast, early-maturing boys have been described as more poised and controlled in their interactions and as more self-confident. These differences have been shown (in at least some studies) to be fairly robust (Clausen, 1975), continuing to appear in adult males in their early 30s.

The effects of early and late maturation in girls have been less clear and probably more variable. Nevertheless, maturational rate is still important to the developmentally sensitive clinician. Early-maturing girls, like their male counterparts, also tend to be more relaxed and confident (Mussen et al., 1984). However, because of early-maturing girls' relative precocity (compared to other girls and to same-age boys), a mismatch between the social demands placed upon them and their level of mental maturity may put them at greater risk for early sexual activity and pregnancy (Neinstein & Kaufman, 1991) and may limit their access to opportunities to develop important same-sex isophillic relationships (Conger & Petersen, 1984). By knowing what to expect from this literature, the clinician can be better prepared to realize the effect of social experiences on the development of behavioral problems, particularly during the adolescent period.

Attributional (Social) Age

How old a child or adolescent may actually *look* suggests yet another line of potentially important developmental concern. Clinicians might be privy to the chronological, mental, and even biomaturational ages of patients, but members of the surrounding social network are not likely to be as informed. Moreover, age-graded expectations for behavior are more typically based on how old others believe a child to be (their attributional age) rather than the child's true chronological age. This point was well illustrated in a clever study published by Fry and Willis in 1971. These investigators positioned children of various attributional ages in a place where they would invade the adults' personal space. They then observed the adults' behavior in response to this invasion. Unaware that the children were actually all the same chronological age, the adults behaved much as the authors had expected; that is, they treating the invasions of the attributionally younger children with informative and affiliative social responses, whereas the attributionally older children were treated more harshly (e.g., actively ignored, or rejected) by the adults.

Clinicians need to be well aware that the meaning attributed by others to the same behavior exhibited by children considered to be of different ages is often not the same (e.g., crying behavior). Even though the behavior may be intended to achieve a similar function, it may meet with a different social response.

Sex Differences

Also related to the issue of developmental change and norms are the important differences that can seen in the behaviors of boys and girls at different age levels. The research literature can be helpful in instructing the clinician about the prevalence of sex differences in general development (e.g., in aggression [Maccoby, 1980]) but can also aid in considering the base rates of sex differences in a broad range of clinical conditions in childhood that have rather large differences of diagnostic incidence by sex (e.g., hyperactivity, speech disorder, delinquency).

SPECIFIC APPLICATIONS

Knowing many of the patterns of child development as illustrated can provide much useful information as a clinician prepares to do a child assessment and begin an intervention. However, strict allegiance to the types of expectations that derive from normal child development frequently can be no more than a helpful guidepost. The following discussion illustrates some of these concerns as clinicians must face them in the psychiatric setting.

Developing Concepts of Health and Illness

Many of a child's attitudes and behaviors about physical and mental health are the results of early socialization patterns. A brief look at the clinical literature shows that so many of the well-entrenched behavior disorders in adolescence and adulthood have their roots in childhood experience and early-life family dynamics (Tinsley, 1992). This is perhaps no more true than in the shaping of the child's health practices, personal beliefs, and attitudes about illness-related behavior.

Health-related behaviors are molded in the contexts of active and dynamic developmental systems. As such, efforts to intervene or prevent the development of later disorders, for example, alcoholism (Brown, 1988; Kaufman, 1986; Tesson, 1990), must of necessity focus on the child's family life and on the personal environment in which early attitudes and behaviors related to disorder are learned. Clinicians who work in this area would do well to acknowledge the role of developing concepts of health and illness in the children that they treat.

Early studies (e.g., Nagy, 1951, 1959), as well as later replications (Bibace & Walsh, 1980; Natapoff, 1982), show that children view concepts of health and illness differently at different ages. Children aged 6 and 7 are likely to perceive of illness (almost regardless of type) as something related to infection but have little understanding of the mechanisms involved. Children aged 8 to 10 are more likely to conceive of illness as causally related to the operation of germs and microorganisms; but it is not until age 11 or 12 that children consistently make a link between different illnesses and different causal agents (e.g., microorganisms, social factors). At what point children consider the possible role of buffering agents in illness (e.g., good health practices) is not well known; nor is it well known how children's conceptions of mental health might take into account the diversity of factors involved. It is known from some studies (Natapoff, 1982; Redpath & Rogers, 1984) that certain aspects of children's health and illness concepts are linked to Piagetian developmental stages. It is also known that the ways in which children cope with stress and pain tend to change as a function of cognitive development (Brown, O'Keeffe, Sanders, & Baker, 1986).

Clinicians might do well to recognize that, in case of illness-related conceptualizations, young children seem to be particularly vulnerable to various types of magical thinking and to the overextension of certain illness concepts, like that of contagion and pain. Young children are also more likely to accept imminent-justice explanations (cf. Kohlberg, 1984) for those persons who have problem behavior and also suffer from illnesses, as well as to believe that misbehavior and illness are causally linked (Ferrari, 1990).

Studies also suggest that other aspects of children's knowledge of healthy behavior and of illness undergo developmental change. Parcel and Meyer (1978) showed that children's "health locus of control" gradually became more internalized with advancing age. General-cognitive-developmental factors and locus-of-control factors have also been found to relate to a child's concept of healing (Neuhauser, Amsterdam, Hines, & Stewart, 1978). Children also tend to perceive of their own health and problem behaviors as initially very focused and distinct and to gradually change their perception so that they view problems as related to one another or as parts of multiple clusters of symptoms. Finally, children progress developmentally toward an increased recognition of the role of internal bodily processes in their health (cf. Whitt, 1982) and how these processes are important aspects and determinants of their behavior.

Developmental Considerations in Treatment

Developmental concerns cannot stop with an assessment alone; instead, they should continue to loom as significant features of the treatment planning process and of its ongoing evaluation. Whether a clinician employs a behavioral picture-card communication system, cognitive self-instructions, or in vivo exposure techniques, the behavioral treatment of children must consider developmental issues because these may be associated with different levels of treatment success.

In the case of cognitive self-instruction (CSI) procedures, research shows that the child's age must be considered. Several studies have documented age-related differences in the effectiveness of CSI procedures across a wide range of childhood problems (Finch, Spirito, Imm, & Ott, 1993; Hobbs, Moguin, Tyroler, & Lahey, 1980). One reason for this may be that developmentally younger children are less likely to spontaneously employ covert speech (Flavell & Markman, 1985). Miller, Weinstein, and Karniol (1978) showed that older children (third graders) were more likely to use spontaneously generated covert speech to help them in a delay-of-gratification task than younger children (kindergarteners), who rarely employ such a strategy. Sawin and Parke (1979) showed that second graders were better than first graders at reducing deviant behavior when the self-instruction used was to redirect their attention to some other permissible activity. This difference might help explain why younger children have a more difficult time with delay-of-gratification tasks. Unless given specific prohibitions, they are more likely to focus their attention on the behavior they are avoiding or on the reward for which they are waiting (Harris & Ferrari, 1983). Other differences in the effectiveness of CSI techniques seem to be related to the level of abstraction of verbal instructions (Copeland, 1981) as well as to the mental or developmental age of the child (Barkley, Copeland, & Sivage, 1980).

Similar developmental concerns can be employed when considering the likelihood of success in other treatment domains, for example, using mental-imagery techniques (LeBaron & Zelter, 1985; Strosahl & Ascough, 1981) or social reward systems (Tremblay, LeBlanc, & Schwartzman, 1988).

SUMMARY

This chapter has focused on the contributions of the empirical and theoretical approaches of developmental psychology to the practice of child behavior therapy. Considerable attention has been paid to how clinicians must gauge their assessments and interventions in developmentally appropriate ways. Most clinicians would find it obvious that a downward extension of an adult-based procedure might not lead to the same result in children; clinicians now must become more sensitive and move to applying this obvious point to the differences between children and adults across a host of developmental variables.

The connections between the developmental data base and the methods of the practicing clinician are far from complete. Many of the questions that clinicians would like to have answered cannot at present be fully addressed by developmentalists. These gaps suggest an ongoing importance of acquainting developmentalists with the kinds of clinical issues that behavioral clinicians regularly confront and the kinds of normative data that they require.

REFERENCES

Achenbach, T. M. (1982). *Developmental psychopathology.* New York: Wiley.

Achenbach, T. M., & Edelbrock, C. S. (1983). *Manual for the Child Behavior Checklist and Revised Child Behavior Profile.* Burlington, VT: University of Vermont.

Arnett, J. (1992). Reckless behavior in adolescence: A developmental perspective. *Developmental Review, 12,* 339–373.

Barkley, R. A., Copeland, A. P., & Sivage, C. (1980). A self-control classroom for hyperactive children. *Journal of Autism and Developmental Disorders, 10,* 75–89.

Batshaw, M. L., & Perret, Y. M. (1992). *Children with disabilities: A medical primer.* Baltimore: Paul H. Brookes.

Benner, S. M. (1992). *Assessing young children with special needs: An ecological perspective.* New York: Longman.

Bibace, R., & Walsh, N. E. (1980). Development of children's concepts of illness. *Pediatrics, 66,* 912–917.

Brown, B. (1979). Beyond separation: Some new evidence on the impact of brief hospitalization on young children. In D. Hall & M. Lacey (Eds.), *Beyond separation: Further studies of children in hospital* (pp. 18–53). London: Routledge & Kegan Paul.

Brown, J. M., O'Keeffe, J., Sanders, S. H., & Baker, B. (1986). Developmental changes in children's cognition to stressful and painful situations. *Journal of Pediatric Psychology, 3,* 343–357.

Brown, S. (1988). *Treating ACOAS: A developmental perspective.* New York: Wiley.

Campbell, S. B. (1990). *Behavior problems in preschoolers.* New York: Guilford Press.

Carter, B., & McGolderick, M. (1989). *The changing family life cycle: A framework for family therapy.* Boston: Allyn and Bacon.

Clausen, J. A. (1975). The social meaning of differential physical and sexual maturation. In S. E. Dragastin & G. H. Elder (Eds.), *Adolescence in the life cycle: Psychological change and social context* (pp. 25–48). New York: Wiley.

Conger, J. J., & Petersen, A. C. (1984). *Adolescence and youth: Psychological development in a changing world.* New York: Harper & Row.

Copeland, A. P. (1981). The relevance of subject variables in cognitive self-instruction programs for impulsive children. *Behavior Therapy, 12,* 520–529.

Crnic, K., & Harris, V. (1990). Normal development in infancy and early childhood. In J. H. Johnson and J. Goldman (Eds.), *Developmental assessment in clinical child psychology: A handbook* (pp. 15–37). New York: Pergamon Press.

Culbertson, J. L., & Gyurke, J. (1990). Assessment of cognitive and motor development in infancy and childhood. In J. H. Johnson & J. Goldman (Eds.), *Developmental assessment in clinical child psychology: A handbook.* New York: Pergamon Press.

Dawes, H. C. (1934). An analysis of two hundred quarrels of preschool children. *Child Development, 5,* 139–157.

Drotar, D. (1986). *New directions in failure to thrive.* New York: Plenum Press.

Erickson, M. T. (1992). *Behavior disorders of children and adolescents.* Englewood Cliffs, NJ: Prentice Hall.

Escalona, S. K. (1987). *Critical issues in the early development of premature infants.* New Haven: Yale University Press.

Ferrari, M. (1986). Fears and phobias in childhood: Some clinical and developmental considerations. *Child Psychiatry and Human Development, 17,* 75–87.

Ferrari, M. (1990). Developmental issues in behavioral pediatrics. In A. M. Gross & R. S. Drabman (Eds.), *Handbook of clinical behavioral pediatrics* (pp. 29–47). New York: Plenum Press.

Ferrari, M., & Matthews, W. S. (1983). Self-recognition deficits in autism: Syndrome-specific or general developmental delay? *Journal of Autism and Developmental Disorders, 13,* 317–324.

Finch, A. J., Spirito, A., Imm, P. S., & Ott, E. S. (1993). Cognitive self-instruction for impulse control in children. In A. J. Finch, W. M. Nelson, III, & E. S. Ott (Eds.), *Cognitive behavioral procedures with children and adolescents: A practical guide* (pp. 148–205). Boston: Allyn and Bacon.

Flake-Hobson, C., Robinson, B. E., & Skeen, P. (1983). *Child development and relationships.* Reading, MA: Addison-Wesley.

Flavell, J. H., & Markman, E. M. (Eds.). (1985). *Handbook of child psychology: Vol. 3. Cognitive development.* New York: Wiley.

Flavell, J. H., Mumme, D. L., Green, F. L., & Flavell, E. R. (1992). Young children's understanding of different types of beliefs. *Child Development, 63,* 960–977.

Fletcher, B. A., & Johnson, C. (1982). The myth of formal operations: Rethinking adolescent cognition in clinical contexts. *Children's Health Care, 11,* 17–21.

Fry, A. M., & Willis, F. N. (1971). Invasion of personal space as a function of age of the invader. *Psychological Record, 21,* 385–389.

Gillberg, C., & Steffenburg, S. (1987). Outcome and prognostic factors in infantile autism and similar conditions: A population-based study of 46 cases followed through puberty. *Journal of Autism and Developmental Disorders, 13,* 153–166.

Gochman, D. S. (1985). Family determinants of children's concepts of health and illness. In D. C. Turk & R. D. Kern (Eds.), *Health, illness and families: A lifespan perspective* (pp. 181–214). New York: Wiley.

Harris, F. C., & Phelps, C. F. (1987). Anorexia and bulimia. In M. Hersen & V. B. Van Hasselt (Eds.), *Behavior therapy with children and adolescents: A clinical approach* (pp. 465–484). New York: Wiley.

Harris, S. L., & Ferrari, M. (1988). Developmental factors and their relationship to the identification and treatment of behavior problems in children. In J. C. Witt, S. N. Elliot, & F. N. Graham (Eds.), *Handbook of behavior therapy* (pp. 323–362). New York: Plenum Press.

Harris, S. L., & Ferrari, M. (1983). Developmental factors in child behavior therapy. *Behavior Therapy, 14,* 54–72.

Hartsough, C. S., & Lambert, N. M. (1985). Medical factors in hyperactive and normal children: Prenatal, developmental, and health history findings. *American Journal of Orthopsychiatry, 55,* 190–210.

Hartup, W. W. (1974). Aggression in childhood: Developmental perspectives. *American Psychologist, 29,* 336–341.

Heller, M. A., & Berndt, T. J. (1981). Developmental changes in the formation and organization of personality attributions. *Child Development, 52,* 683–691.

Hersen, M., & Van Hasselt, V. B. (1987). *Behavior therapy with children and adolescents: A clinical approach.* New York: Wiley.

Hetherington, E. M., Lerner, R. M., & Perlmutter, M. (1988). *Child development in life-span perspective*. Hillsdale, NJ: Lawrence Erlbaum.

Hobbs, S. A., Moguin, L. E., Tyroler, M., & Lahey, B. (1980). Cognitive behavior therapy with children: Has clinical utility been demonstrated? *Psychological Bulletin*, *87*, 147–165.

Ireton, H. (1990). Developmental screening measures. In J. H. Johnson & J. Goldman (Eds.), *Developmental assessment in clinical child psychology: A handbook* (pp. 78–99). New York: Pergamon Press.

Janosik, E., & Green, E. (1992). *Family life: Process and practice*. Boston: Jones and Bartlett.

Johnson, J. H., & Goldman, J. (1990). *Developmental assessment in clinical child psychology: A handbook*. New York: Pergamon Press.

Jones, M. C., & Bayley, N. (1950). Physical maturing among boys as related to behavior. *Journal of Educational Psychology*, *41*, 129–148.

Kaufman, E. (1986). The family of the alcoholic patient. *Psychosomatics*, *27*, 347–360.

Kimball, W., Nelson, W. M., & Politano, P. M. (1993). The role of developmental variables in cognitive-behavioral interventions with children. In A. J. Finch, Jr., W. M. Nelson III, & E. S. Ott (Eds.), *Cognitive-behavioral procedures with children and adolescents* (pp. 25–66). Boston: Allyn and Bacon.

Kohlberg, L. (1984). *Essays on moral development: Volume 2. The psychology of moral development*. New York: Harper & Row.

Kolko, D. J. (1987). Depression. In M. Hersen & V. B. Van Hasselt (Eds.), *Behavior therapy with children and adolescents: A clinical approach* (pp. 137–183). New York: Wiley.

Lapouse, R., & Monk, M. A. (1959). Fears and worries in a representative sample of children. *American Journal of Orthopsychiatry*, *29*, 223–248.

LeBaron, S., & Zelter, L. K. (1985). The role of imagery in the treatment of dying children and adolescents. *Journal of Developmental and Behavioral Pediatrics*, *6*, 252–258.

Lewin, K. (1935). *A dynamic theory of personality*. New York: McGraw-Hill.

MacFarlane, J. W., Allen, L., & Honzik, M. (1954). *A developmental study of the behavior problems of normal children between twenty-one months and fourteen years*. Berkeley, CA: University of California Press.

Maccoby, E. E. (1980). *Social development, psychological growth, and the parent-child relationship*. New York: Harcourt Brace Jovanovich.

Maddux, J. E., Roberts, M. C., Sledden, E. A., & Wright, L. (1986). Developmental issues in child health psychology. *American Psychologist*, *41*, 25–34.

Mans, L., Cicchetti, D., & Sroufe, L. A. (1978). Mirror reactions of Down's syndrome infants and toddlers: Cognitive underpinnings of self-recognition. *Child Development*, *49*, 1247–1250.

McCoy, S. A. (1976). Clinical judgments of normal childhood behavior. *Journal of Consulting and Clinical Psychology*, *44*, 710–714.

Miller, D. T., Weinstein, S. M., & Karniol, R. (1978). Effects of age and self-verbalization on children's ability to delay gratification. *Developmental Psychology*, *14*, 569–570.

Mischel, W. (1979). On the interface of cognition and personality. *American Psychologist*, *34*, 740–754.

Mussen, P. H., Conger, J. J., Kagan, J., & Huston, A. C. (1984). *Child development and personality*. New York: Harper & Row.

Nagy, M. (1951). Children's ideas on the origins of illness. *Health Education Journal*, *9*, 6–12.

Nagy, M. (1959). The child's view of death. In H. Feifel (Ed.), *The meaning of death* (pp. 106–129). New York: McGraw-Hill.

Natapoff, J. N. (1982). A developmental analysis of children's ideas of health. *Health Education Quarterly*, *9*, 34–45.

Neinstein, L. S., & Kaufman, F. R. (1991). Abnormal growth and development. In L. S. Neinstein (Ed.), *Adolescent health care: A practical guide* (pp. 133–161). Baltimore: Urban & Schwarzenberg.

Neuhauser, C., Amsterdam, B., Hines, P., & Stewart, M. (1978). Children's concepts of healing: Cognitive development and locus of control factors. *American Journal of Orthopsychiatry, 48*, 335–341.

Parcel, G. S., & Meyer, M. P. (1978). Development of an instrument to measure children's locus of control. *Health Education Monographs, 6*, 149–159.

Pelligrini, D. S., Galinski, C. L., Hart, K. J., & Kendall, P. C. (1993). Cognitive-behavioral assessment of children: A review of measures and methods. In A. J. Finch, Jr., W. M. Nelson III, & E. S. Ott (Eds.), *Cognitive-behavioral procedures with children and adolescents* (pp. 90–147). Boston: Allyn and Bacon.

Politano, P. M. (1993). A conceptualization of psychotherapy with children and adolescents. In A. J. Finch, W. M. Nelson III, & E. S. Ott (Eds.), *Cognitive-behavioral procedures with children and adolescents* (pp. 372–392). Boston: Allyn and Bacon.

Redpath, C. C., & Rogers, C. S. (1984). Healthy young children's concepts of hospitals, medical personnel, operations, and illness. *Journal of Pediatric Psychology, 9*, 29–40.

Ross, A. O. (1981). *Child behavior therapy.* New York: Wiley.

Sawin, D. B., & Parke, R. D. (1979). Development of self-verbalized control of resistance to deviation. *Developmental Psychology, 15*, 120–127.

Scarr, S. (1982). Development is internally guided, not determined. *Contemporary Psychology, 27*, 852–853.

Sears, R. R., Maccoby, E. E., & Levin, H. (1957). *Patterns of child rearing.* New York: Harper.

Stosahl, K. D., & Ascough, J. C. (1981). Clinical uses of imagery: Experimental foundations, theoretical misconceptions, and research issues. *Psychological Bulletin, 89*, 422–438.

Tesson, B. M. (1990). Who are they: Identifying and treating the adult children of alcoholics. *Journal of Psychosocial Nursing, 28*, 16–21.

Tinsley, B. J. (1992). Multiple influences on the acquisition and socialization of children's health attitudes and behavior: An integrative review. *Child Development, 63*, 1043–1069.

Tremblay, R. E., LeBlanc, M., & Schwartzman, A. E. (1988). The predictive power of first-grade peer and teacher ratings of behavior: Sex differences in antisocial behavior and personality at adolescence. *Journal of Abnormal Child Psychology, 16*, 571–583.

Van Kleek, A., & Schuele, M. (1987). Precursors to literacy: Normal development. *Topics in Language Disorders, 7*, 13–31.

Whitt, J. K. (1982). Children's understandings of illness: Developmental considerations in pediatric intervention. In M. Wolraich & D. K. Routh (Eds.), *Advances in developmental and behavioral pediatrics* (pp. 299–318). Greenwich, CT: JAI Press.

PART 2

General Treatment Considerations

CHAPTER 6

Behavior Therapy and Pharmacological Adjuncts

BENJAMIN L. HANDEN

INTRODUCTION

The use of psychotropic medications in the treatment of childhood psychiatric disorders has increased steadily over the past few decades with the advent of a wide range of agents (Van Hasselt & Hersen, 1993). Some psychotropic agents are quite specific in nature (e.g., low doses of imipramine to treat nocturnal enuresis), while others are rather general in their effect (e.g., the use of clonidine to tread such symptoms as aggression, overactivity, mood swings, and tics). With the increased use of medication for the control of behavior, the nonphysician clinician has a number of important roles to play. First, in many cases, it is the clinician who makes the initial referral for consideration of the use of medication as a treatment adjunct. Second, the clinician may provide an important role both in determining the efficacy of medication and in examining potential adverse side effects. Finally, the clinician must be aware of the effectiveness of the combined use of a pharmacological intervention and nonpharmacological treatment and must use this information in making treatment decisions and recommendations.

Historically, clinicians seem to be better at examining comparative outcomes than examining interactions between two forms of treatment (Hollon & Beck, 1978). This is especially true for the pharmacological and behavioral literatures. Such a state of affairs may reflect a long-standing mind-body debate (Kendall & Lipman, 1991). Like many disciplines, controversy over mind-body interactions has continued for some time and is certainly reflected in issues regarding psychopharmacology and behavior. Behavioral and pharmacological paradigms are conceptually and operationally distinct. While psychology focuses upon the internalization of rules and behavior, pharmacology is based on a more mechanistic/biologic theory of behavior as a somewhat automatic occurrence (Kendall & Lipman). These differing views have tended to limit the development of interactive models.

The purpose of this chapter is to provide an overview of the available literature on the efficacy of pharmacological treatment as an adjunct to behavioral interventions among children. However, because of limited information on combination treatment of children in areas such as depression or obesity, some of the discussion will primarily address the adult literature. The chapter will focus upon four classes of drugs—psychostimulants, antidepressants, neuroleptics, and anxiolytics/sedatives—and their interactions with behavioral interventions. Additionally, the indications for several novel drugs will be discussed. In each case, the literature comparing behavioral and pharmacological treatments will be reviewed for a particular disorder. Then, the available literature on interactive effects when combined treatments are utilized will be examined. Uhlenhuth,

Lipman, and Covi's (1969) model will serve as a guide in which several possible forms of therapy interactions are postulated: (a) addition: combined effects are equal to the sum of the individual contributions of the treatments; (b) potentiation: combined effects are greater than the sum of the individual contributions of the treatments; (c) inhibition: combined effects are less than the sum of the individual contributions of the treatments; and (d) reciprocation: combined effects are equal to the contribution of the most effective treatment. Finally, implications for treatment will be discussed.

OVERVIEW OF DRUG CLASSES

To better understand combined pharmacological and behavioral treatment effects, a brief overview of the various medication classes and the types of behaviors/disorders for which each has been prescribed is provided below. Table 6.1 summarizes the classes of drugs used with children along with their indications.

Neuroleptics

Neuroleptics (also referred to as major tranquilizers) can be divided into six categories: phenothiazines (e.g., Mellaril, Thorazine, Stelazine), butyrophenones (e.g., Haldol), thioxanthenes (e.g., Taractan, Navane), dihydroindolones (e.g., Moban), dibenzosazepines (e.g., Asendin, Loxitane), and dipehnylbutylpiperidines (e.g., Orap). These agents are typically prescribed for schizophrenia and bipolar disorder in adults, disorders that are rarely seen in prepubescent children (Campbell, Green, & Deutch, 1985). Among children, this class of drugs is prescribed for moderately to severely disturbed children who present with a range of disorders, usually after failing to respond to other pharmacological interventions (Campbell et al., 1985). Haloperidol and pimozide have been prescribed for children with Tourette syndrome to treat primary symptoms, such as vocal or motor tics (Comings, 1990). Neuroleptics have also been frequently prescribed for children with mental retardation or autism who exhibit self-injurious or aggressive behaviors (see review by Handen, 1993).

Psychostimulants

Psychostimulants, such as methylphenidate, dextroamphetamine, and pemoline, have been used extensively over the past three decades for the treatment of attention-deficit/ hyperactivity disorder (ADHD). Both methylphenidate and dextroamphetamine are short-acting medications (with clinical effects lasting 4 to 6 hours) that can be prescribed for targeted time periods (e.g., school hours only). Stimulants are extremely effective in increasing attention span and in decreasing impulsivity and overactivity. While the presence of a tic disorder will likely contraindicate the continued use of stimulants, there are a few reports of stimulants being successfully prescribed for the treatment of ADHD-like symptoms among children with Tourette syndrome (Comings & Comings, 1987). Additionally, there are some reports of these same drugs treating ADHD-like symptoms among children with autism (Birmaher, Quintana, & Greenhill, 1988; Strayhorn, Rapp, Donina, & Strain, 1988).

Antidepressants

Antidepressants are divided into two primary groups: monoamine oxidase inhibitors (MAOIs) and trycyclic antidepressants. Many new antidepressants are also prescribed, such as fluoxetine (Prozac). Antidepressants have been used to treat depression, enuresis, school phobia, hyperactivity, obsessive-compulsive disorder, and sleep disorders in children.

Anxiolytics

Anxiolytics include agents such as benzodiazepines, antihistamines, and buspirone (Buspar). While some of these drugs have been successfully used to treat both sleep disorders and anxiety disorders among children, few well-controlled studies have actually been conducted (Bukstein, 1993). Recently, buspirone has been used to treat aggression, self-injurious behavior, and self-stimulatory behavior in children and adults with mental retardation or autism (see review by Aman, 1991).

Other Drugs

A few other drugs will also be discussed in this chapter. The first is fenfluramine (a serotonin-depleting agent), a drug that has been used to treat symptoms of autism and ADHD. The second drug is clonidine, an antihypertensive agent (alpha-adrenergic receptor antagonist) that has been used to treat Tourette syndrome, ADHD, and autism among children. A third drug, propranolol (Inderal), is a beta-adrenergic blocking agent that has been used to treat aggression and self-injury among children with mental retardation or autism. Lithium carbonate, a drug prescribed to treat depression, bipolar disorder, and aggression, will also be discussed. Finally, studies of naloxone and naltrexone, opiate antagonists that have been used to treat self-injurious behavior among children with mental retardation or autism, will be presented.

PHARMACOLOGICAL AND BEHAVIORAL TREATMENTS

Attention-deficit/hyperactivity disorder

Attention-deficit/hyperactivity disorder (ADHD) affects 3% to 5% of school-age children and is characterized by significant deficits in attention span, impulsivity, and overactivity. Secondary characteristics include poor school performance, low self-esteem, and depression as children reach adolescence and adulthood (Barkley, 1990). Behavioral interventions are frequently used to treat children with ADHD. Successful interventions must occur within the child's immediate environment, such as home or school The use of token economies, response cost systems, time out, and consistent rules and expectations can result in significant improvement in behavior. However, treatment effects are typically found only in those environments in which intervention is implemented and although gains in behavior are often noted, they typically fail to fall within the normal range of age-appropriate behavior (Murphy, Pelham, & Greenstein, 1993; Pelham & Murphy, 1986). Cognitive therapy has also been used in a number of studies of children with ADHD in which specific social skills and the ability to control impulsive responding are addressed.

TABLE 6.1. Pharmacologic Agents Used with Children

Drug class	Other names	Examples (Brand names)	Indications
Neuroleptics	Major tranquilizers	Chlorpromazine (Thorazine)	Psychosis, Mania, schizophrenia, aggression
		Thioridazine (Mellaril)	Psychosis, autism, aggression
		Haloperidol (Haldol)	Psychosis, autism, aggression, Tourette syndrome
Psychostimulants	Analeptics	Methylphenidate (Ritalin)	ADHD
		Dextroamphetamine (Dexedrine)	ADHD
		Pemoline (Cylert)	ADHD
Anxiolytics	Minor tranquilizers or benzodiazepines	Clonazepam (Klonopin)	Anxiety reduction, sleep induction
		Alprazolam (Xanax)	Anxiety reduction, sleep induction
		Diazepam (Valium)	Anxiety reduction, sleep induction
	Antihistamines	Diphenhydramine (Benadryl)	Nighttime sedation, antianxiety during the day, motion sickness
	None	Buspirone (Buspar)	Anxiety reduction
Antidepressants —Tricylics	None	Amitriptyline (Elavil)	Major depression, obsessive-compulsive disorder, school refusal or phobia, panic disorder
		Nortriptyline (Pamelor)	Major depression
		Clomipramine (Anafranil)	Major depression, obsessive-compulsive disorder
		Desipramine (Norpramin)	Major depression, ADHD, school refusal or phobia, panic disorder, obsessive-compulsive disorder
		Imipramine (Tofranil)	Major depression, ADHD, school refusal or phobia, panic disorder, obsessive-compulsive disorder, plus enuresis

—New Antidepressants	None	Fluoxetine (Prozac)	Major depression, obsessive-compulsive disorder
		Sertraline (Zoloft)	Major depression, obsessive-compulsive disorder
		Paroxctine (Paxil)	Major depression, obsessive-compulsive disorder
Other drugs	None	Lithium (Eskalith)	Bipolar disorders, aggression
	Alpha-adrenergic receptor antagonist	Clonidine (Catapres)	Tourette syndrome, ADHD, manic episodes, aggression
	Opiate antagonist	Naltrexone	Self-injury
	Serotonin depleting	Fenfluramine (Ponidimin)	Autism
	Beta-adrenergic blocking agent	Propranolol (Inderal)	Aggression, migraine headache
	None	Desmopressin Acetate (DDAVP)	Enuresis

Note. From Bukstein in Van Hasselz & Hersen (Eds.), *Handbook of Behavior Therapy and Pharmacotherapy for Children: A Comparative Analysis* (p. 17), 1993, Boston, MA: Allyn and Bacon, Copyright 1993 by Allyn and Bacon. Adapted with permission.

However, recent reviews of this literature question the generalizability of such an intervention (see review by Abikoff, 1991).

Stimulant medication is the most widely used treatment for ADHD with documented response rates of 73% to 77% (see review by Barkley, 1977). Recent estimates suggest that over 600,000 children are currently prescribed stimulant medication for management of symptoms of ADHD (Safer & Krager, 1983). However, Pelham and Murphy (1986) report a number of important limitations in the use of such drugs. First, stimulants often fail to bring behavior within the normal range on measures of academic, social, and behavioral functioning. Second, effects are only observed during those periods of time in which medication is given and fail to address issues in the home where these drugs are less often prescribed. Finally, there is little evidence that the use of stimulants changes the long-term prognosis for a child (Hechtman, Weiss, & Perlman, 1984). Tricyclic antidepressants such as imipramine and desipramine have also been used to treat children with ADHD who have been nonresponsive to stimulant medications (Campbell, Green, & Deutsch, 1985). Among children with mental retardation and ADHD, stimulants, neuroleptics, clonidine, and fenfloramine have been used to treat inattention and overactivity (see review by Handen, 1993).

Because of some of the limitations noted for both pharmacological and behavioral interventions, combined treatments may be extremely important, especially if interactions are potentially complementary (i.e., each treatment produces change in unique domains) or additive (i.e., combined effects are equal to the sum of the individual treatments). Pelham and Murphy (1986) reviewed the literature on the combined use of psychostimulants and behavioral interventions and found a total of 19 articles in the literature. Several of those studies found children with ADHD to approach normal functioning only with a combined intervention (e.g., Abikoff, 1982; Hinshaw, Henker, & Whalen, 1984). Of the 19 studies, 13 demonstrated superiority of combined treatment on at least one variable. Overall, combined treatment resulted in greater improvement than either treatment alone. However, results were limited to those periods when medication was prescribed and usually involved a treatment period of only 3 weeks. No long-term follow-up data were provided. Finally, these authors noted a number of potentially significant methodological problems that limited their ability to draw definitive conclusions.

A review of *Index Medicus* from the years 1985 through 1992 identified an additional six papers involving combined treatments for ADHD. One recent paper by Carlson, Pelham, Milich, and Dixon (1992) attempted to address many of the aforementioned methodological issues and clearly demonstrated additive effects of two treatment interventions. Twenty-four boys received b.i.d. doses of placebo and two doses of methylphenidate (MPH) (0.3 mg/kg and 0.6 mg/kg) crossed with a behavioral and regular classroom setting. The behavioral intervention included a token economy, time out, and daily report card. Figure 6.1 presents percent-on-task behavior in the two classrooms, indicating that both MPH and behavior modification singly produce significant gains in behavior and that the combined effects of the two treatments at the lower MPH dose are equal to the effects of the higher MPH dose alone. Figure 6.2 shows similar results on a measure of disruptive classroom behavior. The combined effects of these two treatments would allow for a lower dose of medication along with fewer adverse side effects. Yet despite positive reports such as this, Hinshaw and Erhardt (1993) caution that there continues to be a great need to evaluate alternative and adjunctive interventions to stimulant medications in this population.

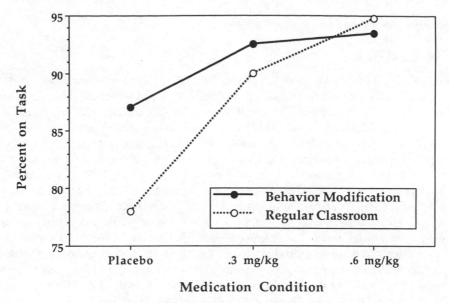

Figure 6.1. The mean percent of on-task behavior as a function of separate or combined behavioral and drug treatment.
Note. From "Single and Combined Effects of Methylphenidate and Behavior Therapy on the Classroom Performance of Children with Attention-deficit/hyperactivity disorder," by C. L. Carlson, W. E. Pelham, R. Milich, and J. Dixon, 1992, *Journal of Abnormal Child Psychology, 20*, pp. 213–232. Copyright 1992 by Plenum Press. Reprinted by permission.

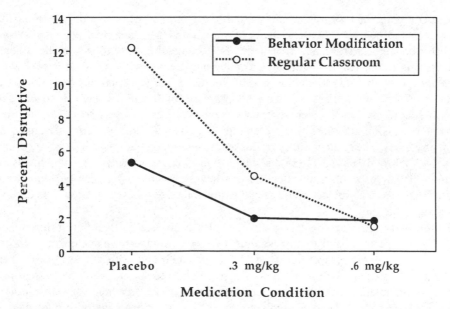

Figure 6.2. The mean percent of disruptive classroom behavior as a function of separate or combined behavioral and drug treatments.
Note. From "Single and Combined Effects of Methylphenidate and Behavior Therapy on the Classroom Performance of Children with Attention-deficit/hyperactivity disorder," by C. L. Carlson, W. E. Pelham, R. Milich, and J. Dixon, 1992, *Journal of Abnormal Child Psychology, 20*, pp. 213–232. Copyright 1992 by Plenum Press. Reprinted by permission.

Tourette Syndrome

Tourette syndrome (TS) is a neuropsychiatric disorder that affects approximately 0.5% of children and is characterized by the presence of both vocal and motor tics. Up to 50% of children with this disorder also exhibit symptoms of ADHD (Comings & Comings, 1988). TS has also been identified in individuals with severe and profound mental retardation (Crews, Bonaventura, Hay, Steele, & Rowe, 1993). Behavioral treatment of TS has generally been found to be unsuccessful for control of tics, although such interventions can be effective in managing associated behavior problems (Comings, 1990). Psychotropic agents used in treatment have included haloperidol, pimozide, and clonidine. Haloperidol, for example, has been found to control tics in about 80% of patients (Shapiro, Shapiro, & Wayne, 1973). Pimozide, another neuroleptic, is closely related to haloperidol and has also been used to successfully treat TS (Shapiro, Shapiro, & Eisenkraft, 1983). Clonidine has fewer side effects than the neuroleptics and can treat both tics and symptoms associated with ADHD. It tends to work in slightly more than half of patients (Comings, 1990). There have been a few reports of the successful use of stimulants to control ADHD symptoms in some children with TS (e.g., Comings & Comings, 1987). Additionally, a recent study involving an open trial of fluoxetine among a group of children with TS and obsessive-compulsive disorder suggests that this agent may also be of some use (Riddle, Hardin, King, Scahill, & Woolston, 1990). The author is unaware of any study examining the combined use of behavioral and pharmacologic treatments for TS.

Autism

Autism is a childhood disorder characterized by severe and pervasive deficits in social attachment and behavior, severe deficits in speech and language, and compulsive and ritualistic behaviors. There is a rich literature documenting the efficacy of behavioral interventions among children with autism addressing areas such as social deficits, speech and language skills, and elimination of self-stimulatory or self-injurious behaviors (see review by Schreibman, 1988). Additionally, the use of functional analysis to identify specific conditions under which aberrant behaviors are most likely to occur has also received increasing attention in the literature (e.g., Iwata, Dorsey, Slifer, Bauman, & Richman, 1982). The clinical utility of this assessment procedure was demonstrated in a study by Carr and Durand (1985) in which two children displayed greater levels of disruptive behavior when adult attention was lowest. Decreases in such behavior were documented when the subjects were taught communicative phrases that could be used to obtain adult attention.

A number of pharmacological agents have also been used to treat both primary and secondary symptoms of autism. For example, two recent studies have documented the use of stimulants to treat symptoms of ADHD among children with autism (Birnmaher, Quintana, & Greenhill, 1988; Strayhorn, Rapp, Donina, & Strain, 1988). There has also been a recent interest in naltrexone, an opiate blocker, for treatment of self-injurious behavior (SIB). Over 18 studies involving the use of naltrexone have been published to date, including five among children with autism. Two prominent but competing theories regarding SIB involve the opiate system. One posits that excessive levels of endogenous opioids in the central nervous system lead to insensitivity to pain, whereas the other suggests that SIB causes the release of endogenous opioids and an euphoric effect. The majority of studies involving naltrexone found decreases in rates of SIB for at least some subjects (see review by Aman, 1991).

Fenfluramine, a serotonin-depleting agent, has also been prescribed to treat symptoms associated with autism (e.g., Geller, Ritvo, Freeman, & Yuwiler, 1982). Based on evidence that children with autism have higher concentrations of serotonin than control groups (Schain & Freedman, 1961), a number of researchers have examined the efficacy of this drug among children with autism. Although data are somewhat conflicting, there is evidence that fenfluramine may have positive effects on problem behaviors such as hyperactivity, inattention, and stereotypy but that it does not lead to improvement in overall cognitive functioning or adaptive behavior (see Aman & Kern, 1989). Clonidine, an alpha-adrenergic receptor antagonist, has also been successfully used in a small number of double-blind, placebo-controlled studies to treat overactivity and social interactions among children and adults with autism (see Fankhauser, Karumanchi, German, Yates, & Karumanchi, 1992; Jaselskis, Cook, Fletcher, & Leventhal, 1992).

In studies involving neuroleptics among individuals with autism, there is some evidence that positive results may be due to secondary effects of sedation, such as increased lethargy or social withdrawal (see review by Schroeder, 1988). However, haloperidol has been used successfully in a number of well-controlled studies among children with autism in which reduction of stereotypies and social withdrawal were noted (e.g., Campbell et al., 1978; Cohen et al., 1980). In fact, one of these studies describes the combined used of behavioral and pharmacological interventions: A group of 40 children with autism, ages 2.6 to 7.2 years, served as subjects in a study examining the efficacy of haloperidol and a placebo in combination with contingent and noncontingent reinforcement of language training (Campbell et al.). Language training involved 30 minutes of individualized programming based on a training package designed by Lovaas (1977). The children were assigned to one of four possible treatment groups: drug or placebo, and contingent or noncontingent reinforcement language training. As shown in Figure 6.3, the combined effects of haloperidol and behavior therapy (contingent reinforcement) were superior to medication or behavior therapy alone in increasing the mean number of words imitated per session.

Mental Retardation

There is a rich literature on the use of behavioral interventions for the treatment of a variety of behavioral and learning difficulties for children with mental retardation (see review by Green & Cuvo, 1993). This population has also been exposed to a wide range of pharmacological agents. A recent paper by Handen (1993) reviews the literature on pharmacotherapy among children with mental retardation or autism. It is important to note that medications have not been prescribed to treat mental retardation per se, but to treat specific behavioral and learning difficulties experienced by some individuals.

In some cases, children with special needs respond in the same manner to pharmacological agents as children without development delays; for example, Handen, Breaux, Gosling, Ploof, and Feldman (1990) and Handen, Breaux et al. (1992) found response rates to methylphenidate among children with moderate to borderline mental retardation and ADHD to be similar to that of the nondelayed population. However, Aman, Marks, Turbott, Wilsher, and Merry (1991) found that children with ADHD who had IQs below 45 rarely responded well to stimulants. One particularly well-designed study documents the combined use of stimulant medication and behavioral interventions with a 5-year-old boy with mild mental retardation, severe dysphasia, and ADHD (Schell et al., 1986). A placebo and 0.3 mg/kg dose of MPH were each used alone and in combination with

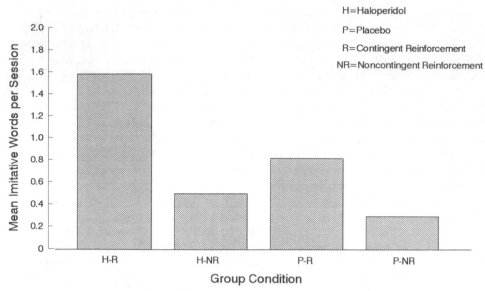

Figure 6.3. The effects of haloperidol, behavior therapy, and their interaction on acquisition of imitative speech in 40 autistic children ages 2.6 to 7.2 years.
Note. From *Child and Adolescent Psychopharmacology* by M. Campbell, W. H. Green, and S. I. Deutsch, 1985, Volume 2 of *Developmental Clinical Psychology and Psychiatry* (A. E. Kazdin, Series Editor), Newbury Park, CA: Sage Publications, Inc. Copyright 1985 by Sage Publications, Inc. Reprinted by permission.

prompts and *prompts plus reinforcement* conditions to teach word identification. MPH was found to reduce both noncompliance and defiance during sessions, whereas only defiance was reduced by reinforcement. Peak performance on word identification occurred with the combination of MPH and reinforcement, as can be seen in Figure 6.4.

Enuresis

Nocturnal enuresis is defined as involuntary urination during sleep. It is fairly normal among infants and toddlers, with 90% of children learning to remain dry during sleep between the ages of 3 and 6 years (Schmitt, 1990). There are a number of possible causal factors involved in nocturnal enuresis, including small functional bladder capacity, deficiency of antidiuretic hormone (ADH), inability to delay micturition urge, large intake of fluids at night, and difficulty awakening when the bladder feels full (Schmitt, 1990). A number of behavioral treatments have documented positive treatment rates of 70% to 90%, including a bell-and-pad enuresis alarm (Fordham & Meadow, 1989) and dry-bed training (Azrin & Thienes, 1978). The use of imipramine, a tricyclic antidepressant, has long been used as a treatment for enuresis, with success rates ranging from 10% to 60% (Schmitt, 1990). Doses typically range from 25 to 75 mg/day, much lower than that prescribed for the treatment of depression. Treatment appears best when imipramine is prescribed for a 3-to-4-month period and then gradually reduced over a 3-to-4-week period (Blackwell & Currah, 1973). Relapse rates when imipramine is discontinued are as high as 90% (Schmitt, 1990).

A second, more recent, pharmacological treatment involves the use of desmopressin

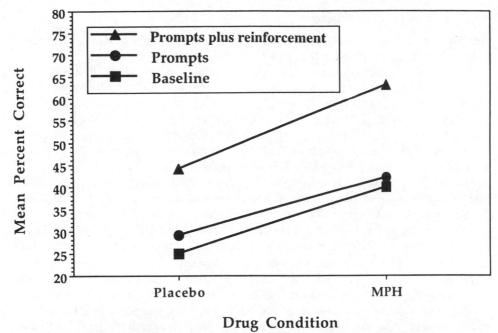

Figure 6.4. The mean percentage of correct word identifications as a function of instructional and drug conditions.

Note. From "The Concurrent Assessment of Behavioral and Psychostimulant Intervention: A Controlled Case Study" by R. M. Schell, W. E. Pelham, M. E. Bender, J. A. Andree, T. Law, and F. R. Robbins, 1986, *Behavioral Assessment, 8*, pp. 373–384. Copyright 1986 by Association for Advancement of Behavior Therapy. Reprinted by permission.

(DDAVP), a drug that increases levels of vasopressin, or ADH. This treatment is based upon data suggesting that ADH normally increases during the night and causes the body to produce smaller volumes of concentrated urine. However, some children with nocturnal enuresis have been found not to have an expected rise in ADH levels with sleep (Norgaard, Rittig, & Djurhuus, 1989). A review of 12 placebo-controlled studies of DDAVP found improvement in 10% to 65% of children (Klauber, 1989). However, as with imipramine, research suggests that up to 80% of children relapse with the discontinuation of medication (Schmitt, 1990).

Only a few studies have compared behavioral and pharmacological treatments. Willie (1986) compared the use of DDAVP and bell-and-pad alarm with 46 children. While improvement was noted in 70% and 86% of children, respectively, almost half the sample using DDAVP relapsed after treatment, whereas only one child relapsed in the bell-and-pad group. An additional study comparing imipramine with enuresis alarms documented higher levels of improvement and lower relapse rates for the alarm versus pharmacological treatment (Wagner, Johnson, Walker, Carter, & Wittner, 1982). The superiority of behavioral treatment over medication is likely due to the educative effects of the former regimen. There are no known studies examining any possible additive effects of behavioral and pharmacological treatments, possibly because the long-term effects of combined treatment might be inhibiting, as drug therapy could decrease the opportunities for a child to experience the consequences of the behavior or to learn alternative toileting behaviors.

Anxiety Disorders and Phobias

Anxiety disorders among children typically include separation anxiety, avoidant disorders, overanxious disorders, and phobias (see DSM-IIIR, American Psychiatric Association, 1987). Prevalence rates of intense fears among children are around 7% to 8% (Strauss, 1987). Behavioral interventions for children have involved a range of techniques, including systematic desensitization, flooding/implosion, operant approaches (e.g., positive reinforcement, shaping, fading, extinction), modeling, and cognitive procedures. The behavioral literature is generally comprised of clinical case reports or single-case studies of the treatment of situation-specific fears or phobias, such as nighttime fears, fear of medical procedures, or school phobias. Few researchers have focused on the treatment of generalized anxiety disorders (Silverman & Kearney, 1993). Examination of the behavioral literature indicates that a range of interventions have generally been successful in treating specific fears or phobias; Barrios and O'Dell (1989), for example, reviewed contingency-management procedures to treat childhood fears and found most studies to have resulted in significant fear reduction for periods ranging from 1 to 12 months. They also found that systematic desensitization evidenced considerable success in the treatment of phobias in children, with gains maintained for periods ranging from 3 to 36 months. Finally, Barrios and O'Dell reviewed 9 studies using flooding/implosion therapy and 30 studies using modeling procedures to treat fears in children and again noted significant clinical effects in the vast majority of studies, with gains continued for extended follow-up periods.

Few medications have been found to be effective in the treatment of anxiety disorders in children (Gislason & Neri, 1993). Antihistamines, such as Benadryl and Atarax, have been found to decrease anxiety in children, mostly via the induction of sedation (Bender & Nichtern, 1956). Benzodiazepines (e.g., Librium, Valium, Xanax) are the most common form of pharmacological treatment for anxiety disorders, especially among adults. Simeon and Ferguson (1985) treated 12 children who had overanxious or avoidance disorders with alprazolam (Xanax), with one child evidencing marked improvement and six showing moderate gains. Biederman (1987) successfully treated three children who had anxiety disorders with panic-like symptoms with clonazepam (Klonopin—a drug with antiepileptic properties).

The possible interactions between behavioral interventions and antianxiety medications, such as benzodiazepines, have received relatively little attention in the literature (Wardle, 1990), despite the fact that these two interventions are often used in combination clinically. In fact, data suggest that up to 65% of adult patients with anxiety who are referred for behavior therapy are already prescribed a minor tranquillizer (Durham & Turvey, 1987). Animal studies indicate that benzodiazepines and barbiturates impair extinction in comparison to placebo, suggesting that combined pharmacological and behavioral interventions among humans would attenuate clinical response (Wardle, 1990). However, in a review of six such studies involving acute drug treatment (i.e., given during exposure trials only), the majority indicated additive interactions when behavioral interventions were combined with medication (Wardle, 1990). In one of the few studies involving continuous and long-term benzodiazepine use, drugs plus behavior therapy had a deleterious effect, with only 8% of subjects improved at 1 year follow-up versus 86% improved with behavior therapy alone. Interestingly, in two groups assigned to a cognitive therapy condition, a 50% response rate at 1-year follow-up was noted with or without the inclusion of drugs (Durham & Turvey, 1987; Wardle, 1990).

Depression

Depression involves the presence of dysphoric or depressed mood that lasts a minimum of 2 weeks and includes symptoms such as a significant change in appetite; sleep disturbance; psychomotor agitation or retardation; anhedonia; loss of energy or excessive fatigue; feelings of worthlessness; diminished ability to think or concentrate; and recurrent thoughts of death, suicidal ideation, or actual suicidal attempts (American Psychiatric Association, 1987). Prevalence rates among children vary greatly. A study of a nonclinic community sample of 9-10-11-year-olds found a rate of 5.2% (Lefkowitz & Tesiny, 1980), whereas the rate among high school adolescents is somewhat higher (8.6%) (Kaplan, Hong, & Weinhold, 1984).

Behavioral interventions for depression among children, as well as adults, have generally focused upon cognitive-behavior therapy. However, although there has been a proliferation of nonpharmacological outcome research among adults with depression, examination of the efficacy of such interventions among children has lagged behind (Kaslow, Celano, & McCarthy, 1993). A number of case reports have examined the effects of social-skills-training packages on the behavior of children with depression, suggesting that such interventions can lead to improved mood and interpersonal functioning (e.g., Frame, Matson, Sonis, Fialkor, & Kazdin, 1982; Schloss, Schloss, & Harris, 1984). A small number of controlled group studies have also been conducted and suggest that cognitive-behavioral interventions are superior to control conditions in the treatment of depressive symptoms among children and adolescents (e.g., Fine, Forth, Gilbert, & Haley, 1990; Lewinsohn, Clarke, Hops, & Andrews, 1990). Gains also appear to be maintained at follow-ups lasting from a few weeks to up to 2 years.

The relatively small number of controlled studies of antidepressants among children make the data difficult to analyze (Grob, 1993). Few studies are methodologically rigorous; sample sizes are small; and there is a high placebo response rate. In fact, several studies of prepubescent children have failed to demonstrate the superiority of drugs such as imipramine and nortriptyline over placebo (Geller, Cooper, McCombs, Graham, & Wells, 1989; Puig-Antich et al., 1987). Among adolescents, only two studies have examined the efficacy of tricyclics for the treatment of depression: One found no difference between placebo and amitriptyline (Kramer & Feiguine, 1983); the other documented a 44% response rate with the use of imipramine (Ryan et al., 1986). Finally, two well-controlled studies of small groups of adolescents who had been refractory to tricyclics have also been conducted: Ryan, Meyer, Cachille, Mazzie, and Puig-Antich (1988) documented a 74% response rate with an MAOI (monoamine oxidase inhibitors), whereas Ryan, Puig-Antich, Rabinovich, et al., (1988) found a 44% response rate when lithium was added to the tricyclic regimen.

There exist a number of studies comparing the efficacy of cognitive therapy (CT) with tricyclic pharmacotherapy for treatment of adults and adolescents with depression (see Dobson, 1989). In general, CT was found to be at least comparable, if not superior, to medication. However, the total number of studies has been small, and sample sizes have been limited. Consequently, it is premature to draw definitive conclusions from the present available literature (Hollon, Shelton, & Loosen, 1991).

A handful of studies have also sought to examine the interactive effects of combined CT and pharmacotherapy. Hollon et al. (1992), for example, compared the efficacy of CT, of imipramine, and of combined CT/imipramine among a group of 107 unipolar depressed adult outpatients. No differences in outcome were observed between the single modalities with a nonsignificant advantage of the combined modality. However, there was an average 40% attrition rate across modalities and an absence of a placebo control. Murphy, Simons, Wetzel, and Lustman (1984) utilized a similar design with the tricyclic nortriptyline and included a CT/placebo-control group. All conditions resulted in significant gains over time with no differences among them. However, absence of a placebo-control group limits interpretation. Beck, Hollon, Young, Bedrosian, and Budenz (1985) compared CT with CT/amitriptyline among a group of unipolar depressed outpatient adults. No differences were observed, although amitriptyline dose levels were relatively low and adverse side effects led to reduced compliance. Covi and Lipman (1987) compared CT/imipramine with CT alone and interpersonal oriented dynamic therapy. No significant differences were found between CT and CT/imipramine, although the combined treatment was favored. Both treatments were more effective than the dynamic-therapy group. Finally, Miller, Norman, Keitner, Bishop, and Dow (1989) compared standard pharmacologic treatment, CT/medication, and social-skills-training/medication among a group of depressed inpatients. No differences were noted at discharge, although the CT/medication and social-skills-training/medication groups maintained lower levels of symptoms in comparison to the standard treatment group following 4 months of outpatient treatment.

At present, there is little evidence to suggest that combined therapies are superior to single-modality interventions for the treatment of depression (Hollon, Shelton, & Loosen, 1991). However, the small yet nonsignificant differences noted in a number of reports in favor of combined therapies suggest that this area warrants further investigation.

Obsessive-Compulsive Disorder

Obsessive-compulsive disorder (OCD) involves the presence of obsessions and/or compulsions. Obsessions are persistent ideas, recurrent thoughts, images, or impulses that are experienced as intrusive and senseless and that the person attempts to ignore or suppress. Conversely, compulsions are repetitive, purposeful, and intentional behaviors performed in response to an obsession. They involve a task or ritual conducted in a repetitive, stereotyped manner that is designed to produce or prevent some dreaded event or situation (American Psychiatric Association, 1993). OCD is a fairly rare disorder among children and adolescents, with estimates ranging from 0.2% to 1.2% of child psychiatric cases (Flament et al., 1985). Recent reviews of the OCD-treatment literature suggest that both behavior therapy and pharmacotherapy are effective interventions (Christensen, Hadzi-Pavlovic, Andrews, & Mattick, 1987; Marks & O'Sullivan, 1988). The most common forms of behavioral intervention involve the use of exposure, in which a patient confronts objects or situations that cause anxiety, and response prevention, which requires that patients delay or diminish rituals used to decrease anxiety. In an examination of 200 OCD patients treated with behavioral interventions, Foa, Steketee, and Ozarow (1985) found 90% to report reduction in symptoms ranging from 31% to 100%. At 1-year follow-up, 76% of patients remained improved.

The most consistent response to drug treatment has involved the use of serotonin uptake inhibitors, such as clomipramine, paroxetine, fluoxetine, and sertraline. The tricyclic clomipramine has received the most attention in the literature. The average reduction in OCD symptoms in adults with clomipramine is 30% to 42% (Greist, 1990). A recent review of the literature found clomipramine to be more effective than placebo as well as other antidepressants (DeVeaugh-Geiss, Katz, Landau, & Katz, 1989). Clomipramine has also been found to be an effective treatment for children and adolescents with OCD. A study conducted by Flament et al. (1985), for example, found 75% of subjects to evidence moderate to marked improvement. Similarly, Leonard, Swedo, Rapoport, Coffey, and Cheslow (1988) found clomipramine to be superior to both placebo and desmethylimipramine (another tricyclic antidepressant). Neuroleptics appear helpful in patients with OCD and schizotypal personality or movement (tic) disorder (Zetin & Kramer, 1992). Also buspirone (Buspar) has been shown to decrease some symptoms of OCD (Pato et al., 1989). However, long-term treatment with medication is often required, and there is a high rate of relapse once medication is discontinued (Greist, 1990).

A small number of studies have examined the combined effects of pharmacologic treatment and behavioral interventions, most frequently involving the use of exposure therapy. O'Sullivan, Noshirvani, Marks, Monteiro, and Lelliot (1991), for example, conducted a 6-year follow-up study of patients treated with 36 weeks of placebo or clomipramine and 3 or 6 weeks of exposure therapy. Improved long-term outcome was associated with longer exposure therapy. Drug treatment during the first year was not correlated with outcome at 6 years. Another study (Rachman et al., 1979) examined the effects of behavioral treatment alone and in combination with clomipramine on OCD symptoms in a group of 40 patients. Although the behavioral treatment resulted in significant gains on most behavioral measures, medication led to improvement on mood scales and some behavioral measures. No interaction effects were noted between the two treatments.

Bulimia Nervosa

Bulimia nervosa is a chronic disorder characterized by binge eating followed by self-induced purging, usually involving vomiting or excessive laxative use. Cognitive-behavioral treatment of bulimia nervosa has been examined in a number of controlled studies, indicating this intervention to be superior to no treatment and to other psychotherapy control conditions. A recent review of this literature found decreases in binge eating and purging ranging from 52% to 96%, with 15% to 90% of patients achieving complete remission of symptoms (Craighead & Agras, 1991). Follow-up data also suggested good maintenance of gains for up to 4 years post-treatment (Agras, 1991). A somewhat different behavioral treatment for bulimia nervosa involves response prevention of vomiting (Leitenberg, Gross, Nudelman, & Vara, 1988). Although controlled studies have demonstrated the treatment efficacy of response prevention (Leitenberg et al., 1988; Wilson, Rossiter, Kleifeld, & Lindholm, 1986), a study combining cognitive-behavioral and response prevention found the latter to inhibit the effectiveness of the cognitive-behavioral approach (Agras, Schneider, Arnow, Raeburn, & Telch, 1989). Behavioral interventions appear to work by decreasing dietary restraint (Craighead & Agras, 1991).

A number of pharmacologic agents have been examined as potential treatments for this disorder. However, only antidepressants have been found to significantly reduce symptoms among depressed and nondepressed individuals with bulimia nervosa. This includes the use of monoamine oxidase inhibitors, tricyclic antidepressants, and new antidepressants such as fluoxetine (Walsh, 1991). It is suggested that the therapeutic mechanism of antidepressants, especially tricyclics, is to increase dietary restraint (Craighead & Agras, 1991). However, most studies have involved adults, and additional work needs to be done to establish the efficacy of antidepressants among adolescents (Walsh, 1991). Short-term efficacy of antidepressants is well documented, with an average decrease in binge frequency of about 50%. However, only about 20% of patients completely discontinue binge eating (Walsh, 1991). Studies examining long-term follow-up have been less promising. Both Pyle et al. (1990) and Walsh, Hadigan, and Devlin (1991) found almost one-third of responders to antidepressants to relapse within 4 months of recovery.

Although both pharmacological and behavioral interventions for bulimia nervosa appear to have somewhat similar initial-response rates, greater drop-out rates due to adverse side effects and to poorer long-term maintenance have been noted with antidepressants. Combining these two treatments may be somewhat problematic, given that the former works by increasing dietary restraint and the latter treatment is designed to decrease dietary restraint. Two recent studies have examined these questions. Mitchell, Pyle, and Eckert (1990) studied a group of 174 women with bulimia nervosa using imipramine or placebo crossed with cognitive-behavioral or no treatment. Following 12 weeks of treatment, both imipramine and cognitive-behavioral treatment were found to be superior to placebo and no treatment. However, cognitive-behavioral treatment alone and combined with imipramine were both superior to drug alone, suggesting that medication added little to the effects of nonpharmacological treatment. A study by Agras et al. (1992) compared desipramine, cognitive-behavioral treatment, and a combined treatment. Similar results were noted as in the Mitchell et al. (1990) study. However, the combined treatment was found to significantly reduce dietary preoccupation. At present, there remain too few studies to draw any definitive conclusions regarding the efficacy of combined therapies in the treatment of bulimia nervosa.

Obesity

Studies suggest that 10% to 15% of young children and 15% to 30% of adolescents are obese (Colley, 1974; Garn & Clark, 1976). The behavioral model of obesity assumes that maladaptive eating patterns and poor exercise habits lead to a positive energy balance and accumulated weight over time (Craighead & Agras, 1991). Consequently, behavioral interventions promote increased activity, enhanced restraint, and the development of normalized eating patterns. Reviews of the considerable amount of behavioral research conducted in this area in the 1970s and early-to-middle 1980s found that 8- to 20-week programs consistently resulted in weight loss and good maintenance for up to 1 year (Brownell & Wadden, 1986). However, follow-up studies that went beyond a 2-year period found a gradual return to weights at or near pretreatment levels (Brownell & Jeffrey, 1987). More recent work suggests that longer and more comprehensive treatment programs may lead to improved long-term maintenance (Perri et al., 1988). Obesity must be seen presently as a chronic condition that requires long-term intervention.

Pharmacological treatment of obesity initially involved the use of anorexiant medications such as amphetamines, based on the assumption that individuals often eat in response to increased hunger or lack of satiety. Although such drugs might initially assist in successful weight loss, weight gain quickly follows the discontinuation of medication (Galloway, Farquhar, & Munro, 1984). Consequently, there seems to be little evidence supporting the efficacy or long-term use of this class of anorexiant drugs. In fact, amphetamines are now felt to be an inappropriate treatment option due to their abuse potential. More recently, the use of drugs such as diethylpropion, fenfluramine (which releases and presents the reuptake of serotonin), maxindol, and phentermine has resulted in weight loss, and these drugs have less abuse potential. A recent review by Gotesman and Hauge (1987) suggests that fenfluramine may be the most promising of these alternative medications.

Many recent studies have also suggested a role for antidepressants in the treatment of obesity. McAnn and Agras (1990), for example, successfully treated a group of compulsive overeaters with desipramine, a tricyclic antidepressant. Three additional studies of nondepressed obese individuals have involved the use of fluoxetine, one of whose side effects is weight loss. Each documented significant weight loss. However, attrition rates ranged from 16% to 40%, and follow-up data are not available (Ferguson & Feighner, 1987; Levine, Enas, et al., 1989; Levine, Rosenblatt, & Bosomworth, 1987). Since patients were not depressed and showed no change on measures of depression during treatment, the effects of fluoxitine are felt to be mediated more by anorexiant effects than by any relationship with mood (Craighead & Agras, 1991).

The literature on combined behavioral and drug treatment for obesity is equivocal. Difficulties in the interpretation of results are often due to poor follow-up and to variable quality of the behavioral interventions (Craighead, 1987). Although adding medication to a behavioral regimen appears to enhance weight loss, there is little evidence of an additive effect over behavioral interventions alone at 1-year follow-up with the use of newer anorexiant medications such as fenfluramine and diethylpropion (Craighead & Agras, 1991). It was initially hypothesized that combined treatments would be not only compatible, but additive. Medication might not only decrease appetite cues, but produce a more conducive environment for the successful teaching of appropriate eating habits and self-control. However, studies suggest that once medication is discontinued, weight gain ensues, leading some to question the additive aspects of the two treatment paradigms. Craighead and Agras (1991) suggest that anorexiant medication is most efficacious when introduced once behavioral treatment has begun. Otherwise, subjects may be less likely to practice behavioral strategies because they can depend upon medication to assist in coping with internal cues of hunger and satiety. Therefore, medication may best be reserved only for those who have difficulty acquiring skills taught in a behavioral intervention. Others have hypothesized that internal cues become more salient when drugs are discontinued. Such a theory is supported by evidence that individuals taking a placebo exhibited responses more similar to those with behavioral interventions alone than to those in a drug condition once medication was discontinued (Rodin, Elias, Silberstein, & Wagner, 1988). Finally, a single study on the combined use of fluoxetine and behavioral interventions was conducted by Marcus et al. (1990). The combined drug and behavioral condition resulted in significantly greater weight loss than the combined placebo and behavioral condition. In fact, the latter condition resulted in a mean weight gain for the group, suggesting this to be a poor comparison with a behavioral intervention alone. An average 20% weight gain was noted at 3- to 6-month follow-up after fluoxetine was discontinued.

SUMMARY

While children have been exposed to a wide range of pharmacological agents, there is relatively little research on the effects of combined drug and behavioral treatments. This is particularly worrisome given the fact that, for many childhood disorders, standard clinical practice is to provide combined treatment interventions. Yet, without a greater understanding of the potential for both additive and inhibitory effects of combined treatments, children and their families have the potential to be poorly served. Data on combined treatments is more readily available for those drugs that have a rich literature for use among children, for example, the over two dozen articles describing the additive effects of stimulants and behavioral interventions for children diagnosed with ADHD. Some literature on combined treatment is available for disorders such as obesity, OCD, and eating disorders for which both pharmacological and behavioral interventions have been used for some time. However, this research has generally focused on adolescents and adults and may not be generalizable for prepubescent children. Finally, novel drugs such as fluoxetine or clonidine have only recently begun to be prescribed and studied in children. Consequently, it will likely be some time before well-controlled combined-treatment studies are available. The clinician, therefore, must draw from the available literature and work closely with a child's physician to assist in monitoring drug effects on behavior because, with few exceptions, medication will most often need to be combined with an appropriate psychosocial intervention to provide the most effective treatment program.

REFERENCES

Abikoff, H. (1982, August). *Normalizing effects of medication and behavior therapy in hyperactive children.* Paper presented at the annual meeting of the American Psychological Association, Washington, DC.

Abikoff, H. (1991). Cognitive training in ADHD children: Less to it than meets the eye. *Journal of Learning Disabilities, 24,* 205–209.

Agras, W. S. (1991). Nonpharmacologic treatments of bulimia nervosa. *Journal of Clinical Psychology, 52,* (Suppl. 10), 29–33.

Agras, W. S., Rossiter, E. M., Arnow, B., Schneider, M.A., Telch, C. F., Raeburn, S. D., Bruce, B., Perl, M., & Koran, L. M. (1992). Pharmacological and cognitive-behavioral treatment for bulimia nervosa: A controlled comparison. *American Journal of Psychiatry, 149,* 82–87.

Agras, W. S., Schneider, J. A., Arnow, B., Raeburn, S. D., & Telch, C. F. (1989). Cognitive-behavioral treatment with and without exposure plus response prevention in the treatment of bulimia nervosa: A reply to Leitenberg and Rosen. *Journal of Consulting and Clinical Psychology, 57,* 778–779.

Aman, M. G. (1991). Pharmacotherapy in the developmental disabilities: New developments. *Australia and New Zealand Journal of Developmental Disabilities, 17,* 183–199.

Aman, M. G., & Kern, R. A. (1989). Review of fenfluramine in the treatment of the developmental disabilities. *Journal of the American Academy of Child and Adolescent Psychiatry, 28,* 549–565.

Aman, M. G., Marks, R. E., Turbott, S. H., Wilsher, C. P., & Merry, S. N. (1991). The clinical effects of methylphenidate and thioridazine in intellectually subaverage children. *Journal of the American Academy of Child and Adolescent Psychiatry, 30,* 246–256.

American Psychiatric Association. (1987). *Diagnostic and statistic manual of mental disorders* (3rd ed., rev.). Washington, DC: Author.

American Psychiatric Association. (1993). *DSM-IV draft criteria.* Washington DC: Author.

Azrin, H. H., & Thienes, P. M. (1978). Rapid elimination of enuresis by intensive learning without a conditioning apparatus. *Behavior Therapy, 9,* 342–354.

Barkley, R. A. (1977). A review of stimulant drug research with hyperactive children. *Archives of General Psychiatry, 36,* 201–208.

Barkley, R. A. (1990). *Attention-deficit/hyperactivity disorder: A handbook for diagnosis and treatment.* New York: Guilford Press.

Barrios, B. A., & O'Dell, S. L. (1989). Fears and anxieties. In E. J. Mash & R. A. Barkley (Eds.), *Treatment of childhood disorders* (pp. 167–221). New York: Guilford Press.

Beck, A. T., Hollon, S. D., Young, J. E., Bedrosian, R. C., & Budenz, D. (1985). Treatment of depression with cognitive therapy and amitriptyline. *Archives of General Psychiatry, 42*, 142–148.

Bender, L., & Nichtern, S. (1956). Chemotherapy in child psychiatry. *New York State Journal of Medicine, 6*, 2791–2795.

Biederman, J. (1987). Clonazepam in the treatment of pre-pubertal children with panic-like symptoms. *Journal of Clinical Psychiatry, 48*, 38–41.

Birmaher, B., Quintana, H., & Greenhill, L. L. (1988). Methylphenidate treatment of hyperactive autistic children. *Journal of the American Academy of Child and Adolescent Psychiatry, 27*, 248–251.

Blackwell, B., & Currah, J. (1973). The psychopharmacology of nocturnal enuresis. In I. Kolvin, R. C. MacKeith, & S. R. Meadow (Eds.), *Bladder control and enuresis* (pp. 231–257). London: W. Heinemann Medical Books.

Brownell, K. D., & Jeffrey, R. W. (1987). Improving long-term weight loss: Pushing the limits of treatment. *Behavior Therapy, 18*, 353–374.

Brownell, K. D., & Wadden, T. A. (1986). Behavior therapy for obesity: Modern approaches and better results. In K. D. Brownell & J. P. Forety (Eds.), *Handbook of eating disorders: Physiology, psychology, and treatment of obesity, anorexia, and bulimia* (pp. 180–197). New York: Basic Books.

Bukstein, O. G. (1993). Overview of pharmacological treatment. In V. B. Van Hasselt & M. Hersen (Eds.), *Handbook of behavior therapy and pharmacotherapy for children: A comparative analysis* (pp. 13–32). Boston: Allyn and Bacon.

Campbell, M., Anderson, L. T., Meier, M., Cohen, I. L., Small, A. M., Samit, C., & Sachar, E. J. (1978). A comparison of haloperidol and behavior therapy and their interaction in autistic children. *Journal of the American Academy of Child Psychiatry, 17*, 640–655.

Campbell, M., Green, W. H., & Deutsch, S. I. (1985). *Child and adolescent psychopharmacology*. Beverly Hills, CA: Sage Publications.

Carlson, C. L., Pelham, W. E., Milich, R., & Dixon, J. (1992). Single and combined effects of methylphenidate and behavior therapy on the classroom performance of children with attention-deficit/hyperactivity disorder. *Journal of Abnormal Child Pshychology, 20*, 213–232.

Carr, E. G., & Durand, V. M. (1985). Reducing behavior problems through functional communication training. *Journal of Applied Behavior Analysis, 18*, 111–126.

Christensen, H., Hadzi-Pavlovic, D., Andrews, G., & Mattick, R. (1987). Behavior therapy and tricyclic medication in the treatment of obsessive-compulsive disorder: A quantitative review. *Journal of Consulting and Clinical Psychology, 55*, 701–711.

Cohen, I. L., Campbell, M., Posner, D., Small, A. M., Trickel, D., & Anderson, L. T. (1980). Behavioral effects of haloperidol in young autistic children. *Journal of American Academy of Child Psychiatry, 19*, 665–677.

Colly, J. R. T. (1974). Obesity in school children. *British Journal of Preventative and Social Medicine, 28*, 221–225.

Comings, D. E. (1990). *Tourette syndrome and human behavior*. Duarte, CA: Hope Press.

Comings, D. E., & Comings, B. G. (1987). A controlled study of Tourette syndrome: I. Attention-deficit disorder, learning disorders, and school problems. *American Journal of Human Genetics, 41*, 701–741.

Comings, D. E., & Comings, B. G. (1988). Tourette's syndrome and attention-deficit disorder. In D. J. Cohen, R. D. Bruun, & J. F. Leckman (Eds.), *Tourette's syndrome and tic disorders: Clinical understanding and treatment* (pp. 119–135). New York: Wiley.

Covi, L., & Lipman, R. S. (1987). Cognitive-behavioral group psychotherapy combined with imipramine in major depression. *Psychopharmacological Bulletin, 23*, 173–176.

Craighead, L. W. (1987). Behavior therapy and pharmacotherapy in the treatment of obesity. In W. G. Johnson (Ed.), *Advances in eating disorders* (Vol. 1, pp. 65–86). Greenwich, CT: JAI Press.

Craighead, L. W., & Agras, W. S. (1991). Mechanisms of action in cognitive-behavioral and pharmacological intervention for obesity and bulimia nervosa. *Journal of Consulting and Clinical Psychology, 59*, 115–125.

Crews, W. D., Jr., Bonaventura, S., Hay, C. L., Steele, W. K., & Rowe, F. B. (1993). Gilles de la Tourette disorder among individuals with severe or profound mental retardation. *Mental Retardation, 31*, 25–28.

DeVeaugh-Geiss, J., Katz, R., Landau, P., & Katz, R. (1989). Preliminary results from a multicenter trial of clomipramine in obsessive-compulsive disorder. *Psychopharmacology Bulletin, 25*, 36–49.

Dobson, K. S. (1989). A meta-analysis of the efficacy of cognitive therapy for depression. *Journal of Consulting and Clinical Psychology, 57*, 414–419.

Durham, R. C., & Turvey, A. (1987). Cognitive therapy vs. behaviour therapy in the treatment of chronic general anxiety. *Behaviour Research and Therapy, 25*, 229–234.

Fankhauser, M. S., Karumanchi, V. C., German, M. L., Yates, A., & Karumanchi, S. D. (1992). A double-blind, placebo-controlled study of the efficacy of transdermal clonidine in autism. *Journal of Clinical Psychiatry, 53*, 77–82.

Ferguson, J. M., & Feighner, J. P. (1987). Fluoxetine-induced weight loss in overweight nondepressed humans. *International Journal of Obesity, 11*, 163–170.

Fine, S., Forth, A., Gilbert, M., & Haley, G. (1990). Group therapy for adolescent depressive disorder: A comparison of social skills and therapeutic support. *Journal of the American Academy of Child and Adolescent Psychiatry, 30*, 79–85.

Flament, M. F., Rapoport, J. L., Berg, C. J., Sceery, W., Kilts, C., Mellstrom, B., & Linnoila, M. (1985). Clomipramine treatment of childhood obsessive-compulsive disorder. *Archives of General Psychiatry, 42*, 977–983.

Foa, E. B., Steketee, G. S., & Ozarow, B. J. (1985). Behavior therapy with obsessive-compulsives: From therapy to treatment. In M. Mavissakalian, S. M. Turner, & L. Michelson (Eds.), *Obsessive-compulsive disorder: Psychological and pharmacological treatment* (pp. 49–129). New York: Plenum Press.

Fordham, K. E., & Meadow, S. R. (1989). Controlled trial of standard pad and bell alarm against mini-alarm for nocturnal enuresis. *Archives of Disease in Children, 64*, 651–565.

Frame, C., Matson, J. L, Sonis, W. A., Fialkor, M. J., & Kazdin, A. E. (1982). Behavioral treatment of depression in a prepubertal child. *Journal of the American Academy of Childhood and Adolescent Psychiatry, 3*, 239–243.

Galloway, S. M., Farquhar, D. L., & Munro, J. F. (1984). The current status of antiobesity drugs. *Postgraduate Medical Journal, 60*, 19–26.

Garn, S. M., & Clark, D. C. (1976). Trends in fatness and the origins of obesity. *Pediatrics, 57*, 443–456.

Geller, B., Cooper, T. B., McCombs, H. G., Graham, D., & Wells, J. (1989). Double-blind, placebo-controlled study of nortriptyline in depressed children using a "fixed plasma level" design. *Psychopharmacology Bulletin, 25*, 101–108.

Geller, E., Ritvo, E. R., Freeman, B. J., & Yuwiler, A. (1982). Preliminary observations on the effects of fenfluramine on blood serotonin and symptoms in three autistic boys. *New England Journal of Medicine, 307*, 165–169.

Gislason, I. L., & Neri, C. L. (1993). Pharmacological treatment. In V. B. Van Hasselt & M. Hersen (Eds.), *Handbook of behavior therapy and pharmacotherapy for children: A comparative analysis* (pp. 55–69). Boston: Allyn and Bacon.

Gotesman, K. G., & Hauge, L. W. (1987). Drug treatment of obesity. In W. G. Johnson (Ed.), *Advances in eating disorder* (Vol. 1, pp. 39–63). Greenwich, CT: JAI Press.

Green, G., & Cuvo, A. J. (1993). Behavioral treatment. In V. B. Van Hasselt & M. Hersen (Eds.), *Handbook of behavior therapy and pharmacotherapy for children: A comparative analysis* (pp. 105–128). Boston: Allyn and Bacon.

Greist, J. H. (1990). Treatment of obsessive-compulsive disorder: Psychotherapies, drugs, and other somatic treatment. *Journal of Clinical Psychiatry, 51*(Suppl. 8), 44–50.

Grob, C. S. (1993). Pharmacological treatment. In V. B. Van Hasselt & M. Hersen, (Eds.), *Handbook of behavior therapy and pharmacotherapy for children: A comparative analysis* (pp. 89–103). Boston: Allyn and Bacon.

Handen, B. L. (1993). Pharmacotherapy in mental retardation and autism. *School Psychology Review, 22*, 162–183.

Handen, B. L., Breaux, A. M., Gosling, A., Ploof, D. L., & Feldman, H. (1990). Efficacy of Ritalin among mentally retarded children with ADHD. *Pediatrics, 86*, 922–930.

Handen, B. L., Breaux, A. M., Janosky, J., McAuliffe, S., Feldman, H., & Gosling, A. (1992). Effects and noneffects of methylpheniadate in children with mental retardation and ADHD. *Journal of the American Academy of Child and Adolescent Psychiatry, 31*, 455–461.

Hechtman, L., Weiss, G., & Perlman, T. (1984). Young adult outcome of hyperactive children who received long-term stimulant treatment. *Journal of the American Academy of Child Psychiatry, 23*, 261–269.

Hinshaw, S. P., & Erhardt, D. (1993). Behavioral treatment of attention-deficit/hyperactivity disorder. In V. B. Van Hasselt & M. Hersen (Eds.), *Handbook of behavior therapy and pharmacotherapy for children: A comparative analysis* (pp. 233–250). Boston: Allyn and Bacon.

Hinshaw, S. P., Henker, B., & Whalen, C. K. (1984). Cognitive-behavioral and pharmacologic intervention for hyperactive boys: Comparative and combined effects. *Journal of Consulting and Clinical Psychology, 52*, 739–749.

Hollon, S. D., & Beck, A. T. (1978). Psychotherapy and drug therapy: Comparisons and combinations. In S. L. Garfield & A. E. Bergin (Eds.), *The handbook of psychotherapy and behavior change: An empirical analysis* (2nd ed.) (pp. 437–490). New York: Wiley.

Hollon, S. D., DeRubeis, R. J., Evans, M. D., Wiemer, M. J., Garvey, M. J., Grove, W. M., & Tuason, V. B. (1992). Cognitive therapy and pharmacotherapy for depression: Singly and in combination. *Archives of General Psychiatry, 49*, 774–781.

Hollon, S. D., Shelton, R. C., & Loosen, P. T. (1991). Cognitive therapy and pharmacotherapy for depression. *Journal of Consulting and Clinical Psychology, 59*, 88–99.

Iwata, B. A., Dorsey, M. F., Slifer, K. J., Bauman, K. E., & Richman, G. S. (1982). Toward a functional analysis of self-injury. *Analysis and Intervention in Developmental Disabilities, 2*, 3–20.

Jaselskis, C. A., Cook, E. H., Jr., Fletcher, K. E., & Leventhal, B. L. (1992). Clonidine treatment of hyperactive and impulsive children with autistic disorder. *Journal of Clinical Psychopharmacology, 12*, 322–327.

Kaplan, S. L., Hong, G. K., & Weinhold, C. (1984). Epidemiology of depressive symptomatology in adolescents. *Journal of the American Academy of Child Psychiatry, 23*, 91–98.

Kaslow, N. J., Celano, M. P., & McCarthy, S. M. (1993). Behavioral treatment. In V. B. Van Hasselt & M. Hersen (Eds.), *Handbook of behavior therapy and pharmacotherapy for children: A comparative analysis* (pp. 71–87). Boston: Allyn and Bacon.

Kendall, P. C., & Lipman, A. J. (1991). Psychological and pharmacological therapy: Methods and modes for comparative outcome research. *Journal of Consulting and Clinical Psychology, 59*, 78–87.

Klauber, G. T. (1989). Clinical efficacy and safety of desmopressin in the treatment of nocturnal enuresis. *Journal of Pediatrics, 114,* 719–722.

Kramer, E., & Feiguine, R. (1983). Clinical effects of amitriptyline in adolescent depression. *Journal of the American Academy of Child Psychiatry, 27,* 636–644.

Lefkowitz, N. N., & Tesiny, E. P. (1980). Assessment of childhood depression. *Journal of Consulting and Clinical Psychology, 48,* 43–50.

Leitenberg, H., Gross, J., Nudelman, S., & Vara, L. S. (1988). Exposure plus response-prevention treatment of bulimia nervosa. *Journal of Consulting and Clinical Psychology, 56,* 535–541.

Leonard, H., Swedo, S., Rapoport, J. L., Coffey, M., & Cheslow, D. (1988). Treatment of childhood obsessive-compulsive disorder with clomipramine and desmethylimipramine: A double-blind crossover comparison. *Psychopharmacology Bulletin, 24,* 93–95.

Levine, L. R., Enas, G. G., Thompson, W. L., Byyry, R. L., Daver, A. D., Kirby, R. W., Kreindler, T. G., Levy, B., Lucas, C. P., McIlwain, H. H., & Nelson, E. B. (1989). Use of fluoxetine, a selective serotonin-uptake inhibitor, in the treatment of obesity: A dose-response study (with a commentary by Michael Weintraub). *International Journal of Obesity, 13,* 635–645.

Levine, L. R., Rosenblatt, S., & Bosomworth, J. (1987). Use of serotonin re-uptake inhibitor, fluoxetine, in the treatment of obesity. *International Journal of Obesity, 11,* 185–190.

Lewinsohn, P. M., Clarke, G. N., Hops, H., & Andrews, J. (1990). Cognitive-behavioral treatment for depressed adolescents. *Behavior Therapy, 21,* 385–401.

Lovaas, O. I. (1977). *Language development through behavior modification.* New York: Wiley.

Marcus, M. D., Wing, R. R., Ewing, L., Kern, E., McDermott, M., & Gooding, W. (1990). A double-blind, placebo-controlled trial of fluoxetine plus behavior modification in the treatment of obese binge-eaters and on-binge eaters. *American Journal of Psychiatry, 147,* 876–881.

Marks, I., & O'Sullivan, G. (1988). Drugs and psychological treatments for agoraphobia/panic and obsessive-compulsive disorders. *British Journal of Psychiatry, 153,* 650–658.

McAnn, U. D., & Agras, W. S. (1990). Successful treatment of non-purging bulimia nervosa with desipramine: A double-blind placebo-controlled study. *American Journal of Psychiatry, 47,* 1509–1513.

Miller, I. W., Norman, W. H., Keitner, G. I., Bishop, S. B., & Dow, M. G. (1989). Cognitive-behavioral treatment of depressed inpatients. *Behavior Therapy, 20,* 25–47.

Mitchell, J. E., Pyle, R. L., & Eckert, E. D. (1990). A comparison study of antidepressants and structured intensive group psychotherapy in the treatment of bulimia nervosa. *Archives of General Psychiatry, 47,* 149–157.

Murphy, D. A., Pelham, W. E., & Greenstein, J. J. (1993). Pharmacological treatment. In V. B. Van Hasselt & M. Hersen (Eds.), *Handbook of behavior therapy and pharmacotherapy for children: A comparative analysis* (pp. 251–271). Boston: Allyn and Bacon.

Murphy, G. E., Simons, A. D., Wetzel, R. D., & Lustman, P. J. (1984). Cognitive therapy and pharmacotherapy, singly and together in the treatment of depression. *Archives of General Psychiatry, 41,* 33–41.

Norgaard, J. P., Rittig, S., & Djurhuus, J. C. (1989). Nocturnal enuresis: An approach to treatment based on pathogenesis. *Journal of Pediatrics, 114,* 705–710.

O'Sullivan, G., Noshirvani, H., Marks, I., Monteiro, W., & Lelliot, P. (1991). Six-year follow-up after exposure and clomipramine therapy for obsessive-compulsive disorder. *Journal of Clinical Psychiatry, 52,* 150–155.

Pato, M. T., Piggott, T. A., Hill, J. L., Grover, G. N., Bernstein, S., & Murphy, D. L. (1989, May). Clomipramine versus buspirone in OCD: A controlled trial. [Abstract NR14, page 34]. *Proceedings of the 142nd Annual Meeting of the American Psychiatric Association.*

Pelham, W., & Murphy, H. A. (1986). Attention-deficit and conduct disorders. In M. Hersen (Ed.),

Pharmacological and behavioral treatment: An integrative approach (pp. 108–148). New York: Wiley.

Perri, M. G., McAllister, D. A., Gange, J. J., Jordan, R. C., McAdoo, W. G., & Nezu, A. M. (1988). Effects of four maintenance programs on the long-term management of obesity. *Journal of Consulting and Clinical Psychology, 56*, 529–534.

Puig-Antich, J., Perel, J. M., Luputkin, W., Chambers, W. J., Tabrizi, M. A., King, J., Goetz, R., Davies, M., & Stiller, R. L. (1987). Imipramine in prepubertal depressive disorders. *Archives of General Psychiatry, 40*, 187–192.

Pyle, R. L., Mitchell, J. E., Eckert, E. D., Hatsukami, D., Pomeroy, C., & Zimmerman, R. (1990). Maintenance treatment and 6-month outcome for bulimic patients who respond to initial treatment. American Journal of Psychiatry, 147, 871–875.

Rachman, S., Cobb, J., Grey, B., McDonald, D., Mawson, G., Sartory, G., & Stern, R. (1979). The behavioural treatment of obsessional-compulsive disorders, with and without clomipramine. *Behaviour Research and Therapy, 17*, 467–478.

Rodin, J., Elias, M., Silberstein, L. R., & Wagner, A. (1988). Combined behavioral and pharmacologic treatment for obesity: Predictors of successful weight maintenance. *Journal of Consulting and Clinical Psychology, 56*, 399–404.

Ryan, N., Puig-Antich, J., Cooper, T., Rabinovich, H., Ambrosini, P., Davies, M., King, J., Torres, D., & Fried, J. (1986). Imipramine in adolescent major depression: Plasma level and clinical response. *Acta Scandinavica Psychiatrica, 73*, 275–288.

Ryan, N. D., Meyer, V. A., Dachille, S., Mazzie, D., & Puig-Antich, J. (1988). Lithium antidepressant augmentation in TCA-refractory depression in adolescents. *Journal of the American Academy of Child and Adolescent Psychiatry, 27*, 371–376.

Ryan, N. D., Puig-Antich, J., Rabinovich, H., Fried, J., Ambrosini, P., Meyer, V., Torres, D., Dachille, S., & Mazzie, D. (1988). MAOIs in adolescent major depression unresponsive to tricyclic antidepressants. *Journal of the American Academy of Child and Adolescent Psychiatry, 27*, 755–758.

Safer, D. J., & Krager, J. M. (1983). Trends in medication treatment of hyperactive school children. *Clinical Pediatrics, 22*, 500–504.

Schain, R. J., & Freedman, D. X. (1961). Studies on 5-hydroxyindole metabolism in autistic and other mentally retarded children. *Journal of Pediatrics, 58*, 315–320.

Schell, R. M., Pelham, W. E., Bender, M. E., Andree, J. A., Law, T., & Robbins, F. R. (1986). The concurrent assessment of behavioral and psychostimulant interventions: A controlled case study. *Behavioral Assessment, 8*, 373–384.

Schloss, P. J., Schloss, C. N., & Harris, L. (1984). A multiple baseline analysis of an interpersonal skills training program for depressed youth. *Behavioral Disorders, 9*, 182–188.

Schmitt, B. D. (1990). Nocturnal enuresis: Finding treatment that fits the child. *Contemporary Pediatrics, 7*, 70–97.

Schreibman, L. (1988). *Autism.* Newbury Park, CA: Sage Publications.

Schroeder, S. R., (1988). Neuroleptic medications for persons with developmental disabilities. In M. G. Aman & N. N. Singh (Eds.), *Psychopharmacology of the developmental disabilities* (pp. 82–100). New York: Springer-Verlag.

Shapiro, A. K., Shapiro, E. S., & Eisenkraft, G. J. (1983). Treatment of Gilles de la Tourette's syndrome with clonidine and neuroleptics. *Archives of General Psychiatry, 40*, 1235–1240.

Shapiro, A. K., Shapiro, E. S., & Wayne, H. (1973). Treatment of Tourette's syndrome with haloperidol, review of 34 cases. *Archives of General Psychiatry, 28*, 92–96.

Silverman, W. K., & Kearney, C. A. (1993). Behavioral treatment of childhood anxiety. In V. B. Van

Hasselt & M. Hersen (Eds.), *Handbook of behavior therapy and pharmacotherapy for children: A comparative analysis* (pp. 33–53). Boston: Allyn and Bacon.

Simeon, J. G., & Ferguson, H. B. (1985). Recent development in the use of antidepressant and anxiolytic medications. *Psychiatric Clinics of North America, 8,* 893–907.

Strauss, C. C. (1987). Anxiety. In M. Hersen & V. B. Van Hasselt (Eds.), *Behavior therapy with children and adolescents: A clinical approach* (pp. 109–136). New York: Wiley.

Strayhorn, J. M., Rapp, N., Donina, W., & Strain, P. S. (1988). Randomized trial of methylphenidate for an autistic child. *Journal of the American Academy of Child and Adolescent Psychiatry, 27,* 244–247.

Uhlenhuth, E. H., Lipman, R. S., & Covi, L. (1969). Combined psychotherapy and pharmacotherapy: Controlled studies. *Journal of Nervous and Mental Disease, 148,* 52–64.

Van Hasselt, V. B., & Hersen, M. (1993). *Handbook of behavior therapy and pharmacotherapy for children: A comparative analysis.* Boston: Allyn and Bacon.

Wagner, W., Johnson, S., Walker, D., Carter, R., & Wittner, J. (1982). A controlled comparison of two treatments for nocturnal enuresis. *Journal of Pediatrics, 101,* 302.

Walsh, B. T. (1991). Psychopharmacologic treatment of bulimia nervosa. *Journal of Clinical Psychiatry, 52* (Suppl. 10), 34–38.

Walsh, B. T. Hadigan, C. M., & Devlin, M. J. (1991). Long-term outcome of antidepressant treatment for bulimia nervosa. *American Journal of Psychiatry, 148,* 1206–1212.

Wardle, J. (1990). Behaviour therapy and benzodiazepines: Allies or antagonists? *British Journal of Psychiatry, 156,* 163–168.

Willie, S. (1986). Comparison of desmopressin and enuresis alarm for nocturnal enuresis. *Archives of Disease in Children, 61,* 30–33.

Wilson, G. T., Rossiter, E., Kleifeld, E. I., & Lindholm, L. (1986). Cognitive-behavioral treatment of bulimia nervosa: A controlled evaluation. *Behaviour Research and Therapy, 24,* 277–288.

Zetin, M., & Kramer, M. A. (1992). Obsessive-compulsive disorder. *Hospital and Community Psychiatry, 43,* 689–699.

CHAPTER 7

Unit Structure and Behavioral Programming

CYNTHIA R. JOHNSON

INTRODUCTION

Within the field of behavior analysis and therapy, there have been tremendous advances in technology. The last 25 years have seen ongoing increases in evaluative efforts to better refine behavioral treatments (Favell & Reid, 1988). Treatments based on behavioral principles have successfully addressed such childhood behaviors and psychiatric problems as aggression and conduct disorder (e.g., Kazdin, 1987; Mace, Page, Ivancic, & O'Brien, 1986), self-injury (e.g., Iwata et al., 1990), disruption (e.g., Santarcangelo, Dyer, & Luce, 1987), noncompliance (e.g., Cataldo, Ward, Russo, Riordan, & Bennett, 1986; Forehand & McMahon, 1981), attention-deficit disorder symptoms (e.g., Barkley, 1981; O'Leary & Wilson, 1987), depression (e.g., Frame, Matson, Sonis, Flakov, & Kazdin, 1982), autistic symptoms (e.g., Lovaas, 1987; Schreibman, 1988), and fear and phobias (e.g., Morris & Kratochwill, 1985) to highlight only a few.

Reports of behavioral interventions implemented in psychiatric inpatient settings first began to appear in the literature in the 1960s. Discontentment with the milieu therapy approach has been attributed to the allowance of behavioral interventions in psychiatric settings (Hersen, 1985). Despite early resistance to behavioral interventions, which initially consisted of simple token economy systems, the demonstrated success of such programs led to further utility of behavioral approaches in these settings. With more recent advances in behavioral technology, this treatment approach has had much to offer inpatient psychiatric units for children and adolescents and has greatly enhanced the effectiveness of the inpatient milieu. Behavioral treatments are now commonplace and are integrated with other treatment modalities in diverse and specialized inpatient psychiatric settings for children and adolescents.

The intent of this chapter is to provide an overview of the structuring and daily management of a child psychiatric inpatient unit and of the implementation of behavioral assessment and treatment procedures in this context. Special considerations and issues related to integration of inpatient psychiatry and behavioral treatment are also discussed. Specific procedures and approaches in structuring a large child-and-adolescent inpatient unit on which behavioral treatment and programming are a strong and often primary treatment focus are offered. The John Merck Multiple Disabilities Program Inpatient Unit at Western Psychiatric Institute and Clinic in Pittsburgh is a specialized 24–bed inpatient unit that serves children and adolescents with development disabilities coupled with behavioral and psychiatric disorders.

UNIT STRUCTURE AND ORGANIZATION

Child Inpatient Structure and Routine Schedules

The framework for both a therapeutic environment and an environment conducive to ongoing, intensive behavioral treatment is structure, consistency, and the establishment of explicit rules and expectations. Structured activity programming has been demonstrated to be inversely related to the occurrence of inappropriate behaviors on an inpatient unit (Wong, Slama, & Liberman, 1985). Closely related to the organization of a structured environment is the institution of consistent routines and schedules. The relationship between routine schedules and the occurrence of behavior problems has been noted (Brown, 1991). Use of a daily routine has long been advocated by child rearing experts (Christophersen, 1988). The purpose of a routine schedule on the psychiatric inpatient unit allows the child inpatients to predict the next activity as well as the subsequent set of expectations (Dalton & Forman, 1992). Brown (1991) asserts that the schedule should be individualized to the extent possible to allow for a sense of control on the part of the patient; for example, the patient may have a choice of the art activity in which to participate or of the time when he or she is seen for individual therapy. A typical daily schedule on a child-and-adolescent inpatient unit is likely to include school time; specialized groups, such as social-skills training and anger-control training; patient education groups; group activities, such as cooking, board games, and gross motor games; mealtimes and snack times; community meetings; and free time. Outings within the hospital, such as the patient library, or out of the hospital might also be scheduled on a regular basis.

A daily or weekly unit schedule is frequently posted for the unit, and individual schedules may be provided for the patients who understand the concept of time. It is also advised that patients be provided with a schedule at the time of their admission so that they will be apprised of what to expect. Even younger children or those children with cognitive or language deficits may benefit from seeing a schedule; this might be depicted with pictures: The morning routine could be represented by pictures of the bathroom and a child brushing his or her teeth and by a picture of a child eating breakfast in the cafeteria. To reiterate, although the daily activities may vary, it is important that a skeleton schedule remain consistent.

Staff: Patient Ratio

Key to the structuring of an inpatient unit is the availability of staff to implement unit programming. Recommendations for optimal staff:patient ratio have been discussed in the child psychiatric literature. Pines, Kupst, Natta, and Schulman (1985) demonstrated that ratios of 2:5 and 3:5 resulted in the lowest rates of problem behavior in the child patients. However, these investigators noted that the ratio in isolation was not related to patient behavior, but, instead, staff behaviors and interactions with the patient concomitant with the ratio were associated with the children's behavior. A staff:patient ratio of 1:3 has been recommended by the American Academy of Child and Adolescent Psychiatry (1990) as a minimum during the daytime. Obviously, an optimal ratio is likely to be dependent on the developmental age of the patients, the presenting problems of the patients, and the types of activities taking place. The need for a high staff ratio in different inpatient settings also varies across patients. It has been the author's experience that although some patients need more staff attention in high-demand situations, such as in the classroom, other patients need more staff attention during less structured, but lower demand situations, such as quiet time, to maintain control and low rates of their target behaviors. Identifying which patients need a high staff ratio and in which settings is based on behavioral intake interviews, behavioral assessment procedures, and baseline observations.

Communication Among Staff Members

Daily Report

Effective communication among those staff responsible for ongoing treatment on the inpatient unit is essential for effective and consistent treatment. Given the often rapid changes in all modalities of treatment (e.g., behavioral, psychopharmacologic, family) inherent in inpatient treatment, a method for daily updating of staff is essential. Typically, this takes place in a nursing report or rounds meeting scheduled at the beginning of each shift. Here, a brief report of the child's progress and of any treatment changes may be made. While this meeting is most often chaired by a charge nurse, it has been found helpful to have other multidisciplinary team members attend the meeting to discuss particular treatment changes related to that discipline or to provide an explanation for a less frequently used treatment strategy. In conjunction with the nursing report, utilization of other written forms of communication is useful. Even though daily notes are written on each patient, staff may not find the time to read the medical charts. Hence, the posting of individual treatment changes, typically with regard to behavioral treatment, on boards on the unit and in the classrooms facilitates communication and leads to consistent treatment implementation. To protect patient confidentially, a unit-developed code is used to communicate the individual patient's behavioral treatment plan, and only first names of patients are used.

Multidisciplinary Team Meetings

Multidisciplinary team meetings, typically held weekly, serve to collaborate with all disciplines involved with the inpatient's treatment. On a child or adolescent unit, the team members commonly are the attending psychiatrist (often a resident in university settings), a primary nurse, other direct-care staff, a social worker, teacher, psychologist, and any other professional providing assessment or treatment services (e.g., speech and language pathologist, occupational therapist). The goal of the team meeting is to review the patient's progress, to address areas where no progress is made, and to develop alternative treatment strategies. It is also an opportunity to gain a fuller account of the patient's functioning across all settings (i.e., in individual therapy, in the classroom during academics, on the unit during free time). On the author's inpatient unit, the behavioral psychologist for the team is responsible for summarizing data collected and for presenting behavioral assessment data, in graphed form. The appropriateness for changes in treatment to include behavioral programming are also discussed.

BEHAVIORAL PROGRAMMING

The sequential steps to behavioral programming on a child-and-adolescent psychiatric inpatient unit are similar to those taken in the development of any behavioral treatment plan. First of all, goals for intervention should be clearly established and delineated. Based on identified treatment goals, behavioral assessment procedures should be chosen to include the appropriate observational systems. From the assimilation of behavioral assessment data, development and implementation of behavioral treatment procedures are the next step. Finally, a systematic method to monitor and evaluate treatment effects should be established. These steps for conducting behavior analysis are widely acknowledged and are considered the framework in which all programs based on applied behavior analysis and behavior therapy follow (Gelfand & Hartmann, 1984; Sulzer-Azaroff & Mayer, 1991).

Behavioral Intervention Goals and Defining Target Behaviorals: Behavioral Intake Information

Prior to or at the time of admission, an intake assessment is typically conducted. Within a psychiatric setting, this involves a psychiatrist and additional multidisciplinary team members, often including a social worker and nurse. The team member who is responsible for the behavioral assessment and treatments optimally participates in the admission procedure and conducts the behavioral intake interview. The purpose of the behavioral intake interview component is to gather specific information about the behavior problems exhibited that warrant admission and the behaviors that will be a focus of inpatient behavioral treatment. In addition to obtaining an operational definition of *target* behaviors, eliciting possible information about possible antecedents and consequences of the problematic behaviors serves to begin making hypotheses about the environmental influences of the behaviors. This information is further helpful in directing behavioral assessment procedures that will be most sensitive in measuring identified behavior problems. Other commonly obtained information during the behavioral intake interview is the trend of the behavior problems and previous approaches that have been carried out. All of this information helps in goal setting and treatment planning. While some of the information gathered may be redundant with information obtained during the psychiatric intake interview or interviews with another professional, the focus on obtaining behavioral information (specifically on those behaviors to be treated while the child or adolescent is an inpatient) assists in developing a behavioral assessment and treatment plan in an efficacious manner. Similarly, information gathered in the behavioral intake interview may be communicated to direct-care staff with respect to likely antecedents of the patient's target behaviors. It has been the author's experience on the inpatient unit that inclusion of the behavioral psychologist in the admission process provides valuable information and data for later behavioral programming.

INPATIENT UNIT ASSESSMENT PROCEDURES

Behavior Rating Scales

To supplement information obtained from the behavioral interview, parents or guardians are often requested to complete standardized behavioral rating tools. The *Child Behavior Checklist* (Achenbach & Edelbrock, 1991), an extensively used multidomain rating scale with excellent psychometric properties, is often administered to the parents to supplement information obtained in the behavioral interview. Obtaining ratings on the *Teacher Rating Form* (Achenbach & Edelbrock, 1991) from the home teacher of the child is also important to adduce in obtaining behavioral information as to the patient's behaviors and interests in the school setting. These premeasures serve both diagnostic and treatment-planning purposes.

On the unit, daily or weekly ratings using various measures are often a component of ongoing behavioral-assessment procedures. A shortened version of the *Child Behavior Checklist*, the *Child Behavior Rating Form* (Edelbrock, 1985), has been used as a repeated measure to evaluate treatment effects on an inpatient unit for children (Kolko, 1988). Other behavior rating scales filled out in the inpatient setting both as an initial assessment and as ongoing measures to monitor progress and behavioral change include the *Abbreviated Symptoms Questionnaire—Teacher Version* (Conners, 1991), the *IOWA Conners* (Loney & Milich, 1982), the *Inpatient Global Rating Scale* (Conners, 1985), and the *Children's Psychiatric Rating Scale* (Fish, 1985). For children and adolescents with mental retardation, the *Aberrant Behavior Checklist* (Aman & Singh, 1986) has utility as a repeated measure to assess inpatient treatment effects (Rojahn & Helsel, 1991).

Unit Direct-Observation Procedures

Behavioral assessment procedures that include direct observations should answer the question: "What is the extent of the child's baseline behaviors?" The measurement used, although dependent on presenting behaviors, is most often the frequency of a discrete behavior, duration of a behavior, or topography of the behavioral response. The decision about what direct observation procedures to use should be based on the information obtained from the behavioral intake. Ease of obtaining and recording this information must also be taken into consideration so that there will be consistent staff implementation. On the author's unit, antecedent-behavior-consequence-data forms are completed and frequency counts are taken during the first few days after admission to begin to develop hypotheses of possible environmental contingencies maintaining or at least influencing the behavior problem. Offering staff various options to record behavioral data often promotes compliance; for example, for high-frequency data, use of hand-held tally counters has proven useful for the immediate recording of each event and the later transcription of this number to a data form. When frequency of a behavior is extremely high, time intervals for observation and recording of a particular target behavior are prespecified.

Staff collection of data is supplemented by observations conducted by behavioral psychologists who serve as nonparticipant observers. Use of partial-interval recording is most typically employed to measure a number of behaviors from on-task behavior to pica. Attempts are made to measure the child's behavior across various settings. It is often the case that various environmental variables are manipulated to determine their influence on the target behaviors (i.e., level of reinforcement, high-demands vs. low-demands task; preferred activity vs. low-preferred activity; high staff ratio vs. low staff ratio). These environmental manipulations in assessing functions of maladaptive behaviors have proven to be essential in the development of effacious treatments (see Carr & Durand, 1985; Cooper, Wacker, Sasso, Reimers, & Donn, 1990; Northup et al., 1991). Direct observations are ongoing and conducted across all treatment phases (i.e., behavioral and pharmacological interventions) to determine the effects of treatment modalities.

Other Assessment Procedures

In addition to the rating scales administered and direct observations conducted, other measures or instruments also add data that have utility in the development of a behavioral treatment plan. Self-informant tools such as the *Child Depression Inventory* (Kovacs, 1981), *Children Manifest Anxiety Scale* (Reynolds & Richmond, 1978), and the *Matson Evaluation of Social Skills with Youngsters* (Matson, Rotatori, & Helsel, 1983) are scales sensitive to inpatient behavioral treatment.

A measure of treatment acceptability is also suggested. Having consumers to rate the acceptability of alternative treatment options was introduced by Kazdin (1980a, 1980b), who also developed the *Treatment Evaluation Inventory* (TEI) (the most widely utilized tool for assessing treatment acceptability). The 15 items of this inventory may be answered on a 7–point Likert scale and have been demonstrated to differentiate treatments effectively by degree of acceptability among inpatient staff, parents, and patients (Kazdin, 1984; Kazdin, French, & Sherick, 1981). This area of literature suggests the need to determine the caregiver's acceptance of treatment approaches, which may lead to increased compliance. In the author's inpatient program, the TEI is administered as part of the parent training initial assessments. Findings from the TEI are considered in designing a patient's individualized behavioral treatment plan. Finally, of particular utility on the inpatient unit for children with developmental disabilities, the administration of a reinforcer inventory to the caregiver, and if possible, to the child yields valuable information about potential reinforcers for the patient that may then be incorporated into the behavioral plan.

Baseline Behavioral Procedures

Though a baseline phase assumes no intervention, this is confounded in the hospital, given that the admission itself is a significant change; therefore, observing a child or adolescent in a hospital setting is far from a true baseline. While conducting a baseline assessment to the extent possible is recommended, the necessity to maintain safety on the unit at all times may preclude the ability to establish a stable baseline before some form of intervention is initiated. Implementation of a contingency management program, such as token economy system, frequently is instituted immediately. For behaviors that are not dangerous or harmful, a simple interrupt-and-redirection program is often implemented for the target behaviors that are to be decreased during this baseline period. Prosocial or adaptive behaviors are reinforced through both the token economy and verbal praise from staff.

Individualized Behavioral Treatment Protocols

Protocols that delineate the purpose and rationale of the behavioral intervention, operational definitions of the behaviors for which the intervention will be used, and the procedures detailing each step are routinely included in the treatment plan on behaviorally oriented units. These protocols allow for the individualization of behavioral procedures.

While space limitations prohibit an in-depth discussion of all behavioral procedures and strategies, the behavioral procedures or approaches most likely to be implemented in the context of a child-and-adolescent inpatient psychiatric unit are discussed in the following paragraphs.

Token Economy Systems

Motivational systems, such as a token economy program, have been successfully implemented to improve various types of behaviors with children and adolescents in numerous settings (Kistner, Hammer, Wolfe, Rothblum, & Drabman, 1982; Wolfe, Boyd, & Wolfe,

1983). Token economies have a long history on inpatient units and were among the first systematic applications of behavioral techniques in inpatient psychiatric settings for adult patients (Ayllon & Azrin, 1968; Carlson, Hersen, & Eisler, 1972; Kazdin, 1977).

Since the earlier reports, design and implementation of token economies (e.g., point systems, star cards), on child units have been widely instituted. On units where the patients are of similar developmental age and similar in presenting problems, a unit-wide program may be successfully used. By contrast, on units with a wide spread in age, cognitive ability, and presenting behavior problems, development of more individualized token economy systems may be warranted.

The mainstay of the token economy is the delivery of tokens, points, stars, and so on, contingent on discrete observable behavior. Accumulated tokens may be cashed in at a later time for tangible reinforcers or privileges. Loss of points, a response cost, is commonly also included within the program—points are removed contingent on specific, problematic behaviors (i.e., aggression, disruption, lying). The point ration should be set to maximize learning of contingencies operating and to ensure some success soon after implementation. For younger children, use of stars or stickers in lieu of points or tokens is the norm. For children of lower developmental levels, more frequent cash-in times may be necessary than for children of higher developmental levels.

Differential Reinforcement

Differential reinforcement of other behaviors (DRO), the least intrusive of interventions, is a reductive method that has proven to be effective in decreasing maladaptive behaviors that include aggression and self-injury (Frankel, Moss, Schofield, & Simmons, 1976; Wong, Floyd, Innocent, Woolsey, 1991), disruptive classroom behavior (Deitz, 1977), and inattentive behavior (Luiselli, Colozzi, & O'Toole, 1980). Variations of this procedure have also been successful, such as differential reinforcement of incompatible behaviors (DRI) and differential reinforcement of low rates (DRL). To illustrate, a DRI schedule was used to treat pica where the incompatible behavior was gum chewing (Donnelly & Olczak, 1990).

Differential reinforcement schedules may be whole-interval or momentary. Whole-interval DRO refers to the delivery of reinforcement for the occurrence of *other* (not the target) behaviors for the full duration of the time interval (e.g., 2 minutes). If delivery of reinforcement is provided when an other behavior and not the target behavior is occurring at the end of the time interval (e.g., at the second minute), this is referred to as momentary DRO (Sulzer-Azaroff & Mayer, 1991). Although Repp, Barton, and Brulle (1983) demonstrated the superior effect of whole-interval differential reinforcement, this may be difficult to implement consistently on an inpatient unit. Of interest is that momentary differential reinforcement has been shown to be more effective if preceded by a whole-interval approach (Barton, Brulle, & Repp, 1986). Hence, it may be advisable to first consider a whole-interval approach but to quickly revise to a momentary approach once acceptable decreases in the target behavior have been observed. Another consideration in using differential reinforcement is the rate or schedule at which reinforcers will be delivered. This rate should be individualized and based on those rates observed during baseline with an initial, obtainable goal set. On an outpatient unit, examples of other or incompatible behaviors should be made explicit so that appropriate behaviors are reinforced. A timer is often used to implement a DRO schedule. As progress is made, reinforcement should be systematically faded to more closely approximate the schedule that will realistically be applied in the child's natural environment.

Extinction

Effectiveness of extinction in reducing or eliminating a problematic behavior is clearly documented in the literature (Brown & Elliot, 1965; Williams, 1959; Rincover, 1978; Wolf, Risely, & Meese, 1964). Extinction is rarely used in isolation and most commonly is implemented in conjunction with a differential reinforcement schedule. These methods taken together are often referred to as *systematic attention/planned ignoring*. Within an inpatient setting, behaviors to be placed on extinction should be those that are nonharmful to others and that can be consistently ignored and those for which there is strong evidence from assessment results that the behavior is motivated and has been maintained by attention. Staff should be reminded of the likelihood of an extinction "burst" before the target behavior decreases. It has been the author's experience that staff commonly interpret use of extinction as "not doing anything," so that continued emphasis that extinction is a legitimate behavioral treatment for some target behaviors may be needed. If extinction does not result in reduction in the target behavior, supervisors should closely observe staff in their responses to ensure that inadvertent attention is not being given to the child in response to the behavior.

Compliance Training

Noncompliance is the most common behavior problem for which parents seek help (Forehand, 1977). Methods for increasing compliance have included reinforcing compliance, issuing the request a second time with an additional prompt for noncompliance after the first request, and then imposing a consequence if the child fails to comply (Forehand & McMahan, 1981; Parrish, Cataldo, Kolko, Neef, & Egel, 1986). This sequence of steps is often referred to collectively as compliance training.

Time Out

A commonly employed behavioral intervention across settings is time out from positive reinforcement. This procedure has been successfully used to reduce an array of behaviors from mild to extremely severe behavior problems (Bostow & Bailey, 1969; Mace et al., 1986), despite ongoing controversy over its use (Foxx & Shapiro, 1978). There are several variations of time out that have been carried out, ranging from the least restrictive (nonexclusionary time out) to more restrictive (exclusionary time out) to the most restrictive (seclusionary time out). *Nonexclusionary time out* refers to moving a child away from a group or situation but having the child remain in view of the group or activity (Porterfield, Herbert-Jackson, & Risely, 1976). A variation of this form of time out was used in an investigation by Foxx and Shapiro (1978) in which children in a classroom with ribbons received edible reinforcers. Contingent on misbehavior, a child's ribbon was removed, and the delivery of reinforcement was withheld. Such a nonexclusionary time out procedure drastically reduced classroom behavior problems. Variations of this procedure have been used with success on the author's unit where "time in" bows, baseball hats, and special jewelry have been used to apply the same principles.

Use of exclusionary time out includes removal of the child to an area away from the group, such as a time-out room (Wilson, Robertson, Herlong, & Haynes, 1979; Wolf, Risely, Johnson, Harris, & Allen, 1967) or a corner (Olson & Roberts, 1987). On inpatient units, use of a seclusion room (open or locked) for time out is frequently employed (Liberman & Wong, 1984; Soloff, 1987). However, caution should be exercised when the decision is made to use the unit seclusion room for time out. A functional analysis of the behavior should have demonstrated that the patient's behavior is not motivated by escape (i.e., the desire to get out of the situation or demand). Otherwise, seclusion could be reinforcing and increase the behavior it is intended to decrease. Furthermore, parameters in the use of a seclusionary time out should be clearly delineated to prevent it being abused. Operational definitions of the behavioral response(s) for use of seclusion and length of time so secluded should be clearly specified. It is helpful to post patient's seclusion programs to ensure proper implementation of the program.

Overcorrection

Overcorrection has been used extensively to suppress numerous maladaptive behaviors, including pica (Foxx & Martin, 1975; Singh & Bakker, 1984), aggression, and disruption (Ollendick & Matson, 1978). Contingent on the target behavior, the individual is required to overcorrect the effects of the behavior and also may be required to practice an appropriate behavior. In developing an overcorrection procedure for a particular behavior, Foxx (1982) advises that it must be related to the target behavior. Moreover, it needs to be implemented swiftly. A fuller account of the use of overcorrection is provided by Azrin and Besalel (1980).

As with all other behavioral procedures, overcorrection procedural steps are delineated in a behavioral protocol on our unit. Modeling of the overcorrection procedure is provided for staff in order to ensure the integrity of the procedure.

Contingent Exercise

Similar to overcorrection procedures, contingent exercise is a mild punishment procedure in which the patient is asked to perform a specified physically effortful exercise contingent on occurrence of the target behavior. This procedure has been effective in reducing verbal and aggressive behaviors in children diagnosed as seriously emotionally disturbed (Luce, Delquadri, & Hall, 1980). Although there has been little research literature about this procedure in comparison to overcorrection, it is amenable to implementation in inpatient unit settings.

Behavioral Physical Restraint

As evident from the name, this procedure involves the brief restraint or immobilization of a patient's limbs (e.g., hands held to the side or on a flat surface) or body for a prespecified time period contingent on the occurrence of the target behavior. Use of a physical restraint procedure has been effective in decreasing pica (Bucher, Reykdal, & Albin, 1976), tantrums (Swerissen & Carruthers, 1987), and self-injury (Favell, McGimsey, & Jones, 1978).

Use of Aversive Stimuli

The contingent presentation of an aversive stimulus as a punisher for a specified behavior has raised many ethical and humanitarian issues, particularly in the treatment of children and individuals with developmental disabilities (see LaVigna & Donnellan, 1986; Matson & DiLorenzo, 1984; Matson & Taras, 1989). Nonetheless, there are empirical data available indicating that such approaches may be effective in reducing or suppressing severe behaviors. Some aversive stimuli that have been applied contingently include water mist (Dorsey, Iwata, Ong, & McSween, 1980), aromatic ammonia (Baumeister & Baumeister, 1978; Rojahn, McGonigle, Curcio, & Dixon, 1987), lemon juice (Sajwaj, Libert, & Agras, 1974), and contingent electrical shock (Foxx, McMorrow, Bittle, &

Bechtel, 1986; Linscheid, Iwata, Ricketts, Williams, & Griffin, 1990). Subjects in these studies were either mentally retarded or psychotic (Tate & Taroff, 1966) who evinced severe behavior problems.

Despite the fact that aversive treatment is never used as a first choice or used in isolation, its use may be appropriate in certain situations and under certain conditions, including documentation that (a) the maladaptive behavior is a serious threat to others or to the child; (b) other treatments have been consistently tried and have had minimal effect; (c) the behavior precludes the child from participating in activities essential for development; or (d) the child is being managed only by the use of restraints (either chemical or physical) (see Foxx, Plaska, & Bittle, 1986; Martin, 1975). Lovaas and Favell (1987) recommended that such techniques be implemented only under the supervision of a professional trained and experienced in the use of aversives. Likewise, procedural safeguards (see Matson & Kazdin, 1981) should be closely adhered to, and informed consent should be obtained before any aversive stimulus is applied.

Evaluation of Behavioral Programming

A distinguishing feature of behavior analysis is not only to evaluate whether the behavior changed but also to determine what changed the behavior. Drawing from single-subject methodology (see Barlow & Hersen, 1984), commonly used strategies in evaluating behavioral treatment include withdrawal or reversal designs, multiple baseline designs, alternative treatment designs, and changing criterion designs. All of these experimental designs may be implemented in the context of an inpatient unit. In designing a behavioral intervention, thought should be given to how the program will be evaluated with consideration of time limits and other limitations of the inpatient unit.

OTHER SPECIAL CONSIDERATIONS

Use of Seclusion and Restraint

Use of seclusion and restraint has received much attention in child psychiatry. Whereas it is not the intention here to provide a comprehensive discussion of legal and ethical issues surrounding the use of seclusion and restraint, relationship of seclusion and restraint to the unit structure and behavioral intervention deserves to be mentioned. As already discussed, use of seclusion and a brief restraint may be one component of a patient's individualized behavioral treatment plan. Seclusion and restraint, as carried out in an inpatient psychiatric setting, may also serve as a crisis management intervention method to safeguard against imminent danger to the patient or others (Gutheil & Tardiff, 1984). These two very different cases should be emphasized to inpatient staff.

Staff Training and Consultations

A noted characteristic of behavioral treatment is that the person actually implementing behavioral treatment is frequently not the same as the individual developing the behavioral program or treatment plan (Berstein, 1984; Milne, 1984). In the psychiatric inpatient setting, the behavioral change agents are often professionals and paraprofessionals with variable training and orientation. On an inpatient unit, these agents are direct-care staff that may include psychiatric nurses, nursing assistants, milieu therapists, clinical assistants (typically holding a bachelor's degree), and child care workers (usually with less education than other staff). Hence, these agents reflect different levels of expertise and treatment orientations. For behavioral assessment and treatments to be implemented accurately and competently, behavioral training of staff is necessary (Hersen & Bellack, 1978; Lovass & Favell, 1987). Training approaches in psychiatric and other settings have varied and, therefore, have resulted in different outcomes.

Inservice training in behavioral treatment has incorporated various formats and has employed a number of different instructional strategies. Within the medical and psychiatric settings, didactic instruction, provided either verbally or written, is common. Milne (1984) described a 5–day in-service course for psychiatric nurses in behavior therapy. More recently, Tynan and Gengo (1992) described a staff behavioral-training program for nurses in pediatric rehabilitation hospitals that involved three 2–hour sessions completed over 9 weeks. The effectiveness of this type of instruction has nonetheless been questioned (Demchak, 1987), with little evidence that the approach leads to change in practices or observed skills (Odom, 1987). On an inpatient psychiatric unit, Delamater, Conners, and Wells, (1984) demonstrated lack of change on nurses' and aides' performance after participating in an inservice training program in behavioral skill. Change in staff behaviors was only observed after the use of role-playing was instituted. Ivancic, Reid, Iwata, Faw, and Page (1981) recommended a multicomponent approach to increase the likelihood of improving staff performance with respect to use of behavioral skills to change client behavior. Their approach involved instruction, modeling, public posting of performance, and verbal feedback. Additionally, recent findings support the need for ongoing consultation to provide on-site feedback necessary for maintenance of staff behavioral change (Harchik, Sherman, Sheldon, & Strouse, 1992). Within a psychiatric setting, much feedback may be incorporated into the regular supervisory routine (Dalton & Forman, 1992).

On the author's unit, efforts have been made to embrace a multicomponent approach to training given the present data in research evaluating behavioral training. When a new staff member is hired, he or she is provided with an orientation to behavioral theory and principles. The new staff member is also acquainted with the most typically employed behavioral procedures and strategies carried out on the unit. After a 2–week orientation that also involves other aspects of unit functioning, staff members are enrolled in a unit inservice-training program that involves the didactic instruction in behavioral assessment and treatment supplemented by case examples. Ongoing role-playing on the unit is provided by behavioral psychologists. Observations of staff by direct supervisors and behavioral psychologists in the implementation of behavioral treatment and procedures are conducted, and corrective feedback using a standardized form with specific behavioral skill areas is also conducted periodically in an effort to maintain training gains.

ADVANTAGES AND LIMITATIONS TO INPATIENT TREATMENT

One of the advantages of inpatient behavioral treatment includes the level of intensity with which such interventions may be applied. This allows for the child or adolescent to come into contact with the behavioral contingencies at higher rates than is likely in their natural environment and, thus, to promote change more rapidly than outpatient behavioral treatment. An obvious advantage is the ability to make observations of the child or adolescent across the day in all types of settings. The ability to complete more comprehensive diagnostic appraisals is another benefit of hospitalization. Lastly, the inpatient setting allows for more extensive control of environmental variables that may influence the patient's behavior.

Limitations of inpatient treatment include the lack of treatment generalizability from the inpatient environment to the patients' environments outside of the hospital. Different contingencies are likely to be operating than are present when a child is in a hospital setting (e.g., peer pressures). Similarly, the capability to engage in specific referral problems are precluded by hospitalization (e.g., shoplifting, firesetting). An obvious and frequently raised concern of inpatient treatment is that of cost-effectiveness. This has become more and more of an issue with the advent of managed-care organizations. Obviously, patients are not admitted for these considerations alone. Rather, dangerousness to self and others is the foremost concern.

SUMMARY

Behavioral programming in inpatient psychiatric settings for children and adolescents serves an important treatment component. To ensure treatment integrity of behavioral intervention with this setting, certain criteria must be met to include the establishment of a routine and consistent schedule, a sufficient staff:patient ratio, mechanisms for ongoing and frequent communications, and ongoing staff training and consultation in behavioral treatment. Not unlike other settings where behavioral interventions are implemented, the steps involved include goal setting, baseline behavioral assessment, development and implementation of behavioral treatment plans, and ongoing monitoring of the effects of treatment.

REFERENCES

Achenbach, T. M., & Edelbrock, C. S. (1991). *The Child Behavior Checklist.* Burlington, VT: University of Vermont, Department of Psychiatry.

Achenbach, T. M., & Edelbrock, C. S. (1991). *The Teacher Rating Form.* Burlington, VT: University of Vermont, Department of Psychiatry.

Aman, M. G., & Singh, N. N. (1986). *Aberrant Behavior Checklist: Manual.* East Aurora, NY: Slosson Educational Publications.

American Academy of Child and Adolescent Psychiatry. (1990, May). *Task force on hospitalization: Model for minimal staffing patterns for hospitalization providing acute inpatient treatment for children and adolescents with psychiatric illnesses.* Washington, DC: American Academy of Child and Adolescent Psychiatry.

Ayllon, T., & Azrin, N. (1968). *The token economy: A motivational system for therapy and rehabilitation.* New York: Appleton.

Azin, N. H., & Besalel, V. A. (1980). *How to use overcorrection.* Lawrence, KS: H&H Enterprises.

Barkley, R. A. (1981). *Hyperactive children: A handbook for diagnosis and treatment.* New York: Guilford Press.

Barlow, D. H., & Hersen, M. (1984). *Single case experimental designs: Strategies for studying behavior change.* (2nd ed.) New York: Pergamon Press.

Barton, L. E., Brulle, A. R., & Repp, A. C. (1986). Maintenance of therapeutic change by momentary DRO. *Journal of Applied Behavior Analysis, 19,* 277–282.

Baumeister, A. A., & Baumeister, A. A. (1978). A suppression of repetitive self-injurious behavior by contingent inhalation of aromatic ammonia. *Journal of Autism and Childhood Schizophrenia, 8,* 71–77.

Bernstein, G. (1984). Training of behavior change agents. In M. Hersen, R. M. Eisler, & P. M. Miller, *Progress in Behavior Modification* (Vol. 17, pp. 167–199). New York: Academic Press.

Bostow, D. E., & Bailey, J. B. (1969). Modification of severe disruptive and aggressive behavior using brief timeout and reinforcement procedures. *Journal of Applied Behavior Analysis, 2,* 31–37.

Brown, F. (1991). Creative daily scheduling: A nonintrusive approach to challenging behaviors in community residences. *The Association for Persons with Severe Handicaps, 16,* 871–889.

Brown, P., & Elliot, R. (1965). Control of aggression in a nursery school class. *Journal of Experimental Child Psychology, 2,* 103–107.

Bucher, B., Reykdal, B., & Albin, J. (1976). Brief physical restraint to control pica in retarded children. *Journal of Behavior Therapy and Experimental Psychiatry, 7,* 137–140.

Carlson, C. G., Hersen, M., & Eisler, R. M. (1972). Token economy programs in the treatment of hospitalized adult psychiatric patients: Current status and recent trends. *Journal of Nervous and Mental Disease, 155,* 192–204.

Carr, E. G., & Durand, M. (1985). Reducing behavior problems through functional communication training. *Journal of Applied Behavior Analysis, 16,* 111–126.

Cataldo, M., Ward, E., Russo, D., Riordan, M., & Bennett, D. (1986). Compliance and correlated problem behavior in children: Effects of contingent and noncontingent reinforcement. *Analysis and Intervention in Developmental Disabilities, 6,* 265–282.

Christophersen, E. R., (1988). *Little people: Guidelines for commonsense child rearing* (3rd ed.). Kansas City, MO: Westport.

Conners, C. K. (1985). IGRS (Inpatient Global Rating Scale). *Psychopharmacology Bulletin, 21,* 832–834.

Conners, C. K. (1991). *Abbreviated Symptoms Questionnaire—Teacher Version.* New York: Multi-Health Systems.

Cooper, L. J., Wacker, D. P., Sasso, G. M., Reimers, T. M., & Donn, L. K. (1990). Using parents as therapists to evaluate appropriate behavior of their children: Application to a tertiary diagnostic clinic. *Journal of Applied Behavior Analysis, 23,* 285–296.

Dalton, R., & Forman, M. A. (1992). *Psychiatric hospitalization of school-age children.* Washington, DC: American Psychiatric Press.

Deitz, S. M. (1977). An analysis of programming DRL schedules in educational settings. *Behavior Research and Therapy, 15,* 103–111.

Delamater, A., Conners, C. K., & Wells, K. (1984). A comparison of staff training procedures: Behavioral applications in the child psychiatric inpatient setting. *Behavior Modification, 8,* 39–58.

Demchak, M. (1987). A review of behavioral staff training in special education settings. *Education and Training in Mental Retardation, 22,* 205–217.

Donnelly, D. R. & Olczak, P. V. (1990). The effect of differential reinforcement of incompatible behaviors (DRI) on pica for cigarettes in persons with intellectual disability. *Behavior Modification, 14,* 81–96.

Dorsey, M. F., Iwata, B. A., Ong, P., & McSween, T. E. (1980). Treatment of self-injurious behavior using a water mist: Initial response suppression and generalization. *Journal of Applied Behavior Analysis, 13,* 343–353.

Edelbrock, C. S., (1985). Child Behavior Rating Form. *Psychopharmology Bulletin, 21,* 835–837.

Favell, J. E., McGimsey, J. F., & Jones, M. L. (1978). The use of physical restraint in the treatment of self-injury and as positive reinforcement. *Journal of Applied Behavior Analysis, 11,* 137–140.

Favell, J. E., & Reid, D. H. (1988). Generalizing and maintaining improvements in problem behavior. In R. H. Horner, G. Dunlap, & R. L. Koegel (Eds.), *Generalization and maintenance: Lifestyle changes in applied setting* (pp. 171–196). Baltimore: Brookes.

Fish, B. (1985). Children's Psychiatric Rating Scale. *Psychopharmacology Bulletin, 21,* 753–770.

Forehand, R. (1977). Child noncompliance to parental requests: Behavioral analysis and treatment. In M. Hersen, R. M. Eisler, & P. M. Miller (Eds.), *Progress in behavior modification 5,* (pp. 111–147). New York: Academic Press.

Forehand, R., & McMahon, R. (1981). *Helping the noncompliant child: A clinician's guide to parent training.* New York: Guilford Press.

Foxx, R. M. (1982). *Decreasing behaviors of severely retarded and autistic persons.* Champaign, IL: Research Press.

Foxx, R. M., & Martin, E. D. (1975). Treatment of scavenging behavior (coprophagy and pica) by overcorrection. *Behavior Research and Therapy, 13,* 153–162.

Foxx, R. M., McMorrow, M. J., Bittle, R. G., & Bechtel, D. R. (1986). The successful treatment of a dually-diagnosed deaf man's aggression with a program that included contingent electric shock. *Behavior Therapy, 17,* 170–186.

Foxx, R. M., Plaska, T. G., & Bittle, R. G. (1986). Guidelines for the use of contingent electric shock to treat aberrant behavior. In M. Hersen, R. M. Eisler, P. M. Miller (Eds.), *Progress in Behavior Modification* (Vol. 20, pp. 1–34). Orlando, FL: Academic Press.

Foxx, R. M., & Shapiro, S. T. (1978). The timeout ribbon: A nonexclusionary timeout procedure. *Journal of Applied Behavior Analysis, 11,* 125–136.

Frame, C., Matson, J. L., Sonis, W. A., Flakov, M. J., & Kazdin, A. E. (1982). Behavior treatment of depression in a prepubertal child. *Journal of Behavior Therapy and Experimental Psychiatry, 3,* 239–243.

Frankel, F., Moss, D., Schofield, S., & Simmons, J. Q. (1976). Case study: Use of differential reinforcement to suppress self-injurious and aggressive behavior. *Psychological Reports, 39,* 843–849.

Gelfand, D. M., & Hartmann, D. P. (1984). *Child behavior analysis and the therapy* (2nd ed.). Oxford: Pergamon Press.

Gutheil, T. G., & Tardiff, K. (1984). Indications and contraindications for seclusion and restraint. In K. Tardiff (Ed.), *The psychiatric uses of seclusion and restraint* (pp. 11–17). Washington, DC: American Psychiatric Press.

Harchik, A. E., Sherman, J. A., Sheldon, J. B., & Strouse, M. C. (1992). Ongoing consultation as a method of improving performance of staff members in a group home. *Journal of Applied Behavior Analysis, 25,* 599–610.

Hersen, M. (1985). Overview. In M. Hersen (Ed.), *Practice of Inpatient Behavior Therapy: A Clinical Guide* (pp. 3–31). New York: Grune & Stratton.

Hersen, M., & Bellack, A. S. (1978). Staff training and consultation. In M. Hersen & A. S. Bellack (Eds.), *Behavior therapy in the psychiatric setting* (pp. 58–87). Baltimore: Williams & Wilkins.

Ivancic, M. T., Reid, D. H., Iwata, B. A., Faw, G. D., & Page, T. J. (1981). Evaluating a supervision program for developing and maintaining therapeutic staff-resident interactions during institutional care routines. *Journal of Applied Behavior Analysis, 14,* 95–107.

Iwata, B. A., Pace, G. M., Kalsher, M. J., Cowdery, G. E., Edward, & Caltaldo, M. F.(1990). Experimental analysis and extinction of self-injurious escape behavior. *Journal of Applied Behavior Analysis, 23,* 11–27.

Kazdin, A. E. (1977). Assessing the clinical or applied significance of behavior change through social validation. *Behavior Modification, 1,* 427–452.

Kazdin, A. E. (1980a). Acceptability of alternative treatments for deviant child behavior. *Journal of Applied Behavior Analysis, 13,* 259–273.

Kazdin, A. E. (1980b). Acceptability of time out from reinforcement procedures for disruptive child behavior. *Behavior Therapy, 11,* 329–344.

Kazdin, A. E. (1984). Acceptability of aversive procedures and medication as treatment alternatives for deviant child behavior. *Journal of Abnormal Child Psychology, 12,* 289–302.

Kazdin, A. E. (1987). Treatment of antisocial behavior in children: Current status and future directions. *Psychological Bulletin, 102,* 187–203.

Kazdin, A. E., French, N. H., & Sherick, R. B. (1981). Acceptability of alternative treatments for children: Evaluation of inpatient children, parents, and staff. *Journal of Consulting and Clinical Psychology, 49,* 900–907.

Kistner, J., Hammer, D., Wolfe, D., Rothblum, E., & Drabman, R. S. (1982). Teacher popularity and contrast effects in a classroom token economy. *Journal of Applied Behavior Analysis, 15,* 85–96.

Kolko, J. D. (1988). Daily ratings on a child psychiatric unit. *Journal of the American Academy of Child and Adolescent Psychiatry, 27,* 126–132.

Kovacs, M. (1981). Rating scales to assess depression in school-age children. *Acta Paedopsychiatry, 46,* 305–315.

LaVigna, G. W., & Donnellan, A. M. (1986). *Alternatives to punishment: Solving behavior problems with non-aversive strategies.* New York: Irvington.

Liberman, R. P., & Wong, S. E. (1984). Behavior analysis and therapy procedures related to seclusion and restraint. In K. Tardiff (Ed.), *The psychiatric uses of seclusion and restraint* (pp. 35–67). Washington, DC: American Psychiatric Press.

Linscheid, T. R., Iwata, B. A., Ricketts, R. W., Williams, D. E., & Griffin, J. C. (1990). Clinical evaluation of the self-injurious behavior inhibiting system (SIBIS). *Journal of Applied Behavior Analysis, 23,* 53–78.

Loney, J., & Milich, R. (1982). Hyperactivity, inattention, and aggression in clinical practice. *Advances in Developmental and Behavioral Pediatrics, 3,* 113–147.

Lovaas, O. I. (1987). Behavioral treatment and normal educational and intellectual function in young autistic children. *Journal of Consulting and Clinical Psychology, 55,* 3–9.

Lovaas, O. I., & Favell, J. (1987). Protection for clients undergoing aversive/restrictive interventions. *Education and Treatment of Children, 10,* 311–325.

Luce, S. C., Delquadri, J., & Hall, R. V. (1980). Contingent exercise: A mild but powerful procedure for suppressing inappropriate verbal and aggressive behavior. *Journal of Applied Behavior Analysis, 13,* 583–594.

Luiselli, J. K., Colozzi, G. A., & O'Toole, K. M. (1980). Programming response maintenance of differential reinforcement effects. *Child Behavior Therapy, 2,* 65–73.

Mace, R. C., Page, T. J., Ivancic, M. T., & O'Brien, S. (1986). Effectiveness of brief timeout with and without contingent delay: A comparative analysis. *Journal of Applied Behavior Analysis, 19,* 79–86.

Martin, R. (1975). *Legal challenges to behavior modification.* Champaign, IL: Research Press.

Matson, J. L, & DiLorenzo, T. M. (1984). *Punishment and its alternatives: A new perspective for behavior modification* (Vol. 13). New York: Springer.

Matson, J. L., & Kazdin, A. E. (1981). Punishment in behavior modification: Pragmatic ethical and legal issues. *Clinical Psychology Review, 1,* 197–210.

Matson, J. L., & Taras, M. E. (1989). A 20–year review of punishment and alternative methods to treat problem behaviors in developmentally delayed persons. *Research in Developmental Disabilities, 10,* 85–104.

Matson, J. L., Rotatori, A. F., & Helsel, W. J. (1983). Development of a rating scale to measure social skills in children: The Matson Evaluation of Social Skills of Youngsters (MESSY). *Behaviour Research and Therapy, 21,* 335–340.

Milne, D. (1984). The development and evaluation of a structured learning format introduction of behavior therapy for psychiatric nurses. *Journal of Clinical Psychology, 23,* 175–185.

Morris, R. J. & Kratochwill, T. R. (1985). Behavioral treatment of children's fears and phobias: A review. *School Psychology Review, 14,* 84–93.

Northup, J., Wacker, D., Sasso, G., Steege, M., Cigrand, K., Cook, J., & DeRadd, A. (1991). A brief functional analysis of aggressive and alternative behavior in an outclinic setting. *Journal of Applied Behavior Analysis, 24,* 509–522.

Odom, S. (1987). The role of theory in the preparation of professionals in early childhood special education. *Topics in Early Childhood Special Education, 7,* 1–11.

Ollendick, T. H., & Matson, J. L. (1978). Overcorrection: An overview. *Behavior Therapy, 9,* 830–842.

O'Leary, K. D., & Wilson, G. T. (1987). *Behavior therapy and outcome* (2nd ed). Englewood Cliffs, NJ: Prentice-Hall.

Olson, R. L., & Roberts, M. W. (1987). Alternative treatments for sibling aggression. *Behavior Therapy, 18,* 243–250.

Parrish, J. M., Cataldo, M. F., Kolko, D. J., Neef, N. A., & Egel, A. L. (1986). Experimental analysis of response covariation among compliant and inappropriate behaviors. *Journal of Applied Behavior Analysis, 19,* 241–254.

Pines, R., Kupst, M., Natta, M., & Schulman, J. (1985). Staff-patient ratio and type of interaction on a child psychiatry inpatient unit. *Child Psychiatry and Human Development, 16,* 14–29.

Porterfield, J. K., Herbert-Jackson, E., & Risley, T. R. (1976). Contingent observation: An effective and acceptable procedure for reducing disruptive behavior of young children in a group setting. *Journal of Applied Behavior Analysis, 9,* 55–64.

Repp, A. C., Barton, L. E., & Brulle, A. R. (1983). A comparison of two procedures for programming the differential reinforcement of other behaviors. *Journal of Applied Behavior Analysis, 16,* 435–445.

Reynolds, C. R., & Richmond, B. O. (1978). What I think and feel: A revised measure of children's manifest anxiety. *Journal of Abnormal Child Psychology, 6,* 271–280.

Rincover, A. (1978). Sensory extinction: A procedure for eliminating self-stimulatory behavior in psychotic children. *Journal of Abnormal Child Psychology, 6,* 299–310.

Rojahn, J., & Helsel, W. J. (1991). The Aberrant Behavior Checklist with children and adolescents with dual diagnosis. *Journal of Autism and Developmental Disorders, 21,* 17–28.

Rojahn, J., McGonigle, J. J.,. Curcio, C., & Dixon, M. J. (1987). Suppression of pica by water mist and aromatic ammonia: A comparative analysis. *Behavior Modification, 11,* 65–74.

Sajwaj, T., Libert, J., & Agras, S. (1974). Lemon-juice therapy: The control of life-threatening rumination in a six-month old infant. *Journal of Applied Behavior Analysis, 7,* 557–563.

Santarcangelo, S., Dyer, K., & Luce, S. C. (1987). Generalized reduction of disruptive behavior in unsupervised settings through specific toy training. *Journal of the Association for Persons with Severe Handicaps, 12,* 281–289.

Schreibman, L. (1988). *Autism.* Newbury Park, CA: Sage Publications.

Singh, N. N., & Bakker, L. W. (1984). Suppression of pica by overcorrection and physical restraint: A comparative analysis. *Journal of Autism and Developmental Disorders, 14,* 331–341.

Soloff, P. H. (1987). Physical controls: The use of seclusion and restraint in modern psychiatric practice. In L. H. Roth (Ed.), *Clinical treatment of the violent person* (pp. 124–144). New York: Plenum Press.

Sulzer-Azaroff, B., & Mayer, G. (1991). *Behavior Analysis for Lasting Change.* Chicago: Holt, Rinehart, and Winston.

Swerissen, H., & Carruthers, J. (1987). The use of a physical restraint procedure to reduce a severely intellectually disabled child's tantrums. *Behavior-Change, 4,* 34–38.

Tate, B. B., & Baroff, G. S. (1966). Aversive conditioning of self-injurious behavior in a psychotic boy. *Behaviour Research and Therapy, 4,* 281–287.

Tynan, W. D., & Gengo, V. (1992). Staff training in pediatric rehabilitation hospital: Development of behavioral engineers. *Journal of Developmental and Physical Disabilities, 4,* 299–306.

Williams, C. D. (1959). The elimination of tantrum behavior by extinction procedures. *Journal of Abnormal and Social Psychology, 59,* 269.

Wilson, C. C., Robertson, S. J., Herlong, L. H., & Haynes, S. N. (1979). Vicarious effects of time out in the modification of aggression in the classroom. *Behavior Modification, 3,* 97–111.

Wolf, M. M., Risley, T. R., Johnson, M., Harris, F., & Allen, E. (1967). Application of operant conditioning procedures to the behavior problems of an autistic child, a follow-up extension. *Behaviour Research and Therapy, 5,* 103–112.

Wolf, M. M., Risley, T. R., & Meese, H. (1964). Application of operant conditioning procedures to the behavior problems of an autistic child. *Behaviour Research and Therapy, 1,* 305–312.

Wolfe, V. V., Boyd, L. A., & Wolfe, D. A. (1983). Teacher cooperative play to behavior-problem preschool children. *Education and Treatment of Children, 6,* 1–9.

Wong, S. E., Floyd, J., Innocent, A. J., & Woolsey, J. E. (1991). Applying a DRO schedule and compliance training to reduce aggressive and self-injurious behavior in an autistic man: A case report. *Journal of Behavior Therapy and Experimental Psychiatry, 22,* 299–304.

Wong, S. E., Slama, K. M., & Liberman, R. P. (1985). Behavioral analysis and therapy for aggressive psychiatric and developmentally disabled patients. In L. H. Roth (Ed.) *Clinical treatment of the violent person* (pp. 22–56). New York: Plenum Press.

PART 3

Treatment of Specific Disorders

CHAPTER 8

Mental Retardation

FRANK H. KOBE AND JAMES A. MULICK

DESCRIPTION OF THE PROBLEM

Mental retardation is usually diagnosed in late infancy or early childhood, but sometimes the condition remains unrecognized until a child begins school. It represents a pervasive failure by the child to acquire age-appropriate skills and knowledge, and it is usually not restricted to only a few domains of learning or skill, such as reading or motor coordination. Formal diagnostic criteria for mental retardation have been offered by several learned associations and are currently under scientific scrutiny; so it can be assumed that details of a generally accepted set of criteria will be shifting in the short term. The most significant differences between major classification systems at the present time relate to the weight given to environmental modifications and supports with respect to the presence of mental retardation (American Association on Mental Retardation, 1992) versus the traditional approach emphasizing individual characteristics of the person with mental retardation (e.g., Grossman, 1983). The DSM-IV draft criteria (American Psychiatric Association, 1993) adhere more to the individual-difference notions of traditional classification systems; retain traditional onset before age 18 and severity levels of mild (IQ 55 to 55 through 70), moderate (IQ 35 to 40 through 50 to 55), severe (IQ 20 to 25 through 35 to 40), and profound (IQ less than 20 to 25); and combine standardized intelligence testing, clinical judgment, and the requirement of a finding of culturally relative impairment in adaptive functioning in at least 2 of 10 areas of life activity (including communication, self-care, home living, social/interpersonal skills, use of community resources, self-direction, functional academic skills, work, leisure, and health and safety) to make the classification. The effect of requiring significant deficits in both IQ and adaptive behavior in diagnostic criteria has been to reduce the prevalence of mental retardation from the theoretical 3%, derived from the distribution of IQ alone, to half that, or about 1.5% of the general population (Baroff, 1986).

Professional interest in the problems of children with mental retardation has grown rapidly since the introduction of P.L. 94-142 in 1975 (the Education of All Handicapped Children Act). This legislation put an end to the educational exclusion of children with mental retardation and marked the true beginning of broad societal recognition of both the special needs and the realistic capabilities of children with significant cognitive impairments. The period since the late 1970s, when the special-education law became universally implemented, has seen an explosion of educational and support services for children with mental retardation, both in school settings and in nonschool medical and social service settings. Consequently, persons with mental retardation have generally become more

---

Supported in part by U.S. Department of Health and Human Services, Maternal and Child Health Bureau Special Project MCJ 009053.

visible; and, with increased visibility, has come the growing realization that adaptation to the various forms of special education, vocational, and residential services can be a difficult process that can embody significant risk factors for emotional disturbance.

Over this same period, there has been a continuing decline in the number of institutional beds and a roughly parallel increase in community-based services. But, the community services that developed for individuals with mental retardation have not been designed to match one for one, in terms of service types, the specific needs of those individuals who were deinstitutionalized. The community-based service system is largely a product, actually an extension, of the preexisting community-based system of education, employment, health care, and social services. It is centered on the school and the family in the childhood years and on work and the family in later years, with some elaboration of nonfamily-based residential options. Professional mental health services, however, have remained a clinic-based ambulatory service with ties to the psychiatric inpatient care system and *not* to community agencies for people with mental retardation. Thus, separation of the mental health and the mental retardation service systems places mental health practitioners at a disadvantage when dealing with the range of new community *institutions* in which both the newer environmental supports and the adaptive difficulties of people with mental retardation are to be seen: school, sheltered work-places, group homes, and public commercial and recreational settings.

Although community programs often serve as a primary resource for the developmental needs of children with mental retardation residing in the family home or community-based residential care, it is not unusual for caregivers to turn to mental health professionals for assessment and treatment services. Unfortunately, the high prevalence of behavioral and emotional problems in this population (Jacobson, 1990) and relative inaccessibility of appropriate psychiatric services (Menolascino & Fleisher, 1992) are well documented, each impacting the delivery of services. Barriers to accessibility include the unfamiliarity of mental health workers with the mental retardation service system, the time consuming special needs of patients with mental retardation and their families, and the need to adapt methods of assessment and treatment for individuals with limited cognitive abilities. Other barriers to mental health service accessibility are similar to those noted by Garrard (1983) in accessing community medical services. These include (a) negative attitudes, (b) lack of training of mental health personnel in mental retardation issues, (c) procedural uncertainties about how to adapt routine practices to a population with limited speech and limited understanding of the purposes of the procedures, (d) consent issues with teenagers and young adults, (e) double standards in clinical decision making based on tacit assumptions about the social worth of individuals with mental retardation, (f) insufficient reimbursement for time actually spent in contact with patients and their families and in adapting services to special needs, (g) turnover of nonfamily caregivers and important third-party informants, (h) architectural barriers for people with physical disabilities and (i) the ironic existence of unstated behavioral requirements for access to waiting areas and treatment facilities that sometimes lead to rejection of low-functioning individuals with markedly atypical behavior.

The full range of mental health problems has been detected and described in the population of persons with mental retardation (Bernstein, 1988). Common presenting complaints referred to mental health professionals involve temper tantrums, aggression, oppositional behavior, self-injury, stereotypy, conduct problems, hyperactivity, destructive behavior at home and at school, anxiety disorders, mood-related disorders, and, perhaps most importantly, their etiological contribution to *other* mental disorders (Helsel

& McGonigle, 1992; Muick, Hammer, & Dura, 1991; Nezu, Nezu, & Gill-Weiss, 1992). Many of these problems can be addressed successfully through outpatient mental health treatment with active recruitment of caregivers as participants in the therapeutic process. There is, however, a shortage of professionals with sufficient training, experience, and, quite possibly, the *interest*, to address the needs of this population (Menolascino & Fleisher, 1992). Consequently, there may be relatively low utilization of community mental health services with resulting overreliance upon inpatient psychiatric care in addressing childhood mental health problems—problems that often result from inadequate educational programs, impoverished environments, or poorly trained program and residential-care personnel.

Jacobson (1990) commented that one of the most "perplexing" aspects of mental disorders among persons with mental retardation is the difficulty discriminating between the constructs "adaptation, maladaptation, behavioral disturbance, and mental or behavioral disorder" (p. 21). This is particularly pertinent as researchers now commonly use the label of *dual diagnosis* (i.e., mental retardation and mental illness) in referring to mentally retarded persons with some form of concomitant mental disorder. Unfortunately, the problems of those referred for inpatient care generally are exceedingly complex and cannot be addressed with a simplistic diagnostic approach. Thus, a multimodal approach to understanding the functional parameters of the presenting problem (Crnic, 1988), along with an adaption of traditional procedures used in assessment and treatment, can be viewed as the norm for children with mental retardation. In addition, the majority of cases will necessitate a behavioral approach in both assessment and treatment.

Hersen and Bellack (1978) were among the first to observe that behavioral treatment models often are the most successful in treating the problems of persons with mental retardation in inpatient settings, a position that certainly corresponds with the authors experience throughout the 1980s to the present time. Nevertheless, psychiatric treatment continues to rely on a traditional medical model of care, thereby limiting the value of psychiatric care in mental retardation. Organic disorders and central nervous system (CNS) insults are, after all, prevalent in mental retardation as elements of etiology; but their effective treatment is often medically and technically impossible, and the presenting complaint often is only partly related to the underlying organic condition(s) (Gunsett, Mulick, Fernald, & Martin, 1989; Mulick & Meinhold, 1994; Mulick, Hammer & Dura, 1991). The other major contributing influence in the psychopathology and maladaptive behavior observed in mental retardation is the inappropriate learning that can result from the effects of disability on the behavior of the patient in some environments and on the behavior of others toward the patient. The effects of disability, whether physical or mental, on others can establish social conditions that favor the acquisition and maintenance of maladaptive behavior. Disability itself is only indirectly causal, however, and complete understanding of the mental or emotional problems of persons with disabilities requires a sophisticated interactionist perspective. Growing recognition of this perspective has essentially led to a progressive decline in the use of unimodal, biologically oriented, inpatient treatment for children with mental retardation, further limiting training opportunities for psychiatrists and other mental health professionals with this population. Most importantly, children with mental retardation served by inpatient settings may not receive services consistent with their needs due to a lack of knowledge about critical aspects of mental illness in this population, as well as poor understanding of community-based services and nonmedical resources for children with mental retardation. Thus, the purpose of this chapter is to provide readers with a broad overview of critical issues concerning psychiatric disorders in youngsters with mental retardation, methods of assessment and treatment, and continuity of care considerations following inpatient treatment.

Psychiatric Disorders and Mental Illness in Persons with Mental Retardation

The diagnosis and treatment of mental health problems in persons with mental retardation has become a significant area of research over the past decade (Jacobson, 1990; Matson & Barrett, 1982; Menolascino & Stark, 1984; Reiss, Levitan, & McNally, 1982). While much of the research in this area has focused upon the needs of adults, it is clear that children with mental retardation not only have a high prevalence of behavioral and emotional disorders, but that impaired cognitive and adaptive skills increase the risk for developing some form of mental illness (Russell, 1988). Although continued research is necessary to improve our understanding of specific risk factors, effective assessment techniques, and the contribution of person-environment interactions in the development of mental illness within this population, an expanding literature on these topics reflects widespread professional attention to the problem (Jacobson, 1982; Menolascino & Fletcher, 1989; Menolascino & Stark, 1984; Matson & Barrett, 1982).

Researchers continue to debate the details of epidemiology, classification, assessment, and treatment. Russell (1988), for example, cites a need to refine diagnostic criteria in order to understand prevalence and interrelationships between psychiatric diagnosis and mental retardation, whereas Thompson (1988) indicates that "the vast majority of behavioral problems of people with mental retardation *are in and of themselves the disorder* and are not symptoms of anything else" (p. 99) [italics in original]. It is, perhaps, this confusing distinction that makes accurate and effective assessment, as well as treatment, such a difficult undertaking.

The assessment, diagnosis, and treatment of mental illness in persons with mental retardation are difficult tasks even for clinicians with direct mental retardation experience (Reiss, et al., 1982). Some experts emphasize that the primary assessment task is to identify symptoms indicative of a mental illness versus those attributed solely to mental retardation (Sovner & Lowry, 1990), whereas others counter that pragmatic concerns dictate the need to address natural-environment features that may maintain or aggravate the maladaptive behavior of the patient (Mulick & Schroeder, 1980).

Distinct categories of psychiatric disorder have been difficult to empirically establish due to the high level of comorbidity in mental retardation. In fact, the diagnostic data base in this field is rather small. Although case descriptions of psychiatric disorders in persons with mental retardation are common, theoretical conceptualization of specific categories of psychiatric disorder has been concentrated primarily in the areas of depression and mood disorders (Dosen, 1984; Matson, 1983; Sovner & Hurley, 1982; Sovner & Hurley, 1983). Until differential diagnosis is refined to the point that differential treatment is much less equivocally supported in this population, pragmatic concerns will outweigh those of classification, and mental health services will continue to focus on the symptom rather than on the substrate (Schroeder, 1989).

Prevalence

All known psychiatric disorders can coexist with mental retardation (Bernstein, 1988; Reid, 1981; Szymanski & Crocker, 1989). However, prevalence data tend to vary according to the definitional parameters utilized and the assessment methods employed (Russell,

1988). Because standards for the assignment of a person with mental retardation to specific psychiatric diagnostic categories based upon specific symptoms have not been firmly established (Mulick, Hammer & Dura, 1991) and because the independence of psychiatric classification procedures generally yields inadequate results in some diagnostic categories (Nihira, Price-Williams, & White, 1988), the best use of psychiatric diagnosis in children with mental retardation is to generate treatment hypothesis enabling the clinician to develop, implement, and assess interventions consistent with these hypotheses and the pragmatic needs of the patient.

Despite differing perspectives on epidemiology, a number of studies provide a starting point to understand mental disorders in persons with mental retardation. In a study of over 30,000 persons with mental retardation residing in both community and institutional settings, Jacobson (1982) reported an overall prevalence of concomitant psychiatric impairment among 11.6% of the total population and among 9.8% of children. Further, large-scale epidemiological studies comprising all 9-, 10-, and 11-year-old children on the Isle of Wight (Rutter, Tizard, Yule, Graham, & Whitmore, 1976) indicated that although the prevalence of psychiatric disorders in those children was 7%, among children with IQs of less than 70, it was 30% based upon parent report, and 42% based on teacher report. These data suggested that children with cognitive disabilities have a four to five times greater prevalence of psychiatric disorders than groups of normal children (Rutter, Graham, & Yule, 1970: Rutter, et al., 1976).

Prevalence has also been shown to vary according to the age and functioning level of the child (Ando & Yosimura, 1978; Benson, 1985), as well as the type of population from which the sample is drawn. Clinical outpatient samples of children with borderline to profound mental retardation exhibiting behavioral and emotional problems range from 25% (Groden, Pueschel, Domingue, & Deignan, 1982) to as high as 87% (Philips & Williams, 1975). In addition, problems are not simply restricted to older children or adolescents. Recently, Varley and Furukawa (1991) reported that 23% of a clinic sample of 524 young children with developmental disabilities (age 6 and under) could be classified with a psychiatric diagnosis.

Although prevalence data pertaining to psychiatric disorder remains difficult to interpret, there are further complications stemming from three issues:

1. There are inconsistent correlations between psychiatric diagnosis and problem behavior (Rojahn, Borthwick-Duffy, & Jacobson, 1993).

2. Severity of some but not all problem behavior tends to increase as IQ declines (Dura, Mulick, & Myers, 1988; Russell, 1988).

3. It is unclear as to the percentage of children actually receiving diagnostic and treatment services for mental disorders because such treatment is not confined to traditional mental health settings, nor is it necessarily carried out by designated mental health workers.

The New York and California Epidemiological Study

As noted, prevalence data are limited to just a few large-scale studies, and the results are difficult to interpret. Until recently, many would have assumed that aberrant behavior would be strongly predictive of psychiatric diagnosis. This assumption may not reflect actual professional practice, however. An important study by Rojahn et al. (1993) is of particular relevance to the epidemiology of mental disorders in mental retardation. The data encompassed huge state data bases from California (n = 89,419) and New York (n = 45,683) and covered an age range of birth to 45 years. Data collection used consistent and standardized formats and seems to reflect the current state of the field. The most startling finding was that *no* consistent association was found between any major classification of psychiatric diagnosis and common types of problem behavior present in persons with mental retardation (e.g., aggression, self-injury, stereotypic behavior, property destruction). This suggests that commonly observed behavior problems in persons with mental retardation are recognized, for the most part, independent of a specific psychiatric diagnosis of record. Thus, differential diagnosis should be practiced cautiously, and special care should be observed in attempting to use common types of behavior problems as markers of underlying mental illness. The New York and California epidemiological study strongly implies that, in practice, treatment services addressing these problems are provided independently to people with mental retardation.

Comment

Despite the substantial limitations in prevalence data, it is clear that children with mental retardation (a) are particularly vulnerable to the development of psychiatric disorders, (b) can exhibit the full range of psychiatric disorders found in intellectually normal populations of children, and (c) will frequently be referred to mental health professionals for assessment and treatment.

Psychiatric Disorders and the Environment of Children with Mental Retardation

Children with mental retardation are subjected to a host of environmental risk factors related to the development of psychiatric disorders. These risk factors include high levels of family stress (Harris & McHale, 1989; Holroyd, 1974; McKinney & Peterson, 1987; Orr, Cameron, & Day, 1991), family dysfunction (Rutter, 1989), repeated learning failure (Reynolds & Miller, 1985, Weisz, 1979), social isolation (Harris & McHale, 1989), social deprivation (Trad, 1987), and, in some cases, institutionalization (Hill & Bruinicks, 1984). In fact, behavior disorders are frequently cited as a primary source of family stress leading to out-of home placement (Hill & Bruinicks, 1984) and to the failure of successful placement in the community (Jacobson & Ackerman, 1989).

For the most part, direct manifestations of behavioral and emotional problems of children with mental retardation can be viewed as similar to those of children with normal intelligence and, in some cases, can be identified with measures developed for use with nonhandicapped populations (Benavidez & Matson, 1993; Matson, Barrett, & Helsel, 1988). However, symptoms are best understood in relation to adverse life experiences influenced, and perhaps potentiated, by cognitive- and adaptive-skill deficits (Philips, 1971; Philips & Williams, 1975). Since mental retardation may result from a multitude of biological, environmental, and social factors, each influencing the presentation and course of symptoms (Rojahn, Hammer, & Marshburn, 1992), the most appropriate focus is a biopsychosocial approach (Matson, 1985) in which psychiatric assessment determines the relative influence of developmental, behavioral, and environmental factors affecting the child and his or her caregivers. Since the *context* in which behavior occurs often proves to be one of the most important developmental influences among children with mental retardation, assessment must *always* examine potential environmental explanations of disordered behavior. This is not to minimize or limit the role of traditional psychiatric diagnosis, but rather to acknowledge that symptoms may have multiple influences, perhaps to a greater extent in the environments of children with mental retardation. Thus, treatment inevitably includes methods that focus upon altering the timing and sequence of environmental events and their contingent relations with behavior (Mulick & Meinhold, 1994).

Although it is clear that children with mental retardation are substantially at risk for developing psychiatric disorders (Russell & Tanguay, 1981; Rutter et al., 1976; Trad, 1987), their needs have traditionally been overlooked by mental health systems. This has resulted in poor access to specialized psychiatric assessment, treatment, and related support services (Helsel & McGonigle, 1992; Matson, 1988a). Psychiatric consultation and, particularly, inpatient care are often nonexistent or very limited for this group of children. In addition, few clinicians at the community level, *including* those working primarily with persons having mental retardation, have the necessary training or experience to recognize psychiatric disorders and provide effective treatment (Tanguay & Szymanski, 1980). Thus, children referred to an inpatient psychiatric setting will most likely present with the most severe level of symptomatology found among this population (Borthwick-Duffy & Eyman, 1990). They will include many children for whom most, if not all, community resources already have been exhausted in an attempt to address psychiatric concerns. These may include severe aggressive behavior and conduct problems, marked withdrawal or psychotic behavior, anxiety and attention disorders that have a severe impact upon daily functioning, self-injurious behavior, suicidal ideation, or other unusual combinations of these behaviors that could not be effectively managed on an outpatient basis or through existing mental retardation services in the community.

With this in mind, two key elements may help clinicians to determine the focus of treatment for the child with mental retardation referred for inpatient care. These are (a) the source of referral and (b) the current living situation of the child. Since there is remarkable variation in living environments for children with mental retardation, there may also be dramatically different presenting concerns based upon unique demands with expectations for behavior that influence the adjustment and conduct of the child with mental retardation. A child residing with his or her biological or adoptive parents, for example, may present markedly different concerns and treatment needs from a child residing in a foster home, group home, or institutional setting in which paid caregivers maintain the ongoing responsibility for care. Similarly, the child's presenting problems must be viewed in context with the environmental characteristics, caregiver strengths and weaknesses, and inherent problems of care associated with the daily life setting. Variables such as the number of persons residing with the child, behavior-management practices employed, accessibility of outside consultation and professional resources, and programmatic focus of the facility (i.e., daytime program or 24-hour residential facility) can influence the assessment and treatment process, both in positive and negative ways. It is important to recognize the strengths as well as the weaknesses of these environments and how they may contribute to the presentation of symptoms and caregiver concerns. While it can be an overwhelming task, consideration of these variables will allow each child's case to be planned in a fashion that is consistent with the resources, skills, and professional practices occurring within each environment.

Inpatient Psychiatric Care for Children with Mental Retardation

Very few general child-psychiatric hospitals actively seek admission referrals from patients with all levels of mental retardation, and there are virtually only a handful of specialized inpatient psychiatric programs for children with mental retardation. Thus, in some cases, a child with mental retardation experiencing a psychiatric crisis may be refused inpatient services or may receive only crisis stabilization if admitted. However, most child inpatient psychiatric facilities *can* play an important role for this group of children. In many respects, their basic treatment needs may be similar to children with normal intellectual capacity in terms of routine services. However, the major difference is that psychiatric facilities providing services to children with mental retardation *must* have a strong behavioral focus, with substantial flexibility in assessment and treatment methods, in addition to biologically based approaches.

Naturally, this leads to the following questions:

1. What is the best use of inpatient psychiatric care for children with mental retardation?

2. What adjustments or additions to assessment approaches and treatment services must occur in order to adequately serve this population?

These questions will guide the presentation of information in the remainder of this chapter.

The Role of Inpatient Care

The most appropriate use of inpatient care for children with mental retardation is serving those with severe and acute symptoms, suicidal ideation or dangerous self-destructive behavior, and assaultive or other extreme forms of aggressive and destructive behavior. Acute problems of this nature may be associated with other symptoms such as sleep disturbance, changes in appetite, extreme withdrawal, or high levels of anxiety and emotional arousal. These children may require a safe, secure, and closely monitored environment to provide temporary relief to parents or caregivers and to allow for a thorough diagnostic workup. While this is generally consistent with services provided for children *without* mental retardation, it is the clinical interpretation of the child's presenting symptoms and caregiver concerns that will determine the specific tasks required of the assessment and treatment process. Thus, the primary goals of the assessment should be to determine whether the presenting symptoms (a) are indicative of an existing psychopathology that is amenable to and appropriate for inpatient treatment, (b) are primarily related to features of the child's environment that might be minimally impacted by inpatient treatment and perhaps best handled on an outpatient basis, or (c) reveal a complex interaction between existing psychopathology and environmental stressors that might benefit from a careful assessment and treatment plan. This information will establish the core of professional recommendations as well as direct the assessment and treatment activities to be completed if the child is admitted.

The ability to answer these questions is largely a function of the admitting psychiatrist's education and training, experience with mental retardation, and personal beliefs about psychiatric disorders and mental retardation, that is, if symptoms are viewed as indicative of an underlying disorder, then it is likely that inpatient care will be used to initiate specific treatment. Inpatient care without this perspective may result in short-term crisis stabilization with little, if any, actual treatment. While both instances may occur in professional practice, it is critically important that the child's caregivers clearly understand the professional's view of the role of hospitalization. Often, parents and caregivers have unrealistic expectations about the outcome that may occur from inpatient treatment and look to psychiatric professionals as the expert source in addressing all the child's problems. Disappointment is likely to follow from such expectations. Honesty about the ability to address the various needs of children with mental retardation is the best starting position. It will save much anguish and dissatisfaction later.

Persistent Issues in Diagnosis and Treatment

The diagnosis of psychiatric disorder among children with mental retardation is a complex task. Often, the challenge is to identify specific psychiatric symptoms that might be overlooked as a consequence of the child's cognitive- or adaptive-skill deficits. Since accurate self-reporting of symptoms may be very limited, the clinician must be able to disassociate features of developmentally appropriate behavior, resulting from the person's functioning level or characteristics of the environment, from behavior that might reflect common symptoms of a mental disorder (Sovner, 1988; Sovner & Hurley, 1986).

Experimental studies confirm that the presence of mental retardation adversely influences the ability of the clinician to identify common psychiatric symptoms (Reiss, Levitan, & Szyszko, 1982; Reiss & Szyszko, 1983: Spengler, Strohmer, & Prout, 1990). Reiss, Levitan & Szyszko (1982) introduced the term *diagnostic overshadowing* to describe instances when common symptoms of psychiatric disorders are mistakenly viewed as part of the clinical manifestation of mental retardation. This research demonstrated, from presentations of case studies to clinicians, that common symptoms of psychiatric disorders are frequently overlooked when the person is described as "mentally retarded." Spengler et al. (1990) summarized this perspective by suggesting that the debilitating influence of an existing psychiatric disorder becomes overshadowed by the clinician's perception of the symptoms as salient features of a person's mental retardation. Reiss and Szyszko (1983) found that professionals, regardless of experience level, often do not make the diagnosis of a coexisting psychiatric disorder, despite the presence of overt symptomatology. Together, these works suggest that even professionals clearly aware of psychiatric issues in mental retardation may not be able to overcome perceptual bias in diagnosis.

From a clinical perspective this overshadowing phenomenon in the assessment of psychiatric disorders is not surprising, given the reliance upon diagnostic criteria primarily developed for use among persons with normal intellectual functioning. Pawlarcyzk and Beckwith (1987), for example, found that criteria in the *Diagnostic and Statistical Manual of Mental Disorders* (DSM-III) (American Psychiatric Association, 1980) for a diagnosis of depression appeared applicable only for persons with mild and moderate mental retardation. Generally, it appears that clinicians use standard diagnostic criteria with persons functioning in the borderline range of mental retardation (Jacobson & Ackerman, 1989). Although there is little research regarding the applicability of standard diagnostic criteria in child populations, correlational data using scores from the Children's Depression Inventory (Kovacs & Beck, 1977) have been associated with significant levels of depressive symptoms in children with mental retardation as well as DSM-III-R (American Psychiatric Association, 1987) qualifying criteria (Kobe & Hammer, 1994; Matson, Barrett, & Helsel, 1988).

Psychiatric Symptoms in Children with Mental Retardation

Children with mental retardation experiencing psychiatric problems may be identified in a variety of community settings. Because they often take part in specialized medical and educational services, staff from many organizations may have contact with these children and begin to recognize a psychiatric component of a given child's problems. These settings may include developmental and early childhood programs, schools, child protective agencies, pediatric and primary-care settings, and community mental health programs.

In many respects, the problem in both identification and treatment of psychiatric problems centers upon comorbidity and the ecobehavioral relationships influencing the presentation of symptoms. While it may seem logical to assume that, as cognitive and adaptive skills decrease, a greater likelihood of mixed disorders of emotion and conduct could occur, professionals are just beginning to understand the ways in which specific psychiatric disorders may present. Much exciting research still remains to be done in this area.

Most persons with mental retardation referred for inpatient care are those displaying behavior such as aggression, unacceptable social behavior, or severe resistance to caregivers' efforts at habilitative programming (Borthwick-Duffy & Eyman, 1990). While these types of behaviors can be associated with a number of psychiatric diagnoses and may have a genetic or biological basis (i.e., family history of psychiatric disorder), it is equally possible that multiple environmental factors may precipitate, potentiate, or maintain the pattern of symptoms. When viewed from this perspective, and as previously noted, it is the *interaction* of the child's symptoms and the environmental contingencies that is generally the most important consideration for the clinician. While it is tempting to follow the dual diagnosis movement in mental retardation, diagnoses are generally most useful in testing hypotheses about behavior. Diagnostic schemes have limited value beyond such ends.

Predisposing Factors in Mental Retardation for Developing Psychiatric Disorders

Several key factors account for the prevalence of psychopathology in children with mental retardation and should be considered in the assessment and treatment approach adopted by the inpatient clinician. These include the following:

1. Neurologic damage affecting both cortical and subcortical systems that can result in diffuse effects on personality and coping responses, as well as damage to temporal, frontal, and limbic systems that subserve behavioral and emotional responses. These may affect the child's ability to effectively process stimuli and result in confusion, frustration, immature reactions, disinhibition, impulsiveness, rigidity in thinking, and poor adaptability to change.

2. Life circumstances of the child resulting from placement in developmentally inappropriate environments (i.e., institutions, congregate care facilities) that leave them poorly equipped to conform to challenges, threats, and expectations posed by these environments.

3. Poor access to psychiatric care, resulting in the overuse of psychotropic medications by nonspecialists and a general lack of attention to behavioral treatment approaches.

Furthermore, genetic factors may play an important role in the development of specific patterns of psychopathology; for example, Bregman (1991), in a review of psychopathology in mental retardation, reported that oppositional and conduct disorders were frequently present in children with Prader-Willi syndrome, a disorder of hyperphagia, obesity, and compulsive food-seeking. Clearly, genetic factors may be directly involved, or indirectly involved via negative life experiences of people who, like so many Prader-Willi patients, are constantly being thwarted by caregivers in their attempts to get at food. Similarly, Bregman, Leckman, and Ort (1988) noted that nearly three-quarters of all

Fragile X affected boys have substantial attention deficits and hyperactivity (X-linked inheritance being the most commonly identified genetic subtype of mental retardation).

PROTOTYPIC ASSESSMENT

An assessment of the child with mental retardation in an inpatient setting must consider four primary domains:

1. Identification of physical and neurological factors affecting the presentation of symptoms.

2. Clarification of the relationship between specific cognitive-, communication-, or social-skill deficits and psychopathology through an assessment of the intellectual and adaptive functioning of the child.

3. A functional analysis of behavior to understand stimulus-response relationships in maintaining the specific types of behavior (e.g., aggressive outbursts, withdrawal, self-injury.

4. A thorough assessment of broad environmental factors present in each child's unique situation as they affect the presentation, maintenance, or severity of symptoms (e.g., family stressors; characteristics of the child's home or other living environment, such as foster homes, institutions, or group homes; or the ability of caregivers to effectively address the child's basic and emotional needs).

Assessment of these variables requires a multimodal approach. The presenting concerns may represent only a small component of the clinical issues relevant to inpatient treatment planning. While it is impossible to anticipate all issues in these patients, a prototypic assessment for the child with mental retardation should include the following elements:

1. A complete history and physical and neurological examination with laboratory testing as indicated.

2. A comprehensive psychological evaluation to determine level of functioning with respect to both intellectual skills and adaptive behavior. The initial workup should include a psychoeducational (including IQ) evaluation appropriate to the developmental skills and the possible sensory and motor handicaps of the child, assessment of organicity, and a mental status examination. These results should be compared with the records of past functioning to determine whether the present difficulties are associated with a change in the overall level of functioning of the patient, often an important marker associated with some mental disorders.

3. A data-based description of the presenting behaviors and an assessment of the functional relationship between these behaviors and environmental antecedents and consequences. This should be combined with behavioral rating scales to allow for easy comparison of behavior across different informants and settings.

4. A complete description and general understanding of the day-to-day settings in which the child functions, in order to be familiar with the expectations and demands of each setting.

5. Clinical interviews with the patient, his or her parents, and other informants, such as residential-program staff, teachers, outpatient clinicians involved to determine prior programming, existing behavior management methods, linkages with professional resources, and previous treatment. In particular, a family history of psychiatric disorders is critical to determine if the child's presenting symptoms are consistent with previously diagnosed psychiatric disorders in the family.

Some key elements of the assessment process must be adapted to account for differences in the child's level of cognitive ability. Among children with borderline, mild, or moderate mental retardation, for example, the clinical interview and mental status exam should consist of several short interview periods (15 to 30 minutes each rather than one period of 60 to 90 minutes) conducted in a relatively informal setting. Interviews with these children should use concrete language and avoid questions that require unrealistically high levels of conceptually driven information (e.g., cognitive interpretation of events, feelings, emotions). Furthermore, there is always a need to be cognizant of suggestibility and the possibility of affirmation or acquiescence to statements that are confusing or poorly understood by the child (Sigelman, Budd, Winer, Schoenrock, & Martin, 1982).

In most cases, children with severe and profound levels of mental retardation may have very limited expressive and receptive language skills that make all components of the psychiatric assessment a difficult undertaking. Direct patient interview may be rendered essentially useless. However, important diagnostic information can be obtained through *direct behavioral observations* and interval recording of problem behaviors (e.g., Touchette, MacDonald, & Langer, 1985), as well as close monitoring of activity level and of sleep and eating patterns (Sovner & Lowry, 1990). Behavioral observations have the potential to determine antecedent cues for behavior. Analog functional analysis can be easily accomplished by videotaping a structured interaction with the child. This can allow for detailed analysis of behavior in order to determine potential operant relationships. When these approaches are combined with interval recording of target behaviors (i.e. aggression toward others, self-injury, property destruction, crying episodes), important environmental-setting events can often be determined (Mulick & Meinhold, 1994; Schroeder, et. al., 1982).

A mental status examination remains an important aspect of the psychiatric assessment for children with mental retardation. However, clinicians should remember that the utility of this information may be a function of the child's level of cognitive deficit. In particular, some individuals with mental retardation may be a poor source of information and, if verbal at all, may respond to language in idiosyncratic ways that are more related to their own social history than to events under discussion (Sigelman et al., 1982). While the mental status areas of interest are generally the same as with children without cognitive delays, clinicians should be careful not to assume that presenting behaviors are simply symptomatic of mental retardation (e.g., affect, activity level, verbalizations). As noted previously, this creates the potential for the child's cognitive delays to overshadow the presence of well-known and overt types of psychiatric symptoms.

Although adaptation in the methods used may be necessary in mental status examination of the child with mental retardation, the specific data obtained may be relevant to diagnosis as well as treatment. General areas such as the reaction to examiner, anxiety, personal hygiene, dress, and eye contact may be evidence of social-skill deficits. The child's response to a novel situation may provide data on coping skills, level of anxiety, and manner of relating to changes in the environment. Retardation or agitation of motor behavior, in the absence of specific antecedent cues, may suggest depression, especially when combined with reported changes in sleep, eating, or activity patterns. Language characteristics such as rate, rhythm, stuttering, or pressured speech, · may indicate situation-specific anxiety or important organic factors contributing to the child's mental retardation and symptom presentation. Thought content may be extremely variable, however, based upon a child's level of functioning. Assessment of the child's primary concern, perception of reality, suicidal ideation, hallucinations, delusions, coherence, linked versus loose associations, flight of ideas, perseveration, blocking, and echolalia is necessary to determine symptoms of schizophrenic, personality, or organic brain disorders. Finally, general behavioral observations during interview may be of great importance in differential diagnosis of problems such as conduct, anxiety, or affective disorders.

All clinical-interview data should be interpreted as to its correspondence with informant reports of previous functioning. As noted, self-report data, commonly used in psychiatric assessment, should be considered extremely suspect unless corroborated by informants. This is due to the difficulties children with mental retardation may have with abstract concepts and in accessing a sufficiently broad fund of information (Sovner & Hurley, 1990). Baseline data obtained from reports of parents, teachers, or caregivers is important to ensure that the observed symptoms are viewed in context. In addition, reports concerning the child's behavior over time are crucial to engender a longitudinal perspective. This alone will help to isolate changes that may help differentiate maladaptive behavior from psychiatric illness. Changes in mood, behavior incidents, cognitive ability, activity level, leisure time interests, and somatic complaints are just several of the areas that may help clarify the nature of presenting symptoms.

Differential Diagnosis

The use of differential diagnosis is a common approach among children with mental retardation referred for inpatient care. Since some form of severe aggressive behavior is often a presenting concern in children with mental retardation, assessment should rule out disorders such as attention-deficit hyperactivity disorder (ADHD), conduct disorder, oppositional defiant disorder, temporal lobe epilepsy, drug-induced aggression, intermittent explosive disorder, mood disorders (unipolar, bipolar, or rapid cycling), psychosis, or panic disorder. The differential may also vary according to the level of mental retardation; for example, children with mild and moderate mental retardation may display aggression directed toward others or property destruction that could reflect symptoms of a depressive disorder, whereas a similar problem in children with severe or profound mental retardation might be inferred from a change in the severity, frequency, or intensity of a longstanding behavior (e.g., self-injury, stereotypies).

Sovner and Hurley (1990) suggest approaches using biographical timelines of critical events (e.g., onset of medical and behavioral issues, personal or environmental stressors, medication changes), and charting of sleep, mood, and behavior incidents as part of a thorough psychiatric assessment in persons with mental retardation. In many respects, this reiterates in a concrete manner the perspective that useful assessment of psychological and psychiatric status must focus upon multiple levels of analysis and employ a microanalytic approach to observing behavior. The authors have found that a case history is enhanced by collection of information about a typical day for the child in his or her family, and classroom; descriptions of routine activities, such as meal times and play times; and detailed narrative characterizations of important social relationships.

A variety of behavioral checklists or screening measures have been developed to assess psychopathology in persons with mental retardation. However, few have been specifically designed for children. General assessment instruments such as the Child Behavior Checklist (CBCL) (Achenbach & Edelbrock, 1983) can be useful, especially among children with mild to moderate mental retardation. The CBCL covers a variety of important behaviors and can be used with different informants to determine the child's behavioral functioning across environments (e.g., school vs. home). Several measures of psychopathology have been created for use in persons with mental retardation, such as the Psychopathology Inventory for Mentally Retarded Adults (PIMRA) (Matson, 1988b) and the Reiss Screen for Maladaptive Behavior (Reiss, 1988). However, few measures have been specifically designed for child populations or have specific research supporting their use. The exceptions are the Reiss Scales for Children's Dual Diagnosis (Reiss & Valenti-Hein, in press), the Emotional Disorders Rating Scale (Feinstein, Kaminer, Barrett, & Tylenda, 1988), and the Aberrant Behavior Checklist (Aman, Richmond, Stewart, Bell, & Kissel, 1987). In addition, some research has shown that the Children's Depression Inventory (Kovacs, 1981), normed with nonhandicapped children, may be useful in assessing depression in children with mental retardation (Kobe & Hammer, 1994; Matson, Barrett, & Helsel, 1988). In addition, the Conners Rating Scale (Conners, 1969) can be useful in the assessment of ADHD. Finally, Kolko (1988) developed a behavioral assessment checklist specifically for a child psychiatric inpatient program, and, in the authors' experience, it can be used effectively by both caregivers and treatment staff to obtain a profile of relevant behaviors. Readers interested in an extensive coverage of this area should obtain the recent comprehensive review of all available assessment instruments for assessing psychopathology in persons with mental retardation by Aman (1991).

Further assessment centered upon adaptive skills is essential information to determine the child's pattern of functional strengths and weaknesses. This can be used in designing both treatment and programming approaches that are matched to the individual skills of the child. Several of the more useful measures include the Matson Evaluation of Social Skills with Youngsters (Matson, Rotatori, & Helsel, 1983), the Vineland Adaptive Behavior Scales (Sparrow, Balla, & Cicchetti, 1984), and the AAMR (American Association on Mental Retardation) Adaptive Behavior Scale (Nihira, Foster, Shellhaas, & Leland, 1969).

ACTUAL ASSESSMENT

The previous section presented a framework for prototypic assessment. However, each child will present a dramatically varied set of presenting problems that require a flexible and creative approach to assessment. This is due to the variation in living environments of children with mental retardation and in the resources available of community-based services to provide appropriate continuity of care following a psychiatric hospitalization. Thus, it is necessary to consider the *most* crucial elements of assessment for children admitted for inpatient psychiatric care. This involves an examination of both medical and behavioral domains. A careful physical examination is necessary to rule out relevant biological factors, such as medication side effects, chronic illness, or changes in physical health, that may contribute to symptoms (Gunsett et al., 1989). All of these have the potential to elicit pain, discomfort, or alteration of sensory systems in a manner that could lead to frustration and varying forms of aggressive or atypical behavior in the child. The presenting problems must also be examined relative to behavioral antecedents and consequences that may serve to maintain the behavior. Although a functional analysis of behavior can yield a wealth of hypotheses related to diagnosis, the core elements of behavioral assessment comprise interviews of the patient, family, and other caregivers involved with the child on a day-to-day basis.

A key element of the assessment, though often omitted, is obtaining a *clear* definition of the presenting problem. The initial assessment by the admitting psychiatrist must provide sufficient information to generate clinical hypotheses that can be tested through medical evaluation and follow-up observations of behavior, social interaction, and activity level. A cognitive and mental status evaluation should be completed in order to clarify the relationship of the presenting problems to specific cognitive-, communication-, or social-skill deficits. Behavioral observation will be required for nearly all children, both to establish the relationship of the symptoms to environmental events and to serve as a baseline against which to measure the effectiveness of treatment interventions. Finally, clinicians should either perform formal cognitive and adaptive testing on each child or obtain this information from existing sources.

During hospitalization, it is important to recognize that differences in environmental demands, expectations, and activities for the child with mental retardation may produce a dramatic contrast in behavior from the presenting concerns: A rapid adjustment to the demands of inpatient care with nearly total elimination of the presenting concerns (e.g., destructive behaviors or conduct disorders) may indicate the presence of stimulus control over behavior. In contrast, consistency in the presentation of symptoms may provide a firm basis for the existence of underlying psychopathology (e.g., psychotic behaviors, depression, or anxiety disorders). Although these are simplified examples that can occur when there is a dramatic contrast between reported and presenting concerns, these areas are important as they suggest equally dramatic differences in the treatment needs of the child.

CASE EXAMPLE: ASSESSMENT

The following case example illustrates the assessment of a nonambulatory adolescent female with severe retardation who was referred due to frequent, high-intensity episodes of screaming, crying, and tantrums. These behaviors had been reported periodically during the previous 3 years but had reportedly increased in frequency and severity over the last several months. She was placed out of her natural home at age 8 and resided in a medical facility for persons with mental retardation. The treatment team, comprised of all facility staff, presented dramatically different perspectives and information regarding the source of the problems upon initial assessment. The nursing and therapy staffs reported frequent periods of depressed mood and irritability combined with a decreased appetite and activity level. In contrast, the direct-care staff (i.e., unit attendants, shift supervisors) suggested that episodes frequently occurred when access to her wheelchair was restricted (a medical necessity to maintain skin integrity) or when one-to-one attention was terminated.

The assessment first ruled out complicating medical factors such as medications or illness accounting for reported changes in mood, appetite, sleep pattern, and activity level. Records obtained on sleep, eating, and activity patterns, based on interval recording of data, confirmed a substantial change from previous levels of functioning. The psychological assessment revealed no change in cognitive or adaptive skills when compared with baseline. While the mental status examination revealed a high interest in social interaction, periods of depressed mood and irritability were present across settings. Expressive language was limited to single-syllable vocal sounds, and no gestures or other functional communication were present. Behavior rating scales corroborated observations of disturbance in mood and of frequent episodes of screaming, crying, and tantrums. To examine these behaviors in detail, a videotaped functional analysis of behavior was completed. This consisted of a systematic alteration in the level of task demands in a 12-by-14 foot area that allowed testing hypotheses regarding stimulus-control relationships. The results of the functional analysis indicated that crying and screaming were part of an escalating sequence of behaviors culminating in severe tantrums.

The assessment results provided two relevant hypotheses. First, data suggested a clinically significant depressive episode that could be appropriately treated with antidepressant medication. Second, the functional analysis suggested a strong behavioral component in which maladaptive behaviors were maintained by operant relationships. Interestingly, both of the initial observations by treatment staff were confirmed through the multimodal data-based assessment. This provided the basis for the treatment intervention to be described in the following treatment section.

PROTOTYPIC TREATMENT

Treatment of children with mental retardation may be a complex clinical undertaking. More often than not, there are likely to be multiple determinants that stem from behavioral, social, and environmental explanations. Nezu et al. (1992) summarized the issue by noting that "any attempt to explain psychopathology that focuses on a single phenomenon is likely to fall short of clinical reality. Similarly, any clinical intervention that uses only a single technique is likely to fall short of success" (p. 30). This indicates the need to balance flexibility, creativity, and clinical reality.

Because clinicians working in the psychiatric setting generally cannot impact directly upon the multiple determinants involved in a given case, a framework should be designed that will give outpatient clinicians a direction and focus in working with the child over time. No one intervention, be it behavioral or pharmacological, will completely address the complexity of psychiatric disorders in the child with mental retardation. As such, treatment becomes a dynamic process in which inpatient care serves as a foundation and guide for follow-up.

Treatment interventions should include a hierarchical approach in relationship to the child's presenting problems. Following assessment, the inpatient clinician should be able to determine the most important problems relative to their current impact on the life of the child. This hierarchical approach may result in individually focused treatment, such as medication, to address psychiatric symptoms (Aman & Singh, 1991; Chandler, Gualtieri & Fahs, 1988; Gadow, 1985) or in behavior management interventions to reduce or increase specific target behaviors (Forehand & Baumeister, 1976; Huguenin & Mulick, 1981; Matson & McCartney, 1981; Mulick, Hammer, & Dura, 1991) or may employ environmentally based changes (Schroeder, Kanoy, et al., 1982) that help to improve the child's life circumstances. This can encompass interventions such as parent training (Baker, 1983), teaching interpersonal skills (Taras, Matson, & Leary, 1988), and improving affect-related expression (Matson, 1982).

Environmentally based treatment can be one of the most useful adjuncts to long-term care of children referred for psychiatric care (Mulick, Hammer, & Dura, 1991). However, this approach varies as a function of the age and cognitive ability of the individual as well as of the setting in which the problem behaviors occur. To obtain any treatment improvement over time, a consideration of generalization issues must occur.

Generalization and maintenance of behavioral gains continue to be one of the most difficult problems in treatment of persons with mental retardation (Favell & Reid, 1988). This is due to competing stimulus-control relationships that create barriers in overcoming problem behavior (Horner & Billingsley, 1988). Stokes and Baer (1977) argued that generalization should be specifically programmed rather than assuming it as a natural outcome of the behavioral change process. From this perspective, inpatient programs for children with mental retardation must specifically address this issue or the effects of treatment are unlikely to be maintained. Although the basic treatment methods should focus upon behavioral excesses (e.g., the specific problem behavior, aggression), skill deficits (e.g., coping strategies, social skills), and medical issues identified during assessment, there also must be attention focused upon simultaneous restructuring of the environment specific to the child's circumstances. In this manner, behavioral excesses either are less likely to be elicited or are actively discouraged through contingency management, and the skill deficits are taught and maintained through positive reinforcement. This will also provide a measure of generalization and maintenance that are so crucial in the treatment of children with mental retardation. A variety of specific behavior modification techniques are effective, and the next section details those most notable.

Contingency management procedures have been applied successfully to modify a large variety of behavior patterns in children with mental retardation. These behavior modification procedures have been thoroughly reviewed in recent years and, for more extensive coverage, the interested reader is referred to the work of Mulick and Schroeder (1980), Repp and Brulle (1981, and Whitman, Scibak, and Reid (1983). Basic decelerative procedures include (a) *time out from positive reinforcement,* in which ongoing sources of reinforcement are temporarily interrupted contingent on misbehavior; (b) *response cost,* in which removal of valued objects is made contingent on misbehavior (Foxx & Shapiro, 1978); (c) *overcorrection,* in which elements of time out and negative reinforcement for incompatible behavior are combined (Foxx & Azrin, 1973); and (d) *punishment,* in which stimuli are systematically programmed following the behavior to be decreased (Matson & Taras, 1989). In addition, reinforcement-oriented token economies can be developed within the inpatient setting and then adapted for use in the child's home environment (see Kazdin, 1977, for a comprehensive review of token economies). Care should be exercised in adapting token economies that are consistent with the diminished cognitive capacities, limited reading ability, and decreased attention span typical of the patient with mental retardation.

Schedules of positive reinforcement are often effective either to reinforce the absence of the target behavior, as in *differential reinforcement of other behavior* (DRO), and targets the performance of appropriate or prosocial behavior as in *differential reinforcement of incompatible behavior* (DRI). *Contingency contracting* is a verbally mediated approach to managing behavioral goals that provides positive and/or negative consequences to produce and maintain the goals. However, it is typically used with children having a sufficient core of cognitive skills (i.e., borderline to mild mental retardation).

Direct decelerative procedures often produce more rapid and complete suppression of specific maladaptive behavior if combined with positive reinforcement procedures. It is very important to build and maintain prosocial skills, or maladaptive behavior may be only temporarily controlled. Decelerative procedures should always be combined with skill building and habilitation-oriented instruction to provide a complete treatment plan. Finally, treatment of oppositional- and conduct-disordered children should include parent training and educational programming in order to teach caregivers appropriate discipline techniques, such as differential attention and planned ignoring (i.e., *extinction* of negative attention seeking behavior) and effective decelerative procedures (e.g., time out from positive reinforcement).

Convincing evidence (Patterson, 1982; Patterson, Dishion, & Bank, 1984) has shown that many parents of antisocial children actually demonstrate a skill deficit in the effective use of punishment, tending to be inconsistent, arbitrary, and poorly controlled in its use. This is particularly pertinent in treatment of children with mental retardation since ag-gressive behavior is a common problem. Baker (1983) describes a successful comprehensive parent-training model for use with parents of handicapped children. In training younger children, prosocial skills can be developed by focusing upon independent play, positive peer interaction, and assertive verbal communication of needs, desires, and intentions.

Incorporating school-based treatment programming is an important aspect of continuity of care and discharge planning. This should detail needed changes in the child's Individualized Education Plan (IEP) that emerge as a result of psychiatric hospitalization or treatment. Collaboration with school authorities and amending the IEP are not just a matter of passing on relevant psychiatric recommendations, but also may require a careful analysis of instructional approaches used in the school. This is because a major source of negative reinforcement for problem behavior, and a major source of stress for the child in school, involve the avoidance of difficult or inappropriate task demands. These problems are amenable to improvement through the use of better instructional techniques (Huguenin, Weidenman, & Mulick, 1991) and become increasingly important because the child is involved in a greater range of settings, such as classrooms, recreational programs, and general community activities.

Medication

The use of medication is often a primary treatment approach for inpatient psychiatric settings. While treatment based upon medication alone is of limited value in terms of reducing symptomatic behavior or improving the general adaptation of persons with mental retardation (Aman & Singh, 1988), the most important clinical issues surround the diagnosis of symptoms and the use of medications that specifically address these symptoms. Systematic and well-controlled research simply has not kept up with practice and is still so sparse that few firm conclusions can be drawn. However, a brief overview of this area will be presented.

Antisocial behavior and aggression remain among the most common reasons for prescribing psychotropic medication to children with mental retardation. Neuroleptics (e.g., chlorpromazine and thioridazine) have been frequently prescribed in a maintenance fashion for aggressive behavior, especially in long-term community residential programs and institutions (Buck & Sprague, 1989; Chadsey-Rush & Sprague, 1989). Despite this, neuroleptics may have their greatest utility only as a very short-term approach to manage an acute problem of aggressive, destructive, or hyperactive behavior in children with mental retardation. Stimulants (see Gadow, 1985) have been used with some success, but clinical response may depend upon the level of the child's cognitive functioning (Aman, 1982). Lithium has been receiving more and more attention in the psychiatric literature and is increasingly used in treatment settings for aggressive behavior, as well as for bipolar disorders, for which it remains the primary medication of choice (Gualtieri, 1989; Sovner & Hurley, 1981). While some clinical improvement has been noted when lithium is used in children (Linter, 1987), diagnostic clarity with respect to manic episodes is often overlooked. Diagnostic clarity is also appropriate in treating anxiety and affective disorders. Although a variety of medications, such as buspirone, desipramine, and imipramine, are commonly used in treating such disorders, there is a relative lack of data on their effectiveness in children with mental retardation. A strict empirical or hypothesis-testing approach is still required with each patient in view of the current state of knowledge.

Novel pharmacologic approaches are sometimes used in treating psychiatric disorders in persons with mental retardation; for example, carbamazepine has been reported as an effective treatment for some forms of affective disorders (Sovner, 1988). Research has also suggested that adrenergic receptor antagonists are helpful in treating some types of aggressive, hyperactive, and self-injurious behaviors. A reduction of hyperactive and impulsive behaviors in children with autism was reported using chlonidine, an alpha-2 blocker (Jaselskis, Cook, Fletcher, & Leventhal, 1992), and research suggests that propranolol, a beta blocker, has been effective in treating some types of aggressive and self-injurious behaviors (Ratey, 1991). However, a lack of systematic research has precluded a definite role for this class of medication (Arnold & Aman, 1991). Finally, recent research suggests that opioid antagonists may have beneficial effects for both self-injurious behavior (Sandman, 1983; Sandman, Barron, & Coleman, 1990), and symptoms of autism (Panksepp & Lensing, 1991; Panksepp, Lensing, Leboyer, & Bouvard, in press).

Overall, caution should be employed in prescribing any psychotropic medications because of the general lack of controlled, systematic research in pharmacotherapy among children with mental retardation. The confounding roles of environmental variables and problems associated with diagnostic clarity indicate a need for inpatient clinicians to conduct a thorough assessment of the presenting problems as well as obtaining baseline data prior to the introduction of medication. A comprehensive text on psychopharmacology issues in developmental disabilities by Aman and Singh (1988) is recommended to readers interested in this area. In addition, Werry and Aman (1993) have written a recent practitioner-oriented guide to psychoactive drugs for children and adolescents that may be helpful.

The Role of Discharge Planning

The most important outcome of psychiatric hospitalization for the child with mental retardation should be a detailed follow-up and *discharge plan*. Instructions regarding medication monitoring should be clearly stated so that primary-care physicians can adequately manage the inevitable number of questions that may occur following hospitalization. Also, the services of a behavioral psychologist from the inpatient program may help with both transition and linkage services (Helsel & McGonigle, 1992). This will provide some help in matching intervention plans with community resources as well as with the characteristics of the child's regular living environment. For the child living in a residential-care program or institution, caregivers must also understand specific recommendations so that resources can be assigned and planning can occur that is consistent with the child's treatment needs. The discharge plan should include professional therapies (e.g., speech, therapy, occupational therapy), support services (e.g., case management, vocational training, expansion of leisure-time alternatives), and, in some instances, a recommendation for specific changes in the child's living environment. In some cases, inpatient clinicians will be able to consult with professionals familiar with the child's home community to address the realities of continuity of care and follow-up services. The discharge plan should include a concise, written set of recommendations that both the parents and/or caregivers are to follow. This will assure that treatment and important follow-up recommendations are not misinterpreted and are completely understood.

Commitment to a continuum of psychiatric treatment services for children with mental retardation would be a worthy societal goal. Unfortunately, it remains as yet unrealized. The options required would include a carefully programmed diagnostic-treatment environment with both day and residential placement capacity. This could be a useful vehicle following inpatient treatment and also could be used to provide respite or crisis intervention services to avoid the need for psychiatric inpatient care for all but the most serious of presenting concerns. Such a facility would allow for the deceleration of dangerous behavior and the development of a long-term plan for prosocial and adaptive-skill development in a sheltered environment where unplanned stressors can be minimized. Such a controlled setting makes it possible to document the effect of treatment, which is often helpful in obtaining follow-up services, and could also provide emergency services that might avoid the need for inpatient care in some instances. Follow-up services must include well-supervised residential options, vocational and recreational options, educational services, and flexible staff deployment to provide consultation and actual intervention in a variety of community settings. These are the minimum structural requirements for planned generalization of the learning achieved in any positive response to comprehensive treatment (e.g., see comments on generalization and maintenance in Schroeder, Kanoy, et al., 1982).

ACTUAL TREATMENT

Since few inpatient psychiatric programs are specifically designed to address the multiple needs of the child with mental retardation, an overreliance upon medication as a primary treatment focus is likely to occur. The authors have presented many potential approaches that have been effective in treating children with mental retardation and cautioned readers about an overreliance upon medications to treat the psychiatric problems of children with mental retardation. However, the constraints upon time and the ability of many psychiatric programs to effectively manage these forms of treatment described is very limited. In spite of this, most parents and caregivers often have high expectations regarding psychiatric treatment and need to clearly understand the role of psychiatric hospitalization in a child's overall plan of care and services available. Too often, parents and caregivers bring unrealistic expectations about the outcome of a psychiatric hospitalization based upon, perhaps, a belief in the presence of underlying psychopathology. Unfortunately, diagnostic clarity generally is elusive among many children with mental retardation referred to psychiatric care. Thus, the inpatient clinician must strive to give effective explanations of treatment recommendations that are clearly based upon assessment data to assure that follow-up services can be planned and monitored.

CASE EXAMPLE: TREATMENT

This case involved an adolescent nonambulatory female with profound mental retardation. The treatment intervention described combined both pharmacological and behavioral strategies presented in a systematic and sequential manner in order to minimize potential confounds in evaluating treatment outcome. First, an antidepressant medication was introduced with no alteration in behavioral or other programming. Data on sleep and eating patterns and activity level, and scatter-plot data on the frequency of screaming, crying, and tantrum episodes were obtained from direct-care staff. Data from the initial assessment phase provided baseline data. Follow-up assessment revealed an improvement in appetite and a decline in disrupted sleep, suggesting a moderate positive response to the antidepressant medication. However, irritability and tantrum episodes remained consistent with the baseline assessment. With medication held constant, a behavioral treatment intervention was then implemented. This comprised one or two teaching sessions per day during which the patient received reinforcement for independent play and the absence of crying or screaming behavior. Reinforcers consisted of access to preferred objects and time in her wheelchair, a preferred location. At the first sign of agitation, the patient was removed from the wheelchair, and all objects were withheld until calm behavior occurred. At that time, objects were reintroduced and she was assisted back to her wheelchair after a short interval of calm behavior. Initially, this was only 1 to 2 minutes, but was systematically increased during the teaching sessions with a target goal of 30 minutes of out-of-chair calm behavior. This goal was reached in 12 sessions, and, at that point, the treatment intervention was transferred to the unit environment and implemented by direct-care staff. The intervention continued concurrent with daily teaching sessions by behavioral treatment staff. Data-based assessment of the frequency and severity of behavior was continued to determine necessary habilitation program changes. In addition, the antidepressant medication was continued with good maintenance of improved sleep and eating patterns.

Discharge Planning Considerations

Routine follow-up regarding general medical care for children admitted to inpatient care is generally adequate. However, linkage with primary physicians often does not occur with any regularity. Parents or caregivers often resort to explaining the results of treatment, and written detailed discharge plans are rare. The lack of experience of psychiatric personnel in effectively addressing the issues of children with mental retardation hinders treatment outcome. It is the interaction between behavioral, social, and environmental variables that comprises the most efficient explanation of psychopathology in persons with mental retardation (Matson, 1985). Thus, inpatient programs that maintain personnel with skills in each area will have the greatest likelihood of success with these patients.

SUMMARY

The assessment and treatment of mental disorders among children with mental retardation are complex tasks that requires flexibility, creativity, and an understanding of the multiple determinants of psychopathology in persons with mental retardation. Fortunately, many children referred for psychiatric inpatient care may already have an extensive array of service providers who can assist the inpatient program in the assessment and treatment process and can assure continuity of care and appropriate follow-up. The authors have argued that the assessment and treatment of these children comprise a strong behavioral focus, especially for those cases that present with a mixed pattern of symptoms in which diagnostic clarity is poor or perhaps even nonexistent. Overreliance upon traditional diagnostic schema in assessment and treatment may minimize the complexity of the problems exhibited by these children. Thus, it is recommended that diagnosis be primarily employed to develop treatment hypotheses that can be systematically evaluated in detail during the hospitalization period. Treatment planning should emphasize a discharge plan in order to account for inherent problems in generalizing and maintaining therapeutic gains and to assure that follow-up services are appropriate to the characteristics of the child's community and living environment.

Caregivers of children with mental retardation should recognize that preventative methods are important in alleviating the development of psychiatric disorders, as well as their debilitating impact. While preventative methods can be generic to all children and families, they are perhaps even more important for children with mental retardation and their families. They include (a) early parent guidance and support groups that address approaches to be used in managing the developmental and emotional needs of children with mental retardation; (b) social-skills training for children, as well as social opportunities with both normal peers and other children with mental retardation; (c) crisis intervention services for children comprised of case management or mental health professionals with specific training in psychiatric approaches for this population; and (d) adequate attention to good medical care, including diet, that may alleviate problems stemming from physiological causes.

Further work in the training of mental health professionals is needed to fully address the complicated needs of these children (Menolascino & Fleisher, 1992). The inpatient treatment program has the potential to tap the resources and personnel necessary to bring more attention to the psychiatric needs of children with mental retardation. Collaborative efforts of psychiatrists, physicians, behavioral psychologist, and other specialty areas are critically needed. The existing university teaching hospitals, in particular, may be one of the best resources to begin this process. Students, interns, and residents must include specific training in serving this population so that community-based efforts can expand critically needed services to this population.

REFERENCES

Achenbach, T., & Edelbrock, C. (1983). *Manual for the Child Behavior Checklist and Revised Child Behavior Profile*. Burlington, VT: University of Vermont, Department of Psychiatry.

Aman, M. G., (1982). Stimulant drug effects in developmental disorders and hyperactivity—toward a resolution of disparate findings. *Journals of Autism and Developmental Disorders, 12*, 385–398.

Aman, M. G. (1991). *Assessing psychopathology and behavior problems in persons with mental retardation: A review of available instruments*. (DHHS Publication No. ADM 91–1712). Rockville, MD: U.S. Department of Health and Human Services.

Aman, M. G., Richmond, G., Stewart, A. W., Bell, J. C., & Kissel, R. C. (1987). The Aberrant Behavior Checklist: Factor structure and the effect of subject variable in American and New Zealand facilities. *American Journal of Mental Deficiency, 91*, 570–578.

Aman, M. G., & Singh, N. N. (Eds.). (1988). *Psychopharmacology of the developmental disabilities*. New York: Springer-Verlag.

American Association on Mental Retardation (1992). *Mental retardation—definition, classification and systems of support*. Washington, DC: Author.

American Psychiatric Association. (1980). *Diagnostic and statistical manual of mental disorders* (3rd ed.). Washington, DC: Author.

American Psychiatric Association. (1987). *Diagnostic and statistical manual of mental disorders* (3rd ed., rev.). Washington DC: Author.

American Psychiatric Association (1993). *DSM-IV draft criteria*. Washington, DC: Author.

Ando, H., & Yosimura, I. (1978). Prevalence of maladaptive behavior in retarded children as a function of IQ and age. *Journal of Abnormal Child Psychology, 6,* 345–349.

Arnold, L., & Aman, M. (1991). Beta blockers in mental retardation and developmental disorders. *Journal of Child and Adolescent Psychopharmacology, 1,* 361–373.

Baker, B.L. (1983). Parents as teachers: Issues in training. In J.A. Mulick & S.M. Pueschel (Eds.), *Parent-professional partnerships in developmental disability services* (pp. 55–74). Cambridge, MA: Academic Guild.

Baroff, G.S. (1986). *Mental Retardation—nature, cause, and management* (2nd ed.). Washington DC: Hemisphere.

Benavidez, D. A., & Matson, J. L. (1993). Assessment of depression in mentally retarded adolescents. *Research in Developmental Disabilities, 14,* 179–188.

Benson, B. (1985). Behavior disorders and mental retardation: Associations with age, sex, and level of functioning in an outpatient clinic sample. *Applied Research in Mental Retardation, 6,* 71–78.

Bernstein, N. (1988). The mentally retarded person. In A. M. Nichols (Ed.), *The new Harvard guide to psychiatry* (pp. 681–684). Cambridge, MA: Belnap Press.

Borthwick-Duffy, S., Eyman, R. (1990). Who are the dually diagnosed? *American Journal on Mental Retardation, 94*(6), 586–595.

Bregman, J. (1991). Current developments in the understanding of mental retardation: Part II: Psychopathology. *Journal of the American Academy of Child and Adolescent Psychiatry, 30,* 861–872.

Bregman, J. D., Leckman, J. F., & Ort, S. I. (1988). Fragile X syndrome: Genetic predisposition to psychopathology. *Journal of Autism and Developmental Disorders, 18,* 343–354.

Buck, J. A., & Sprague, R. L. (1989). Psychotropic medication of mentally retarded residents in community long-term care facilities. *American Journal on Mental Retardation, 93,* 618–623.

Chadsey-Rush, J., & Sprague, R. L. (1989). Maladaptive behaviors associated with neuroleptic drug maintenance. *American Journal on Mental Retardation, 93,* 607–617.

Chandler, M., Gualtieri, T., & Fahs, J. (1988). Other psychotropic drugs: Stimulants, antidepressants, the anxioloytics, and lithium carbonate. In M. Aman & N. Singh (Eds.), *Psychopharmacology of the developmental disabilities* (pp. 111–132). New York: Springer-Verlag.

Conners, K. (1969). A teacher rating scale for use in drug studies with children. *American Journal of Psychiatry, 126,* 884.

Crnic, K. A. (1988). Mental retardation. In E. Mash & L. Terdal (Eds.), *Behavioral assessment of childhood disorders* (pp. 265–302). New York: Guilford Press.

Dosen, A. (1984). Depressive conditions in mentally handicapped children. *Acta Paedopsychiatrica, 50,* 29 -40.

Dura, J. R., Mulick, J. A., & Myers, E. G. (1988). Prevalence of multiple problem behaviors in institutionalized nonambulatory profoundly mentally retarded children. *Behavioral Residential Treatment, 3,* 239–246.

Favell, J., & Reid, D. (1988). Generalizing and maintaining improvement in problem behavior. In R. Horner, G. Dunlap, & R. Koegel (Eds.) *Generalization and maintenance: Life style changes in applied settings* (pp. 171–196). Baltimore: Brookes.

Feinstein, C., Kaminer, Y., Barrett, R., & Tylenda, B. (1988). The assessment of mood and affect in developmentally disabled children and adolescents: The Emotional Disorders Rating Scale. *Research in Developmental Disabilities, 9,* 109–121.

Forehand, R., & Baumeister, A. (1976). Deceleration of aberrant behavior among retarded individuals. In M. Hersen, R. M. Eisler, & P. M. Miller (Eds.) *Progress in Behavior Modification* (Vol. 2) New York: Academic Press.

Foxx, R., & Azrin, N. (1973). The elimination of autistic self-stimulatory behavior by overcorrection. *Journal of Applied Behavior Analysis, 6,* 1–14.

Foxx, R., & Shapiro, S. (1978). The timeout ribbon: A nonexclusionary timeout procedure. *Journal of Applied Behavior Analysis, 11,* 125–136.

Gadow, K. D. (1985). Prevalence and efficacy of stimulant drug use with mentally retarded children and youth. *Psychopharmacology Bulletin, 21,* 291–303.

Garrard, S. D. (1983). Community health issues. In J. L. Matson & J. A. Mulick (Eds.), *Handbook of mental retardation,* (pp. 289–305). New York: Pergamon Press.

Groden, G., Pueschel, S., Domingue, D., & Deignan, L. (1982). Behavioral/emotional problems in mentally retarded children and youth. *Psychological Reports, 51,* 143–146.

Grossman, H. J. (1983). *Classification in mental retardation.* Washington, DC: American Association on Mental Deficiency.

Gualtieri, C. (1989). Antidepressant drugs and lithium. In American Psychiatric Association, *Treatments of psychiatric disorders: A task force report of the American Psychiatric Association* (Vol. 1, pp. 77–85). Washington, DC: Author.

Gunsett, R. P., Mulick, J. A., Fernald, W. B., & Martin, J. L. (1989). Brief report: Indications for medical screening prior to behavioral programming for severely and profoundly mentally retarded clients. *Journal of Autism and Developmental Disorders, 19,* 167–172.

Harris, V., & McHale, S. (1989). Family life problems, daily caregiving activities, and the psychological well-being of mothers of mentally retarded children. *American Journal on Mental Retardation, 94,* 231–239.

Helsel, W., & McGonigle, J. (1992). Children and adolescents with mental retardation in acute inpatient psychiatric care. *Behavioral Residential Treatment, 7,* 121–144.

Hersen, M., & Bellack, A. (1978). Staff training and consultation. In M. Hersen & A. Bellack (Eds.), *Behavior therapy in the psychiatric setting* (pp. 58–87). Baltimore: Williams & Wilkens.

Hill, B. K., & Bruinicks, R. H. (1984). Maladaptive behavior of mentally retarded individuals in residential facilities. *American Journal of Mental Deficiency, 88,* 380–387.

Holroyd, J. (1974). The Questionnaire on Resources and Stress: An instrument to measure family response to a handicapped family member. *Journal of Community Psychology, 2,* 92–94.

Horner, R., & Billingsley, F. (1988). The effect of competing behavior on the generalization and maintenance of adaptive behavior in applied settings. In R. Horner, G. Dunlap, & R. Koegel (Eds.), *Generalization and maintenance: Life style changes in applied settings* (pp. 197–220). Baltimore: Brookes.

Huguenin, N. H., & Mulick, J. A. (1981). Nonexclusionary timeout: Maintenance of appropriate behavior across settings. *Applied Research in Mental Retardation, 2,* 55–67.

Huguenin, N. H., Werdenman, L. E., & Mulick, J. A. (1991). Programmed instruction. In J. Matson & J. Mulick (Eds.), *Handbook of mental retardation* (2nd ed.) (pp. 451–467). New York: Pergamon Press.

Jacobson, J. (1982). Problem behavior and psychiatric impairment within a developmentally disabled population: I: Behavior frequency. *Applied Research in Mental Retardation, 3,* 121–139.

Jacobson, J. (1990). Assessing the prevalence of psychiatric disorders in a developmentally disabled population. In *Assessment of behavior problems in persons with mental retardation living in the community* (pp. 19–70) (DHHS Publication No. ADM 90–1642). Rockville, MD: U.S. Department of Health and Human Services.

Jacobson, J., & Ackerman, L. (1989). Psychological services for persons with mental retardation and psychiatric impairments. *Mental Retardation, 27,* 33 -36.

Jaselskis, C., Cook, E., Fletcher, K., & Leventhal, B. (1992). Clonidine treatment of hyperactive and impulsive children with autistic disorder. *Journal of Clinical Psychopharmacology, 12*, 322–327.

Kazdin, A. E. (1977). *The token economy: A review and evaluation.* New York: Plenum Press.

Kobe, F., & Hammer, D. (1994). Parenting stress and depression in children with mental retardation and developmental disabilities. *Research in Developmental Disabilities, 15* (3), 209–221.

Kolko, D. (1988). Daily ratings on a child psychiatric unit: Psychometric evaluation of the Child Behavior Rating Form. *Journal of the American Academy of Child and Adolescent Psychiatry, 27*, 126–132.

Kovacs, M. (1981). Rating scales to assess depression in school-age children. *Acta Paedopsychiatrica, 46*, 305–315.

Kovacs, M., & Beck, A. (1977). An empirical clinical approach towards a definition of childhood depression. In J. Schulterbrandt & A. Raskin (Eds.), *Depression in children: Diagnosis, treatment, and conceptual models in children* (pp. 1–25). New York: Raven Press.

Linter, C. (1987). Short-cycle manic-depressive psychosis in a mental handicapped child without family history. *British Journal of Psychiatry, 151*, 554–555.

Matson, J. L. (1982). The treatment of behavioral characteristics of depression in mentally retarded. *Behavior Therapy, 13*, 209–218.

Matson, J. L. (1983). Depression in the mentally retarded: Toward a conceptual analysis of diagnosis. In M. Hersen, R. Eisler, & P. Miller (Eds.), *Progress in behavior modification* (Vol. 15, pp. 59–79). New York: Academic Press.

Matson, J. L. (1985). Biosocial theory of psychopathology: A three by three factor model. *Applied Research in Mental Retardation, 5*, 199–227.

Matson, J. L. (1988a). Balanced treatment and assessment approaches. In J. Stark, F. Menolascino, M. Albarelli, & V. Gray (Eds.), *Mental retardation and mental health: Classification, diagnosis, treatment, services* (pp.197–202). New York: Springer-Verlag.

Matson, J. L. (1988b). *Manual for the Psychopathology Inventory for Mentally Retarded Adults.* Orland Park, IL: International Diagnostic Systems.

Matson, J. L., & Barrett, R. (1982). *Psychopathology in the mentally retarded.* New York: Grune & Stratton.

Matson, J. L., Barrett, R., & Helsel, W. (1988). Depression in mentally retarded children. *Research in Developmental Disabilities, 9*, 39–46.

Matson, J. L., Rotatori, A., & Helsel, W. (1983). Development of a rating scale to measure social skills in children: The Matson Evaluation of Social Skills with Youngsters (MESSY). *Behaviour Research and Therapy, 21* (4), 335–340.

Matson, J. L., & Taras, M. (1989). A 20-year review of punishment and alternative methods to treat problem behaviors in developmentally delayed persons. *Research in Developmental Disabilities, 10*, 85–104.

Matson, J. L., & McCartney, J. R. (Eds.). (1981). *Handbook of behavior modification with the mentally retarded.* New York: Plenum Press.

McKinney, B., & Peterson, R. (1987). Predictors of stress in parents of developmentally disabled children. *Journal of Pediatric Psychology, 12* 133–149.

Menolascino, F., & Fleisher, M. (1992). Training psychiatric residents in the diagnosis and treatment of mental illness in mentally retarded persons. *Hospital and Community Psychiatry, 43*, 500–503.

Menolascino F. & Fletcher, R. (1989). *Mental retardation and mental illness: Assessment, treatment, and service for the dually diagnosed.* Lexington, MA: Lexington Books.

Menolascino, F., & Stark, J. (1984). *Handbook of mental illness in the mentally retarded.* New York: Plenum Press.

Mulick, J. Hammer, D., & Dura, J. (1991). Assessment and management of antisocial and hyperactive behavior. In J. Matson & J. Mulick (Eds.), *Handbook for mental retardation* (2nd ed.) (pp. 397–412). New York: Pergamon Press.

Mulick, J., & Meinhold, P. (1994). Developmental disorders and broad effects of the environment on learning and treatment effectiveness. In E. Schopler & G. R. Mesibov (Eds.), *Behavioral issues in autism* (pp. 97–126). New York: Plenum Press.

Mulick, J. A., & Schroeder, S. R. (1980). Research relating to management of antisocial behavior in mentally retarded persons. *The Psychological Record*, *30*, 397–417.

Nezu, C. M., Nezu, A. M., & Gill-Weiss, M. J. (1992). *Psychopathology in persons with mental retardation: Clinical guidelines for assessment and treatment.* Champaign, IL: Research Press.

Nihira, K., Foster, R., Shellhaas, M., & Leland, H. (1969). *Adaptive Behavior Scales: Manual.* Washington, DC: American Association of Mental Deficiency.

Nihira, K., Price-Williams, D. R., & White, J. F. (1988). Social competence and maladaptive behavior of people with dual diagnosis. *Journal of the Multihandicapped Person*, *1*, 185–199.

Orr, R., Cameron, S., & Day, D. (1991). Coping with stress in families of children who have mental retardation: an evaluation of the double ABCX model. *American Journal of Mental Retardation*, *95*, 444–450.

Pankesepp, J., & Lensing, P. (1991). Brief report: A synopsis of an open-trial of naltrexone treatment of autism with four children. *Journal of Autism and Developmental Disabilities*, *21*, 243–249.

Pankesepp, J., Lensing, P., Leboyer, M. & Bouvard, M. P. (in press). Naltrexone and other potential new pharmacological treatments of autism. *Brain Dysfunction*.

Patterson, G. (1982). *Coercive family process.* Eugene, OR: Castalia.

Patterson, G., Dishion, T., & Bank, L. (1984). Family interaction: A process model of deviancy training. *Aggressive Behavior*, *10*, 253–267.

Pawlarcyzk, D., & Beckwith, B. (1987). Depressive symptoms displayed by persons with mental retardation. *Mental Retardation*, *25*, 325–330.

Philips, I. (1971). Psychopathology and mental retardation. In F. Menolascino (Ed.), *Psychiatric aspects of the diagnosis and treatment of mental retardation* (pp. 39–56). Seattle, WA: Special Child Publications.

Philips, I., & Williams, N. (1975). Psychopathology and mental retardation: A study of 100 mentally retarded children: I. Psychopathology. *American Journal of Psychiatry*, *132*, 1265–1271.

Ratey, J., (1991). B-blockers as a primary treatment for aggression and self-injury in the developmentally disabled. In J. Ratey (Ed.,), *Mental retardation: Developing pharmacotherapies* (pp. 51–81). Washington, DC: American Psychiatric Press.

Reid, A. (1981). *The psychiatry of mental handicap.* Oxford, England: Blackwell Scientific Publications.

Reiss, S. (1988). *Manual for the Reiss Screen for Maladaptive Behavior.* Orland Park, IL: International Diagnostic Systems.

Reiss, S., Levitan, G. W., & McNally, R. (1982). Emotionally disturbed mentally retarded people: An underserved population. *American Psychologist*, *37*, 361–367.

Reiss, S., Levitan, G. W., & Szyszko, J. (1982). Emotional disturbance and mental retardation: Diagnostic overshadowing. *American Journal of Mental Deficiency*, *86*, 567–574.

Reiss S.., & Szyszko, J. (1983). Diagnostic overshadowing and professional experience with retarded people. *American Journal of Mental Deficiency*, *87*, 392–402.

Reiss, S., & Valenti-Hein, D. (in press). Development of a psychopathology rating scale for children with mental retardation. *Journal of Consulting and Clinical Psychology*.

Repp, A. C., & Brulie, A. R. (1981). Reducing aggressive behavior of mentally retarded persons. In J. L. Matson & J. R. McCartney (Eds.), *Handbook of behavior modification with the mentally retarded* (pp. 177–210). New York: Plenum Press.

Reynolds, W., & Miller, K. (1985). Depression and learned helplessness in mental retarded and non-mentally retarded adolescents: An initial investigation. *Applied Research in Mental Retardation*, *6*, 295–306.

Rojahn, J., Borthwick-Duffy, S., & Jacobson, J. (1993). The association between psychiatric diagnoses and severe behavior problems in mental retardation. *Annals of Clinical Psychiatry*, *5*, 163–170.

Rojahn, J., Hammer, D., & Marshburn, E. (1993). Mental retardation in children. In R. T. Ammerman and M. Hersen (Eds.), *Handbook of behavior therapy with children and adolescents: Developmental and longitudinal perspectives* (pp. 331 -347). New York: Allyn & Bacon.

Russell, A. T. (1988). The association between mental retardation and psychiatric disorder: Epidemiological issues. In J. Stark, F. Menolascino, M. Albarelli, & V. Gray, (Eds.), *Mental retardation and mental health: Classification, diagnosis, treatment, services* (pp. 41–49). New York: Springer-Verlag.

Russell, A. T. & Tanguay, P. E. (1981). Mental illness and mental retardation: Cause or coincidence? *American Journal of Mental Deficiency*, *85*, 570–573.

Rutter, M. (1989). Isle of Wight revisited: Twenty-five years of psychiatric epidemiology. *Journal of the American Academy of Child and Adolescent Psychiatry*, *28*, 633–653.

Rutter, M., Graham, P. & Yule, W. (1970). *A neuropsychiatric study in childhood*. London: Spastics International Medical Publications.

Rutter, M., Tizzard, J., Yule, W., Graham, P., & Whitmore, K. (1976). Isle of Wight studies, 1964–74. *Psychological Medicine*, *6*, 313 -332.

Sandman, C. A. (1983). Naltrexone attenuates self-abusive behavior in developmentally delayed clients. *Applied Research in Mental Retardation*, *4*, 5–11.

Sandman, C. A., Barron, J.L., & Colman, H. (1990). An orally administered opiate blocker, naltrexone, attenuates self-injurious behavior. *American Journal on Mental Retardation*, *95*, 93–102.

Schroeder, S. R. (1989). Behavior therapy. In American Psychiatric Association, *Treatments of psychiatric disorders: A task force report of the American Psychiatric Association*(Vol. 1, Sec. 1, pp. 111–129). Washington, DC: American Psychiatric Association.

Schroeder, S. R., Kanoy, J. R., Mulick, J. A., Rojahn, J., Thios, S. J., Stephens, M., & Hawk, B. (1982). Environmental antecedents which affect management and maintenance of programs for self-injurious behavior. In J. C. Hollis & C. E. Myers (Eds.), *Life-threatening behavior* (Monograph No. 5). Washington, DC: American Association on Mental Deficiency.

Sigelman, C. K., Budd, E. C., Winer, J. L., Schoenrock, C. M., & Martin, P. W. (1982). Evaluating alternative techniques of questioning mentally retarded persons. *American Journal of Mental Deficiency*, *86*, 511–518.

Sovner, R. (1988). Behavioral psychopharmacology: A new subspecialty. In J. Stark, F. Menolascino, M. Albarelli, & V. Gray (Eds.), *Mental retardation and mental health: Classification, diagnosis, treatment, services* (pp. 229–242). New York: Springer-Verlag.

Sovner, R., & Hurley, A. (1981). The management of chronic behavior disorders in mentally retarded adults with lithium carbonate. *Journal of Nervous and Mental Disease*, *169*, 191–195.

Sovner, R., & Hurley, P. (1982). Diagnosing depression in the mentally retarded. *Psychiatric Aspects of Mental Retardation*, *1*, 1–3.

Sovner, R. & Hurley, P. (1983). Do the mentally retarded suffer from affective illness? *Archives of General Psychiatry*, *40*, 61–67.

Sovner, R. & Hurley, A. (1986). Four factors affecting the diagnosis of psychiatric disorders in mentally retarded persons. *Psychiatric Aspects of Mental Retardation Reviews*, *5*, 45–49.

Sovner, R., & Hurley, A. (1990). Assessment tools which facilitate psychiatric evaluations and treatment. *The Habilitative Mental Health Newsletter*, *9*, 91–98.

Sovner, R., & Lowry, M. (1990). A behavioral methodology for diagnosing affective disorders in individuals with mental retardation. *The Habilitative Mental Health Newsletter, 9*, 55–64.

Sparrow, S. S., Balla, D. E. & Chicchetti, D. V. (1984). *The Vineland Adaptive Behavior Scales.* Circle Pines, MN: American Guidance Service.

Spengler, P., Strohmer, D., & Prout, H. (1990). Testing the robustness of the diagnostic overshadowing bias. *American Journal on Mental Retardation, 95*, 204–214.

Szymanski, L., & Crocker, A. (1989). Mental retardation. In H. Kaplan & B. Sadock (Eds.), *Comprehensive textbook of psychiatry: Vol. 2* (5th ed.) (pp. 1728–1771). Baltimore: Williams & Wilkins.

Tanguay, P., & Szymanski, L. (1980). Training of mental health professionals in mental retardation. In L. S. Szymanski & P. E. Tanguay (Eds.), *Emotional disorders in mentally retarded persons: Assessment, treatment, and consultation* (pp. 19–28). Baltimore: University Park Press.

Taras, M., Matson, J., & Leary, C. (1988). Training social interpersonal skills in two autistic children. *Journal of Behavior Therapy and Experimental Psychiatry, 19*, 275–280.

Thompson, T. (1988). Prevention and early treatment of behavior disorders of children and youth with retardation and autism. In J. Stark, F. Menolascino, M. Albarelli, & V. Gray (Eds.), *Mental retardation and mental health: Classification, diagnosis, treatment, services* (pp. 98–105). New York: Springer-Verlag.

Touchette, P, MacDonald, R., & Langer, S. (1985). A scatter plot for identifying stimulus control of behavior. *Journal of Applied Behavior Analysis, 18*, 343–351.

Trad, P. (1987). Handicapping conditions as a risk factor for infant and childhood depression. In P. Trad (Ed.), *Infant and childhood depression—Developmental factors (p*p. 310–342). New York: Wiley.

Varley, C., & Furukawa, M. (1991). Psychopathology in young children with developmental disabilities. *Children's Health Care, 19*, 86–92.

Weisz, J. (1979). Perceived control and learned helplessness among mentally retarded and nonretarded children: A developmental analysis. *Developmental Psychology, 15*, 311–319.

Werry, J. S., & Aman, M. G., (Eds.). (1993). *Practitioner's guide to psychoactive drugs for children and adolescents.* New York: Plenum Press.

Whitman, T. L. Scibak, J. W., & Reid, D. H. (1983). *Behavior modification with the severely and profoundly retarded.* New York: Academic Press.

CHAPTER 9

Attention-Deficit/Hyperactivity Disorder

BETSY HOZA, GARY VALLANO, AND WILLIAM E. PELHAM, JR.

DESCRIPTION OF THE PROBLEM

Attention-deficit/hyperactivity Disorder (ADHD) is the most commonly diagnosed behavior disorder of childhood and encompasses a heterogeneous group of children. The core symptoms of the disorder are inattention, impulsivity, and hyperactivity, which may be manifested in a variety of specific behavioral difficulties. While the specific behavioral symptom lists that define the disorder have varied slightly from one version of the standard diagnostic system to the next (e.g., *Diagnostic and Statistical Manual of Mental Disorders,* 3rd edition, [DSM-III] [American Psychiatric Association, 1980], and the revised 3rd edition [DSM-III-R] [American Psychiatric Association, 1987]), the major clinical features of the disorder have remained constant. In short, children with the disorder display: (a) a variety of acting-out behaviors indicative of poor impulse control, (b) an impaired ability to pay attention to and/or complete age-appropriate tasks or activities, and (c) excessive motor activity.

As the evolution of the diagnostic system evidences, all children with the disorder may not show difficulties in all these symptom areas. In the DSM-III system, children were required to display problems in all of these areas for a diagnosis of Attention-Deficit Disorder with Hyperactivity to be made, and children who did not display symptoms of hyperactivity were given a separate diagnosis of Attention-Deficit Disorder without Hyperactivity. With increasing awareness of the heterogeneity of the disorder, any 8 of 14 listed symptoms warranted a DSM-III-R diagnosis of ADHD, regardless of the distribution of inattention, impulsivity, and hyperactivity symptoms. In the new DSM-IV diagnostic system (American Psychiatric Association, 1994), the disorder is conceptualized as bidimensional, based on recent empirical studies (Lahey, Pelham, et al., 1988; Pelham, Evans, Gnagy, & Greenslade, 1992; Pelham, Gnagy, Greenslade, & Milich, 1992). Criteria defining the Inattention and Hyperactivity-Impulsivity dimensions under the DSM-IV system are found in Table 9.1. As this table indicates, children are categorized into subtypes of ADHD, including *Predominantly Hyperactive-Impulsive Type*, *Predominantly Inattentive Type*, or *Combined Type*. Hence, despite the fact that the labels for the disorder have changed somewhat as the diagnostic system has evolved, the heterogeneous nature of the disorder has not.

In recent years, the disorder has received increasing attention, largely due to a memorandum issued by the United States Department of Education in September of 1991 (Davila, Williams, & MacDonald, 1991) to clarify federal law with regard to the educational rights of children with attentional problems. Whereas, prior to this date, the legal status and rights of children with the disorder were unspecified, often allowing these children to slip through the cracks of the educational system, this reinterpretation made explicit the rights of these children to adjunctive educational services. Although this

TABLE 9.1.   DSM-IV Listings of Symptoms of Attention-Deficit/Hyperactivity Disorder*

A.   Either (1) or (2):
   (1)   Inattention: At least six of the following symptoms of inattention have persisted for at least six months to a degree that is maladaptive and inconsistent with developmental level:
      (a)   often fails to give close attention to details or makes careless mistakes in schoolwork, work, or other activities
      (b)   often has difficulty sustaining attention in tasks or play activities
      (c)   often does not seem to listen to what is being said to him or her
      (d)   often does not follow through on instructions and fails to finish schoolwork, chores, or duties in the workplace (not due to oppositional behavior or failure to understand instructions)
      (e)   often has difficulties organizing tasks and activities
      (f)   often avoids, expresses reluctance about, or has difficulties engaging in tasks that require sustained mental effort (such as schoolwork or homework)
      (g)   often loses things necessary for tasks or activities (e.g., school assignments, pencils, books, books, or toys)
      (h)   is often easily distracted by extraneous stimuli
      (i)   often forgetful in daily activities
   (2)   Hyperactivity-Impulsivity: At least six of the following symptoms of hyperactivity-impulsivity have persisted for at least six months to a degree that is maladaptive and inconsistent with developmental level:

      Hyperactivity
      (a)   often fidgets with hands or feet or squirms in seat
      (b)   leaves seat in classroom or in other situations in which remaining seated is expected
      (c)   often runs about or climbs excessively in situations where it is inappropriate (in adolescents or adults, may be limited to subjective feelings of restlessness)
      (d)   often has difficulty playing or engaging in leisure activities quietly
      (e)   is always "on the go" or acts as if "driven by a motor"
      (f)   often talks excessively

      Impulsivity
      (g)   often blurts out answers to questions before the questions have been completed
      (h)   often has difficulty waiting in lines or awaiting turn in games or group situations
      (i)   often interrupts or intrudes on others (e.g., butts into other's conversations or games)
B.   Some symptoms that caused impairment were present before age seven.
C.   Some symptoms that cause impairment are present in two or more settings (e.g., at school, work, and at home).
D.   There must be clear evidence of clinically significant impairment in social, academic, or occupational functioning.
E.   Does not occur exclusively during the course of a Pervasive Developmental Disorder, Schizophrenia or other Psychotic Disorder, and is not better accounted for by a Mood Disorder, Anxiety Disorder, Dissociative Disorder, or a Personality Disorder.

Code based on type:

314.00   **Attention-Deficit/Hyperactivity Disorder, Predominantly Inattentive Type:** if criterion A(1) is met but not criterion A(2) for the past six months
314.01   **Attention-Deficit/Hyperactivity Disorder, Predominantly Hyperactive-Impulsive Type:** if criterion A(2) is met but not criterion A(1) for the past six months
314.02   **Attention-Deficit/Hyperactivity Disorder, Combined Type:** if both criteria A(1) and A(2) are met for the past six months

*Reprinted with permission from the American Psychiatric Association.

clarification of the law represented a major milestone in the history of the disorder, the extent to which this policy will translate into improvement in the day-to-day educational experience of children with the disorder is not yet apparent.

The prevalence of the disorder, however, should make it a concern for all mental health, pediatric, and educational professionals. Occurring in 3 to 5% of the childhood population (Pelham, Gnagy, Greenslade, & Milich), it represents the most common child-mental-health referral complaint. The disorder does not appear to affect both genders equally—it occurs approximately six to nine times more often in boys than in girls (Barkley, 1990).

Although diagnostically defined by symptoms of inattention, impulsivity, and hyperactivity, the disorder is characterized also by a number of problems in daily life functioning. These most often include academic difficulties, problems in peer relationships, family problems, and oppositional behavior directed towards adults, although more serious antisocial behaviors (e.g., stealing, truancy, vandalism) also co-occur frequently. Not surprisingly, it is important to consider these associated problems in assessing a child with the disorder and in planning his or her treatment. Thus, in what follows, prototypic approaches to assessing and treating these associated problems, as well as the core disorder, will be considered.

PROTOTYPIC ASSESSMENT

In order to accurately assess and diagnose a child with ADHD, the clinician must consider many factors. These include presence of the core features of the disorder (*inattention, impulsivity, motor overactivity*), age of onset, duration, nature and degree of functional impairment, developmental factors, environmental factors, other psychiatric or medical disorders that may mimic ADHD, and the ability and willingness of the family to participate in treatment. This requires that information be gathered from multiple sources by utilizing multiple methods and necessitates multidisciplinary cooperation.

Assessment Procedures

Prior to beginning the assessment, the clinician must have a thorough knowledge of developmentally appropriate behavior (Cicchetti, Toth, & Bush, 1988) because there is a great deal of age variability with regard to attention span, ability to control impulses, and activity levels. Behavior that is acceptable for a first grader may be considered completely inappropriate for a junior high school student. Therefore, it is important that the clinician interpret the information obtained during the assessment process within a developmental framework.

Frequently, acquisition of information precedes the actual interview with the child and family. There are several commonly used and standardized rating scales that can be mailed to the parents and teachers prior to the initial appointment. The use of rating scales, such as the Iowa Conners Teacher Rating Scale (Loney & Milich, 1982; Pelham, Milich, Murphy & Murphy, 1989), the Conners Parent and Teacher Rating Scales (Goyette, Conners, & Ulrich, 1978), the Disruptive Behavior Disorders Rating Scale for teachers (Pelham, Gnagy, Greenslade, & Milich, 1992), and the parent and teacher versions of the Child Behavior Checklist (Achenbach & Edelbrock, 1983, 1986), is standard practice in many clinics. This is an integral component of the assessment and provides information from multiple informants and from different environments. Information obtained in the child's natural environment is essential because of the unrepresentativeness of observations based on a brief one-on-one office visit (American Psychiatric Association, 1980).

The office-based component of the assessment should include a thorough review of the child's current problems beyond the diagnostic criteria. This allows the clinician not only to establish the presence of the symptoms necessary for an ADHD diagnosis, but also to consider concurrent diagnoses as well. Finally, and perhaps of greatest importance, the clinician should ascertain during assessment the manner in which these symptom patterns translate into functional problems for the ADHD child (Pelham & Hinshaw, 1992). Although presence of symptoms such as difficulty sustaining attention or being easily distracted, for example, are diagnostically important, what is the result of being distracted or not sustaining attention? Is less school work being completed? Is it inaccurate? Does it result in some other functionally impairing behavior? The clinician's primary task in the assessment is to establish a diagnosis *and* determine the child's primary functional problems because it is the child's functional problems that are addressed in treatment (Hoza & Pelham, 1993).

Comorbid Problems

An integral part of an ADHD assessment is to determine other difficulties that may be occurring concurrently with ADHD. Although the range of problems that may co-occur with ADHD is rather broad, spanning most of the childhood disorders, several co-morbid problems are especially common. These include oppositional, conduct, and learning disorders, as well as peer problems.

Oppositional and Conduct Disorders

Commonly, ADHD children manifest other disruptive behavior disorder symptoms, such as aggression, defiance, and noncompliance (Loney & Milich, 1982). Diagnostically, these types of symptoms suggest that the clinician should consider Oppositional Defiant Disorder (ODD) or Conduct Disorder (CD) codiagnoses. As described in the DSM-IV, CD involves violations of the basic rights of others and violation of major age-appropriate social norms. Specifically, CD is defined by behaviors such as theft, truancy, lying, physical cruelty, vandalism, aggression, and other serious violations of others or their property. ODD is described in the DSM-IV as a pattern of negative, hostile, and defiant behaviors without the more serious features of CD. Thus, ODD is defined by behaviors such as frequent loss of temper, arguing, being resentful, defying adult requests, blaming others, being spiteful, annoying others, and being easily annoyed. Children with these comorbid conditions typically require more intensive behavioral and environmental treatments than those with ADHD only.

Peer Difficulties

Another common comorbid problem is poor peer relations. Although not unique to ADHD, peer difficulties may be particularly important prognostic indicators (Parker & Asher, 1987; Cowen, Pederson, Babigian, Izzo, & Trost, 1973). Peer difficulties may take a variety of forms, such as bossiness, teasing, arguing, fighting, and difficulty playing cooperatively with others. These behavioral difficulties are apparent to peers (Pelham & Bender, 1982) and often result in peer rejection (Carlson, Lahey, Frame, Walker, & Hynd, 1987).

Learning Disorders

Additionally, because of the higher incidence of learning disorders (LD) in the ADHD population (Shaywitz & Shaywitz, 1988), recent results of individually administered intelligence and achievement tests should be obtained if such tests were recently conducted by a school psychologist or other qualified educational or mental health professional. If achievement and IQ tests were not recently conducted, psychoeducational testing should be added as part of the assessment for any child for whom poor academic performance is a presenting problem. The importance of this is reflected in the additional services available for children diagnosed with a learning disorder in their specific school system. A comorbid LD diagnosis may make a child eligible for individual classroom assistance and/or specialized classroom placement and may alert the teacher to learning techniques specifically suited for the child. These services represent adjunctive treatment options for a substantial subgroup of ADHD children. In the authors' experience, in most school districts, services for children with concurrent learning disorders are more specific, available, and accessible than services for ADHD children without learning disorders.

In addition to understanding the nature of the child's problems, it is also important to learn as much as possible about how the parents and school are currently managing the problematic behavior, as well as what has been tried in the past and how effective the different management tactics have been. In learning about current and past treatments, it is important to pay specific attention to detail to assure that the intervention was implemented appropriately. With regard to medication, the method of assessment, doses utilized, and side effects reported should be thoroughly explored because they are important factors that will influence current treatment options. With regard to behavioral interventions, the type, intensity, and consistency of implementation should all be explored.

Environmental Factors

The assessment of the family and school environments is critical in determining the feasibility of many treatment recommendations. The current family composition, who provides supervision, the cultural beliefs of the family, the neighborhood in which they live, and current social stressors all impact on treatment options and implementation. Similarly, at school, classroom size, classroom setup, teacher style, state and district rules, and available classroom alternatives will directly impact on treatment recommendations.

Understanding these factors may be facilitated by conducting a functional analysis of the individual problem behaviors. This entails identifying the antecedents and consequences that are promoting or maintaining each individual problem behavior and then determining at what point intervention is likely to be most effective. Environmental factors, then, require close attention at the time of the initial assessment and during the course of treatment.

Family History

Obtaining a family history of psychiatric and medical disorders is important, not only because many disorders are familial, but also because limitations to treatment may occur as a direct result of a parent or significant family member's own illness (Biederman, Faraone, Keenan, Knee, & Tsuang, 1990; Morrison, 1980). A parent with major depression, for example, may not be able to implement behavior programs without additional assistance. Similarly, a parent's alcohol abuse may require treatment prior to initiating treatment for the child. Presence of a stimulant abuser in the home will directly impact on the choice of medication (e.g., desipramine as a first-line option) in those children who may require it. Therefore, these factors must be explored and their potential impact on treatment considered.

Medical Factors

A thorough medical history and recent physical examination are standard components of most psychiatric assessments. The importance of ruling out a treatable medical disorder should not be underestimated. Some medical illnesses that may present with symptoms consistent with ADHD include sensory impairment (hearing or vision loss), lead exposure (Needleman et al., 1979), absence seizures, thyroid disease, or closed-head injury. In addition, if medication is being considered, presence of a medical illness may influence this decision. For example, presence of Tourette's syndrome in an ADHD child may require treatment with medications other than stimulants (Spencer, Biederman, Kerman, Steingard, & Wilens, 1993), and significant cardiac disease may preclude use of tricyclic antidepressants in some children (Tingelstad, 1991).

In summary, a thorough assessment is necessary to establish the diagnosis of ADHD and should be conducted by a professional with knowledge of developmentally appropriate behavior. Such an assessment should include use of standardized rating scales from multiple sources in multiple settings (e.g., parent, teacher), a comprehensive psychiatric interview, and consideration of environmental and family history factors that impact upon the functioning of the caretakers and the child. It is critical to bear in mind that establishing the diagnosis is only one part of the assessment process. Equally important, if not more, is the task of identifying the child's functional problems. It is these functional problems, rather than the core symptoms of the disorder, that are addressed in treatment.

ACTUAL ASSESSMENT

As previously described, the assessment procedure requires cooperation from a variety of professionals and a thorough knowledge not only of childhood psychiatric disorders, but an understanding of adult disorders (which may be present in parents), school systems, developmental issues, and medical illness. This may limit the individual clinician's ability to conduct, single-handedly, a thorough assessment. Consultations with other professionals may be necessary during the assessment process.

Several other factors, however, affect the quality of the assessment conducted. First, the teacher's willingness to complete rating scales may be impacted by their numerous other commitments and responsibilities. The clinician may need to keep the number of rating scales requested at a reasonable number, obtain the information by phone consultation, or rely on parent report until a rapport is established with the school and teacher. This final option should only be exercised after numerous attempts have been made, without success, to gain the teacher's cooperation. The authors' experience has been that the vast majority of teachers will complete our comprehensive rating scale packet once the importance of their participation in the assessment is explained, even though they may initially have expressed reluctance to do so.

A second obstacle to assessment is that parents may be resistant to discuss problems within the home or disorders present in themselves or other significant family members. Thus, the treatment clinician may plan a course of treatment for the child without being fully aware of critical family limitations. These issues may only present during the course of treatment. Therefore, it is important for the clinician to realize that assessment does not end after the initial visit. Rather, new information that is obtained during the course of treatment should be used to fine-tune (or dramatically alter, if necessary) the established treatment. It may be necessary to consult with or refer a family member to a therapist more experienced in the diagnosis and treatment of adult disorders if the presence of a serious disorder (e.g., maternal depression, paternal alcohol abuse) becomes apparent in one of the caretakers during the assessment or course of treatment. Similarly, the need for a thorough understanding of medical illness and developmental issues means that sometimes the psychiatrist or psychologist must consult with a physician more knowledgeable than they are in these areas.

Finally, as was noted, for children who have severe problems with academic skills, it is usually appropriate to administer a psychoeducational battery that includes an individually administered IQ test (e.g., the Wechsler Intelligence Scale for Children-Third Edition; Wechsler, 1991), and achievement tests such as the Wechsler Individual Achievement Test (Wechsler, 1992) or the Woodcock-Johnson Psychoeducational Battery (Woodcock & Johnson, 1989, 1990). Since most psychiatrists are not trained in psychoeducational testing, this would require referral to a psychologist trained in this area. Results of such a test battery should be used to help identify presence of a learning disability and/or to generate hypotheses about the child's academic strengths and weaknesses.

In summary, the actual assessment may vary, but the basic tenets as outlined remain the same. Achieving them may require additional time, effort, and consultation from multiple disciplines. Clinicians should be aware of their own abilities and limitations and familiar with resources available to assist them in the assessment process.

PROTOTYPIC TREATMENT

Only two treatments are well supported by empirical studies as effective for ADHD—behavior therapy and psychostimulant medication (methylphenidate, destroamphetamine, pemoline). The combination of behavior therapy and psychostimulant medication is often needed to effect the result desired within the real-life constraints of the child's situation (see, for example, Atkins, Pelham, & White, 1989). The flow chart that the authors recommend following in order to arrive at the most appropriate treatment is depicted in Figure 9.1. Each step in the progress will be described in more detail in the following discussion:

Step 1. Establishing a Baseline Behavioral Intervention

It is now well established that medication should not be used to treat ADHD in the absence of psychosocial interventions. This is not only recommended by experts in the field (DuPaul & Barkley, 1990; Pelham & Milich, 1991), but by the pharmaceutical companies who manufacture stimulants themselves (*Physician's Desk Reference*, 1994). Thus, the first step in treatment should always be establishment of a standard behavioral intervention. In this way, a standard behavioral intervention serves as the baseline condition against which the need for additional interventions (medication or more intensive behavioral treatments) is evaluated.

The initial standard behavior intervention is ideally a combination of home- and school-

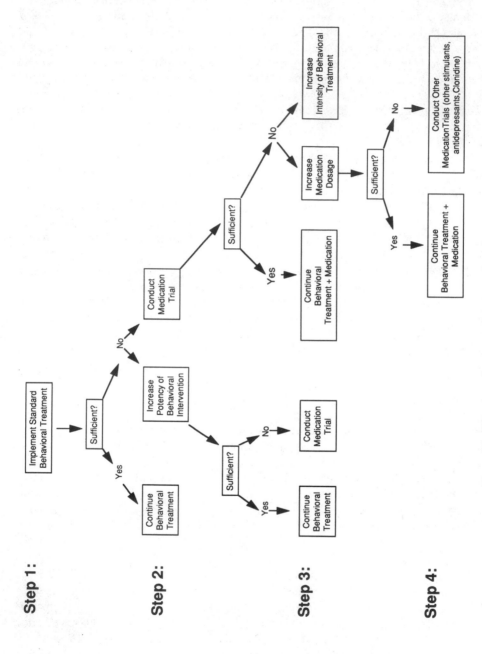

Figure 9.1. Flow chart of recommended progression of treatment of ADHD.

based reward, response-cost, extinction, and punishment procedures (see Carlson & Lahey, 1988, and Pfiffner & O'Leary, in press, for descriptions). These interventions are typically taught to parents in clinic-based parent training classes. Specifically, parents are taught to praise and reward appropriate behavior, ignore minor inappropriate behavior, implement time out for serious negative behaviors, establish and monitor point/token systems that make privileges contingent on behavior, give clear unambiguous commands backed by punishment for noncompliance, and shape appropriate behavior by reinforcing successive approximations to target behaviors. Several excellent parent training books provide step-by-step outlines for parent trainers (examples in Barkley, 1987; Patterson, 1975).

In order for a behavioral intervention to be maximally effective for a given child, his or her teachers must learn these procedures as well. Teachers typically learn these procedures via a behavioral consultant that goes to the school to assist the teacher in developing and implementing a classroom-based behavioral intervention (see Pelham & Hinshaw, 1992, for a review). Such an intervention typically involves establishing classroom rules and consequences for rule violations, setting up a daily report card and assignment sheets, and teaching teachers all of the skills listed above for parent training. Classwide interventions in the form of group contingencies are often used because they assist the teacher in managing all children in the class, not just the target child (Hayes, 1976).

In implementing these standard behavioral procedures, a number of general points must be borne in mind. First, when a behavioral intervention (e.g., extinction) is initially implemented, it is normal to observe an initial, temporary increase in problematic behaviors as the child tests out the new system (Martin & Pear, 1992). Thus, it is important that individuals involved in the treatment (e.g., teachers and parents) be informed that this normal response to treatment may occur so that they do not conclude prematurely that the intervention is not working. Second, all adults in the child's environment should be involved in the intervention (i.e., all caretakers at home, all teachers at school). If not, inconsistent implementation may result in failure of the intervention to make an impact. Third, the research literature indicates that rewards are not a sufficient intervention for most ADHD children—appropriate reprimands and/or punishment in the form of time out and loss of privileges are usually necessary (Rosen, O'Leary, Joyce, Conway, & Pfiffner, 1984; see Pfiffner & O'Leary, in press, for review). For a sizable proportion of ADHD children, these standard behavioral interventions will not be sufficient to bring about the level of change desired; thus, the clinician will have to proceed to step 2 in the flow chart.

Step 2. When Standard Outpatient Behavior Therapy is Not Enough

INCREASE POTENCY OF BEHAVIORAL INTERVENTION. Frequently, the standard behavior therapy approach described is insufficient to effect the desired change in ADHD children's behavior. As Figure 9.1 illustrates, when this occurs, the clinician has to choose which of two possible treatment alterations to make for that child. One possibility is to increase the potency of the behavioral intervention, that is, intensify the intervention. This may be done by adding a more restrictive level system of privileges or by making the child earn the privilege to participate in valued daily activities that were previously a standard part of the daily schedule (e.g., recess, swimming). A description of how to do this in a school setting by providing a consultant (e.g., weekly) to assist the teacher in developing and modifying the behavior program as needed may be found in Atkins, Pelham, and White (1989).

Alternatively, intensifying a child's treatment may take the form of direct contingency management by the treating clinician such as is done in a day-treatment program (see examples in Hoza, Pelham, Sams, & Carlson, 1992, and Hoza & Pelham, 1993). At the Children's Summer Day Treatment Program (STP) at Western Psychiatric Institute and Clinic, for example, a treatment team of five counselors directly implements on a daily basis a point system, time out, and social skills training to children as they participate in recreational activities (e.g., soccer, swimming) that are designed to build competence and self-esteem. In addition, special education teachers implement a similar point system and time out procedure in art, computer, and academic learning centers. On Fridays, those children whose cumulative point totals for the week exceed preset goals earn the privilege of going on a special field trip during which the point system is not employed. Although only preliminary data on the effectiveness of the STP is available, it suggests that this type of intervention may prove to be very efficacious as a short-term treatment for ADHD (see Pelham & Hoza, 1993, for a full description of the STP, as well as for preliminary data).

Of course, in order to employ an intensive behavioral intervention, the persons implementing the intervention must have the time, knowledge, and resources (e.g., personnel) to devote to the intervention in order for the intervention to be carried out adequately. This is more likely to be the case in some settings (e.g., a special education classroom with a high staff-to-student ratio or a day treatment program) than in others (e.g., a mainstream classroom). Also, persons involved must be willing to implement a more intensive, time-consuming intervention. When these conditions are not met, the clinician may want to consider medication as an adjunct to the standard behavioral intervention rather than intensifying the behavioral intervention (see example in Atkins, Pelham, & White, 1989).

MEDICATION AS AN ADJUNCT TO STANDARD BEHAVIORAL TREATMENT.   Methylphenidate (Ritalin and Ritalin SR), pemoline (Cylert), and dextroamphetamine (Dexedrine and Dexedrine Spansules) are central nervous system stimulants and represent the drug(s) of choice in the treatment of ADHD. Each has been shown to be effective in approximately 70% of children with ADHD (Barkley, 1990); and 96% of ADHD children responded to *either* Ritalin or Dexedrine (Elia, Borcherding, Rapoport, & Keysor, 1991). The stimulants are a highly effective treatment intervention but should only be used in combination with behavioral interventions (Pelham & Murphy, 1986; Barkley, 1990; Conners & Wells, 1986).

As was noted, a behavior program (e.g., a daily report card) should typically be established prior to the start of a medication assessment, with the assessment occurring only if the behavioral intervention alone has proven insufficient (Pelham, 1993). An added benefit of this approach is that the data collected from the behavioral intervention may serve as a dependent measure in evaluating the response to medication, along with standardized rating scales and side-effects measures.

The short half-life of Ritalin and Dexedrine allows an assessment of these medications to be conducted in a double-blind placebo trial with medication randomized daily (for specific details, see Pelham & Hoza, 1987; Pelham & Milich, 1991; Pelham, 1993). Cylert requires that randomization occur in blocks of 3 days or more (Pelham, Greenslade, et al., 1990). Although double-blind placebo trials represent one of the most comprehensive methods of assessing medication effects while minimizing environmental errors and bias (Barkley, Fischer, Newby, & Breen, 1988; Pelham, 1982; Swanson, Kinsbourne, Roberts, & Zucker, 1978), they are not common practice. This may be because they require a significant simultaneous commitment from parents, teachers, and clinical staff (Pelham &

Milich, 1991) and because few community-practice physicians know how to do them. Any interested medical practitioner, however, can learn the procedure and implement it in a school setting. Detailed instructions on how to conduct such a medication assessment may be found in Pelham and Milich (1991) and Pelham (1993).

The effective dose range for children is approximately 0.25 to 0.75 mg/kg of body weight for methylphenidate (MPH) and approximately one-half of that range for dextroamphetamine (d-amphetamine). The dose range for pemoline is less clear but approximates four to six times that of a single dose of MPH given once per day in the morning (Pelham et al., 1990; Stephens, Pelham, & Skinner, 1984). The effective spans of action for MPH and d-amphetamine are 3 to 5 hours and 4 to 6 hours, respectively. Long-acting forms of these medications (Ritalin SR and Dexedrine Spansules) are typically given once per day in the morning and typically last twice as long as the short-acting forms of each respective drug (Pelham et al., 1990). It is important to note that the dose ranges for these drugs do not represent the most effective single doses for any one individual, but instead a range for most children. Therefore, an individual assessment is recommended for each child to determine the dose that is the most effective in improving the salient problems of that child while minimizing side effects. It has been the authors' experience that, in combination with a behavioral treatment program, the majority of children respond significantly to the low end of these dose ranges (Carlson, Pelham, Milich, & Dixon, 1992; Pelham, Bender, Caddell, Booth, & Moorer, 1985; Pelham, Schnedler, et al., 1988; Pelham, Carlson, et al., 1993). When a concurrent behavioral treatment is implemented, a minority of children may require a moderate dose, and only a very small number of ADHD children require the higher doses.

If the combination of behavioral interventions and stimulants is insufficient in improving a child's difficulties after an extensive treatment attempt, other medications should be considered. As was noted (Elia et al., 1991), the vast majority of ADHD children respond positively to one of the stimulants. If a child fails to respond to MPH, he or she should be tried on d-amphetamine and pemoline. If the child fails to respond to all three stimulants, then a tricyclic antidepressant should be considered. Imipramine and desipramine are the second line of pharmacologic agents to be considered (Biederman, Baldessarini, Wright, Knee, & Harmatz, 1989; Zametkin & Rapoport, 1983). Other antidepressants, such as bupropion (Simeon, Ferguson, & Van Wyk Fleet, 1986) and fluoxetine (Barrickman, Noyes, Kuperman, Schumacher, & Verda, 1991), have been suggested as alternatives; but, the lack of replicated, well-controlled studies would suggest that these are tertiary alternatives. Clonidine has been reported to be an effective alternative, as well, especially in children with a concurrent diagnosis of Tourette's syndrome (Hunt, Capper, & O'Connell, 1990).

Step 3. Fine-Tuning the Intervention

After the intervention that was implemented at step 2 has been in place for a period of time long enough to determine whether the treatment alteration was sufficient, the clinician should move to step 3. Obviously, if the treatment(s) implemented thus far have been successful in producing the desired change, the treatments as they are should be continued. If, however, there is still a need for behavioral improvement, the clinician should alter the treatment in one of the ways specified at step 3. Specifically, if at step 2 the intensity of the behavioral intervention was increased without achieving the desired results, at step 3 a medication trial is probably indicated. The assessment should be a double-blind placebo-controlled medication trial of the same nature as is described at step 2. If at step 2 a medication assessment was conducted without achieving the desired results, at step 3 the intensity of the behavioral intervention should be increased. This may be accomplished in the same manner described at step 2.

ACTUAL TREATMENT

Under ideal circumstances, the algorithm described by the flow chart in Figure 9.1 works well in guiding the behavioral clinician in determining the course of treatment for an ADHD child. In fact, the algorithm is rather robust and will work in most situations, even given that the prevailing circumstances may not be ideal. Nonetheless, there are certain problems that may arise in implementing the planned treatment, and these will be discussed here. Most commonly, these impediments include the following: poor compliance with the prescribed treatment, inconsistent implementation of treatment across caretakers, parental psychopathology that prevents the parent from participating effectively in the child's treatment, parental life stresses that prevent the parent from participating effectively in the child's treatment, inconsistent attendance of scheduled treatment sessions, apprehension about the use of medication, overdependence on medication, or prohibitive side effects from medication.

Poor Compliance with the Prescribed Treatment

Poor compliance refers to the reluctance or refusal of key adults in the child's life to implement the prescribed treatment. The focus here is on persons who are *able* to implement the treatment fully but who, for any of a variety of reasons, choose not to do so. With regard to behavioral interventions, compliance may be a problem for one or more of the parents (or other caretakers) at home.

At school, noncompliance with behavioral treatment most often refers to the resistance of teachers to implement behavioral interventions in the classroom or other school settings (e.g., the playground). Often teachers state that it takes too much time to implement a behavioral intervention for one child or that they lack the assistance (e.g., in the form of a teacher's aide) necessary. Given that federal law (Davila et al., 1991) now protects the rights of ADHD children to special programming in the schools, parents and clinicians have more leverage in asking for cooperation. Nonetheless, clinicians are advised to keep the program simple and easy to implement if they hope to obtain full cooperation.

As noted previously (Hoza & Pelham, 1993), the authors have found that classroom consultation works best if the clinician asks for the teacher's input as to the behaviors that need to improve and the resources available to assist with implementation. The clinician should then set up the program completely for the teacher, including monitoring sheets, graphs, written instructions, and so on, since teachers appreciate the recognition that they are busy people with limited time and resources. Also, frequent visits to the school by the behavioral consultant are a must so that teachers are not left to troubleshoot alone if the intervention is not running smoothly.

Finally, with regard to psychostimulant treatment, noncompliance refers to the inconsistent administration of medication either at school or at home. Making one person responsible for administration of the medication (e.g., the school nurse) and providing medication compliance cards that are checked off by the administering adult and collected weekly by the clinician may help improve compliance.

Inconsistent Implementation of Treatment Across Caretakers

Inconsistent implementation of treatment across caretakers is a common impediment to successful treatment. For this reason, it is important that all caretakers (e.g., babysitters, grandparents) who regularly monitor the child should be asked to participate in behavioral parent training. When one caretaker (e.g., father) is unable or unwilling to attend the sessions, an effort should be made via handouts or audiotapes to keep him involved in the treatment. When this fails, a family consultation session should be held in which the impact of that caretaker's lack of participation on the effectiveness of treatment should be frankly discussed. If the clinician is still unsuccessful in engaging one caretaker, treatment should proceed, with periodic attempts to offer involvement to the uninvolved person in the hope that he or she will wish to become involved as behavioral changes in the child due to others' efforts become obvious.

Parental (or Family) Psychopathology

Parental or family pathology that co-occurs with the child's problematic behaviors may make it difficult or impossible for the adults at home to implement the child's treatment. Common examples of such problems might be substance abuse, depression, or antisocial behavior (Barkley, 1990). In such cases, it is critical that the clinician help the family obtain assistance with these problems as well. In many cases, it is useful to have a clinician other than the one who trains the parent to manage the child's behavior, work with the parent on his or her problems. In this way, there is less likelihood that one of the two problems will be avoided by the parent (e.g., a substance-abusing parent may always talk about the child's problems, avoiding discussion of his or her own substance abuse). If this type of arrangement is employed, the two clinicians involved should obtain written consent from the parent to converse periodically to make sure they are not working at cross purposes.

Parental Life Stresses

Just as parental psychopathology may serve as an impediment to treatment, stresses on the parent(s) may be a factor as well (Barkley, 1990). Such stresses may include lack of assistance with childcare (especially for single parents), lack of general emotional support from extended family members, divorce, marital conflict, or financial strain due to treatment costs. In these cases, the behavioral management trainer should respond by helping the parent to acknowledge that these difficulties are interfering with treatment and to assist that parent in finding a community resource to provide support or assistance. Often, helping single parents to arrange a trade agreement whereby each watches the other's child once or twice a month to give the other a break may be useful. Often this can be accomplished through parent support groups such as Children with Attention Deficit Disorder (CHADD) or Attention Deficit Disorders Association (ADDA).

Inconsistent Attendance of Scheduled Treatment Sessions

Irregular attendance of treatment sessions by clients is one of the most common complaints of mental health professionals. While there is no absolute solution to this difficulty, establishment of treatment contracts at the outset of intervention that clearly spell out the expectations of the clinician (e.g., at least 80% attendance of scheduled sessions) are often helpful. Consequences for violation of the contract should be spelled out as well.

Medication Issues

Medication for childhood psychiatric disorders, especially stimulants, has received a significant amount of negative media coverage. Unfortunately, this information is frequently misleading and inaccurate. This may result in a parent refusing a medication trial without ever receiving accurate information about the medication. Therefore, parents' perceptions are important, and the treating clinician and physician should carefully inform parents about the use of medication, potential benefits, and side effects and should answer any questions the parents may have about medication. One of the primary clinician's priorities should be to correct misperceptions acquired by the family from the media and other sources.

Equally problematic is the family that prefers to use medication alone to treat their child's ADHD. Sometimes, an initial significant response to stimulants may result in a parent not actively pursuing other treatment options. As noted previously, medication should typically be used only in combination with behavioral treatments. This is because the use of stimulant treatment alone for ADHD has not been found to be effective in long-term outcome studies (Hechtman, Weiss, & Perlman, 1984). Further, medication should typically only be tried after behavioral treatments have proven insufficient. Therefore, it is important to specifically and clearly explain the rationale for the use of behavioral therapy in the treatment of ADHD and to review with parents the importance of not relying solely on medication. Their cooperation in all aspects of treatment should be a prerequisite to the continued use of medication.

Medication side effects are generally not significantly impairing with most children, especially with Ritalin, the most commonly used medication for the treatment of ADHD (Barkley, McMurray, Edelbrock, & Robbins, 1990). Nonetheless, it is important to thoroughly review the most common and most concerning side effects of the medication being assessed. Also, when the prescribing physician is easily available to answer questions and to assist in the management of any side effects that do occur during the initial medication trial, noncompliance is decreased.

SUMMARY

Attention-Deficit/Hyperactivity Disorder is the most common childhood mental health problem today. Fortunately, federal law now requires schools to meet the special needs of children with the disorder. Assessment should occur in a methodic fashion, incorporating information from multiple sources. Assessment should identify the child's functional problems, in addition to confirming the ADHD diagnosis. Prototypic treatment may be thought of as following an algorithm, with treatment decisions made at each step based on practicality and on the child's response to the treatment alteration made at the previous step. A number of problems may interfere with prototypic assessment and treatment; they should be acknowledged and discussed so possible remedies can be suggested.

REFERENCES

Achenbach, T. M., & Edelbrock, C. S. (1983). *Manual for the child behavior checklist and revised child behavior profile.* Burlington, VT: University of Vermont, Department of Psychiatry.

Achenbach, T. M. & Edelbrock, C. S. (1986). *Manual for the teacher's report form and teacher version of the child behavior profile.* Burlington, VT: University of Vermont, Department of Psychiatry.

American Psychiatric Association. (1980). *Diagnostic and statistical manual of mental disorders (3rd ed.).* Washington, DC: Author.

American Psychiatric Association. (1987). *Diagnostic and statistical manual of mental disorders (3rd ed., rev.).* Washington, DC: Author.

American Psychiatric Association. (1994). *Diagnostic and statistical manual of mental disorders (4th ed.).* Washington, DC: Author.

Atkins, M. S., Pelham, W. E., & White, K. J. (1989). Hyperactivity and attention deficit disorders. In M. Hersen Ed.), *Psychological aspects of developmental and physical disabilities: A casebook* (pp. 137–156). Beverly Hills, CA: Sage.

Barkley, R. A. (1987). *Defiant children: A clinician's manual for parent training.* New York: Guilford Press.

Barkley, R. A. (1990). *Attention deficit hyperactivity disorder: A handbook for diagnosis and treatment.* New York: Guilford Press.

Barkley, R. A., Fischer, M., Newby, R. F., & Breen, M. J. (1988). Development of a multi-method clinical protocol for assessing stimulant drug responses in ADHD children. *Journal of Clinical Child Psychology, 17,* 14–24.

Barkley, R. A., McMurray, M. B., Edelbrock, C. S., & Robbins, K. (1990). Side effects of methylphenidate in children with attention deficit hyperactivity disorder: A systematic, placebo-controlled evaluation. *Pediatrics, 86,* 184–192.

Barrickman, L., Noyes, R., Kuperman, S., Schumacher, E., & Verda, M. (1991). Treatment of ADHD with fluoxetine: A preliminary trial. *Journal of the American Academy of Child and Adolescent Psychiatry, 30,* 762–767.

Biederman, J., Baldessarini, R. J., Wright, V., Knee, D., & Harmatz, J. S. (1989). A double-blind placebo controlled study of desipramine in the treatment of ADD: I. Efficacy. *Journal of the American Academy of Child and Adolescent Psychiatry, 28,* 777–784.

Biederman, J., Faraone, S. V., Keenan, K., Knee, D., & Tsuang, M. T. (1990). Family-genetic and psychosocial risk factors in DSM-III attention deficit disorder. *Journal of the American Academy of Child and Adolescent Psychiatry, 29,* 526–533.

Carlson, C. L., & Lahey, B. B. (1988). Conduct and attention deficit disorders. In J. C. Witt, S. M. Elliott, & F. M. Gresham (Eds.), *The handbook of behavior therapy in education* (pp. 653–677). New York: Plenum Press.

Carlson, C. L., Lahey, B. B., Frame, C. L., Walker, J., & Hynd, G. W. (1987). Sociometric status of clinic-referred children with attention deficit disorders with and without hyperactivity. *Journal of Abnormal Child Psychology, 15,* 537–547.

Carlson, C. L., Pelham, W. E., Milich, R., & Dixon, M. J. (1992). Single and combined effects of methylphenidate and behavior therapy on the classroom behavior, academic performance and self-evaluations of children with attention deficit-hyperactivity disorder. *Journal of Abnormal Child Psychology, 20,* 213–232.

Cicchetti, D., Toth, S., & Bush, M. (1988). Developmental psychopathology and incompetence in childhood: Suggestions for intervention. In B. B. Lahey & A. E. Kazdin (Eds.), *Advances in clinical child psychology* (pp. 1–71). New York: Plenum Press.

Conners, C. K., & Wells, K. C. (1986). *Hyperkinetic children: A neuropsychosocial approach.* Beverly Hills, CA: Sage.

Cowen, E., Pederson, A., Babigian, H., Izzo, L., & Trost, M. (1973). Long-term follow-up of early detected vulnerable children. *Journal of Consulting and Clinical Psychology, 41*, 438–446.

Davila, R. R., Williams, M. L., & MacDonald, J. T. (1991). *Clarification of policy to address the needs of children with attention deficit disorders within general and/or special education.* (Memo). Washington, DC: U. S. Department of Education.

DuPaul, G. J., & Barkley, R. A. (1990). Medication therapy. In R. A. Barkley (Ed.), *Attention-deficit/hyperactivity disorder* (pp. 573–612). New York: Guilford Press.

Elia, J., Borcherding, B. G., Rapoport, J. L., & Keysor, C. S. (1991). Methylphenidate and dextroamphetamine treatments of hyperactivity: Are there true nonresponders? *Psychiatry Research, 36*, 141–155.

Goyette, C. H., Conners, C. K., & Ulrich, R. F. (1978). Normative data on revised Conners parent and teacher rating scales. *Journal of Abnormal Child Psychology, 6*, 221–236.

Hayes, L. A. (1976). The use of group contingencies for behavioral control: A review. *Psychological Bulletin, 83*, 628–648.

Hechtman, L., Weiss, G., & Perlman, T. (1984). Young adult outcome of hyperactive children who received long-term stimulant treatment. *Journal of the American Academy of Child Psychiatry, 23*, 261–269.

Hoza, B., & Pelham, W. E. (1993). Attention deficit/hyperactivity disorder. In R. T. Ammerman, C. G. Last, & M. Hersen (Eds.), *Handbook of prescriptive treatments for children and adolescents* (pp. 64–84). Boston: Allyn and Bacon.

Hoza, B., Pelham, W. E., Sams, S. E., & Carlson, C. L. (1992). An examination of the "dosage" effects of both behavior therapy and methylphenidate on the classroom performance of two ADHD children. *Behavior Modification, 16*, 164–192.

Hunt, R. D., Capper, L., & O'Connell, P. (1990). Clonidine in child and adolescent psychiatry. *Journal of Child and Adolescent Psychopharmacology, 1* (1); 87–102.

Lahey, B. B., Pelham, W. E., Schaughency, E. A., Atkins, M. S., Murphy, H. A., Hynd, G., Russo, M., Hartdagen, S., & Lorys-Vernon, A. (1988). Dimensions and types of attention deficit disorder. *Journal of the American Academy of Child and Adolescent Psychiatry, 27* (3), 330–335.

Loney, J., & Milich, R. (1982). Hyperactivity, inattention, and aggression in clinical practice. In M. Wolraich & D. K. Routh (Eds.), *Advances in developmental and behavioral pediatrics* (pp. 113–147). Greenwich, CT: JAI Press.

Martin, G., & Pear, J. (1992). *Behavior modification: What it is and how to do it.* Englewood Cliffs, NJ: Prentice Hall.

Morrison, J. (1980). Adult psychiatric disorders in parents of hyperactive children. *American Journal of Psychiatry, 137* (7), 825–827.

Needleman, H. L. Gunnoe, C., Leviton, A., Reed, R., Peresie, H., Maher, C., & Barrett, P. (1979). Deficits in psychologic and classroom performance of children with elevated dentine lead levels. *New England Journal of Medicine, 300*, 689–695.

Parker, J. G., & Asher, S. R. (1987). Peer relations and later personal adjustment: Are low-accepted children at risk? *Psychological Bulletin, 102*, 357–389.

Patterson, G. (1975). *Families: Application of social learning to family life.* Champaign, IL: Research Press.

Pelham, W. E. (1982). Childhood hyperactivity: Diagnosis, etiology, nature, and treatment. In R. Gatchel, A. Baum, & J. Singer (Eds.), *Handbook of psychology and health: Vol. 1. Clinical psychology and behavior medicine: Overlapping disciplines* (pp. 261–327). Hillsdale, NJ: Lawrence Erlbaum.

Pelham, W. E. (1993). Pharmacotherapy for children with attention-deficit/hyperactivity disorder. *School Psychology Review, 22,* 199–227.

Pelham, W. E., & Bender, M. E. (1982). Peer relationships in hyperactive children: Description and treatment. In K. D. Gadow & I. Bialer (Eds.), *Advances in learning and behavioral disabilities* (pp. 365–436). Greenwich, CT: JAI Press.

Pelham, W. E., Bender, M. E., Caddell, J., Booth, S., & Moorer, S. (1985). The dose-response effects of methylphenidate on classroom academic and social behavior in children with attention deficit disorder. *Archives of General Psychiatry, 42,* 948–952.

Pelham, W. E., Carlson, C., Sams, S. E., Vallano, G., Dixon, M. J., & Hoza, B. (1993). Separate and combined effects of methylphenidate and behavior modification of the classroom behavior and academic performance of ADHD boys. Group effects and individual differences. *Journal of Consulting and Clinical Psychology, 61,* 506–515.

Pelham, W. E., Evans, S. W., Gnagy, E. M., & Greenslade, K. E. (1992). Teacher ratings of DSM-III-R symptoms for the disruptive behavior disorders: Prevalence, factor analyses, and conditional probabilities in a special education sample. *School Psychology Review, 21,* 285–299.

Pelham, W. E., Gnagy, E. M., Greenslade, K. E., & Milich, R. (1992). Teacher ratings of DSM-III-R symptoms for the disruptive behavior disorders. *Journal of the American Academy of Child and Adolescent Psychiatry, 31,* 210–218.

Pelham, W. E., Greenslade, K. E., Vodde-Hamilton, M. A., Murphy, D. A., Greenstein, J. J., Gnagy, E. M., & Dahl, R. E. (1990). Relative efficacy of long-acting CNS stimulants on children with attention deficit-hyperactivity disorder: A comparison of standard methylphenidate, sustained-release methylphenidate, sustained-release dextroamphetamine, and pemoline. *Pediatrics, 86,* 226–237.

Pelham, W. E., & Hinshaw, S. (1992). Behavioral intervention for attention deficit disorder. In S. M. Turner, K. S. Calhoun, & H. E. Adams (Eds.), *Handbook of clinical behavior therapy* (pp. 259–283). New York: Wiley.

Pelham, W. E., & Hoza, B. (1993, February). *Comprehensive and intensive treatment for ADHD: A summer treatment program and outpatient follow-up.* Paper presented at the annual meeting of the Professional Group for Attention and Related Disorders, Santa Fe, NM.

Pelham, W. E., & Hoza, J. (1987). Behavioral assessment of psychostimulant effects on ADD children in a summer day treatment program. In R. Prinz (Ed.), *Advances in behavioral assessment of children and families* (pp. 3–33). Greenwich, CT: JAI Press.

Pelham, W. E., & Milich, R. (1991). Individual differences in response to ritalin in classwork and social behavior. In L. Greenhill & B. P. Osman (Eds.), *Ritalin: Theory and patient management* (pp. 203–221). New York: MaryAnn Liebert.

Pelham, W. E., Milich, R., Murphy, D. A., & Murphy, H. A. (1989). Normative data on the IOWA Conners teacher rating scale. *Journal of Clinical Child Psychology, 18* (3), 259–262.

Pelham, W. E., & Murphy, H. A. (1986). Attention deficit and conduct disorders. In M. Hersen (Ed.), *Pharmacological and behavioral treatment: An integrative approach* (pp. 108–148). New York: Wiley.

Pelham, W. E., Schnedler, R. W., Bender, M. E., Miller, J., Nilsson, D., Budrow, M., Ronnei, M., Paluchowski, C., & Marks, D. (1988). The combination of behavior therapy and methylphenidate in the treatment of hyperactivity: A therapy outcome study. In L. Bloomingdale (Ed.), *Attention deficit disorders* (pp. 29–48). London: Pergamon Press.

Pfiffner, L. J., & O'Leary, S. G. (in press). Psychological treatments: School-based. In J. L. Matson (Ed.), *Hyperactivity in Children: A handbook.* Needham Heights, MA: Allyn & Bacon.

Physician's desk reference (48th ed.). 1994. Montvale, NJ: Medical Economics Date Production Company.

Rosen, L. A., O'Leary, S. G., Joyce, S. A., Conway, G., & Pfiffner, L. J. (1984). The importance of prudent negative consequences for maintaining the appropriate behavior of hyperactive students. *Journal of Abnormal Child Psychology, 12,* 581–604.

Shaywitz, S. E., & Shaywitz, B. E. (1988). Attention deficit disorder: Current perspectives. In J. F. Kavanagh & T. J. Truss (Eds.), *Learning disabilities: Proceedings of the national conference,* (pp. 369–546). Parkson, MD: York Press.

Simeon, J. F., Ferguson, H. B., & Van Wyck Fleet, J. (1986). Bupropion effects in attention deficit and conduct disorders. *Canadian Journal of Psychiatry, 31,* 581–585.

Spencer, T., Biederman, J., Kerman, K., Steingard, R., & Wilens, T. (1993). Desipramine treatment of children with attention-deficit/hyperactivity disorder and tic disorder or Tourette's syndrome. *Journal of the American Academy of Child and Adolescent Psychiatry, 32,* 354–360.

Stephens, R., Pelham, W. E., & Skinner, R. (1984). The state-dependent and main effects of pemoline and methylphenidate on paired-associates learning and spelling in hyperactive children. *Journal of Consulting and Clinical Psychology, 52,* 104–113.

Swanson, J., Kinsbourne, M., Roberts, W., & Zucker, K. (1978). Time-response analysis of the effect of stimulant medication on the learning ability of children referred for hyperactivity. *Pediatrics, 61* (1), 21–29.

Tingelstad, J. B. (1991). The cardiotoxicity of the tricyclics. *Journal of the American Academy of Child and Adolescent Psychiatry, 30,* 845–846.

Wechsler, D. (1991). *Wechsler Intelligence Scale for Children-Third Edition.* San Antonio, TX: Harcourt Brace Jovanovich.

Wechsler, D. (1992). *Wechsler Individual Achievement Test.* San Antonio, TX: Harcourt Brace Jovanovich.

Woodcock, R. W., & Johnson, M. B. (1989, 1990). *Woodcock-Johnson Psycho-Educational Battery-Revised.* Allen, TX: DLM Teaching Resources.

Zametkin, A., & Rapoport, J. L. (1983). Tricyclic antidepressants and children. In G. D. Burrows, T. R. Norman, & B. Davies (Eds.), *Drugs and Psychiatry: Vol. 1. Antidepressants* (pp. 129–147). Amsterdam: Elsevier.

CHAPTER 10

Conduct Disorder

PAUL J. FRICK AND BRIDGET S. O'BRIEN

DESCRIPTION OF THE PROBLEM

Introduction

Severe conduct problems in children and adolescents are a critical mental health concern for researchers, practitioners, and social-policy makers for several reasons. Specifically, conduct problems are not uncommon in the general population; they are highly disruptive to others in a child's environment; and they are chronic and predictive of problems later in life (Frick, Strauss, Lahey, & Christ, 1993). Given the nature of conduct problems, it is clear why so much effort has been directed toward developing a better understanding of this syndrome. Because the purpose of this chapter is to focus on current trends in assessment and treatment of conduct disorders, no attempt is made to provide a comprehensive summary of the many important areas of basic research in this area. However, there are several issues that deserve review because of their impact on the delivery of clinical services to this population.

Classification and Diagnosis

The most commonly used method of classifying conduct problems in children is described in the Task Force on DSM-IV (American Psychiatric Association, 1993). DSM-IV divides conduct problems into two syndromes: oppositional defiant disorder (ODD) and conduct disorder (CD). ODD refers to a pattern of negativistic, oppositional, and stubborn behaviors, whereas CD refers to more severe antisocial and aggressive behaviors that involve serious violations of others' rights or deviations from major age-appropriate norms. A summary of the symptoms included in the diagnostic criteria for each disorder is provided in Table 10.1.

A detailed discussion of the validity of the DSM–IV conduct-problems categories is beyond the scope of this chapter (see Frick, Lahey, Loeber, Tawnenbaum, et al., 1993; Lahey, Loeber, Quay, Frick, & Grimm, 1992). However, the relationship between ODD and CD has several implications for clinical practice. First, there is a hierarchical relationship between the two diagnoses; that is, most children with the more severe symptoms of CD also show the symptoms of ODD (Frick, Lahey, Loeber, Stouthamer-Loeber, et al., 1991; Spitzer, Davies, & Markley, 1990). Furthermore, there seems to be a developmental relationship between ODD and CD (See Loeber, 1990). A 3–year longitudinal study of clinic-referred boys found that 82% of the new cases of CD ($n = 22$) that emerged during the study period had received a diagnosis of ODD in the preceding year (Lahey, Loeber, et al., 1992). Therefore, ODD behaviors can be viewed as a risk factor for the development of CD. This relationship is critical because, as discussed later in the chapter, ODD

TABLE 10.1.   Symptoms Included in the Diagnostic Criteria for Oppositional Defiant Disorder and Conduct Disorder

Oppositional Defiant Disorder	Conduct Disorder
Often loses temper.	Often bullies, threatens, or intimidates others.
Often argues with adults.	Often initiates physical fights.
Often actively defies or refuses to comply with adults' requests or rules.	Has used a weapon that can cause serious physical harm to others.
Often deliberately does things that annoy other people.	Has stolen with confrontation of a victim.
Often blames others for his or her mistakes or misbehavior.	Has been physically cruel to people.
Is often touchy or easily annoyed.	Has been physically cruel to animals.
Is often angry and resentful.	Has forced someone into sexual activity.
Is often spiteful or vindictive.	Often lies or breaks promises to obtain goods or favors or to avoid obligations.
	Often stays out at night despite parental prohibitions, beginning before 13 years of age.
	Has stolen items of nontrivial value without confrontation with the victim either within the home or outside the home.
	Has deliberately destroyed others' property.
	Has run away from home overnight at least twice.
	Often truant from school, beginning before 13 years of age.
	Has broken into someone else's house, building, or car.

Note: These symptoms lists are from the criteria listed in the Task Force on DSM-IV. American Psychiatric Association, 1993, Washington, DC. According to DSM–IV, symptoms must be present for at least 6 months.

behaviors are much more amenable to treatment than are the more severe symptoms of CD. Successful treatment of ODD takes on much greater importance if it is viewed as secondary prevention of CD.

In addition to this division of ODD and CD, several attempts have been made to distinguish between subtypes of CD that also are relevant for clinical practice. Distinctions have been between youths with CD who are capable of maintaining social relationships and/or commit antisocial acts primarily with delinquent peers (socialized/group type) and youths with CD who do not form lasting relationships and/or commit antisocial acts primarily alone (unsocialized/solitary type). Further, distinctions are also made between children who display primarily aggressive or primarily nonaggressive CD symptoms and between children who show an early onset of CD symptoms (prior to age 11) or a late onset of symptoms. The literature on the validity of these methods of subtyping is small and often contradictory (see Lahey, Loeber, et al., 1992). However, undersocialized, aggressive, and early-onset forms of conduct disorders seem to predict a more severe disturbance that is more persistent into adulthood.

Comorbidities

In clinic samples of children with conduct problems, it is clear that comorbidities are the rule. In a large clinically-referred sample with disruptive behavior disorders ($n = 550$), for example, of the 140 children with ODD, only 29 (21%) were free from comorbid mental disorder (Spitzer et al., 1990). Similarly, of the 130 children with CD, only 45 (35%) were free from comorbid diagnosis. Therefore, it is clear that assessment and intervention must be conducted in the context of this high degree of comorbidity. Several types of comorbidity seem especially important to clinical intervention.

The most common comorbidity is with attention-deficit/hyperactivity disorder (ADHD) (American Psychiatric Association, 1993). In clinic-referred samples, 50% to 90% of children with conduct-problem diagnoses are diagnosed with comorbid ADHD (Abikoff & Klein, 1992; Hinshaw, 1987; Spitzer et al., 1990). Such overlap is important because the presence of ADHD usually signals the presence of a more severe (Walker, Lahey, Hynd, & Frame, 1987) and more chronic (Abikoff & Klein, 1992) form of conduct problem in children. Also, there is growing evidence for a reduction of conduct problems among children with ADHD who have been treated with stimulant medication (Hinshaw, 1991).

Children with conduct problems frequently have a comorbid emotional disorder. In a large clinic sample ($n = 177$), 62% of a sample of children with CD had a comorbid diagnosis of an anxiety disorder (Walker, Lahey, Russo, et al., 1991). In contrast to the findings for ADHD, children with CD and a comorbid anxiety disorder tend to be less impaired, to be more amenable to treatment, and to have a better long-term prognosis (Quay & Love, 1977; Walker, Lahey, Russo, et al., 1991). Children with conduct disorders also show a high rate of depression (Harrington, Fudge, Rutter, Pickles, & Hill, 1991; Kovacs, Paulauskas, Gatsonis, & Richards, 1988; Puig-Antich, 1982), although there is no convincing evidence that presence of depression affects the prognosis for CD (Harrington et al., 1991). However, there appears to be a subgroup of children who develop CD secondary to a mood disorder (Kovacs, Paulauskas, et al., 1988; Puig-Antich, 1982) and for whom successful treatment of the depressive symptoms results in the amelioration of the CD symptoms (Puig-Antich, 1982).

Research also indicates that approximately 20% to 25% of children with CD are underachieving in school relative to a level predicted by their age and intellectual abilities (Frick, Kamphaus, et al., 1991). The reason for this association is not clear, possibly because the mechanisms involved may differ depending on the age of the sample studied (Hinshaw, 1992); for example, in elementary-school-aged samples, much of the overlap between CD and academic underachievement seems to be due to the presence of ADHD, which is also associated with learning problems (Frick, Kamphaus, et al., 1991). However, learning difficulties predict adolescent-onset conduct problems (Hinshaw, 1992). Irrespective of the lack of a definitive explanation for this correlation, the simple fact that it occurs so consistently in samples of children with conduct problems warrants the consideration of learning problems in designing assessment and intervention strategies for this population.

Correlates and Causes

Most researchers agree that conduct problems are likely the result of a complex interaction of multiple causal factors (Kazdin, 1987). Determining what the important causal agents are and how they interact to cause conduct problems is still an area in need of more research. Past research has uncovered several factors that are *associated* with conduct disorders and *likely* play a role in their development. These factors can be summarized by four categories: biological factors, family context, social ecology, and peers. The research on the biological correlates of conduct problems in children, while crucial to developing causal theories, is not reviewed here because the current state of knowledge is not sufficiently developed to have clear clinical applications (see Lahey, McBurnett, Loeber, & Hart, in press).

In contrast, the link between family dysfunction and conduct disorders is crucial to clinical intervention. There seem to be at least three dimensions of family functioning that are consistently related to childhood conduct problems: parental psychiatric adjustment, marital instability/divorce, and parental socialization practices (see Frick, 1993). A meta-analysis of the research on the relationship between family functioning and conduct disorders in youth found that parental socialization practices were especially important (Loeber & Stouthamer-Loeber, 1986). To be specific, lack of parental involvement in their child's activities, poor parental supervision of their child, and use of harsh or inconsistent discipline tended to show the highest concurrent and predictive relationships with conduct problems in children, across the studies reviewed.

Another clinically important class of correlates involves factors within the child's larger social ecology. One of the most consistent of these correlates has been low socioeconomic status (Farrington, 1978; Frick, Lahey, Hartdagen, & Hynd, 1989; Wilson, 1975). However, several other ecological factors, many of which are related to low socioeconomic status (e.g., poor housing, poor schools, and disadvantaged neighborhoods), have also been linked to the development of conduct problems in children (see Rutter & Giller, 1983).

Finally, research has documented a relationship between peer rejection in elementary school and the later development of conduct problems (Huessmann, Eron, Lefkowitz, & Walder, 1984; Roff & Wirt, 1984). In addition, peer rejection in elementary school is predictive of an association with a deviant peer group (e.g., one that shows a high rate of antisocial behavior and substance abuse) in early adolescence (Dishion, Patterson, & Skinner, 1989). This relationship is important because association with a deviant peer group leads to an increase in the frequency and severity of conduct problems in adolescence (Patterson & Dishion, 1985). Therefore, peer rejection may be directly related to development of conduct problems, but it also may be indirectly associated with the severity of conduct problems through the child's association with a deviant peer group.

PROTOTYPIC ASSESSMENT

General Assessment Issues

The nature and characteristics of conduct problems are critical for appropriate assessment. Table 10.2 summarizes the issues raised in the introduction and their relevance to the assessment process. As evident from Table 10.2, the complex and pervasive nature of conduct problems requires a comprehensive evaluation that assesses many aspects of the child's functioning and psychosocial environment. To further complicate matters, each domain should ideally be assessed using multiple informants (e.g., parent, child, and teacher), multiple assessment modalities (e.g., rating scales, behavioral observations), and instruments with established psychometric properties (e.g., information on reliability and

TABLE 10.2.   Characteristics of Conduct Problems and Their Implications for Assessment

Characteristic	Assessment Implications
1. Classification and Subtypes	1a. Determine presence of ODD and CD
	1b. Determine undersocialized/socialized and aggressive/non-aggressive type
	1c. Determine age of onset of conduct problems
2. Comorbidities	2a. Assess for the presence of ADHD
	2b. Assess for the presence of anxiety and depression and temporal relationship with depression
	2c. Assess for the presence of learning disabilities
3. Correlates	3a. Assess family functioning, especially parental psychiatric adjustment, marital conflict, and parental socialization practices
	3b. Assess social ecology such as community support, economic stressors, and living environment
	3c. Assess peer relations and association with deviant peer group

Note: ODD refers to Oppositional Defiant Disorder, CD refers to Conduct Disorder, and ADHD refers to Attention-Deficit Hyperactivity Disorder.

validity). The specific methods of accomplishing such an assessment are described in this section.

Assessment of Behavioral and Emotional Functioning

A comprehensive assessment of a child's behavioral and emotional functioning serves three purposes:

1. It assesses the type and severity of conduct problems.
2. It assesses for potential comorbid problems in adjustment.
3. It helps to determine the degree of impairment associated with the child's psychological difficulties.

Given the importance of this assessment domain, the issue of obtaining information from several sources is even more critical than in other areas.

A multiple-informant assessment is required because any one source of information will be imperfect for one or more reasons. First, there is a large body of evidence that a child's behavior, both problematic and normal, varies from setting to setting (see Achenbach, McConaughy, & Howell, 1987). Therefore, information from people who see the child in different settings is necessary to obtain a complete picture of the child's behavioral functioning. Second, self-reports from the child and reports from others are *perceptions* of a child's behavior. These perceptions can be influenced by a number of factors, such as the mood and motivations of the informant. Third, some behaviors and emotions are evident only in certain settings or to certain people; for example, presence or severity of covert conduct problems (e.g., stealing, lying, substance abuse) may not be apparent to a parent or teacher. Therefore, given the imperfection inherent in any one source of information, a combination of sources is the only way to obtain a complete picture of the child's behavioral and emotional functioning. Three primary methods of assessing a child's behavioral and emotional functioning in a multiple-informant format are behavior rating scales, clinical interviews, and behavioral observations.

Behavior Rating Scales

Behavior rating scales have several important characteristics that make them indispensable to the assessment process. First, they allow for collection of information in a reliable and time-efficient format. Second, many rating scales have forms for parents, teachers, and children, so that analogous information on a child's functioning can be obtained from multiple informants. Third, many behavior rating scales allow for a comparison of a child's score on a rating scale with the scores of a large representative sample of children. This information indicates the degree of deviance of a child's behavior, relative to a comparison group.

There are two main types of rating scales. First, there are comprehensive rating scales that assess several areas of a child's behavioral and emotional functioning (see Piacentini, 1993; Witt, Heffer, & Pfeiffer, 1990). The Child Behavior Checklist (CBCL) (Achenbach, 1991) for example, includes forms for parent, child, and teacher and assesses for the presence of emotional difficulties, attentional problems, and social withdrawal, as well as conduct problems. The Comprehensive Behavior Rating Scale for Children (CBRSC) (Neeper, Lahey, & Frick, 1990) is another comprehensive rating scale for teachers that was designed to more closely approximate disorder definitions in the *Diagnostic and Statistical Manual of Mental Disorders* (American Psychiatric Association, 1987). It includes a scale consisting of ODD and CD symptoms, as well as scales designed to assess typical comorbid problems such as attention-deficit disorder, anxiety, peer relations, and behavioral indicators of learning problems and cognitive deficits.

The second type of behavior rating scale assesses behaviors that are specific to one domain of a child's functioning, such as depression (e.g., Kovacs & Beck, 1977), anxiety (e.g., Reynolds & Richmond, 1985), or self-esteem (e.g., Harter, 1982). For many evaluations, a more detailed assessment of a certain area of a child's behavioral or emotional functioning may be required than what is provided by comprehensive rating scales. In these instances, these more specialized rating scales can provide reliable, time-efficient, and norm-referenced information on one specific aspect of a child's functioning.

Clinical Interviews

Like behavior rating scales, clinical interviews can be used to assess for the presence and severity of emotional and behavioral problems using multiple informants. However, there are several important pieces of information that are more readily obtained in an interview format (Frick, 1991). First, interviews can assess for the duration and age of onset of problem behaviors—two parameters that are especially crucial in the assessment of conduct problems. Second, interviews can provide an assessment of the temporal relationship of behaviors; for example, it may be helpful to determine whether or not a child's conduct problems preceded or followed the onset of a depressive episode. Third, interviews allow for an assessment of the degree of impairment (e.g., impairments in social and academic functioning) associated with a child's emotional or behavioral difficulties.

One criticism of unstructured clinical interviews that allow the assessor to determine the method of obtaining information (e.g., what questions to ask, how to word the questions) has been their unreliability. In response to this criticism, there have been a number of structured-interview schedules developed that provide the assessor with a standard format for obtaining information from an informant and with specific rules for rating the information obtained. Length and content of these interview schedules differ, as does the availability of analogous forms to obtain information from different informants (see Gutterman, O'Brien, & Young, 1987; Hodges & Zeman, 1993). Many interview schedules were developed specifically to obtain information necessary to make DSM–III–R diagnoses.

Behavioral Observations

A third way of assessing a child's behavioral and emotional adjustment is through directly observing his or her behavior, either in naturalistic settings (e.g., home or school) or in an analogue setting (e.g., clinic). There are several observational systems available that define specific target behaviors to be observed, define the situations in which the behavior is to be observed, define the observational method (e.g., frequency counts of behavior), and set up training procedures for the observers (see Kazdin, 1993). These observational systems make many unique contributions to the assessment process. First, they allow for an assessment of a child's behavior that is not filtered through the perceptions of an informant. Second, observational systems allow for an assessment of the environmental context of a child's behavior, such as assessing the antecedents and consequences of a child's conduct problem behavior. The context of a child's behavior is critical to several of the most effective behavioral treatments of conduct problems, discussed later in the chapter.

Unfortunately, behavioral observations also have several limitations that have prevented their widespread use in the assessment of conduct problems. First, observations are time-consuming and costly, which makes their use an impossibility in many situations. Second, designing observational situations with ecological validity is difficult, either because the observational situations are so artificial that they do not actually mirror a child's typical environmental context or because the process of observation leads to changes in a child's behavior (or the behavior of others in his or her environment). Third, many types of conduct problems are difficult to assess through observations, either because of their covert nature (e.g., lying and stealing) or because of their infrequent occurrence.

Psycho-Educational Assessment

As was discussed in the introduction, there is a strong association between conduct problems and learning disabilities. In fact, there is some evidence that poor school achievement can contribute to an increase in truancy and acting-out behavior in late childhood and early adolescence (see Hinshaw, 1992). Also, some interventions (i.e., cognitive problem-solving training) seem to require a certain level of intellectual development to be effective. Therefore, a psycho-educational evaluation, which includes a standardized intelligence test and academic achievement screening, should be a part of most evaluations of children with conduct problems (see Kaufman & Ishikuma, 1993; Sattler, 1988).

Assessment of Family Functioning

In the introduction, it was noted that several areas of family dysfunction are common in children with conduct problems. Further, as discussed in greater detail later in this chapter, the most effective treatment of conduct problems is a family-based intervention model. The effectiveness of this intervention model, however, is determined by its ability to address the unique needs of a child's family. Therefore, an assessment of a child's family context is essential for understanding a child's functioning and designing effective treatment programs.

As stated earlier, poor parental adjustment (e.g., antisocial behavior, depression, substance abuse) is highly related to the development of conduct problems in children and should be assessed. There are several structured interviews (e.g., Robins & Helzer, 1985) and rating scales (e.g., Hathaway & McKinley, 1989) that allow for a standardized assessment of parental adjustment. Second, the parents' marital adjustment has been associated with both the development of conduct problems and the success of intervention, and, therefore, the parents' marital satisfaction (e.g., Spanier, 1976) and/or the level of marital conflict (e.g., Porter & O'Leary, 1980) also should be assessed. Third, parents' ability to adequately socialize their child through their involvement in their child's activities and their ability to supervise and monitor their child's behavior through their use of consistent (but not overly harsh) discipline have a strong negative association with conduct problems. Unfortunately, although this dimension of family functioning is likely to be the most critical one for understanding the development of conduct problems and for developing treatment goals, it is also the one area in which a standard and reliable assessment procedure is not readily available.

Assessment of Peer Relationships

As noted in the introduction, peer rejection is predictive of the development of conduct problems and is associated with an adolescent's association with a deviant peer group. Therefore, assessing a child's peer relationships is a critical assessment goal. Several comprehensive rating scales assess a child's peer functioning in addition to emotional and behavioral problems (e.g., CBRSC). Also, there are several rating scales specifically designed to assess peer relationships through either a child's self-report or the report of others in a child's environment (see Hughes, 1990). Unfortunately, these reports often show low correlations with how the child's peers actually view the child (Neeper et al., 1990), and, therefore, some method of actually assessing the perceptions of a child's peers, such as through a sociometric exercise, is often desirable (see Hughes, 1990; Gresham & Little, 1993). Given that a child's association with a deviant peer group is associated with the severity of conduct disorders, some method of assessing this aspect of a child's social functioning (e.g., Elliott, Huizinga, & Ageton, 1985) should also be included in a comprehensive assessment.

ACTUAL ASSESSMENT

The assessment procedures just outlined are quite costly and time-consuming, requiring a large time commitment from the assessor(s), the child, and others in a child's environment (e.g., parents and teachers). Therefore, cost limitations, time constraints, or the lack of motivation or availability of critical sources of information make the ideal assessment impossible in many situations. However, it is believed that the critical elements of this assessment approach—a multiple-informant assessment of multiple dimensions of a child's functioning—should not be sacrificed at any costs. It is the author's contention that many treatment failures are the result of an inadequate assessment.

One way that this procedure is often tailored to a testing situation is by limiting the sources of information to those sources that seem *most* important. Unfortunately, research suggests that the best informant may vary depending on the type of behavior being assessed; for example, parents and teachers may be better informants for overt behaviors (e.g., aggression, defiance, hyperactivity), whereas children may be more important informants for assessing covert behaviors and emotional disturbances (Edelbrock, Costello, Dulcan, Kalas, & Conover, 1985; Hodges, Gordon, & Lennon, 1990: Loeber, Green, Lahey, & Stouthamer-Loeber, 1991). Also, the reliability of information may differ, depending on the child's age. Specifically, children under the age of 10 tend to be unreliable in reporting behaviors in very structured formats (Edelbrock et al., 1985). Further, reliability of teacher information tends to decrease as a child enters adolescence, most likely due to the fact that the knowledge that any one teacher possesses about a child decreases as a child enters high school (Edelbrock et al., 1985).

Another method of tailoring the assessment procedure is to assess the relevant areas of functioning in a less standard format (e.g., using unstructured interviews) than those discussed in previous sections. If situations require obtaining lower quality information, the assessor must be aware of the limitations of this information and appropriately temper his or her interpretations and recommendations. However, the basic principles of a comprehensive multiple-informant assessment must be maintained, even if circumstances prevent the methodological rigor that would be optimal.

PROTOTYPIC TREATMENT

General Treatment Issues

Although carefully controlled outcome research is unavailable for many types of intervention, the existing research suggests that the most promising interventions are those based on social learning principles that fall under the general rubric of behavior therapy (see Dumas, 1989; Garrett, 1985; Kazdin, 1987; McMahon & Wells, 1989). As a result, these interventions, which are the focus of this chapter, should be an integral part of any treatment program for conduct disorders. The following discussion focuses on several of the more promising behavioral techniques, with *promising* defined as "having been shown to be effective in treating children with conduct problems in controlled outcome studies." It should be noted that all of the intervention techniques identify a set of principles that can be utilized in multiple settings (e.g., inpatient hospitals, outpatient clinics, school consultations) and that can be implemented using several different modalities (e.g., individual, group, milieu).

Contingency Management

Contingency management plays a critical role in almost all of the interventions discussed in this chapter, whether the contingencies are designed to teach cognitive problem-solving skills or whether the child's parents are taught appropriate uses of operant techniques. The importance of operant techniques in the treatment of conduct disorders is not simply due to their documented effectiveness (see Garrett, 1985; Kazdin, 1985). A child experiencing appropriate contingencies is also important to many theoretical formulations of the development of conduct problems (e.g., Patterson, 1982; Patterson, Reid, & Dishion, 1992).

Contingency management programs have been successfully utilized in the home, school, and institutional setting to alter conduct problem behaviors in children (for examples and critical reviews, see Kazdin, 1985; McMahon & Wells, 1989). The basic components of an operant program are the designation of target behaviors, both prosocial behaviors (e.g., obeying commands, participating in class, initiating positive interactions) and aversive behaviors (e.g., hitting others, temper tantrums). A structured system of consistently applying positive reinforcement (e.g., praise, attention, privileges, tokens) for a child's display of the prosocial behaviors and consistently applying punishers (e.g., reprimands, time-out, loss of privileges, assignment of work chores) for the negative behaviors is then implemented (Kazdin, 1984; Ross, 1981).

Although these principles appear basic, there seem to be several critical ingredients to a successful contingency management program. Probably the most important step is to develop a program in which contingencies can be *consistently* applied. In fact, the potency of a contingency (e.g., how severe the punishment) is less crucial to its effectiveness than its consistent application. A basic behavioral principle is that behaviors are most likely to change (increase or decrease) when contingencies (reinforcers or punishers) are provided on a continuous schedule (Kazdin, 1984; Ross, 1981). In addition to consistency, using a combination of reinforcement to increase appropriate behaviors and punishment to reduce negative behavior is also critical. There is convincing evidence that the combination is more effective in treating conduct problems than either method used alone (see McMahon & Wells, 1989).

Although these behavioral principles are generally applicable to the treatment of children, there is intriguing research that suggests that both of these characteristics of successful operant programs may be especially important in treating children with conduct disorders. Specifically, many children with conduct disorders exhibit a basic learning style in which they seem to be more motivated to seek reward than to avoid punishment (Daugherty & Quay, 1991; O'Brien, Frick, Lyman, in press). Therefore, contingency programs that emphasize reward for positive behavior and limit the rewarding aspect of antisocial behavior through *consistent* negative consequences would be congruent with this learning style.

Kazdin (1985) summarized the outcome research on contingency management programs for children and adolescents with conduct problems: Operant programs have produced significant changes in aggressive, disobedient, and other antisocial behaviors in many settings (e.g., home, schools, institutions). Unfortunately, there remain several limitations of these techniques. First, most contingency management programs have focused on a few discrete target behaviors, and, unfortunately, the majority of children with conduct problems exhibit multiple problems. Therefore, the *breadth* of change brought about by these programs is questionable. Second, the generalizability of the changes across settings and the long-term maintenance of changes have often been limited.

Cognitive Problem-Solving Training

Cognitive problem-solving training (CPT) is based on the assumption that aggressive and hostile behaviors are the result of a child's perception and interpretation of situations, especially social situations (Kendall & Braswell, 1985; Spivack & Shure, 1982). Research in support of this assumption has indicated that aggressive children are more likely to interpret innocuous events as hostile, to have more difficulty generating nonaggressive solutions to problems, and to have more difficulty taking the perspective of others (see Dodge & Frame, 1982; Dumas, 1989; Spivack & Shure, 1982). Based on this theoretical and empirical literature, several treatment programs have been designed to teach children ways to modify these cognitive processes (e.g., Kazdin, Esveldt-Dawson, French, & Unis, 1987; Kendall & Braswell, 1985; Lochman & Curry, 1986).

The skills that are taught by CPT follow directly from the cognitive problem-solving deficits identified in aggressive children. Children are taught to (a) recognize problem situations, (b) use self-statements to reduce impulsive responses, (c) generate multiple solutions to problems, (d) evaluate possible consequences of actions, and (e) take the perspective of others. These skills are taught by having the child practice a step-by-step problem-solving strategy that incorporates each of the skills using either a group format (Lochman & Curry, 1986) or an individual format (Kazdin, Esveldt-Dawson, et al., 1987). Each skill is first modeled by the experimenter and then practiced by the child using very structured tasks (e.g., games, academic tasks, hypothetical stories). After the child has become competent using these skills in the structured tasks, the child is taught to apply them to real-life situations. Some method of prompting a child's use of the problem-solving strategy and providing reinforcement for its use is usually incorporated into the treatment package.

There are several scholarly reviews of the outcome research on the use of CPT for children with conduct problems, and the authors have generally reached similar conclusions (Dumas, 1989; Kazdin, 1987; McMahon & Wells, 1989). This approach appears promising because its positive effects on child adjustment have been documented in comparison to many types of control groups and to alternative treatments. Furthermore, its effects have been durable up to 1 year follow-up. Unfortunately, these evaluations also indicated that CPT did not typically change a child's behavior sufficiently to bring a child's level of functioning into a normative range. Kazdin, Esveldt-Dawson, et al. (1987) documented the superiority of their individually administered CPT in treating antisocial children on a psychiatric inpatient unit in comparison to antisocial children receiving relationship therapy and a treatment-contact control group. Immediately following treatment, however, only 17.6% of the children receiving CPT had scores on rating scales that were below what is typically considered clinically deviant.

Parent Management Training

Parent management training (PMT) refers to a set of interventions in which the parents are taught methods of interacting with their child in ways that enhance their child's functioning. A primary focus of PMT is on teaching parents appropriate methods of applying contingencies to increase positive child behaviors and decrease negative child behaviors, such as conduct problems. There are numerous PMT treatment packages available for use with children (e.g., Eyberg & Robinson, 1982; Forehand & McMahon, 1981; Patterson, 1976) and adolescents (Patterson & Forgatch, 1987), which can be used in both individual and group formats.

Most PMT interventions are divided into two phases. The first phase involves helping the parents to develop positive ways of interacting with their child, such as attending to their child in appropriate ways while reducing commands and criticisms. This is crucial for changing the negative reaction cycles that often develop between the parents and their children with conduct problems. Also in this first phase of treatment, the parents are educated in basic social learning principles and taught to use positive change strategies (e.g., verbal and physical rewards) to increase positive child behaviors. In the second phase of treatment, parents are taught to use appropriate strategies to reduce problem behavior by ignoring minor problem behaviors, giving appropriate commands, and applying consistent punishment for problem behaviors (e.g., time-out, removal of privileges, work chores). Skills in both phases of treatment are usually taught in a sequential format and through a variety of methods. A skill typically is first modeled by the clinician and then practiced by the parents in a structured setting with the clinician and with their child; finally, home assignments are given to promote use in the actual home environment.

There seem to be several critical considerations in implementing a successful PMT program for families of children with conduct disorders. First, as is the case for any operant program, the program must include methods by which a parent learns *both* to increase the child's positive behaviors and to decrease negative behaviors. Second, teaching the parents general social learning principles, in addition to specific child-management techniques, appears to enhance treatment effectiveness (McMahon, Forehand, & Greist, 1981). Third, involving both parents when possible seems to be critical in enhancing treatment effectiveness, especially in maintaining treatment effects over time (Webster-Stratton, 1985). Fourth, PMT interventions can be enhanced by including long-term follow-up sessions, often termed *booster-sessions*, in which families are seen periodically on a long-term basis and the PMT interventions are reviewed and modified as needed (Kazdin, 1987).

Unlike most other interventions for conduct problems, the effectiveness of PMT programs has been tested in a large number of controlled outcome studies, and this method seems to be the most promising treatment for conduct problems (Dumas, 1989; Kazdin, 1987; McMahon & Wells, 1989; Miller & Prinz, 1990). Outcome research has shown that PMT programs have resulted in significant changes in child behavior compared to the changes found in control groups and to changes brought about by other types of treatment. In fact, PMT often brought the behaviors of treated children into a normative range. Also, these changes tended to generalize to multiple children in a family, and the changes were durable at periods from 1 to 5 years following treatment. Unfortunately, these positive treatment outcomes, while clearly surpassing most other types of intervention, also must be placed in a realistic context. These outcomes were generally found for younger children (8 years of age and under) who exhibited milder conduct problems (oppositional, noncompliant, and mild aggressive behaviors) and who came from families without severe dysfunction (i.e., without such conditions as economic disadvantage, severe parental psychopathology, high levels of marital conflict, or low levels of social support).

ACTUAL TREATMENT

General Considerations

As stated previously, behavioral interventions seem to be the most effective interventions *relative* to other interventions strategies. Therefore, these interventions should be a component of any treatment plan for children with conduct disorders. However, it is also clear from the outcome evidence that these interventions have substantial limitations in terms of the number of clients who benefit and the degree of change brought about by the interventions. As a result, in this section several practical issues in the use of these interventions are discussed, particularly the need for enhancing the effectiveness of these interventions with more broad-based treatment programs.

Enhancing Parent Management Training

Given the several limitations to the effectiveness of PMT programs, this section highlights several possible ways of enhancing the basic PMT model. Miller and Prinz (1990) recommend expanding the skills taught to parents beyond those typically included in current PMT programs: Teaching parents conflict-resolution skills (e.g., expressing feelings, reflective listening, and negotiation) and self-control strategies (e.g., goal setting, self-monitoring, and self-reinforcement) could increase the maintenance of newly acquired parenting skills. Miller and Prinz also highlight the need to incorporate into the PMT model a more broad-based approach to family intervention by intervening into areas of family functioning that transcend parenting behaviors; directly intervening into areas of parental psychiatric adjustment (e.g., depression, substance abuse), marital discord, and extrafamilial stressors (e.g., unemployment, lack of social support) may be required if PMT interventions are to be successful.

Another example of broadening the base of PMT comes from the work of Alexander and colleagues in their development of a model of family intervention labeled functional family therapy (FFT) (Alexander & Parsons, 1982; Barton & Alexander, 1981). This approach to treatment is an attempt to integrate behaviorally oriented PMT with family systems theory. The parent-child interactions are viewed from a broader family systems perspective, and interventions, often similar to the basic techniques of PMT, are tailored to the interactional dynamics of the specific family. Initial outcome research on FFT has generally been favorable and is especially notable for its success in treating delinquent adolescents, a population that has been quite resistant to other treatments (Kazdin, 1987; McMahon & Wells, 1989).

Another way in which PMT can be enhanced is by utilizing it as one part of a multimodal treatment plan. Although pharmacological interventions have not always been promising in the treatment of conduct problems, certain psychotropic medications may be an effective part of a comprehensive treatment plan (Hinshaw, 1991; Stewart, Myers, Burket, & Lyles, 1990). Hinshaw (1991) provided compelling evidence that children with conduct problems *and comorbid attention-deficit disorder* show a reduction in several types of conduct problems, most notably mild aggression, when treated with stimulant medication. Especially for this subgroup of children with conduct problems, it seems that a multimodal treatment package with stimulants and PMT appears warranted.

Whereas the potential benefit of a multimodal intervention combining PMT and medication is largely speculative at present, there is clear outcome data that another combination of approaches is effective. Kazdin, Siegel, and Bass (1992) reported a treatment outcome study of 97 children (ages 7 to 13 years) referred for treatment at a psychiatric outpatient facility for severe aggressive and antisocial behavior. In that study, the authors compared an individually administered PMT program, an individually administered CPT program, and a program that combined both types of treatment (PMT/CPT). It was shown that the multimodal treatment group (PMT/CPT) was clearly superior to either the PMT or the CPT group on most measures of child and family adjustment. In fact, 60% of the children in the PMT/CPT group were rated by parents and teachers in a nondeviant range immediately following treatment, compared to 27% and 18% of the CPT and the PMT groups, respectively.

Child-Focused Interventions

The discussion in the previous section centers around enhancing the effects of PMT in treating children with disorders. This lengthy discussion is important because PMT has shown the most demonstrable effect in treating conduct problems and, when possible, should be the core of any treatment program. However, PMT, with all of the variations and enhancements discussed, requires the presence of a parent who is both willing and able to participate in treatment. As discussed in the introduction, families of children with conduct problems are likely to be so highly dysfunctional (e.g., high rates of psychopathology in the parent(s) that such a parent is often not available.

In these cases, a child-focused intervention often is all that is possible. To add to this unfortunate situation, the most effective child-focused intervention, contingency management, is also difficult without family support. Unless a child shows severe enough behavior to warrant inpatient or residential treatment, it is difficult to sufficiently monitor a child's behavior and control the contingencies on the behavior to implement a successful contingency management program. Therefore, CPT becomes the only option with demonstrated effectiveness.

As already discussed, CPT alone has shown limited effectiveness. However, this approach is still in its infancy, and a great deal of work needs to be done to determine if the treatment effectiveness of this method can be enhanced; for example, combining CPT with other treatment modalities, such as pharmacological intervention, has been untested. There is a critical need for clinical research to continue to refine child-focused interventions, such as cognitive-behavioral approaches, given that in many settings the more successful family-focused options are not feasible.

SUMMARY

Conduct disorders are a major concern in most child psychiatric settings. There are a number of characteristics of conduct disorders that make them particularly difficult to assess and treat. The heterogeneity among children who have conduct problems, the high degree of comorbidity with other problems in adjustment, and the numerous psychosocial correlates combine to make the assessment and treatment of conduct problems a complex undertaking. In this chapter, the authors have attempted to integrate this knowledge of the basic characteristics of conduct problems with the most current clinical research in order to provide some guidelines for clinical practice in a psychiatric setting.

The authors also have attempted to be realistic about the benefits and limitations of the current technology in both assessment and treatment. Sometimes the findings have not been overly optimistic. Whereas this is disheartening to some degree, given the amount of effort that has been placed in trying to develop effective intervention strategies, it is also a challenge to the field to continue to develop and to test the clinical utility of new and innovative types of assessment and intervention. And, as a final note, these findings clearly place paramount importance on prevention efforts so that conduct disorders can be prevented or treated before they develop into a behavior pattern that is less malleable to treatment.

REFERENCES

Abikoff, H., & Klein, R. G. (1992). Attention-deficit/hyperactivity and conduct disorder: Comorbidity and implications for treatment. *Journal of Consulting and Clinical Psychology, 60,* 881–892.

Achenbach, T. M. (1991). *Manual for the Child Behavior Checklist—1991.* Burlington, VT: University of Vermont.

Achenbach, T. M., McConaughy, S. H., & Howell, C. T. (1987). Child/adolescent behavioral and emotional problems: Implications of cross-informant correlations for situational specificity. *Psychological Bulletin, 101,* 213–232.

Alexander, J. F., & Parsons, B. V. (1982). *Functional family therapy.* Monterey, CA: Brooks-Cole.

American Psychiatric Association. (1987). *Diagnostic and statistical manual of mental disorders* (3rd ed., rev.). Washington, DC: Author.

American Psychiatric Association. (1993). *DSM–IV draft criteria.* Washington, DC: Author.

Barton, C., & Alexander, J. F. (1981). Functional family therapy. In A. S. Gurman & D. P. Kniskern (Eds.), *Handbook of family therapy* (pp. 403–443). New York: Brunner/Mazel.

Daugherty, T. K., & Quay, H. C. (1991). Response perseveration and delayed responding in childhood behavior disorders. *Journal of Child Psychology and Psychiatry, 32,* 453–461.

Dishion, T. J., Patterson, G. R., & Skinner, M. S. (March 1989). *A process model for the role of peers in adolescent social adjustment.* Paper presented at the biennial meeting of the Society for Research in Child Development, Kansas City, MO.

Dodge, K. A., & Frame, C. L. (1982). Social cognitive biases and deficits in aggressive boys. *Child Development, 53,* 620–635.

Dumas, J. E. (1989). Treating antisocial behavior in children: Child and family approaches. *Clinical Psychology Review, 9,* 197–222.

Edelbrock, C., Costello, A. J., Dulcan, M. K., Kalas, R., & Conover, N. C. (1985). Age differences in the reliability of the psychiatric interview of the child. *Child Development, 56,* 265–275.

Elliot, D. S., Huizinga, D., & Ageton, S. S. (1985). *Explaining delinquency and drug use.* Beverly Hills, CA: Sage Publications.

Eyberg, S. M., & Robinson, E. A. (1982). Parent-child interaction training: Effects on family functioning. *Journal of Clinical Child Psychology, 11,* 130–137.

Farrington, D. P. (1978). The family backgrounds of aggressive youths. In L. A. Hersov & M. Berger (Eds.), *Aggressive and antisocial behaviour in childhood and adolescence* (pp. 73–94). London: Pergamon Press.

Forehand, R., & McMahon, R. J. (1981). *Helping the noncompliant child: A clinician's guide to parent training.* New York: Guilford Press.

Frick, P. J. (1993). Family dysfunction and the disruptive behavior disorders: A review of recent empirical findings. In T. H. Ollendick & R. J. Prinz (Eds.), *Advances in clinical child psychology* (Vol. 16, pp. 203–226). New York: Plenum Press.

Frick, P. J. (1991). Making the most of structured interview schedules. *Child Assessment News, 1,* 1, 11–12.

Frick, P. J., Kamphaus, R. W., Lahey, B. B., Loeber, R., Christ, M. A. G., Hart, E. L., & Tannenbaum, L. E. (1991). Academic underachievement and the disruptive behavior disorders. *Journal of Consulting and Clinical Psychology, 59,* 289–294.

Frick, P. J., Lahey, B. B., Hartdagen, S., & Hynd, G. W. (1989). Conduct problems in boys: Relations to maternal personality, marital satisfaction, and socioeconomic status. *Journal of Clinical Child Psychology, 18,* 114–120.

Frick, P. J., Lahey, B. B., Loeber, R., Stouthamer-Loeber, M., Green, S., Hart, E. L., & Christ, M.

A. G. (1991). Oppositional defiant disorder and conduct disorder in boys: Patterns of behavioral covariation. *Journal of Clinical Child Psychology, 20,* 202–208.

Frick, P. J., Lahey, B. B., Loeber, R., Tannenbaum, L. E., Van Horn, Y., Christ, M. A. G., Hart, E. A., & Hanson, K. (1993). Oppositional defiant disorder and conduct disorder: A meta-analytic review of factor analyses and cross-validation in a clinic sample. *Clinical Psychology Review, 13,* 319–340.

Frick, P. J., Strauss, C. C., Lahey, B. B., & Christ, M. A. G. (1993). Behavior disorders of children. In P. B. Sutker & H. E. Adams (Eds.), *Comprehensive handbook of psychopathology* (2nd ed., pp. 765–789). New York: Plenum Press.

Garrett, C. J. (1985). Effects of residential treatment on adjudicated delinquents: A meta-analysis. *Journal of Research on Crime and Delinquency, 22,* 287–308.

Gresham, T. M., & Little, S. G. (1993). Peer-referenced assessment strategies. In T. H. Ollendick & M. Hersen (Eds.), *Handbook of child and adolescent assessment* (pp. 165–179). Boston: Allyn and Bacon.

Gutterman, E. M., O'Brien, J. D., & Young, J. G. (1987). Structured diagnostic interviews for children and adolescents: Current status and future directions. *Journal of the American Academy of Child and Adolescent Psychiatry, 26,* 621–630.

Harrington, R., Fudge, H., Rutter, M., Pickles, A., & Hill, J. (1991). Adult outcomes of childhood and adolescent depression: II. Links with antisocial disorders. *Journal of the American Academy of Child and Adolescent Psychiatry, 30,* 434–439.

Harter, S. (1982). The Perceived Competence Scale for Children. *Child Development, 53,* 3–15.

Hathaway, S. R., & McKinley, J. C. (1989). *MMPI-2.* Minneapolis, MN: University of Minnesota.

Hinshaw, S. P. (1987). On the distinction between attentional deficits/hyperactivity and conduct problems/aggression in child psychopathology. *Psychological Bulletin, 101,* 443–463.

Hinshaw, S. P. (1991). Stimulant medication and their treatment of aggression in children with attention deficits. *Journal of Clinical Child Psychology, 20,* 301–312.

Hinshaw, S. P. (1992). Externalizing behavior problems and academic underachievement in childhood and adolescence: Causal relationships and underlying mechanisms. *Psychological Bulletin, 111,* 127–155.

Hodges, K., Gordon, Y., & Lennon, M. P. (1990). Parent-child agreement on symptoms assessed via a clinical research interview for children: The Child Assessment Schedule (CAS). *Journal of Child Psychology and Psychiatry, 31,* 427–436.

Hodges, K., & Zeman, J. (1993). Interviewing. In T. H. Ollendick & M. Hersen (Eds.), *Handbook of child and adolescent assessment* (pp. 65–81). Boston: Allyn and Bacon.

Huessmann, L. R., Eron, L. D., Lefkowitz, M. M., & Walder, L. O. (1984). The stability of aggression over time and generations. *Developmental Psychology, 20,* 1120–1134.

Hughes, J. (1990). Assessment of social skills: Sociometric and behavioral approaches. In C. R. Reynolds & R. W. Kamphaus (Eds.), *Handbook of psychological and educational assessment of children: Personality, behavior, and context* (pp. 364–394). New York: Guilford Press.

Kaufman, A. S., & Ishikuma, T. (1993). Intellectual and achievement testing. In T. H. Ollendick & M. Hersen (Eds.), *Handbook of child and adolescent assessment* (pp. 192–207). Needham Heights, MA: Allyn and Bacon.

Kazdin, A. E. (1984). *Behavior modification in applied settings* (3rd ed). Homewood, IL: Dorsey.

Kazdin, A. E. (1985). *Treatment of antisocial behavior in children and adolescents.* Homewood, IL: Dorsey.

Kazdin, A. E. (1987). Treatment of antisocial behavior in children: Current status and future directions. *Psychological Bulletin, 102,* 187–203.

Kazdin, A. E. (1993). Conduct disorder. In T. H. Ollendick & M. Hersen (Eds.), *Handbook of child and adolescent assessment* (pp. 292–310). Needham Heights, MA: Allyn and Bacon.

Kazdin, A. E., Esveldt-Dawson, K., French, N. H., & Unis, A. S. (1987). Problem-solving skills training and relationship therapy in the treatment of antisocial child behavior. *Journal of Consulting and Clinical Psychology, 55*, 76–85.

Kazdin, A. E., Siegel, T. C., & Bass, D. (1992). Cognitive problem-solving skills training and parent management training in the treatment of antisocial behavior in children. *Journal of Consulting and Clinical Psychology, 60*, 733–747.

Kendall, P. C., & Braswell, L. (1985). *Cognitive-behavioral therapy for impulsive children.* New York: Guilford Press.

Kovacs, M., & Beck, A. T. (1977). An empirical-clinical approach toward a definition of childhood depression. In J. G. Schulterbrandt & A. Raskin (Eds.), *Degression in childhood: Diagnosis, treatment, and conceptual models* (pp. 1–25). New York: Raven Press.

Kovacs, M., Paulauskas, S., Gatsonis, C., & Richards, C. (1988). Depressives disorder in childhood: III. A longitudinal study of comorbidity with and risk for conduct disorders. *Journal of Affective Disorders, 15*, 205–217.

Lahey, B. B., Loeber, R., Quay, H. C., Frick, P. J., & Grimm, J. (1992). Oppositional defiant and conduct disorders: Issues to be resolved for DSM–IV. *Journal of the American Academy of Child and Adolescent Psychiatry, 31*, 539–546.

Lahey, B. B., McBurnett, K., Loeber, R., & Hart, E. L. (in press). Psychobiology of conduct disorder. In G. P. Sholevar (Ed.), *Conduct disorders in children and adolescents: Assessments and interventions.* Washington, DC: American Psychiatric Press.

Lochman, J. E., & Curry, J. F. (1986). Effects of social problem-solving training and self-instruction training with aggressive boys. *Journal of Clinical Child Psychology, 15*, 159–164.

Loeber, R. (1990). Development and risk factors of juvenile antisocial behavior and delinquency. *Cliincal Psychology Review, 10*, 1–41.

Loeber, R., Green, S. M., Lahey, B. B., & Stouthamer-Loeber, M. (1991). Differences and similarities between children, mother, and teachers as informants on disruptive child behavior. *Journal of Abnormal Child Psychology, 19*, 75–95.

Loeber, R., & Stouthamer-Loeber, M. (1986). Family factors as correlates and predictors of juvenile conduct problems and delinquency. In M. Tonry & N. Morris (Eds.), *Crime and justice, 7*, (pp. 29–149). Chicago: University of Chicago Press.

McMahon, R. J., Forehand, R., & Griest, D. L. (1981). Effects of knowledge of social learning principles on enhancing treatment outcome and generalization in a parent training program. *Journal of Consulting and Clinical Psychology, 49*, 526–532.

McMahon, R. J., & Wells, K. C. (1989). Conduct disorders. In E. J. Mash & R. A. Barkley (Eds.), *Treatment of childhood disorders* (pp. 73–134). New York: Guilford Press.

Miller, G. E., & Prinz, R. J. (1990). Enhancement of social learning family interventions for childhood conduct disorder. *Psychological Bulletin, 108*, 291–307.

Neeper, R., Lahey, B. B., & Frick, P. J. (1990). *Manual for the Comprehensive Behavior Rating Scale for Children.* San Antonio, TX: The Psychological Corporation.

O'Brien, B. S., Frick, P. J., Lyman, R. D., in press. Reward dominance among children with disruptive behavior disorders. *Journal of Psychopathology and Behavior Assessment.*

Patterson, G. R. (1976). *Living with children (Revised).* Champaign, IL: Research Press.

Patterson, G. R., (1982). *Coercive family process.* Eugene, OR: Castalia.

Patterson, G. R., & Dishion, T. J. (1985). Contributions of families and peers to delinquency. *Criminology, 23*, 63–79.

Patterson, G. R., & Forgatch, M. S. (1987). *Parents and adolescents living together.* Eugene, OR: Castalia.

Patterson, G. R., Reid, J. B., Dishion, T. J. (1992). *Antisocial boys.* Eugene, OR: Castalia.

Piacentini, J. C. (1993). Checklists and rating scales. In T. H. Ollendick & M. Hersen (Eds.), *Handbook of child and adolescent assessment* (pp. 82–97). Needham Heights, MA: Allyn and Bacon.

Porter, B., & O'Leary, K. D. (1980). Marital discord and childhood behavior problems. *Journal of Abnormal Child Psychology, 8*, 287–295.

Puig-Antich, J. (1982). Major depression and conduct disorder in prepuberty. *Journal of the American Academy of Child and Adolescent Psychiatry, 21*, 118–128.

Quay, H. C., & Love, C. T. (1977). The effect of a juvenile diversion program on rearrests. *Criminal Justice and Behavior, 4*, 377–396.

Reynolds, C. R., & Richmond, B. O. (1985). *Revised Children's Manifest Anxiety Scale (RCMAS)*. Los Angeles, CA: Western Psychological Services.

Robins, L. N., & Helzer, J. E. (1985). *Diagnostic interview schedule (DIS Version III–A)*. St. Louis, MO: Washington University.

Roff, J. D., & Wirt, R. D. (1984). Childhood aggression and social adjustments as antecedents of delinquency. *Journal of Abnormal Child Psychology, 12*, 111–126.

Ross, A. O. (1981). *Child behavior therapy*. New York: Wiley.

Rutter, M., & Giller, H. (1983). *Juvenile delinquency: Trends and perspectives*. London: Penguin.

Sattler, J. M. (1988). *Assessment of children* (3rd ed.). San Diego, CA: Author.

Spanier, G. B. (1976). Measuring dyadic adjustment: New scales for assessing the quality of marriage and similar dyads. *Journal of Marriage and Family, 38*, 15–28.

Spitzer, R. L., Davies, M., & Barkley, R. A. (1990). The DSM–III–R field trials of disruptive behavior disorder. *Journal of the American Academy of Child and Adolescent Psychiatry, 29*, 690–697.

Spivack, G., & Shure, M. B. (1982). The cognition of social adjustment: Interpersonal cognitive problem solving thinking. In B. B. Lahey & A. E. Kazdin (Eds.), *Advances in clinical child psychology* (Vol. 5, pp. 323–372). New York: Plenum Press.

Stewart, J. T., Myers, W. C., Burket, R. C., & Lyles, W. B. (1990). A review of the pharmacotherapy of aggression in children and adolescents. *Journal of the American Academy of Child and Adolescent Psychiatry, 29*, 269–277.

Walker, J. L., Lahey, B. B., Hynd, G. W., & Frame, C. L. (1987). Comparison of specific patterns of antisocial behavior in children with conduct disorder with or without coexisting hyperactivity. *Journal of Consulting and Clinical Psychology, 55*, 666–678.

Walker, J. L., Lahey, B. B., Russo, M. F., Frick, P. J., Christ, M. A. G., McBurnett, K., Loeber, R., Stouthamer-Loeber, M., & Green, S. M. (1991). Anxiety, inhibition, and conduct disorder in children: I. Relations to social impairment. *Journal of the American Academy of Child and Adolescent Psychiatry, 30*, 187–191.

Webster-Stratton, C. (1985). The effects of father involvement in parent training for conduct problem children. *Journal of Child Psychology and Psychiatry, 26*, 801–810.

Wilson, H. (1975). Juvenile delinquency, parental criminality, and social handicap. *British Journal of Criminology, 15*, 241–250.

Witt, J. C., Heffer, R. W., & Pfeiffer, J. (1990). Structured rating scales: A review of self-report and information rating processes, procedures, and issues. In C. R. Reynolds & R. W. Kamphaus (Eds.), *Handbook of psychological and educational assessment of children: Personality, behavior, and context* (pp. 364–394). New York: Guilford Press.

CHAPTER 11

Separation Anxiety Disorder

DEBORA BELL-DOLAN

DESCRIPTION OF THE PROBLEM

Separation anxiety disorder (SAD) is one of the most common childhood psychiatric disorders. Epidemiological studies report that as many as 41% of children experience separation concerns (Lapouse & Monk, 1964), and 2% to 4% of children and adolescents are estimated to show the clinical disorder (Bowen, Offord, & Boyle, 1990; McGee et al., 1990). SAD is often associated with significant impairment in academic, social, and psychological functioning. Many children with SAD stop attending school or only attend sporadically, thus limiting their opportunities for academic and social involvement. They may also experience somatic or physiological distress to an extent that medical treatment is needed. For these reasons, mental health professionals have devoted a great deal of time and attention to identifying and understanding SAD and to developing effective treatments for this disorder. This chapter will overview SAD, describing the disorder and prototypic assessment and treatment. Examples of actual assessment and treatment will also be provided, along with practical considerations that may influence discrepancies between prototypic and actual methods of dealing with SAD.

Symptoms and Diagnosis

The defining feature of SAD is an excessive and unrealistic fear of separation from an attachment figure, usually a parent. This fear is expressed through excessive and persistent worry about separation, behavioral and somatic distress when faced with separation situations, and persistent avoidance of or attempts to escape from such situations. Children with SAD worry about separation resulting from harm to either an attachment figure or themselves. These children might report worrying that a parent will leave and never return or be hurt or killed in a car accident. They might also worry that they themselves will be lost, kidnapped, or killed. Particularly for younger children, repeated nightmares with themes of separation are common (Francis, Last, & Strauss, 1987). Symptoms of subjective distress encompass complaints of physical symptoms, such as headaches or gastrointestinal upset, acting out (having a tantrum), crying, or pleading. These symptoms may occur in the separation situations, as well as in anticipation of such situations.

Avoidance of separation situations may take several forms. Younger children in particular may be very clingy with parents, staying close to or even in physical contact with them when the possibility of separation is present (i.e., in the grocery store). They may also shadow their parents, following them from room to room, or may refuse to play outside unless a parent is present. At night, these children may sleep with their parents rather than in their own rooms. For older children, avoidance of separation may take the form of reluctance to stay home alone or to engage in peer activities where a parent is not present, such as participating in sports or clubs or spending the night with a friend. One of the most frustrating, and often the most debilitating avoidance symptom, is the SAD child's reluctance or refusal to attend school. In mild cases, children may complain about attending school, report physical symptoms such as headaches or stomachaches, or dawdle when getting ready for school. More serious cases may involve children having bouts of vomiting or diarrhea before or during school or refusing to attend school without severe threats or physical force. It is not uncommon to see children with SAD who have not attended school for several weeks or months. Once in a separation situation, children with SAD may exhibit or complain of continued distress and may attempt to escape the situation. When attending school or a slumber party, for example, a child with SAD may phone home repeatedly to check on his or her parents, may become ill and request to be sent home, or may actually leave the school or party and walk home.

The *Diagnostic and Statistical Manual of Mental Disorders* (DSM-III-R) (American Psychiatric Association, 1987) criteria for diagnosis of SAD involve nine symptoms of excessive anxiety concerning separation, including the types of worries, distress, and avoidance as described previously. To be diagnosed with SAD, a child must show at least three of the nine criterion symptoms for at least 2 weeks. Additionally, onset of the separation anxiety must be prior to age 18 and the symptoms may not occur only during a pervasive developmental disorder (autism) or psychotic disorder (e.g., schizophrenia).

The newest DSM revision (DSM-IV, American Psychiatric Association, 1993) increases the stringency of the diagnosis. The presence of three symptoms is still required. However, two of the symptoms listed in DSM-III-R (distress in anticipation of separation, distress upon separation) are combined in the DSM-IV, so that the symptom list now contains eight symptoms. In addition, the 2-week duration required in DSM-III-R is lengthened to 4 weeks in DSM-IV. Further, DSM-IV clarifies that, in order for separation anxiety to be considered pathological, the anxiety needs to be not only excessive, but developmentally inappropriate. These changes should help differentiate between separation anxiety that is developmentally normal or is a transient reaction to change or stress and anxiety that is a more enduring and impairing disorder.

Onset, Course, and Prognosis

SAD is one of the most common anxiety disorders experienced by children, accounting for approximately one-half of children seen for mental health treatment of anxiety disorders (Bowen et al., 1990; Last, Hersen, Kazdin, Finkelstein, & Strauss, 1987; McGee et al., 1990). Although it can occur any time prior to age 18, SAD is seen most often in prepubertal children, with an average onset of 9 years (Kashani & Orvaschel, 1988, 1990; Last, Hersen, Kazdin, Finkelstein, & Strauss, 1987). As already described, symptom expression often varies with age. Younger children may want very close proximity or physical contact with parents, appearing clingy. Older children may be able to tolerate separations that are brief or involve relatively small separation distances, such as the next room or the neighborhood, but may have more difficulty with separations that occur over greater space and time, such as overnight stays with friends or at camp. Several studies have found SAD to occur more frequently in girls than boys (Francis et al., 1987; Last, Hersen, Kazdin, Finkelstein, & Strauss, 1987). However, these differences are small and generally not statistically significant. The course of SAD is variable, with symptoms waxing and waning over time. Periods of stress are high-risk times, often leading to exacerbation of symptoms. In particular, transitions (e.g., family moves, enrollment in a new school) or events that increase the chance of parent-child separation (e.g., parent marital problems or separation/divorce, illness of child or parent) may trigger SAD symptoms (Hersov, 1960; Ollendick & Mayer, 1984). As far as longer term prognosis is concerned, there is some suggestion that children with SAD may develop mood or anxiety disorders (e.g., panic disorder, agoraphobia) in adulthood (Ollendick & Huntzinger, 1990).

Family Characteristics

Certain family characteristics have been shown to be associated with child SAD. Compared to other children seeking treatment for anxiety disorders, children with SAD tend to come from lower socioeconomic status (SES) families (Last, Hersen, Kazdin, Finkelstein, & Strauss, 1987). It is possible that low SES families experience more of the transitions and separation-relevant stressors that are associated with SAD symptoms. Several studies have also shown a link between child SAD and parent anxiety or depression; first degree relatives (especially mothers) of children with SAD are more likely than relatives of normal children or children with disruptive behavior disorders to have experienced an anxiety disorder during their lifetime (Last, Hersen, Kazdin, Finkelstein, & Strauss, 1987; Last, Hersen, Kazdin, Orvaschel, & Perrin, 1991). Although it is currently unclear whether these findings implicate genetic versus environmental factors in families of children with SAD, they do suggest familial transmission of the tendency to experience SAD.

PROTOTYPIC ASSESSMENT

What to Assess

Comprehensive assessment of SAD, as of any disorder or problem behavior, involves making decisions about what, when, and how to assess the phenomenon. In terms of *what* to assess, behaviorally oriented practitioners and researchers consider the problem behavior itself and relevant situational (environmental) factors to be prime assessment targets. Assessment of the problem behavior, or *problem definition*, is a critical starting point, necessary for diagnosis, as well as treatment planning and evaluation. For SAD, defining the problem involves identifying the specific separation anxious behaviors or symptoms that the child exhibits. Problem definition should be as specific as possible. Identification of general classes of symptoms or behavior may be all that is needed to make a diagnosis of SAD; for example, knowing that a 10-year-old worries about harm to self and to his parents, is reluctant to go to school, and does not meet criteria for a pervasive developmental disorder or psychotic disorder is enough to make a diagnosis of SAD. However, a general symptom, such as worry about harm to self, may be expressed differently by different children (i.e., worry about being kidnapped from backyard, worry about being killed in a school bus accident), and knowledge of the specific symptom expression will be helpful in planning individualized treatment. Thus, problem definition should include attention to each of the symptoms identified in DSM-III-R, as well as to child-specific examples of each symptom. It is also important to identify parameters of the separation anxious behaviors, such as their frequency, intensity, and duration; for example, it is useful to know whether a fear of being kidnapped is expressed only occasionally in a fairly casual manner or every day accompanied by crying and tantrums. These parameters provide an index of how severe and pervasive the problem is.

Comprehensive problem definition should also involve assessment of the multiple components of the anxiety response. Anxiety has been characterized as a three-component response, involving thoughts (e.g., worrying, catastrophizing), physiological responding (e.g., headaches, gastrointestinal upset, palpitations), and motor behavior (e.g., avoiding or escaping feared situations, crying) (Delprato & McGlynn, 1984). While all three response components are considered important in the experience of anxiety, their relative importance will vary among individual children. Some children will express primarily cognitive symptoms, while others will complain of physical symptoms but not report worrying. Additionally, the way in which these components influence each other may vary from child to child. One child may worry about her parents, for example, with thoughts becoming increasingly catastrophic, until she feels nauseous, at which point she asks to be sent home from school. Another child may notice his physical symptoms first and then begin to worry that he will die and be separated from his parents. Knowledge of which components are salient for a particular child and which components appear earlier or later in the anxiety experience can aid in selecting treatment approaches.

In addition to problem definition, sound behavioral assessment focuses on situational or environmental factors that may have influenced the development or maintenance of SAD. *Environmental factors* may be broadly classified as antecedents or consequences. Identification of antecedent events that may "trigger," or set the stage for, an anxiety response is vital in determining what situations are problematic for the child and should be addressed in treatment. *Antecedent events* include contextual factors, or setting events, as well as more proximal, immediate situational factors. Contextual factors, such as increased family conflict, illness of a parent, or family members who model separation anxiety, are relevant because they may influence a child's tolerance for separation. A child whose father has recently moved out of the house following legal separation or divorce may feel less comfortable about his or her mother leaving because of concerns that she, too, may move out. Likewise, a child whose parents are overly protective may learn to express similar worries. More immediate antecedents are those that occur shortly or immediately prior to the child's separation anxious behavior; for example, arrival of a school morning is a problem situation for many children with SAD. Another common problem situation is going places where a parent will not be present and having the separation last for hours or days, such as going to day care or being left with a babysitter, going to camp, or going to a friend's house. However, some children's anxiety occurs in response to much more minor antecedent events, such as being left in the house while a parent takes out the trash or being shut out of the bathroom while a parent is bathing. Identification of antecedents to separation anxiety can provide clues about specific themes in the child's anxiety; for example, a child who becomes anxious when a parent goes to the grocery store but not to work may fear not knowing the exact location of the parent or being unable to contact the parent at any time. This information will be useful in designing treatment involving imaginal or in vivo exposure scenes, as will be discussed later.

In addition to identifying antecedents, understanding the consequences of a child's separation anxious behavior is important for complete assessment of separation anxiety. The results of a child's anxious behavior will influence his or her subsequent anxious behavior. If the separation anxious behavior is reinforced or appropriate separation behavior is punished, then a child's separation anxiety will continue and may worsen. When examining possible reinforcing consequences, one should look at both positive and negative reinforcers. An example of a situation that is probably positively reinforcing would be one where a child receives increased attention and comforting from a parent following that child's expression of separation worries. In this case, separation anxious behavior results in what is likely to be an enjoyable outcome (attention, comforting) for the child. Negative reinforcement involves the escape or avoidance of some negative state or event. For a separation anxious child, verbalization of worries, reports of stomachaches, or tantrums may be very effective in escaping or avoiding a separation situation if the parent keeps the child home from school or cancels an evening out to stay with the child. The child may also avoid other unpleasant events, such as spending time with a babysitter or going to school.

A variety of consequences may punish appropriate separation behavior. For example, the same parents who present concerns about their child's separation anxiety may also express disapproval (the punishment) when their child attempts to separate (e.g., fear that child will be hurt, resentment that child prefers peer company to interacting with parent, loneliness when child is gone). This undoubtably is typically not the message that parents intend to send. However, if parent happiness and approval are rewarding to the child, then unhappiness and disapproval following child separation may easily lead to the child becoming more dependent and anxious about separation.

How to Assess

Several procedures and instruments are suitable for assessment of SAD. While only a few allow actual diagnosis of the disorder, several others are helpful in understanding specific components of the child's anxiety, as well as relevant situational factors.

Diagnosis and general symptom description are probably best accomplished via interview. The ability to ask case-relevant questions, clarify as necessary, receive immediate feedback, and follow up accordingly is more characteristic of interviews than any other assessment method. Although clinical interviews are often unstructured, their content guided by the patient's presenting complaint and initial responses and by the clinician's training and interests, more structured interviews are currently considered to be the best means of generating a DSM-III-R diagnosis. Such interviews tend to yield diagnoses that are more reliable than those obtained with unstructured clinical interviews (Last, Hersen, Kazdin, Finkelstein, & Strauss, 1987). Various structured and semi-structured diagnostic interviews have been used for assessment of child anxiety disorders (see Silverman, 1991, in press, for reviews). These interviews focus on DSM-III-R symptoms as reported by children and their parents and cover a variety of child psychiatric disorders. The amount of coverage of particular disorders, specific administration procedures, degree of structure, and reliability of diagnosis vary from interview to interview. The user should evaluate these features in order to select the interview that best meets his or her needs. For the assessment of SAD, two interviews, a modified version of the Schedule for Affective Disorders and Schizophrenia in School-Age Children (K-SADS) and the Anxiety Disorders Interview Schedule for Children (ADIS-C), are especially appropriate. Because of initially modest coverage of anxiety disorders in the original K-SADS (Puig-Antich & Chambers, 1978), Last (1986) modified that interview to include more detailed coverage of the childhood anxiety disorders, as well as phobias, panic disorder with and without agoraphobia, and obsessive-compulsive disorder. In contrast, the ADIS-C (Silverman & Nelles, 1988), developed primarily as a means of assessing anxiety disorders, includes sections on all DSM-III-R anxiety disorders, including some disorders not covered in the K-SADS (e.g., posttraumatic stress disorder, sleep terror disorder). Both interviews also include sections on a variety of other child psychiatric disorders (e.g., mood disorders, disruptive behavior disorders, psychotic symptoms), thus allowing the interviewer to make differential diagnoses and to assess for comorbidity of anxiety and other disorders. Both the K-SADS and the ADIS-C rely on a combination of parent and child report for diagnosis, and both have demonstrated inter-interviewer and test-retest reliability (Last & Strauss, 1990; Silverman, 1991; Silverman & Eisen, 1992).

Despite their similarities, a number of differences between the two interviews suggest that each interview might be useful for slightly different purposes. First, the K-SADS and the ADIS-C differ in the amount of structure, with the ADIS-C being somewhat more structured than the K-SADS. The K-SADS follows a symptom-oriented format, listing a range of possible questions designed to elicit information about diagnostic criteria. The interviewer can select questions that fit the child's developmental level (which influences both cognitive understanding of the questions and expression of the symptoms in question) and the child's or parent's preferred use of descriptors, or language. This format allows a more natural interchange than is often possible with more structured interviews. However, this flexible question format also requires a fair amount of clinical training and judgment on the part of the interviewer and so may not be appropriate for use by paraprofessionals. In contrast, the ADIS-C questions are designed to be asked verbatim, which presumably requires less background in clinical interviewing. Although the increased structure may decrease flexibility in "speaking the child's language," Silverman (1991) does indicate that rewording may be used as necessary to facilitate child understanding. Second, the two interviews differ in the way in which responses are coded. With the K-SADS, responses are scored on rating scales that reflect absence of the symptom, presence at a subclinical level, or presence at varying clinical levels of severity (e.g., mild to extreme). The ADIS-C, on the other hand, elicits yes-no responses to many of the symptom questions and then assesses problem severity separately. The K-SADS' ability to discriminate between clinical and subclinical symptoms and among severity levels can be helpful in classifying children along a separation anxiety continuum. However, it is also more difficult to code reliably with a rating scale than with a dichotomous scale. Third, the extent to which non-DSM-III-R information is assessed varies across the interviews. Because the K-SADS was designed as a general diagnostic tool, its focus is primarily on information directly relevant to making a diagnosis, including diagnostic criteria and onset and duration of the disorder. The ADIS-C, which was developed specifically as a means of assessing anxiety disorders, includes a broader assessment of SAD. In addition to assessing information necessary to determine whether, when, and how long a child has met criteria for the disorder, the ADIS-C includes questions regarding antecedents and consequences, symptom severity, and interference.

These structured diagnostic interviews yield information on the child's psychiatric symptoms and diagnoses. As mentioned earlier, endorsement of diagnostic criteria may result from the child's exhibiting any number of specific behaviors, and the specifics should be noted for future incorporation into treatment planning. Additionally, follow-up with an unstructured interview allows the clinician to assess specific antecedents and consequences; important background factors, such as family history and previous treatment; and functioning in related areas.

Although questionnaire measures alone cannot be used to diagnose SAD, several questionnaires are useful for evaluating SAD symptoms. One such instrument is the Revised Children's Manifest Anxiety Scale (RCMAS) (Reynolds & Richmond, 1978). This self-report measure assesses three factors: worry-oversensitivity, physiological anxiety, and concentration anxiety. One useful feature of the RCMAS is the availability of normative data for children in grades 1 through 12, categorized by age, gender, and race (Reynolds & Paget, 1983), which allows comparison of patient data to relevant norms. Similarly, the Cognitive and Somatic State and Trait Anxiety Scale (CSSTAS) (Fox & Houston, 1983), attempts to specifically measure both the somatic and the cognitive aspects of anxiety. This measure is a modification of the more general State-Trait Anxiety Inventory for Children (Spielberger, 1973). Last (1991) found this measure useful for assessing somatic complaints of children with SAD and school refusal. These children seem to be likely to express such complaints, even more so than children with other types of anxiety. Both measures have demonstrated acceptable reliability and validity (Fox & Houston, 1983; Reynolds, 1980, 1981, 1982; Reynolds & Paget, 1983).

One relatively new questionnaire measure assesses factors that may serve to maintain a child's school refusal. The School Refusal Assessment Scale (SRAS) (Kearney & Silverman, in press) was developed to measure positively reinforcing factors (e.g., attention or tangible rewards) and negatively reinforcing factors (e.g., escape from aversive school-related activities or from fear) in school refusal. The scale, designed to be used as part of a multimethod assessment, is completed by parents, teachers, and children. The SRAS has shown stability over time and across raters. This instrument could be quite valuable in determining the appropriate direction for treatment based on the types of environmental contingencies identified. Additionally, while this measure is specific to school refusal, it is also potentially useful as a model for assessment of factors influencing other types of separation anxious behavior (e.g., preseparation tantrums).

Because interviews and questionnaires may be biased due to their often retrospective nature, the possibility of self-presentation biases, or a child's inability to articulate his or her symptoms, direct observations can be of great help in understanding a child's anxiety. An example of a fairly standardized observation measure is the Observation of Separation-Relevant Play (Milos & Reiss, 1982). This measure has been used to assess motor behavior in SAD children. The number of anxiety-relevant responses during play (e.g., desire to be with mother) provides the basis for an overall separation anxiety score. This observation code is relatively simple, has demonstrated good interrater reliability, and seems to respond to treatment effects. Behavioral avoidance tests can also be used as a more individualized means to observe a child's separation anxious behavior. These tests involve exposing the child to a series of controlled and graduated experiences with a feared situation; for example, a child who fears separation from parents may be observed with a parent in the same room, with a parent in an adjoining room but in sight, with a parent out of sight, and so on. Because behavioral avoidance tests can be designed to fit the situation, they can be quite useful clinically, not only during initial assessment but also as ongoing measures of treatment progress.

In addition to the more formal observations by clinicians, parents' or teachers' observations of a child's behavior in the natural environment can also be a good way of understanding the nature of his or her SAD. Parents and teachers can be asked to observe motor behavior (e.g., escape or avoidance attempts, tantrums) or outward signs that the child is experiencing cognitive or somatic symptoms. Bornstein and Knapp (1981), for example, have demonstrated the utility of parent observations of their SAD children's expression of cognitive symptoms. Parents observed and recorded the number of fear-related statements uttered by their own children every hour. Parents showed good interobserver agreement, and their scores were sensitive to treatment effects, suggesting that this type of participant observation may be useful for clinical assessment. In addition to observing the child's anxious behavior, parents and teachers can also monitor environmental events that may be related to separation anxious behaviors; for example, participant observers can be asked to note situational factors or events, their own reactions, or the behavior of others that may influence the child's anxiety. This information is helpful in the development and testing of hypotheses about the etiology and maintenance of the SAD.

Although observation can be quite useful for providing a detailed picture of a child's anxiety, it is usually an incomplete picture. Because much of the anxiety experience is internal, children themselves may be the only ones who can observe many of their symptoms. Thus, asking children to self-monitor and record their own anxiety on an ongoing basis can flesh out assessment. In particular, children may be asked to monitor their thoughts in separation situations or to track somatic symptoms throughout the week. Self-monitoring is typically most successful with older children (over about 8 or 9) who are more able to carry out the task without frequent reminders and are often more able to describe their subjective experiences.

Although somatic symptoms are recognized as components of several child anxiety disorders, physiological assessment methods have been understudied (Beidel, 1991). Self-report methods asking children to report on their physiological symptoms (e.g., CSSTAS) are available but limited by their indirect nature and by potential response biases common in self-report. Direct measures of physiological responding have begun to be used in research on child anxiety (e.g., see Beidel's [1991] research on differences in physiological responding of test-anxious and non-test-anxious children). However, the utility of these procedures for assessing SAD has not yet been documented.

ACTUAL ASSESSMENT

Practical Considerations

The move from understanding prototypic assessment to implementing actual assessment requires consideration of several practical matters. No matter how knowledgeable, motivated, or resource-rich a clinician or agency is, actual assessment almost never involves optimal use of all of the assessment methods described previously. This may be because (a) some assessment method(s) are not used, or (b) even if a method is used, its results may not be useful. There are several reasons why clinicians may elect not to use a particular means of assessment: First, several of the methods can be fairly time or resource intensive. Effective use of structured diagnostic interviews, for example, requires that the clinician be trained in its use and that he or she take the 2 to 3 hours necessary to administer the complete interview. Second, referral sources (parents, schools) may be reluctant to devote the week or two needed to obtain a reasonable sample of daily naturalistic observation or self-monitoring data, especially in cases of significant impairment, such as prolonged school absence. In this case, it may be helpful to suggest that the cost of missing another week of school for a child who has already missed 8 weeks is probably outweighed by the benefits of a thorough assessment of the problem. Finally, direct physiological assessment may require equipment to which many clinicians may not have access. Given the current uncertainty regarding the utility of physiological assessment, expenditures needed to acquire such equipment may be difficult to justify except in the context of a research setting.

In other cases, assessment methods may not be used because they are not useful. Assessing cognitive symptoms in very young children is unlikely to yield a rich supply of information because these children often simply do not experience (or at least express) specific negative thoughts. Here, reliance on observable avoidance and distress is indicated. Similarly, asking parents, teachers, or children about the child's current or recent behavior in separation situations may prove fruitless if the child is successfully avoiding these situations. In this instance, the clinician may need to rely on parent/teacher reports of past behavior or to set up a behavioral avoidance test to elicit separation anxious behavior.

Even when the clinician plans a well-considered, multimethod assessment protocol, the results may not be of the quality anticipated. General patient-compliance problems can result in incomplete or inaccurate assessment information. Barriers to patient compliance with assessment efforts include instances in which the person misunderstands an interview or questionnaire item, misunderstands the purpose of a particular assessment procedure (e.g., does not understand that the purpose of parent home observation is to get a description of behavior *as it occurs,* rather than a retrospective report at the end of the week), does not see value in the assessment, or finds the assessment task (e.g., talking about a feared event, engaging in a behavioral avoidance task) uncomfortable. The consequences of providing an accurate report may also be uncomfortable for a child or parent; for example, a child may be reluctant to express worries for fear of worrying a parent. Similarly, a child may overreport a stomachache that is relatively minor in order to avoid being sent to school. A parent may underreport symptoms to protect his or her child from being labelled as having a problem or may overreport in order to insure that the child's problem receives attention.

Finally, one should remember that each piece of assessment information represents one point of view about one aspect of the separation anxiety assessed in one situation or point in time. Thus, even information that is accurate will not tell the whole story. Many pieces in combination, considered in the context of their particular sources, are needed for as complete a picture as possible. With these considerations in mind, an example of an assessment of SAD is provided.

Case Illustration

The case involved Darryl, an 11-year-old caucasian male who was referred to a psychiatry clinic due to concerns regarding separation. (Darryl was not an actual patient but rather a fictional character who represents a composite of several cases treated by the author.) Darryl was accompanied to the assessment sessions by his mother, Mrs. Smith. The initial sessions involved a structured diagnostic interview with Darryl and his mother and an unstructured follow-up interview designed to further assess Darryl's functioning in a variety of areas, his family background, and current family situation and to begin to formulate hypotheses as to possible etiological and maintaining factors. The interviews revealed that Darryl met criteria for SAD. Darryl expressed concern that his mother would be kidnapped or hurt in a car accident or that someone would break into their home and that he would not be able to protect his mother. Darryl reported that he also worried about his own safety, although not as often as he worried about his mother. Although he usually attended school, Darryl was often reluctant to do so. He complained of stomachaches before and during school and, once at school, often requested to use the telephone to call his mother at work. Upon arrival at home after school, Darryl also called his mother to be sure that she was safe at work. Darryl avoided a number of peer activities requiring separation (e.g., trips to the mall, staying overnight with friends), and Mrs. Smith reported that although his peer interactions at school were generally appropriate, Darryl had always been shy about making friends. Of greatest concern to Mrs. Smith, however, was that Darryl had not slept in his own bed for over 2 years. Instead, he would sleep in or at the foot of her bed. In addition to SAD, Darryl expressed symptoms of other anxiety disorders (e.g., overanxious disorder, panic disorder), as well as a few depressive symptoms (e.g., insomnia, low interest in age-appropriate peer activities). However, these were not severe enough to warrant separate diagnoses and were considered secondary to the SAD. Darryl and his mother denied problems with school achievement, parent-child relations, or general conduct.

The unstructured interview revealed that Darryl had experienced a number of losses in his lifetime. His parents were divorced shortly after he was born. Visits with his father had become less frequent over the years. Indeed, in the past year, Darryl had not heard from his father and was unsure of his whereabouts. When Darryl was 4 years old, he spent approximately 1 year living with his maternal grandmother while his mother was employed in a job that required frequent travel. Finally, approximately 1 year ago, Darryl and his mother moved from their hometown to their current residence. Of note was that there had been two reported break-ins in their neighborhood in the past year. This information suggested a number of setting events that may have primed Darryl for anxiety regarding separation. Additionally, Mrs. Smith reported experiencing a fair amount of anxiety herself, both currently and during her childhood, suggesting likely familial transmission.

Questions about environmental events more proximal to Darryl's separation anxious experiences identified several likely antecedents, including going to bed after watching the news (where Darryl might hear of burglaries) and his being left alone in the house or leaving his mother alone there. Although it seemed that fear of danger at home was a central feature of Darryl's worries, it had generalized to include almost any situation that he or his mother considered unsafe. A number of consequences also seemed to be reinforcing Darryl's separation anxious behavior. His desire to be physically close to his mother resulted in Darryl and Mrs. Smith spending most of their free time together, which they both reported enjoying. Both Darryl and his mother reported having a very close and satisfying parent-child relationship. In fact, each reported having only one casual outside friend, and both named each other as their primary confidante. Thus, it seemed that avoiding separation allowed Darryl to spend time in a close, comfortable relationship, to please his mother (who also enjoyed the relationship), and to protect her from loneliness and possibly from future relationships that might result in abandonment (as did her marriage). Likewise, the separation avoidance also allowed Darryl to avoid peer activities, which were somewhat difficult for him.

Following the interviews, questionnaires and observations were used to further assess Darryl's motor, cognitive, and physiological symptoms of SAD, as well as relevant environmental factors. Two questionnaires, the RCMAS and the CSSTAS, were completed independently by Darryl and his mother. Darryl's responses indicated a fair number of worries specific to separation dangers and a number of somatic symptoms. Interestingly, when Mrs. Smith completed these questionnaires on her son, she reported more numerous and more varied worries than he did. This type of discrepancy should lead a clinician to search for other bits of evidence that suggest that the child is minimizing or not aware of certain symptoms or that the parent is overreporting. The specific response bias could then be addressed in treatment.

In-session observation was conducted informally when Darryl and his mother were interviewed separately. Darryl displayed very minimal anxiety in the clinic setting, though presumably due to the fact that he did not consider it a dangerous environment for himself or his mother. Thus, further clinic observation was not pursued. However, Mrs. Smith was asked to observe and record Darryl's separation anxious behavior during the week between the first and second assessment sessions. To guide Mrs. Smith's efforts, she was asked to monitor Darryl's behavior during two high-risk times, at night before bed and any time she was preparing to leave Darryl at home alone. During these incidents, Mrs. Smith recorded (a) antecedent situations and events (e.g., news reports of break-ins), (b) specific separation anxious behaviors, and (c) consequent events (e.g., avoidance of unpleasant event, shared parent-child activity). Mrs. Smith's observations indicated that although certain danger cues may have been important in the initial development of Darryl's SAD, the mere suggestion of separation was now enough to increase Darryl's anxiety. It also became apparent that when Darryl slept in his mother's bed, they typically spent time talking and watching television together before they went to sleep. It was not clear that such pleasant interaction occurred when Darryl went to his own room. Mrs. Smith's observation of other separation instances revealed that these never occurred during the week. Mrs. Smith generally asked Darryl if he wanted to accompany her to the store, and so on, and they would choose times when it was convenient to go together.

Finally, Darryl was also asked to monitor his experiences during the same two high-risk situations. Each evening at bedtime, Darryl was to record his behaviors, thoughts, and somatic symptoms and to rate his anxiety level. During the week, Darryl slept in his mother's bed each night. On two nights, however, Mrs. Smith suggested that Darryl go to his own room, at which point Darryl became highly anxious, developed a headache and a stomachache, and became tearful. This lasted only for a few minutes before Darryl went to his mother's bed to sleep. During these two nights, Darryl reported difficulty getting to sleep due to worries about someone breaking in. This information was unique to Darryl's report and had not been noticed by his mother. Darryl's report of the second high-risk time confirmed his mother's report that it did not occur, although he reported that he had wanted to stay home one evening when they instead ran errands. This piece of information implies that Darryl may have desired increased independence from his mother (which would be a good indicator of treatment motivation) or that Mrs. Smith may not have been actively encouraging him to attempt age-appropriate separation (which would be a likely treatment target.)

Other assessment methods could have been used but were not because of the kinds of practical reasons previously described. A clinic-based behavioral avoidance test, for example, was considered to be less useful than home participant observation and self-monitoring. Also, the teacher was not involved in assessment at all for the simple reason that assessment occurred during the summer. However, the assessment procedures used did combine to form a useful picture of Darryl's SAD. Together results of this assessment suggested a situation in which a preadolescent boy had a family history of anxiety and a personal history of loss, lacked close and age-appropriate peer relationships, and had only one close relationship. The relationship with his mother, therefore, was his sole source of support, comfort, and pleasant interaction. Likewise, his mother's support and social life revolved around her son, to the exclusion of adult relationships. Separation anxiety clearly seemed to be serving to maintain the support, closeness, and interpersonal contact that each was receiving. Unfortunately, the parent-child relationship and the separation anxiety were impairing the ability of both parent and child to pursue same-age relationships and, particularly, the ability of the child (who was the identified patient) to engage in the social and educational activities that would facilitate his development. Thus, this was a case in which treatment of SAD was clearly indicated.

PROTOTYPIC TREATMENT

The psychological and psychiatric literatures present a wide array of behavioral and cognitive-behavioral treatments for child anxiety. Many treatment approaches have been designed or implemented for nonseparation fears. However, they are applicable across different types of child anxiety and would seem to be appropriate, possibly with minor modifications, for SAD. Which particular treatment techniques are utilized will depend on the individual child, including the nature of his or her anxiety, age, and developmental level, and on the resources available to the treating clinician.

Behavioral Treatments

Several treatment approaches are based on the notion that SAD is developed or maintained through specific environmental events. *Modeling treatments*, for example, assume that children's behavior, including both separation anxious and nonanxious behavior, is learned by the child observing another person exposed to a fear-producing situation. Thus, such treatments involve having children observe models who cope successfully with the situation that the child fears. Although this treatment has been used most often with fear of medical procedures, it could be used in any instance in which fear-producing stimuli can be identified (Bandura, Blanchard, & Ritter, 1969; Klingman, Melamed, Cuthbert, & Hermacz, 1984; Matson, 1983); for example, for a child who fears having his parent leave for work, modeling might involve observation of a child who copes with a similar separation situation. Modeling appears to be most effective when the treatment requires participation of the anxious child (participant modeling) and when the model is similar to the anxious child in terms of age, level of anxiety, and previous experience with the feared situation or stimulus (Barrios & O'Dell, 1989).

Whereas modeling treatments stress the role of observational or vicarious learning, contingency management approaches assume that a child's separation anxiety is influenced by his or her *direct* experience with environmental contingencies. From this perspective, anxiety, or fearful behavior, exists because it is reinforced or because nonfearful behavior is not reinforced. A SAD child's preseparation tantrums or verbalization of separation worries, for example, may be maintained because they delay or deter a parent's evening out or a child's school attendance. Treatment, thus, involves rewarding the child's nonfearful behavior (e.g., waving good-bye to parents without tantrum earns a special treat with the babysitter) or withdrawing a reward for anxious behavior (e.g., ignoring a child's request to stay home from school) (Ayllon, Smith, & Rogers, 1970; Doleys & Williams, 1977; Neisworth, Madle, & Goeke, 1975). Reinforcement or reward procedures are preferable to punishment or reward-withdrawal procedures because reinforcement procedures help the child to learn adaptive behavior (approach, nonfearful behavior) without the negative emotions often associated with punishment. Additionally, shaping the desired behavior gradually is often preferred, particularly for children who have extreme or long-standing fears.

Exposure-based treatments involve repeated exposure to the feared situation or stimulus. *Systematic desensitization* (Wolpe, 1958) is based on the notion of reciprocal inhibition. This theory suggests that people's anxiety may be reduced by teaching them to exhibit a response (usually relaxation) that is incompatible with anxiety, and, thus, inhibits the anxiety when faced with an anxiety-producing situation. Typically, exposure to the feared situation occurs gradually. The child and therapist develop an anxiety hierarchy, with several anxiety-producing situations rank-ordered from least to most distressing. The child then practices relaxing in each situation, moving to the next situation when anxiety in the current one has decreased to an acceptable level. Variations of systematic desensitization involve using live (in vivo) exposure versus imaginal exposure to the feared situation (Phillips & Wolpe, 1981; Ultee, Griffin, & Schellenkens, 1982), using deep-muscle relaxation versus anger or distraction (e.g., game playing, story telling) as the incompatible response (Bentler, 1962; Croghan & Musante, 1975; Kellerman, 1980), and incorporating support from an imaginary superhero during imaginal densensitization ("emotive imagery") (Jackson & King, 1981; Lazarus & Abramovitz, 1962).

In addition to the reciprocal-inhibition treatments, several researchers have suggested that anxiety may be treated successfully with exposure in the absence of relaxation. These treatment strategies assume that prolonged exposure to a feared situation will eventually lead to habituation and, thus, to decreased anxiety. Similar to systematic desensitization, *flooding* involves construction of an imaginal or in vivo anxiety hierarchy and gradual progression through steps on the hierarchy. In contrast to systematic desensitization, in which relaxation is used to keep anxiety to a minimum, flooding involves having the child experience high levels of anxiety and remain in contact with the feared situation until habituation, or extinction of the anxiety response, occurs. For this reason, flooding generally begins with an intermediate- rather than a low-hierarchy situation.

Finally, Last and Francis (1988) advocate an exposure-based treatment that, although unaccompanied by relaxation, does not necessarily require exposure to the high levels of anxiety required by flooding and implosion. In *graduated exposure*, the child develops an anxiety hierarchy, and exposure assignments are selected by agreement among the child, parent, and therapist. The child practices each assignment until he or she indicates that anxiety has decreased to an acceptable level. Because the child helps to choose the initial assignment and to determine when to move to the next one, he or she is essentially in control of the rate of treatment at all times. Thus, for each individual case, treatment progress may resemble induction of high anxiety levels as in flooding or may look more like the gradual adaptation to small increments in anxiety as in systematic desensitization.

With all of the exposure-based treatments, use of in vivo versus imaginal exposure depends on a variety of factors. Although there is some evidence that in vivo exposure may be more effective than imaginal, especially with younger children (Morris & Kratchowill, 1983; Ultee et al., 1982), practical considerations (e.g., unavailability or uncontrollability of stimulus situations) may prohibit its use, in which case imaginal exposure may be used. Imaginal exposure may be used initially and then followed by in vivo exposure.

Cognitive Treatments

Although behavioral treatment may influence a child's physiological and cognitive experience of anxiety, the major treatment focus is on a successful, nonanxious approach to a fear-producing stimulus or situation, Thus, motor behavior is the primary treatment target, and treatment involves identification of a specific stimulus or situation. Cognitive treatment of SAD can be quite useful when a major component of the child's anxiety is cognitive (e.g., separation worries) or when the child is developmentally mature enough to take responsibility for managing his or her own anxiety. Such self-management is particularly important because the anxiety may often occur in the absence of the treatment agent (therapist, parent), and so the child may have to rely on his or her own coping skills to deal with the anxiety. Cognitive treatments typically include training in self-instruction regarding coping or distraction (e.g., "Just relax; take a deep breath;" "Think about your playhouse"), more realistic appraisal of the anxiety-producing situation (e.g., "Everybody is busy playing, so I don't think they're all looking at me"; "Nothing bad happened last time my mom left me at school, so I bet it won't this time either"), mastery-oriented coping statements (e.g, "I'm pretty brave; I can do this"; "I'm a good student, so I'll do fine on the test"), and self-reinforcement of adaptive coping and approach attempts ("I did it!") (Bankart & Bankart, 1983; Kane & Kendall, 1989; Kendall, Howard, & Epps, 1988; Morris & Kratchowill, 1983).

Physiological Treatment

Finally, relaxation is the only psychological treatment that focuses directly on physiological responding. Relaxation training is typically not employed in isolation to treat children's anxiety disorders, but it is frequently combined with exposure, as in systematic desensitization, or with cognitive self-management. Relaxation training involves teaching the child to tense and relax various muscle groups. For older children, standard progressive-muscle-relaxation training, in which the focus is on the physical sensations associated with relaxation of different muscle groups, can be used (Jacobson, 1938; Morris & Kratchowill, 1983). For younger children, adaptations such as the "turtle technique," which uses imagery (children pretending they are turtles withdrawing and emerging from their shells), may be useful (Kieppen, 1974). Although the relative efficacy of exposure or cognitive treatments with and without a relaxation component is equivocal (Ultee, et al., 1982), inclusion of relaxation does seem promising. This would seem particularly true when the child's SAD symptoms include somatic or physiological complaints.

Pharmacological Adjuncts to Psychological Treatment

To date, the literature on the effectiveness of pharmacological interventions for child anxiety has been quite mixed. Antidepressants, such as imipramine, initially appeared quite promising in treatment of SAD and school refusal (Gittelman-Klein & Klein, 1971, 1973, 1980; Rabiner & Klein, 1969), but more recent work has not supported the superiority of imipramine over placebo (Bernstein, Garfinkel, & Borchardt, 1990; Klein, Koplewicz, & Kanner, 1992). Several anxiolytics have also been tried in the treatment of SAD. Among the benzodiazepines, diazepam has occasionally been used (Lucas & Pasley, 1969); but, because of limited data on its effectiveness and some evidence of side effects, it is difficult to make specific recommendations regarding its application (Klein & Last, 1989). Alprazolam has received somewhat more attention and has shown slight, but nonsignificant, differences from placebo (Bernstein, Garfinkel, & Borchardt, 1990; Klein & Last, 1989). In spite of the equivocal research findings, these medications, particularly imipramine, are often recommended as an adjunct to behavioral treatment, especially in cases with very severe or chronic SAD (American Psychiatric Association, 1988; Last, 1989; Last & Francis, 1988).

ACTUAL TREATMENT

Practical Considerations

As with assessment, the move from prototypic to actual treatment for a particular case will depend on a variety of factors. First, because child anxiety may be expressed motorically, cognitively, and/or physiologically, matching treatment to the relevant mode(s) of expression would seem appropriate. In many cases of SAD with school refusal, for example, motoric components are quite prominent and impairing (e.g., when associated with excessive school absences and missed school work), and treatment should include procedures to increase behavioral or motoric approach to the feared stimulus.

A second selection factor concerns matching treatment with the child's cognitive and developmental level. Young children, for example, would likely have much more difficulty with self-management strategies than older children and so might do better with adult-mediated contingency management. Prior to about 9 years of age, children may also have more difficulty with imaginal procedures, which require use of visual imagery (Morris & Kratchowill, 1983). Similarly, children who are distractible benefit more from imaginal self-control strategies that are relatively uncluttered by fanciful, imaginative descriptors (Ollendick & Mayer, 1984).

Third, treatment choice and efficacy will be influenced by the patient's compliance with the treatment procedures. Many parents and children are reluctant to pursue flooding, for example, in the face of the extreme distress a child is likely to experience. Additionally, it may not be ethical to ask that children experience this distress if other effective treatments are available. One potential benefit of graduated in vivo exposure is that children and their parents may be less likely to drop out of or show resistance to treatment (Last & Francis, 1988). Self-control treatment may also lead to less treatment compliance than other-controlled treatment if a child is too young, too anxious, or not motivated enough to comply with treatment on his or her own. In such a case, a combination of self-control and parent- or therapist-mediated treatment may begin with relatively more control given to the parent or therapist but move toward increasing child self-control. In that way, the child may gradually learn to manage his or her own anxiety. Use of pharmacological treatment may also increase treatment adherence, particularly if medication serves to take the edge off the child's anxiety and, thus, allows him or her to participate more effectively in behavioral treatment. Of course, when using medication, careful attention should be paid to any adverse effects on the child.

Finally, treatment should be conceptualized and delivered in the context of the larger system. The literature suggests that family members of anxious children also display adjustment problems, especially anxiety and mood disorders (Bernstein & Garfinkel, 1988; Last, Hersen, Kazdin, Francis, & Grubb, 1987; Last, Phillips, & Statfeld, 1987). Clinically, it is not uncommon to wonder whether the parent of a child who presents with SAD is actually more separation anxious than the child. Family members may pass on anxiety genetically or environmentally (e.g., through modeling). Failure to incorporate the family into treatment may result in any treatment gains being lost when the child returns to this system. Likewise, anxiety-based school refusal occurs for many reasons (e.g., separation concerns, fear of teacher, fear of failing math), which must be addressed if treatment is to succeed.

Although the various treatment approaches are presented separately here, some of the most effective treatments involve combinations of various components (Blagg & Yule, 1984; Kendall et al., 1988). Selection of components for such compound treatment would involve attention to the same issues as previously described. The compound treatment would, thus, involve components that match the child's modes of anxiety expression, that are appropriate to his or her developmental level, that maximize adherence by the child and any other individuals involved in treatment (i.e., parents), and that incorporate family, school, and other environmental events or issues that are hypothesized to be influenced by the child's anxiety.

CASE ILLUSTRATION

Treatment

Treatment involved three goals: (a) to increase Darryl's ability to comfortably separate from his mother, without excessive worries or somatic distress, (b) to increase Darryl's engagement in age-appropriate social activities, especially those involving independence from his mother, and (c) to maintain a positive parent-child relationship. The first goal paralleled Mrs. Smith's initial concern, while the other two goals were considered integral to the success of separation efforts and to Darryl's social and personal development. An additional goal involved attention to the function that Darryl's SAD seemed to serve for Mrs. Smith. Because her major source of interpersonal support and interaction occurred with Darryl, development of alternative relationships for Mrs. Smith was seen as necessary for successful parent-child separation.

Treatment involved a combination of graduated exposure, cognitive coping, contingency management, and family therapy. Initially, graduated exposure and cognitive coping were employed to address the first goal. Darryl, Mrs. Smith, and the therapist discussed the treatment and agreed to focus first on bedtime. Darryl indicated that physical proximity to his mother's bed was a critical feature in his bedtime anxiety and, thus, generated an anxiety hierarchy with approximately 10 steps that varied on proximity to Mrs. Smith's bed: The first step involved Darryl sleeping at the foot of the bed, an intermediate step involved being outside the bedroom door, and the final step involved Darryl in his own bed. For the exposure assignments, Darryl was to take a sleeping pallet to the assigned location each evening at bedtime. Darryl and the therapist agreed that, initially, Darryl would plan to stay in that location at least 15 minutes before going to his mother's room, with the goal of eventually being able to remain in the assigned location all night. Although the therapist worried that the discomfort of sleeping on the floor might complicate successful separation, Darryl reported that he often slept on the floor. Once Darryl was able to stay at the assigned location all night without excessive anxiety, he proceeded to the next hierarchy step. Thus, the hierarchy was based on both separation distance and time. During this time, frequent contact between Mrs. Smith, Darryl, and the therapist was crucial in order to address problems and setbacks and to plan upcoming assignments. The first few weeks involved one or two midweek telephone calls in addition to weekly sessions.

Darryl's anxiety during graduated exposure assignments was evaluated by having him rate his anxiety on a 0 (not at all scared, do not avoid) to 8 (as scared as I have ever been, always avoid) scale. Each morning, Darryl recorded his anxiety level from the previous night's assignment, along with a brief description of any particular events, thoughts, or feelings that had occurred. (Although it is preferable to have the child record during or immediately after a graduated exposure assignment, in this case, immediate recording would interfere with falling asleep. Morning recording seemed satisfactory.) For Darryl, ratings of 0 to 3 were considered acceptable levels of anxiety and allowed progression to the next hierarchy step. Higher ratings were generally accompanied by worries of a break-in and/or harm to his mother, as well as heart racing, sweating, and difficulty falling asleep.

Approximately 1 week after Darryl began his hierarchy assignments, the therapist introduced cognitive coping. After discussing the concept of cognitive treatment, Darryl and the therapist generated a list of coping self-statements to use during graduated exposure assignments. The list included a combination of self-instructions to breathe deeply, realistic appraisal of the likelihood of a break-in, and mastery-oriented statements (e.g., "I've gone about 15 minutes, and I think I can go another 15"). Additionally, Darryl was taught to self-reinforce his efforts and progress.

After approximately 4 weeks of treatment, Darryl had been progressing reasonably well but seemed to have reached a barrier. Assessment indicated two potential causes: (a) the next hierarchy step involved turning a corner in the hallway so that mother's bedroom would no longer be in sight, and (b) Darryl did not find coping statements helpful once his anxiety had increased. To address the first problem, Darryl and the therapist inserted an intermediate hierarchy step that involved turning the corner but keeping the head of the sleeping pallet in sight of Mrs. Smith's bedroom. Discussion of the second problem revealed that, in the past, Darryl had been able to calm himself by imagining a combination of realistic and heroic coping with a break-in (e.g., calling 911, scaring burglar off by turning on all lights, helping mother stay calm). Thus, this imaginal coping strategy was added to Darryl's list of cognitive strategies.

While graduated exposure was progressing smoothly, it did not require a great deal of session time. After reviewing the week's progress, addressing any problems, and planning the next assignment, session attention was focused on age-appropriate separation in other instances. Initially, the therapist met individually with Mrs. Smith and with Darryl to discuss their feelings regarding their relationship and separation. Both indicated that they wanted to have other age-appropriate relationships and independence from each other but were unsure and somewhat frightened of how to do so. Thus, motivation appeared good. Through both individual and joint discussions, Mrs. Smith and Darryl developed interpersonal goals (e.g., Mrs. Smith: get involved with other single adults; Darryl: have friends outside of school) and means to achieve them (e.g., Mrs Smith: attend a Parents Without Partners social function with friend from work; Darryl: invite school friend to the basketball game). Darryl and Mrs. Smith agreed to each do one independent social activity per week. To reinforce their efforts and simultaneously maintain the parent-child relationship they enjoyed, Darryl and his mother also agreed to reward themselves with special time together (e.g., going for ice cream). Throughout this process, Darryl and Mrs. Smith were encouraged to address their reactions to the changing nature of their relationship (from an exclusive, enmeshed, yet comfortable relationship to a more typical parent-child relationship). For both Darryl and Mrs. Smith, this included discussion of Darryl's father and of general abandonment fears.

Complete assessment and treatment took approximately 6 months. During that time, there were a few setbacks, such as the one following a trip to grandmother's house, where there were only two bedrooms. At the end of treatment, Darryl was sleeping in his own bed comfortably, and there was discussion about the possibility of getting a waterbed and stereo for his room. Mrs. Smith reported that unlike prior to treatment, Darryl was now spending part of each evening in his room doing homework or listening to music ("just like a normal teenager"). Darryl also had two friends with whom he talked on the telephone several times per week and with whom he went places on weekends. Although anxiety at school and frequent phone calls to mother were not addressed specifically in treatment, Darryl and Mrs. Smith indicated that these had decreased to acceptable levels. A closing diagnostic interview indicated that Darryl no longer met criteria for SAD or any other psychiatric disorder. Mrs. Smith reported enjoying her independent time, dividing it between a co-worker with whom she had become friends and her personal hobbies of baking and sewing. A brief follow-up contact 8 months later indicated that treatment gains had been maintained. Darryl was preparing to enter middle school and was excited about it. He had become involved in the school band and a youth group and reported satisfying peer relationships. Darryl also reported that he worried or felt anxious only rarely and that he still used his cognitive coping strategies. Mrs. Smith had begun dating, had completed a stress management course, and was generally satisfied with her life.

Treatment did not involve all possible avenues, such as relaxation training or medication. Relaxation might have been useful for Darryl, given his physiological distress. However, the therapist decided that the time required for relaxation training could be better spent on the family relationship issues, and the treatment outcome was successful without relaxation. Nonetheless, Mrs. Smith benefited from relaxation training in her stress management course, and a similar course could be recommended for Darryl at some point in the future. Medication did not seem indicated in this case due to the relatively mild level of impairment (minimal impairment in school, moderate impairment in peer functioning and independent activities) and high level of motivation. A child with more severe or impairing anxiety might benefit from medication, especially if he or she was reluctant to engage in behavioral treatment.

SUMMARY

Child SAD is clearly an important area in child psychiatry. It is among the most prevalent of the child anxiety disorders and can be associated with considerable distress and impairment in functioning. Behavioral assessment and treatment provide numerous options for addressing the disorder, with choice of specific assessment and treatment approaches dependent on the individual case, as well as pragmatic issues. Although the literature on these disorders is growing, many questions regarding phenomenology, assessment and diagnosis, and treatment remain. In particular, hypotheses as to the etiology of SAD and prognosis for children with the disorder have yet to be empircally verified. Studies that tease apart genetic and environmental factors, as well as longitudinal studies that examine long-term prognosis, are needed. Additionally, at this point, most treatment studies are uncontrolled case studies that provide important information regarding treatment but do not allow as rigorous an assessment of treatment effectiveness as do controlled experiments. The few published controlled studies provide the best evidence regarding effects of various treatment strategies, as well as serving as examples of the type of work that should be pursued in the future. Continued work in child anxiety disorders should bring further refinements in clinicians' understanding and ability to deal effectively with child separation anxiety disorder.

REFERENCES

American Psychiatric Association. (1987). *Diagnostic and statistical manual of mental disorders (3rd ed., rev.)*, Washington, DC: Author.

American Psychiatric Association. (1988). *Treatments of psychiatric disorders.*Washington, DC: Author.

American Psychiatric Association. (1993). *DSM-IV draft criteria.* Washington, DC: Author.

Ayllon, T., Smith, D., & Rogers, M. (1970). Behavioral management of school phobia. *Journal of Behavior Therapy and Experimental Psychiatry, 1*, 125–138.

Bandura, A., Blanchard, E. B., & Ritter, B. (1969). Relative efficacy of desensitization and modeling approaches for inducing behavioral, affective, and attitudinal changes. *Journal of Personality and Social Psychology, 13*, 173–199.

Bankart, C. P., & Bankart, B. B. (1983). The use of song lyrics to alleviate a child's fears. *Child and Family Behavior Therapy, 5*, 81–83.

Barrios, B. A., & O'Dell, S. L. (1989). Fears and anxieties. In E. J. Mash & R. A. Barkley (Eds.), *Treatment of child disorders* (pp. 167–221). New York: Guilford Press.

Biedel, D. C. (1991). Determining the reliability of psychophysiological assessment in childhood anxiety. *Journal of Anxiety Disorders, 5*, 139–150.

Bentler, P. M. (1962). An infant's phobia treated with reciprocal inhibition therapy. *Journal of Child Psychology and Psychiatry, 3*, 185–189.

Bernstein, G. A., & Garfinkel, B. D. (1988). Pedigrees, functioning, and psychopathology in families of school phobic children. *American Journal of Psychiatry, 145*, 70–74.

Bernstein, G. A., Garfinkel, B. D., & Borchardt, C. M. (1990). Comparative studies of pharmacotherapy for school refusal. *Journal of the American Academy of Child and Adolescent Psychiatry, 29*, 773–781.

Blagg, N. R., & Yule, W. (1984). The behavioral treatment of school refusal—comparative study. *Behaviour Research and Therapy, 22*, 119–127.

Bornstein, P. H., & Knapp, M. (1981). Self-control desensitization with a multi-phobic boy: A multiple baseline design. *Journal of Behavior Therapy and Experimental Psychiatry, 12*, 281–285.

Bowen, R. C., Offord, D. R., & Boyle, M. H. (1990). The prevalence of overanxious disorder and separation anxiety disorder. Results from the Ontario child health study. *Journal of the American Academy of Child and Adolescent Psychiatry, 29*, 753–758.

Croghan, L. M., & Musante, G. J. (1975). The elimination of a boy's high-building phobia by in vivo densensitization and game playing. *Journal of Behavior Therapy and Experimental Psychiatry, 6*, 87–88.

Delprato, D. J., & McGlynn, F. D. (1984). Behavioral theories of anxiety disorders. In S. M. Turner (Ed.), *Behavioral theories and treatment of anxiety* (pp. 1–49). New York: Plenum Press.

Doleys, D. M., & Williams, S. C. (1977). The use of natural consequences and a makeup period to eliminate school-phobic behavior: A case study. *Journal of School Psychology, 15*, 44–50.

Fox, J. E., & Houston, B. K. (1983). Distinguishing between cognitive and somatic trait and state anxiety. *Journal of Personality and Social Psychology, 45*, 862–870.

Francis, G., Last, C. G., & Strauss, C. (1987). Expressions of separation anxiety disorder: The roles of age and gender. *Child Psychiatry and Human Development, 18*, 82–89.

Gittelman-Klein, R., & Klein, D. F. (1971). Controlled imipramine treatment of school phobia. *Archives of General Psychiatry, 25*, 204–207.

Gittelman-Klein, R., & Klein, D. F. (1973). School phobia: Diagnostic considerations in the light of imipramine effects. *Journal of Nervous and Mental Disease, 156*, 199–215.

Gittelman-Klein, R., & Klein, D. F. (1980). Separation anxiety in school refusal and its treatment with drugs. In L. Hersov & I. Berg (Eds.), *Out of school* (pp. 321–341). New York: Wiley.

Hersov, L. A. (1960). Persistent non-attendance at school. *Journal of Child Psychology and Psychiatry, 1*, 130–136.

Jacobson, E. (1938). *Progressive relaxation*. Chicago: University of Chicago Press.

Jackson, H. J., & King, N. J. (1981). The emotive imagery treatment of a child's trauma-induced phobia. *Journal of Behavior Therapy and Experimental Psychiatry, 12*, 325–328.

Kane, M. T., & Kendall, P. C., (1989). Anxiety disorders in children. A multiple-baseline evaluation of a cognitive-behavioral treatment. *Behavior Therapy, 20*, 499–508.

Kashani, J. H., & Orvaschel, H. (1988). Anxiety disorders in midadolescence: A community sample. *American Journal of Psychiatry, 145*, 960–964.

Kashani, J. H., & Orvashel, H. (1990). A community study of anxiety in children and adolescents. *American Journal of Psychiatry, 14*, 313–318.

Kearney, C. A., & Silverman, W. K. (1993). Measuring the function of school refusal behavior: The School Refusal Assessment Scale (SRAS). *Journal of Clinical Child Psychology, 22*, 85–96.

Kellerman, J. (1980). Rapid treatment of nocturnal anxiety in children. *Journal of Behavior Therapy and Experimental Psychiatry, 11*, 9–11.

Kendall, P. C., Howard, B. L., & Epps, J. (1988). The anxious child: Cognitive-behavioral treatment strategies. *Behavior Modification, 12*, 281–310.

Kieppen, A. S. (1974). Relaxation training for children. *Journal of Elementary School Guidance and Counseling, 9*, 4–21.

Klein, R. G., Koplewicz, H. S., & Kanner, A. (1992). Imipramine treatment of children with separation anxiety disorder. *Journal of the American Academy of Child and Adolescent Psychiatry, 31*, 21–28.

Klein, R. G., & Last, C. G. (1989). *Anxiety disorders in children*. Newberry Park, CA: Sage Publications.

Klingman, A., Melamed, B. G., Cuthbert, M. I., & Hermacz, D. A. (1984). Effects of participant modeling on information acquisition and skill utilization. *Journal of Consulting and Clinical Psychology, 52*, 414–422.

Lapouse, R., & Monk, M. A. (1964). Fears and worries in a representative sample of children. *American Journal of Orthopsychiatry, 29*, 803–818.

Last, C. G. (1986). *Modification of the K-SADS-P for use with anxiety disordered children and adolescents*. Unpublished manuscript.

Last, C. G. (1989). Anxiety disorders. In T. H. Ollendick & M. Hersen (Eds.), *Handbook of child psychopathology (2nd ed.)* (pp. 219–238). New York: Plenum Press.

Last, C. G. (1991). Somatic complaints in anxiety-disordered children. *Journal of Anxiety Disorders, 5*, 139–150.

Last, C. G., & Francis, G. (1988). School phobia. In B. Lahey & A. Kazdin (Eds.), *Advances in clinical child psychology* (Vol. 11). New York: Plenum Press.

Last, C. G., Hersen, M., Kazdin, A. E., Finkelstein, R., & Strauss, C. C. (1987). Comparison of DSM-III separation anxiety and overanxious disorders: Demographic characteristics and patterns of comorbidity. *Journal of the American Academy of Child and Adolescent Psychiatry, 26*, 527–531.

Last, C. G., Hersen, M., Kazdin, A. E., Francis, G., & Grubb, H. J. (1987). Psychiatric illness in the mothers of anxious children. *American Journal of Psychiatry, 144*, 1580–1583.

Last, C. G., Hersen, M., Kazdin, A. E., Orvaschel, H., & Perrin, S. (1991). Anxiety disorders in children and their families. *Archives of General Psychiatry, 48*, 928–935.

Last, C. G., Phillips, J. E., & Statfeld, A. (1987). Childhood anxiety disorders in mothers and their children. *Child Psychiatry and Human Development, 18*, 103–112.

Last, C. G., & Strauss, C. C. (1990). School refusal in anxiety-disordered children and adolescents. *Journal of the American Academy of Child and Adolescent Psychiatry, 29*, 31–35.

Lazarus, A. A., & Abramovitz, A. (1962). The use of "emotive imagery" in the treatment of children's phobias. *Journal of Mental Science, 108*, 191–195.

Lucas, A. R., & Pasley, F. C. (1969). Psychoactive drugs in the treatment of emotionally disturbed children: Haloperidol and diazepam. *Comprehensive Psychiatry, 10*, 376–386.

Matson, J. L. (1983). Exploration of phobic behavior in a small child. *Journal of Behavior Therapy and Experimental Psychiatry, 14*, 257–260.

McGee, R., Freehan, M., Williams, S., Partridge, F., Silva, P. A., & Kelly, J. (1990). DSM-III disorders in a large sample of adolescents. *Journal of the American Academy of Child and Adolescent Psychiatry, 29*, 611–619.

Milos, M. E., & Reiss, S. (1982). Effects of three play conditions on separation anxiety in young children. *Journal of Consulting and Clinical Psychology, 50*, 389–395.

Morris, R. J., & Kratochwill, T. R. (1983). Childhood fears and phobias. In R. J. Morris & T. R. Kratochwill (Eds.), *The practice of child therapy* (pp. 53–114). New York: Pergamon Press.

Neisworth, J. T., Madle, R. A., & Goeke, K. E. (1975). "Errorless" elimination of separation anxiety: A case study. *Journal of Behavior Therapy and Experimental Psychiatry, 6*, 79–82.

Ollendick, T. H., & Huntzinger, R. M. (1990). Separation anxiety disorder in childhood. In M. Hersen & C. G. Last (Eds.), *Handbook of Child and Adult Psychopathology: A Longitudinal Perspective* (pp. 133–149). New York: Pergamon Press.

Ollendick, T. H., & Mayer, J. A. (1984). School phobia. In S. M. Turner (Ed.), *Behavioral treatment of anxiety disorders* (pp. 367–411). New York: Plenum Press.

Phillips, D., & Wolpe, S. (1981). Multiple behavioral techniques in severe separation anxiety of a twelve-year-old. *Journal of Behavior Therapy and Experimental Psychiatry, 12*, 329–332.

Puig-Antich, J., & Chambers, W. (1978). *The Schedule for Affective Disorders and Schizophrenia for School-Aged Children.* New York: New York State Psychiatric Institute.

Rabiner, C. J., & Klein, D. F. (1969). Imipramine treatment of school phobia. *Comprehensive Psychiatry, 10*, 387–390.

Reynolds, C. R. (1980). Concurrent validity of What I Think and Feel: The revised Children's Manifest Anxiety Scale. *Journal of Consulting and Clinical Psychology, 48*, 774–775.

Reynolds, C. R. (1981). Long-term stability of scores on the Revised Children's Manifest Anxiety Scale. *Perceptual and Motor Skills, 53*, 702.

Reynolds, C. R. (1982). Convergent and divergent validity of the Revised Children's Manifest Anxiety Scale. *Educational and Psychological Measurement, 42*, 1205–1212.

Reynolds, C. R., & Paget, K. D. (1983). National normative and reliability data for the Revised Children's Manifest Anxiety Scale. *School Psychology Review, 12*, 324–336.

Reynolds, C. R., & Richmond, B. O. (1978). What I Think and Feel: A revised measure of children's manifest anxiety. *Journal of Abnormal Child Psychology, 6,* 271–280.

Silverman, W. K. (1991). Diagnostic reliability of anxiety disorders in children using structured interviews. *Journal of Anxiety Disorders, 5,* 105–124.

Silverman, W. K. (in press). Structured diagnostic interviews. In T. H. Ollendick, N. J. King, & W. Yule, (Eds.), *Handbook of Phobic and Anxiety Disorders of Children.* New York: Plenum Press.

Silverman, W. K., & Eisen, A. R. (1992). Age differences in the reliability of parent and child reports of child anxious symptomatology using a structured interview. *Journal of the American Academy of Child and Adolescent Psychiatry, 31,* 117–124.

Silverman, W. K., & Nelles, W. B. (1988). The Anxiety Disorders Interview Schedule for Children. *Journal of the American Academy of Child and Adolescent Psychiatry, 27,* 772–778.

Spielberger, C. D. (1973). *Manual for the State-Trait Inventory for Children.* Palo Alto, CA: Consulting Psychologists Press.

Ultee, C. A., Griffin, D., & Schellekens, J. (1982). The reduction of anxiety in children: A comparison of and effects of 'systematic desensitization in vitro' and 'systematic desensitization in vivo.' *Behaviour Research and Therapy, 20,* 61–67.

Wolpe, J. (1958). *Psychotherapy by Reciprocal Inhibition.* Stanford, CA: Stanford University Press.

CHAPTER 12

Phobia

WALLACE A. KENNEDY

DESCRIPTION OF THE PROBLEM

An acute phobic reaction is probably the most vexing clinical problem of middle to late childhood. It is vexing because phobias ordinarily occur in otherwise well-adjusted families to otherwise well-adjusted children with a suddenness and disruptiveness that absolutely stagger present-day, overscheduled, overcommitted families, who run on very tight schedules or face daunting consequences. Families who start moving with assembly-line precision at 6 in the morning and stay on schedule until 9 at night have little reserves of energy or time to deal with a phobic reaction, particularly one that interferes with vital routines, as do school phobias, social phobias, dentist phobias, and medical-procedure phobias.

Fear versus Phobia: The Distinction

Though the distinction between a mild fear and a phobia seems clear, that between urgent fear and phobia is not. From a treatment point of view, as well as for the basic safety of the child, that distinction is critical. Appropriateness and manipulativeness, rather than severity, are the essential distinctions between phobias and fears.

The diagnostic criteria for *simple phobia,* as stated in the *Diagnostic and Statistical Manual of Mental Disorders*, 3rd edition, revised (DSM-III-R), (American Psychiatric Association, 1987) and DSM-IV (American Psychiatric Association, 1993) contains six elements:

1. A persistent fear of a circumscribed stimulus (object or situation) other than fear of having a panic attack (as in a Panic Disorder) or of humiliation or embarrassment in certain social situations (as in Social Phobia).

2. During some phase of the disturbance, exposure to the specific phobic stimulus (or stimuli) almost invariably provokes an immediate anxiety response.

3. The object or situation is avoided, or endured with intense anxiety.

4. The fear of the avoidant behavior significantly interferes with the person's normal routine or with usual social activities or relationship with others, or there is marked distress about having the fear.

5. The person recognizes that his or her fear is excessive or unreasonable.

6. The phobic stimulus is unrelated to the content of the obsessions of Obsessive Compulsive Disorder or the Post-traumatic Stress Disorder (American Psychiatric Association, 1987, pp. 244–245).

As a practical matter when treating children, making a sharp distinction between fears and phobias is extremely important, since fears of children are relatively common and sometimes quite adaptive, considering the vulnerability of childhood. To be classified as a phobia, the emotion must meet all four of the following differential characteristics (Kennedy, 1983).

1. *The emotion must be inappropriate to the danger of the situation.* A child terrified of a neighbor's vicious and uncontrolled rottweiler loose in the child's neighborhood is not phobic.

2. *The emotion is admittedly irrational.* The inability to tolerate being outside when passenger jets go overhead in a slow ascent from an airport 20 miles away is irrational.

3. *The emotion is involuntary.* The key here in differential diagnosis is the operant quality of the emotion. If the response is dominantly operant, it is not phobic. Children who turn the phobia on and off in any volitional sequence are not phobic. Children who, with a reasonable effort, can control their fears are not phobic. Basically, true phobias are classically conditioned and operantly maintained; that is to say, after a short time, phobic behavior produces a secondary gain; but this secondary gain is truly secondary to the involuntary, reflexive phobia.

4. *The emotion is limiting to life-style.* A snake phobia may not require diagnosis and treatment for a Manhatten-dwelling child, whereas it could be highly significant to a suburban-dwelling child in the southeast United States.

Phobia: Origin and Maintenance

Behavior therapists generally believe the following:

1. *Partial instincts or sign tracking make some stimuli more probably phobic than others.* Seligman (1971) referred to this as *preparedness*. Stimuli with evolutionary significance, such as furriness, are prepared for a phobic response; whereas those with no such significance, such as toy wooden cars, are unprepared. Prepared stimuli are more resistive to extinction.

A number of investigators had trouble replicating Watson's classic study of child phobia (Watson & Rayner, 1920) because Watson, probably inadvertently, picked what the Gestalt psychologists at the time referred to as "pregnant stimuli" and what current psychologists refer to as "prepared stimuli" (which, in the case of little Albert, was a furry object, a rat). When other investigators tried unprepared stimuli, such as wooden toys, conditioning was slow and unstable in contrast to the rapid conditioning and generalization Watson found with his white rat.

It is no accident that, in the general hierarchy of fear, furry animals, snakelike reptiles, and jumping and stinging animals and insects should be very high on a list of stimuli for phobias, with darkness, flashing light, and loud noises following quickly. All of these would probably have evolutionary significance in the history of mankind.

2. *In the early stages of the development of a phobia, reinforcement, or secondary gain, is self-evident.* The principle of partial reinforcement suggests that even when parents are trying to function as effective behavior modifiers, this reinforcement, or the probability of a similar regressive reinforcement, is sufficient to maintain phobias for some time. A child who becomes phobic after a lightning blast in a summer storm is held, cooed to, and protected for some time through several thunderstorms before the

parents identify the thunder phobia as significant. Being held, having a great deal of attention from primary caregivers, sleeping in their bed, and receiving a great deal of reassurance all tend to increase rather than decrease the phobic response in the hierarchy of behavior.

3. *Phobias do not require direct personal encounters with the feared object.* Modeling and vicarious or incidental learning can be the source of a phobic response. Many children have no recollection, nor do their parents recollect their having any encounter with a specific example of an existential issue, such as death, disappearance, or loss. The very fact of being holds with it the possibility or the dread of not being. The very fact of having a parent holds with it the existential possibility of not having a parent.

4. *The preclinical treatment attempts usually consist of inconsistent "weaving and bobbing," with great opportunity for partial reinforcement.* Parents are, as Skinner once remarked, dreadful behavior modifiers, often thinking they are doing quite well when they let a child's phobic response be reinforced only one time in seven, a splendid partial reinforcement schedule that is highly resistive to extinction.

5. *Temporal and sequential tracking of the phobia are poor.* In spite of being constantly under foot, children, in fact, have a great deal of private time and private experience; and often they are not sufficiently well developed cognitively to make reliable informants. Reinforcement histories are very often oversimplified and scrambled. The identification of the origin, course, and reinforcement of the phobia is subject to distortion and outright deception, particularly when the phobia is in any way involved in a split-custody family in the middle of a row.

PROTOTYPIC ASSESSMENT

Because most psychiatric settings not only offer treatment of phobias, but also own the responsibility of teaching and research, prototypic assessment, optimal assessment, is the rule and not the exception. In the case of phobias, the major goal of assessment is to rule out competitive diagnoses. The most critical competing diagnoses are: (a) *fears*, most importantly, appropriate fears of threatening situations; (b) *panic disorder* and *social phobias*, which appear to be much more physiological and biochemical and may require medication even in children; (c) *incipient psychosis*, particularly schizophrenia; (d) *incipient general neurosis*, in which the phobia may be only one, and a minor one, of multiple neurotic symptoms; and (e) *incipient biochemical* or *neurological disorders*, which only get worse if treated as a simple phobia. The importance of correct diagnosis cannot be overemphasized in affecting the outcome of treatment. Five diagnostic steps are essential.

1. *Rule out appropriate fears.* The most critical competing diagnosis is legitimate, appropriate fear. Probably no error in diagnosis has more damage potential than falsely identifying an adaptive fear as a phobia.

A child fearful of being left with what turns out to be an abusive babysitter may be crying out for protection, not demonstrating a phobia.

A child fearful of taking a nap in the late afternoon in a room where the sun's rays are deflected by a slow, wind-driven, window fan may be trying to avoid a strobe seizure, not demonstrating a phobia.

A child fearful of being attacked by rats in his bed after the door is closed is not phobic if he lives in a rat-infested apartment.

Physical and sexual abuse under secret conditions are realistic considerations when diagnosing a phobia.

2. *Rule out panic disorder and social phobia.* This distinction is significant for the DSM-III-R diagnosis, which applies to adults as well as to children, but is a minor problem with children. Characteristic of panic disorder, which typically arises in the late 20s, is a nonspecific panic that occurs immediately before or after exposure to a situation that causes anxiety. Panic disorder is not triggered by situations in which the person was the focus of another person's care and protection. Intense psychophysiological symptoms are the dominant feature, and no avoidant efforts are effective. As in the case of phobia, no organic factor involvement can be established.

Social phobia, on the other hand, arises in late childhood and adolescence and, on some occasions, is more difficult to rule out in the case of simple phobia. The key to the differential diagnosis of social phobia is dominance of fear of public embarrassment, humiliation, or exposure of incompetence. The dominant feature, then is social discomfort, not an object aversion or specific-place aversion.

3. *Rule out incipient psychosis.* A rare but significant competing diagnosis for simple phobia in childhood is the onset of incipient childhood schizophrenia, or secondary autism, which has significant panic or phobic content in the symptom complex. This panic can at one time or another resemble a simple phobia and meet all the criteria for a simple phobia; on the other hand, incipient schizophrenia also carries several symptoms not related to phobias: Simple phobias do not demonstrate hallucinations, delusions, incoherence, or loosening of association; nor do they demonstrate severe regression, infantilism, self-stimulation, loss of continence, or sensory distortions.

4. *Rule out incipient general neurosis or anxiety disorder.* A gradually increasing general neurosis or anxiety disorder usually is a broad spectrum illness, with significant general anxiety and depression. In addition, a general neurosis or anxiety disorder usually involves relatively significant regression and immaturity, as well as habit disturbances, infrequently of a phobic nature. The child with simple phobia is rather tunnel-minded about a very specific place or situation, whereas the incipient neurosis is much broader, with phobias being only a very small part of the symptom complex.

5. *Rule out biochemical or neurological disorder.* The chain of referral in most psychiatric facilities is such that biochemical or neurological disorders have already been ruled out by the pediatric service; but, if not, a specific referral back to pediatrics to rule out unlikely but possible competing medical causes associated with endocrine or infectious diseases is essential. The same may be said regarding brain wave irregularities or abnormal brain growth, but an abundance of caution should make a neurological consultation rather routine if the history of onset is vague or suspect.

Therapeutic Diagnostic Processes

To carry out the five diagnostic steps, behavior therapy requires some specific diagnostic processes.

1. *A thorough history.* An accurate, cross-verified reinforcement history of the behavior, including when it started, its antecedent conditions, when it occurs, what makes it

worse and better, and what remedies have already been exhausted, is absolutely essential. Include the basic theory the parents have adopted, and any family tradition or lore regarding this or similar phobias. Incidental learning is a will-of-the-wisp variable in the development of phobias. Detailed histories are critical, but also invariably time-consuming; a weak history is the major limitation of assessment.

2. *A basic medical assessment.* Medical assessment is necessary to determine that no underlying biochemical or neurological problem is causing the phobia. Borderline epilepsy, hypoglycemia, hypothyroidism, diabetic reactions, and hyperthyroidism can produce intense emotions, including fears, and can be associated with presumed phobic stimuli, such as bedtime and starting out for school. These conditions can and should be ruled out early in the assessment and kept in mind throughout the treatment. Some medical conditions are evolving, insidious, and even intermittent. One of the strengths of behavior therapy is its tenaciousness and aggressiveness of treatment, but it is prudent to always be vigilant and to listen to the patient or the informant for changes in the complexion of the symptom pattern.

3. *A fear assessment inventory.* The administration of a fear assessment inventory, such as the Revised Fear Survey Schedule for Children, to both the child and the parent is necessary for successful assessment to outline the scope as well as the intensity of the phobia. (Wolpe & Lang, 1964).

4. *An in vivo assessment.* The behavior therapist should carry out an in vivo assessment of the phobia through a recreation of the phobic situation or a field visit to the scene of the phobia.

5. *A phobia hierarchy.* The creation of the phobia hierarchy, either through interview or in vivo, is essential.

6. *A storytelling session.* Most helpful in assessment is a storytelling session that affords the child the opportunity, through a projective test like the Roberts Apperception Test for Children (McArthur & Roberts, 1982), to describe the nature of the phobia without reexperiencing its trauma, as required by the in vivo assessment or hierarchy establishment.

7. *A verbal IQ assessment.* To assure successful performance on paper-and-pencil tests, assess the child's cognitive power with a verbal IQ test, such as WISC-R Verbal Scale (Wechsler, 1974).

8. *A reading test.* Assess the child's reading level with a test such as the Wide Range Achievement Test-Revised (WRAT-R) (Jastak & Wilkinson, 1984) to verify that the child can take a self-administered fear inventory.

9. *A sentence-completion test.* Give the child a sentence-completion test, such as the Tendler Sentence Completion (1930), to provide an open-ended description of life as the child sees it.

10. *A test of social maturity.* Administer a test of social maturity, such as the Vineland Adaptive Behavior Scale (Balla, Cicchetti, & Sparrow, 1984), to determine the basic effect of the phobia on the general social maturity of the child and to identify the relative functional strengths and weaknesses of the child.

11. *A problem checklist.* Administer a problem checklist, such as the Child Behavior Checklist (Achenbach & Edelbrock, 1983), to determine whether other significant behavior problems are competing with the phobic behavior for significance.

12. *A depression and anxiety inventory.* Clarify the assessment with the administration of depression and anxiety inventories, such as the Children's Depression Inventory (Kovacs, 1977), the Revised Children's Manifest Anxiety Scale (Reynolds & Richmond, 1984), or the Child Anxiety Scale (Gillis, 1988).

13. *A list of effective positive and negative reinforcers, as well as punishments.* Discovering successful positive and negative reinforcers, as well as punishments, is extremely helpful. These should also be arranged in a hierarchy so that the behavior therapist can pull out an effective reinforcement or punishment at appropriate times and can also empower the parents at critical moments. To be effective, these should have immediate and delayed consequences.

Prototypic Diagnostic Focuses

The prototypic assessment of a child's phobia, then is directly focused on several clearly defined aspects.

1. *Making sure the emotions are inappropriate to the situation the child faces.* The mark of a good intervention is an exhaustive history. Home visits are extremely helpful to assess in vivo phobic responses. Evaluations of the parties involved in the occurrence of the phobias need to be completed. The child needs to be heard out and the behavior needs to be observed and calibrated.

2. *Trying to penetrate the logic of the child's phobic reaction.* The therapist must listen, listen, listen. He or she should try to get into the child's logical system to determine its irrationality from the child's point of view.

3. *Looking for the operant quality of the phobic child's behavior as a totality.* The therapist should ask such questions as: What does the phobia do for the child? What key stimuli precipitate the phobia? Are there situations in which the phobia is not present? Are there situations or stimuli that reduce the dimensions of the phobia?

4. *Discovering the limits the phobia places on the child's life-style.* It is important to find out how the phobia profits the child and what the child would be doing differently if he or she were not phobic.

ACTUAL ASSESSMENT

The difference between a prototypic assessment and an actual, or usual and customary, assessment has to do with the time and referral budget the behavior therapist can commit to the assessment. Cost is a limiting factor in actual assessment. Departmental protocol, case load, and insurance coverage frequently mean that some assessment elements have to be eliminated. The behavior therapist wants to assure that eliminating these elements will not pose a risk to the client's welfare.

First to be eliminated is the luxury of every conceivable medical test that would rule out everything. A pediatric referral, that is, a child's coming from a pediatrician, is usually sufficient safeguard for the behavior therapist to believe the problem is not medical and to go forward with a behavioral approach. An irreversible error in diagnosis of a possible medical cause is extremely unlikely. In the absence of an unexpected and inconsistent physical finding, the primary-care pediatrician is sufficient for the child's medical care.

Second to be eliminated are the home visit and the in vivo assessment. Detailed descriptions of the home situation by both parents or the parent and the child-care supervisor or babysitter are reasonable substitutes for the home visit and save a great deal of time and huge expense. Given case-management restrictions, the behavior therapist should stick to the usual methods: controlled laboratory observations and normed psychological instruments, plus the absolutely essential detailed history.

This decision puts a great deal of emphasis upon the validity of the fear survey and assessment and hierarchal development. The use of picture books and thematic pictures assists greatly with younger children, as do doll- and role-play. When substituting cognitive for behavioral responses, the cognitive material should be as descriptive of the behavior as possible.

Virtually the only reasons for altering the prototypic assessment are the pressures of time and economics. The time-consuming psychometric tests can be sacrificed if there is no real question as to the basic intelligence, cognitive development, and academic and social performance of the child. Having parents fill out questionnaires, hierarchies, and surveys on their own time as homework can save time and cost, as can following structured interviews that involve Gutterman-style severity scales (Gutterman, O'Brien, & Young, 1987). A fear assessment, such as that described by Tasto, Hickson, and Rubin (1971), or the Fear Survey Schedule (Wolpe & Lang, 1964), or the Revised Fear Index (Ollendick, King, & Frary, 1989), saves time. A hierarchal scale, as proposed by Wolpe (1961), also saves time.

PROTOTYPIC TREATMENT

Theories of remedies abound. To believe that responsible parents would stand by and allow their child to remain untreated is unreasonable. A plethora of self-help books and magazine articles are available, and primary-care individuals, including pediatricians, teachers, school counselors, preachers, neighbors, and relatives, as well as the parents, searching their own past, all have ideas about what to do. The question with which this chapter deals is not whether doctors in a psychiatric setting are better than nothing, but rather, can they be better than the usual and customary treatment children receive as a result of folk remedies and less rigorous therapists prior to being referred to behavior therapists. (The reader is referred to the following additional reviews of clinical features of behavioral interventions for child phobias: Barrios and O'Dell [1989], Ferrari [1986], Kennedy [1983], and Marks [1969]).

It is a safe bet that several treatments have been tried and exhausted prior to the child's finding a way to the psychiatric setting. The usual attempts to help include the following:

1. *The tincture of time.* One treatment almost surely exhausted prior to the child's coming to the behavior therapist is the tincture of time, a common and usually incorrect perception that phobic responses fade over time, that children just get over or outgrow phobias. If one basic fact of behavior therapy has been established, it is that forgetting is an extremely weak method of treatment. The literature abounds with examples of phobic responses, latent for half of a lifetime, that can still be potent, particularly when there is disinhibiting or facilitating experience.

2. *Persuasion.* Parents and others often try to talk the child out of a phobia: "That dog won't hurt you," "School is a safe place," "A little thunderstorm is nothing to be afraid of."

With the third criterion, irrationality, being admitted at the onset, this cognitive strategy is simply not going to work. In a somewhat humorous vein, Freud once said that a neurosis is that which follows the "but," as in, "I know thunder won't hurt me, because when I hear the thunder, the lightning is already past, but . . ."

3. *Punishment.* Since secondary gain plays a small part in true phobias, punishment of a phobic response is highly likely to be chained with the phobia and increase its severity.

4. *Bribery.* Bribery usually depends upon a completed counterphobic trial and not successive approximation, as it is used by most parents. Unfortunately, a successfully completed trial seldom occurs. Each uncompleted trial that results in the phobic response being rewarded by survival simply strengthens the response.

Dimensions of the Problem

In the face of the child's continuing misery in spite of their best efforts, the parents have brought the child to the behavior therapist. The assessment has been completed; a clear profile of the phobia has now emerged. The treating doctor, the parents, and the child should now agree on certain dimensions of the problem:

1. *The nature of the stimuli for the phobia.* The objective or subjective elements of the phobic situation should be clear to all concerned. By using the child's language and logic as much as possible, the objects, events, sensations, and perceptions essential for defining the phobia should be specified.

2. *The nature of the response to the phobia.* The intensity, duration, and disruption caused by the phobia in the lives of the child and the parents should now be evident. This information should be quantified, in hierarchal terms when possible, for better ease in assessment of progress during treatment.

3. *The nature of the contingencies of the phobia.* A compilation of a complete behavioral description of all the contingencies related to the maintenance of the phobia, including what happens and does not happen in the child's world as a result of the phobic responses, should now be in hand. Again, it is critical to have these data in as objective and numerical terms as possible, following the scaling technique of Guttman (1944). A complete and power-ordered list of reinforcers and punishers that affect either the phobia, or behavior in general, for the child should be ready at hand.

4. *The nature of the psychometric profile.* A complete picture of the child's intelligence, achievement, social maturity, and symptom range and severity, particularly anxiety and depression, is all important and should be drawn by the time treatment is begun.

5. *The logical stopping point for treatment.* The reasonable therapeutic effect should have been defined and agreed upon by the beginning of treatment.

6. *Effective and ineffective responses to the phobia.* A list of the responses to the phobia that have been somewhat effective, as well as those that have been ineffective, is compiled and ready. Convinced of its ultimate success, the behavior therapist, the parents, and the child are ready now to begin the actual treatment.

Assumptions of the Treatment Plan

The prototypic treatment plan starts with seven underlying assumptions regarding the nature of the phobia.

1. *The phobia interferes with the child's behavior.* The phobia is interfering with a significant and essential behavior of the child, such as going to school, sleeping in one's own bed, playing by one's self, visiting the noncustodial parent, or cooperating with a dental or medical examination or treatment.

2. *The phobia has a preparedness dimension.* The phobia is following a partially instinctive channel and is, therefore, an easily learned reaction to an instinctively provocative situation.

3. *The phobia has a classical learning dimension.* The classical or incidental learning dimension of the phobia is such that the phobic response may have been directly classically conditioned by personal experience or may have been classically conditioned by vicarious or existential learning through cognitive mediation based on the experience of others.

4. *The phobia has an operant conditioning dimension.* It has an operant conditioning dimension and/or an operantly maintained dimension. This secondary gain is a modest factor in true phobias, but, nevertheless, it is eventually an increasing dimension when the phobia has been present for some time. The issue is frequently one of control.

5. *The phobia has a modeling dimension.* It is very often the case that there has been a recent or significant encounter of the child with another significant person who has a tendency toward the same phobia; or, conversely, the child has not been around children with counterphobic behavior patterns; such as the ability to flaunt danger, do dare devil acts, and enjoy the existential thrill associated with phobic objects.

6. *The phobia has an existential or reality dimension.* Practically all phobias have an existential or reality dimension that is generally a low probability but not an impossible risk. The fact is that most phobic events do, indeed, happen with enough frequency in the world to be heard about and cognitively processed. Bad things do happen to some mothers while their children are at school, and bad things do happen at school to some children. What is difficult for the child to understand is that these are very low-frequency events and that a far greater harm and much more probable harm comes from the phobic responses themselves.

The prototypic treatment of the phobia needs to have a strong element of honesty, or the child will be set up for a later severe exacerbation of the condition when he or she finds out that, in truth, the world is a moderately dangerous place that is time-limited.

7. *The phobia has approach-withdrawal chaining.* By the time treatment is to begin, there has been what Delprato and McGlynn (1984) refer to as *approach-withdrawal chaining.* This concept stems from Mowrer's (1939) concept of hope, which refers to the positive conditioning that the chain of avoidance obtains in repeated trials to the extent that the actual connection to the original unconditioned fear stimulus may be lost in the provocative chain of seeking relaxation through the avoidance pattern.

Steps of Treatment

Using school phobia as the example, prototypic treatment then goes through the following steps:

1. *Interpretation, orientation, and training of parents.* The parents are going to be the key therapists in any behavioral treatment. They must be given a significant handout explaining exactly the theoretical and practical dimensions of behavioral treatment as it

applies to phobias. It is very clear that the parents need to be fully in agreement with the basic treatment strategy because of the derailing effect of partial reinforcement. Firmness, confidence, assertiveness, and consistency are key parental characteristics that need to be shaped up during the interpretation and orientation period.

2. *Orientation and training of significant others.* Teachers, bus drivers, principals, school counselors, and school nurses all need to be significantly oriented regarding the theory and practice of behavior therapy as it applies to this program. On rare occasions, the parents may be so tender and so certain that this might be a fear and not a phobia, in spite of an exhaustive review, that they will be poor behavior modifiers; here, a behavior technician assigned to the home from wake-up time until the hand-off to a significant other gives insurance that the system will not break down.

3. *Orientation and training of the phobic child.* Current cognitive behavioral approaches recommend much more cognitive rehearsal, and cognitive processing, on the part of the child. Having the child as a secure ally means that the child has a road map of where the treatment is going and what the key elements are.

The younger the child, the more simplified the plan needs to be. But the child, in the presence of his parents, should hear the total game plan from the top. Part of this orientation should be relaxation training and practice to assist the child in backchaining positive feelings with the phobia stimulus (Delprato & McGlynn, 1984). Here, one begins to work up the hierarchy with the child and does a great deal of positive rehearsal.

4. *Orientation and training of counterphobic models.* Recruiting a child in the same classroom to ride with the phobic child to school after spending the night is a good way to support the child's own counterphobic resolve and efforts.

5. *Developing an errorless or fail-safe behavioral sequence.* This plan should be one that the therapist, the parents, the significant others, and the child all believe can be safely and successfully carried out. Cognitive and behavioral rehearsal of all the key elements of the chain makes the decision of how far to go on the first day; cognitive rehearsal allows the child to understand and accept the behavior expected the following day. For example, on the first day the child may be able to take only the ride to school with a friend in the car. Knowing that getting out of the car will not be required that first day may be necessary for the child's tolerating the car ride to school. Usually, however, with school phobia, the plan can begin with a short stay in the classroom before the child loses confidence.

6. *Producing a high ratio of positive reinforcement to offset the general negative ambience that surrounds the phobia.* This should involve a great deal of recasting by cognitive rehearsal, spotting any mini steps in improvement, diversionary praise, or commenting on irrelevant cues, such as "That's my favorite shirt," "Ann told me yesterday that she is giving a party for Susie this Saturday at the pony farm," or "We are going to have ice cream for dessert tonight." Distraction is a key positive element in the successful treatment of phobias.

7. *Setting and following a fast pace that can reinforce half steps.* Set up a routine for the child, such as getting up a bit late, with one of the parents assigned directly to the task of preparing the child for school with a flow of positive descriptions, actual physical assistance in getting on prearranged clothes, finishing toileting, checking on model child, having a very small breakfast with some treats to take in the car and share. This would be the point where the behavioral technician would be useful if parents lack confidence and assertiveness.

8. *Starting out to school.* The parents, the child, the model, and, where appropriate, the

behavioral technician, all start out for school, usually with the intent of going all the way into the school. The child knows that the parents will hand off the child at the door of the classroom with the model.

9. *Creating success for the first day.* The first day must end in success. The child should be assured that he or she will be picked up early. This arrangement is best made with some slack and generally described as "after lunch." A high-reinforcement activity for immediately after pick-up should be planned involving both parents if at all possible, but certainly one of the parents, with active emotional investment in the activity by the absent parent.

It is imperative that the first day represents an increment or two on the hierarchy, but caution must be made not to go "one bridge too far." Being able to declare a victory on the first day is extremely important, even in the situation where the progress is very modest.

Since the child is bound to cognitively rehearse the phobia, giving him a positive script to rehearse is important. It is also a good move to have the child report his progress to a significant other such as grandparents or a good family friend who has been prepped to be totally positive and to not do any sort of intervention other than enthusiasm for what has happened. Without preparation, the neighbor may suggest that tomorrow will indeed go one bridge too far and could undermine the confidence that the child has that the next step is totally doable.

10. *Providing instant communication.* The essential tool for treatment of most phobias is instant communication over the phone, through the mail, and perhaps home visits by the therapist as well as the behavioral technician. Keeping the parents on track as behavior managers is essential. Often, if the communication is up-to-date, serious variations in the treatment program can be corrected.

11. *Debriefing.* Since everyone wants this miserable experience to have a visible, positive, long-term impact on the child, an extremely positive debriefing should be held in a party atmosphere where the child and the parents and the behavior therapist all bask in the victory and the child incorporates the notion, useful for a lifetime, that phobias are a nuisance that can be overcome.

A Brief Example

The parents, the child, and the behavior therapist are now ready to begin successful treatment of the disruptive phobia. The parents and the role model have been trained; the child has been primed; and the school is ready. The first day of treatment has arrived. An example of the application of this treatment-plan prerequisite uses the most significant phobia of middle to late childhood, Type I school phobia, described by Kennedy (1965, 1983).

A. Overt cues of immediacy of school attendance
   1. Completing dressing
   2. Completing breakfast
   3. Getting in the car
   4. Driving into the school driveway
   5. Getting out of the car
   6. Entering the school

7. Separating from the parent at classroom door
8. Entering the classroom
B. Covert cues of the immediacy of school attendance
   1. Dread and rehearsal
   2. Nausea and/or vomiting
   3. Intrusive thoughts of harm possibility to self or others
   4. Intrusive odors of food, car, school, other children
C. Psychometric profile of child
   1. Usually normal to high normal achievement, IQ, and social maturity
   2. Usually highly focused anxiety, absent significant depression (problem checklist refers exclusively to school attendance)
D. Counterphobic hierarchy
   1. How far the child can go toward school attendance
   2. Point of refusal
   3. Degree of discomfort manifested
E. Exhaustive evaluation determines no reality basis of the fear of school attendance and attending separations and low operant quality of the condition.
F. A survey of assets to influence the child, such as friends, other parent from usual transportation, special foods, special clothes, special trinkets

ACTUAL TREATMENT

The essential difference between the prototypic treatment and the actual treatment has mainly to do with controlling expense. Just as the assessment can be cut by estimation and parent-completed material, so the actual treatment depends more upon the direct effort of the parents and less on the therapist, and particularly less on in vivo treatment and participation in the field of the behavioral technician. Having the parents follow a detailed, written outline of the treatment, keep a detailed log of performance, and report frequently to the therapist is the minimum change that can be made between the prototypic and the actual treatment.

At the minimum, the behavior therapist or behavior technician must be available at crucial periods, such as the morning of the first day of school return. There is no doubt that treatment of a phobia is a front-end-loaded-effort-program. There are no short cuts in the initial effort.

Success in the treatment depends upon a great deal of assertiveness and control on the part of the behavior therapist; and that will occur only if there is a high level of activity, cognitive intervention, and control. Precision in treatment is essential, and nothing must compromise the compliance with the treatment regime.

SUMMARY

Behavioral treatment of phobias requires a behavioral analysis of the contingencies of the phobia, once the diagnosis of phobia has been established. Combining positive reinforcement for counterphobic behavior, mild punishment and blocking of phobic behavior, and modeling of counterphobic behavior leads to a rapid response even in cases of phobias such as school phobia, which results in very serious disruption of life.

REFERENCES

Achenbach, T. M., & Edelbrock, C. (1983). *Child Behavior Checklist.* Burlington, VT: University of Vermont Department of Psychiatry.

American Psychiatric Association. (1987). *Diagnostic and statistical manual of mental disorders* (3rd ed., rev.). Washington, DC: Author.

American Psychiatric Association. (1993). *DSM-IV draft criteria.* Washington, DC: Author.

Balla, D. A., Cicchetti, D. V., & Sparrow, S. S. (1984). *Vineland Adaptive Behavior Scales.* Circle Pines, MN: American Guidance Service.

Barrios, B. A., & O'Dell, S. L. (1989). Fears and anxieties. In E. J. Mash & R. A. Barkley (Eds.), *Treatment of childhood disorders* (pp. 167–221). New York: Guilford Press.

Delprato, D. J., & McGlynn, F. D. (1984). Behavioral theories of anxiety disorder. In S. M. Turner (Ed.), *Behavioral treatment of anxiety disorders* (pp. 63–122). New York: Plenum Press.

Ferrari, M. (1986). Fears and phobias in childhood: Some clinical and developmental considerations. *Child Psychiatry and Human Development, 17,* 75–87.

Gillis, J. S. (1980). *Child Anxiety Scale Manual.* Champaign, IL: Institute for Personality and Ability Testing.

Gutterman, E. M., O'Brien, J. D., & Young, J. G. (1987). Structured diagnostic interviews for children and adolescents: Current status and future directions. *Journal of the American Academy of Child and Adolescent Psychiatry, 26,* 621–630.

Guttman, L. (1944). A basis for scaling qualitative data. *American Sociological Review, 9,* 139–150.

Jastak, S., & Wilkinson, G. S. (1984). *The Wide Range Achievement Test—Revised.* Wilmington, DE: Jastak.

Kennedy, W. A. (1965). School phobia: Rapid treatment of fifty cases. *Journal of Abnormal Psychology, 70,* 285–289.

Kennedy, W. A. (1983). Obsessive-compulsive and phobic reactions. In T. H. Ollendick & M. Hersen (Eds.), *Handbook of child psychology* (pp. 277–292). New York: Plenum Press.

Kovacs, M. (1977). *Children's Depression Inventory.* Philadelphia, PA: University of Pennsylvania School of Medicine.

Marks, I. M. (1969). *Fears and phobias.* New York: Academic Press.

McArthur, D. S., & Roberts, G. E. (1982). *Roberts Apperception Test for Children: A manual.* Los Angeles, CA: Western Psychological Services.

Mowrer, O. H. (1939). A stimulus-response analysis of anxiety and its role as a reinforcing agent. *Psychology Review, 46,* 553–565.

Ollendick, T. H., King, N. J., & Frary, R. B. (1989). Fears in children and adolescents: Reliability and generalizability across gender, age, and nationality. *Behaviour Research and Therapy, 27,* 19–26.

Reynolds, C. R., & Richmond, B. O. (1984). *Revised Children's Manifest Anxiety Scale.* Los Angeles: Western Psychological Services.

Seligman, M. E. P. (1971). Phobias and preparedness. *Behavior Therapy, 2,* 307–320.

Tasto, D. L., Hickson, R., & Rubin, S. E. (1971). Scaled profile analysis of fear survey schedule factors. *Behavior Therapy, 2,* 543–549.

Tendler, A. D. (1930). A preliminary report on a test for emotional insight. *Journal of Applied Psychology, 14,* 122–136.

Watson, J. B., & Rayner, R. (1920). Conditioned emotional reactions. *Journal of Experimental Psychology, 3*, 1–12.

Wechsler, D. (1974). *Wechsler Intelligence Scale for Children—Revised.* San Antonio, TX: Psychological Corporation.

Wolpe, J. (1961). The systematic desensitization treatment of neuroses. *Journal of Nervous and Mental Disease, 132*, 189–203.

Wolpe, J., & Lang, P. J. (1964). A fear schedule for use in behavior therapy. *Behaviour Research and Therapy, 2*, 27–30.

CHAPTER 13

Obsessive-Compulsive Disorder

GRETA FRANCIS

DESCRIPTION OF THE PROBLEM

Obsessive-compulsive disorder (OCD) in children and adolescents is characterized by recurrent obsessive thoughts and/or compulsive behaviors (American Psychiatric Association, 1987). These symptoms are of sufficient severity to cause distress and impairment in functioning or to be excessively time-consuming. The obsessions are perceived, at least initially, in a negative manner, and attempts are made to suppress them. The obsessive thoughts of children parallel those of adults and include worries about germs, physical harm, fear of doing or having done something wrong, doubts, and thoughts of a sexual or violent nature. Compulsive behaviors are purposeful and may be performed as a way to decrease or prevent distress. The most common compulsions of adults and children are checking, cleaning, counting, ordering, touching, hoarding, and repeating rituals. Although adolescents and adults typically are aware of the abnormality of their symptoms, younger children may have difficulty recognizing the irrationality of their thoughts and behaviors.

While the essential features remain unchanged, a number of small modifications have been made to the diagnostic criteria for OCD in the working draft of DSM–IV (American Psychiatric Association, 1993). The criteria for obsessions have been expanded to include a statement that they are not merely excessive worries about everyday problems. The draft defines compulsions as repetitive behaviors or *mental acts* (e.g., repeating words silently, counting). Whereas in the *Diagnostic and Statistical Manual of Mental Disorders*, 3rd edition, revised (DSM–III–R) (American Psychiatric Association, 1987), it was noted that the criterion of recognition that obsessions or compulsions are excessive or unreasonable "may not" apply to children, the draft states more definitively that this criterion "does not apply to children." The draft also specifies that symptoms do not result from direct effects of a substance or medical condition. Finally, a subtype of OCD is proposed called *poor insight type* in which the person usually does not recognize that the obsessions or compulsions are excessive or unreasonable. Though not directly addressed in the draft, one would anticipate that children with OCD would not be specified as "poor insight type" since they are not expected to realize that their symptoms are excessive or unreasonable.

Prevalence of OCD in nonreferred children has been estimated at 0.3% of 10- and 11-year-olds (Rutter, Tizard, & Whitmore, 1970) and 1.0% of adolescents (Flament, Whitaker, et al., 1988). Prevalence of OCD in clinical samples, estimated by retrospective chart reviews, has ranged from 0.2% of outpatients (Hollingsworth, Tanguay, Grossman, & Pabst, 1980) to 1.2 % of inpatients (Judd, 1965). Flament et al. (1988) hypothesized that estimates of the prevalence of OCD in children may be low because of the secretiveness often associated with the disorder.

Although data are limited, there appears to be a greater preponderance of males with OCD among referred children (Despert, 1955; Flament, Rapoport, et al., 1985;

Hollinsworth et al., 1980; Marks, 1987; Rapoport, 1986; Swedo & Rapoport, 1989). In contrast, the male/female ratio in adolescents with OCD is roughly equal (Flament et al., 1988). These findings differ from the adult literature, in which a slightly larger number of females as compared to males has been reported for OCD (Black, 1974; Karno, Golding, Sorenson, & Burnam, 1988; Rasmussen & Tsuang, 1986).

Typical age of onset for OCD is late adolescence or early adulthood (Rachman, 1985), and approximately 65% of patients develop the disorder before the age of 25 years (Rasmussen & Tsuang, 1986). However, cases of OCD have been reported in children as young as 3 years old (Hollingsworth et al, 1980; Judd, 1965). Age of onset for childhood OCD was reported to be between the ages of 3 and 14 years in an NIMH prospective study (Rapoport, 1986).

The prognosis for children and adolescents with OCD is unclear because little prospective data exist. In Rapoport's (1986) longitudinal study of children with OCD, 68% continued to qualify for the diagnosis at follow-up 2 to 5 years later. Similarly, Flament and colleagues found that 68% of their sample of 25 children with OCD still had OCD at follow-up 2 to 7 years later (Flament, Koby, et al., 1990). In contrast, earlier findings by Warren (1960) suggested that approximately 50% of adolescent OCD cases remit. Although the natural history and prognosis of childhood OCD remain empirical questions, the course of OCD in adults typically is chronic and unremitting (Turner & Beidel, 1988).

Many of the psychiatric conditions associated with OCD in adults also have been reported in children and adolescents with OCD. Approximately one-fourth of youngsters with OCD have comorbid affective and anxiety disorders (Flament et al., 1988; Swedo & Rapoport, 1989). In addition, children and adolescents with OCD may evidence symptoms of Tourette's syndrome (Grad, Pelcovitz, Olesn, Matthews, & Grad, 1987) or chronic motor tics (Swedo, Rapoport, Leonard, Lenane & Cheslow, 1989).

Although the etiology of OCD is unclear, a number of studies have examined familial and biological influences. The results of familial studies are mixed. Lenane et al. (1990) found an increased familial rate of OCD as compared to that expected for the general population and to that found in a conduct-disordered population. In contrast, Black, Noyes, Goldstein, and Blum (1992) reported an increased risk of anxiety disorders, but not specifically OCD, in relatives of OCD patients as compared to psychiatrically normal controls.

Rapoport (1991) reviewed the evidence for the association between OCD and neurologic impairment. She indicated that there is growing evidence that OCD is linked to basal ganglia dysfunction and the serotonin system.

PROTOTYPIC ASSESSMENT

A comprehensive assessment of childhood OCD should include a functional analysis of presenting symptoms as well as information about presence of comorbid conditions. Such an evaluation can best be obtained through the use of multiple methods and multiple informants. Among the different methods available to assess OCD in children and adolescents are clinical interviews, self-report inventories, and direct behavioral observations by the clinician.

Teachers and parents also are valuable sources of information toward obtaining a complete clinical picture of the disorder. The role of the family in the assessment of childhood OCD is crucial. Parents typically bring a child to treatment because of his or her level of distress or impairment and/or the deleterious effects of the OCD on family functioning. Children may have difficulty describing their symptoms or may minimize their obsessions and compulsions. Interviewing parents is helpful to gather descriptive information about symptoms, to provide a chronology of events, and to report information of which children and adolescents may be unaware (e.g., developmental history).

The Clinical Interview

The clinical interview of the child and family should be geared towards establishing the diagnosis and conducting a functional analysis of the presenting complaints. Of particular importance in the assessment of obsessions is information regarding external anxiety cues (tangible objects), internal anxiety cues (thoughts, images, or impulses), and worries about disastrous consequences (Steketee & Foa, 1985). It is important to identify the source of anxiety because this information is necessary in the development of a treatment plan that involves habituation to the source of anxiety. The functional relationship of each compulsive behavior to the anxiety cues and avoidance behaviors also should be determined via the behavioral functional analysis. A thorough account of the events surrounding onset of current symptoms may provide information regarding variables associated with maintenance of symptoms. Comorbid conditions, such as depression and anxiety, also need to be assessed as they may be associated with treatment success (Basoglu, Lax, Kasvikis, & Marks, 1988; Steketee & Foa, 1985). Finally, a general history, including information about family and peer relationships, developmental history, and educational progress, should be gathered.

There are several structured and semistructured interviews that are appropriate for use with children and adolescents. These include the Diagnostic Interview for Children and Adolescents—Revised (DICA–R) (Herjanic & Campbell, 1977; Welner, Reich, Herjanic, & Campbell, 1987), Diagnostic Interview Schedule for Children (DISC) (Costello, Edelbrock, Dulcan, Kalas, & Klaric, 1984), Schedule for Affective Disorder and Schizophrenia for School-Age Children (K–SADS) (Puig-Antich & Chambers, 1982), Interview Schedule for Children (ISC) (Kovacs, 1983), Anxiety Disorders Interview Schedule for Children (Kiddie ADIS) (Silverman & Nelles, 1988), and Children's Assessment Schedule (CAS) (Hodges, McKnew, Cytryn, Stern, & Kline, 1982).

Although none of these interviews was designed specifically to assess OCD, each covers a broad spectrum of child psychopathology, including symptoms of OCD. Most of the semistructured, symptom-oriented interviews also allow for behavioral observations during the interview process. An additional advantage of these interviews is that they have parallel forms for collecting information from both children and parents.

A cautionary note on the use of structured interviews for diagnosing OCD is that children may misinterpret questions due to unfamiliarity with unusual behaviors, such as obsessions and compulsions (Breslau, 1987). In clinical practice, it is helpful to clarify initial questions with concrete examples of obsessive thoughts and compulsive behaviors; for example, questions about compulsive behaviors can be clarified by describing them as "habits that are really hard to stop . . . like having to wash your hands over and over again."

Self-Report Measures

The most widely used OCD self-report instruments for children and adolescents are the *Children's Yale-Brown Obsessive-Compulsive Scale* (CY–BOCS) (Goodman,

Rasmussen, et al., 1986), *Leyton Obsessional Inventory—Child Version* (LOI–CV) (Berg, Rapoport, & Flament, 1986), and the *Maudsley Obsessive-Compulsive Inventory* (MOCI) (Hodgson & Rachman, 1977).

The CY–BOCS is a child version of the Yale-Brown Obsessive-Compulsive Scale for Adults (Y–BOCS) (Goodman, Price, et al., 1989). The CY–BOCS assesses core and associated symptoms of OCD, along with global severity and improvement. Items are rated on a 5-point scale that allows the assessment of response to treatment.

LOI–CV assesses the presence of persistent thoughts, fear of dirt and/or dangerous objects, order, cleanliness, checking, repetition, and indecision. Positive responses are then assessed for degree of resistance and interference. The card-sorting method of administration lends itself to direct behavioral observations of behaviors such as slowness of task performance, indecisiveness with questions, and the need to obsess and/or perform rituals. The LOI–CV reportedly discriminates between adolescent obsessive patients and normal controls; obsessive patients and psychiatric controls differ only on the extent of resistance and interference (Berg, Rapoport, & Flament, 1986). There also is a 20-item survey version of the LOI–CV that provides age and gender norms for adolescents aged 13 to 18 years (Berg, Whitaker, Davies, Flament, & Rapoport, 1988).

The MOCI consists of 30 true-false questions that yield a general obsessive-compulsive score as well as five subscales: checking, clearing, slowness, doubting-conscientiousness, and rumination. Adequate reliability and validity have been reported for using the MOCI with adults (Rachman & Hodgson, 1980). Clark and Bolton (1985) found that it distinguished between OCD and anxious adolescents on general OC score and the checking subscale.

There are many self-report questionnaires that provide information about other kinds of anxiety and fear in children. Among these are the Revised Children's Manifest Anxiety Scale (RCMAS) (Reynolds & Richmond, 1978), State-Trait Anxiety Inventory for Children (STAIC) (Spielberger, 1973), Fear Survey Schedule for Children—Revised (FSSC–R) (Ollendick, 1983), Test Anxiety Scale for Children (TASC) (Sarason, Davidson, Lighthall, Waite, & Ruebush, 1960), and the Social Anxiety Scale for Children—Revised (SASCR) (LaGreca, Dandes, Wick, Shaw, & Stone, 1988).

Behavioral Observation

Behavioral monitoring of compulsive behaviors, avoidance and exposure tests, and physiological and cognitive indexes of anxiety have been used in the assessment of OCD in adults. However, there are no reports of the systematic use of these measures with children.

In clinical practice, observing children performing their rituals can be extremely helpful in understanding the topography of such behaviors. This task may be difficult, however, as youngsters often inhibit their symptoms in front of others. As such, behavioral observations may be conducted most productively after the therapist has built rapport with the child.

ACTUAL ASSESSMENT

In order to illustrate the process of actually assessing a youngster with OCD, a case study of a child recently treated by the author will be presented.

CASE ILLUSTRATION

Identifying Information

Russ was an 11-year-old boy who lived with his biological parents and three brothers. He was in the fifth grade, where he received resource services for reading.

Reason for Referral

He had been seen initially at a local community mental health center and was referred to a university affiliated outpatient clinic in a private psychiatric hospital in order to obtain a more comprehensive assessment of compulsive behaviors. The clinic specialized in the assessment and treatment of childhood anxiety disorders.

Course of Assessment

Russ and his parents were seen for a diagnostic evaluation, during which they were interviewed separately by a clinical child psychologist. An unstructured clinical interview was used initially in order to gather general information. Following this, Russ and his parents were administered the CY–BOCS. The parents also completed the CBCL. Upon obtaining permission from the parents, Russ' principal and homeroom teacher were contacted. They provided general information regarding his behavior in school, and then all of his teachers (homeroom, speech, resource, art) completed the teacher-report of the CBCL.

History of Presenting Problem

Russ began to exhibit a variety of compulsive behaviors approximately 6 months prior to the evaluation. He insisted on sleeping with a number of heavy blankets on his bed in a room with the windows closed throughout the summer months, regardless of the hot weather. Russ began to wear the same clothes for several days in a row in order to prevent bad luck. He arranged his belongings in a particular order and became extremely upset and angry if anyone touched or moved them. He became very upset, for example, when his mother changed the sheets on his bed. Russ cried and tried to stop his mother from completing the task. If not supervised, he pulled the clean sheets off the bed and replaced them with the old sheets from the laundry. At school, his books and papers were placed carefully in special places on his desk. Even though coathooks were not assigned in his classroom, he insisted on using one particular hook every day. Russ repeatedly touched things and people to the point that if someone accidently brushed against him he would chase after them in order to touch them again. He often repeated things that he said and frequently asked his parents the same questions over and over again. According to CY–BOCS ratings, Russ's symptoms fell into the moderate range of severity and impairment.

Past Psychiatric and Medical History

Russ was diagnosed with attention-deficit/hyperactivity disorder (ADHD) at the age of 6 years. His symptoms included difficulty sitting still, poor concentration, and impulsivity. He was treated with Ritalin (10 mg) just on school days for approximately 18 months.

Reportedly, his behavior and academic performance improved while he was on the medication. Ritalin was discontinued by the pediatrician when Russ began to display the compulsive behaviors previously described. His medical history was benign. At the time of the evaluation, Russ was a physically healthy boy on no medication.

Family Psychiatric History

Family psychiatric history was positive for panic disorder, agoraphobia, motor tics, and psychosis in maternal and paternal relatives. The mother denied psychiatric difficulties. The father acknowledged that he was somewhat compulsive regarding work functioning.

Mental Status Examination

Russ was quiet throughout the initial interview. Although he answered questions briefly, he offered little spontaneous information. His eye contact was minimal. Russ' verbal presentation was well organized. His affect appeared somber, though Russ described his mood as "good." Russ denied, and did not evidence, symptoms indicative of disorganized thought processes, hallucinations, or delusions. He expressed no thoughts or plans to behave in a dangerous way toward himself or others.

He acknowledged that it was difficult to talk about his problems because he felt embarrassed. Russ described frequent intrusive thoughts about bad luck, such as performing poorly in sports or getting into trouble at home or school. He indicated that he performed rituals either to prevent bad luck or to ensure good luck; he stated that he did not like the rituals but felt as though he could not stop them. Russ reported that these thoughts made it difficult for him to concentrate in school. Furthermore, he stated that he wanted to "do something" to get rid of this problem.

Parent and Teacher Rating Scales

The parents' report of Russ's presenting symptoms yielded a total behavior problem score in the clinical range on the CBCL. His most elevated scores fell on depressed, uncommunicative, obsessive-compulsive, and hyperactive scales.

Teacher reports indicated that Russ was functioning somewhat below grade level in reading, language, spelling, and math and at grade level in social studies and science. They described multiple problems with Russ perseverating on certain topics and repeating behaviors. These behaviors often caused him to be disruptive and noncompliant in the classroom. On the CBCL, his teachers rated his behaviors in school as significantly problematic and described the problems as "obsessive-compulsive" and "nervous-overactive."

Diagnostic Formulation

Based on reports from multiple sources across various settings, Russ was diagnosed with obsessive-compulsive disorder. The extent to which his current difficulty concentrating was indicative of OCD or ADHD or both was not clear at the time of the initial assessment. As such, a diagnosis of ADHD had to be ruled out over the course of therapy.

PROTOTYPIC TREATMENT

The literature on treatment of OCD in children and adolescents is quite limited. Behavioral and psychopharmacological treatment approaches will be reviewed here.

Behavioral Treatment

The study of behavioral treatments for childhood OCD is limited to a small number of single-subject studies and case reports of strategies used successfully with adults. Exposure and response prevention have emerged as the treatments of choice for adults with OCD, with a 70% effectiveness rate (Foa, Steketee, & Ozarow, 1985; Perse, 1988). Although there are no systematic investigations of behavioral procedures to treat childhood OCD, response prevention and exposure are the most frequently reported treatments (Apter, Bernhout, & Tyano, 1984; Bolton, Collins, & Steinberg, 1983; Clark, Sugrim, & Bolton, 1982; Green, 1980; Harris & Wiebe, 1992; McCarthy & Foa, 1988; Mills, Agras, Barlow, & Mills, 1973; Ong & Leng, 1979; Stanley, 1980; Zikis, 1983).

Mills et al. (1973) examined use of response prevention to treat a hospitalized adolescent boy with OCD. The youngster's OCD symptoms included lengthy morning and bedtime rituals. After a 12-day baseline monitoring phase, response prevention was applied to the bedtime rituals. The adolescent was told that he was no longer allowed to engage in bedtime rituals. A staff member remained in the adolescent's bedroom throughout the night. The authors reported that bedtime rituals stopped within 10 days. Frequency of morning rituals also decreased, even though these rituals had not been targeted specifically for treatment. Reportedly, treatment gains were maintained for approximately 8 weeks following the adolescent's discharge from the hospital. During subsequent outpatient treatment, the boy began to demonstrate a number of bathing rituals. The authors reported that parent-administered response prevention was successful in reducing frequency of these bathing rituals.

Other types of behavioral treatment used for childhood OCD include extinction (Francis, 1988; Hallam, 1974), positive reinforcement (Dalton, 1983; Queiroz, Motta, Madi, Sossai, & Boren, 1981), and thought stopping (Campbell, 1973; Ownby, 1983). Francis (1988), for example, used extinction to treat compulsive reassurance-seeking in an 11-year-old boy with OCD. An ABAB single-case experimental design was used, and treatment was conducted on an outpatient basis. The child repeatedly asked questions such as "Am I going to die?", "Am I going blind?", and "Do you think I will throw up?" Parents were instructed to ignore all reassurance-seeking questions and redirect the conversation. Results indicated that the extinction procedure was successful in decreasing the frequency of reassurance-seeking questions. The child's behavior worsened notably during the withdrawal phase but improved again with the reimplementation of treatment.

An example of the use of positive reinforcement was a study by Dalton (1983). The author described the treatment of a 9-year-old boy with checking and washing rituals. Treatment included positive reinforcement of appropriate behaviors combined with planned ignoring of rituals. The author reported success using these procedures, with treatment gains being maintained at 1 year follow-up.

The most commonly used treatment strategy for obsessive thoughts in children with OCD is thought stopping. Campbell (1973) used thought stopping to treat a 12-year-old boy's repetitive thoughts about his sister's death. The boy was encouraged to engage in the obsession and then disrupt it by counting backwards loudly. This was followed by thinking of a pleasant scene. The author reported that frequency of obsessions decreased quickly and obsessions were eliminated within 4 weeks.

Although the majority of the clinical reports of treatment of childhood OCD describe treatment successes, there is a need for more systematic research before generalizations about the effectiveness of behavioral treatments can be made. The literature is hampered by the small number of patients treated in each study, lack of reference to standardized diagnostic criteria, absence of baseline observations, and varying outcome criteria. Furthermore, most studies describe short-term successful outcomes. Given the chronic nature of OCD, demonstration of long-term treatment success is critical.

Pharmacological Treatment

The use of pharmacotherapy for treating childhood OCD also has received some research attention. Clomipramine is the only pharmacological treatment that has been evaluated systematically for treating youngsters with OCD (Flament, Rapoport, et al., 1985; Leonard, Swedo, Rapoport, Coffey, & Cheslow, 1988; Leonard, Swedo, Lenane, Rettew et al., 1991; Rapoport, Elkins, & Mikkelson, 1980). Flament, Rapoport et al. (1985) conducted a double-blind, crossover-design study comparing clomipramine and placebo. Clomipramine reportedly yielded a decrease in obsessional symptoms that was independent of baseline depression levels. However, clomipramine did not produce full recovery of obsessive symptoms.

Leonard, Swedo, Rapoport, et al. (1988) completed a double-blind crossover study comparing clomipramine (CMI) and desipramine (DMI). Results indicated that CMI was superior to DMI in alleviating OCD symptoms. DMI produced little or no improvement from baseline, and relapse was apparent within 2 weeks when DMI followed CMI.

The only other pharmacological agent reported in the literature for the treatment of childhood OCD is fluoxetine. Riddle, Hardin, King, Scahill, and Woolston (1990) described preliminary clinical experience using fluoxetine to treat children and adolescents with OCD. Out of 10 youngsters studied, 5 were characterized as *responders* as indicated by "much improved" ratings by their clinician. As the authors readily acknowledge, data in this study must be viewed cautiously given the lack of placebo control.

Prescribing Treatment

The current literature suggests that the most effective behavioral treatment for childhood OCD includes exposure and response prevention coupled with positive reinforcement techniques. For OCD children exhibiting obsessions only, thought stopping would be an appropriate initial intervention. CMI may also be effective in diminishing obsessive symptoms in youngsters with OCD.

In order to develop an appropriate treatment plan, information about presence or absence of compulsions and obsessions is needed. The degree of distress and impairment must be taken into consideration in order to evaluate whether there is a need for pharmacological intervention and if such a need is immediate. Furthermore, symptoms may require in vivo or imaginal exposure, depending on their content; that is, certain obsessions cannot easily be exposed in vivo, such as those related to aggressive thoughts. Finally, a determination must be made about the child's and the parents' ability to implement the treatment aimed at OCD symptoms. Often, parents first require teaching of basic child-management techniques. Children with poor self-control skills may need a more extensive system of external supports than children with adequate self-control skills.

ACTUAL TREATMENT

In order to illustrate the process of actually treating a youngster with OCD, the case of Russ again will be presented.

CASE ILLUSTRATION

Russ and his family began treatment on an outpatient basis. The first step in therapy was to educate them about obsessive-compulsive disorder and the treatments available. An overview of behavioral treatment (exposure, response prevention, positive reinforcement) and pharmacological treatment was provided. The family elected to begin with behavior therapy, saving pharmacotherapy as an adjunct if needed.

In the early phase of treatment, parents were encouraged to remove themselves from Russ' rituals, and parents were warned that his behavior would likely worsen. Russ often asked his mother not to change his sheets, and, if his father touched him once, Russ asked his father to touch him twice. Over the course of the first few sessions, parents disengaged themselves from these rituals by requiring Russ to adhere to basic cleanliness and hygiene rules. Mother went ahead and changed Russ' sheets and removed soiled clothing from his room. In addition, parents refused to engage in repetitive touching. Russ' response to these changes was to become increasingly angry and upset. His behavior escalated to the point that parents became concerned that he could not be managed safely. Russ was irritable and noncompliant and began to destroy property at home. He reported constantly worrying about bad luck.

During this escalation in negative behavior, parents met with a child psychiatrist to discuss the pharmacological therapies available to treat childhood OCD in more detail. Parents decided to go ahead with medication treatment because of their concerns about the extent of Russ's angry reaction to response prevention. It was agreed that response prevention would continue even with the addition of medication.

CMI was selected as the medication of choice. Potential benefits and side effects were explained to Russ and his parents. A pediatric examination was completed, as were routine bloodwork and a baseline EKG. Results of these evaluations were negative. Russ was eager to take medication as he reported feeling as though he had no control over his obsessive thoughts. Over the course of 6 months, CMI was titrated from a daily dose of 25 mg to 100 mg. Russ experienced few side effects other than dry mouth.

Over the course of the 6 months of treatment with CMI, Russ and his parents continued to be involved in weekly behavior therapy. Russ was able to practice touching things once in the office and participated in developing an incentive program to be used at home. Each week he selected three behaviors to practice, and parents administered weekly rein-forcements such as special snack or access to a favored activity. Progress was slow, as Russ had difficulty self-monitoring consistently, and parents had difficulty waiting until tasks were completed before allowing him to access reinforcers. Typically, Russ was highly motivated during the 2 or 3 days following therapy sessions, but he then lost interest over the remainder of the week. Midweek phone calls from the therapist were imple-mented without noticeable improvement in compliance. Finally, a series of home visits was conducted in order to facilitate practice of response prevention at home. Russ was compliant with the therapist's instructions to complete response prevention tasks but was very argumentative with parents when they intervened with him. Parents found it ex-tremely difficult to ignore his verbal arguments and often became sidetracked from the task of response prevention.

During the fifth month of treatment with CMI, Russ and his parents began to question the effectiveness of the medication. While they understood that an adequate trial was neces-sary in order to rule out CMI as a treatment, they were frustrated by his lack of response. At home, Russ was increasingly irritable and noncompliant.

Russ' behavior also began to escalate at school. He was being teased by peers about his repetitive touching and often acted out in a negative manner. A meeting was held between Russ' teachers, mother, and the therapist in order to evaluate his decline in performance at school. Teachers reported feeling hesitant to redirect Russ because they were not sure whether he was misbehaving because he was noncompliant or because of OCD. Teachers were given some basic education regarding OCD and were encouraged to redirect and consequate inappropriate behaviors in school, regardless of etiology.

By the sixth month after beginning treatment with CMI, parents requested a more restric-tive level of care for Russ. His irritability had increased steadily, and he began to talk about wishing he would die. His appetite was poor and he was easily fatigued. Russ's motivation to try to prevent his rituals was almost nonexistent. Consultation between the therapist, child psychiatrist, and parents yielded a recommendation to pursue a brief inpatient admission.

Russ was admitted to the inpatient unit of a children's psychiatric hospital for 10 days. He continued to work with his therapist and child psychiatrist. During that time, his clomipramine dose was increased to 125 mg per day. Inpatient treatment did not go smoothly. It was very difficult for inpatient staff to administer response prevention, even after repeated explanations of the rationale and role modeling of the procedure; for example, when Russ refused to shake someone's hand, staff did not intervene to require him to do so "because it made him nervous." Given these difficulties, the therapist arranged for response prevention to be implemented by a trainee research assistant. The research assistant was experienced in implementing response prevention and was under the supervision of the treating therapist. Russ participated in 2 hours of individual response prevention each day. During these sessions, he was required to touch things and people just once.

Within about 5 days, there was a decrease in Russ's touching rituals. Release from the hospital was made contingent upon him practicing response prevention with his parents and at home because there was concern about the extent to which gains would be maintained outside of the inpatient setting. He was given the task of showing that he would practice during family visits on the unit. As practicing during these brief visits was mastered successfully, visits were extended and subsequently moved off the unit and eventually home. Russ complied with the task of practicing response prevention while away from the unit. Parents reported that he seemed less "compelled" to perform the rituals. Russ's final task was to practice response prevention during an overnight visit home, and he did so successfully. He was discharged after 10 days with a plan to resume outpatient therapy.

Not surprisingly, Russ' touching rituals worsened upon discharge from the inpatient unit. He was angry about having been hospitalized and became reluctant to disclose the extent of his relapse for fear of rehospitalization. Parents were extremely discouraged.

Within 2 weeks after discharge from the inpatient unit, a referral was made for partial hospitalization in order to provide intensive behavior therapy over a longer period of time. In addition, Russ' child psychiatrist recommended changing medication because it was clear that CMI had not been effective. Once CMI was discontinued, Russ began treatment with sertraline. His initial dose was 25 mg per day. Sertraline was titrated to 100 mg per day over a 4-week time period. Russ reported no side effects and indicated that he liked the new medicine better than the CMI. Parents reported that his mood brightened, and he appeared to have more energy. During therapy, Russ's affect was brighter and he was more verbal.

A 6-week partial hospitalization program was secured for Russ. Again, he continued to work with his therapist and child psychiatrist while in the partial program. The program consisted of a classroom-based milieu that he attended on school days. He was placed in a small classroom with two adult staff members and six other students. An individualized behavior program was developed in which Russ was required to follow directions and touch things only once. This included things he typically avoided (e.g., shaking hands, passing plates at mealtimes) as well as things he usually touched repeatedly (e.g., when a peer bumped into him, he was not permitted to chase after the peer to touch him again). Initially, Russ required use of timeouts when he refused to follow directions to touch things once. In addition, he had difficulty remaining seated and was distractible. He was very motivated by the positive reinforcement system in the classroom in which he earned points for compliance with his target behaviors. These points were cashed in at the end of each day for reinforcers such as computer time or outside play time.

The combination of intensive behavior therapy and sertraline appeared to be effective for Russ. He reported feeling "back to my old self" and parents indicated a 50% decline in touching rituals within the first few weeks of the partial program. Parents reported that they found it easier to be consistent with discipline at home because of a decrease in the volatility of Russ's mood. They implemented a basic time out procedure for noncompliance and described it as successful. Russ reported feeling much less compelled to perform rituals at home and at school. Of note, he continued to have difficulty with self-administered response prevention. Russ required direction from adults and incentives in order to complete response prevention tasks. His diagnoses upon discharge from the partial program included both OCD and ADHD.

Russ returned to public school following completion of the partial hospitalization. An individualized educational planning (IEP) meeting was held with his teachers, principal, parents, and partial hospital staff. The need for structure and consistency in the classroom was emphasized. Public school teachers again were encouraged to provide positive incentive for appropriate behavior while redirecting and consequating negative behavior (including noncompliance associated with rituals). He was maintained on 100 mg of sertraline per day. Outpatient therapy was conducted once per month.

SUMMARY

The purpose of this chapter has been to review the prototypic assessment and treatment strategies for childhood OCD and to then contrast them with the actual assessment and treatment of a youngster with OCD. As reflected in the case illustration presented, there can be significant differences between ideal and real. Ideally, Russ and his parents would have self-monitored OCD symptoms consistently, waited to complete an adequate trial of response prevention before beginning medication, and been able to participate in response prevention more successfully. In reality, Russ's course of treatment did not evolve in this manner.

Treating children with OCD often is time-consuming, labor intensive, and messy. Multiple interventions, involving the child, family, and school, and the need for coordination among treating professionals are typical. One rather unusual aspect of Russ's case was the ability of this therapist and child psychiatrist to work with him and his family and to carry out treatment through various levels of care. Often, with different levels of care come different treatment providers. Such discontinuity of providers can complicate the treatment of a child with a chronic condition. In such circumstances the child may be reassessed at each level of care rather than treated in accordance with a long-term plan. In Russ's case, this tendency was reflected in the inability of inpatient unit staff to implement response prevention. Fortunately, his primary-treatment providers were able to intervene on the inpatient unit, thus circumventing the discontinuity problem.

In summary, the assessment and treatment of youngsters with OCD should strive for the prototypes reviewed in this chapter. These prototypes provide overarching goals within which much flexibility is needed in order for therapists to be responsive to the changing needs of the OCD child and his or her family.

REFERENCES

American Psychiatric Association. (1987). *Diagnostic and statistical manual of mental disorders (3rd ed., rev.)*. Washington, DC: Author.

American Psychiatric Association. (1993). *DSM–IV draft criteria*. Washington, DC: Author.

Apter, A., Bernhout, E., & Tyano, S. (1984). Severe obsessive-compulsive disorder in adolescence: A report of eight cases. *Journal of Adolescence, 7*, 349–358.

Basoglu, M., Lax, T., Kasvikis, Y., & Marks, I. M. (1988). Predictors of improvement in obsessive-compulsive disorder. *Journal of Anxiety Disorders, 2*, 299–317.

Berg, C. J., Rapoport, J. L., & Flament, M. (1986). The Leyton Obsessional Inventory—Child Version. *Journal of the American Academy of Child Psychiatry, 25*, 84–91.

Berg, C. J., Whitaker, A., Davies, M., Flament, M. F., & Rapoport, J. L. (1988). The survey form of the Leyton Obsessional Inventory—Child Version: norms from an epidemiological study. *Journal of the American Academy of Child and Adolescent Psychiatry, 27*, 759–763.

Black, A. (1974). The natural history of obsessive neurosis. In P. H. Hoch & J. Zubin (Eds.), *Obsessional states* (pp. 19–54). London: Methuen.

Black, D. W., Noyes, R., Goldstein, R. B., & Blum, N. (1992). A family study of obsessive-compulsive disorder. *Archives of General Psychiatry, 49*, 362–368.

Bolton, D., Collins, S., & Steinberg, D. (1983). The treatment of obsessive-compulsive disorder in adolescence: A report of fifteen cases. *British Journal of Psychiatry, 142*, 456–464.

Breslau, N. (1987). Inquiring about the bizarre: False positives in Diagnostic Interview Schedule for Children (DISC) ascertainment of obsessions, compulsions, and psychotic symptoms. *Journal of the American Academy of Child and Adolescent Psychiatry, 26*, 639–644.

Campbell, L. M. (1973). A variation of thought-stopping in a twelve-year-old boy: A case report. *Journal of Behavior Therapy and Experimental Psychiatry, 4*, 69–70.

Clark, D. A., & Bolton, D. (1985). An investigation of two self-report measures of obsessional phenomena in obsessive-compulsive adolescents: Research note. *Journal of Child Psychology and Psychiatry, 26*, 429–437.

Clark, D. A., Sugrim, I., & Bolton, D. (1982). Primary obsessional slowness: A nursing programme with a 13-year-old male adolescent. *Behaviour Research and Therapy, 20*, 289–292.

Costello, A. J., Edelbrock, C., Dulcan, M. K., Kalas, R., & Klaric, S. H. (1984). *Development and testing of the NIMH Diagnostic Interview Schedule for Children (DISC) in a clinic population: Final report.* (Contract No. RFP-DB-81-0027). Rockville, MD: Center for Epidemiological Studies, NIMH.

Dalton, P. (1983). Family treatment of an obsessive-compulsive child: A case report. *Family Process, 22*, 99–108.

Despert, L. (1955). Differential diagnosis between obsessive-compulsive neurosis and schizophrenia in children. In P. H. Hoch & J. Zubin (Eds.), *Psychopathology of childhood* (pp. 240–253). New York: Grune & Stratton.

Flament, M. F., Koby, E., Rapoport, J. L., Berg, C. J., Zahn, T., Cox, C., Denckla, M., & Lenane, M. (1990). Childhood obsessive-compulsive disorder: A prospective follow-up study. *Journal of Child Psychology and Psychiatry, 31*, 363–380.

Flament, M. F., Rapoport, J. L., Berg, C. J., Sceery, W., Kilts, C., Mellstrom, B., & Linnoila, M. (1985). Clomipramine treatment of childhood obsessive-compulsive disorder. *Archives of General Psychiatry, 42*, 977–983.

Flament, M. F., Whitaker, A., Rapoport, J. L., Davies, M., Berg, C. Z., Kalikow, K., Sceery, W., & Shaffer, D. (1988). Obsessive-compulsive disorder in adolescence: An epidemiological study. *Journal of the American Academy of Child and Adolescent Psychiatry, 27*, 764–771.

Foa, E. B., Steketee, G. S., & Ozarow, B. J. (1985). Behavior therapy with obsessive-compulsives: From theory to treatment. In M. Mavissakalian, S. M. Turner, & L. Michaelson (Eds.), *Obsessive-compulsive disorder: Psychological and pharmacological treatment* (pp. 49–129). New York: Plenum Press.

Francis, G. (1988). Childhood obsessive-compulsive disorder: Extinction of compulsive reassurance-seeking. *Journal of Anxiety Disorders, 2*, 361–366.

Goodman, W. K., Rasmussen, S. A., Price, L. H., Mazure, C., Rapoport, J. L., Heninger, G. R., & Charney, D. S. (1986). *Children's Yale-Brown Obsessive-Compulsive Scale (CY-BOCS).* Unpublished scale.

Goodman, W. K., Price, L. H., Rasmussen, S. A., Mazure, C., Fleischmann, R. L., Hill, C. L., Heninger, G. R., & Charney, D. S. (1989). The Yale-Brown Obsessive Compulsive Scale: I. Development, use, and reliability. *Archives of General Psychiatry, 46*, 1006–1011.

Grad, L. R., Pelcovitz, D., Olsen, M., Matthews, M., & Grad, W. (1987). Obsessive-compulsive symptomatology in children with Tourette's syndrome. *Journal of the American Academy of Child Psychiatry, 26,* 69–73.

Green, D. (1980). A behavioral approach to the treatment of obsessional rituals: An adolescent case study. *Journal of Adolescence, 3,* 297–306.

Hallam, R. S. (1974). Extinction of ruminations: A case study. *Behavior Therapy, 5,* 565–568.

Harris, C. V., & Wiebe, D. J. (1992). An analysis of response prevention and flooding procedures in the treatment of adolescent obsessive-compulsive disorder. *Journal of Behavior Therapy and Experimental Psychiatry, 23,* 107–115.

Herjanic, B., & Campbell, W. (1977). Differentiating psychiatrically disturbed children on the basis of a structured psychiatric interview. *Journal of Abnormal Child Psychology, 5,* 127–135.

Hodges, K., McKnew, D., Cytrynn, L., Stern, L., & Kline, J. (1982). The Child Assessment Schedule (CAS) diagnostic interview: A report of reliability and validity. *Journal of the American Academy of Child Psychiatry, 21,* 468–473.

Hodgson, R. J., & Rachman, S. (1977). Obsessive-compulsive complaints. *Behavior Research and Therapy, 15,* 389–395.

Hollingsworth, C. E., Tanguay, P. E., Grossman, L., & Pabst, P. (1980). Long-term outcome of obsessive-compulsive disorder in childhood. *Journal of the American Academy of Child Psychiatry, 19,* 134–144.

Judd, L. L. (1965). Obsessive-compulsive neurosis in children. *Archives of General Psychiatry, 25,* 298–304.

Karno, M., Golding, J., Sorenson, S., & Burnam, A. (1988). The epidemiology of obsessive-compulsive disorder in five US communities. *Archives of General Psychiatry, 45,* 1094–1099.

Kovacs, M. (1983). The Interview Schedule for Children (ISC): Interrater and parent-child agreement. Unpublished manuscript. University of Pittsburgh, Pittsburgh, Pennsylvania.

LaGreca, A. M., Dandes, S. K., Wick, P., Shaw, K., & Stone, W. L. (1988). Development of the Social Anxiety Scale for Children: Reliability and concurrent validity. *Journal of Clinical Child Psychology, 17,* 84–91.

Lenane, M. C., Swedo, S. E., Leonard, H., Pauls, D. L., Sceery, W., & Rapoport, J. L. (1990). Psychiatric disorders in first-degree relatives of children and adolescents with obsessive-compulsive disorder. *Journal of the American Academy of Child and Adolescent Psychiatry, 29,* 407–412.

Leonard, H. L., Swedo, S. E., Levane, M. C., Rettew, D. C., Cheslow, D. L., Hamburger, S. D., & Rapoport, J. L. (1991). A double-blind desipramine substitution during long-term clomipramine treatment in children and adolescents with obsessive-compulsive disorder. *Archives of General Psychiatry, 48,* 922–927.

Leonard, H. L., Swedo, S. E., Rapoport, J. L., Coffey, M. L., & Cheslow, D. L. (1988). Treatment of childhood obsessive-compulsive disorder with clomipramine and desmethylimipraime: A double-blind crossover comparison. *Psychopharmacological Bulletin, 24,* 93–95.

McCarthy, P. R., & Foa, E. B. (1988). Obsessive-compulsive disorder. In M. Hersen & C. G. Last (Eds.), *Child Behavior Therapy Casebook* (pp. 55–69). New York: Plenum Press.

Marks, I. M. (1987). *Fears, phobias and rituals.* New York: Oxford Press.

Mills, H. L., Agras, W. S., Barlow, D. H., & Mills, J. R. (1973). Compulsive rituals treated by response prevention: An experimental analysis. *Archives of General Psychiatry, 28,* 524–529.

Ollendick, T. H. (1983). Anxiety-based disorders in children. In M. Hersen (Ed.), *Outpatient Behavior Therapy: A clinical guide.* New York: Grune & Stratton.

Ong, S. B. Y., & Leng, Y. K. (1979). The treatment of an obsessive-compulsive girl in the context of Malaysian Chinese culture. *Australian New Zealand Journal of Psychiatry, 13,* 255–259.

Ownby, R. L. (1983). A cognitive behavioral intervention for compulsive handwashing with a thirteen-year-old boy. *Psychology in the Schools, 20,* 219–222.

Perse, T. (1988). Obsessive-compulsive disorder: A treatment review. *Journal of Clinical Psychiatry, 49*, 48–55.

Puig-Antich, J., & Chambers, W. (1982). *Schedule for Affective Disorders and Schizophrenia for School-Age Children* (6–16 years)—Kiddie-SADS. New York: New York State Psychiatric Institute.

Queiroz, L., Motta, M., Madi, M., Sossai, D., & Boren, J. (1981). A functional analysis of obsessive-compulsive problems with related therapeutic procedures. *Behavior Research and Therapy, 18*, 377–388.

Rachman, S. J. (1985). An overview of clinical and research issues in obsessive-compulsive disorders. In M. Mavissakalian, S. M. Turner, & L. Michelson (Eds.), *Obsessive-Compulsive Disorders: Psychological and Pharmacological Treatment* (pp. 1–47). New York: Plenum Press.

Rachman, S. J., & Hodgson, R. J. (1980). *Obsessions and Compulsions.* Englewood Cliffs, NJ: Prentice-Hall.

Rapoport, J. L. (1986). Childhood obsessive-compulsive disorder. *Journal of Child Psychology and Psychiatry, 27*, 289–295.

Rapoport, J. L. (1991). Recent advances in obsessive-compulsive disorder. *Neuropsychopharmacology, 5*, 1–10.

Rapoport, J., Elkins, R., & Mikkelson, E. (1980). Clinical controlled trial of chlorimipramine in adolescents with obsessive-compulsive disorder. *Psychopharmacological Bulletin, 16*, 61–63.

Rasmussen, S. A., & Tsuang, M. T. (1986). Epidemiology and clinical features of obsessive-compulsive disorder. In M. A. Jenike, L. Baer, & W. E. Minichiello (Eds.), *Obsessive-Compulsive Disorders: Theory and Management* (pp. 23–44). Littletown, MA: PSG Publishing.

Reynolds, C. R., & Richmond, B. O. (1978). Factor structure and construct validity of What I Think and Feel: The Revised Children's Manifest Anxiety Scale. *Journal of Personality Assessment, 43*, 281–283.

Riddle, M. A., Hardin, M. T., King, R., Scahill, L., & Woolston, J. L. (1990). Fluoxetine treatment of children and adolescents with Tourette's and obsessive-compulsive disorders: Preliminary clinical experience. *Journal of the American Academy of Child and Adolescent Psychiatry, 29*, 45–48.

Rutter, M., Tizard, J., & Whitmore, K. (1970). *Education, Health, and Behavior.* London: Longmans.

Sarason, S. B., Davidson, K. S., Lighthall, F. F., Waite, R. R., & Ruebush, B. K. (1960). *Anxiety and Elementary School Children.* New York: Wiley.

Silverman, W. K., & Nelles, W. B. (1988). The Anxiety Disorders Interview Schedule for Children. *Journal of the American Academy of Child and Adolescent Psychiatry, 27*, 772–778.

Spielberger, C. D. (1973). *Manual for the Strait-Trait Inventory for Children.* Palo Alto, CA: Consulting Psychologists Press.

Stanley, L. (1980). Treatment of ritualistic behavior in an eight-year-old girl by response prevention: A case report. *Journal of Child Psychology and Psychiatry, 21*, 85–90.

Steketee, G., & Foa, E. B. (1985). Obsessive-compulsive disorder. In D. H. Barlow (Ed.), *Clinical Handbook of Psychological Disorders* (pp. 69–144). New York: Guilford Press.

Swedo, S. E., & Rapoport, J. L. (1989). Phenomenology and differential diagnosis of obsessive-compulsive disorder in children and adolescents. In J. L. Rapoport (Ed.), *Obsessive-Compulsive Disorder in Children and Adolescents* (pp. 13–32). New York: American Psychiatric Press, Inc.

Swedo, S., Rapoport, J. L., Leonard, H., Lenane, M., & Cheslow, D. (1989). Obsessive-compulsive disorder in children and adolescents: Clinical phenomenology of 70 consecutive cases. *Archives of General Psychiatry, 46*, 335–341.

Turner, S. M., & Beidel, D. C. (1988). *Treating Obsessive-Compulsive Disorders.* New York: Pergamon Press.

Warren, W. (1960). Some relationships between the psychiatry of children and of adults. *Journal of Mental Science, 106*, 815–826.

Welner, A., Reich, T., Herjanic, B., & Campbell, W. (1987). Reliability, validity and parent-child agreement studies of the Diagnostic Interview for Children and Adolescents. *Journal of the American Academy of Child Psychiatry, 26*, 649–653.

Zikis, P. (1983). Treatment of an 11-year-old obsessive-compulsive ritualizer and Tiqueur girl with in vivo exposure and response prevention. *Behavior Psychotherapy, 11*, 75–81.

CHAPTER 14

Depressive Disorders

KEVIN D. STARK, SUSAN SWEARER, MICHELLE DELAUNE, LYNDEE KNOX,
AND JASON WINTER

DESCRIPTION OF THE PROBLEM

Many children who are hospitalized due to a psychiatric illness are suffering from depressive disorders. Research indicates that between 6.2% (Olsen, 1961) and 17.8% (Strober, Green, & Carlson, 1981) of inpatient adolescents and between 37% (Alessi, 1986) and approximately 59% (Carlson & Cantwell, 1980; Kashani et al., 1981; Petti, 1978) of inpatient children have been diagnosed with a depressive disorder. The clinical picture of depressed children is complicated by the fact that most of them are experiencing additional psychiatric disturbances (Anderson, Williams, McGee, & Silva, 1987), including externalizing disorders (Asarnow, 1988) such as conduct disorders (Carlson & Cantwell, 1979; Jensen, Burke, & Garfinkel, 1988; Marriage, Fine, Moretti, & Haley, 1986; Rutter, Tizard, & Whitmore, 1970) and attention-deficit/hyperactivity disorder (Bierdman & Steingard, 1989). Internalizing disorders such as anxiety disorders are the most common coexisting disorders (Kovacs, Feinberg, Crouse-Novak, Paulaskos, & Finkelstein, 1984). Further complicating the clinical picture may be a history of child maltreatment, substance abuse, parental psychopathology, and family dysfunction. Moreover, as a result of the many disturbances in the depressed youngster's life, he or she often has experienced school failure and interpersonal difficulties. The complexity of childhood depression calls for a well-coordinated, integrated, multidisciplinary, and multimodal approach to treatment.

Childhood depression is a syndrome that is comprised of a number of symptoms that consistently co-occur (Carlson & Cantwell, 1980). Depression during childhood is manifested in a manner similar to adulthood depression, but the symptoms are expressed in a developmentally appropriate fashion. The most common symptoms of depression are reported in Table 14.1 and are divided into affective, cognitive, motivational, and physical manifestations (Kovacs & Beck, 1977). According to the *Diagnostic and Statistical Manual of Mental Disorders*, third edition, revised, (DSM-III-R) (American Psychiatric Association, 1987), there are two primary diagnoses of unipolar depressive disorders including major depression and dysthymic disorder. The diagnostic criteria as well as issues in the diagnosis of depressive disorders in children were described in the previous paragraph. (For further discussion, the interested reader is referred to Stark, Christopher, and Dempsey [1993].)

However, a few of the differences between the diagnostic criteria in DSM-III-R and the new DSM-IV (American Psychiatric Association, 1993) should be noted here. While the changes are not dramatic, they appear to better represent the nature of depressive disorders in youths and the clinical realities of diagnosing these youngsters. The two major diagnostic categories of unipolar depressive disorders, major depression and dysthymic disorder, continue to be used, and the diagnostic criteria for each disorder have changed

TABLE 14.1. Symptoms of Depression Commonly Reported by Children

Affective symptoms	Cognitive symptoms	Motivational symptoms	Physical and vegetative symptoms
Dysphoric mood	Negative self-evaluations	Social withdrawal	Fatigue
Anger and irritability	Excessive guilt	Suicidal ideation and behavior	Change in appetite/weight
Anhedonia	Hopelessness	Decreased academic performance	Aches and pains
Excessive weepiness	Difficulty concentrating		Sleep disturbance
Loss of mirth response	Indecisiveness		Psychomotor agitation
Feeling unloved	Morbid ideation		Psychomotor retardation
Self-pity			

only slightly. The primary change in the diagnostic criteria for major depression is the addition of rule-out criteria for medical conditions that present as depressive disorders; for example, withdrawal from substance abuse and hyperthyroidism. Another change is the delineation of a time frame for differentiating between a depressive disorder and the natural grieving that follows the loss of a loved one: if the depressive symptoms occur within 2 months of the loss of a loved one, the depressive symptoms are not considered to be a reflection of a depressive disorder, but a reflection of the normal grieving process.

Some significant changes are evident in the diagnostic criteria for dysthymic disorder. In DSM-III-R, the youngster had to demonstrate a mood disturbance plus two of six possible additional symptoms. In the DSM-IV, in addition to the mood disturbance, the individual has to experience three of nine possible symptoms. The pool of additional symptoms has been both changed and expanded. The physical or vegetative symptoms of a disturbance in eating and sleeping have been dropped. The new symptoms include social withdrawal, anhedonia, excessive guilt, irritability or anger, and decreased activity, effectiveness, or productivity. The last symptom would be especially evident in a youngster's behavior in school. In general, the changes are consistent with the authors' research on the nature of depressive disorders among youths and assist in the often difficult process of diagnosing youngsters with possible depressive disorders.

Assessment of a child to determine the presence and severity of a depressive disorder should go beyond a measurement of symptom presence or absence to include an assessment of variables that have relevance for treatment. Thus, the assessment battery includes measures of cognition, interpersonal and academic behavior, family functioning, parenting behavior, and parental psychopathology. Results of this multifaceted assessment serve as a road map for effective treatment.

PROTOTYPIC ASSESSMENT

The prototypic assessment for childhood depressive disorders involves the use of multiple raters to assess for the presence and severity of depressive symptoms. In addition, there is a need to assess variables that impact treatment, for example, parental psychopathology, parenting skills, and the family's beliefs, rules, and interaction patterns. Since depression and family maladjustment may stem from prolonged exposure to stress, it is also important to assess the child's and family's exposure to stressful life events and chronic strains. Finally, following the behavioral tradition, it is important to assess the severity of the child's depressive symptoms over the course of treatment to determine whether treatment is effective. To complete such an assessment battery, both the identified child-patient and his or her parents will be asked to complete a number of measures and to participate in a few assessment activities, for example, an observation of the family trying to resolve a hypothetical conflict.

Assessment of the Child

The identified child is asked to complete several measures that assess the presence and severity of depression as well as measures of variables that might impact and are relevant to treatment. The child is considered to be the primary source of information about his or her subjective experience of depression. In addition, since it is believed that children respond to family members according to their perceptions of them rather than to the objective behavior of family members, a child's perceptions of the family as well as the actual characteristics of the family are considered to be important variables for assessment.

Depression

It is imperative to use a clinical interview to assess the presence and severity of depressive symptoms and to obtain a diagnosis (Kazdin, 1988). A variety of semi-structured clinical-interview schedules have been developed, including the Child Assessment Schedule (Hodges, McKnew, Cytryn, Stern, & Kline, 1982), Diagnostic Interview for Children and Adolescents (Herjanic & Reich, 1982), Diagnostic Interview Schedule for Children (Costello, Edelbrock, & Costello, 1985), Interview Schedule for Children (Kovacs, 1978), and the Schedule for Affective Disorders and Schizophrenia for School-Age Children (Puig-Antich & Ryan, 1986). All of these measures have demonstrated solid psychometric properties and assess a breadth of depressive symptoms as well as the symptoms that comprise most of the other major DSM-III-R disorders.

The clinical interview provides the clinician with face-to-face contact with both the child and parents. This provides the interviewer with the opportunity to observe the youngster's appearance (i.e., to see if the child looks depressed) and to inquire about assessment-related behavior and interpersonal behavior. In addition, the interviewer can obtain unlimited information about the parents, their mental health, attitudes toward the child and mental health services, and so on, during the course of the interview. Of particular concern for determining the presence of a depressive disorder is historical information, for example, the time of onset of the disorder, presence and nature of any precipitating events, previous episodes of the disorder, evidence of a prior manic episode, degree of suicidal risk, and presence of other disorders. The typical procedure is to interview the child and parents separately and then to combine the information from both sources to determine whether a diagnosis is warranted.

In addition to completing a diagnostic interview with the youngster, the child is asked to complete a self-report measure of depression. This provides the examiners with some additional information about the youngster's subjective experience of depression. The youngster's responses to these paper-and-pencil questions are often used as a basis for additional probing through an interview.

Treatment-Relevant Constructs

Research on childhood depression has identified a number of disturbances that appear to be related to depressive disorders and have implications both for the child's motivation for treatment and for what areas should be addressed during treatment. Hopelessness and self-evaluations are assessed because they have implications for the youngster's involvement in treatment as well as for the level of supervision required within the hospital. A depressed youngster who is hopeless is unlikely to believe that treatment is going to help or that his or her situation is going to change. Hopelessness also is highly related to suicidal behavior (Kazdin, French, Unis, Esveldt-Dawson, & Sherick, 1983) and, if it is accompanied by suicidal ideation, agitation, and sufficient energy to act on an impulse, the child's safety must be ensured through heightened supervision. Kazdin, French, et al. (1983) have developed the Hopelessness Scale for Children, which is a 17-item measure that assesses the severity of hopelessness. This measure has demonstrated acceptable psychometric properties (Kazdin, Colbus, & Rogers, 1986), and it can be completed in 5 to 10 minutes.

The child's self-evaluations are assessed for a number of reasons. Not only are self-evaluations highly related to suicidal ideation (Robbins & Alessi, 1985), but also, as research indicates, they tend to be unrealistically negative (Kendall, Stark, & Adam, 1990) and, thus, lead to information-processing errors and low self-esteem. The My Standards Questionnaire is a 30-item measure that assesses the child's (a) self-evaluations, (b) ideal standards, and (c) perceptions of parental standards (Stark, 1990). The instrument yields five scores: (a) an indication of the magnitude of the standards the child sets, (b) a measure of perceived parental standards, (c) a measure of the child's self-evaluations, (d) a discrepancy score between self-imposed standards and self-evaluations, and (e) a discrepancy score between perceived parentally imposed standards and the child's self-evaluations. Finally, the child rank orders 10 self-evaluation areas from most to least personally important.

The authors' research (Stark, Linn, MacGuire, & Kaslow, 1993) indicates that depressed children experience a disturbance in interpersonal functioning that is due to disturbances in social skills, the child's cognitions in social situations, and aversive emotional arousal in social situations. It appears as though these disturbances inhibit the youngster's enactment of appropriate social behavior. Consequently, it is useful to identify deficient or maladaptive social skills as well as the accompanying negative cognitions and aversive emotional arousal for intervention. A number of social skills measures exist, but the authors have used the Matson Evaluation of Social Skills for Youths (MESSY)(Matson, Rotatori, & Helsel, 1983). The MESSY is a paper-and-pencil measure that can be completed either by the child and/or his or her teacher.

In addition to assessing social skills, the youngster's academic skills and abilities should be assessed for a variety of reasons noted later in this chapter in the section on the hospital school. Briefly, the information is used to guide the modification of curriculum behavior and classroom environment. Typically, the assessment involves the administration of an intelligence test (Wechsler Intelligence Scale for Children, WISC-III), a measure of academic skills (e.g., Wechsler Individual Achievement Test), and a variety of other tests of cognitive skills and abilities that may be related to any academic difficulties the child is experiencing.

The youngster's automatic thoughts, processing errors, and schemata are targets for intervention and should be assessed. Unfortunately, few empirically validated measures exist for assessing such constructs. Consequently, the authors recommend combining extended inquiry during treatment sessions with paper-and-pencil self-report measures, projective techniques, such as the Roberts Apperception Test, and drawings to assess these cognitive constructs.

Ratings Completed by Significant Others

While the child usually is the best source of information about his or her subjective experience of depressive symptoms, the youngster's parents may be more accurate reporters of time-related information, such as when the current episode began, how long it has lasted, how often symptoms are present over an average week, and how long symptoms last over the course of a day. Parents also can report time-related information about previous episodes. In instances when the child believes that it is in his or her best interest to report inaccurate information (e.g., when the youngster is trying to avoid hospitalization), the child's parents may be the only reliable source of information. Thus, it is important to interview the child's parents with the same semi-structured interview that was completed with the child.

Assessment for Parental Psychopathology

Depressed youths are at greater risk than nondepressed youths for having a parent with a psychological disorder, especially a depressive disorder (Hammen, 1991). Depressed parents are likely to be more irritated by their child's behavior and more punitive than they would be if they were not depressed; and they do not have the energy and proper emotional state to provide their child with adequate nurturance. A depressed parent may model maladaptive information processing and may contribute to the child acquiring depressogenic schemata and processing errors. In addition to concerns about the ways that the parents may be contributing to their child's pathology through their own, the presence of parental pathology has implications for the role that the parents can play in their child's treatment. Dependent on the type of disorder, it may preclude using the parents as lay therapists for their child. Furthermore, it has implications for family therapy. Moreover, given the genetic basis to many disorders, knowledge of parental pathology may have implications for the child's long-term prognosis. Consequently, it is important to assess the youngster's parent(s) to determine whether either one is currently suffering from or has suffered from a psychological disorder. If the parent is currently experiencing a psychological disorder, then the parent will also need therapy, and the family system is likely to be more severely disturbed. In addition to gathering the usual demographic information from the parents, the therapist commonly asks the parents to complete the Beck Depression Inventory (BDI; Beck, Ward, Mendelsohn, Mock, & Erlbaugh, 1961) and the MMPI-2.

Assessment of Family Pathology

While several measures have been developed for assessing the family milieu, the authors have relied on a combination of a paper-and-pencil measure like the Self-Report Measure of Family-Functioning—Child and Parent (Stark, Humphrey, Crook, & Lewis, 1990) and observations of the family to gain an initial understanding of the family's functioning. The paper-and-pencil measure is completed by each family member who is old enough to do so; the results are used to gain an understanding of their perceptions of the family. Observations of the family during therapy sessions and during therapist contrived situations are the primary assessment tools.

Since family interactions are so complex, the primary form of assessment involves joining the family, observing them, and interpreting the interactions. All family members are observed with an eye toward identification of maladaptive behavior patterns that contribute to the child's distress. In addition to observing other family members, the child-patient is observed to identify the behaviors that he or she is enacting that contribute to the maladaptive sequence of interactions. Also of interest are the skills the family demonstrates in such areas as dealing with conflict, problem solving, decision making, and communication; and interactions are evaluated for the messages they send to the depressed child that lead to and maintain the child's negative sense of self, the world, and the future. These messages may be communicated through words, through nonverbal reactions, or, more subtly, through patterns of behaviors. Likewise, the therapist is concerned with determining what thoughts and beliefs underlie various maladaptive behaviors of family members. On a broader level, family interactions are observed to try to identify maladaptive rules that may be governing the family's interactions and communications. These rules have to be deduced from observing and interacting with the family.

During observations of the family, a number of structural characteristics are evaluated (Stark & Brookman, 1992), including subsystems, boundaries, alignment, and power. It is hypothesized that the families of depressed children are characterized by a weak marital subsystem, diffuse parent/child boundaries, low levels of supportive alliance behaviors, unstable and detouring coalitions, and rigid interaction patterns.

Ongoing Assessment

Assessment of the impact of treatment while the child is in the hospital allows the treatment team to learn whether the intervention is effective and what modifications may need to be made. In addition, it alerts the team to any setbacks that the child is experiencing and any changes in the clinical picture. Weekly and biweekly administrations of the CDI (Children's Depression Inventory) have been tried with some success. However, this has proven too time-consuming and too annoying for the children. Consequently, the authors have used a 21-item symptom checklist. The child indicates which symptoms were experienced between sessions by placing a check mark in front of the symptom.

ACTUAL ASSESSMENT

The authors' experience with psychiatric hospitals suggests that most of the prototypic assessment is completed. The youngster and his or her parent(s) are interviewed with nothing more than the interviewer's knowledge of psychopathology guiding the interview. Usually, it is only in university or medical school hospitals where research is being conducted that a semi-structured interview such as those noted previously is used. During the interview, the clinician obtains a psychosocial history, completes a mental status exam, and forms his or her impressions of both the youngster and his or her parent(s) and family. Following the interview, the hospital often contracts with a psychologist to complete a psychoeducational assessment and a psychological assessment that include a number of projective measures such as drawings, storytelling procedures, incomplete sentences, and the Rorschach test. When projectives are administered, the youngster's responses are commonly interpreted within a psychodynamic framework. Dependent on the age of the youngster, he or she may also complete the MMPI-A. Parent(s) commonly complete a rating scale such as the Child Behavior Checklist. Parents are rarely formally assessed for their own psychopathology. Only in research institutions are the treatment-relevant constructs assessed. Ongoing assessment is usually based on the clinician's and/or clinical team's judgment of the patient as he or she progresses through the hospital program. Weekly assessments of symptom severity are rare.

PROTOTYPIC TREATMENT

Therapeutic Milieu

Children who have been hospitalized for a psychiatric disturbance spend most of their time within the therapeutic milieu and the hospital school. Typically, they receive 1 to 2 hours of individual psychological therapy per week, their psychiatrist makes regular brief visits to monitor the effects of medication and overall progress, and the youngsters participate in a variety of therapeutic groups. Given this limited contact with professional clinical staff and the fact that the children are immersed within the therapeutic milieu for almost the whole day (i.e., acute and residential care) or most of the day (i.e., day treatment), the therapeutic milieu plays a central role in treatment and needs to be designed so that it supports and fosters attainment of the goals of individual, group, and family therapy.

The milieu must be fully integrated with the other modes of intervention, and the staff should all be working toward common goals, which in the case of depressed youths typically include (a) alleviation of depressive symptoms, (b) development of a positive sense of self, (c) remediation of faulty information processing and development of more adaptive schemata, (d) development of more appropriate coping and interpersonal skills, (e) development of more appropriate parenting behaviors that will support the changes the child makes in treatment, and (f) development of a healthy family system. If the milieu is going to foster the accomplishment of these goals, certain conditions must be met:

1. It must be a safe and supportive environment.
2. It must be problem-solving oriented.
3. There must be a well-designed and powerful behavior management system in place that motivates the child to change.
4. Staff must be consistent in their implementation of the system and in their dealings with the child.
5. The staff must be supportive and genuinely concerned about each child.
6. The community of children must be supportive of each other and their treatment programs.

A milieu that supports therapy and fosters attainment of the aforementioned therapeutic goals is one that models and fosters a problem-solving orientation, is strongly grounded in positive reinforcement, sets consistent limits, emphasizes and models adaptive coping and social skills, promotes the development of a positive self-schema and adaptive information processing, is flexible enough that each child can attain success, and promotes generalization of change to the home environment. A point system can also be used as a means of encouraging the children to acquire and use new skills and ways of thinking. Changing one's behavior and ways of deriving meaning from everyday life is a difficult and anxiety-producing process for children. They often need some additional incentives that provide them with positive feedback and rewards for their efforts. These rewards serve as a bridge of encouragement between the trial-and-error process of acquiring new skills and the natural reinforcement that accompanies the successful implementation of the skills outside of the hospital.

Problem-Solving

Stark (1990) has noted the importance of teaching problem solving to depressed youths. It helps them gain a sense of self-efficacy rather than hopelessness, and it breaks their rigid and often black-and-white thinking. It takes an extended period of training for a youngster to internalize a problem-solving orientation to daily life. This internalization process can be speeded up if the youngster is immersed within an environment that continually models and supports the use of problem solving. The therapeutic milieu is designed to have a problem-solving orientation. Staff continually look for opportunities to model the use of problem solving for the children. Any time they face a problem, they model the problem-solving process by verbalizing the steps and involving the children in the generation of alternatives and consequential thinking. Early in treatment, when a child is in the midst of a problem, staff will help the youngster identify that a problem exists and identify the nature of the problem. This is a very important first step because most depressed children have a hard time cognitively removing themselves from the situation to recognize that they are in the midst of a problem. In addition, staff can help keep track of the problem situations that each child faces. They can then be reviewed by the clinical staff in an attempt to identify any patterns. If a problem pattern is identified, then an intervention strategy is devised.

As children learn the problem-solving steps, they need assistance from staff with the generation of alternative, and especially new, solutions to their problems. Depressed youths have a very difficult time objectively evaluating the potential consequences of the solutions they generate. Thus, staff can help them combat their pessimism by helping them see potentially positive consequences. In addition, staff can help children follow through with their plans until completion. Depressed children often need this assistance because they short circuit their plans before they are carried through to the finish. Finally, staff help children process the outcome of their problem-solving plan. This helps prevent them from distorting and negatively evaluating the outcome of their plans. It helps them see and experience their success. As the children progress through treatment, they are progressively expected to independently use problem solving. Countless problems arise within the milieu every day. Any time a conflict or decision has to be resolved, the children are encouraged to use problem solving to arrive at a solution plan.

Another time when problem solving is systematically used within the milieu is after a child behaves inappropriately. When this occurs, staff problem solve with the child to develop a plan for preventing the future occurrence of the behavior. Thus, the milieu is solution oriented rather than punitive or focused on the negative behavior that may be exhibited. This is important for helping the children develop self-esteem. Children gain a sense of self-efficacy by successfully handling their own difficulties and developing effective plans.

As part of the solution orientation, a prominent disturbance in mood is identified as a problem, and staff assist the child in using problem solving to develop a plan for coping with it. Managing anger is an important coping skill that many depressed children need to learn. The first step in the process of helping children manage anger is to teach them to recognize cues that they are angry. Staff cue children that they are seeing signs of anger. This is done quite delicately through the use of carefully chosen verbal and nonverbal cues. Then staff direct the angry child to use an anger reducer, that is, an activity used to decrease the amount of anger that he or she is experiencing (e.g., taking a self-time-out leaving the situation alone and sitting quietly, throwing a kooshball against the wall, or doing physically demanding exercises). A staff member then accompanies the child to a room where the child can complete the anger reducer. Children also are encouraged to verbalize their angry feelings and to problem solve about situations involving anger. It also is important to help the children identify their angry thoughts and to help the children alter these thoughts either within the milieu, if appropriate, or during individual therapy.

Point System

TARGET BEHAVIORS.   A number of rules are followed for choosing the behavioral categories that form the cornerstone of a point system for depressed youths. Emphasis is placed on using the point system to help create a positive environment in which adaptive and desirable behaviors are "caught" and reinforced socially as well as through receipt of points. To create this positive environment, more categories of positive/adaptive behaviors than negative/maladaptive behaviors are included within the point system. This seems to keep everyone focused on positives and makes it more difficult for children to lure the staff into negative interactions.

A positive environment is one in which the children are safe and feel safe; thus, categories for behaviors that contribute to a safe and supportive therapeutic community are included. It should also be kept in mind that target behaviors should be ones that naturally draw reinforcement in the child's extrahospital environment. They should help the child to be successful both personally and interpersonally. Thus, behavioral categories are included that help children to manage their behavior (e.g., keeping hands and feet to self) and to develop new and appropriate behaviors (e.g., express feelings). The point system also needs to be flexible enough that it responds to individual therapeutic needs as well as to the needs of the overall hospital community. This can be accomplished through the inclusion of a few categories of "target" behaviors (e.g., "social target," "treatment target," "school target") that reflect individual treatment needs and especially targets of cognitive restructuring. Finally, it is important to include a number of bonus categories that foster the development of problem solving (e.g., problem-solved), self-control (e.g., agrees with staff ratings) and coping skills (e.g., coped with anger).

As was mentioned, through the creative development of behavioral categories in a point system, the treatment program is individualized through the use of target behaviors. The clinical team identifies the particular needs of each child in the program and develops target behaviors for that child. Typical target behaviors for a depressed child are those that will build self-esteem and/or decrease sadness; for example, "Say a nice saying to yourself," "Name one thing you liked during the prior point period," or "Name one thing you did well during the prior point period" can be used to help the depressed youngster learn how to self-monitor the positive things going on in his or her life. As a result of completing the self-monitoring, the child's depressogenic beliefs, such as "Nothing is ever fun" or "I can't do anything right," are countered. Another common target behavior is "Express feelings." Even though "Express feelings" is a common and almost cliche category, it is used with depressed children because (a) it helps them learn to use dysphoria or other unpleasant mood states as a cue to use coping skills; (b) it helps them recognize the continuum of feelings they experience; and (c) it helps them recognize the thoughts they have that accompany their unpleasant feelings.

The number and specificity of the behavioral categories reflect a balance between therapeutic objectives and the practical realities of the hospital setting. In settings where there is a low child/staff ratio, the behavioral categories can be defined in more specific terms and a larger number of categories can make up the system. This is made possible by the fact that each staff member divides his or her attention across fewer children. When the child/staff ratio is higher, fewer and more broadly defined behavioral categories are used. Another variable that determines the specificity and number of behavioral categories is the amount of structure present in the environment. In a more structured environment where the children are in close proximity to the staff member who is rating them, more refined and specific categories can be used. In a more loosely structured setting such as that found in a residential treatment center, children are likely to be spread apart and not in close proximity to the staff member who is rating them; then broader categories are useful.

A key ingredient to establishing a positive milieu is the stance of the staff that are managing it on a day-to-day basis. Staff are taught to take a proactive approach to the point system; in that approach, they try to catch the children enacting appropriate and therapeutically relevant behaviors and to socially reinforce them through verbalizing what they have observed. This social reinforcement takes the form of staff praise that includes a statement of the exact behavior that a child exhibited (e.g., "Nice job of following the five problem-solving steps") rather than vague words (e.g., "Good"). This labeling of the appropriate behavior serves an additional purpose: it makes the child aware of what he or she is doing, which, in turn, helps the child learn to self-monitor and self-evaluate. In addition, it provides the child with evidence that he or she can behave in a positive fashion. Appropriate behaviors that the child enacts that are not included in the point system are also recognized and socially reinforced. Thus, depressed children are confronted with behavioral evidence indicating that they have demonstrated appropriate behavior and are capable of being successful.

The point system should produce a milieu that is rich in reinforcement, including praise and verbal acknowledgment. As alluded to in the previous paragraph, ongoing, consistent positive reinforcement for adaptive behavior is particularly important in the treatment of depressed children not only because it promotes the enactment and acquisition of appropriate behavior, but also because it leads to cognitive restructuring. The consistent reinforcement of appropriate behavior communicates a positive message to the children. As the children experience social reinforcement, the message they perceive is that they can be successful and personally efficacious, which leads to a more positive self-schema and the development of a coping schema.

The point system gains its motivating properties through its relationship to an incentive described in the next section. Each behavioral category has a point value attached to it, with the higher point values attached to behaviors that are more therapeutically desirable and that require greater effort for the child to enact. Thus, the problem-solving, coping-skills, and target categories are typically assigned higher point values.

LEVEL SYSTEM.   The point system serves as a motivator because it is tied to a level system, access to special twice-weekly activities, and purchase at a hospital store. The program has four levels that differ according to the number and desirability of daily recreational activities, the amount of self-control the child has, and the amount of independence the child has within the milieu. Ideally, access to all recreational activities is tied into the point system. This creates a powerful incentive system. Children on the lower levels (levels 1 and 2) have minimal access to enjoyable recreational activities or access to less desirable activities, whereas children on the higher levels (levels 3 and 4) have greater access to more desirable activities. Twice a week, the children on the higher levels have an opportunity to participate in special recreational activities within and outside the hospital. In addition, the points they earn translate into money that can be used during the outing to purchase snacks or to purchase something from the hospital store. The levels are set on Monday and Thursday and are based on the average number of points earned during the preceding interval.

As children move up through the level system, they are given greater self-control over the point system. On the lower levels, the child and staff both simultaneously and independently rate the child's behavior and compare ratings for agreement. The comparison time is designed to be a time when the staff help educate the child about what was observed. It is not a time for bickering about ratings. When children are able to maintain level 4 for 2 consecutive weeks and when they have demonstrated the ability to accurately self-monitor and self-evaluate, as evidenced by consistent agreement in the ratings between the child and staff, then the child is given the responsibility for self-monitoring and recording of his or her behavior. Staff no longer complete ratings on the child; but they will enforce consequences when necessary and will continue to recognize and socially reinforce appropriate behavior. If the child is on level 4 for 2 additional consecutive weeks, then the youngster is placed on a revised point sheet that consists of four therapeutic target behaviors that are determined through collaboration between the child and his or her clinical team.

A potential problem with having the children carrying their point sheets is that they might destroy them when they get upset. To help prevent this, if a child destroys his or her point sheet then he or she loses all points earned to that point. In addition, on the opposite side of the point sheet is a certificate. This certificate serves as their money for spending at the hospital store or on recreational trips outside of the hospital. At the end of the day, staff complete the certificate by filling in total point earnings for the day, and the youngsters deposit the certificate in the hospital bank night deposit box.

The amount of independence the child has within the hospital also is tied to the level system. Children on level 1 are constantly monitored by staff. Children on level 2 are allowed to maintain greater distance from staff. Children on level 3 are allowed more freedom, such as the opportunity to independently walk to and from the hospital school. Children on level 4 are given the privilege of walking independently around campus.

GOALS GROUPS.   In a further attempt to help the children to set appropriate standards for their behavior, the children meet as a group with their unit director at the start of each shift to set goals for the number of points each child wants to earn during the shift. This time serves as an opportunity for the children to use problem solving as a means of developing plans for achieving their goals. Difficulties that the children faced during the previous day or shift are brought up by staff, and problem solving is used to develop solutions to prevent the difficulty from arising again. Long-term goals, such as achieving a higher level, are discussed, and progress toward achieving goals is monitored. In addition, the children provide one another with encouragement and support for progress toward goal attainment.

During the course of this meeting, staff are vigilant for expressions of perfectionism, negative expectations, and the tendency to make negative self-evaluations. When they occur, staff help the children to recognize them and to adopt a healthier approach. With time, the children help each other recognize expressions of perfectionism, negative expectations, and negative self-evaluations. In addition, staff help the children learn more adaptive ways of thinking.

CONSEQUENCES.   The point system also includes limits and consequences for negative behavior. Children lose points for each negative behavior that they exhibit during the specified time interval. However, to prevent the children from digging too deep a hole, if there are more than two instances of maladaptive behavior within the same interval, the youngster is instructed to take a time-out. The loss of points for negative behaviors is completed in a matter-of-fact, consistent manner, with the focus clearly on the child's behavior rather than on the child. This helps buffer the child's sense of self, which, in the case of depressed children, reflects low self-esteem and a fragile self-image. In addition, to help the children learn how to cope with disappointment and frustration, they are given the opportunity to earn positive points for "good acceptance" of the loss of points or other consequence.

The limits and consequences in the milieu are consistently and immediately delivered. When an inappropriate behavior occurs, staff label it, and negative points are given. When a time-out is given, the child is initially instructed to take a 5-minute self-time-out. If the child refuses to take a time-out, a 10-minute time-out is required, although the child can extend the time-out by acting out or refusing to problem solve about the situation after the time-out has been served. At the end of the time-out, the child is required to use problem-solving to generate alternative ways of dealing with the situation in the future. Children also can be assigned think time as a less punitive way to help them problem solve program issues. Children also can receive structure time, which involves being placed away from peers in a one-on-one situation with staff for a prescribed minimum duration time. The children can only work on schoolwork during this time. Structure time is a clinical team decision and usually occurs for major infractions. In order to complete individual structure time, the child must problem solve about solutions to the situation and must explain to the community during a group meeting what happened and what he or she intends to do about it.

The consistent, supportive manner of staff when dealing with negative behavior is important in the treatment of depressed children. Children are not treated punitively, and negative behavior is framed in a problem-solving light such that the children see their behavior as something they can work on and change. Additionally, staff help children implement the plans they have developed in order to avoid future negative consequences. The children also receive positive reinforcement for successfully resolving a problem. With depressed children, it is especially important that they identify the thoughts they had during the incident. The goal is to identify the patterns of thoughts that may reflect a maladaptive schema. Once the maladaptive schema is identified, the child's individual therapist works with the child to change it, and the milieu and point system are used to help the child restructure the maladaptive schema.

PROMOTION OF ADAPTIVE COPING SKILLS AND SOCIAL SKILLS.   As noted earlier, the point system is designed to promote the acquisition of skills for managing anger and for promoting appropriate interpersonal behavior. In addition, children are encouraged to learn to cope with disappointment through a bonus category entitled "Coping with Disappointment." When the youngster earns negative points for inappropriate behavior but handles this disappointment appropriately, he or she earns these bonus points.

Staff within the milieu use problem solving to teach the children how to cope with frustration, disappointment, and the other hassles children face on a daily basis. During the process of identifying multiple solutions to each problem, staff teach the children coping skills; for example, a child who appears highly anxious may be directed to go to a quiet spot with a comfortable chair and listen to a relaxation tape.

Daily interactions within the milieu provide the staff with countless opportunities to teach the children appropriate social skills. As the children display inappropriate social behavior, they are informed in a nonjudgmental manner of the problematic behavior, and then they are taught more appropriate behavior. In addition, when they behave in a socially skillful fashion, staff recognize this and socially reinforce it. Staff also might cue the youngsters to use certain social behaviors that they are trying to acquire. Moreover, through the relationships the children develop with staff, they learn about appropriate social behavior.

PROMOTION OF A POSITIVE SENSE OF SELF.   The milieu promotes a positive sense of self through the emphasis on positives and success. Alterations to the program and school that help each child experience success lead to a positive sense of self. Staff continually remain alert for examples of distorted information processing and help the children perceive things more accurately and realistically. Staff also may be informed by the youngster's individual therapist about maladaptive schemata that the child is working to change. They may be asked to help the youngster recognize and process schema-inconsistent evidence. A child may believe, for example, that the other kids are unsupportive and untrustworthy; then staff would help the youngster recognize times when the other children are supporting him or her and times when they are demonstrating that they are trustworthy.

GENERALIZATION TO THE HOME ENVIRONMENT.   During the course of treatment, the therapeutic milieu has to be extended into the home environment. Initially during treatment, this is necessary to promote the acquisition of skills and to manage the child's behavior when he or she is at home. Later in treatment, it becomes necessary for the promotion of the generalization and maintenance of treatment gains. The extension into the home environment is accomplished through parent training and family therapy as the parents are taught ways to create an appropriate and supportive milieu at home and also appropriate skills for managing their child's behavior. A number of steps are taken to accomplish this. The children's parents are taught how to use a simplified home version of the point system that has parallel behavioral categories. The parents learn the point system while they are completing the required parent-training modules. Videotapes, direct coaching, and role-playing are used to help the parents learn what to observe and how to deliver reinforcement, response cost, and time-out. The children take home and subsequently return the home version of the point sheet on a daily basis. Depending on the nature of the family milieu and the child's specific therapeutic needs, his or her level may be partially determined by behavior at home. In addition, a child may be given think time or structure time for inappropriate behavior at home.

Communication

In order to maximize the effectiveness of the treatment program, an effective system must be in place for communication among milieu staff, the individual therapist, the psychiatrist, the group therapist, and the family therapist. This system must reflect both daily developments and long-term goals, and it has to be readily accessible to all of the individuals who are working with the child and his or her parents and family. In addition, there must be a system in place for ongoing monitoring of the effectiveness of the treatment program. This system must be objective and capable of measuring tangible, measurable, and meaningful changes. To accomplish this, staff are taught to write regular case notes that include treatment-relevant information and especially new information that has relevance to the overall treatment plan. Staff note what they are working on from the child's master treatment plan and also note progress toward treatment goals. A communication log book is maintained, and staff write notes to each other regarding each youngster's treatment. Weekly treatment-team meetings are conducted, and all members of the child's treatment team are required to attend. During this time, the child's master treatment plan and progress are discussed. Changes are discussed and agreed upon and responsibilities are designated.

Hospital School

A child spends 40% of his or her waking hours in school, yet when a child begins to have emotional problems, the school's role in the child's life is frequently overlooked. This is especially true in a hospital setting where the school may be seen merely as the place the child goes when he or she is not receiving therapy. This is an unfortunate conception because the hospital-based school and its teacher can be very powerful players in the child's treatment.

The hospital school has a number of strengths when it comes to working with depressed children. First, it typically has a low teacher/child ratio, which allows for a highly individualized curriculum that promotes success. Second, it has the resources of the entire hospital to draw upon, which can lead to effective and creative educational programs. Third, given the school's size, the teacher is more able to create an artificially safe environment for the children to help them reengage in the learning process and to develop a new sense of self as learner.

Depression's Impact on the School Setting

Based on their symptom picture, depressed children have a number of special needs in the classroom. These needs are determined by how a child's particular symptoms interact with the academic setting. Table 14.2 outlines possible needs and effects.

Assessment

As discussed in the previous sections, depression has many different presentations. Therefore, the teacher should conduct a thorough classroom-based assessment. Assessment should address three areas: academic, behavioral, and cognitive abilities. The youngster should complete a thorough psychoeducational assessment upon entry into the hospital. The teacher also might complete a number of academic screening tests to measure the child's academic level and learning abilities. The information obtained from this formal and informal testing is used for planning the child's hospital curriculum and to check the appropriateness of the child's prehospital placement. The teacher also conducts a thorough behavioral assessment including an interview of the child's out-school teacher to get an

TABLE 14.2.   Symptoms of Depression and Their Impact on the Academic Setting

Symptoms	Impact
Motivational impairment	Reduced interest in school work
Anhedonia	Behavioral reinforcers hard to identify
Fatigue	Difficulty finishing assignments
Impaired concentration	Difficulty attending and finishing assignments
Lack of persistence	Failure to complete work
Impaired social relationships	Lack of engagement with teacher or students
Sadness/Tearfulness	Withdrawal, alienation from peers, lack of energy for learning
	Teasing by other children
Cognitive biases	Overperception of failures; tendency to interpret feedback as negative; grades become reinforcers of negative set
Heightened self-consciousness	Difficulty participating in group activities
Irritability/Aggression	Disruptive to rest of class; not engaged in learning process; failure to complete work; becomes central focus to exclusion of other symptoms
Withdrawal	Lack of engagement with others or process; tendency to be ignored

idea of the problems the child might have been having in the classroom prior to hospitalization.

The teacher completes a behavioral observation of the child and collects baseline data. This information is most helpful if presented in graphic form because it can become a powerful communication tool with both staff and the child's family. Because of the extended time a child spends in the hospital classroom, the effects of different medications on the child's academic performance and school behavior can be uniquely evaluated by the teacher. Baseline data greatly facilitate this process. The teacher interviews the child to obtain information in the following areas: the child's strengths academically/behaviorally in the classroom; the child's weaknesses; the child's actions that result in trouble, or, in the case of a non-acting-out depressed child, the causes of a child's trouble at school; the child's actions to stay out of or resolve trouble; the child's thoughts on what the problem is and on what the teachers say the problem is; the child's expectations of the classroom; and what if anything he or she would like to change about him- or herself in school. The interview should also be used as a time to orient the child to the classroom and for the teacher to define his or her role as authority but ally to the child.

Depressed children are notoriously difficult to engage, so the teacher concentrates on connecting with the child during the interview. Other methods for engaging depressed children include one-to-one discussions at least once a class; lunching with each child outside the classroom once a week, assigning special tasks to each child, allowing the children to earn adult-like privileges (e.g., drinking decaffeinated coffee which one teacher reports is an astounding motivator), and taking "service walks" in which the children and teacher take a break to visit a geriatric or neonatal unit to bring, for example, flowers. In addition, the teacher should conduct an assessment of reinforcers for use with the child in the classroom. Depressed children often have difficulty generating these, so the teacher may need to observe the child for ideas. Initially, sleep may be the primary reinforcer. A brief assessment should also be made of the child's cognitions about school and himself or herself as a learner. The teacher uses the information to begin to modify the children's academic self-image.

A thorough assessment of the child in the academic environment will go a long way toward helping the teacher plan interventions for the child in the hospital. The assessment data will also prove invaluable in suggesting posthospital placements, modifying individual education plans (IEP) and teaching approaches, preparing future teachers, and educating the parents about the child as learner.

Process

The hospital classroom is a unique environment in which many variables can be controlled. However, for the child's long-term success, many aspects of the hospital school must approximate those of the out-school. For this reason, the hospital school treatment of the child takes place in a number of stages. The first is highly controlled and orchestrated to increase the child's academic self-esteem and feelings of success. However, as the child progresses through treatment, the teacher should arrange the child's experience in the classroom to more closely approximate the real world and, as a final step, set up a practice version of the selected posthospital classroom.

Curriculum

The overall goal in developing a curriculum for depressed children is to create a learning experience in which the children are successful. To facilitate this, the teacher makes a number of modifications. First, during the initial stages of hospitalization, the teacher designs a curriculum that is one to two grades below the child's current level. Assignments are shortened and draw as much as possible on areas of interest to each child. All of these modifications combat the impaired concentration and motivation of the depressed child and ensure that the child experiences success in school. This, in turn, boosts the child's self-esteem. Grades have traditionally proven to be ineffective motivators for depressed children, either resulting in anxiety and obsession or in reinforcement of the child's negative cognitive set. For this reason, grades are downplayed as much as possible in the initial stages of treatment.

Behavior Management

The teacher employs the same behavior management program used in the hospital milieu. However, the teacher may choose to modify the system slightly to focus on academic behaviors and goals. Again, the objective is to create experiences in which the child is successful. This means that initially the teacher sets behavioral goals that are easily achieved by the child. Any positive behavior is reinforced. Special procedures should also be in place to deal with crisis situations, such as suicide threats. In the classroom, the policy should be that all threats will be taken seriously and handled not just by the teacher but the entire treatment team.

Transitioning

Perhaps the most overlooked element of the child's school intervention is transitioning from the hospital school to the out-school. The major rule of thumb when transitioning the depressed child is to never discharge a child until the out placement has been secured. There is nothing as detrimental to the child's treatment as being discharged into the old setting and then being changed again into a new one. This requires the child to go through two anxiety-provoking transitions. Determining proper placement prior to the child returning to the out-school is necessary but can present a dilemma, especially when planning for the withdrawn or compliant depressed child. The question becomes whether to place the child in a classroom for emotionally disturbed (ED) children, which will most likely include behaviorally disordered children, or to place the child directly back into the regular class where there is less support and fewer curricular modifications. The jury is still out on the best strategy; however, several teachers recommend placing the child in the ED classroom so that the transition is less drastic and the classroom is more supportive. If this is the chosen course of action, the hospital teacher should visit the ED teacher to discuss possible modifications to the program, the tendency to neglect a compliant child, and the need to move the child back into the regular classroom as soon as possible.

Once placement is decided, the teacher must prepare the setting, the child, and the child's parents. To prepare the setting, the hospital teacher should set up a meeting with the new teacher and provide him or her with an educational discharge summary outlining the child's progress in the program and successful teaching strategies. To prepare the child, the teacher and child should go on a field trip to the new (or old) school, meet the teacher and other relevant staff, and observe the classroom. During transition, the child is usually anxious and often defensive. A staged conversation between the hospital teacher and the new teacher in which they discuss the similarities between the hospital school and the anticipated placement can go a long way toward quelling this anxiety. Upon returning to the hospital, the teacher and the child should recreate the new system, complete with anticipated stumbling blocks, so the child can practice them in the safety of the hospital. During this time, the teacher must also help the child detach from the hospital classroom. This process is often more difficult with the depressed child than the nondepressed child as depressed children have a tendency to be more dependent. The teacher can facilitate detachment through the procedures just mentioned, discussing the progress the child has made and talking up the new placement. The teacher should also arrange for the child to attend the new school for half a day and the hospital school for half a day for a while so the child can process any difficulties with staff and so the transition is less traumatic. The teacher should also let the child know that he or she can write to the teacher at any time.

The hospital teacher has a unique role in preparing the parents for the transition. First, if it is being suggested that the child be qualified as ED for the first time, then it is preferable for the parents to learn of this recommendation from the treatment team and not from the out-school. The parents should be included in the decision-making process, and the process should begin as soon as the teacher sees that it is the preferred course of action. The hospital teacher is in a unique position because he or she can function as an advocate for the child and parents with minimal concern for the politics of the out-school. Therefore, the teacher teaches the parents how to advocate for their child within the out-school. This might include coaching them about what to look for in classroom settings for their child, describing the Assessment, Review, and Dismissal (ARD) process, informing them of their rights within the ARD and helping them to decide what to request, and, finally, attending the ARD if the parents request they do so. The ultimate goal is that the parents function as an advocate for the child, not the hospital teacher.

Parental Involvement

The teacher's involvement with the parents is critical to a successful intervention. It is often tempting to leave family matters to the therapists, but the teacher should be prepared to work with the parents on school issues connected to the child. The teacher should conduct weekly conferences with the parents to update them on their child's progress, discuss their concerns, and begin to prepare them for posthospital placement. If warranted, the teacher should also use the conference time to help parents modify inaccurate academic expectations of their child and should be willing to bring in the family therapist for a consultation should it be needed.

Psychiatric Intervention

Psychiatric intervention represents an important component of the multimodal approach employed in the hospital setting to treat depressive disorders in youths. Issues related to the use of psychopharmacological medications have been discussed elsewhere (see Stark et al., 1993). However, it is important to note that the hospital setting provides the children, their families, and the psychiatrist with an opportunity to try medications in a highly controlled environment where external confounds to gauging effectiveness are minimized. Often, it is the first time that the children have been very carefully stabilized on an antidepressant medication. The most commonly prescribed antidepressant medication is Tofranil, but Wellbutrin seems to be growing in its usage. Prozac and Zoloft are also used with adolescents. In addition to prescribing and monitoring medication, the psychiatrist's medical expertise is tapped to identify any possible medical basis to the youngster's depressive disorder, and the psychiatrist commonly heads the child's treatment team, runs the staffings, and communicates with the insurance carriers. Furthermore, his or her diagnostic and therapeutic expertise are valued sources of input into the assessment and treatment planning.

Individual Therapy

In this section, a cognitive-behavioral approach to treating depressed youths is briefly described. (The interested reader is referred to Stark [1990] and Stark, Dempsey, and Christopher [in press] for more detailed descriptions of the treatment program.) The treatment program is based on research that has direct implications for treatment (e.g., Stark, Humphrey, Laurent, Livingston, & Christopher, in press) and on research that has evaluated the efficacy of components of the program (e.g., Stark, Reynolds, & Kaslow, 1987). During the course of treatment, children are taught a number of coping and self-control skills, as well as cognitive strategies. While the intervention program emphasizes the acquisition of coping skills, it is recognized that a solid therapeutic relationship and productive therapy groups are the basis for the acquisition of these skills. Individual and group treatment support one another and often overlap in content. They each serve as the vehicle for the children to acquire the skills and to try them out in safe and relatively structured environments. The therapeutic milieu and point system are designed to encourage children to use coping skills in a more natural and less structured setting. Individual therapy also has to be coordinated with parent training and family therapy. Most of the time, it is necessary to produce changes in the family that will support the acquisition and use of the skills as well as the more realistic and positive ways of thinking about the self, the world, and the future that the child is acquiring.

Therapeutic Relationship

Establishment of a solid therapeutic relationship between the individual therapist and depressed child in a hospital setting is very important for therapeutic success and contributes to a more rapid improvement in the symptom picture. This relationship often serves as leverage that helps the child overcome fears and other road blocks to trying new skills and to challenging his or her comfortable way of thinking and behaving. Furthermore, in a program where therapeutic homework is so crucial, it also serves as a source of motivation for the child completing it. Moreover, the cognitive procedures cannot be used with maximum efficacy without the empathic understanding of the youngster that comes from having a solid therapeutic relationship with the child. Establishing such a relationship with the depressed child-patient often is difficult because of depressive symptoms such as hopelessness, social withdrawal, fatigue, and anhedonia. In addition, the youngster's propensity to distort information and establish coercive/destructive relationships with significant others can often impede or destroy the relationship. Consequently, direct, clear, open communication with plenty of feedback is necessary.

Affective Education

Children are taught a variety of coping skills and cognitive strategies for moderating their depressive symptoms during individual therapy. In order for the children to be able to use these skills, they first have to be able to recognize their emotions. Recognition that they are experiencing certain specific emotions serves as the cue to use various coping strategies. Thus, one of the first objectives of treatment is to help the children become more knowledgeable about and sensitive to their own emotional experiences. Children are taught to recognize affective, physical, and cognitive cues that they are experiencing various emotions and a vocabulary for communicating what they are experiencing. This is most effectively accomplished through the affective education groups described in a later section of this chapter. However, there usually is a need to supplement the group experience with individual therapy. The individual therapist helps the children recognize fine distinctions in mood, thinking, and physiological cues between the various emotions and the therapist can reinforce the notion that each emotion is experienced along a continuum of severity. This can be best accomplished through working with each child's own experiences and helping the child recognize the continuum of experience from examples in his or her own life.

Once children are able to recognize variations and changes in their emotions, they begin collecting information that helps guide intervention. They are taught to catch themselves when they are feeling better and to use this improvement in mood as a cue to note what they are doing and thinking. Staff can help children with this by cueing them that they have noticed a positive change in affect and by helping the children remember to record what is happening and what they are thinking. The information gained from this self-monitoring is combined with information gathered through an interview of the child and parents to construct pleasant-events schedules. Once constructed, the children use the pleasant-events schedules to guide their self-monitoring. This forces the children to attend to the positive and enjoyable things occurring in their lives, which produces an improvement in depressive symptoms. Over the course of treatment, the children are taught to self-monitor a variety of other variables.

Self-Monitoring & Problem-Solving

Due to the depressed youngster's proclivity for distorting information in a negative way, it is important for the therapist to remain actively involved in the self-monitoring process as he or she helps the child process the results. The child may quite accurately record the occurrence of a variety of pleasant events over the course of a day, for example, but when asked for an evaluation of how the day went, the child replies "Awful! Nothing went right," and proceeds to describe a disappointing event. A closer look at the child's pleasant-events diary reveals that a variety of positive things also happened. However, due to the processing error of selective abstraction, the youngster has focused on the one negative thing that happened to the exclusion of the positives. The therapist can correct this error and help the youngster recognize other times when the error occurs through the cognitive restructuring procedures described in the following paragraphs. With the previous example of the "awful" day, the therapist might first ask the child to define an awful day. Then, based on the definition, they would check the child's diary for the evidence to determine whether the day in question was awful or OK.

Once children are able to recognize and identify their unpleasant emotions, children are taught problem solving as a general coping strategy, and the unpleasant emotion or other depressive symptom is viewed as a problem to be solved. Once the symptom is identified as a problem, the youngster is taught to identify possible solutions/coping strategies for handling the problem. After generating possible solutions/coping strategies, each one is evaluated for its possible effectiveness. The strategy with the greatest opportunity for success is chosen, implemented, and evaluated for its success.

Problem solving is taught and honed as a skill during individual therapy sessions, and its use is modeled and encouraged within the milieu. Problem solving is initially taught through playing games that require consideration of multiple alternatives for each move (e.g., Checkers, Connect Four). As the children gain an understanding of each step and master the use of the steps during game play, they are taught to use problem solving to develop plans for coping with depressive symptoms and to better deal with interpersonal difficulties and daily hassles. This is accomplished through role-playing relevant hypothetical situations. The hypothetical situations are derived from information obtained from staff who have observed the youngster experiencing difficulties within the milieu. Children also keep problem-solving diaries. In these diaries, they define the problem and write down their response for each of the five steps.

Youngsters are taught a variety of coping skills to use when they identify a depressive symptom as a problem. As was noted, the child is initially taught to self-monitor pleasant events in response to various symptoms. In addition, the child may be taught to use activity scheduling. In other words, an unpleasant experience is used as a cue to get up and do something "fun." These activities commonly are noted on the youngsters' pleasant-events schedules. A list of fun activities within the hospital can be generated, and the child and therapist can contract for their enactment (given that they are appropriate for the child's level of supervision). A feeling of anger is used as a cue to get staff and go to a room to use anger reducers. Anxiety serves as a cue to use relaxation. The youngster checks out a portable tape player and relaxation tape and uses them while sitting back in an overstuffed chair. Regular, strenuous physical exercise is encouraged and rewarded as a general coping strategy for depressed youngsters. Children are encouraged to use other coping strategies including talking with staff, talking with a peer, or expressing oneself through writing or artwork.

Later in treatment, as children have gained some distance from their thinking and mastered a number of coping skills, self-monitoring is used as an assessment tool to identify depressogenic thoughts and to serve as a cue for using cognitive restructuring. The youngsters are instructed to use a change in mood as a cue to focus on their thinking and then to record it. Particularly difficult situations that are associated with dysphoria may also be used by children as cues to tune in to their thoughts.

Self-Reinforcement

Children are taught self-reinforcement (a) as a means of enhancing mood, (b) as a means of reinforcing the child's use of coping skills, (c) as a motivational bridge between acquiring and using skills and the natural reinforcement of symptom improvement, and (d) as a procedure that remediates a deficit that typically exists among depressed youths. Youngsters are taught to reinforce themselves after completing steps of a therapeutic homework assignment, after enactment of an adaptive behavior, and as a means of enhancing mood.

Cognitive restructuring procedures are used throughout treatment and may be used in every session. Initially, the therapist takes responsibility for identifying and helping the children modify depressogenic thoughts. As therapy progresses, the children are taught to identify and restructure their maladaptive thoughts. In addition, they progress from applying the techniques to their individual thoughts to applying them to themes in their thinking. Behavioral assignments that directly test the premises that underlie the child's maladaptive beliefs appear to be the most powerful procedures for changing his or her thinking.

A number of cognitive restructuring procedures are used and taught to the children, for example, What's the evidence?, What's another way of thinking about it?, and What if . . . ? (Beck, Rush, Shaw, & Emery, 1979; Stark, 1990). The essence of the procedures is that they are designed to help youngsters acquire more adaptive and realistic ways of thinking about the self, the world, and the future. The goal is to help the children complete the cognitive restructuring independently from the therapist. Children require some extra structure to be able to do this on their own. This is accomplished by having staff and their parents help them acquire and implement the procedures.

In addition to the therapist's spontaneous use of cognitive restructuring that goes on throughout treatment, a number of sessions are devoted to teaching the children how to use cognitive restructuring. Children can learn to tune in to their thoughts during individual therapy sessions. A change in mood during a session is used as a cue to tune in to their thoughts. The therapist can help the children recognize mood changes by pointing them out. Then the child is asked to think out loud as a means of learning to tune in to his or her thinking. Once the child is able to tune in to his or her thinking, then the therapist educates the child about how to use cognitive restructuring. Staff facilitate the independent use of cognitive restructuring outside of the office by cueing the children to use it and by providing the children with an incentive for using it through the point system.

Self-evaluation training is introduced late in treatment because of the heavy overlay of distorted thinking surrounding the child's self-evaluations. There are two primary objectives to the self-evaluation training: (a) the identification and modification of standards and self-evaluations, and (b) working toward self-improvement. Late in treatment, the youngster has acquired a number of valuable coping skills that can be used to produce additional improvements in the youngster's life. The therapist and the child work together to identify areas where the child would like to change and where it is realistic to expect some change to occur. Each area of desired change is translated into objective goals and then broken down into subgoals. The child and the therapist create a plan for achieving the subgoals, and all of the relevant skills the child has acquired are used to help the child achieve the desired goals. The child, the therapist, and milieu staff monitor progress.

Group Therapy

Group therapy is an integral part of the treatment of depressed youths in the hospital. However, due to a number of characteristics of depressed children, consideration has to be given to altering the process of the group to meet some of their special needs. Depressed youths tend to be self-centered and have difficulty decentering enough to be able to empathize with and support their fellow group members. An entire group of depressed youths can be very demanding on the therapist and difficult to engage in productive process. Due to their fragile self-concepts and their tendency to put themselves in victim roles, they can be devastated by the actions of other group members. Confrontations are misunderstood to be personal attacks that confirm a negative self-image, and direct cutting comments can be devastating for a depressed child. Some of these difficulties can be avoided by structuring the groups and setting specific rules that prohibit personal attacks.

Children participate in a number of topic-centered groups that emphasize skill acquisition; the topics include affective education, problem solving, cognitive distortions, social skills, and anger management. Children meet once or twice a week for these skills groups. They also attend less structured groups (process groups) twice a day to process what has transpired over the course of the day or evening. These process groups are solution oriented and also aid the team in their quest to identify the thoughts and schemata that underlie each group member's problematic behaviors and symptoms. In addition, they provide the team with a good opportunity to observe the children's interactions in a less structured environment.

Although there are a variety of skills that can be taught during group sessions, social skills and assertiveness skills are those best taught in groups because the group provides a natural medium for assessing and teaching social skills. Disturbances in social behavior can be observed and appropriate behaviors can be taught and rehearsed with other children. Through their reactions and comments, the other children can provide very powerful reinforcement for improved social behavior. Distorted cognitions that occur before, during, and after interpersonal situations and the accompanying aversive physiological arousal can be assessed while they are hot. Similarly, new behaviors can be rehearsed in a real interpersonal situation.

Group social-skills training is coordinated with individual therapy to maximize the impact of both. The skills deficits are identified during group sessions, and more appropriate skills are taught during individual sessions and subsequently enacted during future group sessions. Feedback is provided to the children during individual and group therapy, and the skills are fine-tuned during individual sessions. However, the most powerful feedback is provided by other group members rather than the therapist.

Group therapy also plays a very important role in teaching the children how to use cognitive restructuring procedures. It is easier for children to initially identify an example of another child's distorted thinking than it is to identify their own. Thus, during the cognitive distortions group, the children identify examples of other children's distorted thinking and talk about their own examples. As the group progresses in their acquisition of the skills, they model the therapist's behavior and help each other use cognitive restructuring. This process seems to help the children gain some distance from their own thinking, which enables them to begin to use cognitive restructuring to change their own depressive thoughts.

Parent Training

A major component of the hospital treatment program for depressed youths is an evening of parent training once or twice a week. Research has shown that parent training programs improve parent-child relations (Seymour, Levy, & Ushaw, 1989); and when individual therapy with the child is combined with parent training, the improvements tend to be maintained over an extended period of time and they appear to generalize to home and school environments (Kazdin, Esveldt-Dawson, French, & Unis, 1987). A number of parent training programs have been developed for children with serious externalizing disorders (e.g., Barkley, 1987; Kazdin, 1990) and for general parenting issues (e.g., Dinkmeyer & McKay, 1989; Gordon, 1975), but nothing has been specifically developed for parents of children who have internalizing disorders such as depression. Thus, based on research with families of depressed children, the authors have combined components of various parent training programs (e.g., Barkley, 1987; Guerney & Guerney, 1989; Phillips & Bernstein, 1989) with their own ideas to create a program for parents of depressed youths.

A couple of additional issues have to be kept in mind when developing and implementing such programs. The literature on families of depressed youth indicates a greater chance that the parents are also depressed. In fact, 40% to 70% of depressed children were found to have depressed mothers (Kaslow & Racusin, 1990). Thus, the parents' mental health needs to be considered when deciding on the nature of their involvement in their child's treatment. Furthermore, methods for encouraging the disturbed parent to obtain treatment become important. Another concern is the high rate of comorbidity among depressed youths. Dependent on the nature of the co-occurring disorder, certain procedures may become more or less critical to the success of the overall program. The training program for the parent of a child who has a co-occurring anxiety disorder, for example, would be very different from one for the parent of a child with a co-occurring conduct disorder or attention-deficit disorder. Thus, some individualization of the program to meet the child's and parents' specific needs becomes important (Spitzer, Webster-Stratton, & Hollinsworth, 1991). Because the parent training sessions are conducted with groups of parents whose children may exhibit a variety of psychiatric disturbances in addition to depression, the family therapist often is the one who is responsible for helping the parents individualize the parent training to meet their specific needs and situation. However, much of this is done during the discussion portion of the parent training meetings.

Unfortunately, while parent training is a critical component of treatment and may be crucial for the generalization and maintenance of the skills being acquired in the hospital, attendance at the parent training sessions is not good. Furthermore, it often seems as though the parents that need training the most do not attend on a regular basis. Parents who live out of town cannot make it to the hospital as frequently as would be ideal. In these cases, they are asked to watch videotaped demonstrations of the crucial skills.

Initial sessions are designed to recreate the problem-solving oriented environment and point system at home. To do this, parents are taught how to use a simplified version (fewer categories) of the point sheet that also includes categories that are more specific to situations that arise at home. The point system and category labels are parallel to the hospital point system. Emphasis is placed on consistently catching appropriate behavior, recognizing it, and recording it on the home point sheets. Similarly, the parents are taught to actively watch for the early signs of undesirable behavior and to consistently enact the appropriate consequences. A parallel objective is to teach the parents the same skills at home. Parents are taught the same five-step problem-solving sequence that the children have learned. They learn how to help their children recognize when a problem has arisen and how to use problem solving to deal with it. In addition, parents are taught how to use and model problem solving to manage problems that the family faces. Subsequently, parents are taught how to help their children use coping skills and anger reducers to moderate the impact of depressive symptoms. Similarly, parents are kept abreast of the social skills their children are learning and how to encourage their children to use them. In addition, they are encouraged to facilitate their child having play time with other children. They provide their child with encouragement and praise for appropriate social behavior and enactment of new social skills.

During recreation therapy in the hospital, children learn to have fun. Parents of depressed children are encouraged to help their children engage in enjoyable activities at home. In addition, the parents are taught to involve the whole family in recreational activities. Oftentimes, cognitive restructuring procedures have to be used to help the parents overcome misbeliefs that prevent parents from engaging their families in recreational activities. Problem solving also is brought to bear on the problems of creating a win-win situation for all family members.

The most difficult skill to teach parents is cognitive restructuring. Once again, the objective is to teach the parents how to help their child use cognitive restructuring. Parents can quickly learn how the children are supposed to use the cognitive restructuring procedures, but they have difficulty identifying when a child is exhibiting a negative cognition or belief. They often give a few examples of their children's maladaptive thinking; these, combined with examples from other parents and the therapist, serve as the base for identifying additional cues that their child should use one of the cognitive restructuring procedures.

Family Therapy

The goal of family therapy is to identify and to help the family alter interaction patterns, communications, and family rules that support the child's depressogenic behavior, information processing, and schemata. Treatment begins by working with the family to help them understand how their family fits into a cognitive behavioral model of depression. The therapist joins the family and observes the family for examples of maladaptive interactions while he or she is establishing a relationship with the family. The therapist explores the thoughts and beliefs that underlie the maladaptive interactions of family members and the cognitive restructuring procedures that might be used. The family, like the depressed youngster, is given specific homework assignments to work on between meetings.

The individual and group therapists, the psychiatrist, and other members of the treatment team communicate with the family therapist and each other to provide information about the child's depressogenic behavior and thinking that might be based in the family. Based on this information, the therapist looks for behaviors and verbalizations from other family members, especially parents, that may have led to the development of the child's depressogenic behavior and currently support it. Once identified, the therapist may use therapeutic directives, education, coaching, modeling, feedback, behavioral rehearsal, and contracting to help the family change. The family is taught a variety of skills, including communication skills, conflict resolution skills, democratic decision-making skills, and recreation skills. With some very inactive families, activity scheduling may be used to increase their involvement in pleasant activities.

ACTUAL TREATMENT

The actual treatment of depressed youths in the hospital setting varies widely from hospital to hospital, with most programs reflecting a psychodynamic or medical mode. A level system may be used to manage the children's behavior, but that is the extent of the behavioral program. Rarely are the programs as integrated as the prototypic program, and it is very unusual to find a program that integrates a cognitive perspective into the point system and milieu. Equally rare are psychiatric hospitals that take a cognitive-behavioral approach to the individual, group, parent training, and family therapy components of treatment. Currently, the authors are involved in evaluating two treatment programs that have served as the model for the prototypic program described in this chapter. One of them is a day treatment program (St. David's Pavilion, Austin, Texas) that has been designed by Larry Bachus, Ph.D., who has been developing and running the program for 8 years.

The other program is in a residential treatment center and is in the process of being implemented and modified with experience.

Point System

The point system within the day treatment program consists of 15 objectively defined behaviors that earn positive points and 10 behaviors that earn negative points. The behaviors are discrete, specific, and readily observable. In addition, each child has one or two therapeutic target behaviors that are set by the clinical team. The point system includes bonus points for accurate self-monitoring and self-evaluation, enactment of all positive behaviors during an interval, using problem solving, using anger reducers, and coping with the loss of points.

Children earn advancement to different levels according to their success within the point system. The level that children are on determines their independence in self-monitoring behavior. On level 1, children check in with staff at the end of each 30-minute interval, and they are expected to remember whether or not they earned the points for each behavioral category. The children are allowed to ask staff for the negative points they earned. To earn level 2, children must earn an average of 50% of the total possible positive points and 50% of the agreement points (points earned for agreeing with staff about the occurrence or nonoccurrence of each behavior) for 10 days. At level 2, children carry their own point sheets and record points as they earn them. At the end of each 30-minute interval, staff check the children's point sheets for accuracy, and children earn agreement points for accurate self-monitoring. To move to level 3, children must earn 70% of the total possible positive points and 70% of the agreement points for 10 consecutive days. Once on level 3, the children record their own points on a point sheet, and staff check the points at midday and again at the end of the day. To move to level 4, children must once again earn 70% of the total possible points and 70% of the agreement points for 10 consecutive days. These youngsters are assigned additional therapeutic target behaviors and do not have to have their point sheets checked for agreement with staff. Thus, it is expected that the child will self-monitor without having to be rewarded for it. To remain on level 3 or 4, the children must earn 70% of agreement points for 4 days out of each week. Children can lose their level permanently or temporarily by behaving in a manner that is not commensurate with the level they have earned, such as being aggressive. In addition to the independence the children have within the point program, the privileges the children earn are determined by the level they are on. Each successive level includes access to more and more desirable recreational activities as well as to greater freedom within the hospital setting.

Activity Time

In addition to the privileges earned from being on higher levels, the children earn twice-daily activity rewards based on the number of points they earn in the morning and in the afternoon. The number of points determines to which toys or games the children have access during the reward times, with access to the more desirable games requiring more points. The children also are rewarded through a store time during which time they use the points they earned during the previous day to "buy" privileges, such as extra video game time or the use of an adult-sized chair for group therapy. In addition to the activities, free recreation time, weekly lunch visits to the cafeteria, and special outings for fun are built into the program.

Generalization to the Home

While children are in the day treatment program, they spend every evening and night at home; therefore, the extension of the milieu into the home environment becomes crucial. The home point system is individualized to meet each child's and family's needs. Similar to the procedure for completing point sheets within the program, the children on level 2 and higher self-monitor their behavior at home, and their ratings will be compared to parents' ratings. During this comparison time, discrepancies are discussed. If consequences are not consistently or effectively delivered at home, then consequences for home behavior may be established within the program; for example, a child will earn think time in the hospital for physical aggression against a sibling during the previous evening at home. Children who are having difficulty controlling their anger at home use problem solving during the day in the hospital to develop plans for managing anger at home. In addition to serving as an extension of the milieu into the home, the daily home point sheet is a valuable tool for helping staff communicate with parents.

Goal Setting

To help the children learn how to self-evaluate, the day begins with each child choosing a goal or challenge for the day. Typically, the goal is to earn a certain number of points within a behavioral category; for example, a child might want to earn 70% of the agreement points in a day. The children learn how to set more reasonable standards for their own behavior through the staff making sure that the challenges are neither too easy nor too difficult. Each day concludes with the children reviewing their day and listing things they liked and did not like.

Problem-Solving Environment

The milieu is designed to have a problem-solving orientation and, thus, facilitate the acquisition of problem-solving skills. Any time a conflict or decision has to be resolved within the milieu, the children are encouraged to use problem solving to arrive at a plan. If a child behaves inappropriately, staff problem solve with the child to develop a plan for preventing the future occurrence of the behavior. Early in treatment, staff assist the children in the generation of alternative solutions to their problems by helping them generate new solutions. In addition, they help the children follow through with their plans until completion.

Anger management training is an important part of the intervention program for most of the children. Children are taught to use anger as a cue to use anger reducers. Anger reducers that the children learn to use while they are at the program include taking a self-time-out, shooting baskets, throwing a ball against the wall, and lifting weights. Generally, the children are allowed to ask to leave the milieu and complete an anger reducer with a staff member. They also are encouraged to verbalize their angry feelings and to problem solve about situations involving anger.

Consequences

The limits and consequences in the milieu are consistently and immediately delivered. When an inappropriate behavior occurs, staff label it, and negative points are given. If a child receives negative points three times in the same category during an interval, the child is placed in time-out. A 5-minute time-out is required, although the child can extend the time-out by acting out or refusing to problem solve about the situation after the time-out has been served. The child is required to use problem solving to generate alternative ways of dealing with the situation. Children also can be assigned think time instead of time-out when they have something they need to think about or talk about with staff. Children also can receive structure time, which involves the child being placed away from peers in a one-on-one situation with staff for a prescribed minimum duration of time. The children can only work on schoolwork during this time. In order to complete individual structure time, the child must problem solve about solutions to the situation and must explain to peers during a group meeting what happened and what he or she intends to do about it.

Individual Therapy

The type of individual therapy that the child receives in the day hospital varies widely from one child to the next because the children commonly enter the program under the care of their own outside therapist. Consequently, they continue to work with this individual while they are in the day treatment program. The maximum outcome usually occurs in those instances where the therapist has a background and understanding of cognitive behavioral therapy. Such individuals know how to derive for their patient the maximum benefit from the program. Individual therapists who are not familiar with the program do not understand how to coordinate efforts and may be working toward different goals from those of the program. With the exception of graduate students who have taken specific training in the treatment program described by Stark (1990), few of the individual therapists have implemented the cognitive-behavioral treatment program described earlier in this chapter.

Group Therapy

Children attend group therapy for 1 hour every day. Group rules are reviewed at the beginning of each meeting. Since these meetings can be rather anxiety producing, children can choose a stuffed animal to hold during the meeting. Each child has an opportunity to talk, usually about the topic they chose during the morning planning-for-the-day meeting. Children are encouraged to express their feelings, and they obtain empathy and guidance from the leader. In addition, group therapy is used as an opportunity for peers to give each other feedback, and the leader of the group actively solicits the opinions and input of other children when one child brings up an issue or a problem. Often group problems arise, such as who is going to talk first, and the group must problem solve to resolve the conflict.

Children attend half-hour social skills groups every day. The social skills taught include skills for interacting with peers, for self-control, and for school-related social behaviors. To teach the skills, the following general strategy is employed: The children are educated about the skill; the group leaders model the skill; the children role-play and practice the skill; and the group, as well as the group leaders, provide constructive feedback and coach the children in the appropriate enactment of the skill. The desired social skill is written on each youngster's point sheet and monitored and reinforced by staff.

Hospital School

In an earlier section of the chapter, the prototypic hospital school was described. Unfortunately, the ideal hospital school is rarely found, not even in the day treatment program that has been described here. In hospital schools, realities such as limited time, budget, and problems with the integration of school and hospital agendas invariably taint the ideal picture. Teachers, due to time constraints, often fail to do the types of assessments described earlier. Instead, they may do part or rely heavily on testing already completed for the hospital. Curriculum is frequently based on what the child was doing prior to admission and so is not designed to orchestrate success. The behavior management system usually focuses on the acting-out behavior of certain children to the exclusion of other problems associated with depression. The transition process is often truncated due to time demands on the teacher. Rarely do the teacher and child make an on-site visit to the out-school, and communication between hospital teacher and out-school often fails to extend beyond paper contacts. Parental involvement in the academic intervention with the child often falls to the wayside in lieu of more pressing issues or as a result of lack of interest. Finally, although the school may be successfully integrated into the larger hospital, there are always glitches. The most frequent of these is the exclusion of the teacher from the treatment milieu and a tendency to undervalue his or her role in the child's treatment.

Family Therapy and Parent Training

Each patient's family is required to be involved in family therapy, either from an outside therapist who has already been conducting the family therapy or from one of the program therapists. The orientation of the family therapist varies widely and commonly does not overlap with the treatment the child is receiving within the hospital, although efforts are made to impact the nature of the family therapy by involving each patient's family therapist in the weekly treatment-team meetings. Parents also are required to attend weekly parent training meetings. The topics covered during parent training include giving positive reinforcement, setting limits and time-out, consistently following through with limits, utilizing problem solving at home, and utilizing anger reducers. Parent training also is a time for the parents to gain support and encouragement from professionals and other parents. Although the format is partially didactic in nature, plenty of time is left for empathizing with parent concerns and for addressing specific parenting problems.

SUMMARY

The behavioral approach to the assessment and treatment of depressed children in the hospital setting holds much promise. A multimethod multi-informant model of assessing depressed children was described. The proposed assessment model went beyond the assessment of depressive symptoms to the assessment of variables that have implications for treatment. In addition, ongoing assessment of the child within the hospital to gauge the impact of treatment was proposed. A multimodal treatment model was described. This model is currently being implemented in a residential treatment center, and most of the program is being successfully employed in a day treatment program. The prototypic treatment program described in this chapter emphasizes an integrated approach to treatment in which the therapeutic milieu, hospital school, individual therapy, group therapy, psychiatric intervention, parent training, and family therapy are all integrated and support the overall objectives of treatment. Each mode of intervention is complementary to each other and enhances the effectiveness of the other modes of intervention. To make such a program work, there has to be a system for communicating among members of the treatment team, and each member of the team must trust the professional abilities of each other member. Furthermore, every member of the hospital staff that comes into contact with the child must understand the program and support it. The therapeutic milieu was emphasized in the description of the program because the authors believe that this portion of the treatment program is very powerful and often overlooked in its importance. The milieu and point system that were described were somewhat unique in that they represented a cognitive-behavioral hospital milieu program.

REFERENCES

Achenbach, T. M., & Edelbrock, C. (1983). *Manual for the Child Behavior Checklist and Revised Child Behavior Profile.* Burlington, VT: University of Vermont, Department of Psychiatry.

Alessi, N. E. (1986). *DSM-III diagnosis associated with childhood depressive disorders.* Paper presented at the American Academy of Child Psychiatry, Los Angeles.

American Psychiatric Association. (1987). *Diagnostic and statistical reversal of mental disorders.* (3rd ed., rev.). Washington, DC: Author.

American Psychiatric Association. (1993). *DSM-IV draft criteria.* Washington, DC: Author.

Anderson, J. C., Williams, S., McGee, R., & Silva, P. A. (1987). DSM-III disorders in preadolescent children: Prevalence in a large sample from the general population. *Archives of General Psychiatry, 44,* 69–76.

Asarnow, J. R. (1988). Peer status and social competence in child psychiatric inpatients: A comparison of children with depressive, externalizing, and concurrent depressive and externalizing disorders. *Journal of Abnormal Child Psychology, 16,* 151–162.

Barkley, R. A. (1987). *Defiant children: A clinician's manual for parent training.* New York: Guilford Press.

Beck, A. T., Rush, A. J., Shaw, B. F., & Emery, G. (1979). *Cognitive therapy of depression.* New York: Guilford Press.

Beck, A. T., Ward, C. H., Mendelson, M., Mock, J., & Erbaugh, J. (1961). An inventory for measuring depression. *Archives of General Psychiatry, 4,* 561–571.

Bierdman, J., & Steingard, R. (1989). Attention-deficit/hyperactivity disorder in adolescents. *Psychiatric Annals, 19,* 587–596.

Carlson, G. A., & Cantwell, D. P. (1979). A survey of depressive symptoms in a child and adolescent psychiatric population: Interview data. *Journal of American Academy of Child Psychiatry, 18,* 587–599.

Carlson, G. A., & Cantwell, D. P. (1980). A survey of depressive symptoms, syndromes, and disorders in a child psychiatric population. *Journal of Child Psychology and Psychiatry, 21,* 19–25.

Costello, E. J., Edelbrock, C. A., & Costello, A. J. (1985). Validity of the NIMH Diagnostic Interview Schedule for Children: A comparison between psychiatric and pediatric referrals. *Journal of Abnormal Child Psychology, 13,* 579–595.

Dinkmeyer, D., & McKay, G. D. (1989). *Systematic training for effective parenting. The parent's handbook.* Circle Pines, MN: American Guidance Service.

Gordon, T., (1975). *Parent effectiveness training.* New York: Plume.

Guerney, L., & Guerney, B. (1989). Child relationship enhancement: Family therapy and parent education. *Person-Centered Review, 4*, 344–357.

Hammen, C. (1991). *Depression runs in families: The social context of risk and resilience in children of depressed mothers.* New York: Springer-Verlag.

Hathaway, S. R., & McKinley, J. C. (1989). *MMPI-2: Minnesota Multiphasic Personality Inventory-2.* Minneapolis, MN: The University of Minnesota Press.

Herjanic, B., & Reich, W. (1982). Development of a structured psychiatric interview for children: Agreement between child and parent on individual symptoms. *Journal of Abnormal Child Psychology, 10*, 307–324.

Hodges, K., McKnew, D., Cytryn, L., Stern, I., & Kline, J. (1982). The Child Assessment Schedule (CAS) diagnostic interview: A report on reliability and validity. *Journal of the American Academy of Child Psychiatry, 21*, 468–473.

Jensen, J. B., Burke, N., & Garfinkel, B. D. (1988). Depression and symptoms of attention deficit disorder with hyperactivity. *Journal of American Academy of Child and Adolescent Psychiatry, 27*, 742–747.

Kashani, J. H., Husain, A., Shekim, W. O., Hodges, K. K., Cytryn, L., & McKnew, D. H. (1981). Current perspectives on childhood depression: An overview. *American Journal of Psychiatry, 138*, 143–153.

Kaslow, N. J., & Racusin, G. R. (1990). Childhood depression: Current status and future directions. In A. S. Bellack, M. Hersen, & A. E. Kazdin (Eds.), *International handbook of behavior modification and therapy* (2nd ed.) (pp. 649–667). New York: Plenum Press.

Kazdin, A. E. (1988). The diagnosis of childhood disorders-assessment issues and strategies. *Behavioral Assessment, 10*, 67–94.

Kazdin, A. E. (1990). Conduct disorders. In A. S. Bellack, M. Hersen, & A. E. Kazdin (Eds.), *International handbook of behavior modification and therapy* (2nd ed.) (pp. 669–706). New York: Plenum Press.

Kazdin, A. E., Colbus, D., & Rogers, A. (1986). Assessment of depression and diagnosis of depressive disorders among psychiatrically disturbed children. *Journal of Abnormal Child Psychology, 14*, 499–515.

Kazdin, A. E., Esveldt-Dawson, K., French, N. H., & Unis, A. S. (1987). Effects of parent management training and problem-solving skills training combined in the treatment of antisocial child behavior. *Journal of the American Academy of Child and Adolescent Psychiatry, 26*, 416–424.

Kazdin, A. E., French, N. H., Unis, A. S., Esveldt-Dawson, K., & Sherick, R. E. (1983). Hopelessness, depression, and suicidal intent among psychiatrically disturbed inpatient children. *Journal of Consulting and Clinical Psychology, 51*, 504–510.

Kendall, P. C., Stark, K. D., & Adam, T. (1990). Cognitive deficit or cognitive distortion in childhood depression. *Journal of Abnormal Child Psychology, 18*, 255–270.

Kovacs, M. (1978). *Interview Schedule for Children (ISC) (10th Version).* Pittsburgh, PA: University of Pittsburgh School of Medicine.

Kovacs, M., & Beck, A. T. (1977). An empirical clinical approach toward a definition of childhood depression. In J. G. Schulterbrandt & A. Raskin (Eds.), *Depression in childhood: Diagnosis, treatment, and conceptual models* (pp. 1–25). New York: Raven Press.

Kovacs, M., Feinberg, T. L., Crouse-Novak, M. A., Paulaskos, S. L., & Finkelstein, R. (1984). Depressive disorders in childhood: A longitudinal prospectus study of characteristics and recovery. *Archives of General Psychiatry, 41*, 229–237.

Marriage, K., Fine, S., Moretti, M., Haley, G. (1986). Relationship between depression and conduct disorder in children and adolescents. *Journal of the American Academy of Child Psychiatry, 25*, 687–691.

Matson, J. L., Rotatori, A. F., & Helsel, W. J. (1983). Development of a rating to measure social skills in children: The Matson Evaluation of Social Skills with Youngsters (MESSY). *Behavioural Research and Therapy, 41*, 335–340.

McArthur, D. S., & Roberts, G. E. (1982). *Roberts Apperception Test for Children: Manual.* Los Angeles: Western Psychological Services.

Olsen, T. (1961). Follow-up study of manic-depressive patients whose first attack occurred before the age of 19. *Acta Psychiatrica Scandinavia, 162*, 45–51.

Petti, T. (1978). Depression in hospitalized child psychiatry patients: Approaches to measuring depression. *Journal of the American Academy of Child Psychiatry, 12*, 49–59.

Puig-Antich, J., & Ryan, N. (1986). *Schedule for Affective Disorders and Schizophrenia for School-Age Children.* Pittsburgh, PA: Western Psychiatric Institute and Clinic.

Pyillips, D., & Bernstein, F. (1989). *How to give your child a great self-image.* New York: Random House.

Robbins, D. R., & Alessi, N. E. (1985). Depressive symptoms and suicidal behavior in adolescents. *American Journal of Psychiatry, 142*, 588–592.

Rutter, M., Tizard, J., & Whitmore, K. (1970). *Education, health, and behavior.* New York: Wiley.

Seymour, F. W., Levy, D., & Ushaw, S. (1989). Parent skill training in groups. *Community Mental Health in New Zealand. 4*, 41–59.

Spitzer, A., Webster-Stratton, C., & Hollinsworth, T. (1991). Coping with conduct-problem children: Parents gaining knowledge and control. *Journal of Clinical Child Psychology, 20*, 413–427.

Stark, K. D. (1990). *Childhood depression: School-based intervention.* New York: Guilford Press.

Stark, K. D., & Bookman, C. (1992). Childhood depression: Theory and family-school intervention. In M. Fine & C. Carlson (Eds.), *Handbook of family-school intervention: A systems perspective* (pp. 247–271). Orlando, FL: Grune & Stratton.

Stark, K. D., Christopher, J., & Dempsey, M. (1993). Depression. In A. S. Bellack & M. Hersen (Eds.), *Handbook of behavior therapy in the psychiatric setting.* New York: Plenum Press.

Stark, K. D., Dempsey, M., & Christopher, J. (1993). Depressive disorders. In R. T. Ammerman, C. G. Last, & M. Hersen (Eds.), *Handbook of prescriptive treatments for children and adolescents.* Needham, MA: Allyn and Bacon.

Stark, K. D., Humphrey, L. L., Laurent, J. L., Livingston, R., & Christopher, J. C. (1993). Cognitive, behavioral, and family factors in the differentiation of depressive and anxiety disorders during childhood. *Journal of Consulting and Clinical Psychology.*

Stark, K. D., Humphrey, L. L., Crook, K., & Lewis, K. (1990). Perceived family environments of depressed and anxious children: Child's and mother's perspectives. *Journal of Abnormal Child Psychology, 18*, 527–547.

Stark, K. D., Linn, J. D., Macguire, M., & Kaslow, N. J. (1993). *The interpersonal functioning of depressed and anxious children: Social skills, social knowledge, automatic thoughts, and physical arousal.* Manuscript submitted for publication.

Stark, K. D., Reynolds, W. M., & Kaslow, N. J. (1987). A comparison of the relative efficacy of self-control therapy and a behavioral problem-solving therapy for depression in children. *Journal of Abnormal Child Psychology, 15*, 91–113.

Strober, M., Green, J., & Carlson, G. (1981). Phenomenology and subtypes of major depressive disorder in adolescence. *Journal of Affective Disorders, 3*, 281–290.

CHAPTER 15

Eating Disorders

CHRISTINE SHAFER AND DAVID M. GARNER

DESCRIPTION OF THE PROBLEM

A key feature of anorexia and bulimia nervosa is a persistent overconcern with body size and shape that is indicated by behavior, such as prolonged fasting, strenuous exercise, and self-induced vomiting, aimed at decreasing body weight and fat. The etiology of these eating disorders is generally assumed to be multifactorial. According to this view, symptom patterns represent a final common pathway resulting from the interplay of individual (biological and psychological), familial, and cultural predisposing factors (Garner, 1993a; Garner & Garfinkel, 1980). It is often difficult to determine if the wide range of psychological symptoms associated with these disorders are etiological, incidental, or even sequelae of starvation and chaotic eating patterns. However, regardless of their psychological origin, symptoms such as vomiting and laxative abuse must be brought under control since they can perpetuate the eating disorder, can lead to serious medical complications, and can even lead to death.

Eating disorders have been documented across a range of age groups and social classes, with bulimia nervosa being more common than anorexia nervosa (Hoek, 1991; Lucas, Beard, O'Fallon, & Kurland, 1991). Eating disorders may occur in males; however, the preponderance of cases occur in females (90%–95%). When eating disorders do present in men, their clinical picture is similar to that of women (Andersen, 1990). The prevalence of eating disorders is approximately 1% to 4% among adolescent and young adult women (Hoek, 1991: Lucas et al., 1991). First-degree relatives of eating disorder patients have a greater risk of having anorexia nervosa (Strober, Lampert, Morrell, Burroughs, & Jacobs, 1990). Monozygotic twins have a concordance rate of about 50%, compared to about 10% for dizygotic twins (Holland, Sicotte, & Treasure, 1988). There is evidence that certain athletes, especially those in sports that emphasize leanness to improve performance or appearance (e.g., gymnastics, figure skating, ballet) are at risk of developing an eating disorder (Garner & Rosen, 1991). Sexual abuse is found in the history of approximately 20% to 50% of eating disorder patients. However, this rate does not appear to differ from that present in other psychiatric disorders (Pope & Hudson, 1992); Welch & Fairburn, in press). Although there are case reports of anorexia nervosa in young children (Fosson, Knibbs, Bryant-Waugh, & Lask, 1987) and in the elderly (Kellett, Trimble, & Thorley, 1976), it is generally considered rare at the extreme ends of the age spectrum (Jaffe & Singer, 1989). Chronic dieting and eating disorder symptoms are common in adolescent girls (Hoek, 1993). Eating disorders appear to be most common in Western society but have been identified in different cultural groups. (Dolan, 1991).

The clinical features and related psychopathology of anorexia nervosa and bulimia nervosa have been well documented since the early 1980s. Most clinicians agree that the premorbid personality of patients with eating disorders is characterized by emotional instability; however, much of the research aimed at documenting the role of personality factors in the development of eating disorders has been plagued by serious methodological limitations. Nevertheless, there is a lifetime prevalence of major depression ranging between 25% to 80% across different samples of patients with eating disorders (Halmi et al., 1991). Similarly, anxiety symptoms are common, with obsessive-complusive symptoms observed in 11% to 83% of anorexia nervosa patients either during the active phase of the disorder or after weight restoration (Hsu, Kaye, & Welzin, 1993). Data on the incidence and prevalence of personality disorders are inconsistent (Halmi, et al., 1991; Herzog, Keller, Sacks, Yeh, & Lavori, 1992). However, personality disturbances do occur in a significant subset of patients with eating disorders, and this may be associated with poor prognosis.

Conceptual and empirical advancements have led to recent changes in the diagnostic criteria for eating disorders (American Psychiatric Association, 1993). The new diagnostic criteria will be briefly reviewed because they have important clinical implications.

Anorexia Nervosa

The DSM-IV (American Psychiatric Association, 1993) diagnostic criteria for anorexia nervosa are summarized as follows:

1. Refusal to maintain a body weight at or above a minimally normal weight for age and height (e.g., weight loss leading to maintenance of a body weight less than 85% below norms or failure to achieve expected weight during a period of growth)
2. Intense fear of gaining weight or becoming fat, even though underweight
3. Disturbance in the way that body weight, size, or shape are experienced
4. Amenorrhea in females

Patients with anorexia nervosa are further subdivided into *restricting type* (i.e., those who lose weight by rigidly restricting food intake) and *binge eating/purging type* (i.e., those who avoid weight gain or lose weight after binge eating by purging (through self-induced vomiting or the misuse of laxatives or diuretics). This represents a departure from earlier conventions in which binge eating was the exclusive marker for differentiating subtypes of anorexia nervosa (Casper et al., 1980; Garfinkel, Moldofsky, & Garner, 1980). The change is empirically justified since purging, rather than the amount eaten prior to purging, defines a subgroup of patients who share important clinical features and who may be differentiated from pure restricters (Garner, Garner, & Rosen, 1993). Subtyping on the basis of purging behavior has additional merit because these target behaviors are not complicated by the many measurement problems associated with binge eating (Garner, 1993b). Finally, focusing on the presence or absence of purging is more clinically relevant because there are serious physical health consequences and metabolic abnormalities associated with vomiting and laxative abuse (Beumont, 1988; Comerci, 1990; Halmi, 1985; Mitchell, & Boutacoff, 1986; Mitchell, Pomeroy & Huber, 1988).

In sum, children who have been socialized to overvalue thinness are vulnerable to inappropriate dieting and weight loss. It is the deliberate intent to lose and/or maintain the inappropriate weight that distinguishes anorexia nervosa from other childhood syndromes presenting with weight loss as a result of a psychological symptom such as a food phobia, food refusal, or ritualistic or bizarre eating preferences (Jaffe & Singer, 1989). Sometimes, anorexia nervosa develops following a medical illness that has resulted in weight loss. In these cases, inappropriate weight is maintained because of the self-satisfaction and social reinforcement it generates. Again, diagnosis of an eating disorder requires the presence of the deliberate intent to lose or maintain an inappropriate weight. Any interruption in a child's anticipated growth and development should be cause for concern and should prompt careful investigation. Although psychopathology is often the focus of investigations, it is important to recognize that weight loss may also have lasting physical consequences, such as the failure to grow to anticipated stature and osteoporosis (Rigotti, Nussbaum, Herzog, & Neer, 1985).

Bulimia Nervosa

According to the DSM-IV diagnostic criteria for eating disorders (American Psychiatric Association, 1993), the essential features of bulimia nervosa are as follows:

1. Recurrent episodes of binge eating (i.e., the consumption of an amount of food that is definitely larger than most people would eat during a similar period of time and with a sense of lack of control over eating)
2. Recurrent inappropriate compensatory behavior in order to prevent weight gain (i.e., self-induced vomiting; misuse of laxatives, diuretics, or other medications; fasting; or excessive exercise)
3. Binge eating and inappropriate compensatory behaviors both occurring at least twice a week on average for 3 months
4. Self-evaluation unduly influenced by body weight and shape
5. Disturbance not occurring exclusively during episodes of anorexia nervosa

These criteria also specify that bulimia nervosa is subdivided into *purging* and *nonpurging* types based on the presence or absence of self-induced vomiting or misuse of laxatives or diuretics.

Bulimia nervosa is usually preceded by strict dieting and, in some cases, by frank anorexia nervosa (Abrahams & Beumont, 1982). Food cravings and the tendency to binge eat can be understood, in part, as normal compensatory responses to prolonged periods of dieting and weight suppression (Polivy & Herman, 1985; Russell, 1979). Purging becomes a way to eliminate the caloric consequences of perceived overeating. This leads to a vicious cycle in which binge eating is actually perpetuated by purging because the patient comes to depend on these behaviors to reverse the effects of overeating. The binge-purge cycle may also be maintained because it serves psychological needs in some patients who experience elation, sedation, tension release, or other functional responses to these behaviors (Heatherton & Baumeister, 1991). In some cases, the behaviors are perpetuated by their interpersonal consequences. Once the binge-purge cycle becomes established, it is associated with intense feelings of remorse, shame, and guilt. Laboratory research has shown that purging has limited effectiveness because diuretic and laxative abuse lead to dehydration rather than nonabsorption of calories (Bo-Lynn, Santa-Ana, Morawski, & Fordtran, 1983) and because a significant number of calories are retained in the gastrointestinal tract after vomiting (Kaye, Welzin, Hsu, McConaha, & Bolton, 1993).

Binge Eating Disorder

The pattern of binge eating in individuals who did not have anorexia or bulimia nervosa was clearly described many years ago by Strunkard (1959). In recent years, the topic has received much growing attention in different diagnostic subgroups (Fairburn & Wilson, 1993). DSM-IV has specified that a diagnosis of *binge eating disorder* be given when such eating occurs in the absence of inappropriate compensatory behaviors characteristic of bulimia nervosa. This diagnosis falls under the general category of *Eating Disorders Not Otherwise Specified.*

Relationship Between Diagnostic Groups

Even though distinctions between eating disorder syndromes have been emphasized, there are limitations in thinking of these eating disorders as completely separate entities. Anorexia nervosa and bulimia nervosa share many core features, and, within each diagnostic category, there is extraordinary variability on a wide range of demographic, clinical, and psychological dimensions (Garner, Garner, & Rosen, 1993; Welch, Hall, & Renner, 1990). Patients have been observed to move between eating disorders and their subtypes over time, and chronicity leads to an increased risk of binge eating and purging (Hsu, 1988). Many individuals present with some but not all of the features required for an eating disorder diagnosis as specified by DSM-IV (e.g., binge eating on *small* amounts of food; all criteria for anorexia nervosa, but insufficient weight loss or no amenorrhea). Although these individuals may be thought of as "subthreshold" cases, they deserve careful evaluation because it may only be due to improved recognition that they have been identified at an early stage in the course of their eating disorder.

Primary Versus Secondary Symptoms

While it is obvious that anorexia nervosa patients restrict their food intake and lose weight, it is important to recognize that extreme caloric restriction and periods of weight loss are also common features in patients with bulimia nervosa (Russell, 1979). Experimental semistarvation studies indicate that sustained caloric restriction and weight loss can lead to food preoccupation, abnormal taste preference, food hoarding, and binge eating in normal volunteers (Keys, Brozek, Henschel, Michelson, & Taylor, 1950). These studies also indicate that psychological changes (e.g., impaired concentration, lability of mood, depressive features, obsessional thinking, irritability, difficulties with decision making, impulsivity, and social withdrawal) are common responses to sustained caloric restriction and weight loss. Thus, in the initial assessment with an eating disorder patient, it may not be apparent whether psychological distress, cognitive impairment, and behavioral symptoms signal fundamental emotional disturbance or are secondary elaborations resulting from weight loss and chaotic dietary patterns (Fairburn, Cooper, Kirk, & O'Connor, 1985; Garner, Olmsted, Davis, et al., 1990). In this sense, the patient's response to brief, educationally oriented therapy can be a valuable assessment tool because many patients show marked improvement simply with more consistent eating patterns and weight restoration (Olmsted, Davis, Garner, Eagle, & Rockert, 1991).

PROTOTYPIC ASSESSMENT

A biopsychosocial model understanding of eating disorders leads to a broad assessment framework. A thorough medical history and physical examination are the initial steps in most cases. Assessment must also include evaluation of specific symptoms to permit diagnosis and to determine the most likely course of treatment. To these areas are added the assessment of the patient's overall psychological and personality functioning, as well as the characteristics of the family and the home environment.

Format and Style of the Assessment

It is important that the format and style of assessment interviews be aimed at the development of a sense of openness and trust between patient and clinician. These early meetings are particularly crucial with younger eating disorder patients who may have been brought to the assessment against their wishes. They are often threatened by the assessment, which they see as intrusive and aimed at convincing them to abandon symptoms they see as desirable or even vital to their self-esteem. Thus, it is particularly important to communicate sincere respect for the young patient's perspective on the circumstances surrounding symptom development. Under most circumstances, when assessments are being performed with young patients who are living at home, all members of the family should participate in the evaluation. However, there should also be respect for the patient's autonomy and privacy. It may be useful to devote a portion of the assessment to meeting separately with the identified patient and with the parents. This denotes respect for the patient's basic autonomy (even though an enmeshed interpersonal style may be evident in the family), and it allows the clinician to gather information regarding eating symptoms that either the patient or the parents might be reluctant to share in the presence of each other.

Content Areas for Assessment

Several specific content areas should be covered in initial assessments of patients with eating disorders. These areas will be briefly reviewed; however, further details as well as specific probe questions for their assessment have been provided elsewhere (Fairburn, 1987; Foreyt & McGavin, 1988; Garner, 1991; Wilson, 1993).

Physical Complications

A medical evaluation of patients with eating disorders is necessary to determine overall physical status and to identify or rule out physical complications associated with starvation or with certain extreme weight-losing behaviors (Comerci, 1990). Despite the patient's claim to feel fine and certain normal laboratory values, the anorexic patient will often have physical complications that include hypotension, hypothermia, bradycardia, orthostatic pulse, postural edema, dehydration, and overall reduced metabolic rate. Self-induced vomiting and purgative abuse may cause various symptoms or abnormalities, such as weakness, muscle cramping, postural edema, constipation, cardiac arrhythmias, and paraesthesia. Additionally, general fatigue, constipation, depression, various neurological abnormalities, kidney and cardiac disturbances, swollen salivary glands, oesophageal irritation, electrolyte disturbances, edema, dental deterioration, finger clubbing or swelling, and dehydration can occur. Laboratory studies may reveal electrolyte disturbances, hypomagnesia, and hyperamylasemia. Large bowel abnormalities may result from laxative abuse. Peripheral muscle weakness and cardiomyopathies may result from ipecac abuse. Importantly, prolonged amenorrhea may produce infertility and potentially irreversible osteopenia (Stewart, Robinson, & Goldbloom, 1990). These and other complications have been the subject of several thoughtful reviews (Comerci, 1990; Mitchell, 1990:

Mitchell & Boutacoff, 1986; Mitchell, Pomeroy, Huber, 1988; Schocken, Holloway, Powers, 1989).

Weight History

A thorough weight history provides important information regarding the nature and temporal sequence of events as they relate to the patient's struggle with weight. A weight history should include information regarding purposeful or inadvertent gains or losses.

Overconcern for Weight and Shape

One of the key features of eating disorders is the way that weight, shape, and/or thinness become the sole or predominant referent for inferring personal value or self-worth (Fairburn & Garner, 1986; Garner & Bemis, 1982; Wilson, 1993). The patient's beliefs and feeling about weight, body size, and fat should be elicited sensitively because this may challenge his or her values and perhaps those of the parents. Assessment should include questions regarding the manner that the patient uses in judging his or her body, such as weighing, viewing in a mirror, comparing shape with that of others, and techniques of measuring physical dimensions. Frequency, meaning, emotional reactions, and response to these measurements should also be noted. In exploring the specific meaning that weight and shape has for the patient, it is important to try to elicit his or her understanding of the derivation of these beliefs. In some cases patients appear to display actual distortion of their size or shape; however, disparagement of the body or of particular areas is the most common observation. Specific questions regarding weight and shape not only provide valuable information on this topic but also reveal the more general belief structure and conceptual style of the patient. Through this type of questioning, the meaning of weight and shape and the intensity of the patient's convictions can be explored.

Binge Eating, Dieting, and Weight-Losing Behaviors

The frequency and intensity of binge eating, dieting efforts, and types of weight-losing behaviors employed should be assessed in an initial interview (Fairburn & Cooper, 1993; Garner, 1991). A dieting history should pinpoint when dieting and binge eating first began, as well as the different methods that have been used to reduce or control weight. Questions should be asked regarding weight-controlling behaviors, such as laxative and diuretic abuse, diet pills or other drugs to control appetite, use of emetics, chewing and spitting food out before swallowing, prolonged fasting, and vigorous exercise for the explicit purpose of controlling body weight. In each case, probes should elicit information regarding onset frequency, and severity of each method and any associated reactions, such as pleasure, satisfaction, relief, guilt, or increased energy. Since binge eating can have psychological meaning, the functional relationships between binge eating and affective state should be assessed (Heatherton & Baumeister, 1991).

General Psychological and Family Functioning

A complete psychological assessment should include assessment of personality functioning, psychological distress, depression, anxiety, family functioning, history of sexual abuse, self-esteem, social and vocational adaptation, and impulse-related features that may be relevant to the development and maintenance of eating disorders. Reassessment during the course of treatment is desirable because it may provide a more meaningful picture of personality dimensions that endure once the acute symptoms of the eating disorder are resolved.

Individual, familial, and sociocultural background factors have collectively and in combination been implicated in the development of anorexia nervosa and bulimia nervosa. These background factors have formed the basis for different theoretical approaches to eating disorders, which have resulted in treatment orientations that may be characterized as primarily behavioral, cognitive-behavioral, educational, psychodynamic, and family systems in focus. Full discussion of the range of determinants and the psychological orientations that they represent have been reviewed elsewhere (Garfinkel & Garner, 1982; Garner & Garfinkel, 1985; Johnson & Connors, 1987; Vandereycken, Kog, & Vanderlinden, 1989). While certain core features may be common to many patients with eating disorders, individual differences in premorbid personality and in levels of psychological functioning contribute to major differences in the manifestation of key symptoms.

A thorough evaluation should also include attention to potential physical and psychological trauma. Prenatal or perinatal risk factors, including infections, trauma, convulsions, exposure to alcohol, older maternal age, and low birth weight, appear to be relatively common in selected patient samples and have been linked to a poor prognosis in anorexia nervosa (Bakan, Birmingham, & Goldner, 1991). A high rate of gastrointestinal problems has been identified in the early feeding history of anorexia nervosa patients (Rastam, 1992). The level of safety that the young eating disorder patient feels within his or her environment should be carefully evaluated. Sexual abuse has been identified as common in eating disorder patients. While this does not appear to be a specific risk factor for eating disorders (Welch & Fairburn, 1994), when it is part of the clinical picture, it should be addressed once a therapeutic alliance has been formed.

The presence of other psychiatric disorders should be determined for the patient and the family. Depression and anxiety disorders (particularly obsessive-compulsive traits) have been documented in many clinical samples (Halmi et al., 1991; Herzog, et al., 1992). Family history should be reviewed carefully for mood and anxiety disorders, as well as drug and alcohol abuse.

In addition to the usual measures of psychological distress and developmental history, standardized psychometric instruments have been developed specifically to tap psychological and behavior themes that are particularly relevant to eating disorders. Two widely used self-report measures are the Eating Attitudes Test (EAT) (Garner & Garfinkel, 1979) and the Eating Disorder Inventory (EDI) (Garner, 1991; Garner, Olmsted, & Polivy, 1983). The most widely used interview method is the Eating Disorder Examination (EDE) (Fairburn & Cooper, 1993). The advantages and disadvantages of the respective methods have been reviewed elsewhere (Garner, 1991; Wilson, 1993). Whereas these methods have been developed and validated on adolescents and adults, their utility with children is not known.

ACTUAL ASSESSMENT

CASE ILLUSTRATION

Kristen Peters was almost 13 years old and in the seventh grade when she was referred for treatment. She was four feet eleven inches tall and weighed 79 pounds. She had lost approximately 24 pounds during the previous 4 months. Despite concerns raised by her pediatrician and pleading by her parents, she had refused to restore the lost weight. Kristen also appeared to be developing emotional problems. Her mother made the initial appointment, which was their first contact with a psychiatric service.

In retrospect, Mrs. Peters believes that Kristen may have become concerned about her weight about 6 months previously after a routine sports physical provided at school. Kristen had experienced a growth spurt over the preceding summer, and she became upset to learn that her weight was 103 pounds. She had tearfully reported that all of the other girls weighed under 100 pounds and that the boys had teased her about her weight. Mrs. Peters had reassured Kristen that she was just growing up and, as long as she adhered to a proper diet and exercised, she would be fine.

This appeared to mitigate Kristen's concerns. However, she showed signs of being increasingly conscious of diet, exercise, and health. In addition to participation in girls' basketball, Kristen began jogging and using her mother's aerobic workout video on a daily basis. She began reading food labels and questioning her mother about recipes in order to restrict her dietary fat intake. Mrs. Peters saw this as a positive step because she did not want her daughter to become fat. Kristen was forced to drop basketball midseason due to a broken finger. She responded by increasing other exercise, such as stair climbing and jumping in place, stating that she was "getting ready for volleyball season." At the time of evaluation, Kristen was consuming only small portions of the family dinner, despite being offered all of her favorite foods. Mrs. Peters was shocked to see how thin Kristen had become when she saw her daughter one morning in her underwear. She immediately took Kristen to the doctor, who documented a weight of 70 pounds.

A review of Kristen's medical history revealed that she had been healthy throughout her development. She had shown continuous progress along the growth curve and began breast development during the summer; however, she had not yet experienced menarche. She indicated no strong food preferences or intolerances prior to the onset of her weight loss.

Mrs. Peters reported that Kristen had always been friendly, responsible, and even-tempered. Now, she was irritable, with frequent crying spells. Kristen recently began describing her friends as "snobs," and she abruptly stopped taking phone calls. She spent most of her time alone in her room studying, exercising, or scrutinizing herself in the mirror. She weighed herself several times each day on the bathroom scale. She would stand when watching television in the family room. Although Kristen's grades at school had continued to be excellent, she became fretful about her homework, spending long hours doing and redoing assignments. There was no evidence of vomiting or laxative use.

Kristen is the eldest of three healthy and, reportedly, well-adjusted children. Mrs. Peters was unaware of any emotional or physical trauma or abuse in the family. Siblings include a brother, Kevin, age 11, described by Mrs. Peters as "all boy," and a sister Katie, age 5, described as a "pixie." Both parents are college educated. Mrs. Peters has remained at home with the children while Mr. Peters has worked as an accountant. He described his job as demanding and stressful. The family attends the Catholic Church on a regular basis, and the older children are in parochial school. There was no diagnosis of any psychiatric disorder in the family. However, neither parent uses alcohol or other intoxicating substances due to a strong history of alcoholism on both sides of the family. Mr. Peters recalled a period of excessive double-checking over several months during his adolescence. There is no history of obesity in the family.

Upon examination, Kristen was a pale, very thin girl with dry, curly hair. She sat clothed in leggings, sweatpants, a turtleneck, and two sweatshirts, jiggling her legs up and down. When questioned about her movements, she stated that they were aimed at "losing fat." She looked alertly about the room but avoided direct eye contact. Her speech was clear, coherent, and delivered at a brisk pace. She reported that she was the only healthy one in the family and cited evidence of her low-fat diet, daily exercise, and normal lab values recorded from her visit to the doctor. She reported that 6 months previously, she decided that she wanted to weigh less than 100 pounds. Once she achieved this goal, she decided that 95 pounds was preferable, "just to be safe." She now felt compelled to weigh 70 pounds since 79 pounds now felt fat. She described her brother as a "pig," eating whatever he wanted. She was angry with her mother for bringing her to the assessment interview; however, she conceded that she understood her parents' concern. Nevertheless, she stated that she did not want to become fat again and felt that she could not tolerate gaining any weight. She denied having an appetite, saying that what she ate filled her up. She denied episodes of binge eating or any use of laxatives, diuretics, or other medications. She admitted to being less happy than usual, worrying, spending more time on homework, often feeling lightheaded, being cold all the time, and sleeping poorly most nights. Suicidal ideation or intent was denied.

At the initial assessment interview, Kristen was informed that she met all of the diagnostic criteria for anorexia nervosa. She was reassured that the primary aim of any treatment would be to help her feel better about herself. While weight gain would be necessary to achieve this goal, particularly because many of her symptoms were secondary to starvation, at no time would the treatment lose sight of her own needs and wishes. She was given two self-report measures to complete, the Eating Disorder Inventory-2 (EDI-2) and the EAT, with the explanation that, although she had anorexia nervosa, all patients were different. These measures were to assist in learning a bit about the particular issues that were important to her. A second assessment interview was scheduled to review the information on the EDI-2 and EAT, as well as to explore issues that may have occurred to her or her parents as important in the intervening week. Kristen's EDI-2 profile indicated subscale scores above the 75th percentile on the Ineffectiveness, Perfectionism, Maturity Fears, and Asceticism subscales, using adolescent female norms (Garner, 1991). Her EAT score was at the 40th percentile for anorexia nervosa patients (Garner, Olmsted, Bohr, & Garfinkel, 1982). These scores were consistent with the clinical impressions at the initial assessment interview. The second assessment interview focused on further review of historical information, treatment recommendations, and a brief review of educational material in preparation for treatment.

PROTOTYPIC TREATMENT

General Guidelines

The clinician treating eating disorders should possess the accepted qualities of all skilled therapists: warmth, genuineness, empathy, honesty, and acceptance. The fact that many of the symptoms evinced by the eating disorder patient are ego-syntonic requires that the therapist have the ability to be firm, authorative, and directive while maintaining a collaborative therapeutic style. It is important for the clinician to be knowledgeable in several areas outside the typical training in general psychotherapy. These include an understanding of (a) biological and psychological consequences of dieting and semistarvation, (b) consequences of extreme weight-control methods such as vomiting and laxative abuse, (c) attitudes and beliefs toward the body and food that are specific to eating disorder patients, and (d) extraordinary cultural pressures for thinness that impinge especially on women today and how dealing with those pressures needs to be integrated into the psychotherapy.

Establishing a working relationship with the family is essential with the younger patient, as well as with some older patients who are living at home. However, family therapy may not always be a realistic option because experienced therapists are unavailable or because of insurance limitations or the family's unwillingness to participate. Reluctant family members may become motivated to participate in family therapy once they recognize that they are not being blamed for the eating disorder or once they find the intervention to be helpful to the overall functioning of the family.

Educational Material

Early in treatment, patients often benefit from a review of studies describing starvation symptoms. These studies can convey the notion that body weight appears to be homeostatically regulated and that deviations from a certain levels (i.e., "set point") result in the activation of powerful biological compensatory mechanisms designed to restore body-weight equilibrium (Garner, Rockert, Olmsted, et al., 1985). Education plays an important role in cognitive-behavioral treatment because it provides a benchmark in reality from which it is possible to determine the degree to which behavior is driven by simple lack of information or by distorted beliefs.

Family Therapy

The specific components of family therapy are beyond the scope of the present chapter and have been reviewed in detail elsewhere (Humphrey, 1989; Minuchin, Rosman, & Baker, 1978; Root, Fallon, & Friedrich, 1985; Vandereycken et al., 1989). However, there are several fundamental issues that are appropriate to most family interventions:

1. The identified patient and his or her parents often need help in overcoming denial regarding the seriousness of the eating disorder. Parents may need assistance in accurately labeling eating disorder behaviors; for example, behaviors that were identified as *healthy* when they occurred in moderation must be reinterpreted as *eating disordered*, given the current context.

2. Parents may need help in developing an effective parenting style. Guilt and fear may have prohibited them from being firm and effective in establishing guidelines of behavior consistent with recovery. Parents should be encouraged to maintain usual expectations in areas unrelated to food and eating (bedtime, chores, language, treatment of siblings), except when unrealistic parental expectations are directly contributing to the problem. Treatment recommendations should be consistent with family's value system. Parenting style appropriate to the developmental stage of the child should be encouraged.

3. Parents may need assistance in accepting the patient's intrinsic value as a person irrespective of objective performance standards such as weight, school achievement, or athletic competition.

4. Parental attitudes about weight and shape should be identified, and inappropriate emphasis on thinness or fitness that does not take into account the patient's condition need to be challenged. Inappropriate family eating patterns, beliefs about food, or eating rituals should be identified, and practical interventions need to be designed that address areas of potential conflicts.

5. Problematic family interactional patterns need to be addressed, such as enmeshment, overprotectiveness, inadequate mechanisms for resolving conflicts, and inappropriate parent-child allegiances that undermine the marital relationship (Minuchen et al, 1978). The identified patient's symptoms may be functional within a disturbed-family context, and the meaning systems that underlie the resulting interactional patterns need to be identified and corrected; for example, weight loss, with its effects on shape, emotional maturity, and dependence on the family, may lead to maturational arrest, thereby reducing fears associated with separation (Crisp, 1980).

Behavioral Principles

Behavioral treatment should be based on a systematic analysis of contingencies that maintain the eating disorder (Bemis, 1987; Garner & Bemis, 1982, 1985). The behavioral principles should be well integrated with other individual and family therapies. Behavioral contingencies should be rational and understandable. Careful inquiry into the patient's understanding of behavioral contingencies is essential. They should be described as consistent with the overall goal of recovery and based on the same reinforcement principles that guide most people's behavior. The need for external control in the initial stages of treatment can be explained as a response to the patient's current state of *loss* of control. This loss of control is evidenced by absence of choice (i.e., the anorexic experiences little choice in eating and exercise patterns, and the bulimic experiences little choice regarding eating and purging behaviors). The patient can be enlisted to participate in treatment planning with the understanding that he or she is valued as an individual and that the goal is to help him or her return to a state of autonomous functioning. Reasonable objections to contingencies should be met with problem solving and with the development of alternative strategies, always with the proviso that more external control is needed if more lenient behavioral objectives are not met. With patients who have the complication of binge eating, it is important to anticipate slips and to develop a strategy for getting back on track after these setbacks (Fairburn, Marcus, & Wilson, 1993; Garner, Rockert, Olmsted, et al., 1985).

Normalizing Weight and Nutritional Rehabilitation

Normalizing eating and weight depends heavily on education (Garner, Rockart, Olmsted, et al., 1985). An initial acceptable weight range should be established at a level that will allow adequate caloric intake and nutritional balance, that will support moderate exercise, and that will permit growth in the younger patient. This weight range can be approximated by a projection on an established growth curve or by using the weight at which menarche occurred in the post-menarcheal female. Reward should be reserved for weight gain, rather than actual food intake, in the anorexic patient, and for elimination of pathogenic weight-control measures when the symptom of binge eating is present. This will minimize inadvertent reinforcement for hiding food, lying about food intake, and the use of purging methods. Some patients will be unable to make progress because of extreme fears that they might become accustomed to eating the large volume of food required during the weight-regain phase of treatment. In these cases, fears may be allayed by using a liquid food supplement during weight restoration, limiting the amount of solid-food intake to that anticipated for weight maintenance. The merits of this method should be balanced against the risk of not allowing the patient to experience the fact that the intense food cravings experienced while emaciated generally disappear spontaneously with weight gain. It is also important not to reinforce anorexic eating patterns and inappropriate food phobias. Patients without a personal or family history of obesity generally require more calories during weight regain. On the other hand, those with a personal or family history of obesity usually require fewer calories to restore weight, and they may feel hungry even when eating normal amounts of food. The emotional reactions and potential misinterpretation of these different caloric needs can impede the therapeutic progress.

Cognitive Behavioral Methods

Cognitive behavioral treatment (CBT) for eating disorders has been described in numerous clinical reports and research articles since 1980, and the reader is encouraged to consult original sources for detailed descriptions (Agras, Schneider, Arnow, Raeburn, & Telch, 1989; Edgette & Prout, 1989; Fairburn, Marcus, & Wilson, 1993; Garner & Bemis, 1982, 1985; Garner & Rosen, 1990). Most of these depend heavily upon the principles developed originally by Beck and colleagues for depression and anxiety disorders (Beck & Emery, 1985; Beck, Rush, Shaw, & Emery, 1979). While there is debate regarding the active ingredients of CBT in the treatment of eating disorders, it is generally recognized that the primary points of emphasis are (a) analyzing the functional relationships between current distorted beliefs and symptomatic behaviors related to eating, weight, and body shape and (b) assisting the patient in challenging inappropriate or distorted beliefs and assumptions that have led to the development and maintenance of the eating symptoms. Although there is general agreement that self-monitoring is an important component of CBT, there are different points of emphasis in the target behaviors for this procedure. Some reports emphasize monitoring of affective and interpersonal antecedents of binge eating, whereas others focus more on dietary management and on the attitudes toward weight and shape that are presumed to underlie extreme weight-controlling behaviors. Both of these approaches can play a valuable role in treatment, although there is some consensus that self-monitoring should, at the very least, focus on normalizing food intake.

Descriptions of CBT have typically focused on beliefs and assumptions related to weight and shape; however, cognitive methods are also ideally suited for addressing developmental and interactional themes best described by psychodynamic and family theorists. Themes such as fears of separation, engulfment or abandonment, failures in the separation-individuation process, false self-adaption, transference, overprotectiveness, enmeshment, conflict avoidance, inappropriate involvement of the child in parental conflicts, and symptoms as mediators of family stability all involve distorted meaning on the part of the individual, the family, or both.

Hospitalization

Improvements in outpatient care have reduced the need for hospitalization for most patients with anorexia nervosa. However, there are circumstances in which brief or even extended hospitalization is beneficial or necessary. The main objectives of hospitalization for eating disorder patients are (a) weight restoration or, in the case of anorexia nervosa, interruption of steady weight loss; (b) interruption of unremitting bingeing and vomiting; (c) evaluation and treatment of medical complications; (d) management of associated conditions, such as severe depression, suicidal behavior, or substance abuse; (e) addressing psychological and interpersonal factors that have initiated or maintained the eating disorder, and (f) occasionally, disengagement of patients from a social system that both contributes to the maintenance of the disorder and disrupts outpatient treatment (Garner & Sackeyfio, 1993).

ACTUAL TREATMENT

After completion of the assessment discussed earlier, Kristen Peters entered treatment.

CASE ILLUSTRATION

Treatment began with feedback from the assessment and with review of basic educational material with both Kristen and her parents. The occurrence of anorexia nervosa was described in relation to an interplay between cultural pressures to be thin and factors within the family or the individual that may predispose to the disorder. Symptoms of semistarvation and associated symptoms in anorexia nervosa were outlined with specific reference to Kristen's own experiences. Nutritional rehabilitation, measured by weight restoration, was labeled as the essential first step in recovery. Psychological hypotheses that might account for Kristen's weight loss and failure to regain were initiated by several examples of common themes in adolescent anorexia nervosa (Crisp, 1980; Strober, 1993; Strober & Yager, 1985). This was intended to provide a nonthreatening introduction to psychological issues possibly relevant to the development of the disorder in Kristen's case. Kristen and her parents were then asked if they thought that the weight loss might have had any positive effects on any member of the family. Kristen suggested that it seemed to be associated with a reduction in the amount of time that her parents argued; however, the parents disagreed with this formulation. The plan was to return to this issue after outlining the treatment options. Treatment options, including family, individual, or marital therapy, were described, as were the criteria for determining if hospitalization would be required. Hospitalization was described as necessary if weight dropped further or if outpatient therapy was ineffective in the gradual weight restoration. Hospitalization was characterized not as a threat but as a logical and humane option for an adolescent who remained ill. If hospitalization became necessary, it should not be interpreted as a sign of failure on the part of Kristen or her parents. It was emphasized that the family should consider the eating disorder as a serious illness that has made Kristen temporarily unable to make healthy decisions for herself. Kristen expressed the concern that no one really understood her and that it was unfair to make her do things that she did not want to do. It was explained that the adults in her life had moral and legal responsibility to care for her when she was ill and that their level of control over her daily routine would naturally decline once she could care for herself. Treatment was designed to provide greater structure around eating, while focusing attention on psychological and family issues that might be playing a role in the maintenance of the disorder. Maintaining factors, rather than etiology, were the initial focus of therapy because they might be much more easily tied to weekly behavioral objectives. It was also assumed that discussions of possible maintaining factors would likely lead to the emergence of more fundamental beliefs, underlying assumptions, and developmental issues that might have played a role in the original unfolding of the eating disorder.

Kristen indicated that she was reluctant to participate in treatment because she felt the primary objective was to make her fat. She was reassured that weight gain was a necessary but insufficient goal of treatment. It was crucial that she feel better about her body and herself in general, but this would probably not occur until after initially feeling much worse during the weight restoration phase. Some of the practical benefits of treatment were reviewed, including better sleep, energy, concentration, and mood and an end to feeling cold all the time. Kristen seemed reassured by the idea that calories were a measure of heat not fat.

The format of treatment included both individual and family meetings, underscoring the fact that Kristen was both an autonomous person and a member of a larger family system. The individual meetings began with a review of Kristen's eating behavior and weight, as well as her thoughts and feelings about her body. She was encouraged to keep notes in a journal and to record the foods that she ate at each meal, along with her feelings at mealtimes, her exercise patterns, and her more general thoughts and feelings about herself. The importance of this written record was emphasized. It would provide documentation of her efforts and would be of interest to her in looking back on the recovery process.

Initially, appointments were scheduled twice weekly with the intention to see Kristen for half of the session and the parents, with or without Kristen, for the remainder. In both the individual and family sessions, behavioral expectations were clearly outlined and then negotiated. It was decided that there should be a temporary moratorium on exercise, with the agreement that it could be gradually reintegrated once weight restoration was well under way. Her parents were to intervene if exercise occurred. Kristen was allowed to watch television only if she remained seated. She would be allowed to attend school, which she desired, only if she maintained her weight. It was agreed that the bathroom scale would be removed from the home and that weight would be determined at the weekly therapy meetings. Kristen's parents were encouraged to keep a journal relating any of their concerns or questions, which would be addressed in weekly meetings.

It became clear in the initial family meeting that Kristen resented her mother's attempts to "fatten her up" with cookies and chips and by surreptitiously adding butter and oil to meals. It was agreed that the mother would immediately stop any covert attempts to supply extra calories and that only the amount of food specified in advance of the meal would be provided. Kristen continued to consume foods that she viewed as safe, such as skim milk and diet yogurt in the mornings; however, she was to be served the usual family foods at dinner. Foods with which Kristen felt most comfortable were identified, and these were to be packed for lunch at school. She was to begin consuming two snacks, one in the afternoon and one after dinner. The caloric intake was to begin at 1,500 calories a day and would increase gradually to a level that would achieve a weekly weight gain of 2 to 3 pounds.

Problem solving related to several potentially difficult scenarios was rehearsed in the family sessions. Discussion regarding Kristen's actual food intake was reserved for the individual therapy sessions unless she made inadequate progress with her weight. The rationale was that her eating was a matter of personal concern unless she was incapable of controlling her weight. Similarly, the parents were instructed to make no positive reference to Kristen's weight or eating (e.g., "You are doing so much better"), because this made Kristen feel like she was acquiescing in what she described as "a power struggle over food."

Kristen's weight was stable over the first week and dropped 2 pounds during the second week. Inquiries were made concerning the availability of a hospital bed in the children's psychiatric unit. At the same time, Kristen was kept home from school, in bed, with assurances that she could go back to her normal routine once her medical condition (i.e., weight) improved. She complained that she could not eat because she felt full after consuming only small amounts of food. In addition, she described panic at the sight of her postprandial protruding abdomen. She was reassured that this was a symptom of her eating disorder and was provided with evidence that her weight would redistribute normally with time (see Garner, Rockert, Olmsted, et al., 1985). To address the feelings of fullness, it was suggested that she try consuming two cans of a liquid supplement, in addition to the proposed meal plan. She was not discouraged from complaining about how hard it was to eat and how uncomfortable she felt. Her progress and the decision regarding hospitalization would be reviewed the following week based on her weight.

In the initial family meeting, Mrs. Peters revealed that she was plagued by the fear that she had not been a good mother to Kristen. She felt that she had been unable to spend enough time with Kristen when she was a toddler because Kevin had required so much attention at that time. She also wondered how much she had contributed to Kristen's illness because her feelings about herself were also highly determined by her own weight and shape. Her belief about being a neglectful parent was explored in detail, and she admitted that she had never neglected her children. In fact, she had been an extremely dedicated mother. With further probing, it became clear that an underlying assumption that guided much of Mrs. Peters' behavior was that she *must* always do her best as a mother and that any shortcomings in her children were direct testimony to her inadequacy as a mother. Her inflated sense of responsibility caused her to become depressed when one of her children had even minor difficulties at home or at school. When there were no apparent problems, she was highly anxious in anticipation of future difficulties. Thus, she lived in a continuous state of guilt or fear of personal failure. Mrs. Peters was able to see that this view was not only self-defeating, but also somewhat grandiose. She was encouraged to take practical steps to minimize her sense of responsibility for the mental health of her children and to gradually begin to widen her definition of her own worth to include nonmothering activities. It was explained that this would likely result in her improved confidence in her ability to parent. She was prompted to take time for herself and for the younger children and to try to participate with her husband in activities that did not involve the children. She was relieved to learn that she really was not solely responsible for the well-being of the entire family and that she had the option to engage in normal activities without feeling guilty if Kristen's condition did not improve.

Despite repeated attempts to engage Mr. Peters in treatment, he attended only one session. He indicated that he was extremely busy because it was tax season. When his priorities were sharply challenged, he proclaimed that his daughter's eating disorder was "illogical" and that the entire experience was simply too frustrating for him to continue to participate. He stated that he felt that Kristen was in control of her eating and that all she had to do was try and she would improve. He indicated that he felt unable to help his daughter at that point and that he could not attend future meetings. Mrs. Peters became tearful then and revealed her sense of abandonment by him over their years. He indicated that this was simply the way it had to be at this point since he could not make a commitment to therapy.

Kristen was kept home from school for 3 weeks, and she slowly began to increase her food intake. This was accompanied by improvement in her mood, fewer requests for reassurance, and improved sleep. Her mother reported that Kristen engaged in less crying, fewer frantic outbursts, and better tolerance of being directed away from eating disorder behavior. Kristen showed a small, progressive weight gain so the plans for hospitalization were deferred. Mrs. Peters worked with the school to reintegrate Kristen according to recommendations made in treatment. Several practical steps were taken at school: Kristen did not participate in gym, and she was transferred from the cooking section of home economics to the sewing section. She agreed to give up her involvement in the upcoming science unit on nutrition and eating disorders. Kristen admitted to throwing her lunches away at school, so supervision of meals was provided by one of the school counselors. She began consuming a liquid supplement in the morning and afternoon at the nurse's office and was helped to see this as "medicine."

Kristen was able to identify the fact that feeling fat was associated with other more vague unhappy feelings of being unlovable, defective, and generally not good enough. This schema and its associated feelings were activated by other situations, such as her interactions with friends. She felt that her lack of popularity at school meant that there was something fundamentally wrong with her. She was able to identify that her intense need to be accepted by peers made her behave in an unnatural manner and put excessive pressure on friendships. She also admitted that she saw no advantage in growing up. Her younger brother had more freedom and privileges than she was given. He was given permission to attend coed public high school. Although she also wanted to attend public high school, she had been afraid to ask her parents. Kristen was surprised to find out that they were willing to consider enrolling her in public school once she had achieved a normal weight. This activated another basic schema and its associated fears which were probably at the heart of Kristen's reluctance to broach the topic of public school earlier. She was frightened about the potential social expectations associated with a mixed-gender classroom. She was worried that she would not know how to react. She was reassured that her fears were quite normal but that their intensity might indicate a problem. Her fears in this area were addressed using cognitive-behavioral methods; however, it was explained that it would be impossible to determine if the issues had really been covered adequately until she was actually enrolled in the public school and at a normal body weight. Some patients report their concerns increase with the biological and psychological changes associated with weight restoration, and others indicate that anticipated fears simply do not materialize (Crisp, 1980). Because of this uncertainty, it was recommended that she reinitiate therapy once she began public school so that issues could be addressed if they emerged.

After 4 months of treatment, Kristen's weight was consistently above 87 pounds. She was allowed to resume modest physical activity with others such as bike riding. However, she was advised to continue refraining from isolated or strenuous aerobic activity because this would almost certainly reactivate her sense of internal competitiveness with its escalating demands for performance. She wanted to attend a 2-week summer camp in 2 months, and it was agreed that this would be possible only if she could document her ability to eat foods likely to be served at camp under social conditions and if she could maintain a weight of not less than 92 pounds for the 2 weeks prior to camp. Kristen found passing 90 pounds traumatic, and she admitted trying to vomit, unsuccessfully. Kristen was permitted to go to camp. The camp nurse agreed to weigh her every other day and to dispense the liquid supplement supplied to her upon Kristen's request. Upon return from camp, Kristen was more socially confident and rather proud of what she had accomplished. She was eager to make her mother keep the promise of new school clothes if she maintained a healthy weight.

In anticipation of the end to therapy meetings, Mrs. Peters revealed her awareness of her changing role with her younger daughter starting school and of her loneliness that resulted from husband's long hours and reclusive nature. She was encouraged to seek therapy for herself to deal with these issues.

Kristen continued in weekly meetings, and her weight steadily increased with reassurance in therapy and at home. After 11 months, her weight was 110 pounds, and the frequency of meetings was reduced to once a month. She began menstruating 1 year after commencement of therapy. Therapy was terminated, and she was encouraged to reinitiate therapy if her concerns about weight worsened or if other problems emerged, particularly surrounding enrollment in public school.

SUMMARY

Anorexia nervosa and bulimia nervosa represent serious problems in childhood and adolescence. These eating disorders are associated with significant morbidity and mortality. They usually begin with a diet and successful weight loss that are reinforced by peers and parents. Unchecked, in vulnerable individuals, continued weight loss stimulates physiological, psychological, and environmental perpetuating mechanisms. Vomiting, laxative abuse, and other extreme measures may be enlisted in the interest of weight control, greatly increasing medical risk. The evaluation of the usually reluctant patient and family must be comprehensive. The patient's medical status must be determined at the beginning of treatment and monitored throughout. The multifactorial nature of eating disorders should be taken into active consideration in performing an adequate evaluation and to design a meaningful treatment. A trusting and collaborative therapeutic relationship is important for treatment to be successful. Support and education are also important components of treatment. Treatment must address the biological and the evolving psychological needs of the child or adolescent. Individualized behavioral contingencies can be effective in achieving nutritional rehabilitation and weight stabilization. It is important to combine these with psychotherapy that addresses distorted beliefs and meaning systems that often operate with these patients and their families. When anorexia nervosa or bulimia nervosa occurs in adolescence or childhood, family therapy is the preferred modality of treatment, and it is often integrated with individual therapy for the identified patient. Inpatient treatment is necessary for some patients who are at immediate medical risk or who display severely disrupted psychosocial functioning. As eating disorders are often chronic in nature and marked by relapse, long-term maintenance treatment is needed in many cases.

REFERENCES

Abraham, S. F., & Beumont, P. J. V. (1982). How patients describe bulimia or binge eating. *Psychological Medicine, 12*, 625–635.

Agras, W. S., Schneider, J. A., Arnow, B., Raeburn, S. D., & Telch, C. F. (1989). Cognitive-behavioral and response-prevention treatments for bulimia nervosa. *Journal of Consulting and Clinical Psychology, 57*, 215 –221.

American Psychiatric Association. (1993). *DSM-IV draft criteria.* Washington, DC: Author.

Andersen, A. E. (1980). *Males with eating disorders.* New York: Brunner/Mazel.

Bakan, R., Birmingham, C. L., & Goldner, E. M. (1991). Chronicity in anorexia nervosa: Pregnancy and birth complications as risk factors. *International Journal of Eating Disorders, 10*, 631–645.

Beck, A. T., & Emery, G. (1985). *Anxiety disorders and phobias: A cognitive perspective.* New York: Basic Books.

Beck, A. T., Rush, A. J., Shaw, B. F., & Emery, G. (1979) *Cognitive therapy of depression: A treatment manual.* New York: Guilford Press.

Bemis, K. M. (1987). The present status of operant conditioning for the treatment of anorexia nervosa. *Behavior Modification, 11*, 432–463.

Beumont, P. J. V. (1988). Bulimia: Is it an illness entity? *International Journal of Eating Disorders, 7*, 167–176.

Bo-Lynn, G., Santa-Ana, C. A., Morawski, S. G., & Fordtran, J. S. (1983). Purging and calorie absorption in bulimic patients and normal women. *Annals of Internal Medicine, 99*, 14–17.

Casper, R. C., Eckert, E. D., Halmi, K. A., Goldberg, S. C., & Davis, J. M. (1980). Bulimia: Its incidence and clinical importance in patients with anorexia nervosa. *Archives of General Psychiatry, 37,* 1030–1034.

Comerci, G. D. (1990). Medical complications of anorexia nervosa and bulimia nervosa. *Medical Clinics of North America, 74*, 1293–1310.

Crisp, A. H. (1980). *Anorexia nervosa.* New York: Grune & Stratton.

Dolan, B. (1991). Cross-cultural aspects of anorexia nervosa and bulimia: A review. *International Journal of Eating Disorders, 10*, 67–79.

Edgette, J. S., & Prout, M. F. (1989). Cognitive and behavioral approaches to the treatment of anorexia nervosa. In A. Freeman, K. M. Simon, L. E. Beutler, & H. Arkowitz (Eds.), *Comprehensive handbook of cognitive therapy* (pp. 367–384). New York: Plenum Press.

Fairburn, C. G. (1987). The definition of bulimia nervosa: Guidelines for clinicians and research workers. *Annals of Behavioral Medicine, 9*, 3–7.

Fairburn, C. G., & Cooper, Z. (1993). The Eating Disorder Examination (12th ed.). In C. G. Fairburn & G. T. Wilson (Eds.), *Binge eating: Nature, assessment, and treatment* (pp. 317–360). New York: Guilford Press.

Fairburn, C. G., Cooper, P. J., Kirk, J., & O'Connor, M. (1985). The significance of the neurotic symptoms of bulimia nervosa. *Journal of Psychiatric Research, 19,* 135–140.

Fairburn, C. G., & Garner, D. M. (1986). The diagnosis of bulimia nervosa. *International Journal of Eating Disorders, 5,* 403–419.

Fairburn, C. G., Marcus, M. D., & Wilson, G. T. (1993). Cognitive-behavioral therapy for binge eating and bulimia nervosa. In C. G. Fairburn & G. T. Wilson (Eds.), *Binge eating: Nature, assessment, and treatment* (pp. 361–404). New York: Guilford Press.

Fairburn, C. G., & Wilson, G. T. (1993). *Binge eating: Nature, assessment, and treatment.* New York: Guilford Press.

Foreyt, J. P., & McGavin, J. K. (1988). Anorexia nervosa and bulimia. In E. J. Marsh & L. G. Tudal (Eds.), *Behavioral assessment of childhood disorders* (pp. 776–805). New York: Guilford Press.

Fosson, A., Knibbs, J., Bryant-Waugh, R., & Lask, B. (1987). Early onset anorexia nervosa. *Archives of Disease in Childhood, 62,* 114–118.

Garfinkel, P. E., & Garner, D. M. (1982). *Anorexia nervosa: A multidimensional perspective.* New York: Brunner/Mazel.

Garfinkel, P. E., Moldofsky, H., & Garner, D. M. (1980). The heterogeneity of anorexia nervosa. *Archives of General Psychiatry, 37,* 1036–1040.

Garner, D. M. (1991). *Eating Disorder Inventory-2: Professional manual.* Odessa, FL: Psychological Assessment Resources.

Garner, D. M. (1993a). Pathogenesis of anorexia nervosa. *Lancet, 341,* 1631–1635.

Garner, D. M. (1993b). Binge eating in anorexia nervosa. In C. G. Fairburn & G. T. Wilson (Eds.), *Binge eating: Nature, assessment, and treatment* (pp. 50–76). New York: Guilford Press.

Garner, D. M. & Bemis, K. M. (1982). A cognitive-behavioral approach to anorexia nervosa. *Cognitive Therapy and Research, 6,* 123–150.

Garner, D. M. & Bemis K. M. (1985). Cognitive therapy for anorexia nervosa. In D. M. Garner & P. E. Garfinkel (Eds.), *Handbook of psychotherapy for anorexia nervosa and bulimia* (pp. 107–146). New York: Guilford Press.

Garner, D. M. & Garfinkel, P. E. (1979). The Eating Attitudes Test: An index of the symptoms of anorexia nervosa. *Psychological Medicine, 9,* 273–279.

Garner, D. M. & Garfinkel, P. E. (1980). Socio-cultural factors in the development of anorexia nervosa. *Psychological Medicine, 10,* 647–656.

Garner, D. M., & Garfinkel, P. E. (1985). *Handbook of psychotherapy for anorexia nervosa and bulimia.* New York: Guilford Press.

Garner, D. M., Garner, M. V., & Rosen L. W. (1993). Anorexia nervosa "restricters" who purge: Implications for subtyping anorexia nervosa. *International Journal of Eating Disorders, 13,* 171–185.

Garner, D. M., Olmsted, M. P., Bohr, Y., & Garfinkel, P. E. (1982). The Eating Attitudes Test: Psychometric features and clinical correlates. *Psychological Medicine, 12,* 871–878.

Garner, D. M., Olmsted, M. P., Davis, R., Rockert, W., Goldbloom, D., & Eagle, M. (1990). The association between bulimic symptoms and reported psychopathology. *International Journal of Eating Disorders, 9,* 1–15.

Garner, D. M., Olmsted, M. P., & Polivy, J. (1983). Development and validation of a multidimensional eating disorder inventory for anorexia nervosa and bulimia. *International Journal of Eating Disorders, 2,* 15–34.

Garner, D. M., Rockert, W., Olmsted, M. P., Johnson, C. L. & Coscina, D. V. (1985). Psychoeducational principles in the treatment of bulimia and anorexia nervosa. In D. M. Garner & P. E. Garfinkel (Eds.), *Handbook of psychotherapy for anorexia nervosa and bulimia* (pp. 513–572). New York: Guilford Press.

Garner, D. M., & Rosen, L. W. (1990). Anorexia nervosa and bulimia nervosa. In A. S. Bellack, M. Hersen, & A. E. Kazdin (Eds.), *International handbook of behavior modification and therapy* (pp. 805–817). New York: Plenum Press.

Garner, D. M., & Rosen, L. W. (1991). Eating disorders in athletes: Research and recommendations. *Journal of Applied Sports Research, 5,* 100–107.

Garner, D. M. & Sackeyfio, A. H. (1993). Eating disorders. In A. S. Bellack & M. Hersen (Eds.). *Handbook of behavior therapy in the psychiatric setting* (pp 477–497). New York: Plenum Press.

Halmi, K. A. (1985). Classification of the eating disorders. *Journal of Psychiatric Research, 19,* 113–119.

Halmi, K. A., Eckert, E. Marchi, P., Sampugnaro, V., Apple, R., & Cohen, J. (1991). Comorbidity of psychiatric diagnoses in anorexia nervosa. *Archives of General Psychiatry, 48* 712–718.

Heatherton, T. F., & Baumeister, R. F. (1991). Binge-eating as escape from self-awareness. *Psychological Bulletin, 110,* 86–108.

Herzog, D. B., Keller, M. B., Sacks, N. R., Yeh, C. J., & Lavori, P. W. (1992). Psychiatric morbidity in treatment-seeking anorexics and bulimics. *Journal of the American Academy of Child and Adolescent Psychiatry, 31,* 810–818.

Hoek, H. W. (1991). The incidence and prevalence of anorexia nervosa and bulimia nervosa in primary care. *Psychological Medicine, 21,* 455–460.

Hoek, H. W. (1993). Review of the epidemiological studies of eating disorders. *International Review of Psychiatry, 5,* 61–74.

Holland, A. J., Sicotte N., & Treasure, J. (1988). Anorexia nervosa: Evidence for a genetic base. *Journal of Psychosomatic Research, 32,* 561–571.

Hsu, L. K. G. (1988). The outcome of anorexia nervosa: A reappraisal. *Psychological Medicine, 18,* 807–812.

Hsu, L. K. G., Kaye, W., & Weltzin, T. E., (1993). Are the eating disorders related to obsessive-compulsive disorder? *International Journal of Eating Disorders, 14,* 305–318.

Humphrey, L. L. (1989). Is there a causal ink between disturbed family processes and eating disorders? In W. G. Johnson (Ed.), *Bulimia nervosa: Perspectives on clinical research and therapy.* New York: JAI Press.

Jaffe, A. C., & Singer, L. T. (1989). Atypical eating disorders in young children. *International Journal of Eating Disorders, 8,* 575–582.

Johnson, C. L., & Connors, M. E. (1987). *The etiology and treatment of bulimia nervosa: A biopsychosocial perspective.* New York: Basic Books.

Kaye, W. H., Welzin, T. E., Hsu, L. K. G., McConaha, C., & Bolton, B. (1993). Amount of calories digested after bingeing and vomiting. *American Journal of Psychiatry, 150,* 969–971.

Kellett, J., Trimble, M., & Thorley, A., (1976). Anorexia nervosa after the menopause. *British Journal of Psychiatry, 128,* 555–558.

Keys, A., Brozek, J., Henschel, A., Michelson, O., & Taylor, H. L. (1950). *The biology of human starvation.* Minneapolis, MN: University of Minneapolis.

Lucas, A. R., Beard, C. M., O'Fallon, W. M., & Kurland, L. T. (1991). 50-year trends in the incidence of anorexia nervosa in Rochester, MN: A population-based study, *American Journal of Psychiatry, 148,* 917–922.

Minuchin, S., Rosman, B. L., & Baker, L. (1978). *Psychosomatic families: Anorexia nervosa in context.* Cambridge, MA: Harvard University Press.

Mitchell, J. E. (1990). *Bulimia nervosa.* Minneapolis, MN: University of Minnesota Press.

Mitchell, J. E., & Boutacoff, M. A. (1986). Laxative abuse complicating bulimia: Medical and treatment implications. *International Journal of Eating Disorders, 5,* 325–334.

Mitchell, J. E., Pomeroy, C., & Huber, M. (1988). A clinician's guide to the eating disorders medicine cabinet. *International Journal of Eating Disorders, 7,* 211–233.

Olmsted, M. P., Davis, R., Garner, D. M., Eagle, M., & Rockert W. (1991). Efficacy of brief psychoeducational intervention for bulimia nervosa. *Behaviour Research and Therapy, 29,* 71–83.

Polivy, J., & Herman, C. P. (1985). Dieting and bingeing: A causal analysis. *American Psycholgist, 40,* 193–201.

Pope, H. G., & Hudson, J. I. (1992). Is childhood sexual abuse a risk factor for bulimia nervosa? *American Journal of Psychiatry, 149,* 455–463.

Rastam, M. (1992). Anorexia nervosa in 52 Swedish adolescents: Premorbid problems and comorbidity. *Journal of American Academy of Child and Adolescent Psychiatry, 31,* 819–829.

Rigotti, N. A., Nussbaum, S., Herzog, D., & Neer, R. M. (1985). Osteoporosis in women with anorexia nervosa. *New England Journal of Medicine, 311,* 1601–1606.

Root, M. M. P., Fallon, P., & Friedrich, W. N. (1985). *Bulimia: A systems approach to treatment.* New York: W. W. Norton.

Russell, G. F. M. (1979). Bulimia nervosa: An ominous variant of anorexia nervosa. *Psychological Medicine, 9,* 429–448.

Schocken, D. D., Holloway, J. D., & Powers, P. S. (1989). Weight loss and the heart: Effects of anorexia nervosa and starvation. *Archives of Internal Medicine, 149,* 877–881.

Stewart D. E., Robinson, E., & Goldbloom, D. S. (1990). Infertility and eating disorders. *American Journal of Obstetrics and Gynecology, 163,* 1196–1199.

Strober, M. (1993). Disorders of the self in anorexia nervosa: An organismic-developmental perspective. In C. Johnson (Ed.), *Psychodynamic treatment of anorexia nervosa and bulimia* (pp. 354–373). New York: Guilford Press.

Strober, M. Lamper, C., Morrell, W., Burroughs, J., & Jacobs, C. (1990). A controlled family study of anorexia nervosa: Evidence of familial aggregation and lack of shared transmission with affective disorders. *International Journal of Eating Disorders, 9,* 239–253.

Strober, M. & Yager, J. (1985). A developmental perspective on the treatment of anorexia nervosa in adolescents. In D. M. Garner & P. E. Garfinkel (Eds.), *Handbook of psychotherapy for anorexia nervosa and bulimia* (pp. 363–390). New York: Guilford Press.

Stunkard, A. J. (1959). Eating patterns and obesity. *Psychiatric Quarterly, 33,* 284–295.

Vandereycken, W., Kog, E., & Vanderlinden, J. (1989). *The family approach to eating disorders.* New York: PMA Publishing.

Welch, G. W., Hall, A., & Renner, R., (1990). Patient subgrouping in anorexia nervosa using psychologically-based classification. *International Journal of Eating Disorders, 9,* 311–322.

Welch, S. L., & Fairburn, C. G. (1994). Sexual abuse and bulimia nervosa: Three integrated case control comparisons. *American Journal of Psychiatry, 151,* 402–407.

Wilson, G. T. (1993). Assessment of binge eating. In C. G. Fairburn & G. T. Wilson (Eds.), *Binge eating: Nature, assessment, and treatment* (pp. 227–249). New York: Guilford Press.

CHAPTER 16

Tic Disorders

IRWIN J. MANSDORF

DESCRIPTION OF THE PROBLEM

Tics are behaviors that are particularly well suited for intervention by behavior therapists because tics are viewed by most medical and psychiatric experts as a phenomenological rather than pathological concept (Weingarten, 1968). While there are several theoretical bases for tic disorders, the tic activity itself is usually well defined, observable, and discrete.

Tics can be present in a variety of forms and in a variety of people. They can range from simple habitual responses that are often disregarded by others to more complex and serious disturbances, such as those found in Gilles de la Tourette's syndrome. They are often accompanied by other behaviors, such as obsessive-compulsive disorders, that require intervention as well. When tics are present, they often cause the individual much distress and require behavioral intervention to help that individual adjust to the problems that the disorder has caused. In most cases, they are exacerbated by stress. Thus, treatment of tic disorders requires not only direct intervention with the actual behavior, but also collateral intervention with other disorder-related behaviors.

The multiplicity of symptoms in tic disorders is very nicely described by Ostfeld (1988). In describing psychological interventions for Tourette's syndrome, she discusses several areas of intervention that do not deal directly with the tic behavior. With Tourette's, psychological intervention should include facilitation of social adjustment; enhancement of skills for self-esteem; treatment for attendant behavioral, personality, or learning disorders; and reduction of the need of medication. While behavior therapy methods may be appropriate for the tic behavior, the underlying symptoms that play a role in the phenomena should be addressed first.

Lerer (1987) stated that while tics themselves are often self-limiting, most children with Tourette's syndrome have learning disabilities and attentional disorders. Determining appropriate behavioral and psychological interventions is especially important with such children because traditional drug therapy for attention-deficit disorders often exacerbates symptoms of the tics themselves.

Behavior therapists, whose daily work includes dealing with measurable and observable behavior, should be particularly well trained in treating tic disorders in psychiatric settings. The diagnostic category *Tic Disorders* as described in DSM-IV (American Psychiatric Association, 1993) presents distinctly behavioral descriptions of the phenomena.

Diagnostically, a *tic* is an involuntary movement characterized by sudden, rapid, recurrent, nonrhythmic, stereotyped movements or vocalizations. Tics can be either motor or vocal and are classified as either simple or complex. Table 16.1 describes several forms of behaviors common in tic disorders.

Some of the more common manifestations of tic disorders involve transient behaviors.

TABLE 16.1. Behavioral Examples of Tic Disorders

Motor		Vocal	
Simple	Complex	Simple	Complex
Eye blink	Facial gestures	Coughing	Coprolalia
Neck jerk	Grooming behaviors	Throat clearing	Echolalia
Shoulder shrug	Jumping	Grunting	Palilalia
Facial grimace	Touching objects	Snorting	
	Hitting self	Sniffing	

Diagnostically, the category *Transient Tic Disorder* (DSM-IV, 307.21) contains five criteria:

1. Single or multiple motor tics and/or vocal tics.
2. Tics occurring many times daily for at least 4 weeks, but no longer than for 12 consecutive months.
3. Onset prior to age 18.
4. No history of Tourette's syndrome or chronic motor or vocal tic disorder.
5. Not related to substance use or any general medical condition.

The category *Chronic Motor or Vocal Tic Disorder* (DSM-IV, 307.22) contains five specific criteria:

1. Either (but not both) motor tics or vocal tics have been present.
2. The tics occur many times daily, nearly every day for a period of over 1 year, with no period of remission over 2 months at a time.
3. Onset prior to age 18.
4. No history of Tourette's syndrome.
5. Not related to substance use or any general medical condition.

Perhaps the most serious tic disorder involves Tourette's syndrome (DSM-IV, 307.23). The four criteria applicable here are:

1. The presence of both multiple motor tics and vocal tics, although not necessarily concurrently.
2. Frequent occurrence, often in bouts, daily or intermittently for a period of over 1 year, without any period of remission longer than 2 months at a time.
3. Onset prior to age 18.
4. Not related to substance use or any general medical condition.

A fourth diagnostic category of tic disorder is classified by the DSM-IV. This category, *Tic Disorder Not Otherwise Specified* (307.20), includes those tics that do not meet the criteria for one of the other disorders. Tics that occur for periods of less than 1 year or tics occurring first in adulthood would be included under this category.

Because the psychiatric definition of *tic disorder* rules out a neurological condition, some professionals feel that behavioral treatment for tic disorders that fall into one of the diagnostic categories just presented would be limited to non-central-nervous-system (CNS) manifestations. However, because a tic is a symptomatic concept, it can occur in both non-CNS and CNS diseases. While the etiology of tic disorders is often described in both organic and psychological terms, some (e.g., Wilson, 1955) feel that the widespread occurrence of tics in many types of conditions argues against a clear organic/nonorganic dichotomy.

While a vast literature exists on tics, there does not appear to be a common etiological thread in describing the problem. Perhaps because of the lack of definitive explanations, most descriptions and discussions appear to focus on overt symptomatology rather than pathogenesis. In general, tic disorders appear to be described either in terms of simple or complex motor tics or in terms of Tourette's syndrome (a more intense and serious form of the disorder). While common traits exist between Tourette's syndrome and more simple tics, Tourette's is lifelong and characterized by the appearance of multiple motor and vocal tics. Both treatment and description of all tic disorders, however, appear to be based in large part on work with Tourette's patients. In many cases, the most important distinction between Tourette's syndrome and a tic disorder in any form is that the latter is a transient phenomenon, while the former is not.

For the most part, tics first appear during childhood. This is especially true of tics that are not known to have any clear organic basis. The period of modal occurrence appears to be between the ages of 6 and 12. Epidemiologically, tics affect about 0.03% to 0.05% of the population of the United States (Shapiro & Shapiro, 1982). As with many other behavioral disorders, more males than females are affected, with the male/female ratio being approximately 3:1. Psychologically, children with tics are not known to have any particular psychopathology, although arguments have been made both for the existence and the absence of predisposing psychological factors. What is known, however, is that environmental factors, such as stress and family strife, contribute to distinct exacerbation of tics. In discussing treatment of the disorder, one cardinal component would be the assessment and treatment of attendant environmental factors as well as direct assessment and treatment of the morphological characteristics of the tic itself.

Heredity as well is mentioned by some as a factor in tic disorders. Nee, Polinsky, and Ebert (1982) quote other studies as well as their own findings that suggest a familial factor in Tourette's syndrome.

Tics vary widely in terms of form and expression. Such variability is noted both between patients and within the same patient (Fahn, 1982). A typical tic is a patterned, involuntary movement ranging from the simple (e.g., eye blink) to the more complex (intricate body movements). Motor tics are most commonly observed in the face and the neck region. Other tics extend to the shoulders and arms, often combining with facial tics. Tics in the lower portion of the body are rare, but jumping and stamping tics have been described in the literature.

Vocal tics are most common in Tourette's syndrome. These are characterized by grunts, snorts, and throat clearing as well as by more linguistic manifestations, such as coprolalia, palilalia, and echolalia. Nonlinguistic sounds, such as grunts, squeals, and hisses, appear to be related to involuntary diaphragmatic contractions and may be actual extensions of motor tics. Even linguistic tics may have more of an organic than psychological component. Coprolalia, which is reported to occur in over 60% of Tourette's syndrome patients, shows a distinctly different cadence, pitch, context, and volume with Tourette's patients as opposed to other emotionally charged situations. The linguistic vocalizations of Tourette's patients are spontaneous, explosive, and involuntary. While coprolalia is widespread with Tourette's, other vocalizations that involve phrases, words, or even syllables are also seen.

PROTOTYPIC ASSESSMENT

While many psychiatric and behavioral problems can be assessed by using as a base the characteristics (or diagnostic criteria) in the *Diagnostic and Statistical Manual of Mental Disorders* (DSM-III-R) (American Psychiatric Association, 1987), tic disorders require a somewhat modified approach. In describing tic disorders, the DSM-III-R criteria refer to categories of behavior rather than discrete behavioral units. Describing the behavior itself is sufficient only in understanding the overt morphology of the tic. It does not, however, serve as an adequate source for planning the details of treatment. In assessing a tic disorder, attention must be paid to the wide variety of situational, psychological, and cognitive components that accompany the disorder, as well as to the actual type of motor and/or vocal tics presented. In practical terms, assessing the overt tic itself is not as critical in treatment as assessing the behavioral unit in which the tic disorder is contained.

For the purpose of assessment of tic disorders, a *behavioral unit* consists of both the overt symptomatology and the psychological and behavioral context that surrounds the symptoms. The contextual, surrounding factors are often more important in treatment than the actual physical expression of the tic. An inaccurate assessment of the behavioral unit in a tic disorder can lead to treatment that would be inappropriate.

The importance of accurate assessment of the contextual factors in behavioral disorders occurs in other areas of behavior therapy as well. In weight control, for example, not only are the actual eating behaviors considered modifiable targets, but so are the moderating cognitive variables that determine when and how overeating takes place. While the actual treatment of the target behavior may be similar across individuals, cognitive variables are by definition individual, private, and variable. Since these cognitive variables present in many forms, assessment of them must be individual in order to be accurate.

Tic disorders, therefore, can be assessed concretely by following a procedural outline that addresses specific variables. These variables can be molded into a decision tree that, in effect, serves as a map to aid the clinician in assessment. What follows is a guide in carrying out this assessment process.

Assessing the Tic

Observing the overt behavioral manifestations of a tic is an appropriate first step in assessment. Notwithstanding the actual diagnostic category (e.g., Tourette's syndrome), behavioral treatment can be introduced that would address an aspect or aspects of specific tic activity within a particular category. By initially targeting activity within a tic disorder rather than addressing a diagnostic category, a more molecular approach to treatment takes place. As noted by Caine, Margolin, Brown, and Ebert (1978), such an approach avoids possible errors in diagnosis. In discussing the case of a child who developed tardive dyskinesia after treatment with neuroleptics for Tourette's, the authors stress that care must be taken to differentiate Tourette's from other forms of childhood tics for which nondrug treatments would be effective.

What is the Type of Tic Observed?

As noted earlier, tics can be either motor or vocal and can be either simple or complex. Initial assessment should clearly describe the actual problem tic. Observations of the tic should include reports of activity from various environmental settings as well as direct observation by the clinician. The goal of this aspect of assessment is not to analyze the specific components of the behavior, but rather to simply determine what the behavior is. Assessments of children should take into account three major sources of information: parental observations, teacher observations, and direct clinical observations.

This portion of the assessment should provide the clinician with information concerning what aspect of overt tic activity will be changed. Typically, a measurement of the behavior that initially prompted the referral for treatment will be assessed.

What is the Frequency of Tic Behavior Observed?

Once the description of the tic is completed, the measurement of its frequency provides baseline data with regard to severity and intensity of the problem. As with other behavioral problems, baseline measurement provides the clinician with a mechanism with which to assess progress in treatment. Measurement that would provide the type of data that simulates laboratory studies is often not possible to gather in clinical situations. However, clinical treatment (as opposed to research) does not always require technical data measurements. The clinician should nevertheless attempt to take some sort of measure of what is observed and can even instruct significant others (e.g., parents or teachers) in ways to conduct such unobtrusive measurement.

During clinical work whereby a child would be observed in simple verbal interaction, the use of a hand-held counter would be ideal. The counter can be held by the clinician and used to record frequency of the tic or tics in questions. With simple motor tics, recording is fairly straightforward. With complex motor tics, where several types of tics coexist, a random sampling of each type of tic within a particular time period would suffice to provide clinical data that can be used to assess treatment progress. If a counter is not available, a simple pad and pencil are often adequate substitutes.

In determining frequency of tics in the natural environment, it is impractical and unrealistic to expect most parents to provide consistently accurate measures of tic activity. The typical parent is neither proficient in behavioral measurement nor willing to serve as what many would view as a paraprofessional in therapy. While many parents may not object to the task of providing discrete behavioral measurements of tic frequency, the clinician must take into consideration the fact that such measurements should be used prudently because they may not be accurate.

Parents can, however, provide appropriate subjective data that are clinically appropriate and that can have clinical utility. Early behavioral measurement of phobic behavior typically followed this approach (e.g., SUDS, subjective units of desensitization). Similarly, subjective units of tic intensity or severity can be adequate in clinical situations. These subjective units may be assessed by both outside observers (e.g., parents and/or teachers) as well as the child. Using scales of 1 to 10 or 1 to 100 can provide satisfactory clinical methods of measuring tic intensity.

Where Does the Tic Take Place?

The situational variables of any behavior are critical in any behavioral assessment. Tics are known to wax and wane, often in response to environmental stimuli, such as stress

(Pray, Kramer, & Lindskog, 1986). Where external, observable stimuli control frequency of behavior, the assessment of those stimuli provides an important clue to planning effective and targeted treatment.

Asides from periods of sleep, when tics are generally not active, delineating the environmental components of the disorder can provide the clinician with information on where to begin and on focus treatment. The most practical assessment device is the clinical interview with the child and with significant others (parents, teachers) who would come into contact with the behavior.

The interview should be in the form of an information-gathering session. In questioning parents, care should be taken to avoid the impression of ascribing blame or causality to any particular person or situation. Building a behavioral framework should be as matter-of-fact as possible, covering the various overt cues surrounding the child's day. Questions should review the child's activities from morning to bedtime, guiding the interviewees in describing the day. The ultimate measure in these sessions is frequency of behavior, which is often an elusive and inaccurate variable when lay observers are charged with its determination. Exact measurements, however, are not critical clinical factors in treatment. Assessing general frequency in different situations yields important information even without pure, exact measures of behavior.

The answer to the question of where the tic takes place lies in the child's world. Assessment of the behavior at home should focus on times of the day (e.g., at school versus at home), household activities (e.g., family activities versus eating alone), areas of occurrence (e.g., own room versus family room), and other factors that can be considered as general stimulus variables.

When Does the Tic Take Place?

The final environmental element in the behavioral unit of a tic is the question of when the tic takes place. As noted earlier, periods of sleep usually are devoid of tic activity. Otherwise, time of day as well as day of week may be an important aspect in assessment. Once frequency and location data are determined, they should be charted in terms of time period. The goal here is to determine if any pattern of occurrence is linked to time. The focus should be on day of week (e.g., weekend versus weekday), time of day (e.g., morning versus evening), and activity (e.g., lunchtime, school recess, school dismissal).

Assessing the Ticquer

Once the environmental assessment of the overt tic behavior is completed, an assessment of the individual child, or "ticquer," takes place. This usually involves a cognitive assessment in which the child's emotions and thoughts regarding and during tic behavior are determined.

Theoretically, the function of the cognitive assessment is to provide clues to internal stimuli that relate to the tic. While assessment of environmental events, such as external stressors, is important in analyzing tics, internal events also play a key role in control. While cognition may not necessarily be the major factor in the etiology of any particular tic, it nevertheless plays a role in the maintenance of the behavior. Even the medical management of severe tic behavior calls for an understanding of such attendant factors in tic management (Kurlan, 1989).

In assessing cognitive factors, the goal is to attempt to determine any factors that may exert control on the behavior. As with any assessment, the ultimate aim is to incorporate what is learned into a treatment program; therefore, determining appropriate cognitions paves the way to using those cognitions in treatment.

What is the Child Thinking About?

The simplest approach in cognitive assessment is to ask what the child is thinking about. Approaching the child should typically be carried out only after a preliminary assessment of potential cognitive material is determined. By interviewing parents and teachers, the clinician can get a feel for the types of thoughts and emotions that may be critical. Since children are not always able to adequately express what they feel or think, a preliminary interview can provide information that is clinically important.

In approaching the child directly, a cognitive assessment is best carried out in the form of a nondirective clinical interview. Questions of the "What types of things . . . " variety help in breaking the ice with these typically anxious and, at times, insecure children. Instead of initially asking, "What do you think about when you tic?", a more effective initial approach may include the question "What kinds of things are on your mind during the day?" By gradually approaching the situations that environmental analysis has indicated might be relevant to tic activity, the appropriate cognitive substrates for each environmental element can be determined. Table 16.2 outlines the relationship between environmental events and cognitive analysis of the child.

How Can the Child Begin to Exercise Control?

While control of the tic is a skill that the ticquer typically does not fully enjoy, there are other types of behaviors and situations over which the child has greater control. Determining the types of cognitions that accompany these behaviors and situations helps in creating a treatment program that can utilize effective self-control methods.

In determining these methods, analysis of the child's perception of what happens during periods of tic waning is important. Since these periods are times of relative quiescence, accompanying cognitions either may be responsible for or may acquire characteristics of

TABLE 16.2.   The Relationship Between Environmental and Cognitive Analysis

Environmental Events			
Where	When	How	How Much
Place of occurrence	Time of day	Form of tic	Frequency
People	Day of week	Type of tic	Intensity
Situations			

What is the child thinking about?

Cognitive Analysis

control. Tapping into the child's cognitive control system serves to provide a means with which to plan treatment. Since cognitions vary from child to child, the determination of individual cognitive factors requires individual analysis.

Determining how the child exercises control may not appear to be an issue related to assessment; however, the ultimate purpose of all assessment is to map out an effective base with which to approach treatment. Since self-control is one type of treatment technique for tic disorders, the determination of its parameters is important. Thus, assessment for self-control should include what the child currently uses and what the child could use for control.

A critical component here is fantasy material. In younger children, this would take the form of inquiring about whom the child looks up to or admires. Incorporating the perceived features of these figures into the child's repertoire would be used in treatment. In older children, an inquiry into the cognitive components of specific behaviors that the child lacks would serve as a basis for assessing features in self-control.

Assessing Attendant Behaviors

Tic disorders often are accompanied by a host of attendant behaviors that also require treatment. While treatment approaches to each of these behaviors are often independent of the tic, much of the stress that is associated with tic exacerbation is often part of the behavioral unit of the disorder itself (Bronheim, 1991).

While assessment and treatment of these associated or attendant behaviors are significant in total treatment of tics, the clinician should refer to individual aspects of the specific disorder for guidance on how to incorporate them into a comprehensive approach to the problem.

ACTUAL ASSESSMENT

The difference between prototypic and actual assessment may appear to be the difference between the real and the ideal. While there may be some truth to this, behavioral approaches to actual clinical assessment take a far more functional approach. The prototypic outline of assessment of tic disorders could be best viewed as a guideline or map for the practitioner in planning treatment. How this map is used depends largely on the actual clinical presentation of the case.

In conducting actual assessment of a tic disorder, the guiding element for the clinician should be the formulation of a proposed treatment plan. Prototypic guidelines are merely suggested steps to take in the assessment. Treatment considerations with the actual child will determine the aspects of assessment that will be applied in any individual case.

The case to be analyzed here is based in part on unpublished aspects of previously published clinical material (Mansdorf & Friedman, 1980).

CASE EXAMPLE: THE EYE BLINKER

Method of assessment and clinical background

The young boy presented here, Daniel, was a 6 ½-year-old first grader. Assessment took place utilizing clinical interviews of both the child and the parents. The child and parents were observed and interviewed both together and individually. Phone interviews with the child's pediatrician and teacher also took place. The presenting problem was an eye-blink tic that had been present for over 4 years. As with other tics, there was some waxing and waning, but the tic itself never disappeared. To this point, the only formal intervention had been psychoanalytically oriented family therapy, recommended to deal with observed marital tension that was assumed by previous clinicians to be maintaining tic behavior.

Assessing the Tic

What was the type of tic observed?
Daniel's eye-blink tic was a simple, motor tic that occurred daily for the past 4 $\frac{1}{2}$ years. Diagnostically, the tic qualified as a chronic motor tic disorder (DSM-IV 307.22). Both behavioral observations and interview material yielded no evidence of any other motor or vocal tics. No organic etiology was present. While there was no evidence of any current marital difficulties, the parents did report that they had had a period of marital difficulty in the past, which was now resolved.

What was the frequency of the behavior observed?
Initial assessment took place during the clinical interview with the parents and child. Using pencil and pad, the clinician marked the pad each time an eye blink occurred. In order to stratify measurements, these markings took place during six 2-minute intervals throughout the session. Total number of marks was divided by number of minutes of observation to yield a measure of eye blinks per minute.

Parents were instructed to use a subjective method of assessment in measurement. Using a scale of 1 to 100, where higher numbers correlate with greater frequency, the parents were asked to give their impressions of tic frequency in a number of settings. Since both parents were involved in observations, a weighted measure was taken of individual parental scores.

The child's teacher was also requested to present her observations in subjective numerical form. She was instructed by the clinician how to use subjective measures and was asked to note intensity/frequency on three different school days.

Subjective measurement has the disadvantage of being an inexact and primitive means of assessment. However, in the practical world of clinical reality, it is often the best that one can expect. In any case, it serves the purpose of giving a fundamental baseline impression, albeit an inexact one, of the behavior in question.

Where and when did the tic take place?
A complete behavioral analysis includes looking at frequency of behavior in a variety of settings. In Daniel's case, clinical assessment required comparing frequency in different environmental contexts. Since frequency was assessed in several situations, the question of where the tic took place was easy to answer. The in-office clinical assessment of Daniel showed a very high rate of behavior, averaging 78 eye blinks per minute. The parents rated the data as an 85 on the subjective scale of 1 to 100. The parents' other subjective assessments showed that the tic was present in almost all aspects of Daniel's life. Tics were noted at home, at school, at play, and even during sleep, an unusual (if questionable) observation. Subjective ratings by parents and teachers in other settings yielded similar intensity/frequency scores.

Assessing Daniel—The ticquer

Since assessment is the initial link in a treatment plan, data gathered from clinical assessment serve to create appropriate clinical hypotheses about treatment. Accordingly, behavioral analysis should include evaluation of characteristics of the ticquer that play a role in tic maintenance. In Daniel's case, evaluation was made of critical cognitive components of self-control.

What is the child thinking about?
Tics are often linked to the child's specific cognitions. Since stress exacerbates tics, certain stressful thoughts may be linked to the appearance or maintenance of tics. Daniel was assessed in a series of brief interviews that included play, fanatasy, and structured questioning. The history of the tic appears to have been related to family tensions over marital problems some years earlier. If the tic was still exacerbated by these tensions, some hint of this may have been present in Daniel's cognitive constellation. In assessment, however, Daniel gave no sign of any feelings or problems relating to his parents. A sentence-completion technique with questions such as "The thing that worries me most about my parents is . . . " and "When my parents are together they . . . " yielded no evidence of any cognitive distress related to his parents' relationship. An analysis of other sentence-completion material also showed that, although Daniel was concerned over his tic, there did not appear to be any specific cognitive trigger or correlate to the problem.

Based on assessment material gathered, it appeared that although cognitive factors may have been responsible for the original triggering of tic behavior, other factors were related to actual maintenance of the tic. The range of situations in which the tic was noted and the lack of any clear cognitive component argued for the view that the tic was a conditioned habit response. Originally exacerbated by the previously reported parental stress, the tic may have become conditioned to the multiple environmental cues that accompanied the child's cognitive distress. While cognitive factors may not be present in tic maintenance, they very well may have been in originally establishing the tic.

How can the child exercise cognitive control?
Daniel's tic represented a loss of control over a group of voluntary muscles. Reestablishing control can be aided by use of cognitive elements. While no cognitive element may be responsible for the present tic, there may be some cognitive control that the child can exert.

Daniel's assessment revealed him to be a child of above average intelligence who was doing well scholastically despite his tic. While self-esteem may have been affected somewhat because of the tic, he nevertheless displayed an independent presence of mind. This appeared to suggest that cognitive self-control may be an effective tool for him. A feedback technique was utilized in the treatment program that was designed for Daniel. Cognitive control served as a mechanism to augment much feedback training. In interviewing and observing Daniel, his independent nature appeared to suggest that he would be successful in employing cognitive messages that emphasized his ability to control. Adaptation of a "Superman" figure with which Daniel would "make believe" was tested. Daniel appeared to be excited over this and seemed to relish his role as "Superman." Use of the cognitive figure of Superman, combined with self-instruction messages urging control (e.g., "I can do it"), seemed opportune in this case.

Link to Treatment

While assessment of a situation is critical, it is only one element in the approach to tic disorders. Effective assessment will often yield specific elements of a child's behavioral repertoire that would aid in treatment planning. For example, when a child is assessed to have independent thinking, a self-control technique is helpful in treatment. If the child's cognitive assessment shows a more submissive and passive behavioral pattern (e.g., Mansdorf, 1986), treatment may involve reversing this pattern by helping the child develop more assertive behavior.

Assessment should be viewed, therefore, both as a means with which to establish baseline measurements for clinical comparisons and as a method to determine possible effective treatment plans for the child in question.

PROTOTYPIC TREATMENT

Treatment for tic disorders encompasses a wide range of behavioral or nonbehavioral techniques. While pharmacological intervention is the most popular nonbehavioral intervention, it often results in exacerbating tics rather than diminishing their frequency (Gualtieri & Patterson, 1986). Since most behavioral interventions serve to augment or replace drug therapy, the focus in this section will be on nonpharmacological interventions.

Tic behavior can be treated using both directive approaches, where the behavior itself is attacked, and indirect approaches, where the contingencies maintaining the behavior are dealt with. Prototypic treatment involves following specific procedures based on "techniques." While actual treatment requires a more comprehensive approach to cases, a fundamental knowledge of these behavioral techniques gives the clinician the basic repertoire required for effective intervention.

Direct Approaches

Motor and vocal tics are discrete, observable, and measurable behaviors. As such, they lend themselves easily to classic behavioral approaches in which operant and classical conditioning approaches are applied directly.

Negative or Massed Practice

Yates (1958) spoke of tics as learned responses. Tics may arise as avoidant responses that are conditioned during a traumatic or anxiety-producing event. They assume drive-reducing qualities and acquire strength through subsequent reinforcement. Through a process of stimulus generalization, a variety of situations and conditions can elicit the tic, leading to its become an even stronger habit.

According to this model, a tic can be extinguished by building up a negative or incompatible response that is antagonistic to the tic. Treatment of tics using this model would rely on having the ticquer perform the response *voluntarily* to the point of building up a good degree of inhibition. By massing this type of voluntary response (i.e., having the tic performed over and over again), negative inhibition is created. The ticquer will eventually be forced to cease voluntary performance as reactive inhibition builds up. When this occurs, a natural period of rest will follow—the tic does not occur and the ticquer rests. Such a period of rest serves a drive-reducing quality and is associated with not performing the tic. Since nonperformance is reinforced, continued massed practice leads to extinction of the tic.

Treatment with massed practice is discrete and practical. As a rule, the ticquer is asked to practice the tic over a period of time. While the actual technique varies, ticquers are invariably asked to repeat the tic in massed form over short periods of time; for example, an eye-blinker would be asked to voluntarily and continuously blink for 5-minute periods, resting only for a brief time between the blinking periods. Others have varied this procedure to include gradual lengthening of practice sessions. Walton (1961) treated a child who practiced the tic for periods that increased from 15 to over 30 minutes at a time.

In general, where massed practice is successful, it results in a decrease over time of ability to voluntarily elicit the tic. The tic is ultimately extinguished, with generalization extending beyond the treatment setting. There have been reports in which massed practice has been combined with other methods, particularly negative feedback, in which some sort of aversive stimulus is avoided by refraining from the tic (Rafi, 1962).

Operant Techniques

Use of operant techniques is based on the theory that the tic is ultimately under environmental control and is maintained by some sort of external stimulus. Following this model, contingency management techniques are employed for intervention.

Simply stated, these approaches build on a behavioral assessment that determines which contingencies appear to be involved in tic maintenance. Restructuring these consequences would lead to a change in tic frequency. In some cases, a potential reinforcer can be introduced into a situation in order to help increase or decrease the frequency of a tic. Barrett (1962) used such a technique in structuring music as an element that served as reinforcer for periods of abstinence from tic behavior. While attention to music was not observed to be a high-frequency behavior, it was assessed to be a response that could serve as a reinforcer.

Operant models of treatment point out the importance of accurate behavioral assessment in actual intervention. The clinical selection of reinforcers can be based on two methods: first, the observation of what follows tic behavior with any frequency, and, second, the observation of what in the person's environment occurs with frequency in other situations and can be classified as a positive reinforcer.

By structuring contingencies, the clinician can create a framework that subsequently can increase or decrease frequency of tic activity. Reinforcement can be negative as well as positive, such as occurs in the absence of a certain event.

Schulman (1974) used this approach in simply but elegantly treating a child with multiple motor tics. During behavioral assessment, a clinical interview indicated that tics were occurring in the presence of the child's mother. Furthermore, it appeared that the mother actually paid a certain amount of attention to the tics, but that the child's father ignored them. What was observed was a diminution of tic frequency in the presence of the father.

The clinical treatment plan in this operant format called for a rearranging of environmental events and used parental reinforcement to control tic activity. A family-therapy framework was employed whereby instruction and feedback to the parent was given as to how to extinguish the tic and reinforce nontic behavior. Intervention clearly showed a relationship between attention and tic behavior. While tics certainly were reduced in frequency as a result of this intervention, maternal attention was not completely controlled. After a period of total remission, some tic activity returned as family tension rose. With the rise in family tension, tic behavior exacerbated and maternal attention increased. While the authors did not explicitly mention it, this phenomenon is a good example of why a combination of techniques (including behavioral and general psychotherapeutic) is often important in the comprehensive treatment of tics.

Miller (1970) used this very combination of techniques in an operant program that controlled tic activity in a young child suffering from Tourette's syndrome. Reinforcement for not producing tics was initially introduced in structured clinical sessions. When it became evident that the tics were under operant control, a thorough analysis of the child's home environment was conducted. This analysis showed that parental attention was involved in the problem. A family therapy framework was used to systematically teach the parents how to attend to positive behavior and to ignore negative behavior. Counseling continued over an extended period, with parental behavior monitored and supervised by professionals.

The ultimate success of the operant programs described is not in the simple application of techniques, but rather in the judicious combination of techniques.

Habit Reversal

Habit reversal is a technique originally implemented by Azrin and Nunn (1973). The technique is really a combination of methods used to decrease and eventually eliminate the occurrence of tics. Habit reversal is a five-component treatment consisting of awareness training, situations and habit inconvenience review, relaxation, competing response, and social support.

The habit reversal procedure begins with a review of the type of tic and with attempts to insure that the ticquer is aware of its presence. The negative aspects of the tic are then reviewed, with an emphasis on the inappropriateness of the behavior in social situations and contexts. Relaxation training is introduced to set the stage for the most critical component of the technique, namely, teaching the ticquer a competing response. The method here resembles another behavioral technique: overcorrection (Gross & Mendelson, 1982). As in overcorrection, where the goal is the substitution of an appropriate response for an inappropriate response, habit reversal chooses a topographic reversal of the tic to be repeated in sets of trials; for example, if the particular tic is a shoulder shrug, the "reversal" would be practice in forcibly keeping the shoulders down.

Several successful approaches to habit reversal have been reported in the literature, including Azrin, Nunn, and Frantz (1980) and Zikis (1983). The major advantage to the technique is the adaptiveness of the procedure to almost all forms of motor tics and the ability for a clinician to improvise in the reversal procedure.

Indirect Approaches

The direct approaches previously described are characterized by application of formal behavioral techniques directly to the behavior in question. Indirect approaches, on the other hand, use behavioral techniques in an attempt to deal with situational factors that are related to or exacerbate the tic.

Relaxation Training

As noted earlier, stress is a factor that has been observed to increase tic frequency. It would stand to reason, therefore, that relaxation would be effective in reducing tic frequency. Rarely used alone, relaxation is often combined with other treatment techniques to help suppress tic movements. While most relaxation techniques take the form of a muscle relaxation procedure, several authors emphasize approaches labeled *multifaceted* or *combination* (Teichman & Eliahu, 1986) to describe the use of other stress-reducing modalities.

Brunn (1984) described treatment of several cases of Tourette's syndrome. She describes the feelings of inner tension that are reported by most patients. In reviewing treatment methodology, she emphasizes multiple factors in therapy and the importance of psychotherapy and general support. While not directly used as a specific relaxation technique, these interventions nonetheless serve a function similar to the stress-managing aspects of relaxation.

Most cases of tic treatment in which family therapy or social support is involved can only presuppose some sort of stress-mediating and relaxation function. However, relaxation has a specific function of acting on the musculature involved in the tic. Poth and Barnett (1983) describe the case of a 3-year-old child who suffered from a shuddering tic. The child was taught a relaxation technique that served to counter the shuddering and also was instructed to induce this state whenever possible. In a series of planned activities and in combination with other reinforcements for nontic behavior, incidence of tic frequency decreased.

Relaxation, at times, may work when other techniques do not. This was illustrated by O'Brien and Brennan (1979) with an adult who responded to relaxation and other techniques after specific behavioral techniques alone were not successful.

Self-Instruction and Self-Monitoring

Originally described by Meichenbaum and Goodman (1971), self-instruction is a method used to develop self-control in children. The technique consists of teaching children to essentially speak to themselves subvocally in an effort to map out specific strategies. Applied mainly for treating impulsive children, self-instruction allows for a control device to be cognitively rehearsed by the children and to be practiced and repeated over many trials. Through constant cognitive review, a child learns to internalize a specific technique with which to counter the tic.

Self-monitoring is a form of self-instruction in which the child is taught to observe and attend to the tic behavior. Ollendick (1981) found that self-monitoring alone was as successful as self-administered overcorrection with several children for reducing tics.

Fuata and Griffiths (1982) used a form of cognitive therapy in conjunction with more formal operant methods in treating a vocal tic. In combining habit-reversal training with cognitive self-control methodology, tic behavior was significantly reduced, with gains maintained after follow-up at 6 months.

Self-instruction and self-monitoring are typically used in self-control programs in which both internal (cognitive) and external (environmental) variables are manipulated in order to effect certain behavioral changes. In self-instruction, whatever behavioral strategy is applied is often mentally rehearsed in an effort to strengthen it. This type of cognitive intervention is especially important in dealing with the attendant variables to tic behavior. With anxiety and other stressors serving to exacerbate tic activity, clinical intervention that takes into account cognitive strategies serves to address an important aspect of the problem.

Use of self-control strategies with children has been reported by Keat (1972), who described broad-spectrum approaches to a variety of problems. Mansdorf (1986) used self-instruction to embellish the treatment effects of behavioral approaches in reducing tic activity.

In using self-control, several techniques are combined to bring about reduction of tic frequency. In general, the prototypic treatment of tic disorders would involve an assessment and intervention into the variety of dimensions that relate to the behavior. Kivalo (1979) points out the relationship between environmental stress and tic frequency. Insofar as the sources of stress can be multiple (e.g., family, school, etc.), the treatment approach should take into account the need to influence environmental stress.

ACTUAL TREATMENT

While several techniques exist for treatment of tics, actual treatment of the behaviors involved will be determined largely by the behavioral assessment conducted. In most cases, a combination of techniques may be necessary in order to effectively target the various factors that may be responsible for the tic.

Extremely difficult cases, especially cases of Tourette's syndrome, are often treated with a combination of medication and psychotherapy. As noted by Golden (1982), however, side effects are often found in 50% of the children treated with haloperidol, the most commonly prescribed drug for the disorder. Ferre (1982) used clonidine in treating an adolescent boy but suggested that a major focus in treatment should be on reduction of anxiety and on improving coping skills.

Behavioral intervention in this regard can be extremely productive. In most cases, the comprehensive treatment of a tic disorder will more than likely involve a combination of techniques rather than a specific technique.

Self-Control

The term *self-control* refers to situations in which the individual, rather than the external environment, effects control over the behavior. Some techniques used in self-control involve cognitive self-instruction, self-monitoring, and assertiveness training. Use of self-control, however, encompasses techniques that may include both environmental and cognitive modalities. Hence, actual treatment will often involve part or all of the techniques reviewed in the previous section on prototypic treatment.

Link to Assessment

Determining if any particular treatment is appropriate is actually a function of the behavioral assessment. In the following case (Mansdorf, 1986), the child, a 10-year-old boy, experienced facial grimacing tics for a period of about 9 months. The assessment was conducted along operant, behavioral, and cognitive lines. As a result of the behavioral analysis, a clinical hypothesis was formulated that linked tic activity to a behavioral trait, namely unassertiveness. Repeated observations showed that the child's tic activity increased during periods when he felt psychologically threatened or when he appeared to be unable to cope with some social situations.

Besides formulating an appropriate treatment plan, actual behavioral assessment must focus on those types of tics that would be most responsive to behavioral intervention. Accordingly, those tics that appear to be a function of stress or some sort of psychological variable would be most responsive to behavioral interventions. In the case at hand, assessment showed two distinct areas where intervention was required. The first was the operant area, where it was observed that tics increased following maternal criticism. The second area was cognitive-behavioral, as tic activity seemed to be a function of un-assertive behavior.

Treatment focused on training the child in assertive responses to psychologically threatening situations and on training the mother to use responses other than criticism when tics were evidenced. Assertiveness training followed a cognitive-behavioral plan whereby the child underwent behavioral rehearsal once weekly. During these rehearsal sessions, self-instruction training took place in which the child was given specific responses to rehearse in carrying out threatening behavioral tasks. Assessment showed that school dismissal time, for example, generated anxiety and increased tic activity. This was linked to difficulty in joining a group of classmates with whom to walk home. Training consisted of rehearsing behaviors that would counter this problem, along with self-statements of appropriate remarks to make in setting the stage for this behavior. Thus, self-statements such as "I'll just walk over and ask those kids directly. They won't bite me" and "So what if they make a remark. Words can't hurt me" were used to aid in augmenting assertive behavior.

Operant intervention consisted of parallel training of the child's mother to seek out situations where tics did not take place and to appropriately praise and verbally reinforce her child. A gradual shift from attention to tic behavior to attention to nontic behavior then followed.

This treatment combined three distinct approaches in controlling tic behavior: Operant intervention was used to help in controlling external environmental variables (maternal reinforcement); behavioral intervention was used to elicit alternative responses to situations that generated anxiety and then led to increased tic activity; and cognitive intervention (self-instruction training) was used to help create attitudes and methods through which the appropriate responses could be carried out. The combination of these approaches in a treatment package of overall self-control resulted in marked reduction in tic behavior over a period of 2 months with little or no recurrence of activity 1 year later.

SUMMARY

The diagnostic category *tic disorders* is a class of behavior of which form and content vary a great deal. Often accompanied by other behavioral problems, the observable and mea-surable nature of tic activity makes it an ideal target for behavioral intervention.

While no agreed-upon etiology exists for the disorder, several types of treatment, including pharmacological, general psychotherapeutic, and behavioral, have been studied and applied to tics. In general, the disorder can be described in terms of overt motor and/ or vocal tics that vary in intensity from transient to more lasting phenomena. Tourette's syndrome, a particularly well-researched form of tic disorder, is a category thought by many to be a distinctly separate and more severe form of the problem.

Behavioral approaches to tic disorders with children have largely been applied to motor tics. In general, the approaches described in the literature focus on specific techniques of intervention rather than general approaches to treatment.

While specific techniques serve as the basic tools for any treatment for tic disorders, a more comprehensive approach requires that a broad behavioral and cognitive analysis take place. By viewing tic activity as a specific behavior that exists in the context of more extensive environmental personal variables, intervention can be tailored more specifically to the child rather than to the tic. Focusing on overt tic activity alone may lead to temporary suppression of a specific response but would not in all likelihood serve as a lasting solution to the problem.

Comprehensive clinical intervention to tic disorders in children requires a behavioral analysis that includes assessment of both the tic and the ticquer. Hence, cognitive variables and attributes figure prominently. By linking the overt manifestations of the disorder with the cognitive and behavioral components that often accompany it, the clinician can target both the child and the behavior, resulting in actual treatment that appropriately mirrors the child's environment.

Linking assessment to treatment is not a novel concept in behavior therapy. While many nonbehavioral approaches often seek to first explain behavior and then to treat it, behavioral interventions reach explanation through a focus on behavioral description. Accurate description of all the variables in a particular disorder serves to map out the approaches that would be necessary for treatment and for effective intervention. Tic activity, as both a class of symptoms and a unique disorder, has been responsive to this integrated approach. Cognitive and behavioral intervention following comprehensive behavioral assessment would include use of the specific techniques described earlier and would treat the child rather than the problem itself. Such an approach would provide a practical and effective mechanism for actual intervention in tic disorders.

REFERENCES

American Psychiatric Association. (1987). Diagnostic and statistical manual of mental disorders (3rd ed., rev.) (DSM-III-R). Washington, DC: Author.

American Psychiatric Association. (1993). DSM-IV draft criteria. Washington, DC: Author.

Azrin, N. H., & Nunn, R. G. (1973). Habit-reversal: A method of eliminating nervous habits and tics. *Behaviour Research and Therapy, 11*, 619–628.

Azrin, N. H., Nunn, R. G., & Frantz, S. E. (1980). Habit reversal vs. negative practice treatment of nervous tics. *Behavior Therapy, 11*, 169–178.

Barrett, B. H. (1962). Reduction in rate of multiple tics by free operant conditioning methods. *Journal of Nervous and Mental Disease, 135*, 187–195.

Bronheim, S. (1991). An educator's guide to Tourette's syndrome. *Journal of Learning Disabilities, 24*, 17–22.

Brunn, R. D. (1984). Gilles de la Tourette's syndrome: An overview of clinical experience. *Journal of the American Academy of Child Psychiatry, 23*, 126–133.

Caine, E. D., Margolin, D. I., Brown, G. L., & Ebert, M. H. (1978). Gilles de la Tourette syndrome, tardive dyskinesia, and psychosis in an adolescent. *American Journal of Psychiatry, 135*, 241–243.

Fahn, S. (1982). The clinical spectrum of motor tics. *Advances in Neurology, 35*, 314–344.

Ferre, R. C. (1982). Tourette's disorder and the use of clonidine. *Journal of the American Academy of Child Psychiatry, 21*, 294–297.

Fuata, P., & Griffiths, R. A. (1982). Cognitive behavioral treatment of a vocal tic. *Behavior Change, 9*, 14–18.

Golden, G. S. (1982). Movement disorders in children: Tourette syndrome. *Journal of Developmental and Behavioral Pediatrics, 3*, 209–216.

Gross, A. M., & Mendelson, A. N. (1982). Elimination of an eye-blink tic using self-administered overcorrection. *Behavioral Engineering, 8*, 1–4.

Gualtieri, C. T., & Patterson, D. R. (1986). Neuroleptic-induced tics in two hyperactive children. *American Journal of Psychiatry, 143*, 1176–1177.

Keat, D. B. (1972). Broad-spectrum behavior therapy with children: A case presentation. *Behavior Therapy, 3,* 454–459.

Kivalo, A. (1979). An evaluation and follow-up study of children with tics. *Psychiatric Anniki,* 59–63.

Kurlan, R. (1989). Tourette's syndrome: Current concepts. *Neurology, 39,* 1625–1630.

Lerer, R. J. (1987). Motor tics, Tourette syndrome and learning disabilities. *Journal of Learning Disabilities, 20,* 266–267.

Mansdorf, I. J. (1986). Assertiveness training in the treatment of a child's tics. *Journal of Behavior Therapy and Experimental Psychiatry, 17,* 29–32.

Mansdorf, I. J., & Friedman, S. (1980). Sensory feedback training to eliminate eye tics: A study in self-control. *The Behavior Therapist, 3,* 23–24.

Meichenbaum, D. E., & Goodman, J. (1971). Training impulsive children to talk to themselves: A means of developing self-control. *Journal of Abnormal Psychology, 77,* 115–126.

Miller, A. L. (1970). Treatment of a child with Gilles de la Tourette's syndrome using behavior modification techniques. *Journal of Behavior Therapy and Experimental Psychiatry, 1,* 319–321.

Nee, L. E., Polinsky, R. J., & Ebert, M. H. (1982). Tourette syndrome: Clinical and family studies. *Advances in Neurology, 35,* 291–295.

O'Brien, J. S., & Brennan, J. H. (1979). The elimination of a severe long term facial tic and vocal distortion with multi-facet behavior therapy. *Journal of Behavior Therapy and Experimental Psychiatry, 10,* 257–261.

Ollendick, T. H. (1981). Self-monitoring and self-administered overcorrection: The modification of nervous tics in children. *Behavior Modification, 5,* 75–84.

Ostfeld, B. M., (1988). Psychological interventions in Gilles de la Tourette's syndrome. *Psychiatric Annals, 18,* 417–420.

Poth, R., & Barnett, D. W. (1983). Reduction of a behavioral tic with a preschooler using relaxation and self-control techniques across settings. *School Psychology Review, 12,* 472–476.

Pray, B., Kramer, J. J., & Lindskog, R. (1986). Assessment and treatment of tic behavior: A review and case study. *School Psychology Review, 15,* 418–429.

Rafi, A. A. (1962). Learning theory and the treatment of tics. *Journal of Psychosomatic Research. 6,* 71–76.

Schulman, M. (1974). Control of tics by maternal reinforcement. *Journal of Behavior Therapy and Experimental Psychiatry, 5,* 95–96.

Shapiro, A. K., & Shapiro, E. (1982). Tourette syndrome: History and present status. *Advances in Neurology, 35,* 17–23.

Teichman, Y., & Eliahu, D. (1986). A combination of structural family therapy and behavior techniques in treating a patient with two tics. *Journal of Clinical Child Psychology, 15,* 311–316.

Walton, D. (1961). Experimental psychology and the treatment of a ticquer. *Journal of Child Psychology and Psychiatry, 2,* 148–155.

Weingarten, K. (1968). Tics. In R. J. Vinker & G. W. Bruyn (Eds.), *Handbook of clinical neurology: Vol. 6. Diseases of the basal ganglia* (pp. 782–808). New York: Wiley.

Wilson, S. A. K. (1955). *Neurology.* Vol. 3. London: Butterworth.

Yates, A. J. (1958). The application of learning theory to the treatment of tics. *Journal of Abnormal and Social Psychology, 56,* 175–182.

Zikis, P. (1983). Habit reversal treatment of a 10-year-old school boy with severe tics. *The Behavior Therapist, 6,* 50–51.

CHAPTER 17

Elimination Disorders

MICHAEL W. MELLON AND ARTHUR C. HOUTS

This chapter presents a biobehavioral perspective on the assessment and treatment of functional childhood enuresis and encopresis. Although both of these elimination disorders have traditionally been treated by medical professionals, psychologists have developed and tested intervention strategies that show considerable promise. Assessment and treatment of functional elimination disorders is one of the most promising areas of behavioral medicine and health psychology because true collaboration between psychologists and physicians is required to achieve the best results for care of children with these disorders. Throughout this chapter, we emphasize the theme of collaboration between psychology and medicine as a necessity for understanding how to conceptualize the problems of functional enuresis and encopresis. We believe that future advances in the assessment and treatment of functional elimination disorders will be made by interdisciplinary teams comprised of professionals who know how to relate the physiological mechanisms of these disorders to the larger context of social learning and child development.

The chapter is organized in accord with the theme of this volume. For each disorder we (a) provide a description of the problem and epidemiological information, (b) present what we consider to be an ideal or prototypic assessment, (c) discuss problems associated with implementation of an ideal assessment, (d) present evidence for what should be considered an ideal or prototypic treatment course, and (e) discuss what may be done when problems arise with implementation of prototypic treatment. For nocturnal enuresis, the case is made that ample research evidence is now in hand to recommend some type of urine alarm treatment. We offer some practical suggestions about our approach to urine alarm treatment, which is known as Full Spectrum Training. For functional encopresis, the research evidence is not adequate to make comparably strong recommendations about treatment. We offer broad suggestions about the treatment of encopresis and note some of the problems frequently encountered.

DESCRIPTION OF THE PROBLEM: NOCTURNAL ENURESIS

Enuresis is a general term that refers to accidental or uncontrolled wetting. Current diagnostic criteria set an age of 5 years old as a cutoff for formal diagnosis (American Psychiatric Association, 1987). *Diurnal enuresis* refers to daytime wetting, and *nocturnal enuresis* refers to nighttime bed-wetting. Children who wet during the daytime, regardless of whether or not they also wet at night, have significantly more medical problems than

---

Partial support for this research was provided by a Centers of Excellence grant from the State of Tennessee to the Department of Psychology at Memphis State University and also by a National Institutes of Health grant R01 HD21736 to Arthur C. Houts.

do children who simply wet at night (Arnold & Ginsberg, 1973; Schmitt, 1982a). Children who present with daytime wetting will most likely need extensive medical evaluation and will benefit from drug treatments for urinary tract infection or from antispasmodic medications that reduce spontaneous bladder contractions. The focus of this section of this chapter is nocturnal enuresis without daytime wetting.

Although epidemiological estimates of prevalence vary (see review by De Jonge, 1973), even the most conservative estimates indicate that about 7% of all 8-year-old children wet their beds (Essen & Peckham, 1976; Fergusson, Horwood, & Shannon, 1986; Jarvelin, Vikevainen-Tervonen, Moilanen, & Huttunen, 1988; Verhulst et al., 1985). A majority of that 7% wet the bed every night of the week. Less than 10% of these children have any organic complications of the urinary tract (American Academy of Pediatrics Committee on Radiology, 1980; Jarvelin, Huttunen, Seppanen, Seppanen, & Moilanen, 1990; Kass, 1991; Redman & Siebert, 1979; Rushton, 1989; Stansfeld, 1973), so most are called *functional enuretics*. Bed-wetting runs in families, and enuretic children show signs of delayed maturation of the nervous system (Jarvelin, 1989: Jarvelin, Moilanen, Kangas, et al., 1991). Approximately 80% of these children are called *primary enuretics* because they have never attained at least 6 months of continuous nighttime continence. *Secondary*, or onset, *enuresis* characterizes a minority of these children and has been associated with delayed acquisition of initial nighttime continence, as well as a higher incidence of stressful life events (Fergusson, Horwood, & Shannon, 1990; Jarvelin, Moilanen, Vikevainen-Tervonen, & Huttunen, 1990). Up to the age of 11 years, more than twice as many males as females suffer from enuresis.

The publication of the DSM-IV by the American Psychiatric Association brings about minor changes to the current definition and classification of enuresis. Specifically, the criteria necessary for wetting episodes to be considered clinically significant are that they occur with either a frequency of twice a week for at least 3 consecutive months or that the presence of wetting episodes produces considerable distress or impairment in social, academic (occupational), or other important areas of the child's functioning (American Psychiatric Association, 1993). Further, the *primary* versus *secondary* distinction has been dropped from the criteria. The utility of removing this traditional distinction remains to be empirically supported.

Epidemiological surveys indicate that the prevalence of enuresis declines with age. This decline has contributed to a belief among some professionals and parents that bed-wetting is a problem children will simply outgrow (e.g. Burke & Stickler, 1980; Novello & Novello, 1987; see also surveys by Haque et al., 1981; Shelov et al., 1981.) Although most children do eventually stop bed-wetting, cessation without treatment can take several years. Forsythe and Redmond (1974), for example, found that only 15% of 8-year-old children stop bed-wetting in any year if they are not treated and that the annual rate of remission among adolescents is only 16%. Moreover, as many as 3% of young adults may continue bed-wetting (Forsythe & Redmond, 1974; Levine, 1943; Thorne, 1944).

Considering the social stigma and disruption to family life involved, it is not surprising that continued bed-wetting has been associated with problems of emotional and social adjustment among enuretic children (Essen & Peckham, 1976; Kaffman & Elizur, 1977; Rutter, Yule, & Graham, 1973; Stromgren & Thomsen, 1990). In fact experimental studies have demonstrated that enuretic children treated for bed-wetting improve more than untreated controls on measures of self-concept and peer relations (Baker, 1969; Lovibond, 1964; Moffatt, Kato, & Pless, 1987).

Although a variety of etiological hypotheses for bed-wetting can be found in the literature, none have proven to be adequate to explain the problem. At the present time, the two leading etiological hypotheses are (a) deficiency in nocturnal secretion of anti-diuretic hormone and (b) deficiency of muscular responses needed to inhibit urination during sleep (see review by Houts, 1991). The problem of enuresis is clearly a physical problem with behavioral and psychological consequences. However, to say that enuresis is a physical problem does not necessarily imply that effective treatment consists of pharmacological interventions. In fact, the most effective treatment for bed-wetting is some form of the urine alarm (see review by Houts, Berman, & Abramson, 1993). As with other physical problems such as headache, obesity, and diabetes, the problem of enuresis is best conceptualized as a biobehavioral problem in which changes of behavior brought about by application of learning and conditioning principles may alter the physiological mechanisms that cause or maintain the problem.

PROTOTYPIC ASSESSMENT: NOCTURNAL ENURESIS

A medical screening and an in-depth clinical interview are important to determine if a child can be treated with the urine alarm or if pharmacotherapy is needed. Ongoing assessment is needed to maintain treatment gains and to make rational decisions about alternative approaches if the first treatment fails. In the following sections is presented an overview of the ideal research-based assessment that should be conducted. Following this protypic assessment are presented some practical points about what may be done when such ideals cannot be met.

Medical Screening

Because a small percentage of nocturnal enuretics suffer from organic pathologies that can promote or prolong the problem, all children presenting for urinary incontinence need to have a basic physical exam that includes a urinalysis and, ideally, a sonogram of the bladder and kidneys. In about 3% to 5% of cases, poor bladder control that results in both daytime and nighttime wetting is caused by diseases like nephritis and diabetes. Such diseases cause incomplete processing of urine and result in excessive urination or polyuria. Careful questioning about excessive fluid intake, dramatic changes in weight, and family history of diabetes or kidney problems can help determine if more extensive tests are needed.

At a minimum, all children with wetting problems need a basic urinalysis. Examination of the urine and reliable urine cultures can be performed quickly and inexpensively in outpatient settings. As many as 5% of boys and 10% of girls who wet the bed have urinary tract infections (Stansfeld, 1973). Symptoms can include a painful burning sensation when the child urinates and periodic unexplained fevers. Unfortunately, a child can have a urinary tract infection without any obvious symptom. If left untreated, urinary tract infections can cause progressive renal damage and reduce functional bladder capacity, which can make bed-wetting more difficult to treat. Most urinary tract infections can be treated successfully with 7 to 10 days of antibiotic therapy (Margileth, Pedreira, Hirschman, & Coleman, 1976). Among the small number of bed-wetting children who have urinary tract infections, roughly 40% of those treated stop wetting the bed when the infection is cleared (Schmitt, 1982b). In most cases, however, urinary tract infections are more likely a result, rather than a cause, of enuresis (Shaffer, 1985), and the bed-wetting will still have to be treated once the infection has been eliminated.

The availability of outpatient ultrasonography has made it unnecessary to perform routine invasive medical examinations such as cystoscopy and intravenous pyelogram. Previous research with such invasive procedures typically produced diagnostic yields as low as 2% to 5% among monosymptomatic bed-wetters. In the absence of significant warning signs such as a history of disease, daytime wetting, and current signs of infection, medical researchers generally agree that bed-wetting alone does not warrant the routine use of these invasive examinations (American Academy of Pediatrics Committee on Radiology, 1980). Some researchers have been using noninvasive medical procedures like uroflowmetric studies (Toguri, Uchida, & Bee, 1982) and renal sonography (Poston, Joseph, & Riddle, 1983) to identify those children who may have medical problems associated with simple bed-wetting. From a practical standpoint of ruling out structural abnormalities, bladder and renal ultrasound examination should be considered a necessary precaution before commencing treatment for bed-wetting.

In the rare cases where ultrasound exams identify physical defects, complete urological examinations including invasive procedures need to be conducted. Physical defects such as urinary tract obstructions or lesions are found primarily in children with diurnal symptoms or infections. Children who have demonstrable organic pathologies, such as meatal stenosis or urethral stricture, are generally treated surgically. In most cases, however, surgical treatments to correct structural abnormalities do not correct concomitant bed-wetting (Arnold & Ginsberg, 1973).

Clinical Interview

If a child's bed-wetting is not accompanied by medical problems, the treatment of choice is typically some version of urine alarm treatment. Such treatments require a substantial investment of time and energy from the whole family. An in-depth clinical interview with the parents and the child is essential to determine if a family can implement such a demanding procedure. Of primary importance is the assessment of factors that may predict treatment outcome as well as maintenance of treatment gains for those who cease bed-wetting. Information should be gathered about the history of enuresis and previous treatment, parental attitudes and beliefs, family and home environment, behavioral problems, and the child's current wetting pattern.

By taking a thorough history, the type of enuresis can be determined. If a child has started bed-wetting after an extended period of continence (6 months to 1 year), medical or emotional factors may be involved. Parents of secondary enuretics should be questioned about any kind of distress that may have coincided with the onset of wetting. Especially for secondary enuretics, it may be necessary to focus attention on minimizing current stressful events before implementing treatment for bed-wetting.

Behavioral, pharmacological, or even surgical interventions provided by health care practitioners may have been tried with limited or no success. Parents need to be questioned about what methods were tried and with what results. It is important to reach some mutual understanding about why these methods may have failed to correct the problem. Often, previous failure with the urine alarm is due to the fact that parents were not properly instructed to awaken the child, and they did not understand that treatment can take up to 16 weeks before it is effective. In such cases, frequent contact with the family and careful monitoring during treatment can prevent repeating a disappointing experience. Previous drug treatment failures are the norm rather than the exception, and parents can be reassured that their child's continued bed-wetting is not due to some failure of parenting.

Parents' attitudes and beliefs about bed-wetting are important. In a survey of parents of 346 enuretics, Haque et al. (1981) showed that 35% of those surveyed dealt with bed-wetting by punishing the child for wet nights. Clearly, some parents view bed-wetting as a problem that the child should be able to control. Butler, Brewin, and Forsythe (1986) found that a greater perceived burden on the mother and attribution of the cause of enuresis to the child were associated with greater parental intolerance as assessed by Morgan and Young's (1975) Tolerance for Enuresis Scale. These findings are important in view of the fact that high scores on this scale (indicative of intolerance) have predicted treatment dropout. Getting parents to view the child's problem as a deficit of physical learning rather than a willful act or the result of laziness can promote the needed supportive family environment to begin behavioral treatment. With some families, correcting false beliefs, modifying negative attitudes, and eliminating punishment for bed-wetting may be necessary before commencing behavioral treatment.

A child who wets the bed is likely to have parents or siblings who were themselves enuretic. Young and Morgan (1973) reported a relationship between treatment dropout and positive family history of enuresis, and Fielding and Doleys (1989) have suggested that these findings may be indicative of complacency or poor motivation in these families. Parents and children need to understand how difficult it can be for everyone to implement behavioral treatment with a urine alarm. Since the treatment can be easily disrupted by noncooperation within the family, it is important to assess the child's and parents' motivation. The authors' behavioral-contracting approach requires parents and child to sign explicit agreements of cooperation between themselves, and if they cannot honestly do that, treatment does not proceed.

A global assessment of stress, family disturbance, and the physical home environment is important. Although family stresses may not cause bed-wetting, parents of children who seek help for enuresis are likely to experience more stress than those who do not seek treatment (Couchells, Johnson, Carter, & Walker, 1981). Morgan and Young (1975) reported that family disturbances and high levels of maternal anxiety characterized their group of slow responders. Dische, Youle, Corbett, and Hand (1983) noted that family distress and discord were significant predictors of treatment failure and relapse. Relevant problem areas included marital discord, mental or physical handicap of family members, poor maternal coping skills, and unusual family living arrangements. Single parents often need therapeutic and social support to implement behavioral treatment. Easy access to a bathroom and private bedroom for the enuretic child are essential for successful treatment.

Because some research has suggested that children with behavior problems are more likely to experience relapse after successful treatment (Dische et al., 1983; Sacks & De Leon, 1973), a careful assessment that includes parent and teacher self-report measures can identify children who need additional attention. In cases of extreme noncompliant behavior, treatment for bed-wetting may need to be postponed until parents first learn to manage oppositional behavior and noncompliance. Noncompliant children and children who are forced into treatment by their parents have the worst prognosis for remaining in urine alarm treatment.

A 2-week baseline of wetting frequency should be established. Parents can keep record forms that include columns for wet nights and dry nights, the size of the wet spot, and whether or not the child spontaneously awakened to go to the bathroom. As a rule, the more frequently a child wets, the longer it will take for the child to cease bed-wetting (Hallgren, 1957). In this regard, it is important to determine if a child is a multiple wetter, that is, wets more than once per night. Accurate assessment of this may have to wait until the child uses a urine alarm for 1 week. Multiple wetters typically take longer to reach a criterion of 14 consecutive dry nights. Parents of multiple wetters need to be given realistic expectations about their child's progress to avoid discouragement and possible dropout from treatment.

ACTUAL ASSESSMENT: NOCTURNAL ENURESIS

It is not always possible to carry out all the elements of the assessment one would ideally like to have for any given case. The following sections follow those aforementioned elements but present what may go wrong with assessment and what may be done to correct these problems.

Medical Screening Pitfalls

In the absence of daytime wetting, the probability that a bed-wetting child has any significant medical complications of enuresis is rather low. Nevertheless, the probability is not zero, and failure to conduct the minimal screening of a physical exam and a urinalysis may be considered failure to meet accepted standards of care. Urinalysis conducted within 2 weeks of starting a treatment regimen is simply required and cannot be overlooked. If parents make arrangements to get a urinalysis but fail to make the appointment, treatment should be postponed until the test is completed.

In the ideal setting, children should receive a renal and bladder ultrasound to rule out any structural abnormalities related to enuresis. Once again, the probability of such structural abnormalities is less than 5% if a child is otherwise symptom free, but standards of care in medicine may require this level of examination. The cost of ultrasound examination may be prohibitive in some areas. In such situations, it is possible to proceed with urine alarm treatment on the assumption that there is a 95% chance or greater that a monosymptomatic bed-wetter has no structural anomalies. For legal reasons, it is probably advisable to obtain a release from the parents to proceed without ultrasound examination because regional standards of care may vary.

Problems in Psychological and Behavioral Assessment

To assess those variables that have been previously related to the course of treatment with a urine alarm, it is preferable to use some standardized assessment questionnaires along with a clinical interview. Such questionnaires have sometimes been viewed as a substitute for clinical judgment when responses to them have been accurately predictive of treatment outcome. Although the authors strongly favor this actuarial approach to such decisions (as opposed to the clinical judgment), the current state of knowledge does not permit the kind of prediction that is needed. Thus, in using questionnaires to supplement a clinical interview, an attempt is being made to conduct the clinical interview more efficiently.

As a screening questionnaire to assess child-noncompliance problems that may interfere with full implementation of behavioral treatment with a urine alarm, the Child Behavior Checklist (CBCL) (Achenbach & Edelbrook, 1983) has been found useful. If one or both parents indicate that they view their child as having significant problems of externalizing behaviors (Externalizing T score greater than 70), then this needs to be followed up in the interview. Children who are generally noncompliant with parental requests are likely to be noncompliant with the demands of behavioral treatment, especially the demand for the child to awaken to the urine alarm rather than to disconnect the alarm and go back to sleep. A decision has to be made whether to train parents in contingency management before commencing behavioral treatment for enuresis. Failure to assess noncompliance can result in the family making a significant emotional investment in carrying out the treatment only to discover that the treatment cannot be implemented. Such a failure experience is likely to add to the child's already diminished sense of confidence and self-efficacy that is typically associated with bed-wetting.

Failure to assess family distress can also lead to preventable negative outcomes for parents and children. As a screening measure of family distress, it is useful to have parents complete the Locke-Wallace Marital Adjustment Test (MAT) (Locke & Wallace, 1959). When spouses indicate significant marital distress (MAT scores below 85 for either person), this needs to be addressed further in the clinical interview. Once again, marital or family therapy may need to precede implementation of behavioral treatment for enuresis. Among single parents, typically mothers, the Beck Depression Inventory (BDI) (Beck, Rush, Shaw, & Emery, 1980) is a useful measure of current general distress. Researchers of conduct disorders have reported that mothers' BDI scores predicted dropout from behavioral treatment (McMahon, Forehand, Griest, & Wells, 1981). The authors consider elevations on the BDI (scores above 15) to be indicative of parental distress that may need therapeutic attention prior to engaging in behavior therapy for bed-wetting.

PROTOTYPIC TREATMENT: NOCTURNAL ENURESIS

A quantitative analysis of treatments indicates clearly that some form of urine alarm treatment is the treatment of choice for medically uncomplicated bed-wetting (see review by Houts, Berman, & Abramson, 1993). The authors' preference is for multicomponent treatments that address the problems of speed of response and relapse in standard urine alarm treatment by adding other behavioral procedures to the basic urine alarm approach. For the past 12 years, the authors' research group has developed and modified one such treatment, Full Spectrum Treatment.

Full Spectrum Treatment (FST) was designed to provide parents and children with an inexpensive, easy-to-use, and effective treatment for primary nocturnal enuresis. The components of the treatment are (a) basic urine alarm treatment, (b) cleanliness training, (c) retention control training, and (d) overlearning. For *basic urine alarm treatment*, children are instructed to follow the rule of getting out of bed and standing up before turning off the urine alarm. Parents are told never to turn off the alarm for the child. The newer urine alarm devices (e.g., Palco Wet Stop) that are worn on the body have been found to be more reliable than the older devices that required use of a bedpad and free-standing alarm box. Most of these newer alarm devices are turned off by removing from the underwear and drying the urine sensitive probe that acts as switch when urine contacts it.

The steps involved in *cleanliness training* are displayed on a wall chart ("Daily Steps to A Dry Bed") that is placed in the child's room. The chart also displays a record of the child's progress and is marked by the child as either *wet* or *dry* for each night of the training. In order to make sure that the child is fully awake after a wetting episode, parents are instructed to have the child go through with the full procedure of remaking the bed even if the sheets are not wet. Newer alarm devices make it possible for children to trigger the alarm before getting the bed completely wet. This is, in fact, a sign of progress when a child wets only the underwear and stops urinating before getting the bed wet.

Retention control training is done once a day, and the child is given money for holding, or postponing urination, for increasing amounts of time in a step-by-step fashion up to a 45-minute holding time. This practice in holding is a useful adjunctive procedure because it speeds the acquisition of the inhibitory response believed to be conditioned by the urine alarm procedure (Houts, Peterson, & Whelan, 1986).

Although procedures such as intermittent alarm schedules have been shown to reduce relapse from basic urine alarm treatment (Finley, Rainwater, & Johnson, 1982), FST uses the simpler procedure of *overlearning* (Young & Morgan, 1972) to prevent relapse. The authors initially implemented overlearning by having the child drink 16 ounces of water during the hour before bedtime once the child had attained 14 consecutive dry nights in the treatment program (Houts, Liebert, and Padawer, 1983). In the initial field trial, this nightly drinking continued until the child attained 14 more consecutive dry nights while drinking water.

Whereas this initial way of implementing overlearning consistently resulted in reducing relapse by 50% compared to basic urine alarm treatment without overlearning, it was also noted that some children who failed to achieve 14 more consecutive dry nights in overlearning also failed to recover from the relapse induced by overlearning (Houts, Peterson, & Whelan, 1986). Recently, better success has been achieved with a *modified form of overlearning*, in which the amount of water that a child drinks is gradually increased rather than having all children drink a very large amount of water. The first step in this gradual approach to overlearning is to determine the maximum amount of water for a child to drink. This is done by a formula: 1 ounce for each year of age plus 2 ounces (Berger, Maizels, Moran, Conway, & Firlit, 1983). Thus, for an 8-year-old child, the maximum amount would be 8 plus 2, or 10 ounces. Children then begin the overlearning process by drinking 4 ounces of water 15 minutes before bedtime. If they remain dry for two nights while drinking 4 ounces, then amount increases by 2 ounces to 6 ounces. If they remain dry for two nights at 6 ounces, then the water is increased to 8 ounces. The water increases continue in this fashion, 2 ounces more for every 2 consecutive dry nights, until the child's maximum amount is reached. If at any point the child wets, the child drinks the same amount of water consumed on the previous dry night until the child is dry for five nights in a row. The amount increases in 2-ounce increments until the maximum amount is reached. Overlearning stops when the child attains a criterion of 14 consecutive dry nights under conditions of drinking before bedtime. The results from this modified overlearning suggest that the rate of relapse can be reduced up to yet another 50%, making the average relapse from FST between 10% and 15% rather than the typical 41% observed in urine alarm treatment without any adjunctive procedures.

The authors have experimented with delivering FST by didactic videotape (Houts, Whelan, & Peterson, 1987) and with adding other procedures, such as nightly waking procedure, to the FST package (Whelan & Houts, 1990). They have not been able to improve upon the overall effectiveness of FST. Overall, the complete FST is effective for about 7 out of every 10 cases. That makes the treatment very good, but not perfect. Most of the problems with FST are problems of achieving full implementation in the home by parents and children. Some of these problems and possible solutions to them are presented in the next section.

ACTUAL TREATMENT: NOCTURNAL ENURESIS

As was noted with the assessment of nocturnal enuresis, so too there are some important problems that can arise with treatment. The two most important difficulties with implementing FST are problems in waking the child and problems in the delayed response of some children, each of which can lead to frustration and termination of treatment before the child becomes continent.

Waking Problems

Urine alarm treatments such as FST will only work if a child is systematically awakened immediately after a wetting episode begins. Although numerous studies have failed to find a reliable relationship between depth of sleep (as measured by electroencephalography) and wetting episodes; the authors have found that some children are more difficult to arouse than others. Some of the most difficult cases are those where a child fails to wake up to the sound of the urine alarm. In these cases, it is crucial to establish a waking routine early in the treatment. This requires having the child get out of bed and get to his or her feet before disconnecting and turning off the urine alarm. With younger children who are especially difficult to arouse, it may be necessary for one parent to sleep in the child's room in order to ensure that the child is awakened immediately when the alarm sounds.

It is also important to make sure that the child is fully awake. Children can do rather remarkable things in a sleep-walking state. It has been found useful to check the child's mental alertness by asking the child to perform short-term memory tasks such as repeating the home phone number backwards. Families also find it useful to establish a wake-up password that is decided on just before the child goes to bed. If the alarm sounds, the child is asked to repeat the password as a test to see if the child is fully awake.

If after 2 weeks of assistance a child is still not waking to the urine alarm, it is useful to implement a waking schedule (Azrin, Sneed, & Foxx, 1974) to disrupt the child's sleep pattern. Parents are instructed to wake the child hourly using minimal prompts throughout the first night. At each awakening, the child is praised for a dry bed and encouraged to void in the toilet. The second night, the child is awakened only once, 3 hours after falling asleep. From the second night forward, the waking schedule continues with the child being awakened once each night. Following a dry night, the parents wake the child 30 minutes earlier than the previous night. If the child wets during the night, then the time of waking remains the same as the previous night. The nightly waking ends when the scheduled time for waking the child has moved forward to within 30 minutes immediately following bedtime. This procedure is very demanding for the whole family and should be used only if absolutely necessary to train a child to awaken to the alarm. It should also be remembered that urine alarm treatments for bed-wetting are not perfect and that between 1 and 2 of every 10 children will fail to cease bed-wetting with this treatment.

Delayed Response Problems

In FST, the first goal is for the child to attain 14 consecutive dry nights. Overlearning is then started, and the child completes the treatment when 14 additional consecutive dry nights are attained while drinking water before bedtime. Most children reach the first goal within 8 weeks of treatment, and they take an average additional 4 weeks to complete overlearning. Some children will not attain the first 14 consecutive dry nights even after

12 weeks of treatment, and their delayed response is often frustrating to them and to their parents.

One way to deal with the problems of delayed response is to keep parents and children focused on the progress that is being made. This requires regular follow-up and supportive therapy sessions with a family. Even though children may not attain 14 consecutive dry nights in the first 8 weeks of treatment, they almost always show evidence of progress. Signs of progress include (a) a reduction in the number of nights that the child needed adult assistance to awaken, (b) a reduction to wetting once per night among children who started out wetting two or three times each night, (c) a reduction in wetting frequency, (d) a reduction in the size of the wet spot, and (e) an increase in the interval between bedtime and the first wetting episode.

Children who are multiple wetters are especially likely to be delayed responders. These children may also be good candidates for combined behavorial and pharmacotherapy. To date, the research on combined treatments is very sparse. More research is needed to test the efficacy of such combinations, especially with difficult cases such as multiple wetters. At present, only two investigations have considered such combinations, and both report positive findings. Philpott and Flasher (1970) initially intended to compare imipramine with basic urine alarm treatment but decided that, if the urine alarm was not producing a satisfactory result, imipramine would be added. Thus, 27 boys and 6 girls received this combination treatment. Of those children, 21 boys and 4 girls experienced some positive change, and those authors concluded that the addition of imipramine to the urine alarm enhanced the therapeutic effect. In the second investigation, Sukhai, Mol, and Harris (1989) compared the combination of the urine alarm and desmopressin (DDAVP)to the alarm and a placebo pill. The combined treatment was more effective than the alarm with placebo in terms of increasing the number of dry nights during treatment. Neither of these studies provided long-term follow-up, and, as is typical of outcome studies of pharmacological treatments for enuresis, outcome was reported in average reductions of wet nights rather than the percentage of children who ceased bed-wetting. Nevertheless, they both pointed to the potential usefulness of combining the immediate effects of pharmacological agents with the more lasting effects of multicomponent behavioral treatments. Combining FST with DDAVP for multiple wetters may reduce the frustration of parents and children who would otherwise be delayed in reaching success criteria. How and at what point to withdraw the pharmacotherapy are questions that need to be answered by future research.

DESCRIPTION OF THE PROBLEM: FUNCTIONAL ENCOPRESIS

Childhood encopresis is but one variety of fecal incontinence in children and is considered a distinct disorder because of its functional aspects. The authors believe that functional encopresis, like enuresis, is a biobehavioral problem. According to this view, inasmuch as behavior can be determined by biological constraints, these biological constraints may themselves be altered when behavior change is brought about by social learning based treatments. Therefore, the prototypic care of the child with functional encopresis should include a multidisciplinary and multimethod approach. This section of the chapter describes the problem and highlights the relevant literature on encopresis as it pertains to prototypical versus actual assessment and treatment.

The most widely accepted definition of functional childhood encopresis is ". . . the repeated involuntary (or, more rarely, intentional) passage of feces into places not appropriate for that purpose (e.g., clothing or floor) . . . occurring at least once a month for at least six months; the chronologic and mental age of the child must be at least four years, and physical disorders that can cause fecal incontinence, such as aganglionic megacolon, must be ruled out" (American Psychiatric Association, 1987, p. 82). To avoid excluding children in need of treatment, Houts and Abramson (1990) have recommended a broader definition that lowers the age to 3 years old and includes only soiling that occurs with a regularity sufficient to result in moderately negative social and emotional consequences for the child. The negative emotional consequences of withholding treatment (Landman, Rappaport, Fenton, & Levine, 1986) and current social pressures to toilet train at an earlier age (e.g., the demands of day-care centers) are also reasons to favor a lower age limit.

Classification

Traditionally considered a medical condition, the many classification systems that have been proposed for encopresis have been consistent with the medical model of taxonomically describing problems. In terms of implications for treatment, two distinctions are quite useful. The first has been referred to as *primary* versus *secondary* encopresis (Easson, 1960) or *continuous* versus *discontinuous* encopresis (Anthony, 1957), and it distinguishes children who have never achieved bowel control from those who have at one time attained continence. The second distinction is between children whose soiling is accompanied by constipation compared to those who soil without retention of feces. Labels for this difference include *retentive* versus *nonretentive* encopresis Gavanski, (1971) and soiling in the presence of *bowel control* versus soiling in the *absence of bowel control* (Hersov, 1977).

Similar to enuresis, the American Psychiatric Association (1993) has made minor changes to the definition and classification of encopresis in the upcoming DSM-IV. These changes include reducing the duration of the soiling (at least once a month) from 6 months to 3 months and the removal of the *primary* versus *secondary* distinction. The latter change reflects the treatment utility of the *retentive* versus *nonretentive* distinction by specifying fecal soiling associated *with* constipation and overflow incontinence versus soiling *without* constipation and overflow incontinence.

Boon and Singh (1991) have proposed a parsimonious model of classification that attempts to combine the aforementioned distinctions in an effort to match specific treatment protocols to the type of encopretic child. The *retentive* encopretic has the primary symptom of constipation (often chronic by history) with fecal impaction of the colon, periodic reports of abdominal pain, the painful passage of large diameter stool, and frequent daily accidents. Boon and Singh further divide the nonretentive encopretic into the *primary-nonretentive* and the *secondary-nonretentive*. Both the primary and secondary nonretentive encopretic have one to two accidents per day with normal stool size and consistency. However, the primary nonretentive encopretic child is alleged to have not been adequately toilet trained and has been incontinent for more than 1 year, whereas the secondary nonretentive encopretic possesses basic toileting skills and has demonstrated a period of fecal continence of greater than 1 year.

Epidemiology

Estimates of the incidence of nonorganically based childhood encopresis have been quite variable and range from 0.5% to 10.0% with most figures ranging between 2% and 3%.

This variability is related to the contention that estimates from clinic-referred populations tend to be higher than those from nonreferred samples. Incidence is higher in males, with male/female estimates ranging from 6:1 (Levine, 1982) to 2:1 (Bellman, 1966).

Most investigators agree that the incidence of encopresis tends to diminish with age. Bellman (1966), for example, reported a sharp decline in incidence from 8.1% to 2.8% between the ages of 3 and 4 years old. Consistent with Bellman's findings, Rutter, Tizzard, and Whitmore (1970) have noted that the incidence of encopresis gradually levels off to approximately 0.75% between ages 10 and 12 years old. As might be expected from gender differences, incidence levels off to 0.3% for girls and to 1.2% for boys. Such figures suggest that most children will eventually outgrow soiling.

Regarding taxonomic distinctions, greater than 75% of these children are retentive as opposed to nonretentive, and 40% are continuous as opposed to noncontinuous soilers (Levine, 1975). The distinction between retentive and nonretentive encopresis is probably the most useful in terms of treatment implications as well as etiology of soiling.

Physiology and Etiology

For an in-depth account of normal bowel function and physiology, the reader is referred to Whitehead and Schuster (1985). For present purposes, it is important to understand that normal bowel function involves a complex interaction between physiology and learned motor responses. In the case of functional encopresis, in which, by definition, there is normal anatomy and physiology, physiological *function* may be disrupted due to nonorganic causes.

There are several redundant physiological mechanisms that contribute to continence, and their interaction involves a complex balance between expulsive and retentive forces. No single physiological mechanism is both necessary or sufficient for continence. Mass peristalsis, which occurs approximately twice daily, moves fecal material from the transverse or descending colon to the sigmoid colon and finally to the rectum. How quickly and rapidly fecal material enters the rectum is determined by the motility of the descending colon and sigmoid colon. At the extremes, increased numbers, durations, and intensities of contractions contribute to diarrhea, whereas less activity contributes to constipation.

The rectum, being quite elastic, stretches in response to filling and acts as a reservoir for feces prior to defecation. Distention of the rectal wall leads to increased peristalsis and reflexive relaxation of the internal anal sphincter for about 25 seconds. When the compliance of the rectum is either abnormally high or low, incontinence may result (De Vroede, 1982). Increased compliance is associated with the occurrence of large hard fecal masses that can be difficult and painful to defecate. Fecal masses that chronically dilate the internal anal sphincter can reduce its protective tone. This may reduce the child's awareness of an impending bowel movement. Such impaction often presents as the passage of liquid fecal material around a hardened mass. Abnormally low rectal compliance leading to incontinence is often related to organic etiology. As stool is pushed toward the distal end of the rectum, it is allowed to pass into the upper end of the anus where it contacts the upper anoderm, which is densely packed with sensory receptors. Passage of feces into this region prompts awareness of the urge to defecate.

The passage of feces during normal defecation changes from an entirely reflexive process to one that is under the control of the child as the rectum becomes full. Under normal conditions, the levator ani muscles contract and push the stool upward to preserve temporary continence as an overlearned response. This is coordinated with voluntary contractions of the pelvic floor and external sphincter, which pull the anus upward and pinch the anal canal (Whitehead, Orr, Engel, & Schuster, 1981). Defecation then occurs through a predetermined sequence of events. Voluntary relaxation of the levators again opens the anal canal to fecal contents and pressure. Pressure in the anal canal is increased through the valsalva maneuver in which thoracic and abdominal muscles are voluntarily contracted when the child's legs are flexed toward the abdomen. Automatic pelvic floor contractions that occur after feces have already passed into the anus force the bolus outward. Simultaneously, the external anal sphincter is relaxed, allowing feces to leave the body.

The voluntary mechanisms of defecation can be disrupted in a number of ways to produce functional encopresis. One way this can happen is if the child's pelvic floor is tightened either voluntarily or reflexively, causing retention of feces in the colon even if the levator ani are relaxed. Because feces cannot reach the anoderm, smooth muscle in the rectum eventually accommodates to tension created by the fecal mass. The urge to defecate and the sense of pelvic fullness eventually pass and may not return for up to 24 hours when mass peristalsis begins again (Doleys, 1983). Pressure created by a continually building fecal mass and loss of the warning of when defecation is imminent eventually result in passage of feces at inappropriate times and places. This can take the form of passage of large stools and overflow soiling. Incontinence without impaction can result when the child fails to exert pressure on the pelvic floor. Under such circumstances the levator ani are prematurely relaxed, allowing for easy passage of fully formed stools. Whereas most etiologic theories agree that these are the physiological events that ultimately produce encopresis, the interaction of physiological and behavioral aspects of the problem provides the best explanation.

Biobehavioral Perspectives

Viewing the etiology of functional encopresis from a biobehavioral perspective appears to be most useful. Unitary medical or learning explanations of the problem fail to acknowledge the importance of the other's impact. Traditional medical theories postulate that soiling results from problems with neurological integrity, anatomical abnormalities, and organically caused malfunction of the physiological mechanisms involved in defecation. These problems are explained as stemming from developmental delay or predisposing physiological, constitutional factors such as family tendency toward the development of constipation. Some of these theories also consider dietary intake to be a precipitating or maintaining factor (Davidson, 1958). Whereas unitary medical theories may at first appear to provide the most parsimonious explanation, they are problematic because they are poorly defined and inconsistent. Moreover, interventions suggested by these theories are, at best, only marginally effective and often do not by themselves lead to resumption of normal toileting (Doleys, 1981).

In general, behavioral theories view the acquisition of bowel control as a muscular-coordination skill that must be learned. However, the teaching process involved in toilet training is slightly different from the process for most skills a child learns. Bowel control cannot be directly taught without the use of sophisticated biofeedback equipment. In children undergoing toilet training, only the prerequisite skills that allow the body to regulate itself can be taught. These include learning to (a) use bodily cues to discriminate when there is a need for defecation, (b) find the appropriate place to go, (c) undress and sit on the toilet, and (d) execute the valsalva maneuver. Reinforcement for this complex chain of behaviors is necessary for acquisition of bowel control. Encopresis results when the sequence of behaviors is disrupted.

Behavioral theories can account for differences that may exist between various subtypes of encopresis. Nonretentive encopresis, for example, has been conceptualized as resulting from faulty learning of prerequisite toileting skills and from the inability of the child to use discriminative cues of rectal distention, contact of feces with the anoderm, and internal anal sphincter relaxation for temporary retention of bowel movements. These deficits in learned muscular coordination and physiological discrimination may be remediated through direct training of appropriate responses. In contrast, retentive encopresis has been viewed as resulting from pain or from fear-arousing events that a child wishes to hold back, thereby escaping immediate aversive consequences. In this way, the retention response becomes habitual and overgeneralized through negative reinforcement. It is as if holding back is functionally autonomous.

Unitary behavioral explanations and their subsequent treatment implications will also prove to be inadequate if they fail to address the often severe and chronic constipation in the encopretic child. In a retrospective, descriptive study of 227 children presenting at their gastroenterology clinic, Partin, Hamill, Fischel, and Partin (1992) documented complaints of difficult defecation, fecal soiling, fecal impaction, and severe withholding behavior. Of the children younger than 36 months, 86% presented with pain, 71% with impaction, and 97% with severe withholding. Of the children older than 36 months ($M = 7.3$ years), 85% were soiling, 57% complained of painful defecation, 73% had fecal impaction, and 96% exhibited withholding; difficult defecation persisted an average of 4.52 years before presentation. Of children who soiled, 63% reported painful defecation beginning before age 36 months. Without the use of bowel cathartics to initially remove a fecal impaction or the use of laxatives or dietary changes to prevent its recurrence, the proper sensory and mechanical functioning of the bowel and sphincters is not likely to be achieved, and soiling will continue.

PROTOTYPIC ASSESSMENT: FUNCTIONAL ENCOPRESIS

Examining encopresis from a functional-analytic perspective that utilizes the S-O-R-C method (Goldfried & Sprafkin, 1974) can provide a comprehensive conceptualization of the problem. The overall goals of this method are to determine for each child, the situation (S) in which the soiling occurs, the relevant characteristics of the organism or encopretic child (O), an exact description of the soiling response (R), and the consequences (C) of soiling that influence its strength and frequency. As is the case with functional enuresis, both medical and psychological assessment are necessary.

Medical Assessment

The principal aims of medical assessment are to identify the organismic (O) and difficult-to-observe response (R) variables influencing the soiling by differentiating organic from functional encopresis, determining what purgatives should be used (how much and how long), and whether dysfunctional defecation dynamics exist. Researchers have noted that an organic cause may be found in from 2% to 15% of children presenting with bowel problems (Liebman, 1979; Schmitt, 1984). Organic problems are more common in retentive than nonretentive encopresis (Schmitt, 1984). Common types of organic syndromes that can result in soiling and need to be ruled out are Hirschsprung's disease (Ravitch, 1958), congenital hypothyroidism, and anorectal anomalies (Hendren, 1978; Leape & Ramenofsky, 1978). Although these disorders present with similar symptomatic behavior, their proper management is quite different from that of functional encopresis.

Most professionals agree that a clinical and medical history and full physical, complete with rectal exam, should be performed to exclude organic involvement and to determine the causes of soiling. Different professionals have emphasized different areas in the history, but all do agree that it should include review of medications that could result in constipation and overflow soiling (Sondheimer, 1985; Suberman, 1976), as well as a description of the frequency and type of accidents. The complete physical has usually included a routine check of all systems, examination of stool for occult blood, and, in the case of females, a urinalysis due to a high incidence (2.72% to 20%) of urinary tract infection caused by soiling and fecal bacterial infiltration (Sondheimer, 1985). At a minimum, the rectal exam involves palpation of the abdomen for fecal masses and examination of the anus for rectal stenosis (Liebman, 1979; Nisley, 1976). In addition, it has been suggested that the exam include checking for the presence of a prominent posterior shelf behind the sphincter, which is indicative of anterior ectopic anus (Leape & Ramenofsky, 1978). It is also important to inspect the anus for fissures that may be causing or exacerbating soiling by encouraging the child to withhold stools for fear of pain (Fleisher, 1976; Mercer, 1967; Schmitt, 1984). Use of abdominal X-rays has been defended on the grounds that they lead to more accurate determination of whether retention and physical anomalies are involved and that they can be reliably scored for degree of impaction (Barr, Levine, Wilkinson, & Mulvihill, 1979; Levine, 1975).

When organic causes have been suspected a number of additional procedures have been used. These include barium enemas and rectal biopsy. Barium enemas have been commonly used when rectal examination leads to suspicion of Hirschsprung's disease. Liebman (1979) reported that in a sample of 123 children with bowel-problem onset before the age of 1 year, this procedure was diagnostic in two of three cases. More invasive procedures include suction biopsy or a full-thickness surgical biopsy of the rectal wall and may be used to verify a diagnosis of Hirschsprung's disease (Fitzgerald, 1975; Liebman, 1979). Levine (1982), however, has cautioned that, even with this method, false positive misdiagnosis is possible because an apparent decrease in ganglionic cells may be due to chronic stretching of the rectal wall that can occur in functional encopresis.

Contemporary assessment efforts have focused upon dysfunctional defecation dynamics via anorectal manometry. Dysfunctional defecation dynamics may play a role in both etiology and maintenance of encopresis (Loening-Baucke & Cruikshank, 1986; Wald, Chandra, Gabel, & Chiponis, 1987; Whitehead & Schuster, 1985). The anorectal manometric abnormalities that have been described in encopretics with constipation are (a) decreased relaxation response of the internal and sphincter with rectal distention (Abrahamian & Lloyd-Still, 1984; Loening-Baucke, 1984), (b) decreased sensitivity of rectum and sigmoid colon (Goligher & Hughes, 1951; Loening-Baucke, 1984), and (c) abnormal contraction of the external anal sphincter during defecation (Loening-Baucke & Cruikshank, 1986; Wald et al., 1987). Controlled studies have also demonstrated that treatment resistance was related to severe constipation, abnormal contraction of the external anal sphincter and pelvic floor during defecation, and inability to defecate 100 ml balloons (Loening-Baucke, 1989; Loening-Baucke, Cruikshank, & Savage, 1987).

Loening-Baucke (1990) and Wald et al. (1987) found that children trained to produce normal defecation patterns through biofeedback were more successful with traditional cathartic and laxative protocols.

Psychological Assessment

Behavioral assessment for functional encopresis includes both a clinical interview with parents and the child and direct observations and records of relevant target behaviors. The aims of the assessment are to (a) determine if appropriate toileting behaviors are present or need to be learned (i.e., stimulus conditions, S); (b) identify parental and child responses (R) that may be maintaining soiling; and (c) evaluate parental motivation for compliance to the treatment regimen (i.e., consequences, C). The last issue is particularly important, considering current evidence that links parental compliance with remission of soiling (Levine & Bakow, 1976).

The interview should include a review of developmental milestones and previous attempts at toilet training. Information about failed attempts at toilet training or treatment for soiling may reveal problems with parental responses, such as placing excessive pressure on the child to have bowel movements, delivering inconsistent or excessive punishment for soiling accidents, and failing to attend to appropriate toileting behavior. As in the case of assessment for enuresis, some evaluation of marital discord and inconsistent parental expectations of the child is needed. Often, these latter problems need to be remediated before a treatment program can be successfully implemented. In those families in which there has a history of ineffective punishment, it is usually beneficial to assist parents to view the soiling as a response the child cannot control rather than as a behavior that the child performs deliberately. Occasionally, soiling may be part of a general response class of oppositional behavior, and this can be assessed through broad-band behavior checklists like the CBCL (Achenbach & Edelbrock, 1983). Finally, an accurate count of the child's underpants is needed to prevent hiding of soiled pants.

Interview with the child can assess whether or not the child experiences the need to have a bowel movement. Among retentive encopretics, it is not uncommon for the child to report that he or she does not feel the urge to defecate. Reports of fear of the toilet and of painful bowel movements may indicate a need for gradual exposure and in vivo desensitization-type procedures. Finally, because many behavioral interventions rely on use of tangible reinforcers to promote proper toileting practice, an inventory of rewards and pleasant events for the child needs to be obtained.

Behavioral observations by the clinician and parents are needed to individualize a treatment program. Direct observation of the child's toileting behavior is instructive and should include how the child undresses, approaches the toilet, and executes the valsalva maneuver and whether the child wipes completely. Information about the frequency and type of the accidents is needed to determine whether laxatives are appropriate and to establish a baseline of at least 2 weeks for measuring progress (Doleys, 1983). Parents can be instructed to keep daily records of both soiling accidents and bowel movements (BMs) in the toilet. The frequency of soiling and BMs in the toilet, the size of the accident or of appropriate BMs, the consistency of the stool (i.e., whether the stool was loose or hard, smooth or grainy), and the time and place that accidents or appropriate BMs occurred should be included in the record. Records also need to indicate the number of self-initiated bathroom visits and BMs in the toilet, as well as parental response to accidents. Recording the time of day that bowel activity (either accidents or appropriate toileting) typically occurs is necessary to establish times for scheduled toileting practice. For those interventions that require manipulation of diet, it is important to have parents record complete details of the child's food intake.

This assessment process is a continual one of monitoring the effects of encopresis treatment. Both researchers and clinicians have found it helpful to view treatment as a single case design where functional analysis of appropriate toileting behavior and soiling accidents leads to systematic interventions based on recorded frequencies of those two classes of behavior. Fortunately, as in the case of enuresis, the relevant variables are highly salient and can be measured reliably when parents are properly instructed.

ACTUAL ASSESSMENT: FUNCTIONAL ENCOPRESIS

The difference between the prototypic assessment and the actual assessment of functional encopresis varies according to where the child presents for services (i.e., gastroenterology service vs. general pediatric clinic vs. psychological services clinic) and the treatment orientation of the provider (i.e., physiologic vs. psychoanalytic vs. behavioral). The components of assessment that have been found to be useful in terms of successful treatment outcome and practical use are emphasized in this section.

Debates about the value of various medical diagnostic strategies will remain academic in the absence of empirical evidence from large-scale studies regarding the effectiveness of procedures in accurately distinguishing functional from organic encopresis and different types of organic encopresis from each other. Standards need to be set and tested more adequately before any firm conclusions can be drawn in this area. Despite the scientific limitations of current medical assessment, physician consultation is still needed to provide some reasonable estimates as to whether or not encopresis may be due to medical causes, to determine the extent of constipation or fecal impaction, and to evacuate the bowel if needed.

A thorough medical and clinical history combined with a physical exam of all systems, including a rectal exam, abdominal palpation, and X-ray film of the abdomen is generally all that is necessary to rule out organic causes of fecal incontinence (Hatch, 1988; Levine, 1982). Invasive assessment procedures such as barium enemas, colonic tissue biopsies, and colonoscopy generally produce a low diagnostic yield and are, therefore, impractical (Levine, 1982). Coekin and Gairdner (1960) have pointed to the dangers of exposing gonads to radiation and of barium exacerbating preexisting constipation. They have argued that this procedure should only be used when pseudo Hirschsprung's disease due to organic and obstruction is a possible diagnosis. This condition is suspected in the presence of colonic inertia combined with signs of physical obstruction of the flow of feces, and it often requires surgery (Hendren, 1978).

Although considered an invasive procedure, anorectal manometry may prove to be an important component in a complete medical assessment because of the large percentage of encopretics with abnormal defecation dynamics. The procedure has also been used to identify those children who are likely to fail laxative treatments (Loening-Baucke, 1989).

The usefulness of developing a topography of soiling and toileting behavior in a functional analytic perspective is clear. The major obstacle to obtaining this information is enlisting the encopretic's parents in maintaining complete and accurate records. Designing simple records, making careful efforts in training the parents in data recording, and emphasizing the importance of the records in order to tailor the treatment to the child and in monitoring its effectiveness will usually ensure that a complete soiling topography is available to the clinician. As with most psychological interventions, there is simply no substitute for a good working relationship with parents. Regular supportive contacts and problem-solving sessions are needed to collect the information necessary for effective treatment monitoring.

PROTOTYPIC TREATMENT: FUNCTIONAL ENCOPRESIS

The authors believe that functional encopresis is a biobehavioral problem that is best treated through the collaboration of physicians and health psychologists. This conclusion is based upon the evidence that between 75% (Levine, 1975) and 95% (Christopherson & Rapoff, 1983) of clinic-referred children with soiling are classified as retentive encopretics. Further, 63% have a history of painful defecation that began in infancy and that led to the pain-avoidance response of external anal sphincter contraction during defecation, and this continued response maintains the constipation (Partin, et al., 1992). Treatment of functional encopresis must address, therefore, the physiological aspects of constipation, fecal impaction, and frequent soiling. It must also address the pain-avoidance response and retention that interfere with normal defecation. A minority of children presenting with encopresis do not have histories of constipation, painful defecation, and withholding, and, therefore, most of these children do not require cathartic and laxative therapies.

In the following sections, the reader is cautioned against drawing firm conclusions about what is the treatment of choice for encopresis. The research on encopresis treatment is not nearly as extensive nor as clear as outcome research on enuresis. The treatment-outcome literature for functional encopresis is limited by the fact that only 1% of published reports detailed results of randomized trials that compared two or more interventions, and 91% involved case studies or simple pre/post group designs (see review by Houts & Abramson, 1990). The combined use of cathartics and laxatives, complex behavioral interventions, and biofeedback is reviewed here because these are the existing treatments for which there are some promising outcome data.

Medical treatments have involved use of purgatives and laxatives (Berg & Jones, 1964; Loening-Baucke & Younoszai, 1982), dietary manipulation (Loening-Baucke & Cruickshank, 1986), and pharmacological compounds assumed to affect musculature involved in defecation (Gavanski, 1971). Typically, these interventions include regular potting of the child once any fecal impaction has been removed. The overall effectiveness of medical approaches indicates that the upper-bound estimate of permanent cure (defined as percent cured minus percent relapsed) has been 60% (Houts & Abramson, 1990). In comparison to other treatment options that have been researched, in most cases, medical intervention alone may not be the treatment of choice. Nevertheless, the assumption that some substance may be necessary for cleansing the encopretic of fecal impaction should not be discarded because some children may be so impacted that initial evacuation is necessary before an alternative treatment can be successful.

In general, behavioral treatments have focused on teaching prerequisite skills for toileting and on changing contingencies of reinforcement so that soiling cannot be maintained and appropriate toileting can occur. Specific behavioral procedures that have been used are (a) toileting-skills training (Crowley & Armstrong, 1977) (b) discrimination training (Olness, McParland, & Piper, 1980), (c) overcorrection and punishment for soiling (Ayllon, Simon, & Wildman, 1975; Rolider & Van Houten, 1985), (d) positive reinforcement for sitting on the toilet (Neale, 1963), (e) positive reinforcement for defecation in the toilet (*Type I reinforcement*) (Keehn, 1965), and (f) positive reinforcement for clean underwear (*Type II reinforcement*) (Pedrini & Pedrini, 1971). Some of these methods have been used alone (e.g., reinforcement for clean pants, negative reinforcement), and, more frequently as individual cases required, they have been combined into treatment packages that appear to be more effective than isolated procedures. Overall, Houts and Abramson (1990) estimated that behavioral treatments resulted in an upper-bound estimate of 63% permanently cured. Simple behavioral methods are estimated to have resulted in 59% being permanently cured, in contrast to 67% being permanently cured for complex behavioral programs. This manner of organizing the literature certainly suggests that combined behavioral procedures are more effective than behavioral procedures used in isolation. Obviously, randomized controlled studies are needed to develop a reliable behavioral treatment package.

Various behavioral procedures have been used in conjunction with cathartics and diet modification. These treatment packages are based on the assumption that reinforcement and punishment procedures to produce appropriate bowel habits will be ineffective if longstanding constipation and fecal impaction of the colon and rectum are left untreated. Approaches that combine reinforcement with cathartics are more effective when they involve Type I reinforcement (Doleys, 1983). Houts and Abramson (1990) estimated that cathartics combined with Type I reinforcement produced an upper-bound estimate of 72% permanently cured versus 48% for cathartics combined with Type II reinforcement. Interestingly, when laxatives alone or laxatives with purgatives have been used with a combination of Type I reinforcement and Type II reinforcement, results have been less promising, with overall estimates of 62% permanently cured. Houts and Abramson also noted that, compared to those protocols that used initial evacuation with enemas, those that did not use evacuation resulted in lower estimates of permanent cure (85% versus 30%). This trend is consistent with the recommendation of Parker and Whitehead (1983) who have advocated the use of water enemas over laxatives because enemas clean out the colon and rectum more immediately and thoroughly.

Several investigations included dietary-fiber increase alone or together with laxatives or in combination with behavioral interventions (Hein & Beerends, 1978; Houts, Mellon, & Whelan, 1988; Houts & Peterson, 1986; Sluckin, 1981; Taitz, Wales, Urwin, & Molnar, 1986; Wakefield, Woodbridge, Steward, & Croke, 1984). The use of diet modifications in place of laxatives was prompted by reports of laxative dependency and patterns of passive defecation associated with long-term use of laxatives (Schaefer, 1979). Overall, these diet-modification procedures appear to be less effective than procedures involving cathartics and laxatives. Houts and Abramson (1990) estimated the upper-bound estimate for permanent cure to be 60% for these diet-modification treatments.

The overall effectiveness of interventions that combined cathartic and behavioral treatments can be estimated to have an upper-bound estimate of permanent cure of 66%. Whereas this overall estimate is somewhat lower than for other types of treatment strategies, the studies reviewed by Houts and Abramson (1990) suggested that addition of cathartics to certain types of multifaceted behavioral interventions resulted in substantial gains over use of behavioral intervention alone. Specifically, a combination of cathartics and enema with Types I and II reinforcement and a combination of laxatives and diet with support for parents have been quite successful. At the very least, Type I reinforcement should be included in combined cathartic and behavioral treatments.

Several researchers have documented the increased risk of failing conventional cathartic and laxative treatment when abnormal defecation dynamics exist. These investigators have also shown that retraining encopretic children to make the appropriate response through biofeedback leads to greater treatment efficacy (Loening-Baucke, 1990; Wald et al., 1987). Biofeedback treatment of up to six 1-hour training sessions has been viewed as complementary to a conventional cathartic and laxative regimen. Biofeedback training most likely assists with the molecular responses involved in defecation and may shorten the length of time it takes to achieve a resolution of soiling problems with more conventional treatments such as those previously described.

Although the evidence is only suggestive given the current state of research knowledge, the authors speculate that an ideal treatment for encopresis would combine the biofeedback training of anorectal response competency with cathartics and diet manipulation (or laxatives) as well as behavioral treatment that includes Type I reinforcement. The aim of such treatment would be to immediately and completely evacuate the bowel and to ensure that future constipation is prevented through the use of a high fiber diet or laxatives. Biofeedback training of anorectal musculature would lead to more efficient control of the molecular responses needed to attain continence, and behavioral intervention would establish regular toileting habits.

ACTUAL TREATMENT: FUNCTIONAL ENCOPRESIS

There are several obvious practical challenges to the use of an ideal treatment for encopresis. As with problems implementing a prototypic assessment for functional encopresis, implementation of treatment varies according to the treatment setting and the orientation of the clinicians. Encopretics that present to a physician in a pediatric office will often receive cathartics, laxatives, and recommendations for regular daily sitting on the toilet. Encopretics that present at a mental health clinic often are treated with simple contingency management that includes reinforcement for appropriate toileting, clean underwear, and some response cost for soiling accidents. These trends are dictated by the equipment and services available to the clinician and by the training of the service provider.

The cost, for example, of anorectal manometry and of the equipment and training to provide it is likely to be prohibitive for the pediatrician or psychologist in a private practice setting. Likewise, the increased time and effort to do a functional analysis of the soiling behavior, to develop a treatment plan from this information, and to conduct an ongoing evaluation through a single case design is also unlikely to be implemented in most private practice settings.

The simplest solution to these incomplete approaches has been the call for increased collaboration between physicians and health psychologists (Houts & Abramson, 1990). Because of a history of professional turf issues, collaboration between independent physicians and psychologists even in the same city is still rare. Perhaps the best solution to the problem is to develop specialty clinics for functional encopresis in pediatric psychology settings. A medical school department of pediatrics with a faculty of physicians specializing in general pediatrics and gastroenterology and of pediatric psychologists trained in behavior therapy would not only have the means and methods to provide the ideal treatment, but would also be able to conduct the necessary research that is currently needed.

SUMMARY

The functional elimination disorders of children present a challenge to clinicians and researchers in the fields of medicine and psychology. Both enuresis and encopresis can be conceptualized as biobehavioral problems that require a new kind of thinking for both disciplines. On the one hand, clinicians and researchers need to understand the basic physiology of micturition and defecation if they are to solve these problems. On the other hand, and because of the functional nature of the problems, they also need to understand principles of conditioning and learning if they are to provide sociopsychological interventions that restore basic physiological mechanisms to their proper functioning. This biobehavioral approach to the problem is likely to lead to new knowledge about how changes in human behavior at the molar and socially influenceable level can alter the behavior of bodily systems at the molecular and physiological level.

REFERENCES

Abrahamian, F. P., & Lloyd-Still, J. (1984). Chronic constipation in childhood: A longitudinal study of 186 patients. *Journal of Pediatric Gastroenterology and Nutrition, 3*, 460–467.

Achenbach, T. M., & Edelbrock, C. (1983). *Manual for the Child Behavior Checklist.* Burlington, VT: Department of Psychiatry, University of Vermont.

American Academy of Pediatrics Committee on Radiology. (1980). Excretory urography for evaluation of enuresis. *Pediatrics, 65*, 644–655.

American Psychiatric Association. (1987). *Diagnostic and statistical manual of mental disorders* (3rd ed., rev.) Washington, DC: Author.

American Psychiatric Association. (1993). *DSM-IV draft criteria.* Washington, DC: Author.

Anthony, E. J. (1957). An experimental approach to the psychopathology of childhood encopresis. *British Journal of Medical Psychology, 30,* 146–175.

Arnold, S. J., & Ginsberg, A. (1973). Enuresis: Incidence and pertinence of genitourinary disease in healthy enuretic children. *Urology, 2*, 437–443.

Ayllon, T., Simon, S. J., & Wildman, R. W. (1975). Instructions and reinforcement in the elimination of encopresis: A case study. *Journal of Behavior Therapy and Experimental Psychiatry, 6*, 235–238.

Azrin, N. H., Sneed, T. J., & Foxx, R. M. (1974). Dry-bed training: Rapid elimination of childhood enuresis. *Behaviour Research and Therapy, 12*, 147–156.

Baker, B. L. (1969). Symptom treatment and symptom substitution in enuresis. *Journal of Abnormal Psychology, 74*, 42–49.

Beck, A. T., Rush, A. J., Shaw, B. F., & Emery, G. (1980). *Cognitive therapy of depression.* New York: Guilford Press.

Bellman, M. (1966). Studies on encopresis. *Acta Pediatrica Scandinavica.* (Suppl. 170), 7–151.

Berg, I., & Jones, K. V. (1964). Functional fecal incontinence in children. *Archives of Disease in Childhood, 39*, 465–472.

Berger, R. M., Maizels, M., Moran, G. C., Conway, J. J., & Firlit, C. F. (1983). Bladder capacity (ounces) equals age (years) plus 2 predicts normal bladder capacity and aids in diagnosis of abnormal voiding patterns. *The Journal of Urology, 129*, 347–349.

Boon, F., & Singh, N. (1991). A model for the treatment of encopresis. *Behavior Modification, 15*, 355–371.

Burke, E. C., & Stickler, G. B. (1980). Enuresis—Is it being overtreated? *Mayo Clinic Proceedings*, *55*, 118–119.

Butler, R. J., Brewin, C. R., & Forsythe, W. I. (1986). Maternal attributions and tolerance for nocturnal enuresis. *Behaviour Research and Therapy*, *24*, 304–312.

Christophersen, E. R., & Rapoff, M. A. (1983). Toileting problems of children. In C. E. Walker & M. C. Roberts (Eds.), *Handbook of clinical child psychology* (pp. 593–615). New York: Wiley.

Coekin, M., & Gairdner, D. (1960). Fecal incontinence in children. *British Medical Journal*, *2*, 1175, 1807.

Couchells, S. M., Johnson, S. B., Carter, R., & Walker, D. (1981). Behavioral and environmental characteristics of treated and untreated enuretic children and matched nonenuretic controls. *The Journal of Pediatrics*, *99*, 812–816.

Crowley, C. P., & Armstrong, P. M. (1977). Positive practice, overcorrection, and behavior rehearsal in the treatment of three cases of encopresis. *Journal of Behavior Therapy and Experimental Psychiatry*, *8*, 411–416.

Davidson, M. (1958). Constipation and fecal incontinence. *Pediatric Clinics of North America*, *4*, 749–757.

De Jonge, G. A. (1973). Epidemiology of enuresis: A survey of the literature. In I. Kolvin, R.C. MacKeith, & S.R. Meadow (Eds.) *Bladder control and enuresis* (pp. 39–46). London: Heinemann.

DeVroede, G. (1982). Anal incontinence. *Diseases of the Colon and Rectum*, *25*, 90–95.

Dische, S., Yule, W., Corbett, J. & Hand, D. (1983). Childhood nocturnal enuresis: Factors associated with outcome of treatment with an enuresis alarm. *Developmental Medicine and Neurology*, *25*,67–80.

Doleys, D. M. (1981). Encopresis. In J. M. Ferguson & C. B. Taylor (Eds.) *The comprehensive handbook of behavioral medicine* (pp. 145–157). New York: Spectrum.

Doleys, D. M. (1983). Enuresis and encopresis. In T. H. Ollendick & M. Herson (Eds.), *Handbook of child psychopathology* (pp. 201–226). New York: Plenum Press.

Easson, W. M. (1960). Encopresis: Psychogenic soiling. *Canadian Medical Association Journal*, *82*, 624–627.

Essen, J., & Peckham, C. (1976). Nocturnal enuresis in childhood. *Developmental Medicine and Child Neurology*, *18*, 577–589.

Fergusson, D. M., Horwood, L. J., & Shannon, F. T. (1986). Factors related to the age of attainment of nocturnal bladder control: An 8-year longitudinal study. *Pediatrics*, *78*, 884–890.

Fergusson, D. M., Horwood, L. J., & Shannon, F. T. (1990). Secondary enuresis in a birth cohort of New Zealand children. *Paediatric and Perinatal Epidemiology*, *4*, 53–63.

Fielding, D., & Doleys, D. M. (1989). Elimination problems: Enuresis and encopresis. In E. J. Mash & L. G. Terdal (Eds.), *Behavioral assessment of childhood disorders* (pp.586–623). New York: Guilford Press.

Finley, W. W., Rainwater, A. J., & Johnson, G. (1982). Effect of varying alarm schedules on acquisition and relapse parameters in the conditioning treatment of enuresis. *Behaviour Research and Therapy*, *20*, 69–80.

Fitzgerald, J. F. (1975). Encopresis, soiling, constipation: What's to be done? *Journal of Pediatrics*, *56*, 348–349.

Fleisher, D. R. (1976). Diagnosis and treatment of disorders of defecation in children. *Pediatric Annals*, *5*, 71–101.

Forsythe, W. I. & Redmond, A. (1974). Enuresis and spontaneous cure rate: Study of 1129 enuretics. *Archives of Disease in Childhood*, *49*, 259–263.

Gavanski, M. (1971). Treatment of non-retentive secondary encopresis with imipramine and psychotherapy. *Canadian Medical Association Journal*, *104*, 46–48.

Goldfried, M. R. & Sprafkin, J. N. (1974). *Behavioral personality assessment.* Morristown, NJ: General Learning Press.

Goligher, J. C., & Hughes, E. S. (1951). Sensibility of the colon and rectum. *Lancet, 1,* 543–548.

Hallgren, B. (1957). Enuresis: A clinical and genetic study. *Acta Psychiatrica et Neurologica Scandinavica, 32* (Suppl. 114), 1–159.

Haque, M., Ellerstein, N. S., Gundy, J. H., Shelov, S. P., Weiss, J. C., McIntire, M. S., Olness, K. N., Jones, D. J., Heagarty, M. C., & Starfield, B. H. (1981). Parental perceptions of enuresis: A collaborative study. *American Journal of Diseases of Children, 135,* 809–811.

Hatch, T. F. (1988). Encopresis and constipation in children. *Pediatric Clinics of North America, 35,* 257–280.

Hein, H. A., & Beerends, J. J. (1978). Who should accept primary responsibility for the encopretic child?: A successful pediatric program based on dietary control, bowel training, and family counseling. *Clinical Pediatrics, 17,* 67–70.

Hendren, W. H. (1978). Constipation caused by anterior location of the anus and its surgical correction. *Journal of Pediatric Surgery, 13,* 505–512.

Hersov, L. (1977). Faecal soiling. In M. Rutter & L. Hersov (Eds.), *Child psychiatry: Modern approaches* (pp. 613–627). Philadelphia: Blackwell Scientific Publications.

Houts, A. C. (1991). Nocturnal enuresis as a biobehavioral problem. *Behavior Therapy, 22,* 133–151.

Houts, A. C. & Abramson, H. (1990). Assessment and treatment for functional childhood enuresis and encopresis: Toward a partnership between health psychologists and physicians. In S. B. Morgan & T. M. Okwumabua (Eds.), *Child and adolescent disorders: Developmental and health psychology perspectives* (pp. 47–103). Hillsdale, NJ: Lawrence Erlbaum.

Houts, A. C., Berman, J. S., & Abramson, H. (in press). The effectiveness of psychological and pharmacological treatments for nocturnal enuresis. *Journal of Consulting and Clinical Psychology.*

Houts, A. C., Liebert, R. M., & Padawer, W. (1983). A delivery system for the treatment of primary enuresis. *Journal of Abnormal Child Psychology, 11,* 513–519.

Houts, A. C., Mellon, M. W., & Whelan, J. P. (1988). Use of dietary fiber and stimulus control to treat retentive encopresis: A multiple baseline investigation. *Journal of Pediatric Psychology, 13,* 435–445.

Houts, A. C., & Peterson, J. K. (1986). Treatment of a retentive encopretic child using contingency management and diet modification with stimulus control. *Journal of Pediatric Psychology, 11,* 375–383.

Houts, A. C., Peterson, J. K., & Whelan, J. P. (1986). Prevention of relapse in Full-Spectrum home training for primary enuresis: A components analysis. *Behavior Therapy, 17,* 462–469.

Houts, A. C., Whelan, J. P., & Peterson, J. K. (1987). Filmed vs. live delivery of Full-Spectrum home training for primary enuresis: Presenting the information is not enough. *Journal of Consulting and Clinical Psychology, 55,* 902–906.

Jarvelin, M. R. (1989). Developmental history and neurological findings in enuretic children. *Developmental Medicine and Child Neurology, 31,* 728–736.

Jarvelin, M. R., Huttunen, N., Seppanen, J., Seppanen, U., & Moilanen, I. (1990). Screening of urinary tract abnormalities among day and nightwetting children. *Scandinavian Journal of Urology and Nephrology, 24,* 181–189.

Jarvelin, M. R., Moilanen, I., Kangas, P., Moring, K., Vikevainen-Tervonen, L., Huttunen, N. P., & Seppanen, J. (1991). Aetiological and precipitating factors for childhood enuresis. *Acta Pediatrica Scandinavica, 80,* 361–369.

Jarvelin, M. R., Moilanen, I., Vikevainen-Tervonen, L., & Huttunen, N.P. (1990). Life changes and protective capacities in enuretic and non-enuretic children. *Journal of Child Psychology and Psychiatry, 31*, 763–774.

Jarvelin, M.R., Vikevainen-Tervonen, L., Moilanen, I., & Huttunen, N. P. (1988). Enuresis in seven-year-old children. *Acta Pediatrica Scandinavica, 77*, 148–153.

Kaffman, M., & Elizur, E. (1977). Infants who become enuretics: A longitudinal study of 161 kibbutz children. *Monographs of the Society for Research in Child Development, 42*, (2, Serial No. 170), 1–54.

Kass, E. J. (1991). Approaching enuresis in an uncomplicated way. *Contemporary Urology, 3*, 15–24.

Keehn, J. D. (1965). Brief case-report: Reinforcement therapy of incontinence. *Behavior Research and Therapy, 2*, 239.

Landman, G. B., Rappaport, L., Fenton, T., & Levine, M. D. (1986). Locus of control and self-esteem in children with encopresis. *Developmental and Behavioral Pediatrics, 7*, 111–113.

Leape, L. L., & Ramenofsky, M. L. (1978). Anterior ectopic anus: A common cause of constipation in children. *Journal of Pediatric Surgery, 13*, 627–630.

Levine, A. (1943). Enuresis in the navy. *American Journal of Psychiatry, 100*, 320–325.

Levine, M. D. (1975). Children with encopresis: A descriptive analysis. *Pediatrics, 56*, 412–416.

Levine, M. D. (1982). Encopresis: Its potentiation, evaluation, and alleviation. *Pediatric Clinics of North America, 29*, 315–330.

Levine, M. D., & Bakow, H. (1976). Children with encopresis: A study of treatment outcome. *Pediatrics, 58*, 845–852.

Liebman, W. M. (1979). Disorders of defecation in children: Evaluation and management. *Postgraduate Medicine, 66*, 105–110.

Locke, H.J., & Wallace, K. M. (1959). Short marital adjustment and prediction tests: Their reliability and validity. *Marriage and Family Living, 21*, 251–255.

Loening-Baucke, V. A. (1984). Sensitivity of the signoid colon and rectum in children treated for chronic constipation. *Journal of Pediatric Gastroenterology and Nutrition, 3*, 454–459.

Loening-Baucke, V. A. (1989). Factors determining outcome in children with chronic constipation and faecal soiling. *Gut, 30*, 999–1006.

Loening Baucke, V. A. (1990). Modulation of abnormal defecation dynamics by biofeedback treatment in chronically constipated children with encopresis. *Journal of Pediatrics, 116*, 214–222.

Loening-Baucke, V. A., & Cruikshank, B. M. (1986). Abnormal defecation in chronically constipated children with encopresis. *Journal of Pediatrics, 108*, 562–566.

Loening-Baucke, V. A., Cruikshank, B. M., & Savage, C. (1987). Defecation dynamics and behavior profiles in encopretic children. *Pediatrics, 80*, 672–679.

Loening-Baucke, V. A., & Younoszai, M. K. (1982). Abnormal and sphincter response in chronically constipated children. *Journal of Pediatrics, 100*, 213–218.

Lovibond, S. H., (1964). *Conditioning and enuresis*. New York: Macmillan.

Margileth, A. M., Pedreira, F. A., Hirschman, G. H., & Coleman, T. H. (1976). Urinary tract bacterial infections: Office diagnosis and management. *Pediatric Clinics of North America, 23*, 721–734.

Mercer, R. D. (1967). Constipation. *Pediatric Clinics of North America, 14*, 175–185.

McMahon, R. J., Forehand, R., Griest, D. L., & Wells, K. C. (1981). Who drops out of treatment during parent behavioral training? *Behavioral Counseling Quarterly, 1*, 79–85.

Moffatt, M. E. K., Kato, C., & Pless, I. B. (1987). Improvements in self-concept after treatment of nocturnal enuresis: A randomized clinical trial. *The Journal of Pediatrics, 110*, 647–652.

Morgan, R. T. T., & Young, G. C. (1975). Parental attitudes and the conditioning treatment of childhood enuresis. *Behaviour Research and Therapy, 13,* 197–199.

Neale, D. H. (1963). Behaviour therapy and encopresis in children. *Behaviour Research and Therapy, 1,* 139–149.

Nisley, D. D. (1976). Medical overview of the management of encopresis. *Journal of Pediatric Psychology, 4,* 33 -34.

Novello, A. C., & Novello, J. R., (1987). Enuresis. *Pediatric Clinics of North America, 34,* 719–733.

Olness, K., McParland, F. A. & Piper, J. (1980). Biofeedback: A new modality in the management of children with fecal soiling. *Journal of Pediatrics, 96,* 505 -509.

Parker, L., & Whitehead, W. (1983). Treatment of urinary and fecal incontinence in children. In D. C. Russo & J. W. Varni (Eds.), *Behavioral pediatrics: Research and practice* (pp. 143–174). New York: Plenum Press.

Partin, J. C., Hamill, S. K., Fischel, J. E., & Partin, J. S., (1992). Painful defecation and fecal soiling in children. *Pediatrics, 89,* 1007–1009.

Pedrini, B. C., & Pedrini, D. T. (1971). Reinforcement procedures in the control of encopresis: A case study. *Psychological Reports, 28,* 937–938.

Philpott, M. G., & Flasher, M. C. (1970). The treatment of enuresis: Further clinical experience with imipramine. *The British Journal of Clinical Practice, 24,* 327–329.

Poston, G. J., Joseph, A. E. A., & Riddle, P. R. (1983). The accuracy of ultrasound in the measurement of changes in bladder volume. *British Journal of Urology, 55,* 361–363.

Ravitch, M. M., (1958). Pseudo Hirchsprung's disease. *Annals of Surgery, 147,* 781–795.

Redman, J. F., & Siebert, J. J. (1979). The uroradiographic evaluation of the enuretic child. *The Journal of Urology, 122,* 799–801.

Rolider, A., & Van Houten, R. (1985). Treatment of constipation-caused encopresis by a negative reinforcement procedure. *Journal of Behavior Therapy and Experimental Psychiatry, 16,* 67–70.

Rushton, H. G. (1989). Nocturnal enuresis: Epidemiology, evaluation, and currently available treatment options. *The Journal of Pediatrics, 114,* 691–696.

Rutter, M., Tizzard, J., & Whitmore, K. (Eds.). (1970). *Education, health, and behavior.* London: Longman.

Rutter, M., Yule, W., & Graham, P. (1973). Enuresis and behavioral deviance. In I. Kolvin, R. C. MacKeith, & S. R. Meadow (Eds.), *Bladder control and enuresis* (pp. 137–147). London: Heinemann.

Sacks, S., & DeLeon, G. (1973). Case histories and shorter communications: Conditioning of two types of enuretics. *Behaviour Research and Therapy, 11,* 653–654.

Schaefer, C. E. (1979). *Childhood encopresis and enuresis: Causes and therapy.* New York: Van Nostrand Reinhold.

Schmitt, B.D. (1982a). Daytime wetting (diurnal enuresis). *Pediatric Clinics of North America, 29,* 9–20.

Schmitt, B. D. (1982b). Nocturnal enuresis: An update on treatment. *Pediatric Clinics of North America, 29,* 21–37.

Schmitt, B. D. (1984). Encopresis. *Primary Care, 11,* 497–511.

Shaffer, D. (1985). Enuresis. In M. Rutter & L. Hersov (Eds.), *Child and adolescent psychiatry: Modern approaches* (pp. 465–481). Oxford: Blackwell Scientific Publications.

Shelov, S. P., Gundy, J., Weiss, J. C., McIntire, M. S., Olness, K., Staub, H. P., Jones, D. J., Haque, M., Ellerstein, N. S., Heagarty, M. C., & Starfield, B. (1981). Enuresis: A contrast of attitudes of parents and physicians. *Pediatrics, 67,* 707–710.

Sluckin, A. (1981). Behavioural social work with encopretic children, their families and the school. *Child Care, Health, and Development, 7,* 67–80.

Sondheimer, J. M. (1985). Helping the child with chronic constipation. *Contemporary Pediatrics*, 2, 12–22.

Stansfeld, J. M. (1973). Enuresis and urinary tract infection. In I. Kolvin, R. C. MacKeith, & S. R. Meadow (Eds.), *Bladder control and enuresis* (pp. 102–103). London: Heinemann.

Stromgren, A., & Thomsen, P.H. (1990). Personality traits in young adults with a history of conditioning-treated childhood enuresis. *Acta Psychiatrica Scandinavica*, 81, 538–541.

Suberman, R. I. (1976). Constipation in children. *Pediatric Annals*, 5, 32–48.

Sukhai, R. N., Mol, J., & Harris, A. S. (1989). Combined therapy of enuresis alarm and desmopressin in the treatment of nocturnal enuresis. *European Journal of Pediatrics*, 148, 465–467.

Taitz, L. S., Wales, J. K. H., Urwin, O. M., & Molnar, D. (1986). Factors associated with outcome in management of defecation disorders. *Archives of Disease in Childhood*, 61, 472–477.

Thorne, F. C. (1944). The incidence of nocturnal enuresis after age of 5 years. *American Journal of Psychiatry*, 100, 686–689.

Toguri, A. G., Uchida, T., & Bee, D. E. (1982). Pediatric uroflow rate nomograms. *The Journal of Urology*, 127, 727–731.

Verhulst, F. C., van der Lee, J. H., Akkerhuis, G. W., Sanders-Woudstra, J. A. R., Timmer, F. C., & Donkhorst, I. D. (1985). The prevalence of nocturnal enuresis: Do DSM-III criteria need to be changed? A brief research report. *Journal of Child Psychology and Psychiatry*, 26, 989–993.

Wakefield, M. A., Woodbridge, C., Steward, J., & Croke, W. M. (1984). A treatment program for faecal incontinence. *Developmental Medicine and Child Neurology*, 26, 613–616.

Wald, A., Chandra, R., Gabel, S., & Chiponis, D. (1987). Evaluation of biofeedback in childhood encopresis. *Journal of Pediatric Gastroenterology and Nutrition*, 6, 554–558.

Whelan, J. P., & Houts, A. C. (1990). Effects of a waking schedule on primary enuretic children treated with Full-Spectrum Home Training. *Health Psychology*, 9, 164–176.

Whitehead, W. E., & Schuster, M. M. (1985). *Gastrointestinal disorders: Behavioral and physiological basis for treatment*. New York: Academic Press.

Whitehead, W. E., Orr, W. C., Engel, B. T., & Schuster, M. M. (1981). External anal sphincter response to rectal distension: Learned response or reflex. *Psychophysiology*, 19, 57–62.

Young, G. C., & Morgan, R. T. T. (1972). Overlearning in the conditioning treatment of enuresis: A long-term follow-up study. *Behaviour Research and Therapy*, 10, 419–420.

Young, G. C., & Morgan, R. T. T. (1973). Rapidity of response to the treatment of enuresis. *Developmental Medicine and Child Neurology*, 15, 488–496.

CHAPTER 18

Substance Use and Abuse

ERIC F. WAGNER AND JON D. KASSEL

DESCRIPTION OF THE PROBLEM

Substance use by adolescents has become one of the most pressing health concerns in America. This is reflected in marked increases in media reports, governmental mandates, and granting agencies' requests for proposals concerning adolescent substance use (Renz, 1989; Public Health Service, 1990). The U.S. Public Health Service (1990), for instance, recently issued a report concerning health goals for the year 2000 that included 18 objectives directly addressing adolescent substance use and another 10 objectives involving aspects of physical health related to the use of substances by youth. This level of attention to adolescent alcohol and drug use is unprecedented and mirrors growing public awareness of the substance use problem among American youth.

Several survey studies have confirmed that the vast majority of adolescents have experimented with one or more substances (e.g., Johnston, O'Malley, & Bachman, 1991; National Institute of Drug Abuse, 1990). Data indicate that, among high school seniors, more than 90% have imbibed alcohol and over 40% have tried at least one illicit drug. Of those youth who have used drugs, 32% reported at least one episode of excessive drinking during the previous 2 weeks, and 10% reported having used marijuana daily for at least 1 month at some point in their life. Furthermore, one study (Levy & Deykin, 1989) suggested that a sizeable proportion of these individuals will develop a substance use problem prior to entering the third decade of life; and that nearly 10% of 18- and 19-year-old college students were found to meet the diagnostic criteria for substance abuse from the *Diagnostic and Statistical Manual of Mental Disorders* (DSM-III) (American Psychiatric Association, 1980).

Lack of Knowledge

Despite widespread recognition that a significant minority of adolescents use substances excessively and as a result are at great risk for incurring serious harm, there is a paucity of research and theory concerning the assessment and treatment of substance abuse among youth. Donovan and Marlatt's (1988) influential book, *Assessment of Addictive Behaviors*, for example, includes only *one paragraph* about the specifics of assessing adolescents. A similar state of affairs exists in the substance abuse treatment literature.

This dearth of knowledge concerning adolescent substance abuse has led to unfortunate consequences. The lack of standardized and widely accepted diagnostic criteria for adolescent substance abuse has resulted in disparate and atheoretical attempts to assess and treat substance abuse problems among youth (Harrell & Wirtz, 1989; Winters, 1990). As Blum (1987) has noted, most adolescent substance-abuse treatment programs base their services primarily on their own specific philosophical orientation (e.g., multidimensional vs. unitary etiology of drug use), using procedures extrapolated from adult substance abuse treatment models. For reasons described in the following sections, this is inappropriate and has compromised attempts to address adolescent substance abuse.

Adults Versus Adolescents

As any developmental psychopathologist would be quick to point out, adolescents differ significantly from adults in the processes that lead to and the manifestations of mental disorders. This is particularly true in the case of psychoactive substance use disorder. The progressive nature of the disorder, medical complications, physical dependence, and other chronic symptoms are less clearly associated with adolescent substance use problems than with adult substance abuse (Blum, 1987; Kaminer, 1991; White & Labouvie, 1989). Another difference is that adolescents who use substances tend to do so less often than adults but also tend to use in larger amounts, increasing their risk for suffering from acute effects (e.g., blackouts and hangovers) as well as for displaying behavioral concomitants of intoxication (e.g., belligerence) (White & Labouvie, 1989). An additional consideration is that substantial proportions of adolescent chemical abusers mature out of their problem-use patterns by early adulthood without exposure to formal intervention or treatment (Blum, 1987; Winters & Henly, 1988). This, in combination with the tendency of health professionals to overpathologize adolescent behavior and to view any adolescent drug use as pathologic (Blum, 1987), makes the diagnosis and treatment of psychoactive substance use disorder among adolescents especially confusing.

Developmental Factors

Equally important are developmental factors unique to adolescence that affect the risk of substance abuse (Botvin & Botvin, 1992). First is the *ascendancy of the peer group*, which increases adolescents' vulnerability to peer-related influences to use alcohol and drugs. As adolescents become more socially oriented and dependent upon the peer network, there is a concomitant rise in *conformity behavior*, which can independently influence substance use. Third are factors related to *cognitive development*. Adolescents, as they acquire formal operations, become exquisitely aware of contradictions and gray areas in the previously unquestioned actions of adults. Such cognitive changes can undermine previously acquired knowledge of the potential risks of using substances. Finally, issues related to *identity formation* and *public image* may substantially increase general susceptibility to advertising appeals and other social influences promoting substance use (e.g., drinking helps me look cool, drinking helps me look older).

DSM-IV Diagnostic Criteria

At the time of the writing of this chapter, DSM-IV draft criteria for the diagnosis of substance-related disorders were available (American Psychiatric Association, 1993). Given that the diagnosis of *substance dependence* is based primarily on clinical manifestations of tolerance and withdrawal, the progressive nature of the disorder, medical complications, and other chronic symptoms, adolescents are unlikely to meet criteria for this diagnosis. Adolescents with substance use problems are much more likely to meet *substance abuse* diagnostic criteria, which involve "a maladaptive pattern of substance use leading to clinically significant impairment or distress" (DSM-IV, p. H:3). "A maladaptive pattern of substance use" is defined by one or more of the following occurring at any time during the same 12-month period: (a) recurrent substance use resulting in a failure to meet major role obligations; (b) recurrent substance use in situation in which it is physically dangerous; (c) recurrent substance-use-related legal problems; or (d) continued substance use despite persistent social problems caused by or exacerbated by the effects of the substance. Adolescents are also likely to meet diagnostic criteria for *substance intoxication*, which involves clinically significant yet reversible behavioral or psychological changes due to the recent ingestion of a substance.

PROTOTYPIC ASSESSMENT

Fundamental Questions

Skinner (1981) outlined three intersecting questions fundamental to substance abuse assessment:

1. What are the important variables to assess?
2. How can the variables best be measured?
3. How can the assessment findings be used best to make treatment decisions?

In response to the first question, it is believed that the substance abuse problems are best conceptualized as resulting from interactions among biological, psychological, and social factors (see Donovan & Marlatt, 1988). Some of the implications of this biopsychosocial model are that reductionist views of substance abuse problems are inappropriate; that the concept of substance abuse is not categorical and, thus, not easily defined by a set of consensually agreed-upon criteria; and that one can gain the best understanding of the clinical condition of substance abuse by considering the interaction of variables that cut across biological, psychological, and social domains (Donovan, 1988). Within this framework, Tarter, Ott, and Mezzich (1991) have suggested that the ideal adolescent substance abuse assessment should include evaluation of the following domains: (a) the substance use behavior itself; (b) the type and severity of psychiatric morbidity that may be present and whether it preceded or developed after the substance use disorder; (c) cognition, with specific attention to neuropsychological functioning; (d) family organization and interactional patterns; (e) social skills; (f) vocational adjustment; (g) recreation and leisure activities; (h) personality; (i) school adjustment; (j) peer affiliation; (k) legal status; and (l) physical health.

In regard to the second question on the measurement of biological, psychological, and social factors related to adolescent substance abuse, a biopsychosocial conceptualization suggests the need for broad-spectrum assessment (Donovan, 1988). Ideal assessment data should include self-reports of the client (gained through self-monitoring, clinical interview, and/or structured reporting forms); reports from significant others (e.g. parents, teachers); direct observation of the client's behavior in laboratory, quasi-naturalistic,or naturalistic settings; physiological measure; and, psychometric testing.

The third question, concerning the best way to use substance abuse assessment findings, has only recently begun to receive the attention that it deserves. Frequently identified purposes behind assessment include (a) screening for problems; (b) establishing a diagnosis; (c) establishing eligibility and appropriateness for treatment; (d) understanding the individual more comprehensively, and (e) determining which form of treatment, if any, is most appropriate. The authors would like to add the following purposes, taken from Miller and Rollnich (1991), to the list: (f) providing pretreatment scores that later can be compared with status on these same dimensions after treatment in order to assess and document improvement; and (g) building motivation (ie., *motivation* defined as the probability that a person will enter into, continue, and adhere to a specific change strategy) and strengthening commitment for change.

Performing the Assessment

Performing a substance abuse assessment begins with the preparation of the patient and her or his parents for the evaluation. Racusin and Moss (1991) recommend initially discussing the assessment with the parents. The purpose of testing should be explained in a clear, forthright manner. The referring clinician should clarify her or his ongoing relationship with the family and should facilitate contact with the clinician who will perform the assessment. Parents should also be encouraged to share the preparatory information with their adolescent, and the referring clinician should be prepared to help with this task. Among points to emphasize are that testing is being pursued in an effort to provide relevant interpersonal or educational help and that the assessment professional is a "talking doctor" who will not perform any physically invasive procedures. Preparatory information should be reiterated to the adolescent immediately prior to initiating testing.

The assessment clinician is likely to take one or two approaches to evaluating substance abuse (Donovan, 1988). The first approach, termed *clinical hypotheses testing*, involves generating several hypotheses about the identified problem that cut across biological, psychological, and social domains, and then examining each in turn. This approach is preferred when it is relatively certain prior to the assessment that the adolescent is experiencing substance-use-related difficulties. A second approach, called *sequential evaluation*, involves beginning with a substance abuse screen followed by a basic substance use assessment if the screen is positive, and moving on to specialized assessment (e.g., neurophsychological evaluation) if indicated. This approach is preferred when, prior to the assessment, little is known about whether the adolescent has been involved with substances.

Once the assessment is complete, it is important to provide parents and the adolescent with feedback about the results. As Miller and Rollnick (1991) noted, personalized feedback can be persuasive input for convincing clients that they are not where they ought to be. Miller and Rollnick recommended not trying to prove things to clients. Each important finding from the assessment should be described, along with information necessary to understand what the finding means. In order to avoid eliciting defensiveness, results can be presented in a manner that underscores freedom of choice (e.g., "I don't know what you will make of this result, but . . ."). An accusatory or scare-tactic tone, especially with adolescents, should be expressly avoided. Once the results have been presented, the clinician should solicit and reflect the adolescent's and her or his parents' reactions to this information. Occasionally, assessment feedback will arouse strong emotions from adolescents and/or their parents, and the clinician should be prepared to deal with such reactions. The feedback session should conclude with a summary of what has transpired, including risks and problems that have emerged from assessment findings, the clients' (i.e., the adolescent and her or his parents) own reactions to the feedback, and self-motivational statements that have been made, and an invitation for the clients to add to or to correct the summary.

ACTUAL ASSESSMENT

Strains and Confounds

Winters (1990) has identified five factors that strain attempts to accurately and comprehensively assess adolescent substance abuse: First, there are significant gaps in scientific knowledge concerning substance abuse among adolescents. Among important questions that remained unanswered are (a) Can adolescents be meaningfully differentiated in terms of problem severity (e.g., abuse vs. dependence)? (b) What other problems accompany adolescent chemical involvement? and (c) Can the identification of distinct diagnostic subgroups lead to client-treatment "matches"? Second, the demand for treatment and intervention continues to expand. At present, there are more adolescents in need of treatment than there are treatment slots available. Third, the *chemical dependency* label has become increasingly popular. Parents and/or treatment facilities often find the diagnosis of chemical dependency more acceptable than mental illness or delinquency, which may lead to the inappropriate labeling of certain individuals as substance abusers. Fourth are the concerns of watchdog groups, including questions about the ethics of adolescent treatment providers and difficulties that third-party payers have with the cost of treatment. Fifth and finally, adolescents inherently pose problems for assessment. Developmental issues, such as identity formation and cognitive changes, complicate the assessment process.

A more general factor that muddles attempts to assess adolescent substance abuse is the varied and multidimensional nature of substance use and misuse among youth (Farrell & Strang, 1991). Adolescent substance abusers differ in the type of frequency of chemicals used, the actual and anticipated effects and consequences resulting from that use, the contexts and motivations in which use occurs, and the factors that have contributed to or accompany their involvement with chemicals (Henly & Winters, 1989). Moreover, it is important to realize that, just as there may be a variety of paths into alcohol and drug abuse among adolescents, there may be different paths leading out of substance involvement (Henly & Winters, 1989).

Another factor that confounds the assessment of adolescent substance abuse is the tendency among treatment professionals to rely primarily on self-report data. While several investigators have found such data to be a reliable indicator of substance use among adolescents (Polich, 1982; Rouse, Kozel, & Richard, 1985: Single, Kandel, & Johnson, 1975), attempts to validate self-report data (e.g., collecting response-distortion data, biochemical measures, and/or collateral reports) are often neglected. Bailey, Flewelling, and Rachal (1992) have identified two additional problems with using self-reports of adolescent substance use: (a) the reliability of data concerning the age of first use is questionable and remains underinvestigated, and (b) reliability estimates are mathematically constrained to be high because they reflect a consistent pattern of reported nonuse (i.e., such estimates are spuriously high because they include nonusers).

Assessment Measures

As noted earlier in this chapter, there is a general lack of research concerning the assessment of adolescent substance abuse. It is important to recognize, however, that a valid and clinically relevant assessment is essential to effective intervention with adolescent substance abusers (Tarter, 1990). Until recently, clinicians have relied mostly on clinical judgment or locally developed procedures to diagnose adolescent substance use problems (Owen & Nyberg, 1983). Hopefully, this will change as standardized and clinically valid instruments are introduced into the literature. It should be noted that standardized assessment offers several advantages over more traditional approaches, including providing a benchmark against which clinical decisions can be compared and validated, immunity to rater bias and inconsistencies, providing a common language from which improved communication in the field can develop, and permitting the pooling of data from descriptive and evaluation studies (Henly & Winters, 1989). The following is a summary of some of the more promising measures.

Self-Reporting Screening Measures

1. *Adolescent Alcohol Involvement Scale* (AAIS) (Mayer & Filstead, 1979; Robertson, 1989). The AAIS is a 14-item self-report scale that evaluates the degree to which drinking interferes with psychological functioning, social relations, and family living. It is designed to identify adolescents who are misusing alcohol, but it does not provide for discrimination between different types and configurations. The instrument has not been independently validated, but it is noteworthy for being among the first attempts to develop a standardized measure of adolescent alcohol use problems.

2. *Youth Diagnostic Screening Test* (YDST) (Alibrandi, 1978). The YDST is quite similar to the AAIS in that it is a brief screening instrument and does not discriminate between different problem types and configurations. It, too, has not been independently validated, but it is among the early attempts to develop a standardized measure of adolescent alcohol abuse.

3. *Adolescent Drinking Inventory: Drinking and You* (ADI) (Harrell, Sowder, & Kapsak, 1988; Harrell & Wirtz, 1989). The ADI is a 24-item self-report inventory, designed for use by clinicians without specialized training in substance abuse assessment. It is intended to determine whether adolescents should be referred for further alcohol evaluation; it utilizes multidimensional conceptualization of adolescent drinking, and possesses good psychometric properties.

4. *Rutgers Alcohol Problem Index* (RAPI) (White & Labouvie, 1989). The RAPI is an empirically derived 23-item self-report scale that covers all the criteria required for a DSM-III-R diagnosis (American Psychiatric Association, 1987), with the exception of reasons for use. White and Labouvie omit reasons for use because they believe those reasons may be most associated with *heavy* use and, thus, may not fit clearly into an operationalization of problem drinking among adolescents. Psychometric data support the validity and reliability of the instrument; however, data have not yet been published on clinical samples and clinical versus nonclinical sample comparisons.

5. *Perceived-Benefit-of-Drinking Scale* (Petchers & Singer, 1987: Petchers, Singer, Angelotta, & Chow, 1988). This five-item self-report scale was developed to address the need for a quick, easy-to-administer screening instrument that could be used in health care settings to enhance the detection of adolescent alcohol abuse. Recently, the measure has been updated to include five similar statements with reference to drugs (i.e., the Percieved-Benefit-of-Drugs Scale). A potential advantage of the Perceived-Benefit scales, in comparison to other brief measures, is that they are not dependent upon directly eliciting information about drinking/drug use patterns or negative consequences resulting from such patterns. Psychometric data support the reliability and validity of the scales in high school samples, but no data have been published on clinical samples.

6. *Drug and Alcohol Problem Quick Screen* (DAP) (Schwartz & Wirtz, 1990). The DAP is a 30-item self-report scale that is designed to detect adolescent substance misuse. Schwartz and Wirtz have also developed a 14-item short version of the measure. The DAP appears to be an adolescent-acceptable, reasonably sensitive means of detecting substance-use-problem behaviors in primary care settings. However, it has not been independently validated, and data have not been published on clinical samples.

7. *Personal Experience Screening Questionnaire* (PESQ) (Winters, 1991): This 40-item self-report inventory is designed to identify adolescents in need of a drug abuse assessment referral. It includes a problem-severity scale, two response-distortion scales, and a supplemental information section providing data about the respondent's psychosocial status and drug-use history. The PESQ shares many items in common with more comprehensive Personal Experience Inventory (Winters & Henly, 1989; see next section). Published psychometric data support the reliability and validity of the PESQ in both nonclinical and clinical populations.

Self-Report Multidimensional Measures

1. *Personal Experience Inventory* (PEI) (Henly & Winters, 1989). The PEI is a self-report instrument that includes 15 clinical scales measuring the severity of drug use and 17 additional scales measuring psychosocial functioning (i.e., self-esteem, peer relationships, family functioning, behavioral disturbance, achievement motivation, and social adjustment). The PEI attempts to (a) measure the adolescent's behavioral involvement with alcohol and drugs; (b) assess the frequency, style, duration, and sequelae of drug use; (c) evaluate personality characteristics and environmental circumstances of the user; (d) assist in the formulation of DSM-III-R diagnoses; (e) identify psychosocial stressors; and (f) examine for the presence of other disorders besides drug abuse. Extensive psychometric data have been published about the PEI, and the validity and reliability of the scale have received strong support.

2. *Drug Use Screening Inventory* (DUSI) (Tarter, 1990). The DUSI is a self-report measure that profiles substance-use involvement in conjunction with the severity of disturbance in nine spheres of everyday functioning (e.g., school adjustment, social skills, family functioning). Unique to the DUSI is an explicit attempt to link assessment findings to treatment; the DUSI produces a needs assessment and diagnostic summary intended to lead directly to the development of a treatment plan. Published psychometric data support the validity and reliability of the instrument. Additional standardization data are currently being collected.

Interview-Based Measures

1. *Guided Rational Adolescent Substance Abuse Profile* (Addiction Recovery Corporation, 1986). This interview collects information regarding family interactional patterns, drug and alcohol involvement, behavior, and personality disorder that can be used to yield a DSM-III diagnosis. Supporting psychometric studies have not been published.

2. *Drug Taking Evaluation Scale* (DTES) (Holsten & Waal, 1980; Waal & Hostein, 1980). The DTES evaluates older adolescents and young adults on four dimensions: (a) drug-use behavior, including frequency, type of drug use, and control over substance consumption; (b) social functioning and adjustment, work or educational performance, perceived social acceptance, and personal autonomy; (c) social role identification, particularly as it relates to family relationships; and (d) maturity, psychopathology, personality

disorder, and treatment needs. This measure was developed on a Norwegian sample; data from an American sample have not been published.

3. *Adolescent Drug Abuse Diagnosis* (Friedman, 1987). This interview evaluates drug- and alcohol-use patterns, medical and legal status, family problems and background, school or employment record, psychological well-being, and social as well as peer relationships. It is intended for use in clinical settings to aid treatment planning. However, the interview and supporting data have not been published.

4. *Teen Addiction Severity Index* (T-ASI) (Kaminer, Bukstein, & Tarter, 1991; Kaminer, Wagner, Plummer, & Seifer, 1993). This interview is an adaption of the Addiction Severity Index (ASI) (McLellan, Luborsky, Woody, & O'Brien, 1980), an interview concerning substance use widely used with adults. The T-ASI evaluates seven domains, including substance use, school, employment, family, peer/social, legal, and psychiatric disturbance. Initial validity and reliability data support the use of the measure with clinical populations.

5. *Home, Education, Activities, Drug Use and Abuse, Sexual Behavior, and Suicidality and Depression* (HEADSS) (Cohen, MacKenzie, & Yates, 1991). HEADSS is a screening interview intended to provide a psychosocial data base from which to draw information in a clinical setting. It begins with less emotionally charged issues and moves to more sensitive ones; it is designed to be administered by a physician or nurse practitioner. Supporting psychometric studies have not been published.

Research Surveys

Several epidemiologically-oriented surveys of adolescent substance use have been developed primarily for research purposes. These measures tend to be quite lengthy and have limited utility from a clinical perspective. However, data from these instruments have contributed significantly to the knowledge about substance use in adolescence. Among the most influential of these measures are the following:

1. Youth Experience Questionnaire (Dunnette et al., 1980)
2. Research Triangle Institute's Study of Adolescent Drinking Behavior and Attitudes (Rachal et al., 1980)
3. Institute of Social Research's Annual High School Senior Survey Questionnaire (Johnston, O'Malley, & Bachman, 1991)
4. National Household Survey (National Institute of Drug Abuse, 1990)
5. American Drug and Alcohol Survey (ADAS) (Oetting & Beauvais, 1986)
6. Chemical Dependency Assessment Survey (CDAS) (Oetting, Beauvais, Edwards, & Waters, 1984)
7. Instruments developed by Jessor (1976); Gossett, Lewis, and Phillips (1972); and Single, Kandel, and Johnson (1975)

Other research-oriented surveys that may have more applicability in clinical settings include (a) a measure developed by Cohen, Karras, and Hughes (1977) that evaluates drug-use severity and that includes the assessment of the history, effects, usage patter, utility, and social basis for substance consumption; (b) a six-item questionnaire developed by Smart and Jones (1970) that measures the frequency of drug use, availability, source, and history of professional contacts for drug-use problems; and (c) Client Substance Abuse

Index (Moore, 1980), which focuses on drug-use severity within the DSM-III diagnostic scheme.

Semi-Structured Diagnostic Interviews

Several semi-structured psychiatric diagnostic interviews have been developed for use with children and adolescents. While not solely intended for the evaluation of substance abuse, many of these interviews include portions that can aid in the diagnosis of psychoactive substance use disorder. Further, many have complementary versions that can be administered to parents or other collaterals. Among the most prominent of these instruments are the (a) Diagnostic Interview Schedule for Children and Adolescents (Herjanic & Reich, 1982; Reich, Herjanic, Welner, & Gandhy, 1982); (b) Kiddie Schedule for Affective Disorders and Schizophrenia-E (Orvaschel, Puig-Antich, Chambers, Tabrizi, & Johnson, 1982); (c) National Institutes of Mental Health Diagnostic Interview Schedule for Children (Costello, Edelbrock, & Costello, 1984, 1985; Robins, Helzer, Croughan, & Ratcliff, 1981); and (d) Child Assessment Schedule (Hodges, Kline, Stern, Cytryn, & McKnew, 1982).

PROTOTYPIC TREATMENT

General Concerns

In the 1970s and 1980s, interest in treating adolescent substance abuse rose dramatically. Commensurate with this boost in concern has been the development of multiple treatment approaches and orientations. Unfortunately, little attention has been given to an examination of their differential effectiveness. All too often, treatment services are provided to adolescents without being adequately adapted to the client's specific needs (for exceptions, see Babor, et al., 1991; Institute of Medicine, 1990; Tarter, 1990). Indeed, research has suggested that a treatment that is helpful to one client may actually be harmful to another (Annis & Chan, 1983). Clearly, matching an appropriate treatment to the unique characteristics of the adolescent substance abuser becomes imperative. Put simply, "adolescents who are appropriately matched to treatment will show outcomes superior to those who are unmatched or mismatched" (Hester & Miller, 1988, p. 27).

Correspondingly, only treatment approaches that have been subject to empirical scrutiny and validation should be implemented with adolescent substance abusers. However, a review of the literature reveals a dearth of research addressing this important issue (for exceptions, see Friedman & Glickman, 1986; Friedman, Glickman, & Kovach, 1986). For instance, Schinke, Botvin, and Orlandi (1991) remarked, "Surprisingly, few clinical studies have investigated the effectiveness of treatment programs for adolescents" (p. 49). Kaminer (1991) similarly noted, "Paucity of reports from treatment services, scarce treatment quality assessments, and, above all, much disagreement about major treatment approaches account for the difficulty in suggesting optimal treatment strategies for substance-abusing adolescents" (p. 337). Finally, the most extensive review to date of controlled evaluations of adolescent substance treatment programs concluded only that some treatment is better than none and that no particular treatment method has emerged as superior to any other (Catalano, Hawkins, Wells, Miller, & Brewer, 1990–1991). Evidently, the very foundation upon which to build and institute efficacious adolescent substance abuse treatment is weak.

It is important to note that, in addition to the field's limited knowledge about differential treatment effectiveness, even less is known about the mechanisms of change underlying successful — or for that matter, unsuccessful — treatment. Clinicians' perceptions of the treatment processes believed to be curative are clearly dependent on their own particular orientation (e.g., behavioral model vs. 12-Step disease model; Morgenstern & McCrady, 1992). Delineation of the processes through which treatment has its impact is crucial in order to enhance treatment efficacy (Miller, 1992; see also Kassel & Wagner, 1993). Miller (1992) summarizes, "Once the key processes of a treatment method are identified, treatment efficacy can be increased by ensuring that the essential elements have been included" (p. 96).

As discussed earlier, a properly conducted assessment consists of appraising each client's unique characteristics and presenting problems, thus setting the stage for provision of appropriate treatment. Implicit in this strategy is the belief that adolescent substance abusers are not a homogeneous population. They likely come to use, and abuse, drugs for a variety of reasons. The observation that numerous risk factors for drug abuse have been identified is consistent with the notion of heterogeneity among adolescent substance abusers (for an extensive review, see Hawkins, Catalano, & Miller, 1992). As noted earlier, it follows that, when formulating and implementing a treatment plan, the clinician should not only assess substance use behavior, but, when applicable, should also treat other related domains (e.g., coexisting psychiatric disorders, school adjustment, family organization and functioning) that might very well contribute to and sustain the client's drug use (see Tarter, 1990). Put simply, "The modal adolescent patient in chemical dependency treatment has multiple problems" (Hoffmann, Sonis, & Halikas, 1987, p. 453).

Given that treatment approaches used with adolescents often mirror those used with adults, the question arises as to whether such approaches are necessarily appropriate for the adolescent substance abuser. In all likelihood, the answer is an equivocal "No." Adolescence is often a time of tremendous upheaval and transition in biological, psychological, and social domains. It follows that the motives underlying and the factors associated with adolescents' drug-taking behavior may be markedly different from those governing adult substance abuse. When viewed within this developmental framework, "drug use may be seen as a way to consolidate with peers, as a way to establish autonomy, as a way to separate from the family, and as a way to address the emerging questions and hypotheses adolescents have about themselves" (Murray & Perry, 1985, p. 248). More generally, then, drug use can be viewed as a coping strategy (albeit a maladaptive one) with which adolescents deal with the vicissitudes of youth (Murray & Perry, 1985; see also Wills & Shiffman, 1985). Plainly, the developmental differences between adults and adolescents must be taken into account when treating the adolescent substance abuser (Wheeler & Malmquist, 1987).

In summary, ideal treatment of adolescent substance abuse should (a) embrace empirically validated interventions; (b) identify the key curative factors, or mechanisms of change, that underlie positive behavioral change; (c) assess and, when necessary, treat other relevant domains of the client's life (e.g., comorbid psychopathology); (d) match the client's needs to and intervention strategy best suited to meet those needs; and (e) recognize the unique developmental issues and problems inherent in adolescence.

Specific Strategies

Despite limitations in the state of current knowledge, several behavioral interventions hold promise for effectively treating the adolescent substance abuser. First, it has been empirically demonstrated that some methods are more effective than others when treating adult substance abusers (see Miller, 1992). While the limitations of extrapolations from the adult literature are acknowledged, several of these approaches may be appropriate for treating adolescent substance abuse. Secondly, based on an examination of situational factors associated with relapse among adolescents, several treatment strategies emerge as potentially beneficial (Catalano et al, 1990–1991). Drawing upon both the adult and adolescent literatures, the following paragraphs briefly outline some of the more encouraging strategies.

Based on the assumption that some adolescents engage in drug use as a way of coping with stress (Wills, 1985), one treatment approach consists of teaching clients to use more adaptive coping skills. Indeed, *stress management* is emerging as a promising strategy with which to treat substance abuse problems (e.g., Rohsenow, Smith, & Johnson, 1985; see also Stockwell & Town, 1989). Examples of stress management techniques include relaxation training, biofeedback, deep breathing exercises, autogenic training, aerobic exercise, meditation, deep muscle relaxation, coping-skill rehearsal, and desensitization. A host of controlled trials have supported the efficacy of these interventions with adults (e.g., Lanyon, Primo, Terrell, & Wener, 1972; Murphy, Pagano, & Marlatt, 1986; Rohsenow et al., 1985).

A related area of inquiry has suggested that coping in the face of temptation (craving) to use drugs is integrally related to outcome (Brown, Stetson, & Beatty, 1989). These coping skills can be broadly categorized as either *behavioral* (e.g., physical activity, deep breathing, escaping the situation) or *cognitive* (e.g., thinking about positive consequences of not using drugs, thinking about negative consequences of using drugs, thoughts related to delay; see Shiffman, 1985). It has been demonstrated, for example, that, among adult smokers trying to quit, the performance of a coping response when tempted to smoke is the single best predictor of outcome (Shiffman, 1984). Clearly, effective treatment programs should include a component that communicates to the adolescent substance abuser the importance of coping, via cognitive and/or behavioral strategies, when confronted with the urge to drink or use drugs.

Correspondingly, *social skills training* (SST) has emerged as another potentially efficacious intervention (see Chaney, 1989; Van Hasselt, Hersen, & Milliones, 1978). A variant of coping skills training, SST has been used widely as a behavioral technique for treating a wide range of populations with social skills deficits, including drug dependent individuals (e.g., Chaney, O'Leary, & Marlatt, 1978; Oei & Jackson, 1982; Sanchez-Craig & Walker, 1982). SST involves teaching more effective interpersonal communication skills, as well as how to cope with negative intrapersonal situations. Hence, clients practice ways of responding to potentially problematic situations (e.g., parties, dates, negative emotional states) in new and more effective ways. When viewed from a developmental perspective, SST becomes particularly pertinent as drug use may actually supplant or retard the mastery of such social skills (Pentz, 1985; Van Hasselt, Null, Kempton, & Bukstein, 1993). Additionally, SST appears to produce decreases in adolescent drug use when implemented as part of a prevention program (Pentz, 1985).

From the perspective of family systems theory, adolescent substance abuse may be most related to family characteristics (see Bry, 1988; Bry & Krinsley, 1990). Broadly defined, *behavioral family therapy* (BFT) includes the use of techniques borrowed from family systems theory (e.g., "joining" the family, reenactment, reframing) and from behavior theory (e.g., functional analysis, modeling, provision of reinforcement, contingency contracting). The therapist evaluates behavioral sequences in order to delineate interpersonal functions, reframes those sequences in order to change attributions, and then identifies areas in which the family lacks necessary skills (see Gordon & Arbuthnot, 1987). Several studies have suggested that family therapy can be an effective mode of treatment for adolescent substance abusers (e.g., Szapocznik, Kurtines, Foote, Perez-Vidal, & Hervis, 1986; Szapocznik et al., 1988).

An alternate treatment strategy aimed particularly at problem drinkers is *behavioral self-control training* (BSCT). Guided by principles of self-management, BSCT can be used with outcome goals of either abstinence or moderation. Briefly, BSCT employs various behavioral techniques aimed at instilling a sense of personal control over drinking behavior. These techniques include goal setting, self-monitoring, rate control, drink/drug refusal, self-reward for success, alternative coping skills, and functional analysis of drinking situations (see Hester & Miller, 1988; Miller & Munoz, 1982). A growing research literature supports the efficacy of BSCT (e.g., Harris & Miller, 1990; Sanchez-Craig, Annis, Bornet, & MacDonald, 1984). The idea of endorsing controlled use as an outcome, while certainly controversial, may be suitable in some cases given that (a) many adolescents in treatment subsequently relapse anyway (Catalano et al., 1990–1991) and (b) the natural history of the disorder suggests that many adolescents mature out of substance use without any formal treatment (Blum, 1987; see also Peele, 1987). However, this approach has not yet been systematically examined in an adolescent sample.

A relatively new approach to treating substance abuse is *motivational enhancement* (ME). Developed by William Miller (Miller, 1983, 1985; Miller & Rollnick, 1991), this intervention aims to bolster clients' motivation to modify their destructive behavior. Miller (1989) expresses, "[motivation] involves recognizing a problem, searching for a way to change, and then beginning, continuing, and complying with that change strategy" (p. 69). Some of the strategies employed by ME include giving advice, removing barriers to change, instilling a sense of choice, decreasing the attractiveness of substance using behavior, establishing external contingencies designed to persuade the client to seek help, providing personal feedback, setting up goals for change, and expressing optimism and empathy about the client's situation (see Miller & Rollnick, 1991). While evidence has suggested that ME has potential for treating adolescent substance abusers as well as adult substance abusers (Tober, 1991), there have been no controlled outcome trials to date.

Conclusions

Promising strategies for treating adolescent substance abuse include stress management, coping-with-temptation-skills training, social skills training, behavioral family therapy, behavioral self-control training, and motivational enhancement. These approaches have received ample empirical validation in adult populations and have potential for treating substance abuse among adolescents. Furthermore, these treatment regimens utilize mechanisms, or processes, of change that are well delineated and reliable, facilitating empirical validation of the effectiveness of these approaches with teens.

ACTUAL TREATMENT

Strains and Confounds

Currently, several unresolved issues act as barriers to effective treatment. First, the ongoing debate as to whether controlled substance use is a desirable, or even a possible, outcome rages on (Marlatt, 1985; Peele, 1988; Wallace, 1989). The notion of what constitutes a successful treatment outcome is questionable. Any of the following general outcomes might or might not be deemed successful: (a) retention in treatment; (b) abstinence; (c) abstinence plus improvement in other pertinent domains; (d) moderate nonproblematic substance use. While often viewed as an ideologic dilemma, the authors believe that the judgment of what comprises treatment success must ultimately be an empirical one.

Second, high rates of coexisting psychopathology among adolescents presenting for substance abuse treatment introduce potential problems with respect to how the psychopathology should concurrently be treated, as well as the extent to which it is a secondary or primary disorder. Indeed, among adolescents presenting with a substance abuse problem, 42% to 70% meet DSM-III-R criteria for conduct disorder, 35% to 52% meet criteria for major depression, and more than 40% have a comorbid anxiety disorder (Bukstein, Glancy, & Kaminer, 1992; Dimileo, 1989; Stowell & Estroff, 1992).

Third, while family therapy is clearly emerging as a treatment of choice, the fact that many adolescent substance abusers are estranged from their families becomes problematic. Correspondingly, dysfunctional families are less likely to comply with, and adhere to, treatment.

Fourth, the question of which treatment level (inpatient, residential community, or outpatient) is most effective with which particular client is not yet fully understood. For a host of conceptual as well as pragmatic reasons (e.g., cost effectiveness), the authors believe that the least intensive level should be the first choice (see Miller & Hester, 1986a, 1986b). However, if initial treatment proves ineffective, then the client should be moved to a more intensive level of intervention.

Fifth, evidence that the majority of adolescents identified as problem drinkers or drug users no longer demonstrate such problematic behavior after age 22 (e.g., Kandel & Logan, 1984; Yamaguchi & Kandel, 1984a, 1984b) has implications for both assessment and treatment. One can question, for instance, whether adolescent drug abusers should be given a lifelong label *chemically dependent* when in fact many are likely to mature out of substance abuse. Correspondingly, there may be a tendency among professionals to overpathologize drug-and alcohol-related behaviors (Blum, 1987) when instead "experimental use of various drugs, both licit and illicit, may be considered a normative behavior among United States teenagers in terms of prevalence and from a developmental-task perspective" (Newcomb & Bentler, 1988, p. 214).

The Minnesota Model

While there are multiple treatment philosophies and modalities currently available for treating adolescent substance abuse, virtually all programs expose abstinence as the desired outcome (Hoffmann, Sonis, & Halikas, 1987). Adherents to an abstinence-based orientation frequently employ the *Minnesota Model* of substance dependence treatment (see Cook, 1988a, 1988b; Laudergan, 1982). Cook (1988a) ascribes four key tenets to the Minnesota Model philosophy. The first is the belief that substance dependent individuals can modify and change their beliefs, attitudes, and behavior; this allegedly engenders feelings of hope in individuals who might otherwise feel hopeless about their condition. Second, the goals of treatment include abstinence from *all* mood-altering chemicals and a general improvement in life-style. Third, the model endorses the "disease" concept of substance dependence. From the disease perspective, the hallmark of substance abuse is loss of control over use, and substance abuse is viewed as chronic and progressive, inevitably resulting in death if left untreated (Morrison & Smith 1987).

Perhaps the most salient feature of the Minnesota Model is its association with, and endorsement of, the principles of Alcoholics Anonymous (AA) and other 12-Step programs (e.g., Narcotics Anonymous). AA views alcoholism as a four-fold illness comprised of physical, emotional, spiritual, and mental factors (Alcoholics Anonymous, 1976). According to AA, critical aspects of successful recovery include (a) admitting one is powerless over alcohol; b) accepting the concept of a "higher power"; (c) writing, and expressing to another person, a "fearless moral inventory" of oneself; (d) making amends to all those whom the alcoholic harmed; and (e) "passing on" the AA message to others who suffer from substance abuse and dependence (see Alcoholics Anonymous, 1984, for an in-depth discussion of the 12 Steps and 12 Traditions of AA).

As pervasive as AA is, it remains controversial in that there are little data to support its claims of success (McCrady & Irvine, 1989). Further, while there has been a great deal of armchair speculation as to what makes AA work, virtually no empirical study has yet examined the processes of change associated with success in AA (see Kassel & Wagner, in press). AA is unquestionably ideologically bound, and, while many have suggested that its powerful ideology is central to its alleged success, it may also act as a deterrent to potential initiates (Kassel & Wagner, 1993). Correspondingly, as AA was initially developed to serve the needs of older, *chronic* alcoholics, one must also question the appropriateness of this approach in treating adolescent substance abusers.

When compared to the proposed characteristics of ideal adolescent substance abuse treatment outlined earlier, additional problems with the Minnesota Model emerge. First, while there is some evidence to suggest that the Minnesota Model is an effective treatment modality for adults (see Cook, 1988b; Hoffman & Miller, 1992), most studies of this approach are hampered by methodological limitations (Cook, 1988b). Second, little is known about the processes (both inter- and intrapersonal) underlying change in this form of treatment. Third, with the emphasis on substance abuse as a primary disease, there is a danger that critical problem areas may go untreated. Fourth, inherent in AA philosophy is the belief in relative homogeneity among substance abusing individuals; they abuse drugs because they have a disease. Moreover, clinical lore holds that certain characteristics, such as denial and omnipotence, are universally present among adolescent substance abusers (Wheeler & Malmquist, 1987). The result is that it becomes difficult to match a client's specific needs to an appropriate intervention when all clients are believed to have the same needs. A corollary is that the onus of recovery is placed entirely on the patient; if the treatment does not work, it is the client's fault. Finally, as noted earlier, the Minnesota Model may not recognize the unique developmental needs of the adolescent.

It is noteworthy, however, that the Minnesota Model does incorporate many *behavioral* strategies in its approach to adolescent substance abuse. More specifically, Kassel (1992) identifies the following tactics as intrinsic to AA: (a) *stimulus control*: avoid drinking environments, develop interests and habits incompatible with drinking; (b) *behavioral coping*: "don't drink, and go to meetings," call your sponsor; (c) *cognitive coping*: recite the "serenity prayer," tell yourself to take it "one day at a time"; (d) *covert sensitization*; remember the *consequences* of your drinking, tell your "story" at meetings; (e) *self-management*: stress delayed reinforcers versus immediate reinforcers despite initial punishments (e.g., craving, social anxiety); (f) *expanding behavioral repertoire*: learn social skills, establish social support, implement new reinforcers; and (g) *modeling*: watch and learn from successful AA members. Thus, behavioral strategies clearly complement, and may be essential to, a 12-Step Minnesota Model approach. Correspondingly, the clinician working with adolescent substance abusers should be knowledgeable of the 12-Step orientation because it can be an effective adjunct to therapeutic intervention (Chappel, 1992).

SUMMARY

Adolescent substance abuse is currently a significant health concern in the United States. Despite widespread recognition of the adolescent substance abuse problem, there is little research and theory concerning the assessment and treatment of substance abuse among youth. As a result, most adolescent substance abuse treatment programs currently base their services on their own specific philosophical orientation, using procedures extrapolated from adult substance abuse treatment models. However, adolescents differ from adults in many fundamental respects that are likely to influence the manifestation, assessment, and treatment of substance use problems.

Adolescent treatment programs tend to consider adolescent substance abusers to be a relatively homogeneous group and treat each client similarly. However, research has shown that teens who abuse substances differ in the type and frequency of chemicals used, the actual and anticipated effects and consequences resulting from that use, the contexts and motivations in which use occurs, and the factors that have contributed to or accompany their involvement with chemicals. Moreover, there may be different paths leading out of substance involvement for different individuals.

Regarding the assessment of adolescent substance abuse, standardized assessment offers several advantages, including providing a benchmark against which clinical decisions can be compared and validated, immunity to rater bias and inconsistencies, providing a common language from which improved communication in the field can develop, and permitting the pooling of data from descriptive and evaluation studies. Some of the more promising measures were reviewed in this chapter, and points to consider when actually conducting an assessment were discussed.

Given the dearth of research concerning the treatment of substance abuse among teens, the adult literature was drawn upon, and some of the more encouraging treatment strategies were presented. Numbered among them were stress anxiety management, coping-with-temptation-skills training, social skills training, behavioral family therapy, behavioral self-control training, and motivational enhancement. Given the hegemony of the Minnesota Model in actual clinical practice, the strengths and weaknesses of disease-model approaches were reviewed in some detail. Further, an attempt was made to demonstrate how the Minnesota Model may be conceptualized from a behavioral perspective.

To summarize, the current state of adolescent substance abuse assessment and treatment, while far from ideal, shows some promise. However, integration of empirically validated assessment and intervention approaches into clinical practice remains critical to address the growing need for efficacious adolescent substance abuse intervention. Clinicians can no longer afford to be steeped in dogma to the exclusion of promising new approaches. Scientific rigor and scrutiny must be applied to begin to conquer the formidable problem of adolescent substance abuse.

REFERENCES

Addiction Recovery Coporation. (1986). *Guided Rational Adolescent Substance Abuse Profile.* Waltham, MA: Author.

Alcoholics Anonymous. (1976). *Alcoholics Anonymous: The story of how many thousands of men and women have recovered from alcoholism.* New York: AA World Services.

Alcoholics Anonymous. (1984). *Twelve steps and twelve traditions.* New York: AA World Services.

Alibrandi, T. (1978). *Young alcoholics.* Minneapolis, MN: Comp Care Publications.

American Psychiatric Association. (1980). *Diagnostic and statistical manual of mental disorders* (3rd ed.). Washington, DC: Author.

American Psychiatric Association. (1987). *Diagnostic and statistical manual of mental disorders* (3rd ed., rev.). Washington, DC: Author.

American Psychiatric Association. (1993). *DSM-IV draft criteria.* Washington, DC: Author.

Annis, H. M., & Chan, D. (1983). The differential treatment model: Empirical evidence from a personality typology of adult offenders. *Criminal Justice and Behavior, 10,* 159–173.

Babor, T. F., Del Boca, F. K., McLaney, M. A., Jacobi, B., Higgins-Biddle, J., & Hass, W. (1991). Just say Y.E.S.: Matching adolescents to appropriate interventions for alcohol and other drug-related problems. *Alcohol Health and Research World, 15,* 77–86.

Bailey, S. L., Flewelling, R. L., & Rachal, J. V. (1992). The characterization of inconsistencies in self-reports of alcohol and marijuana use in a longitudinal study of adolescents. *Journal of Studies on Alcohol, 53,* 636–647.

Blum, R. W. (1987). Adolescent substance abuse: Diagnostic and treatment issues. *Pediatric Clinics of North America, 34,* 523–537.

Botvin, G. J., & Botvin, E. M. (1992). Adolescent tobacco, alcohol, and drug abuse: Prevention strategies, empirical findings, and assessment issues. *Developmental and Behavioral Pediatrics, 13,* 290–301.

Brown, S. A., Stetson, B. A., & Beatty, P. (1989). Cognitive and behavioral features of adolescent coping in high risk drinking situations. *Addictive Behaviors, 14,* 291–300.

Bry, B. H. (1988). Family-based approaches to reducing adolescent substance use: Theories, techniques, and findings. In E. R. Rahdert & J. Grabowski (Eds.), *Adolescent drug abuse: Analysis of treatment research* (NIDA Research Monograph No. 77, pp. 39–68). Washington, DC: U.S. Government Printing Office.

Bry, B. H., & Krinsley, K. A. (1990). Adolescent substance abuse. In E. L. Feindler & G. R. Kalfus (Eds.), *Adolescent behavior therapy handbook* (pp. 275–302). New York: Springer.

Bukstein, O. G., Glancy, L. G., & Kaminer, Y. (1992). Patterns of affective comorbidity in a clinical population of dually diagnosed adolescent substance abusers. *Journal of the American Academy of Child and Adolescent Psychiatry, 31,* 1041–1045.

Catalano, R. F., Hawkins, J. D., Wells, E. A., Miller, J., & Brewer, D. (1990–1991). Evaluation of the effectiveness of adolescent drug abuse treatment, assessment of risks for relapse, and promising approaches for relapse prevention. *International Journal of the Addictions, 25,* 1085–1140.

Chaney, E. F. (1989). Social skills training. In R. K. Hester & W. R. Miller (Eds.), *Handbook of alcoholism treatment approaches: Effective alternatives* (pp. 206–221). New York: Pergamon Press.

Chaney, E. F., O'Leary, M. R., & Marlatt, G. A. (1978). Skill training with alcoholics. *Journal of Consulting and Clinical Psychology, 46,* 1092–1104.

Chappel, J. N. (1992). Effective use of Alcoholics Anonymous and Narcotics Anonymous in treating patients. *Psychiatric Annals, 22,* 409–418.

Cohen, E., MacKenzie, R. G., & Yates, G. L. (1991). HEADSS, a psychosocial risk assessment instrument: Implications for designing effective intervention programs for runaway youth. *Journal of Adolescent Health, 12*, 539–544.

Cohen, M., Karras, A., & Hughes, R. (1977). The usefulness and reliability of a drug severity scale. *International Journal of the Addictions, 12*, 417–422.

Cook, C. C. H. (1988a). The Minnesota Model in the management of drug and alcohol dependency: Miracle, method, or myth? Part 1. The philosophy and the programme. *British Journal of Addiction, 83*, 625–634.

Cook, C. C. H. (1988b). The Minnesota Model in the management of drug and alcohol dependency: Miracle, method or myth? Part II. Evidence and conclusions. *British Journal of Addiction, 83*, 735–748.

Costello, J., Edelbrock, C., & Costello, A. (1984). *The reliability of the NIMH Diagnostic Interview for Children: A comparison between pediatric and psychiatric referrals*. Pittsburgh, PA: Western Psychiatric Institute and Clinic.

Costello, J., Edelbrock, C., & Costello, A. (1985). Validity of the NIMH Diagnostic Interview for Children: A comparison between psychiatric and pediatric referrals. *Journal of Abnormal Child Psychology and Psychiatry, 13*, 579–595.

Dimileo, L. (1989). Psychiatric syndromes in adolescent substance abusers. *American Journal of Psychiatry, 146*, 1212–1214.

Donovan, D. M. (1988). Assessment of addictive behaviors: Implications of an emerging biopsychosocial model. In D. M. Donovan & G. A. Marlatt (Eds.), *Assessment of addictive behaviors*. New York: Guilford Press.

Donovan, D. M., & Marlatt, G. A. (Eds.). (1988). *Assessment of addictive behaviors*. New York: Guilford Press.

Dunnette, M. D., Peterson, N. G., Houston, J. S., Rosse, R. L., Bosshardt, M. J., & Lammlein, S. E. (1980). *Causes and consequences of adolescent drug experiences: A final report* (Tech. Rep. No. 58). Minneapolis, MN: Personnel Decisions Research Institute.

Farrell, M., & Strang, J. (1991). Substance use and misuse in childhood and adolescence. *Journal of Child Psychology, Psychiatry, and Allied Disciplines, 32*, 109–128.

Friedman, A. S. (1987). *Adolescent Drug Abuse Diagnosis*. Unpublished manuscript, Philadelphia Psychiatric Center, Philadelphia, PA.

Friedman, A. S., & Glickman, N. W. (1986). Program characteristics for successful treatment of adolescent drug abuse. *The Journal of Nervous and Mental Disease, 174*, 669–679.

Friedman, A. S., Glickman, N. W., & Kovach, J. A. (1986). The relationship of drug program environmental variables to treatment outcome. *American Journal of Drug and Alcohol Abuse, 12*, 53–69.

Gordon, D. A., & Arbuthnot, J. (1987). Individual, group, and family interventions. In H. C. Quay (Ed.), *Handbook of juvenile delinquency* (pp. 290–324). New York: Wiley.

Gossett, J., Lewis, M., & Phillips, V. (1972). Psychological characteristics of adolescent drug abusers and abstainers: Some implications for preventive education. *Bulletin of the Menninger Clinic, 36*, 425–435.

Harrell, A. V., Sowder, B., & Kapsak, K. (1988). *Field validation of Drinking and You: A screening instrument for adolescent problem drinking* (Contract No. ADM 281–85–0007). Rockville, MD: National Institute on Alcohol Abuse and Alcoholism.

Harrell, A. V., & Wirtz, P. W. (1989). Screening for adolescent problem drinking: Validation of multidimensional instrument for case identification. *Psychological Assessment: A Journal of Consulting and Clinical Psychology, 1*, 61–63.

Harris, K. B., & Miller, W. R. (1990). Behavioral self-control training for problem drinkers: Components of efficacy. *Psychology of Addictive Behaviors, 4*, 82–90.

Hawkins, J. D., Catalano, R. F., & Miller, J. Y. (1992). Risk and protective factors for alcohol and other drug problems in adolescence and early adulthood: Implications for substance abuse prevention. *Psychological Bulletin, 112*, 64–105.

Henly, G. A., & Winters, K. C. (1989). Development of psychosocial scales for the assessment of adolescents involved with alcohol and drugs. *International Journal of the Addictions, 24*, 973–1001.

Herjanic, B., & Reich, W. (1982). Development of a structured interview for children: Agreement between child and parent on individual symptoms. *Journal of Abnormal Psychology, 10*, 307–324.

Hester, R. K., & Miller, W. R. (1988). Empirical guidelines for optimal client-treatment matching. In E. R. Rahdert & J. Grabowski (Eds.), *Adolescent drug abuse: Analyses of treatment research* (NIDA Research Monograph No. 77, pp. 27–38). Washington, DC: U.S. Government Printing Office.

Hodges, K. K., Kline, J., Stern, L., Cytryn, L., & McKnew, D. (1982). The development of a child assessment interview for research and clinical use. *Journal of Abnormal Child Psychology, 10*, 173–189.

Hoffmann, N. G., & Miller, N. S. (1992). Treatment outcomes for abstinence-based programs. *Psychiatric Annals, 22*, 402–408.

Hoffmann, N. G., Sonis, W. A., & Halikas, J. A. (1987). Issues in the evaluation of chemical dependency treatment programs for adolescents. *Pediatric Clinics of North America, 34*, 449–459.

Holsen, F., & Waal, H. (1980). The DTES — Drug Taking Evaluation Scale: A simple scale for the evaluation of drug taking behavior. *Acta Psychiatrica Scandanavica, 61*, 275–305.

Institute of Medicine (1990). *Broadening the base of treatment for alcohol problems.* Washington, DC: National Academy Press.

Jessor, R. (1976). Predicting time and onset of marijuana use: A developmental study of high school youth. *Journal of Consulting and Clinical Psychology, 44*, 125–134.

Johnston, L. D., O'Malley, P. M., & Bachman, J. G. (1991). *Drug use among American high school seniors, college students and young adults, 1875–1990* (DHHS Publication No. ADM 91–1813). Washington, DC: National Institute of Drug Abuse.

Kaminer, Y. (1991). Adolescent substance abuse. In R. J. Frances & S. I. Miller (Eds.), *Clinical textbook of addictive disorders.* New York: Guilford Press.

Kaminer, Y., Bukstein, O. G., & Tarter, R. E. (1991). The Teen Addiction Severity Index: Rationale and reliability. *International Journal of the Addictions, 26*, 219–226.

Kaminer, Y., Wagner, E. F., Plummer, B. A., & Seifer, R. (1993). Validation of the Teen Addiction Severity Index (T-ASI): Preliminary findings. *The American Journal on Addictions, 3*, 250–254.

Kandel, D., & Logan, J. (1984). Patterns of drug use from adolescence to young adulthood: I. Period of risk for initiation, continued use and discontinuation. *American Journal of Public Health, 74*, 660–667.

Kassel, J. D. (1992). *A cognitive-behavioral analysis of Alcoholics Anonymous.* Unpublished manuscript, University of Pittsburgh, Pittsburgh, PA.

Kassel, J. D., & Wagner, E. F. (1993). Processes of change in alcoholics anonymous: A review of possible mechanisms. *Psychotherapy, 30*, 222–234.

Lanyon, R. I., Primo, R. V., Terrell, F., & Wener, A. (1972). An aversion-desensitization treatment for alcoholism. *Journal of Consulting and Clinical Psychology, 38*, 394–398.

Laudergan, J. C. (1982). *Easy does it! Alcoholism treatment outcomes, Hazelden and the Minnesota Model.* Center City, MN: Hazelden.

Levy, J. C., & Deykin, E. Y. (1989). Suicidality, depression, and substance abuse in adolescence. *American Journal of Psychiatry, 146*, 1462–1467.

Marlatt, G. A. (1985). Controlled drinking: The controversy rages on. *American Psychologist, 40*, 374–375.

Mayer, J., & Filstead, W. J. (1979). The Adolescent Alcohol Involvement Scale: An instrument for measuring adolescents' use and misuse of alcohol. *Journal of Studies on Alcohol, 3*, 291–299.

McCrady, B. S., & Irvine, S. (1989). Self-help groups. In R. K. Hester & W. R. Miller (Eds.), *Handbook of alcoholism treatment approaches: Effective alternatives* (pp. 153–169). New York: Pergamon Press.

McLellan, A. T., Luborsky, L., Woody, G. E., & O'Brien, C. P. (1980). An improved diagnostic evaluation instrument for substance abuse patients. *Journal of Nervous and Mental Disease, 40*, 620–625.

Miller, W. R. (1983). Motivational interviewing with problem drinkers. *Behavioral Psychotherapy, 11*, 147–172.

Miller, W. R. (1985). Motivation for treatment: A review with special emphasis on alcoholism. *Psychological Bulletin, 98*, 84–107.

Miller, W. R. (1989) Increasing motivation for change. In R. D. Hester & W. R. Miller (Eds.), *Handbook of alcoholism treatment approaches: Effective alternatives* (pp. 67–80). New York: Pergamon Press.

Miller, W. R. (1992). The effectiveness of treatment for substance abuse. *Journal of Substance Abuse Treatment, 9*, 93–102.

Miller, W. R., & Hester, R. K. (1986a). Inpatient alcoholism treatment: Who benefits? *American Psychologist, 41*, 794–805.

Miller, W. R., & Hester, R. K. (1986b). The effectiveness of alcoholism treatment: What research reveals. In W. R. Miller & N. Heather (Eds.), *The addictive behaviors: Processes of change* (pp. 121–174). New York: Plenum Press.

Miller, W. R., & Munoz, R. F. (1982). *How to control your drinking* (rev. ed.). Albuquerque, NM: University of New Mexico Press.

Miller, W. R., & Rollnick, S. (Eds.). (1991). *Motivational interviewing: Preparing people to change addictive behavior*. New York: Guilford Press.

Moore, D. (1980). *Client Substance Abuse Index*. Unpublished manuscript, Olympic Counseling Services, Tacoma, WA.

Moore, R. H. (1988). The concurrent validity of the MacAndrew Alcoholism Scale among at-risk adolescent females. *Journal of Clinical Psychology, 44*, 1005–1008.

Morgenstern, J., & McCrady, B. S. (1992). Curative factors in alcohol and drug treatment: Behavioral and disease model perspectives. *British Journal of Addiction, 87*, 901–912.

Morrison, M. A., & Smith, Q. T. (1987). Psychiatric issues of adolescent chemical dependence. *Pediatric Clinics of North America, 34*, 461–480.

Murphy, T. J., Pagano, R. R., & Marlatt, G. A. (1986). Lifestyle modification with heavy alcohol drinkers: Effects of aerobic exercise and meditation. *Addictive Behaviors, 11*, 175–186.

Murray, D. M., & Perry, C. L. (1985). The prevention of adolescent drug abuse: Implications of etiological, developmental, behavioral, and environmental models. In C. L. Jones & R. J. Battjes (Eds.), *Etiology of drug abuse: Implications for prevention* (NIDA Research Monograph No. 56, pp. 236–256). Washington, DC: U.S. Government Printing Office.

National Institute of Drug Abuse. (1990). *National Household Survey on drug abuse: Main findings 1988*. (DHHS Publication No. ADM 91–1813). Washington, DC: U.S. Government Printing Office.

Newcomb, M., & Bentler, P. (1988). *Consequences of adolescent drug use: Impact on the lives of young adults*. Newbury Park, CA: Sage Publications.

Oei, T. P. S., & Jackson, P. R. (1982). Social skills and cognitive behavioral approaches to the treatment of problem drinking. *Journal of Studies on Alcohol, 43*, 532–547.

Oetting, E. R., & Beauvais, F. (1986). *The American Drug and Alcohol Survey*. Fort Collins, CO: Rocky Mountain Behavioral Sciences Institute.

Oetting, E., Beauvais, F., Edwards, R., & Waters, M. (1984). *The Drug and Alcohol Assessment System*. Fort Collins, CO: Rocky Mountain Behavioral Sciences Institute.

Orvaschel, H., Puig-Antich, J., Chambers, W., Tabrizi, M. A., & Johnson, R. (1982). Retrospective assessment of prepubertal major depression with the Kiddie-SADS-E. *Journal of the American Academy of Child Psychiatry, 21,* 392–397.

Owen, P., & Nyberg, L. (1983). Assessing alcohol and drug problems among adolescents: Current practice. *Journal of Drug Addiction, 13,* 249–254.

Peele, S. (1987). What can we expect from treatment of adolescent drug and alcohol abuse? *Pediatrician, 14,* 62–69.

Peele, S. (1988). Can alcoholism and other drug addiction problems be treated away or is the current treatment binge doing more harm than good? *Journal of Psychoactive Drugs, 20,* 375–383.

Pentz, M. A. (1985). Social competence and self-efficacy as determinants of substance use in adolescence. In S. Shiffman & T. A. Wills (Eds.), *Coping and substance use,* (pp. 117–142). New York: Academic Press.

Petchers, M. K., & Singer, M. I. (1987). Perceived-Benefit-of-Drinking: An approach to screening for adolescent alcohol abuse. *Journal of Pediatrics, 110,* 977–981.

Petchers, M.K. Singer, M. I., Angelotta, J. W., & Chow, J. (1988). Revalidation and expansion of an adolescent substance abuse screening measure. *Journal of Developmental and Behavioral Pediatrics, 9,* 25–29.

Polich, J. M. (1982). The validity of self-reports on alcoholism research. *Addictive Behaviors, 7,* 123–132.

Rachal, J. V., Guess, L. L., Hubbard, R. L., Maisto, S. A., Cavanaugh, E. R., Waddell, R., & Benrud, C. H. (1980). *Adolescent drinking behavior.* Research Triangle Park, NC: Research Triangle Institute.

Racusin, G. R., & Moss, N. E. (1991). Psychological assessment of children and adolescents. In M. Lewis (Ed.), *Child and adolescent psychiatry: A comprehensive textbook.* Baltimore, MD: Williams & Wilkins.

Reich, W., Herjanic, B., Welner, Z., & Gandhy, P. R. (1982). Development of a structured psychiatric interview for children: Agreement on diagnosis comparing child and parent interviews. *Journal of Abnormal Child Psychology, 10,* 325–336.

Renz, L. (1989). *Alcohol and drug abuse funding: An analysis of foundation grants.* New York: The Foundation Center.

Robertson, J. F. (1989). A tool for assessing alcohol misuse in adolescence. *Social Work, 34,* 39–44.

Robins, L. N., Helzer, J. E., Croughan, J., & Ratcliff, K. S. (1981). National Institutes of Mental Health Diagnostic Schedule: Its history, characteristics and validity. *Archives of General Psychiatry, 38,* 381–389.

Rohsenow, D. J., Smith, R. E., & Johnson, S. (1985). Stress management training as a prevention program for heavy social drinkers: Cognitive, affect, drinking and individual differences. *Addictive Behaviors, 10,* 45–54.

Rouse, B. A., Kozel, N. J., & Richards, L. G. (1985). *Self-report methods of estimating drug use: Meeting current challenges to validity.* Rockville, MD: U.S. Department of Health and Human Services.

Sanchez-Craig, M., Annis, H. M., Bornet, A. R., & MacDonald, K. R. (1984). Random assignment to abstinence and controlled drinking: Evaluation of a cognitive-behavioural program for problem drinkers. *Journal of Consulting and Clinical Psychology, 52,* 390–403.

Sanchez-Craig, M., & Walker, K. (1982). Teaching coping skills to chronic alcoholics in a coeducational halfway house: I. Assessment of programme effects. *British Journal of Addiction, 77,* 35–50.

Schinke, S. P., Botvin, G. J., & Orlandi, M. A. (Eds.). (1991). *Substance abuse in children and adolescents: Evaluation and intervention.* Newbury Park, CA: Sage Publications.

Schwartz, R. H., & Wirtz, P. W. (1990). Potential substance abuse: Detection among adolescent patients: Using the Drug and Alcohol Problem (DAP) Quick Screen, a 30-item questionnaire. *Clinical Pediatrics, 29,* 38–43.

Shiffman, S. (1984). Coping with temptations to smoke. *Journal of Consulting and Clinical Psychology, 52,* 261–267.

Shiffman, S. (1985). Coping with temptations to smoke. In S. Shiffman & T. A. Wills (Eds.), *Coping and substance use* (pp. 223–252). New York: Academic Press.

Single, E., Kandel, D., & Johnson, B. (1975). The internal validity and reliability of drug use response in a large-scale longitudinal survey. *Journal of Drug Issues, 5,* 426–443.

Skinner, H. (1981). Assessment of alcohol problems. In Y. Israel (Ed.), *Research advances in alcohol and drug problems.* New York: Plenum Press.

Smart, R., & Jones, D. (1970). Illicit LSD users: Their personality characteristics and psychopathology. *Journal of Abnormal Psychology, 75,* 286–292.

Stockwell, T., & Town, C. (1989). Anxiety and stress management. In R. K. Hester & W. R. Miller (Eds.), *Handbook of alcoholism treatment approaches: Effective alternatives* (pp. 222–230). New York: Pergamon Press.

Stowell, R. J. A., & Estroff, T. W. (1992). Psychiatric disorders in substance-abusing adolescent inpatients: A pilot study. *Journal of the American Academy of Child and Adolescent Psychiatry, 31,* 627–634.

Szapocznik, J., Kurtines, W. M., Foote, F. H., Perez-Vidal, A., & Hervis, O. (1986). Conjoint versus one-person family therapy: Further evidence for the effectiveness of conducting family therapy through one person with drug abusing adolescents. *Journal of Consulting and Clinical Psychology, 54,* 395–397.

Szapocznik, J., Perez-Vidal, A., Brickman, A. L., Foote, F. H., Santisteban, D., & Hervis, O. (1988). Engaging adolescent drug abusers and their families in treatment: A strategic structural systems approach. *Journal of Consulting and Clinical Psychology, 56,* 552–557.

Tarter, R. E. (1990). Evaluation and treatment of adolescent substance abuse: A decision tree method. *American Journal of Drug and Alcohol Abuse, 16,* 1–46.

Tarter, R. E., Ott, P. J., & Mezzich, A. C. (1991). Psychometric assessment. In R. J. Frances & S. I. Miller (Eds.), *Clinical textbook of addictive disorders.* New York: Guilford Press.

Tober, G. (1991). Motivational interviewing with young people. In W. R. Miller & S. Rollnick (Eds.), *Motivational interviewing: Preparing people to change addictive behavior* (pp. 248–259). New York: Guilford Press.

U. S. Public Health Service. (1990). *Healthy people 2000: The national health promotion and disease prevention objectives.* Washington, DC: U. S. Government Printing Office.

Van Hasselt, V. B., Hersen, M. & Milliones, J. (1978). Social skills training for alcoholics and drug addicts: A review. *Addictive Behaviors, 3,* 221–233.

Van Hasselt, V. B., Null, J. A., Kempton, T., & Bukstein, O. G. (1993). Social skills and depression in adolescent substance abusers. *Addictive Behaviors, 18,* 9–18.

Waal, H. & Holsten, F. (1980). Evaluation of drug taking behaviour. *Acta Psychiatrica Scandanavica, 61,* 127–134.

Wallace, J. (1989). Can Stanton Peele's opinions be taken seriously? A reply to Peele. *Journal of Psychoactive Drugs, 21,* 259–271.

White, H. R. & Labouvie, E. W. (1989). Towards the assessment of adolescent problem drinking. *Journal of Studies on Alcohol, 50*, 30–37.

Wheeler, K., & Malmquist, J. (1987). Treatment approaches in adolescent chemical dependency. *Pediatric Clinics of North America, 34*, 437–447.

Wills, T. A. (1985). Stress, coping, and tobacco and alcohol use in early adolescence. In S. Shiffman & T. A. Wills (Eds.), *Coping and substance use* (pp. 67–94). New York: Academic Press.

Wills, T. A., & Shiffman, S. (1985). Coping and substance use: A conceptual framework. In S. Shiffman & T. A. Wills (Eds.), *Coping and substance use* (pp. 3–24). Orlando, FL: Academic Press.

Winters, K. D. (1990). The need for improved assessment of adolescent substance use involvement. *Journal of Drug Issues, 20*, 487–502.

Winters, K. C. (1991). *The Personal Experience Screening Questionnaire*. Los Angeles: Western Psychological Services.

Winters, K. C. & Henly, G. A. (1988). Assessing adolescents who abuse chemicals: The Chemical Dependency Assessment Project. *NIDA Research Monograph Series, 77*, 4–18.

Winters, K. C. & Henly, G. A. (1989). *Personal Experience Inventory*. Los Angeles, CA: Western Psychological Services.

Yamaguchi, K., & Kandel, D. (1984a). Patterns of drug use from adolescence to young adulthood: II. Sequences of progression. *American Journal of Public Health, 74*, 668–672.

Yamaguchi, K. & Kandel, D. (1984b). Patterns of drug use from adolescence to young adulthood: III. Predictors of progression. *American Journal of Public Health, 74*, 673–681.

CHAPTER 19

Posttraumatic Stress Disorder

CATHERINE KOVEROLA

DESCRIPTION OF THE PROBLEM

Posttraumatic stress disorder (PTSD) is a relatively new disorder within the psychiatric and psychological literatures. It is unique in that it is in part defined by an etiological event: namely, exposure to a traumatic event. PTSD is further characterized by symptoms of intrusive reexperiencing of the trauma in the form of flashbacks, nightmares, or reenactment of the traumatic event. In children, the reenactment is most commonly manifested in play. A second category of PTSD symptoms is avoidance. More specifically, the individual engages in active attempts to avoid the trauma through such manifestations as avoidance of thoughts and feelings associated with the event, an inability to recall aspects of the event, decreased interest in significant activities, or regression. In children, the regression may present in various areas of development, such as toilet training or speech. Finally, the individual experiences symptoms of physiological hyperarousal. This is characterized by irritability, difficulty concentrating, or physiological reactivity to trauma-related cues. This cluster of symptoms must have been present for at least 1 month in order for the the diagnosis of PTSD to be made. This chapter will endeavor to review the empirical literature on PTSD in children and will highlight the specific issues that must be considered in the assessment and treatment of this disorder in children.

PTSD was first acknowledged as a distinct diagnostic entity in the *Diagnostic and Statistical Manual of Mental Disorders* (third edition, DSM-III) (American Psychiatric Association, 1980). Previous to this, there were some efforts to explore and describe the relationship between traumatic life experiences and psychological sequelae in the psychiatric and psychological literatures. It was, however, the designation of PTSD as a specific syndrome that marked the beginning of its being researched. The initial research focused primarily upon PTSD in adults, most notably combat veterans and rape victims. Research on PTSD in children has lagged behind, and unfortunately much of the present understanding of PTSD in children is based upon extrapolations from findings with adults. This, once again, sadly betrays the adult-centered focus of the majority of psychiatric and psychological research efforts.

Age-specific features of PTSD have, however, been incorporated into the diagnostic criteria in the *Diagnostic and Statistical Manual of Mental Disorders* (third edition, revised, DSM-III-R) (American Psychiatric Association, 1987). This came about largely as a result of consulting psychiatrist Lenore Terr's investigation of the impact of the Chowchilla kidnapping incident. This incident involved the kidnapping and 16-hour entombment of 26 schoolchildren in 1976 in Chowchilla, California. Terr (1979) noted that, although many of the symptoms exhibited by the children were similar to those exhibited by traumatized adults, several symptoms appeared unique to children (e.g., the reexperiencing of the event through stereotyped repetitive posttraumatic play, regressive behaviors, and the sense of a foreshortened future). These age-specific factors were then incorporated into the DSM-III diagnostic criteria. With regard to the issue of the applicability of this adult diagnostic category being utilized with children, Schwarz and Kowalski (1990) compared PTSD symptomatology in a sample of children and adults exposed to the same trauma: a school shooting. These authors contended that the diagnostic criteria adequately assessed the response of children to a catastrophic event. They noted that there appeared to be developmentally based variations in symptom presentation between adults and children, but they felt that these were insufficient to warrant separate and distinct diagnostic categories for adults and children. Finally, there has been one study that attempted to empirically establish the diagnostic validity of the DSM criteria of PTSD as applied to children: Saigh (1989a) concluded that the results do support the validity of the classification in the particular sample he utilized.

Diagnostic Criteria

DSM-III-R criteria for PTSD are as follows:

A. The person has experienced an event that is outside the range of usual human experience and that would be markedly distressing to almost anyone; e.g., serious threat to one's life or physical integrity; serious threat or harm to one's children, spouse, or other close relatives and friends; sudden destruction of one's home or community; or seeing another person who has recently been or is being seriously injured or killed as the result of an accident or physical violence.

B. The traumatic event is persistently reexperienced in at least one of the following ways:

1. Recurrent and intrusive distressing recollections of the event (in young children, repetitive play in which themes or aspects of the trauma are expressed)
2. Recurrent distressing dreams of the event
3. Sudden acting or feeling as if the traumatic event were recurring (includes a sense of reliving the experience, illusions, hallucinations, and dissociative [flashback] episodes, even those that occur upon awakening or when intoxicated)
4. Intense psychological distress at exposure to events that symbolize or resemble an aspect of the traumatic event, including anniversaries of the trauma

C. Persistent avoidance of stimuli associated with the trauma or numbing or general responsiveness (not present before the trauma), as indicated by at least three of the following:

1. Efforts to avoid thoughts or feelings associated with the trauma
2. Efforts to avoid activities or situations that arouse recollections of the trauma
3. Inability to recall an important aspect of the trauma (psychogenic amnesia)
4. Markedly diminished interest in significant activities (in young children, loss of recently acquired developmental skills, such as toilet training or language skills)
5. Feeling of detachment or estrangement from others
6. Restricted range of affect, e.g., unable to have loving feelings
7. Sense of a foreshortened future, e.g., does not expect to have a career, marriage, or children, or a long life

D. Persistent symptoms of increased arousal (not present before the trauma), as indicated by at least two of the following:

1. Difficulty falling or staying asleep
2. Irritability or outbursts of anger
3. Difficulty concentrating
4. Hypervigilance
5. Exaggerated startle response
6. Physiologic reactivity upon exposure to events that symbolize or resemble an aspect of the traumatic event

Because PTSD is a relatively new disorder with regard to the DSM classification system, there are ongoing controversies with respect to diagnostic criteria. A number of changes in PTSD diagnostic criteria are implemented in DSM-IV.

One of the recommended changes in DSM-IV involved the stressor criterion (American Psychiatric Association, 1993), but this has been criticized as being vague and unreliable. Initially, three options were proposed:

1. Providing a specific description of the nature of allowable stressors.
2. Adding a subjective component to the definition by requiring that the stressor provoke a response in the person, such as fear, helplessness, or horror.
3. Stating that the stressor must be exceptional.

After considerable debate, it was decided that DSM-IV should have the following stressor criteria:

1. The person has experienced, witnessed, or has been confronted with an event or events that involve actual or threatened death or serious injury or a threat to the physical integrity of oneself or others.
2. The person's response involved intense fear, helplessness, or horror. *Note:* In children, the response may be expressed instead by disorganized or agitated behavior.

In some cases, identifying the types of stressors that result in PTSD in children is straightforward, for example, exposure to a sniper attack (Pynoos et al., 1987). In other situations, such as in cases of physical and sexual abuse, it is potentially more ambiguous. Children may be unwilling or unable to describe their traumatic experiences. The literature has documented the emergence of PTSD in children in response to experiencing such trauma as concentration camps (Kinzie, Sack, Angell, Mason, & Rath, 1986); severe burns (Stoddard, Norman, Murphy, & Beardslee, 1989); fatal shipwrecks (Yule & Williams, 1990); the murder (Malmquist, 1986) or rape of a parent (Pynoos & Nader, 1988a); a hurricane (Saylor, Swenson, & Powell, 1992); kidnapping (Terr, 1979, 1981); and sexual abuse (Deblinger, McLeer, Atkins, Ralphe, & Foa, 1989; Goodwin, 1988; Kiser et al., 1988; Kiser, Heston, Millsap, & Pruitt, 1991; Koverola, 1992; Koverola & Foy, 1993; Wolfe, Gentile, & Wolfe, 1989). In the present literature, the single most common traumatic event documented as precipitating the onset of PTSD in children is sexual abuse. This is also perhaps the most controversial of the precipitating events and will be discussed at length later in the chapter.

A second major change recommended for DSM-IV pertains to the duration for symptomatology (American Psychiatric Association, 1993). The criterion in DSM-III-R is *at least 1 month*. The literature suggests that there is a high prevalence of brief periods of PTSD-like symptomatology that occur in the immediate aftermath of exposure to severe stressors: There are two differing perspectives with regard to the implications of these findings. In one camp are those who argue that such symptoms are expectable outcomes and do not constitute a mental disorder and, therefore, should not be diagnosed as such. In the alternate camp are those who emphasize the importance of early detection and intervention in order to alleviate the symptomatology and to prevent PTSD from becoming chronic. This debate has not as yet been settled. From a clinical child point of view, both arguments have merit. The problem of inappropriate labeling has long been a concern for clinicians working with children, and one could argue strongly for the lengthening of the symptom-duration period in order to avoid mislabeling transient symptoms as a disorder, particularly in children. Similarly, the importance of early detection and diagnosis of disorders in children is a position taken by many. Particularly in disorders that can become very debilitating, early detection is critical and certainly desirable. This then would lead one to argue for maintaining the shorter duration criterion. DSM-IV makes the following changes with respect to symptom duration. PTSD will be diagnosed as *acute* if the duration of symptoms is less than 3 months and as *chronic* if the duration of symptoms is 3 months or more. PTSD will be diagnosed as *delayed onset* if the onset of symptoms occurs at least 6 months after the traumatic experience.

There was a proposal to remove PTSD from the Anxiety Disorders section and to place it in a newly created Stress-Related Disorders section. Instead, in DSM-IV, a new disorder, Acute Stress Disorder, is added to the Anxiety Disorders section. The symptoms parallel those of PTSD but are somewhat less intense, and the duration of symptoms is less. More specifically, the symptoms must have occurred for a minimum of 2 days and a maximum of 4 weeks, within 4 weeks of the traumatic experience.

Finally, there were proposed changes to further refine the age-specific features in the Reexperiencing Symptom category. DSM-IV includes the following additions/revisions: (a) in young children, repetitive play may occur in which themes or aspects of the trauma are expressed; (b) in children, there may be frightening dreams without recognizable content; (c) in young children, trauma-specific reenactment may occur.

A further diagnostic controversy not addressed by DSM-IV with regard to PTSD in children is whether there are two types. On the basis of her extensive clinical experience, Terr (1991) has proposed Type I and Type II PTSD. Type I results from a single-impact traumatic event, whereas Type II results from a series of traumatic events or from chronic exposure to a prolonged stressor. Type I PTSD is characterized by classic reexperiencing symptoms. Type II PTSD is typified by denial, dissociation, and numbing and is associated with the subsequent development of dissociative, borderline, and multiple personality disorders. In view of the fact that children are particularly susceptible to Type II stressors (e.g., in the form of ongoing abuse), the distinction between Type I and Type II PTSD may become of particular relevance to clinicians working with children. The issue at present remains unresolved (McNally, 1991).

Theories Regarding Posttraumatic Stress Disorder

There have been numerous attempts to explain theoretically how PTSD symptoms develop and why they are maintained. Despite the diversity in theories, the one consistency is the etiological event: namely, the trauma. It is interesting to note further that each theoretical viewpoint focuses on certain aspects of the symptomatology that it can most easily explain and largely ignores the remaining features. From a psychodynamic perspective, for example, PTSD symptoms are explained as the ego being overwhelmed or in terms of *information overload*. The individual is overwhelmed by input for which he or she has no internal schemata to assimilate or accommodate the new information. The individual then alternates between two phases: (a) denial of the incomprehensible situation and (b) intrusive reexperiencing of the encapsulated traumatic image. Central to psychodynamic formulations is the notion that the impact of trauma is related to the individual's developmental stage. Symptoms are considered in light of regression or disruption of psychosocial development (Lyons, 1987). A weakness of the psychodynamic model to explain PTSD symptomatology is that it virtually ignores the physiological arousal component of PTSD symptoms.

From a behavioral perspective, PTSD is conceptualized from both classical/Pavlovian and instrumental/operant conditioning theories (Keane, Zimmering, & Caddell, 1985). Classical conditioning takes place when an individual is traumatized. The individual becomes reflexively distressed by the threatening aspects of the traumatic event, which is the unconditioned stimulus (UCS). Other neutral cues (CS) that happen to be present at the time of the traumatic event become classically conditioned such that they, too, become anxiety eliciting, even though they are not inherently dangerous. The second component of the behavioral model incorporates instrumental/operant conditioning. Essentially, the individual learns to behave in such a way as to bring about a desired consequence; in PTSD, the desired consequence is relief from anxiety. Thus, the individual learns that avoidance of trauma-related cues minimize anxiety. The behavioral model accounts for PTSD symptoms as follows: Symptoms of arousal are viewed as involuntary responses associated with UCS/CS conditioning, and symptoms of avoidance are viewed as instrumentally conditioned avoidance responses. The behavioral perspective largely ignores PTSD symptoms of reexperiencing the trauma.

A cognitive behavioral formulation of PTSD that incorporates the cognitive element of "meaning," with a specific focus on the fear structures, was proposed by Foa and Kozak (1986). They proposed that the fear structure consists of cognitive and affective components. The etiological variable that distinguishes PTSD from other anxiety disorders is the attribution of dangerous meaning to stimuli that had previously been natural or safe. A critical feature of the cognitive behavioral formulation is the predictability and controllability of the traumatic event. The fear structure provides the means by which the individual can process information about the potential danger and, hence, the need for avoidance. According to this formulation, the less predictable and controllable the world appears, the greater the intensity of PTSD symptoms. This formulation accounts primarily for avoidance symptoms in PTSD but does not account for reexperiencing symptoms nor the physiological symptoms of arousal.

Several researchers have begun to explore PTSD from a biological viewpoint. Van der Kolk (1987) proposed a neurobiological learning model based upon the animal model of inescapable shock (Maier & Seligman, 1976) to explain the etiological mechanisms of PTSD in humans. Van der Kolk argues that the limbic system is affected by the extended acute shock and that norepinenphrine depletion becomes a conditioned response that leads to an increase in norepinenphrine receptor hypersensitivity. The PTSD symptoms of numbing and constriction of affect reflect the norepinenphrine depletion resulting from the inescapable stress of the trauma. Symptoms of hyperactivity, such as nightmares, startle response, and intrusive thoughts, reflect a chronic hypersensitivity of the norepinenphrine receptors that is similar to that observed in animals confronted with extended and inescapable trauma. Kolb (1988) has criticized Van der Kolk's model for failing to account for the symptoms of avoidance or for chronic PTSD. Kolb has proposed an alternative neurobiological model, which some believe has heuristic value but which has not been subjected to empirical investigation (Foy, Osato, Houskamp, & Neumann, 1992).

It is evident from this brief consideration of the various theoretical perspectives that there is no one theory that adequately accounts for all of the symptoms evident in PTSD. Furthermore, most of the theories lack strong empirical research to substantiate their arguments. Nevertheless, they do provide clinicians with a way of beginning to conceptualize how PTSD develops and with some direction as to how to intervene. At this point in the understanding of PTSD, it is most prudent to embrace the richness of the various theoretical viewpoints and to attempt to integrate knowledge, rather than to approach the disorder from one narrow, circumscribed viewpoint.

Comprehensive Model of Trauma Impact

The Comprehensive Model of Trauma Impact (CMTI), developed by Koverola (1992), delineates the multiplicity of variables and contexts that must be considered when evaluating the impact of trauma upon a child as well as upon how to proceed with intervention (see Figure 19.1). The CMTI is not wed to any specific theory; rather, it encourages the clinician and researcher alike to take a wholistic perspective on the question of how trauma impacts on the individual. The model begins with a consideration of the interactive areas of functioning in the child: namely, affective, cognitive, interpersonal, moral, sexual, and physical. These areas are continuously affecting each other and are integrally related. The second component of the model is the trauma. The trauma itself is often a multifaceted experience with a number of identifiable characteristics. In some situations, the trauma is clear-cut and identifiable, such as in the case of a sniper attack or acute illness; in other situations, it may be less salient and difficult to assess, such as in the cases of sexual and physical abuse. Trauma characteristics, or more specifically the degree to which the individual has been exposed to the trauma, have been found to be related to symptomatology. The third component of the model is the systemic context in which the child develops: the family, the community, and society. In each of these systemic contexts, there are identifiable variables that interact with the child's development and so mediate the impact upon his or her adjustment. Within the family system, for example, parental response to the child's traumatic experience has been found to be a significant predictor of the severity of that child's symptomatology. Further, within the context of the family, the child will be affected by the parents' overall psychological functioning, parent and sibling support/rejection, family communication styles, and generational boundaries. The community context includes friends, school, church and community groups, and law enforcement, child protection, and medical personnel. The relative degree of support or rejection experienced by the child in the community will interact with his or her adjustment. The societal context refers to the underlying values and beliefs that determine how society responds to the type of trauma experienced by the child, for example, societal values and beliefs about trauma such as sexual abuse. The societal context encompasses cross-cultural issues as well. The means by which the societal context impacts on the child are more indirect than the others and occur largely via the community and the family; however, it is a context that nonetheless, most be borne in mind. The final component of the CMTI addresses the context of time. The child is continually changing across time.

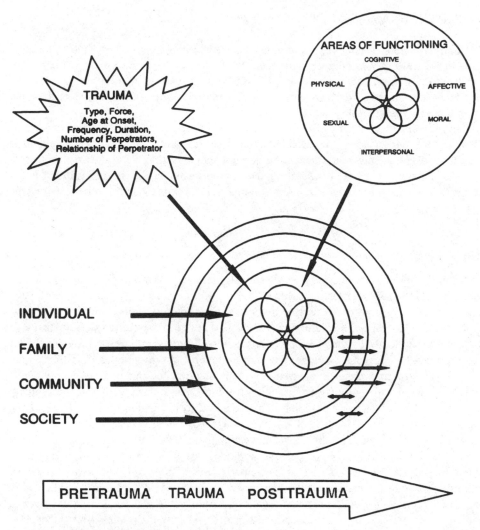

Figure 19.1. Comprehensive model of trauma impact.
Note. From The Psychological Effects of Child Sexual Abuse (p. 26) by C. Koverola, 1992, in A. H. Herger and
S. J. Emans (Eds.), *Evaluation of the Sexually Abused Child*, New York: Oxford University Press. Copyright
1992 by Oxford University Press. Reprinted by permission.

One must consider where in the continuum of pretrauma, trauma, and posttrauma the
evaluation is being conducted and how the passage of time may have impact on the child's
adjustment.

In summary, the CMTI addresses four major areas: the child's functioning, the nature
of trauma, the systemic contexts, and the passage of time. Each of these areas identifies
a number of interactive variables that impact on the child and so mediate the child's
adjustment to the trauma. This model can serve as a useful organizational format from
which to consider variables that have impacted on the child in the past and will continue
to do so in the future.

PROTOTYPIC ASSESSMENT

Evaluating whether a child has symptoms consistent with a diagnosis of PTSD should be done in the context of a comprehensive assessment of his or her emotional and behavioral functioning. In this context, assessment of PTSD involves the evaluation of the traumatic event and the identification of symptoms of reexperiencing the trauma, avoiding the trauma, and hyperarousal.

Children suffering from PTSD generally present to the clinician in one of two ways. They have experienced an identifiable traumatic event, and their parent or caregiver is concerned about the potential impact of this event upon the child. Alternatively, the parent or caregiver may have noted behavioral and/or emotional changes in the child but is not aware that the child has been exposed to trauma. It is rare for the child to be self-referred to the clinician.

Assessing the Trauma

As previously noted, the criterion for what constitutes a trauma is somewhat controversial. The current DSM-III-R criterion includes "experiences that are outside the range of usual human experience and that would be markedly distressing to almost anyone." This has been criticized as vague. Evaluating whether a child has been exposed to a traumatic event is further complicated by the child's inability or unwillingness at times to articulate his or her experiences. The parent or caregiver may be helpful in providing clarification on the child's exposure to trauma, or, alternatively, they may impede this process. Many adults deny or downplay the impact of trauma upon a child, particularly if they are personally responsible for his or her well-being. This can lead to distortions in the nature of the trauma.

While there are some readily identifiable traumatic events that are easily verifiable, such as public incidents of violence, war, natural disasters, and so forth, some traumatic events are much less clear. This is particularly true of physical and sexual abuse of children, as well as of exposure to domestic violence. The issue is further complicated in cases that become litigious in nature. Clinicians, in the course of their assessment, may be suddenly thrust into the position of investigators and may ultimately find themselves defending their assessment procedures in a court of law.

Types of details about the characteristics of the traumatic event will vary greatly depending upon the nature of the trauma. Sexual abuse is the most commonly documented precipitating event of PTSD in children. In general, one should attempt to obtain the following information about the abuse: age at onset, duration of abuse, frequency of abuse, type of abuse (i.e., fondling, attempted penetration, completed penetration), use of force, number of perpetrators, and relationship of the perpetrator. In situations in which the traumatic event is a physical illness and/or medical procedure, the clinician would obtain information such as type of illness, chronic or acute, anticipated duration, nature of impairment, prognosis, and nature of procedures. In the more refined adult literature on PTSD, particularly PTSD arising from combat-related activities, checklists are available to evaluate the specific nature of exposure to trauma. There are not as yet any psychometrically sound measures of children's exposure to specific types of trauma available, with the exception of the trauma characteristics questions included in the structured interviews discussed in the following section.

Assessing Symptoms of PTSD

There are three major areas of symptoms that must be evaluated. These include reexperiencing, avoidance, and hyperarousal. In general, these symptoms can be assessed through verbal inquiry of the child, observation of the child's play, and parental verbal report. Additional methods include questionnaires and psychophysiological measures.

There are a number of structured clinical interviews for assessing childhood PTSD. The most widely reported instrument is the Post-Traumatic Stress Disorder Reaction Index (PTSD-RI) (Frederick, 1985, 1986; Pynoos et al., 1987). This is a 20-item measure that can be administered verbally to children. It allows for DSM-III-R diagnosis. It is also available in a modified form suitable for administration to adults. This measure awaits further research to establish its psychometric integrity. A second instrument is the Children's Posttraumatic Stress Disorder Inventory (CPTSDI), developed by Saigh (1989a, 1989b). Similar to the PTSD-RI, this provides a DSM-III-R diagnosis of PTSD. The measure has been demonstrated to distinguish between PTSD and other forms of psychological distress in children; however, the psychometric integrity of the measure has not yet been established. A third alternative is the modified form of the Diagnostic Interview for Children and Adolescents (DICA) (Welner, Reich, Herjanic, Jung, & Amado, 1987). PTSD items from the Diagnostic Interview Schedule (DIS) (Robins & Smith, 1984) have been added to the DICA in order to allow for PTSD diagnosis. This measure has been used to diagnose children with PTSD. Some (McNally, 1991) have criticized this measure for its use of DIS-based PTSD assessment because the DIS has a low sensitivity for identifying PTSD. Furthermore, the psychometric properties of the DICA for assessing PTSD have not been established (Lipovsky, 1991). In the absence of psychometrically valid and reliable interview schedules, some researchers have utilized DSM-III and DSM-III-R criteria directly and developed their own interviews and checklists to assess for PTSD. This is similarly an option for clinicians.

The child's developmental level and language development, as well as the degree to which he or she is able to respond meaningfully to direct interview methods, can limit the information the clinician can obtain. In these cases, the clinician is well advised to directly observe the child's play. Evidence of intrusive symptoms may be evident in drawings or repetitive play. Similarly, avoidant responses can be identified if the child is unable to engage in play when cues remind him or her of the trauma. Further, the clinician should be alert to overt behavioral manifestations of hyperarousal, such as a startle response.

As in all assessments of children, obtaining information from as many cross-informants as possible is always desirable. The interviews noted previously can be administered in a modified form to the parent or caregiver in order to obtain additional information on the child's symptomatology.

There are several questionnaires that a clinician can elect to utilize in addition to interviewing and observing the child and interviewing the parent. However, the majority of questionnaires that have been used to assess children who have been traumatized evaluate a broad range of distress symptoms. These include depression (e.g., Child Depression Inventory [CDI]), anxiety (e.g., State-Trait Anxiety Inventory for Children [STAIC] [Spielberger, 1973]); low self-esteem (e.g., Self-Esteem Inventory [SEI] [Coopersmith, 1986]); sexualized behavior (e.g., Child Sexual Behavior Inventory [CSBI] [Friedrich, Grambasch, et al., 1989]) or general behavioral disturbance (e.g., Child Behavior Checklist [CBCL] [Achenbach & Edelbrock, 1983]). These measures do not provide specific diagnostic information about PTSD per se, but they do provide the clinician with additional information about distress symptomatology. Some investigators have added PTSD-like items to these standardized questionnaires and found this to be useful. The psychometric properties of the revised measures are, of course, unknown (McNally, 1991). Further, some researchers have selected specific items from a standardized measure such as the CBCL and have constructed a PTSD subscale (Wolfe, Gentile, & Wolfe, 1989). Unfortunately, this subscale does not evaluate the full continuum of PTSD symptomatology, and the psychometric properties have not been well established.

A final exploratory method of evaluation of PTSD is psychophysiological assessment. In the only psychophysiological study on childhood PTSD reported to date, Ornitz and Pynoos (1989) evaluated the startle reflex in children exposed to sniper fire in comparison to children who had not been traumatized. They found that, in comparison to nontraumatized children, the traumatized children failed to exhibit inhibition of startle following brief prestimulation and exhibited facilitation of startle following sustained prestimulation. Psychophysiological assessment of PTSD may prove to be a fruitful avenue of assessment in the future, although, at present, it is likely practical only in the research domain.

PTSD is unlike many of the more well-researched disorders impacting on children, such as attention-deficit/hyperactivity disorder and conduct disorder, for which there are established protocols for assessment. In the case of PTSD, the guidelines are much more vague. The clinician must essentially evaluate whether the child has been traumatized and, secondly, whether the child presents with three categories of symptoms, namely, reexperiencing the trauma, avoiding the trauma, and hyperarousal. Unfortunately, there are no psychometrically sound measures available to evaluate exposure to trauma. In fact, the types of questions to be asked depend largely upon the nature of the trauma. The means to evaluate the presence of the three remaining categories of symptoms are also somewhat vague. Several structured questionnaires for interviewing both child and parent are available; however, the psychometric integrity of these instruments has not been well established. Further, it appears that even many researchers rely upon their own idiosyncratically derived questionnaires based on DSM-III-R criteria. The clinician is also encouraged to observe the child's behavior and play in order to evaluate for further evidence of these symptoms. Finally, the clinician may elect to utilize any number of child- or parent-report questionnaires that assess for a broad range of distress symptoms that overlap with PTSD symptomatology. Nevertheless, upon following this somewhat vague protocol, the clinician will be able to determine within a relative degree of certainty whether a child presents with symptoms that can be diagnosed as PTSD. However, the clinician then has to ask, "How useful is this information?" or, more pragmatically, "So what do I do now?"

In order for the assessment procedure to move beyond arriving simply at a diagnosis of PTSD, the clinician must evaluate a much broader context than the presence or absence of PTSD symptomatology. The CMTI can serve as a useful guide in evaluating various factors that will be important to consider in developing a treatment plan.

The model begins with a consideration of the child's functioning in a number of areas: cognitive, affective, interpersonal, moral, sexual, and physical. The clinician must have a good understanding of how the child has been developing in each of these areas and how each area may have been affected by the trauma. PTSD symptomatology can be evident in may of these areas. In the cognitive domain, for example, the child may be experiencing either difficulty concentrating or intrusive thoughts of the traumatic events or, an ability to recall an important aspect of the trauma. In the affective domain, the child may experience intense psychological distress when exposed to cues that symbolize or resemble aspects of the trauma, as well as a restricted range of affect, irritability, or outbursts of anger. In the interpersonal domain, the child may feel detached and estranged from others. With respect to moral development, the child may experience an intense degree of guilt or responsibility for the trauma, particularly if the child witnessed violent acts being perpetrated upon others but was not physically injured him- or herself. In the sexual domain, a child who has been sexually abused may manifest sexualized behaviors, which can represent a reenactment of the abuse itself. Finally, in the physical domain, PTSD symptomatology may be manifested in the form of hyperarousal, such as an exaggerated startle response or physiological reactivity upon exposure to events that remind the child of the traumatic event. Children may be affected to different degrees in the different areas depending upon their developmental level in each of the areas at the time of the trauma. Further, because each of the areas interacts with the others, it is important to consider the interaction effects.

The second component of the CMTI involves assessing the nature of the traumatic event. This has been previously discussed and will not be elaborated upon further here, other than to note that it is important to evaluate how the specific trauma impacts upon the various areas of functioning. Different types of traumas may have more powerful impacts on specific areas of functioning. Sexual abuse, for example, is more likely to impact on the child's sexual development than is witnessing a fatal car accident.

The third component of the model is the systemic context in which the child develops. It is very important to ascertain whether the family is serving a protective, supportive function for the child in coping with the trauma or whether the family has put the child at risk for exposure to the trauma and is, in fact, exacerbating the child's distress. In some cases, the family may be doing both. Two studies have documented that the family's emotional environment and parental reaction to the child's exposure to trauma have been significant predictors of the child's adjustment (Green et al., 1991; Saylor, Swenson, & Powell, 1992). Children whose parents reacted in a negative, nonsupportive manner and whose families were depressed and/or irritable were significantly more likely to have a diagnosis of PTSD following a community disaster than were children from supportive families. It is important to consider how the traumatic event has affected the family as a whole, that is, whether the family's stability has been threatened or impacted negatively, whether the financial situation has changed, and so forth. There are innumerable ways in which traumatic events can impact on a formerly high functioning family, rendering it unable to provide even the most basic emotional resources for a child. With respect to the community context, it is important for the clinician to evaluate which potential supports and resources can be activated to facilitate the child's coping with the trauma. Further, it is important to identify any potential ongoing factors within the community that may be exacerbating or maintaining the child's distress. In cases of community disasters, the community itself may be in a state of chaos or general distress, and one may need to look beyond the community for support. In other types of traumatic events, the community may provide a rich range of support services that can be activated to strengthen both the family and the child. Finally, the clinician should consider the traumatic event in light of the applicable societal context and should ask such questions as: Is the traumatic event of such a nature that it cannot be dealt with openly in the given community or family? Are there cross-cultural issues, religious issues, and so on, that need to be taken into consideration prior to intervening with the child? Appropriate and acceptable intervention in one societal context may not be appropriate in another.

The final component of the CMTI addresses the continuum of time. The clinician must endeavor to obtain information about the child's functioning prior to the trauma in order to have a realistic sense of appropriate treatment goals. Further, it is important to have a clear understanding of the time frame in which the traumatic event occurred in order to assess the chronicity of the symptoms. The minimal treatment literature that exists on PTSD in children suggests that early intervention is highly desirable in order to prevent PTSD symptomatology from being chronic.

In conclusion, a clinician evaluating a child with PTSD symptoms is advised to evaluate the child comprehensively. This includes determining whether the child's symptoms are consistent with a diagnosis of PTSD, as well as the variables outlined in the CMTI. This includes the child's development in the areas of cognitive, affective, interpersonal, moral, sexual, and physical functioning; the nature of the trauma; the systemic context in which the child exists; and the continuum of time in which the trauma has occurred.

ACTUAL ASSESSMENT

As is evident in the preceding section, assessment of PTSD in children is clearly in its infancy. The literature does provide the clinician with general directives of how one should assess this particular disorder; however, psychometrically sound measures and procedures are sorely lacking. In addition to this, there are a number of inherent pitfalls that can face the clinician endeavoring to complete a thorough assessment of a child who presents with PTSD.

Evaluation of the parent's or caregiver's perception of the traumatic event, as well as the child's functioning, is a critical component of the assessment. The relative psychological health or psychopathology of the parent often can make this a very challenging component of the assessment. This is of particular concern if the parent has likewise been traumatized by the event and has a need to either exaggerate or minimize its severity and impact upon the child. This is especially true in a case of sexual or physical abuse in which parents may have been actively colluding with the perpetrator, may have placed the child at risk because of their own needs, or may be in acute distress because of their own traumatization.

Avoidance symptoms of PTSD can, in some situations, pose a unique problem for assessment. If the child is actively experiencing the avoidance phase of PTSD, he or she may present as highly resistant to assessment. Alternatively, the child may be compliant but unable to provide any information whatsoever about the traumatic event. In child sexual abuse evaluations, it is a very common phenomenon for children to minimize, deny, or retract previous disclosures of abuse, particularly after they have been subjected to numerous interviews about the abuse or when they are required to testify in court. This has been a very perplexing problem for both clinicians and lawyers and has led to allegations that children lie about abuse and cannot be believed. Koverola and Foy (1993) have presented the thesis that minimization, denial, or retraction of abuse may simply reflect PTSD avoidance symptoms. This thesis is consistent with the fact that avoidance seems to typically occur after the child has been exposed to highly anxiety-eliciting cues and to demands to face the distressing traumatic event, such as in court. One would predict that, in these situations, children suffering from PTSD would be likely to avoid memories of the abuse and would, thus, be unable to provide disclosures. Further, with respect to evaluations of sexually abused children, the clinicians must always be prepared for the possibility that she or he will be required to testify in court in regard to the child's disclosure of abuse. For most clinicians, this is a highly aversive prospect, one that is unfamiliar, often hostile, time-consuming, and at cross-purposes with therapeutic goals. The clinician is in a very difficult position, particularly because an assessment conducted for clinical purposes has different goals than interviews conducted for legal purposes and the issue of confidentiality becomes essentially a moot point once one's records have been subpoenaed.

The following is an example of the types of situations that are particularly distressing for the clinician:

A fearful female child discloses for the first time to a clinician that her father repeatedly raped her. She begs the clinician not to tell anyone because she fears for her safety. The abuse is reported to the appropriate child protection agency, and the case goes to court. The clinician is later subpoenaed and required to testify about the child's disclosure. The child is then viciously interrogated by the defense attorney and recants the disclosure. The perpetrator is not convicted; the child is returned home and does not return to therapy.

This kind of experience is common when one assesses large numbers of sexually abused children. This example does not imply that clinicians should not take appropriate measures to report child abuse. Child abuse reporting is clearly an important component of intervention and a means to work towards providing safety for the child. Rather, the example highlights the potential implications of exploring the nature of the trauma a child has experienced. The legal system all too often fails the children it claims to protect. Clinicians are often powerless to intervene and are left to witness the child being traumatized yet again.

Specific situations such as the one just described can be traumatic for the clinician as can the process of assessing high numbers of traumatized children. Further, there is the traumatizing element of simply being chronically exposed to account after account of unpredictable human tragedy. Clinicians have begun to identify this as an area of concern, and there is currently a move to undertake research in this area.

PROTOTYPIC TREATMENT

In the literature to date, there are no controlled-outcome studies of treatment of PTSD in children. There are, however, anecdotal case reports of interventions used successfully with children suffering from PTSD (Deblinger, McLeer, & Henry, 1990; Lyons, 1987; Nir, 1985; Pynoos & Eth, 1986; Terr, 1979, 1985). Further, many have argued that the treatment approaches used to treat adults with PTSD are applicable to children (Foy, Resnick, & Carroll, 1989).

Central to virtually all treatment strategies advocated is an emphasis on reexposing the individual to the traumatic cues in a supportive manner. With children, particularly younger children, there are innumerable techniques whereby this can be accomplished. Some of these include art activities, writing, storytelling, music puppetry, and drama. The aim of exposure techniques is for the child to approach uncomfortable thoughts, feelings, and memories in a supportive, emotionally safe setting. The goal of these procedures is two-fold: first, to disconnect the association between trauma-related stimuli and anxiety, and second, to minimize the avoidance response so that the child is able to deal with the trauma-related cues and still remain comfortable. Saigh (1989b) described a systematic protocol for utilizing in vitro exposure with children and adolescents exposed to war-related incidents. This treatment included therapist-directed relaxation and imaginal flood-ing. Saigh (1989b) reported significant reduction in the children's self-report of emotional distress and specific PTSD symptomatology. Pynoos and Eth (1986) described an inter-view approach in which drawings were incorporated as a way of engaging the child in exposure to trauma-related cues relating to witnessing violence. Deblinger, McLeer, and Henry (1990) included an exposure component in their treatment for sexually abused children presenting with PTSD. They utilized a flexible approach, in that the therapist offers the child a range of exposure methods from which to choose. They stressed that this was important in order for the child to maintain a sense of control. The methods included confronting and addressing abuse-related issues through imagery, doll play, drawing, reading, letter writing, poetry, and singing.

A component of the exposure techniques is relaxation, or at least of exposing the child to the trauma-related cues in a relaxed manner. Anxiety-reduction techniques have also been recommended as a procedure in their own right (Lipovosky, 1991). Deep muscle relaxation techniques can be taught successfully to children (Ollendick & Cerny, 1981). The techniques involve having the child close his or her eyes, sit comfortably, and follow the direction of the therapist. The therapist instructs the child to systematically proceed through a series of tensing and relaxing of various muscle groups. In addition, the child is taught cue-controlled breathing. The child can then utilize the relaxation as a means to cope with the distressing recollections of the traumatic event.

Cognitive restructuring approaches have been used increasingly with adults exper-iencing PTSD and have been recommended for use with children (Frederick, 1985; Lipovosky, 1991; Pynoos & Nader, 1988b). In these approaches, the meaning assigned to the traumatic event is explored. Distortions that are negatively affecting the individual are challenged and reframed. These approaches require an exploration of the child's be-lief system and then providing alternative cognitions that are more adaptive and healthy. Cognitive restructuring can, however, be very difficult, particularly if the child is ex-periencing avoidance symptoms to any degree. In this situation, anxiety-reduction and exposure techniques may be more appropriate. Clearly, the degree to which these tech-niques can be used with a given child will depend upon the child's cognitive-development level.

Finally, intervention must address the role of the parent or caregiver. It has been suggested that the strongest outcome predictor for a traumatized child is the ability of the adults in the child's life to be supportive and to deal with the traumatic event (Friedrich, 1990; Green et al., 1991; Koverola, 1992; Lyons, 1987). As previously noted in the assessment section, parents or caregivers may be unable to be supportive of the child because of their personal sense of responsibility and their guilt over the fact that the trauma occurred, their own experience of traumatization, or, potentially, their role in perpetrating the trauma. If the parent is unwilling or unable to talk with the child about the traumatic event, this can reinforce the avoidance symptomatology and further deprive the child of social support. Teaching parents and other involved adults appropriate ways of commu-nicating with the child about the trauma can be a very important component of treatment (Deblinger et al., 1989; Koverola, 1992; Lipovosky, 1991; Lyons, 1987). At minimum, parents and involved adults should be educated about the symptoms of PTSD and about the normal reactions of the child who is suffering from PTSD.

The treatment program for sexually abused children experiencing PTSD that was developed by Deblinger, McLeer, and Henry (1990), illustrates how a parent-intervention component is included as part of the treatment for the child. The parent intervention is designed for a nonoffending parent. The intervention included three modules: The first provides an educational component to enlighten parents about issues related to abuse and to potential consequences for the child; the second provides parents with guidelines for effective parent-child communication, particularly regarding child sexual abuse (modeling and gradual exposure are utilized); the third is a sequence of sessions on behavior-management skills that are designed to facilitate the management by parent(s) of behavior problems that arise as a result of the abuse.

In summary, while there is no empirical literature on which to base these directives, the existing clinical literature would suggest the following prototypic treatment approach for children suffering from PTSD: the treatment should include exposure, anxiety management strategies, cognitive restructuring, and parent intervention.

The clinician can further use the assessment findings based on the CMTI as a guide in developing a treatment plan specific to each child. First, the clinician must consider the child's developmental level in each of the six areas of functioning: cognitive, affective, interpersonal, moral, sexual, and physical. Assessment findings will guide the clinician in developing an appropriate intervention to facilitate growth and development in those areas most significantly impacted by the trauma. If the child, for example, exhibits significant difficulty in affective expression, then affective expression would clearly be an appropriate target for intervention. Alternatively, if the child is highly symptomatic in the physical domain (e.g., significant hyperarousal symptoms), relaxation training would likely be a key component of intervention.

Second, the clinician must carefully consider the nature of the trauma. In cases of abuse, for example, a component of the intervention might include taking measures to ensure that the child does not continue to be reexposed to the abuse/perpetrator. In cases of medical illness, it may not be possible for the clinician to ensure that the child does not continue to be exposed to the trauma. The illness may be essentially ongoing, and the child might be continuing to receive traumatizing medical interventions. The focus of intervention in this case would clearly need to include a component that would enhance the child's ability to cope with the ongoing trauma.

Third, with regard to the child's systemic context, the clinician's treatment plan will depend to some extent on factors within the various contexts that can be used as supports and resources for the child. Further, the clinician will need to address those factors in the systemic contexts that may be exacerbating and maintaining symptoms in the child.

ACTUAL TREATMENT

The prototypic treatment plan as outlined might seem relatively simple and straightforward. The clinician has a number of behavioral treatment options to use that must be tailored to the child's appropriate developmental level. Further, the clinician engages the parent(s) in intervention and provides the parent(s) with appropriate educational and therapeutic guidelines on how to deal with the child's symptoms at home.

In the present author's experience and that of numerous other clinicians, PTSD symptoms in some children are very difficult to treat. They do not respond to the types of interventions as outlined. While there are cases in which the child does respond to very brief, structured therapy that utilizes the interventions described, many children remain symptomatic. In considering what might be the difference between those who do respond to this type of treatment and those who do not, it seems that two significant factors are the

(a) chronicity of trauma exposure and (b) the relative psychological health of the family, in particular, the parents.

The proposed distinction between Type I and Type II PTSD (Terr, 1988) may be a particularly useful construct in understanding why some children are responsive to focused, brief therapy for PTSD and others are not. Based upon the author's clinical experience, it appears that, in those children who have been exposed to chronic trauma, the level of dysfunction is of a more profound nature than that of children exposed to short-term acute trauma. Children exposed to chronic trauma are more likely to need long-term psychotherapy in addition to brief focused intervention targeted specifically at PTSD symptomatology. Children exposed to more acute brief traumas can benefit from more focused brief interventions and do not need long-term therapy. This comparison of children exposed to acute trauma, versus chronic trauma, is consistent with Terr's observations in that it is Type II PTSD that is more resistant to brief focused interventions.

The degree of family pathology, specifically parental psychopathology, also seems related to the degree of disturbance in the child and in the response to treatment. Children who are exposed to ongoing chronic trauma are more likely to have parents and families that are more dysfunctional. The family dysfunction may have been a contributing factor in putting the child at risk for exposure to the trauma, as well as in impeding therapeutic progress.

Other problems that may thwart the success of actual treatment have been previously highlighted in the assessment section. These include constraints imposed by legal implications of intervention and the clinician's own traumatization, which ensues as a result of working with this population.

SUMMARY

As has become apparent throughout this chapter, PTSD is a newly identified disorder, and, as such, the existing empirical literature particularly on the assessment and intervention of PTSD in children is very minimal. Those who approach assessment and intervention with children from a developmental perspective are undoubtedly further dismayed by the tendency in the literature to conceptualize children as miniature adults and to make only minor modifications in interventions used with adults and to apply them to children.

Nevertheless, the existing literature provides the clinician with important guidelines on how to assess and treat children who experience PTSD. It is important, however, to bear in mind that the present understanding of PTSD is in its infancy and that the currently recommended procedures for assessment and intervention await empirical validation.

In summary, PTSD is a unique disorder, in that it is in part defined by an identifiable etiological event. However, despite the fact that there is an identifiable etiological event, the attempt to provide a comprehensive theory of the underlying mechanism of PTSD symptomatology has been more elusive. At present, there is no one comprehensive theory that can account for all of the symptomatology observed. The majority of initial research on PTSD focused on psychological explanations. There is increasing evidence to suggest that PTSD has a significant neurobiological component. A further important issue that remains unresolved is whether there are, in fact, two types of PTSD, as proposed by Terr (1988). This issue is of particular relevance to clinicians working with children.

The Comprehensive Model of Trauma Impact has been presented as a guide for clinicians in the assessment and treatment of children who have been traumatized. The model highlights a number of major areas of functioning, namely, cognitive, affective, interpersonal, moral, sexual, and physical development; (a) the nature of the trauma; (b) the child's systemic context, namely, family, community, and society; and (c) the passage of time. By considering the multiplicity of variables that are simultaneously impacting on the child, the clinician is in a good position to evaluate the child's functioning and to develop a workable treatment plan.

In the context of the CMTI, the specific evaluation of PTSD in a child should include an assessment of the nature of the trauma and of the presence of symptoms of reexperiencing the trauma, avoidance of the trauma, and hyperarousal. The assessment can be accomplished by interviewing the child through use of a structured interview, by observation of the child's play, by interviewing the parent or caregiver, and by using a broad range of questionnaires.

Recommended treatment approaches for children with PTSD include exposure, anxiety management strategies, cognitive restructuring, and intervention with the parent. The clinician is further encouraged to use the assessment findings based on the CMTI as a guide to developing a treatment plan specific for each child.

There are a number of impediments to both assessment and treatment of children with PTSD. These include parental psychopathology or distress, avoidance symptoms prohibiting treatment progress, legal implications of assessment and treatment findings, and the clinician's becoming traumatized in the process of providing services.

As is clearly evident, there are significant gaps in the knowledge of PTSD in children. There is, however, a growing body of literature that will undoubtedly, in the next decade, illuminate many of the questions that at present remain unanswered.

REFERENCES

Achenbach, T. M., & Edelbrock, C. S. (1983). *Manual for the Child Behavior Checklist and Revised Child Behavior Profile.*

American Psychiatric Association. (1980). *Diagnostic and statistical manual of mental disorders* (3rd ed.) Washington, DC: Author.

American Psychiatric Association. (1987). *Diagnostic and statistical manual of mental disorders* (3rd ed., rev.). Washington, DC: Author.

American Psychiatric Association. (1993). *DSM-IV draft criteria.* Washington, DC: Author.

Coopersmith, S. (1986). *Manual for the Self-Esteem Inventories.* Palo Alto, CA: Consulting Psychologists Press.

Deblinger, E., McLeer, S. V., Atkins, M., Ralphe, D., & Foa, E. (1989). Posttraumatic stress in sexually abused, physically abused, and nonabused children. *Child Abuse and Neglect: The International Journal, 13*, 403–408.

Deblinger, E., McLeer, S. V., & Henry, D. (1990). Cognitive behavioral treatment for sexually abused children suffering post-traumatic stress: Preliminary findings. *Journal of the American Academy of Child and Adolescent Psychiatry, 29*, 747–752.

Foa, E. B., & Kozak, M. J. (1986). Emotional processing of fear: Exposure to corrective information. *Psychological Bulletin, 99*, 20–35.

Foy, D. W., Osato, S. S., Houskamp, B. M., & Neumann, D. (1992). Etiology of posttraumatic stress disorder. In P. A. Saigh (Ed.), *Posttraumatic stress disorder: A behavioral approach to assessment and treatment* (pp. 28–49). Needham Heights, MA: Allyn and Bacon.

Foy, D. W., Resnick, H. S., & Carroll, E. M. (1989). Behavior therapy with PTSD. In A. S. Bellack & M. Hersen (Eds.), *Handbook of comparative treatments.* New York: Wiley.

Frederick, C. J. (1985). Selected foci in the spectrum of posttraumatic stress disorders. In J. Laube & S. A. Murphy (Eds.), *Perspectives on disaster recovery* (pp. 110–130). East Norwalk, CT: Appleton-Century-Crofts.

Frederick, C. J. (1986). Posttraumatic stress disorder and child molestation. In A. Burgess & C. Hartman (Eds.), *Sexual exploitation of clients by mental health professionals* (pp. 133–142). New York: Praeger.

Friedrich, W. N. (1990). *Psychotherapy of sexually abused children and their families.* New York: Norton.

Friedrich, W. N. (1989). Behavior problems in sexually abused children: An adaptation perspective. In G. E. Wyatt & G. J. Powell (Eds.), *Lasting effects of child sexual abuse* (pp. 171–191). Newbury Park, CA: Sage Publications.

Friedrich, W. N., Grambasch, P., Broughton, D., Koverola, C., Damon, L., Hewitt, S., & Lemond, T. (1989). *The Child Sexual Behavior Inventory: Preliminary normative data.* Unpublished manuscript.

Goodman, G. S. (1984). The child witness: Conclusions and future directions for research and legal practice. *Journal of Social Issues, 40,* 157–175.

Goodman, G., Aman, C., & Hirschman, J. (1987). Child sexual and physical abuse: Children's testimony. In S. J. Ceci, M. P. Toglia, & D. F. Ross (Eds.), *Children's eyewitness memory.* New York: Springer-Verlag.

Goodwin, J. (1988). Posttraumatic symptoms in abused children. *Journal of Traumatic Stress, 1,* 475–488.

Green, B. L., Korol, M., Grace, M. C., Vary, M. G., Leonard, A. C., Gleser, G. C., & Smithson-Cohen, S. (1991). Children and disaster: Age, gender, and parental effects on PTSD symptoms. *Journal of the Academy of Child and Adolescent Psychiatry, 30,* 945–951.

Keane, T. M., Zimmering, R. T., & Caddell, J. M. (1985). A behavioral formulation of posttraumatic stress disorder in Vietnam veterans. *The Behavior Therapist, 8,* 9–12.

Kinzie, J. D., Sack, W. H., Angell, R. H., Mason, S., & Rath, B. (1986). The psychiatric effects of massive trauma on Cambodian children: I. The children. *Journal of the American Academy of Child Psychiatry, 25,* 370–376.

Kiser, L. J., Ackerman, B. J., Brown, E., Edwards, McColgan, E., Pugh, R., & Pruitt, D. B. (1988). Posttraumatic stress disorder in young children: A reaction to purported sexual abuse. *American Academy of Child and Adolescent Psychiatry, 27,* 645–649.

Kiser, L. J., Heston, J., Millsap, P. A., & Pruitt, D. B. (1991). Physical and sexual abuse in childhood: Relationship with post-traumatic stress disorder. *Journal of the American Academy of Child and Adolescent Psychiatry, 30,* 776–783.

Kolb, L. C. (1988). A critical survey of hypotheses regarding post-traumatic stress disorders in light of recent findings. *Journal of Traumatic Stress, 1,* 291–304.

Kovacs, M. (1985). The Children's Depression Inventory (CDI). *Psychopharmacology Bulletin, 21,* 995–998.

Koverola, C. (1992). The psychological effects of child sexual abuse. In A. H. Heger & S. J. Emans (Eds.), *Evaluation of the sexually abused child.* Boston: Oxford University Press.

Koverola, C. & Foy, D. (1993). Posttraumatic stress disorder in sexually abused children: Implication for legal proceedings. *Journal of Child Sexual Abuse, 2,* 119–127.

Koverola, C., Foy, D., & Heger, A. (1990, October). *Relationship of posttraumatic stress disorder to child disclosure and medical evidence in sexually abused children.* Paper presented at the Sixth Annual Meeting of the Society for Traumatic Stress Studies, New Orleans, LA.

Lipovsky, J. A. (1991). Posttraumatic stress disorder in children. *Family Community Health, 14,* 42–51.

Lyons, J. A. (1987). Posttraumatic stress disorder in children and adolescents: A review of the literature. *Developmental and Behavioral Pediatrics, 8*, 349–356.

Maier, S. F., & Seligman, M. E. P. (1976). Learned helplessness: Theory and evidence. *Journal of Experimental Psychology: General, 105*, 3–45.

Malmquist, C. P. (1986). Children who witness parental murder: Posttraumatic aspects. *Journal of the American Academy of Child Psychiatry, 25*, 320–325.

McNally, R. J. (1991). Assessment of posttraumatic stress disorder in children. *Psychological Assessment: A Journal of Consulting and Clinical Psychology, 3*, 531–537.

Nir, Y. (1985). Posttraumatic stress disorder in children with cancer. In S. Eth & R. S. Pynoos (Eds.), *Post-traumatic stress disorder in children*. Washington, DC: American Psychiatric Press.

Ollendick, T. H., & Cerny, J. A. (1981). *Clinical behavior therapy with children*. New York: Plenum Press.

Ornitz, E. M., & Pynoos, R. S. (1989). Startle modulation in children with posttraumatic stress disorder. *American Journal of Psychiatry, 146*, 866–870.

Pynoos, R. S., & Eth, S. (1986). Witness to violence: The child interview. *Journal of the American Academy of Child Psychiatry, 25*, 306–319.

Pynoos, R. S., Frederick, C., Nader, K., Arroyo, W., Steinberg, A., Eth, S., Nunez, F., & Fairbanks, L. (1987). Life threat and posttraumatic stress in schoolage children. *Archives of General Psychiatry, 44*, 1057–1063.

Pynoos, R. S., & Nader, K. (1988a). Children who witness the sexual assaults of their mothers. *Journal of the American Academy of Child and Adolescent Psychiatry, 27*, 567–572.

Pynoos, R. S., & Nader, K. (1988b). Psychological first aid and treatment approach to children exposed to community violence: Research implications. *Journal of Traumatic Stress, 1*, 445–473.

Robins, L. N., & Smith, E. M. (1984). *Diagnostic Interview Schedule/Disaster supplement*. St. Louis, MO: Washington University School of Medicine.

Saigh, P. A. (1989a). The validity of the DSM-III posttraumatic stress disorder classification as applied to children. *Journal of Abnormal Psychology, 98*, 189–192.

Saigh, P. A. (1989b). The development and validation of the Children's Posttraumatic Stress Disorder Inventory. *International Journal of Special Education, 4*, 75–84.

Saylor, C. F., Swenson, C. C., & Powell, P. (1992). Hurricane Hugo blows down the broccoli: Preschoolers' post-disaster play and adjustment. *Child Psychiatry and Human Development, 22*, 139–149.

Schwarz, E., & Kowalski, J. M. (1990). Malignant memories: PTSD in children and adults after a school shooting. *Journal of the American Academy of Child and Adolescent Psychiatry, 30*, 936–944.

Stoddard, F. J., Norman, D. K., Murphy, J. M., & Beardslee, W. R. (1989). Psychiatric outcome of burned children and adolescents. *Journal of the American Academy of Child and Adolescent Psychiatry, 28*, 589–595.

Spielberger, C. D. (1973). *Manual for the State-Trait Anxiety Inventory for Children*. Palo Alto, CA: Consulting Psychologists Press.

Terr, L. C. (1979). Children of Chowchilla: A study of psychic trauma. *Psychoanalytic Study of Child, 34*, 547–623.

Terr, L. C. (1981). Psychic trauma in children: Observations following the Chowchilla school-bus kidnapping. *American Journal of Psychiatry, 138*, 14–19.

Terr, L. C. (1985). Psychic trauma in children and adolescents. *Psychiatric Clinics of North America, 8*, 815–835.

Terr, L. C. (1988). What happens to early memories of trauma? A study of twenty children under age five at the time of documented traumatic events. *Journal of the American Academy of Child and Adolescent Psychiatry, 27,* 96–104.

Terr, L. C. (1991). Childhood traumas: An outline and overview. *American Journal of Psychiatry, 148,* 10–20.

Van der Kolk, B. A. (1987). *Psychological trauma.* Washington, DC: American Psychiatric Press.

Yule, W., & Williams, R. M. (1990). Post-traumatic stress reactions in children. *Journal of Traumatic Stress, 3,* 279–295.

Welner, Z., Reich, W., Herjanic, B., Jung, K. G., & Amado, H. (1987). Reliability, validity and parent-child agreement studies of the Diagnostic Interview for Children and Adolescents (DICA). *Journal of the American Academy of Child and Adolescent Psychiatry, 26,* 649–653.

Wolfe, V. V., Gentile, C., & Wolfe, D. A. (1989). The impact of sexual abuse on children: A PTSD formulation. *Behaviour Therapy, 20,* 215–228.

CHAPTER 20

Obesity

JOHN P. FOREYT AND G. KEN GOODRICK

DESCRIPTION OF THE PROBLEM

It has been estimated that obesity, *defined as an excess of body fat*, is a problem in 5% to 10% of preschool children (Maloney & Klykylo, 1983), 27% of children aged 6 to 11 years, and 22% of children aged 12 to 17 years (Gortmaker, Dietz, Sobol, & Wehler, 1987). Over the last two decades, the prevalence of obesity has increased 54% in children and 39% in adolescents (Gortmaker et al.). These rapid changes in prevalence indicate that environmental causes are to blame. Over the last few decades, there has been a dramatic increase in the availability of high-fat foods for children. Concurrently, there has been a reduced demand for activity for children. Today's child may expend only one-half to one-fourth as many calories in exercise as did a child of 1930 (Griffiths & Payne, 1976). It is not difficult to see why childhood obesity is epidemic and increasing.

Since the consequences of eating high-fat foods and inactivity are delayed, it may be difficult for the young child to learn the association between eating, exercise, and obesity. Also, social influences that pressure the child to avoid overweight may not occur until behavioral patterns and obesity are well established.

The need to intervene as early as possible is evident. A 12-year-old obese child has only a 1-in-4 chance of becoming a normal-weight adult; if obesity continues through adolescence, the chances of becoming a normal-weight adult are 1 in 28 (Stunkard & Burt, 1967). Health risks due to childhood obesity have been reviewed by LeBow (1984). The psychological damage has been outlined by Coates and Thoresen (1980). Given the lack of effective treatments for adults (Bennett, 1987; Foreyt, Goodrick, & Gotto, 1981; Goodrick & Foreyt, 1991), prevention or reduction of obesity in childhood is clearly indicated.

Research has focused on the apparent multideterminant nature of obesity, which shows possible contributions from genetic factors (Bouchard et al., 1990; Epstein & Cluss, 1986; Stunkard, Harris, Pedersen, & McClearn, 1990), biochemical factors, and physiological factors. It is not clear, however, how this research on these factors will lead to more successful treatments. The focus for behavioral treatment is limited to manipulable, environmental risk factors (Klesges & Hanson, 1988). Hence, this chapter will cover the assessment of obesity, the factors known to directly or indirectly influence a child's eating or activity behavior, and the cognitive-behavioral methods that can be applied in the psychiatric setting.

The following is known about the behavioral treatment of childhood obesity: (a) behavioral treatments are more effective than health education efforts; (b) parents should be included in the treatment process; and (c) life-style exercise may be associated with better maintenance than aerobic exercise (Epstein, 1988). It should be recognized that targeting obesity in a child is treating a symptom largely caused by familial and societal

Preparation of this chapter was supported by National Institutes of Health Grant No. R01-DK43109.

factors. Behavioral therapy for childhood obesity competes with culture-bound high-fat eating and inactivity. The long-term success rate in nonpsychiatric settings is measured as 33% of those treated and categorized as *nonobese* at 5-year follow-up (Epstein, 1988). If the same pressures and food/exercise environment exist in the psychiatric setting, the level of success will be no greater.

The relationship between obesity and psychiatric problems in children has not been well researched. In nonpsychiatric populations, self-esteem and family functioning do not appear to be related to obesity in preschool children (Klesges, et al., 1992). Body-fat distribution and adiposity are not related to mental retardation (Murphy, Allison, Babbitt, & Patterson, 1992), and sibling studies show that obesity in Down syndrome is a function of family and other environmental factors (Sharav & Bowman, 1992). Morbidly obese women may be more likely to have a lifetime history of mood disorders, anxiety disorders, and bulimia and to have personality disorders (Black, Goldstein, & Mason, 1992). Research is needed to determine when and how the relationship between obesity and psychopathology begins and progresses in childhood. Certainly, obesity can be a factor in determining a child's self-esteem and social integration and, hence, will need to be addressed along with any psychiatric problems.

PROTOTYPIC ASSESSMENT

Ideally, assessment in the treatment of obesity should be comprehensive because of the multidetermined nature of obesity maintenance. The target *behaviors* are eating lower fat foods and increasing exercise. The target *cognitions* should reflect a reduced drive for thinness, a realization that dietary restriction is harmful, and the belief that physical appearance and self-worth are not connected. Obesity and aerobic fitness are the target outcome variables to be assessed as they relate directly to physical health. In addition, eating behaviors, exercise behaviors, and sedentary behaviors should be assessed. Other factors that control or interact with eating, exercise, and sedentary behaviors need to be evaluated. These include child factors, environmental/treatment-unit factors, and family factors. Such variables may interact within a complex system that involves the child, peers, family, treatment setting, school, and community (Foreyt & Goodrick, 1988).

Assessment of Obesity

Obesity becomes a problem when percent body fat (PBF) is excessive in terms of physical and/or mental health. The level of childhood obesity at which health risks become unacceptable needs further longitudinal epidemiological research in addition to the risk for adulthood obesity previously discussed. The level of obesity at which psychological health is affected may be estimated by patient interview and by observation of the child and the interactions with peers. Children begin to worry about being too fat at an early age—before age 10, they are concerned with becoming fat and begin restrictive eating (Gustafson-Larson & Terry, 1992).

Direct assessment of body fat is not possible. Laboratory techniques involving complex equipment and invasive or aversive methods have been reviewed by Bandini and Dietz (1987). Triceps skinfolds and body mass index (BMI) (BMI = weight in kilograms/height^2 in meters) are the most practical measures that have reasonably high correlations with laboratory-measured percent body fat. Care must be taken to get reliable skinfolds.

Standards for skinfold measurements have been published (Tanner & Whitehouse, 1975). Marking skinfold sites (Bray, 1976) and using averages of repeated measures may increase reliability. Calipers with pressure calibrations are required. In extremely fat subjects, skinfolds cannot be accurately measured. As a basis for setting treatment goals, health-fitness standards have been published by the American Alliance for Health, Physical Education, Recreation, and Dance (McSwegin, Pemberton, Petray, & Going, 1989). These standards list acceptable ranges of skinfold and body-mass indexes for children aged 5 to 18 years.

Himes and Bouchard (1989) used densitometry to determine percent body fat (PBF) in children and found that triceps skinfolds is the most accurate single anthropometric indicator of obesity in boys, while BMI is the preferred measure for girls. Total body electrical conductivity assessment estimates PBF by passing the body through an electro-magnetic field (Van Loan, Belko, Mayclin, & Barbieri, 1987). This procedure requires an expensive instrument; however, the technique is quick, involving a 2-minute scan.

Indicators based on height and weight can be used during treatment to assess progress. BMI has been found to correlate well ($r > 0.90$) with *percentage overweight*, which is defined as the ratio weight/ideal weight. *Ideal weight* can be defined as the weight for height, age, and sex from normal growth charts (National Center for Health Statistics, 1988). Upper limits of BMI for school children have been recommended by the American Alliance for Health, Physical Education, Recreation, and Dance (McSwegin et al., 1989).

Use of BMI over time may be problematic because it is not independent of height over the range 5 to 12 years (Michielutte, Diseker, Corbett, Schey, & Ureda, 1985). Indexes of weight/height$^{1.6}$ for children aged 1 to 5 years and of weight/height$^{2.4}$ for children aged 6 to 12 years have been found to be relatively independent of age and sex (Dugdale & Lovell, 1981). Such independence would allow these indexes to be used for serial estimations of the same child.

An index based on normative changes in height and weight calculates an adjusted weight change as a ratio of expected changes to actual changes in height (Brownell, Kelman, & Stunkard, 1983). Rate of weight gain during a pretreatment period has been used to project expected weight gain during treatment (Kahle et al., 1982). An adjusted weight (Adj. Wt.) (Kirschenbaum, Harris, & Tomarken, 1984) for children has been suggested that adjusts children's weight for estimated growth in height and weight and is defined as:

$$\text{Adj. Wt.} = \text{current wt.} + \text{initial wt.} - (\text{initial wt.} \times (100\% + \text{normal \% wt. gain}))$$

Over the last decade, the need for standardization of childhood obesity assessment has become evident. Major researchers in this area recommend using both triceps skinfolds, which is sensitive to changes in fat, and percentage overweight (Epstein & Wing, 1987). Triceps skinfold percentiles for children aged 6 to 17 years have been published (Lauer, Conner, Leaverton, Reiter, & Clarke, 1975). These measures are practical and, in addition to assessment of physical appearance using photographs, are sufficient for tracking of progress in clinical work.

Assessment of Cardiorespiratory Fitness

Physical-fitness measures of endurance of physical working capacity are related nega-tively to indicators of obesity (Boulton, 1981; Epstein, Koeske, Zidansek, & Wing, 1983;

Clark & Blair, 1988). However, a child may lose an appreciable amount of excess fat at the expense of health by using excessively restrictive diets or even by purging (see section on Assessment of Eating Behavior). Such children tend to have low endurance; fitness tests can serve as one way to detect this form of malnutrition.

Although confirmatory longitudinal research has not been carried out, cross-sectional data indicate that inactivity may lead to childhood obesity (Office of Disease Prevention and Health Promotion, 1985). Degree of childhood obesity has been correlated to hours of television viewing (Dietz & Gortmaker, 1985). Children aged 6 to 11 years average 25 hours per week watching television (Dietz, 1988). Children who watch less TV score higher on fitness measures than those who watch more (Tucker, 1986). The inference to be made is that non-TV time is spent in more active pursuits that build fitness.

An interactive process may be at work between inactivity and increasing obesity. A child who eats too much food and exercises too little will add excess body fat and reduce fitness. Both changes may make exercise seem more aversive. Obese children have been found to value sedentary behavior more than nonobese children (Epstein, Smith, Vara, & Rodefer, 1991). The child may be caught in a vicious cycle of less exercise and more body fat. An accumulation of fat in the chest and abdomen may lead to respiratory limitations in obese children; obese children may have lung functions at 60% below normal-weight peers (Ho, Tay, Yip, & Rajan, 1989). Such reduced lung function would make exercise seem more strenuous. Obese children have the same level of maximal oxygen consumption as their normal-weight siblings when the measure is standardized for fat-free mass (Eliot, Goldberg, Kuehl, & Hanna, 1989). However, their lower level of participation in sports may be due to the effort required to carry excess fat, as well as to psychosocial inhibitions.

Estimates of cardiorespiratory fitness can be made using submaximal bicycle ergometry (Adams, Linde, & Miyake, 1961). This requires a calibrated stationary bicycle. For children who have been walking or running, an estimate of fitness is how far they can go in a 12-minute run-walk test (Cooper, 1977). This test is obviously subject to error through motivational differences and should be repeated over several weeks to control for variability of mood and perceived energy. Norms for children aged 8 to 19 years have been established (Governor's Commission on Physical Fitness, 1974). The test protocol outlines details of administration and prescreening criteria (Governor's Commission on Physical Fitness, 1986). Fitness standards and assessment methodology for school children have been developed by McSwegin et al. (1989), which include run-walk tests, flexibility, and upper-body strength tests.

Assessment of Activity

To get an accurate assessment of physical activity, continuous monitoring of caloric expenditure would be required. Monitors could record heart rate as an indicator of activity, but such activity-measurement instruments worn by the child are generally too expensive and cumbersome for clinical use. Pedometers have been found to be too unreliable for more than rough estimations of activity (Klesges, Klesges, Swenson, & Pheley, 1985).

Observation and coding of activity would be a rather inaccurate enterprise unless a trained observer followed a child during waking hours. For aerobic exercises, Cooper's (1977) point system can be used to estimate the fitness value of various activities. To assess aerobic activities, exercise heart rate is used to measure intensity; exercise producing a heart rate within a training range will lead to aerobic conditioning. Attendance at exercise sessions may not be a good measure of exercise because obese children may try to avoid exercise involvement; one study found obese children spending only 3 minutes in vigorous activity during a 40-minute physical education class (Parcel et al., 1987).

Blair (1984) has developed a formula that categorizes activities into four levels of intensity and provides an estimate of energy expenditure. A similar method developed for children is the Fargo Activity Timesampling Survey (FATS) (Klesges, Coates, Moldenhauer-Klesges, et al., 1984). It allows the recording of a child's activities in terms of body movements, ranging from sleeping to fast running.

The current state of the art in assessing childhood activity lacks reliability and validity (Clark & Blair, 1988). An alternative is to use a measure of physical fitness instead of activity assessment because this measure is objective and reflects the health goals of exercise. Ross and Gilbert (1985) found a significant correlation between scores on a run-walk test and self-reported activity.

Recording of general categories of exercise and activities in a Daily Habit Book (Epstein, Wing, Woodall, et al., 1985) can be done by children with the help of hospital staff. Since sedentary behaviors seem to be related to obesity, assessment of these is included. An electronic motion-sensing device that could be set to sound an alarm when kept still for various periods would be helpful in monitoring sedentary behavior patterns.

Child Factors Affecting Exercise

Normal children spontaneously engage in and seem to enjoy vigorous activity. Longitudinal research is needed to discover by what processes a child becomes obese and less active. Using a 5-point hedonic scale, researchers have assessed perceived enjoyment of exercise in children; they found no differences between obese and lean children on perceptual ratings of activities (Epstein, Valoski, et al., 1989). However, obese children may have rated activities as more enjoyable than they actually perceived them to be because they probably were aware that the obese are often labeled as lazy. Duration of sedentary behavior (e.g., TV viewing) has been related to degree of obesity (Dietz & Gortmaker, 1985); this behavior pattern affects activity by taking time away from more active pursuits.

Other child factors having the potential to affect activity but as yet not well-researched include: knowledge and attitudes about the beneficial effects of exercise, skill in self-regulating exercise intensity to maximize enjoyment, perceived energy level, effects of sugar and high-fat foods on energy level, and attitudes towards sports and competitiveness.

Environmental Factors Affecting Exercise

Opportunities for exercise in the psychiatric setting need to be assessed. There is generally a gymnasium in a child psychiatric facility, but the obese child may need an opportunity to take long walks. Many children in psychiatric settings prefer frenetic games; the obese child may not be able to participate at this level.

Family Factors Affecting Exercise

Family factors can be assessed when parents visit the child at exercise time. Parental prompts have been correlated with activity level (Klesges, Coates, Moldenhauer-Klesges, et al., 1984; Klesges & Hanson, 1988) and parental discouragement to be active (e.g., "Go watch TV") has been found to be inversely related to activity (Klesges, Coates, Holzer, et al., 1983).

In addition to these parental influencing factors, it would be valuable to assess the parents' knowledge of and attitudes toward exercise for their children and the parents' experience of exercise as a child and as an adult. Parents may perceive exercise to be aversive rather than an enjoyable activity, and these values could be transmitted to their children. These assessments will be useful in structuring the aftercare plan for the child released back into his family.

Assessment of Eating Behavior

Research has yet to find consistent differences between obese children and normal children in total food intake or dietary factors (Klesges & Hanson, 1988). This may be due in part to the difficulty in getting accurate assessments, as well as to the confounding factors of exercise differences that are also unreliably assessed. Some risk factors for obesity in children have been found, including snacking (Locard et al., 1992) and parental permissiveness regarding eating (Breum, Lissau, Sorensen, Holst, & Friis-Hasche, 1990). Obese children have been found to eat more rapidly, and their rate of eating does not slow down near the end of a meal as it does in normal-weight children (Barkeling, Ekman, & Rossner, 1992). Children at high risk for obesity because of parents' weight status were found to gain more weight than other children and to obtain more calories from fat and fewer from carbohydrates, than low-risk children (Eck, Klesges, Hanson, & Slawson, 1992).

Careful monitoring is required to gather food-intake data. Even in adults, self-monitoring is a rather unreliable endeavor (Nelson, Black, Morris, & Cole, 1989). With children and relatively untrained parents, programs have been successful by approximating total calories and categorizing foods by caloric density. *The Stoplight Diet for Children* (Epstein & Squires, 1988), for example, categorizes foods into three groups: "Red foods" have the highest caloric density and are avoided; "yellow foods" are basic foods of average calorie density needed for good nutrition; and "green foods" are very low in calories and can be eaten ad libidum (Epstein, Masek, & Marshall, 1978). Self-recording in a daily habit book by children and staff can track foods eaten by color category, portion size, and calories.

Monitoring of food intake should be continuous, rather than only at mealtimes. Children may ingest a large part of their daily calories while snacking (Frank, Webber, & Berenson, 1982). Much of this snacking occurs during the average American child's 25 hours of weekly television viewing. Television viewing has been correlated to children's caloric intake (Taras, Callis, Patterson, Nader, & Nelson, 1989). On a psychiatric unit, snacking and TV viewing can easily be recorded on a child's chart as access is controlled.

There are many inventories of child eating behavior and related factors, such as the Eating Behavior Inventory (O'Neil et al., 1979), The Eating Habits Checklist (Israel, Stolmaker, & Andrian, 1985), The Eating Analysis and Treatment Schedule (Coates & Thoresen, 1981), The Food Intake Record (Wheeler & Hess, 1976), and Bob and Tom's Method of Assessing Nutrition (BATMAN) (Klesges, Coates, Brown, et al., 1983). Such a cornucopia of assessment inventories begs for standardization of effort across studies.

Child Factors Affecting Eating

In order to modify a child's eating habits to reduce high-fat, high-sugar foods, it is helpful to measure food preferences to assess the effects of treatment on preferences. It is also useful to identify healthful foods the child likes. Food preferences have been assessed in children using a 5-point rating scale with anchors of *Like* and *Dislike*; enjoyment ratings of food were consistently lower for offspring of obese rather than lean parents. These researchers also found that perception of sweetness and fatness of foods was less intense in obese rather than lean children (Epstein, Valoski, et al., 1989). These characteristics may play a part in destabilizing the energy balance by affecting eating behavior. Further longitudinal research on individual differences on these dimensions is needed to see whether abnormal food perceptions are risk factors for obesity. It has been shown in adults that an increase in fat in the diet tends to increase hedonic preferences for fat and that a reduction of fat in the diet reduces this hedonic response to fat (Mattes, 1993).

An extremely important evaluation to make of all children is an assessment of symptoms that may be behavioral risk factors for eating disorders. In a survey of girls, 50% of 9-year-olds and 80% of 10- and 11-year-olds were dieting to lose weight (Mellin, 1990). In this survey, 58% felt they were overweight, but only 17% were overweight by objective criteria. Of 9-to-11-year-old girls, 9% were practicing purging as a weight-management method (Mellin).

Use of a child's version of the Eating Attitudes Test showed that among children aged 9 to 12 years, 45% wanted to be thinner, 37% had tried to lose weight, and 6.9% scored in the anorexic range (Maloney, McGuire, Daniels, & Specker, 1989). Among high school students, 26% of males and 57% of females have been identified as compulsive overeaters (Marston, Jacobs, Singer, Widaman, & Little, 1988).

Further longitudinal research is needed to determine which children end up as obese and which as normal weight. The two outcomes may both be different results of the same social-influence processes; the amount of excess body fat may depend on the coping response of the child to perceived obesity. The coping could range from restrictive dieting leading to compulsive overeating and obesity, to strategies of bingeing and dieting or purging, or to anorexia, depending upon characteristics of the child's family of origin.

Family Factors Affecting Eating

Studies of obesity correlations between parents and children, and of the degree of obesity in children of different parental fatness combinations, show that obesity follows a family line; even in unrelated persons who live together as a family, there are synchronies in fatness change over time (Garn, LaVelle, & Pilkington, 1984). Klesges, Coates, Moldenhauser-Klesges, et al. (1984) have reported that in 2-to-3-year-old children, parental prompts correlated with food intake and weight. Mothers have been observed consistently giving their obese offspring larger food portions than received by leaner children (Waxman & Stunkard, 1980). These findings indicate that training parents in behavioral-management techniques should have an effect on childhood obesity.

Because of the importance of family influences, the behavioral-treatment model focuses on using parents as behavioral-change agents for their children. The counseling staff in a psychiatric setting can begin to model appropriate parenting behaviors and help the family establish new eating and exercise norms, because parental involvement is needed for lasting weight reduction in children (Epstein, 1988).

Behavioral family factors are related to childhood obesity in terms of family determination of food and activity availability, modeling of eating and exercise behaviors, and reinforcement of these behaviors by parents or siblings. Hence, treatment should include the parents who can manipulate the variables that affect child eating and activity when the child returns home.

Behavioral-management training may not be successful unless the family system is in a state of relative health. Childhood obesity has been related to family conflict and maternal depression (Klesges & Hanson, 1988). Children in families lacking a clear hierarchy of control were found to lose less weight in a behavioral treatment program (Kirschenbaum, Harris, & Tomarken, 1984). Longitudinal research in Sweden revealed that degree of psychosocial stress assessed in 7-year-old children predicted the rate of weight gain from ages 7 to 10 years (Mellbin & Vuille, 1989a). A retrospective study found that increases in relative weight from ages 7 to 15 years correlated with psychosocial stress as assessed by school records and school nurses over the years (Mellbin & Vuille, 1989b). It can be assumed that children with excessive psychosocial stress have a higher probability of having dysfunction in their families. The disturbance of eating behavior due to family dysfunction is manifested even in early childhood. Christoffel and Forsyth (1989) studied cases of severe obesity in early childhood. They found family disorganization, maternal separation, maternal depression, and denial of the growth abnormality. In all cases, parental limit setting was impaired.

These findings demonstrate that there is a need to view and treat childhood obesity within the context of family therapy; however, family therapists and researchers have paid relatively little attention to obesity, and a theoretical framework for guiding research and treatment has yet to be developed (Foreyt & Cousins, 1989). According to family-systems theory, treatment would require changing the patterns of family interaction in which symptomatic behaviors (imprudent eating and inadequate exercise) are imbedded. Studies in this area have found that obese families are characterized by lack of organization and by social isolation; unfortunately, the obese child may serve as scapegoat for the frustrations and anger found in such families (Bullen, Monello, Cohen, & Mayer, 1963; Dietz, 1988; Hammar et al., 1972).

It is easy to understand why children in dysfunctional families would have difficulty in weight-management attempts. The low long-term success rate of family-based treatment for childhood obesity may be due in part to the inability of poorly functioning family systems to maintain prudent eating and exercise behaviors. Hence, it is important to assess family functioning and to apply whatever therapy seems necessary to bring the family to a level of functioning at which self-management is effective. This process should start while the child is still in a psychiatric setting so that family interactions can be monitored in a controlled fashion.

In order to assess family functioning, the Family Environment Scale (Moos, 1974) can be used. A pilot study showed relations between family food-intake patterns and scores on this scale (Kintner, Boss, & Johnson, 1981). The methodology for studying "psychosomatic families" developed by Minuchin et al. (1975) might prove to be appropriate in the study of obese families. These families are characterized by enmeshment, overprotection, rigidity, and lack of conflict resolution. This approach has been applied to anorexia but not to obesity.

Family factors in childhood obesity have been reviewed (Venters & Mullis, 1984; Loader, 1985). Areas for assessment specific for childhood obesity include degree of paternal control of eating, ability of family members to communicate, and appropriateness of and parental agreement on child-rearing practices. Loader has developed the Family Task Interview and the Family Health Scales to assess specific features that distinguish families of obese children.

ACTUAL ASSESSMENT

In a psychiatric setting, there are limitations placed on assessment for childhood obesity. Because most of health-care providers' energy is spent on the psychiatric problems and because of the resources generally available on a psychiatric unit, efforts at obesity assessment and treatment often get short shrift.

Assessment of obesity is usually limited to weight/height measures, and the Adjusted Weight Formula (Kirschenbaum et al., 1984) can be used to track progress. Cardiorespiratory fitness can be assessed most easily using the 12-minute run-walk test (Cooper, 1977). The child's enjoyment of exercise can be logged on an exercise-monitoring form using a 5-point hedonic scale (Epstein, Valoski, et al., 1989). This should be recorded in the progress notes. Minutes spent in sedentary activity can be estimated by careful attention to the elements of the treatment plan, and vigorous exercise can be assessed through the reward system to be described under treatment.

As part of the assessment interview, parents should be asked about the child's exercise and eating habits at home and the child's attitudes toward exercise. They should also be asked if the child's self-esteem seems to be linked to body image.

Assessment of eating behavior can be facilitated if each child is given access only to an appropriate menu (i.e., low-fat meals and snacks adjusted for calorie needs). Children in a typical psychiatric setting, especially adolescents, have access to high-fat snack food in vending machines and are frequently given fried foods, pizza, and so on, for special occasions, such as Friday-night movies. If treatment involves giving the child cards that can be exchanged for prudent foods, then the spent cards will reveal purchase habits, if not actual consumption. These cards will need to be identified with the patient's name, and rules about trading such cards will need to be enforced. For younger children for whom food control is easier, the color coding of foods can be used to keep track of intake (Epstein & Squires, 1988). As part of the assessment, a child can be asked to list favorite foods. A shaping program gradually replaces high-fat, high-sugar items with substitutes.

Parents can be interviewed regarding any unusual eating habits, cravings, or bingeing. In particular, risk factors for eating disorders, such as self-restrictive dieting or an abnormal focus on body image or food, should be noted. If the parents are obese, assessment of their willingness and ability to manage their own weight and to provide a good home environment for their child should be assessed.

At a minimum, weight/height measures, food amount and type (high-fat vs. low-fat), and minutes of vigorous exercise should be recorded. Percent overweight can be calculated from growth-curve norms.

PROTOTYPIC TREATMENT

Based on the research to date, the following treatment components emerge as the most likely candidates for inclusion into a comprehensive approach: (a) parental involvement,

(b) increased activity, (c) reduction in calorie density of food, and (d) use of behavioral approaches. Several excellent resources are available as treatment guides for programs that include these components: a practitioner guidebook (Kirschenbaum, Johnson, & Stalonas, 1987), *The Stoplight Diet for Children* (Epstein & Squires, 1988), and the SHAPEDOWN program (Mellin, Slinkard, & Irwin, 1987).

Ideally, treatment is a team effort of psychologists, dietitians, and pediatricians. The aftercare plan should emphasize management of the exercise and the food environments both in and outside the home, involving schools and communities. Health education and behavioral therapy form the core of this broad view.

First, an intake medical screening (Turner, 1980) is performed to rule out organic dysfunction. Problems with gait or running kinesiology should also be assessed to avoid complications with exercise.

Family members are interviewed individually and observed interacting during a meal and while solving a game puzzle together. Family dysfunction in terms of communications, isolation of target child, inability to cooperate, or history of recent severe stress is an indication that family therapy for dysfunction should precede intervention for obesity. Minor dysfunction, on the other hand, may be helped through the behavioral training and family cooperation emphasized in treatment of childhood obesity. Family assessment scales (Loader, 1985; Moos, 1974) and family therapy can be helpful if questions of readiness for behavioral therapy of weight loss arise.

Preteen children have group therapy with their parents, whereas the teenagers meet separately because older children seem to do better with greater opportunity to display self-reliance and independence from parents (Brownell, Kelman, & Stunkard, 1983).

Health Education

Obese children are taught how to exercise and how to eat for fun and enjoyment so that they do not think of exercise programs and changes in their eating as punitive. Parents are taught to teach their children these eating and exercise skills, together with behavioral management skills. The emphasis is on promoting family cohesion. The family is guided away from the tendency to use the obese child as a scapegoat to absorb the frustrations of other members in a dysfunctional environment.

Only aerobic activity will help improve low fitness levels of the obese child. However, many obese children are opposed to the idea of vigorous activity, and adherence has been better for life-style activity recommendations, such as taking stairs rather than an elevator and walking to the corner store rather than driving there (Epstein, Wing, Koeske, & Valoski, 1985). Despite their reluctance to engage in vigorous activity, children can be taught to make aerobic exercise enjoyable by helping them develop an aerobic regimen very gradually. Rapid walking, using techniques of self-regulation to ensure that exercise is perceived as invigorating rather than exhausting, is usually experienced as enjoyable (Goodrick & Iammarino, 1982). Whether the child engages in an aerobic regimen or not, assessment of physical fitness is done at least quarterly using run-walk tests to document progress and to help detect low fitness due to excessive dietary restriction.

The aftercare plan involves helping the patient's family find exercise/walking paths in the neighborhood. Advice on shoes, apparel, when to walk, and precautions in cold or hot weather are given. Family games requiring moderate activity are suggested. Home exercise equipment is recommended, such as stationary bicycles or the newer cross-country skier machines, which require less coordination than earlier models.

Perhaps as important as helping children increase activity is motivating them to decrease inactivity. They are told of the relationship between TV viewing and body fat. For aftercare, families are encouraged to work together to develop rules regarding TV. One hour a day should be the limit for any child, unless the child is exercising on a stationary exercise machine while watching. In a psychiatric treatment setting, excessive sedentary behavior can be controlled with careful treatment planning.

Dietitians train patients and their families to lower the fat content of their diets through awareness of nutritional food labels and lower fat cooking techniques and recipes (DeBakey, Gotto, Scott, & Foreyt, 1984). Home food surveys are given to families for self-assessment.

The recommended eating plan is based on *The Stoplight Diet for Children* (Epstein & Squires, 1988), described previously under Assessment of Eating Behavior. This plan results in satisfactory fat loss without affecting height (Epstein, Wing, Koeske, & Valoski, 1987).

The hospital cafeteria should promote a prudent diet, and high-fat snack foods should not be available. The exercise program should ensure that each child is aerobically active for at least 45 minutes a day. The activities should be individualized to adapt to the needs of the very obese.

Behavior Therapy

The first step is to train the children to self-monitor eating, exercise, and sedentary behaviors. Self-monitoring booklets are used for this purpose; younger children record activities with the assistance of staff. The monitoring booklets have a space to record reasons why exercise was not done or why imprudent eating occurred. Possible solutions to problems are also recorded for discussion at the next therapy session.

Staff negotiate weekly contracts with the children. Stars are used as token reinforcers for achievements. Stars are awarded for progress in prudent eating (increased number of low-calorie-density meals or snacks per day) and for completion of activities or avoidance of TV. At the end of the week, stars are redeemed for nonfood privileges.

Cognitive-behavioral methods are used with children to help them develop alternatives to negative self-statements and to assist them in feeling good about initiating social interaction. Exploration of self-evaluations, role-playing, imagery, and modeling are used to help build self-esteem (Foreyt & Cousins, 1989). Parents are instructed to communicate unconditional love of the obese child, explaining that their excess body fat does not affect the relationship between parent and child. Future research may show that this approach is helpful in preventing eating disorders, which seem to have their basis in distorted self-image and parental relationships.

Parents are trained in the use of behavioral principles to influence the behavior of their child upon return home. In addition to the use of contracts, prompts and positive attention are encouraged for appropriate eating and exercise behaviors. Parents are trained to respond to inappropriate behaviors by helping the child understand why the behavior occurred and what might be done to prevent a recurrence. The approach is mutual problem solving, with parents of younger children giving more coaching and parents of older children adopting the role of consultants.

ACTUAL TREATMENT

In a psychiatric setting, more attention will be paid to the child's main diagnosis than to obesity. The obesity and presenting disorder are no doubt linked in that self-esteem is damaged by poor body image and excessive eating may be a way of coping with stress. Sedentary behavior needs to be replaced with regular exercise, which can have antidepressant and antianxiety effects, as well as positively affecting body image and sense of accomplishment.

At a minimum, obese children in a psychiatric setting should be given the opportunity to learn that exercise is fun and invigorating; this is taught by gradual, self-regulated-intensity aerobic exercises, preferably in groups with other obese children. They should also be taught which foods have too much fat and how to substitute lower fat alternatives. The treatment environment should include a walking path as well as plenty of healthful food items in the cafeteria and vending machines.

Charting of exercise and eating behavior should be used, with increasing goals for rewards. A chart of progress can be posted on the patient's wall. In group, other patients should be encouraged to point out that the obese child is worthwhile and should not be judged on appearance. The obese child may have a fragile ego; when placed in a psychiatric setting, this may be even more serious. Peers left to their own devices may ridicule the obese child; every effort should be made to ensure that the treatment environment is not countertherapeutic.

Parents should be taught about prudent exercise and eating (Foreyt & Goodrick, 1992) and about praising the child for prudent behaviors, not for weight loss. They should also be instructed to communicate with the child in ways that are nurturing to self-esteem, making sure not to criticize the child's appearance.

SUMMARY

Behavior therapy with parental involvement can produce significant and long-term reductions in obesity for about one-third of children treated (Epstein, 1988). For children who begin treatment in a psychiatric setting, outcomes may be less favorable because the child's disorder may inhibit learning, and the family's dysfunction will limit how much can be achieved through family influences. This situation can be improved if the psychiatric treatment plan has an emphasis on health promotion through nutritional and exercise training.

Childhood obesity needs to be studied within the broader context of eating disorders (Brownell & Foreyt, 1986), especially as this framework encompasses the arena of family-systems approaches. As previously discussed, family dysfunction seems to be related to childhood obesity in ways similar to those found in eating disorders; that is, families of both anorexics and the obese are frequently characterized by overprotectiveness and enmeshment (Brone & Fisher, 1988). Family behavior therapy approaches can identify overprotective and enmeshment behaviors; interventions then are aimed at increasing more healthful interaction patterns. This approach might be helpful in applications with families of obese children. Treatment of such children in a psychiatric setting can benefit from intense involvement with parents; the authors' experience is that, all too often, parental involvement in treatment is minimal. Indeed, low parental involvement seems to predict many childhood psychiatric disorders.

In addition to greater depth of intervention in families, use of peer approaches has potential, at least with older children. Peer-group diet and exercise problem solving has shown some promise with diabetic adolescents (Anderson, Wolf, Burkhart, Cornell, & Bacon, 1989). Peer approaches can help obese children with social skills and provide them with an environment of acceptance.

Further treatment-outcome research is needed to determine whether the integration of treatment of obesity improves the outcome of treatment for psychiatric disorders in obese children. Improvement in overall treatment can be expected due to the beneficial effects of exercise and the improvement in self-esteem derived from an enhanced body image.

REFERENCES

Adams, F. H., Linde, L. M., & Miyake, H. (1961). The physical working capacity of normal school children. 1. California. *Pediatrics, 28*, 55–64.

Anderson, B. J., Wolf, F. M., Burkhart, M. T., Cornell, R. G., & Bacon, G. E. (1989). Effects of peer-group intervention on metabolic control of adolescents with IDDM. Randomized outpatient study. *Diabetes Care, 12*, 179–183.

Bandini, L. G., & Dietz, W. H., Jr. (1987). Assessment of body fatness in childhood obesity: Evaluation of laboratory and anthropometric techniques. *Journal of the American Dietetic Association, 87*, 1344–1348.

Barkeling, B., Ekman, S., & Rossner, S. (1992). Eating behavior in obese and normal weight 11-year-old children. *International Journal of Obesity, 16*, 355–360.

Bennett, W. (1987). Dietary treatments of obesity. *Annals of the New York Academy of Sciences, 499*, 250–263.

Black, D. W., Goldstein, R. B., & Mason, E. E. (1992). Prevalence of mental disorder in 88 morbidly obese bariatric clinic patients. *American Journal of Psychiatry, 149*, 227–234.

Blair, S. N. (1984). How to assess exercise habits and physical fitness. In J. D. Matarazzo, S. M. Weiss, J. A. Herd, N. E. Miller, & S. M. Weiss (Eds.), *Behavioral Health* (pp. 424–447). New York: Wiley.

Bouchard, C., Tremblay, A., Despres, J. P., Nadeau, A., Lupien, P. J., Theriault, G., Dussault, J., Moorjani, S., Pinault, S., & Fournier, G. (1990). The response to long-term overfeeding in identical twins. *New England Journal of Medicine, 322*, 1477–1482.

Boulton, J. (1981). Physical fitness in childhood and its relation to age, maturity, body size, and nutritional factors. *Acta Paediatrica Scandinavica, 70* (Suppl. 284), 80–84.

Bray, G. A. (1976). *The obese patient*. Philadelphia: W. B. Saunders.

Breum, L., Lissau, L. S., Sorensen, T. I. A., Holst, D., & Friis-Hasche, E. (1990). Sweets habits in childhood and the risk of adult obesity: A 10-year prospective study of 552 families. *International Journal of Obesity, 14*(Suppl. 2), 87.

Brone, R. J., & Fisher, C. B. (1988). Determinants of adolescent obesity: a comparison with anorexia nervosa. *Adolescence, 23*, 155–169.

Brownell, K. D., & Foreyt, J. P. (1986). The eating disorders: Summary and integration. In K. D. Brownell & J. P. Foreyt (Eds.), *Handbook of eating disorders* (pp. 503–513). New York: Basic Books.

Brownell, K. D., Kelman, J. H., & Stunkard, A. J. (1983). Treatment of obese children with and without their mothers: Changes in weight and blood pressure. *Pediatrics, 71*, 515–523.

Bullen, B. A., Monello, L. F., Cohen, H., & Mayer, J. (1963). Attitude toward physical activity, food and family in obese and non-obese adolescent girls. *American Journal of Clinical Nutrition, 12*, 1–11.

Christoffel, K. K., & Forsyth, B. W. (1989). Mirror image of environmental deprivation: severe childhood obesity of psychosocial origin. *Child Abuse and Neglect, 13*, 249–256.

Clark, D. G., & Blair, S. N. (1988). Physical activity and prevention of obesity in childhood. In N. A. Krasnegor, G. D. Grave, & N. Kretchmer (Eds.), *Childhood obesity: A biobehavioral perspective* (pp. 121–142). Caldwell, NJ: Telford Press.

Coates, T. J., & Thoresen, C. E. (1980). Obesity in children and adolescents: The problem belongs to everyone. In B. Lahey & A. Kazdin (Eds.), *Advances in child clinical psychology: Vol. 3* (pp. 215–264). New York: Plenum Press.

Coates, T. J., & Thoresen, C. E. (1981). Treating obesity in children and adolescents: Is there any hope? In J. M. Ferguson & C. B. Taylor (Eds.), *The comprehensive handbook of behavioral medicine: Vol. 2. Syndromes and special areas* (pp. 103–129). New York: SP Medical and Scientific Books.

Cooper, K. H. (1977). *The aerobics way.* New York: M. Evans.

DeBakey, M. E., Gotto, A. M., Jr., Scott, L. W., & Foreyt, J. P. (1984). *The living heart diet.* New York: Raven Press.

Dietz, W. H. (1988). Childhood and adolescent obesity. In R. T. Frankle & M-U Yang (Eds.), *Obesity and weight control* (pp. 345–359). Rockville, MD: Aspen.

Dietz, W. H., Jr., & Gortmaker, S. L. (1985). Do we fatten our children at the TV set? Obesity and television viewing in children and adolescents. *Pediatrics, 75*, 807–812.

Dugdale, A. E., & Lovell, S. (1981). Measuring childhood obesity. *Lancet, 2*, 1224.

Eck, L. H., Klesges, R. C., Hanson, C. L., & Slawson, D. (1992). Children at familial risk for obesity: An examination of dietary intake, physical activity and weight status. *International Journal of Obesity, 16*, 71–78.

Eliot, D. L., Goldberg, L., Kuehl, K. S., & Hanna, C. (1989). Metabolic evaluation of obese and nonobese siblings. *Journal of Pediatrics, 114*, 957–962.

Epstein, L. H. (1988). The Pittsburgh childhood weight control program: An update. In N. A. Krasnegor, G. D. Grave, & N. Kretchmer (Eds.), *Childhood obesity: A biobehavioral perspective* (pp. 199–216). Caldwell, NJ: Telford Press.

Epstein, L. H., & Cluss, P. A. (1986). Behavioral genetics of childhood obesity. *Behavior Therapy, 17*, 324–334.

Epstein, L. H., Koeske, R., Zidansek, J., & Wing, R. R. (1983). Effects of weight loss on fitness in obese children. *American Journal of Diseases of Children, 137*, 654–657.

Epstein, L. H., Masek, B. J., & Marshall, W. R. (1978). A nutritionally based school program for control of eating in obese children. *Behavior Therapy, 9*, 766–778.

Epstein, L. H., Smith, J. A., Vara, L. S., & Rodefer, J. S. (1991). Behavioral economic analysis of activity choice in obese children. *Health-Psychology, 10*, 311–316.

Epstein, L. H., & Squires, S. (1988). *The Stoplight Diet for children: An eight-week program for parents and children.* Boston: Little, Brown.

Epstein, L. H., Valoski, A., Wing, R. R., Perkins, K. A., Fernstrom, M., Marks, B., & McCurley, J. (1989). Perception of eating and exercise in children as a function of child and parent weight status. *Appetite, 12*, 105–118.

Epstein, L. H., & Wing, R. R. (1987). Behavioral treatment of childhood obesity. *Psychological Bulletin, 101*, 331–342.

Epstein, L. H., Wing, R. R., Koeske, R., & Valoski, A. (1985). A comparison of lifestyle exercise, aerobic exercise, and calisthenics on weight loss in obese children. *Behavior Therapy, 16*, 345–356.

Epstein, L. H., Wing, R. R., Koeske, R., & Valoski, A. (1987). Long-term effects of family-based treatment of childhood obesity. *Journal of Consulting and Clinical Psychology, 55*, 91–95.

Epstein, L. H., Wing, R. R., Woodall, K., Penner, B. C., Kress, M. J., & Koeske, R. (1985). Effects of family-based behavioral treatment on obese 5-to-8-year-old children. *Behavior Therapy, 16,* 205–212.

Foreyt, J. P., & Cousins, J. H. (1989). Obesity. In E. J. Mash & R. A. Barkley (Eds.), *Treatment of childhood disorders* (pp. 405–422). New York: Guilford Press.

Foreyt, J. P., & Goodrick, G. K. (1988). Childhood obesity. In E. J. Mash & L. G. Terdal (Eds.), *Behavioral assessment of childhood disorders* (2nd ed.) (pp. 528–551). New York: Guilford Press.

Foreyt, J. P., & Goodrick, G. K. (1992). *Living without dieting.* Houston, TX: Harrison.

Foreyt, J. P., Goodrick, G. K., & Gotto, A. M. (1981). Limitations of behavioral treatment of obesity: Review and analysis. *Journal of Behavioral Medicine, 4,* 159–174.

Frank, G. C., Webber, L. S., & Berenson, G. S. (1982). Dietary studies of infants and children: The Bogalusa Heart Study. In T. J. Coates, A. C. Peterson, & C. Perry (Eds.), *Promoting adolescent health* (pp. 329–354). New York: Academic Press.

Garn, S. M., LaVelle, M., & Pilkington, J. J. (1984). Obesity and living together. In D. J. Kallen & M. B. Sussman (Eds.), *Obesity and the family* (pp. 33–47). New York: Haworth Press.

Goodrick, G. K., & Foreyt, J. P. (1991). Why treatments for obesity don't last. *Journal of the American Dietetic Association, 91,* 1243–1247.

Goodrick, G. K., & Iammarino, N. K. (1982). Teaching aerobic lifestyles: New perspectives. *Journal of Physical Education, Recreation and Dance, 53,* 48–50.

Gortmaker, S. L., Dietz, W. H., Sobol, A. M., & Wehler, C. A. (1987). Increasing pediatric obesity in the United States. *American Journal of Diseases of Children, 141,* 535–540.

Governor's Commission on Physical Fitness. (1974). *The Texas Physical Fitness-Motor Ability Test.* Austin: State of Texas.

Governor's Commission on Physical Fitness. (1986). *Fit Youth in Texas (FYT) Test.* Austin: State of Texas.

Griffiths, M., & Payne, P. R. (1976). Energy expenditure in small children of obese and nonobese patients. *Nature, 260,* 698–700.

Gustafson-Larson, A. M., & Terry, R. D. (1992). Weight-related behaviors and concerns of fourth-grade children. *Journal of the American Dietetic Association, 92,* 818–822.

Hammar, S. L., Campbell, M. M., Campbell, A., Moores, N. L., Sareen, C., Gareis, F. J., & Lucas, M. P. H. (1972). An interdisciplinary study of obesity. *Journal of Pediatrics, 80,* 373–383.

Himes, J. H., & Bouchard, C. (1989). Validity of anthropometry in classifying youths as obese. *International Journal of Obesity, 13,* 183–193.

Ho, T. F., Tay, J. S., Yip, W. C., & Rajan, U. (1989). Evaluation of lung function in Singapore obese children. *Journal of the Singapore Paediatric Society, 31,* 46–52.

Israel, A. C., Stolmaker, L., & Andrian, C. A. G. (1985). The effects of training parents in general child management skills on a behavioral weight loss program for children. *Behavior Therapy, 16,* 169–180.

Kahle, E. B., Walker, R. B., Eisenman, P. A., Behall, K. M., Hallfrisch, J., & Reiser, S. (1982). Moderate diet control in children: The effects on metabolic indicators that predict obesity-related degenerative diseases. *American Journal of Clinical Nutrition, 35,* 950–957.

Kintner, M., Boss, P. G., & Johnson, N. (1981). The relationship between dysfunctional family environments and family member food intake. *Journal of Marriage and the Family, 43,* 633–641.

Kirschenbaum, D. S., Harris, E. S., & Tomarken, A. J. (1984). Effects of parental involvement in behavioral weight loss therapy for preadolescents. *Behavior Therapy, 15,* 485–500.

Kirschenbaum, D. S., Johnson, W. G., & Stalonas, P. M. (1987). *Treating childhood and adolescent obesity.* New York: Pergamon Press.

Klesges, R. C., Coates, T. J., Brown, G., Sturgeon-Tillisch, J., Moldenhauer-Klesges, L. M., Holzer, B., Woolfrey, J., & Vollmer, J. (1983). Parental influences on children's eating behavior and relative weight. *Journal of Applied Behavior Analysis, 16*, 371–378.

Klesges, R. C., Coates, T. J., Holzer, B., Moldenhauer, L. M., Woolfrey, J., & Vollmer, J. (1983). Parental influences on children's eating behavior. *Journal of Applied Behavior Analysis, 16*, 371–378.

Klesges, R. C., Coates, T. J., Moldenhauer-Klesges, L. M., Holzer, B., Gustavson, J., & Barnes, J. (1984). The FATS: An observational system for assessing physical activity in children and associated parent behavior. *Behavioral Assessment, 6*, 333–345.

Klesges, R. C., Haddock, C. K., Stein, R. J., Klesges, L. M., Eck, L. H., & Hanson, C. L. (1992). Relationship between psychosocial functioning and body fat in preschool children: A longitudinal investigation. *Journal of Consulting and Clinical Psychology, 60*, 793–796.

Klesges, R. C., & Hanson, C. L. (1988). Determining the environmental causes and correlates of childhood obesity: Methodological issues and future research directions. In N. A. Krasnegor, G. D. Grave, & N. Kretchmer (Eds.), *Childhood obesity: A biobehavioral perspective* (pp. 89–118). Caldwell, NJ: Telford Press.

Klesges, R. C., Klesges, L. M., Swenson, A. M., & Pheley, A. (1985). A validation of two motion sensors in the prediction of child and adult physical activity levels. *American Journal of Epidemiology, 122*, 400–410.

Lauer, R. M., Conner, W. E., Leaverton, P. E., Reiter, M. A., & Clarke, W. R. (1975). Coronary heart disease risk factors in school children: The Muscatine study. *Journal of Pediatrics, 86*, 697–706.

LeBow, M. D. (1984). *Child obesity: A new frontier of behavior therapy.* New York: Springer.

Loader, P. J. (1985). Childhood obesity: The family perspective. *International Journal of Eating Disorders, 4*, 211–225.

Locard, E., Mamelle, N., Billette, A., Miginiac, M., Munoz, F., & Rey, S. (1992). Risk factors of obesity in a five-year-old population. Parental versus environmental factors. *International Journal of Obesity, 16*, 721–729.

Maloney, M. J., & Klykylo, W. M. (1983). An overview of anorexia nervosa, bulimia and obesity in children and adolescents. *Journal of the American Academy of Child Psychiatry, 22*, 99–107.

Maloney, M. J., McGuire, J., Daniels, S. R., & Specker, B. (1989). Dieting behavior and eating attitudes in children. *Pediatrics, 84*, 482–489.

Marston, A. R., Jacobs, D. F., Singer, R. D., Widaman, K. F., & Little, T. D. (1988). Characteristics of adolescents at risk for compulsive overeating on a brief screening test. *Adolescence, 23*, 59–65.

Mattes, R. D. (1993). Fat preference and adherence to a reduced-fat diet. *American Journal of Clinical Nutrition, 57*, 373–381.

McSwegin, P., Pemberton, C., Petray, C., & Going, S. (1989). *The AAHPERD guide to physical fitness education and assessment.* Washington, DC: American Alliance for Health, Physical Education, Recreation, and Dance.

Mellbin, T., & Vuille, J. C. (1989a). Further evidence of an association between psychosocial problems and increase in relative weight between 7 and 10 years of age. *Acta Paediatrica Scandinavica, 78*, 576–580.

Mellbin, T., & Vuille, J. C. (1989b). Rapidly developing overweight in school children as an indicator of psychosocial stress. *Acta Paediatrica Scandinavica, 78*, 568–575.

Mellin, L. M. (1990). Unpublished survey, University of California, San Francisco.

Mellin, L. M., Slinkard, L. A., & Irwin, C. E. (1987). Adolescent obesity intervention: Validation of the SHAPEDOWN program. *Journal of the American Dietetic Association, 87*, 333–338.

Michielutte, R., Diseker, R. A., Corbett, W. T., Schey, H. M., & Ureda, J. R. (1985). The relationship between weight-height indices and the triceps skinfold measure among children 5 to 12. *American Journal of Public Health, 74*, 604–606.

Minuchin, S., Baker, L. L., Rosman, B. L., Liebman, R., Milman, L., & Todd, T. C. (1975). A conceptual model of psychosomatic illness in children. *Archives of General Psychiatry, 32,* 1031–1038.

Moos, R. H. (1974). *Family Environment Scale manual.* Palo Alto, CA: Consulting Psychologists Press.

Murphy, C. M., Allison, D. B., Babbitt, R. L., & Patterson, H. L. (1992). Adiposity in children: Is mental retardation a critical variable? *International Journal of Obesity, 16,* 633–638.

National Center for Health Statistics. (1988). Growth charts for boys and girls. *American Dietetic Association, Manual of clinical dietetics* (pp. 582–599). Chicago: American Dietetic Association.

Nelson, M., Black, A. E., Morris, J. A., & Cole, T. J. (1989). Between- and within-subject variation in nutrient intake from infancy to old age: Estimating the number of days required to rank dietary intakes with desired precision. *American Journal of Clinical Nutrition, 50,* 155–167.

Office of Disease Prevention and Health Promotion. (1985). *Summary of findings from National Children and Youth Fitness Study.* Washington, DC: U.S. Department of Health and Human Services.

O'Neil, P. M., Currey, H. S., Hirsch, A., Malcolm, R. J., Sexaver, J. D., Riddle, F. E., & Taylor, C. I. (1979). Development and validation of the Eating Behavior Inventory. *Journal of Behavioral Assessment, 1,* 123–132.

Parcel, G. S., Simons-Morton, B., O'Hara, N., Baranowski, T., Kolbe, L., & Bee, D. (1987). School promotion of healthful diet and exercise behavior: An integration of organizational change and social learning theory interventions. *Journal of School Health, 57,* 150–156.

Ross, J. G., & Gilbert, G. G. (1985). A summary of findings. *Journal of Physical Education, Recreation, and Dance, 56,* 45–50.

Sharav, T., & Bowman, T. (1992). Dietary practices, physical activity, and body-mass index in a selected population of Down syndrome children and their siblings. *Clinical Pediatrics, 31,* 341–344.

Stunkard, A. J., & Burt, V. (1967). Obesity and the body image: Age at onset of disturbances in the body. *American Journal of Psychiatry, 123,* 1443–1447.

Stunkard, A. J., Harris, J. R., Pedersen, N. L., & McClearn, G. E. (1990). The body-mass index of twins who have been reared apart. *New England Journal of Medicine, 322,* 1483–1487.

Tanner, J. M., & Whitehouse, R. H. (1975). Revised standards for triceps and subscapular skinfolds in British children. *Archives of Disease in Childhood, 50,* 142–145.

Taras, H. L., Sallis, J. F., Patterson, T. L., Nader, P. R., & Nelson, J. A. (1989). Television's influence on children's diet and physical activity. *Journal of Developmental and Behavioral Pediatrics, 10,* 176–180.

Tucker, L. A. (1986). The relationship of television viewing to physical fitness and obesity. *Adolescence, 21,* 795–799.

Turner, T. J. (1980). Obesity in children and adolescents. *Developmental and Behavioral Pediatrics, 1,* 43–47.

Van Loan, M. D., Belko, A. Z., Mayclin, P. L., & Barbieri, T. F. (1987). Use of total-body electrical conductivity for monitoring body composition during weight reduction. *American Journal of Clinical Nutrition, 46,* 5–8.

Venters, M., & Mullis, R. (1984). Family-oriented nutrition education and preschool obesity. *Journal of Nutrition Education, 16,* 159–161.

Waxman, M., & Stunkard, A. J. (1980). Caloric intake and expenditure of obese boys. *Journal of Pediatrics, 96,* 187–193.

Wheeler, M. E., & Hess, K. W. (1976). Treatment of juvenile obesity by successive approximation control of eating. *Journal of Behavior Therapy and Experimental Psychiatry, 7,* 235–241.

CHAPTER 21

Somatization Disorder

JOHN V. CAMPO

DESCRIPTION OF THE PROBLEM

Medically unexplained symptoms are quite common in children and adolescents, although a review of the available pediatric literature highlights the lack of systematic research on the psychological attributes of children and adolescents with medically unexplained symptoms, the course of such problems, and their treatment (Campo & Fritsch, in press). Such patients are often referred to as suffering from or exhibit evidence of somatization, a term that may generate some confusion. In concert with terms such as *conversion* and *hysteria*, the term *somatization* has been used in a variety of ways: as a descriptive term, as the name of a presumed psychological process or mechanism of symptom production, and as the defining label for a categorical psychiatric disorder characterized primarily by unexplained physical symptoms. Somatization may be said to occur (a) when there are one or more physical complaints and medical evaluation reveals no explanatory pathophysiologic mechanism or physical pathology or (b) when there is related physical pathology, but the physical complaints or resulting impairment are grossly in excess of what would be expected from the medical findings (Kellner, 1991). Lipowski (1988) emphasized the importance of seeking help with somatization occurring not simply when patients experience medically unexplained physical symptoms, but when they specifically attribute them to physical disease and seek medical help for them.

As just defined, somatization can be viewed in a variety of ways that may be complementary (Simon, 1991). Some clinicians have focused on somatization as the product of a physiological process associated with emotional arousal and distress, which may not be detectable by the usual means of medical investigation in the clinical setting (Kellner, 1991). Others have viewed somatization from a cognitive perspective, essentially seeing it as a system of perception and cognition, patients showing an increased focus on bodily sensations, misinterpreting or amplifying bodily sensations or signs of emotional arousal as being evidence of physical disease (Barsky, 1992; Barsky, Goodson, Lane, & Cleary, 1988). Somatization can also be viewed as learned interpersonal or social behaviors that are produced or maintained by the benefits or gains attached to attainment of "the sick role" (Slavney, 1990). Family systems theorists have conceptualized somatization as serving a homeostatic or communicative function within families (Mullins & Olson, 1990). Psychodynamic thinkers may view somatization as the manifestation of an intrapsychic process or dynamic psychological defense in which physical symptoms might allow the expression of a wish or distress, while keeping troubling emotions, impulses, memories, or thoughts out of awareness (Lask & Fosson, 1989; Nemiah, 1977). Finally, most relevant to the title of this chapter, somatization can be considered a manifestation of psychiatric disorder, with somatization being associated with a variety of psychiatric

The assistance of Ms. Tammy McLaughlin in the preparation of this manuscript is gratefully acknowledged.

diagnoses across a number of current categorizations (American Psychiatric Association, 1987).

As defined in the *Diagnostic and Statistical Manual of Mental Disorders*, third edition, revised (DSM-III-R), *somatization disorder* refers to a chronic disorder of several years' duration characterized by recurrent and multiple somatic complaints for which medical attention has been sought, but for which the physical complaints are apparently not due to any physical disorder (American Psychiatric Association, 1987). The disorder should have begun prior to age 30 and requires 13 symptoms from a list of 35 somatic symptoms grouped into subcategories as follows: pseudoneurologic (12 symptoms), gastrointestinal (6 symptoms), pain (5 symptoms), cardiopulmonary (4 symptoms), sexual (4 symptoms), and reproductive (4 symptoms). In order for a symptom to be judged significant, it should be the result of no known pathophysiologic mechanism or pathology, and it must be grossly in excess of what would be expected from the physical findings. The symptom must also result in functional impairment and seeking medical help or self-medication, and it must not occur exclusively during a panic attack. Somatization disorder has been viewed by many as the core disorder in the DSM-III-R broad category of somatoform disorder, which addresses clinical situations for which there are physical symptoms suggesting physical disorder but for which there are no demonstrable organic findings or known pathophysiologic mechanisms and for which there is a strong presumption that the symptoms are linked to psychological factors. In somatoform disorder, the reported physical symptoms should not appear to be intentionally produced, and the patient is viewed as not experiencing a sense of controlling the production of the physical symptoms. It is not clear whether the diagnosis of somatization disorder identifies a distinct population or whether it identifies the far end of a spectrum along a continuum of patients with multiple somatic symptoms (Bass & Murphy, 1990).

The criteria for somatization disorder are modified in DSM-IV (American Psychiatric Association, 1993), with a move away from the extensive symptom counts that characterized prior definitions. The diagnosis requires the presence of the following symptoms at some point during the course of the disorder:

1. *Four pain symptoms:* A history of pain related to at least four different bodily sites or functions (e.g., head, abdomen, back, joints, extremities, chest, or rectum, or during sexual intercourse, menstruation, or urination)

2. *Two gastrointestinal symptoms:* A history of at least two gastrointestinal symptoms other than pain (e.g., nausea, diarrhea, bloating, vomiting other then during pregnancy, or intolerance of several different foods)

3. *One sexual symptom:* A history of at least one sexual or reproductive symptom other than pain (e.g., sexual indifference, erectile or ejaculatory dysfunction, irregular menses, excessive menstrual bleeding, vomiting throughout pregnancy)

4. *One pseudoneurologic symptom:* A history of at least one symptom or deficit suggesting a neurological disorder not limited to pain (e.g., sensory impairment, aphonia, impaired coordination or balance, localized weakness or paralysis, difficulty swallowing, difficulty breathing, urinary retention, pseudoseizures, or dissociative symptoms such as amnesia or loss of consciousness other then fainting)

In addition to somatization disorder, there are six other diagnostic subcategories of somatoform disorder in DSM-III-R: *Body dysmorphic disorder* is the diagnosis applied when there is a preoccupation with some imagined physical defect in a person who appears normal or when there is an actual physical defect present but the concern generated is judged excessive. In *conversion disorder*, an alteration or loss of physical functioning is present, with the physical symptom being judged to express a psychological conflict or need. Traditionally, this diagnosis had been applied to symptoms that were primarily pseudoneurologic in nature, essentially those suggesting neurologic disease, though DSM-III-R allows for a broader interpretation of when the diagnosis might be applied, with an emphasis primarily on the mechanism of symptom production. Indeed, it is the only diagnosis in DSM-III-R where a psychological etiology is part of the diagnosis. A return to the more narrow focus on pseudoneurologic symptoms for conversion disorder is found in DSM-IV. *Hypochondriasis* is diagnosed when an individual fears that they have a serious disease or believes that such a disease is present, with persistence of his fears or beliefs despite the reassurance of a physician. *Somatoform pain disorder* is present when there is preoccupation with pain for at least 6 months in the absence of physical findings to account for its presence or intensity. Pain is dealt with somewhat differently in DSM-IV; that is, the diagnosis of pain disorder is made in situations where psychological factors are judged to play an important role in the onset, severity, exacerbation, or maintenance of the pain. The disorder may be judged *acute* (of less than 6-month duration) or *chronic* (duration of 6 months or greater). *Undifferentiated somatoform disorder* is diagnosed when one or more somatic complaints or symptoms are present for at least 6 months and when the patient does not meet criteria for the diagnosis of another somatoform disorder. When somatoform symptoms are present that do not meet criteria for any of the more specific somatoform disorders or adjustment disorder with physical complaints, *somatoform disorder, not otherwise specified* is diagnosed.

Medically unexplained physical symptoms are prominent features across a number of diagnostic categories within DSM-III-R. Physical symptoms are important diagnostic features in the anxiety disorders, particularly panic disorder and generalized anxiety disorder. Children and adolescents with previously diagnosed anxiety disorders frequently exhibit prominent physical symptoms (Beidel, Christ, & Long, 1991; Last, 1991). Last (1991) found that anxiety disordered patients who suffered from prominent somatic symptoms were more likely to exhibit school refusal. A variety of somatic complaints, most notably fatigue, have been noted to be present in depressed children and adolescents (Carlson & Kashani, 1988; Ryan, Puig-Antich, Ambrosini, Nelson, & Krawiec, 1987). Somatic complaints may occur with increasing frequency as the severity of depression increases, perhaps independent of the presence of coexisting anxiety (McCauley, Carlson, & Calderon, 1991). Work with psychiatrically hospitalized children, however, suggests that unexplained physical complaints are common across a variety of psychiatric diagnoses with little specific relation to the type of psychiatric disorder (Livingston, Taylor, & Crawford, 1988).

Other psychiatric disorders for which physical symptoms may be an essential feature include factitious disorder and malingering. *Factitious disorder with physical symptoms* is diagnosed when physical symptoms are feigned or deliberately produced by a patient, with the incentive being internal, essentially the psychological gains associated with being granted the sick role. *Factitious disorder by proxy*, in which a caretaker inflicts or simulates disease for his or her own internal incentives, is a DSM-IV category relevant to children and adolescents, but it is not included in DSM-III-R. In *malingering*, physical symptoms are feigned or deliberately produced with the hope of an external incentive, such as financial gain or avoiding school or punishment. Some patients with diagnosable physical conditions may also experience an exacerbation of their physical symptomatology in relation to emotional or psychological stress. *Psychological factors affecting medical condition* is the diagnosis applied when psychological factors adversely affect the course of an identified physical condition with a demonstrable pathology or known pathophysiologic process (American Psychiatric Association, 1987, 1993).

In examining the prevalence of somatization in children and adolescents, the available studies rarely employ a systematically made psychiatric diagnosis, but rather focus on describing particular physical symptoms, with the literature exhibiting a variety of methodological difficulties (Campo & Fritsch, in press). Recent work has resulted in the development of a promising new instrument, the Children's Somatization Inventory (Walker & Greene, 1989; Walker, Garber, & Greene, 1991), a questionnaire with parent and child self-report versions that provides a list of 36 somatic symptoms based on the DSM-III symptoms list for somatization disorder and on items from the Hopkins Symptoms Checklist (Derogatis, Lipman, Rickels, Ulenhuth, & Covi, 1974), both with modifications made for use in children. The instrument was administered to a community sample of 540 children and adolescents in grades 3 through 12, with nearly one-half of the sample reporting one physical symptom during the preceding 2-week period (Garber, Walker, & Zeman, 1991). Headache was the most commonly reported symptom (25%), followed by low energy (23%), sore muscles (21%), and abdominal discomfort (at least 17%). Fifteen percent of the sample reported four or more symptoms, and approximately 1% endorsed 13 symptoms or more, although a medical assessment was not included in this study, thereby making it difficult to determine whether the reported symptoms were truly medically unexplained (Garber, Walker, & Zeman, 1991). Factor analysis identified four symptom clusters: cardiovascular, gastrointestinal, pain/weakness, and pseudoneurologic.

Review of the available literature supports the finding that headaches are the most commonly reported of painful somatic symptoms across a variety of studies, with 10% to 30% of children and adolescents reporting headaches frequently or at least weekly. Other commonly observed symptoms in the pediatric age group include recurrent abdominal pain, present in 10% to 25% of school-age children and adolescents; limb pain, reported in approximately 5% to 20%; chest pain, in 7% to 15%; and fatigue (see Campo & Fritsch, in press). Indeed, fatigue is an especially common complaint in adolescents, with approximately 15% of adolescents endorsing fatigue on a daily basis (Belmaker, Espinoza, & Pogrund, 1985; Larson, 1991). Other commonly reported symptoms include dizziness or lightheadedness and gastrointestinal complaints such as nausea and vomiting, although all manner of unexplained physical symptoms and complaints have been reported throughout the medical and psychiatric literature. Interestingly, despite the preponderance of reports of pseudoneurologic symptoms or conversion symptoms in the clinical literature, such symptoms appear to be quite rare in community samples of children and adolescents, at least in the English language literature (Garber, Walker, & Zeman, 1991; Rutter, Tizard, & Whitmore, 1970; Stefansson, Messina, & Meyerowitz, 1976). Such symptoms may be more common in other cultures: Turgay (1980) reports that pseudoneurologic symptoms were the fourth most common presentation at a child psychiatry clinic in Turkey.

Somatic symptoms appear to cluster in the pediatric age group. There is empirical evidence for a somatic complaints syndrome derived from principal components analysis performed on parent ratings of over 8,000 children and adolescents aged 6 to 16 years referred for mental health services (Achenbach, Conners, Quay, Verhulst, & Howell, 1989). Approximately one-third of pediatric patients with recurrent complaints of pain will experience more than one variety of pain or will suffer other somatic symptoms (Apley,

1958; Oster, 1972). Multiple and frequent somatic complaints have been reported in 10% to 15% of adolescents (Belmaker, Espinoza, & Pogrund, 1985; Garrick, Ostrov, & Offer, 1988). A somatization syndrome characterized by multiple physical complaints was identified by 4.5% of the boys and 10.7% of the girls aged 12 to 16 years in the Ontario Child Health Study (Offord, et al., 1987). Although somatization is frequently polysymptomatic (Garber, Walker, & Zeman, 1991) and cases of full-blown somatization disorder have been described in children and adolescents (Kriechman, 1987; Livingston & Martin-Cannici, 1985), most children and adolescents are unlikely to report the number of symptoms necessary to make this diagnosis. This is especially true in younger children (Offord et al., 1987). Given the focus on symptom counts in the DSM-III-R diagnostic scheme, one might reasonably expect that children would be less likely to accumulate the number of symptoms necessary to be diagnosed with somatization disorder. In addition, of the 35 somatic symptoms listed in the DSM-III-R criteria, a total of eight are sexual or reproductive in nature and not likely to be developmentally appropriate for use in prepubertal children. Similarly, the DSM-IV criteria require at least one sexual or reproductive symptom. It has been suggested that less restrictive and more developmentally appropriate criteria be developed (Campo & Fritsch, in press; Garber, Walker, Zeman, 1991; Livingston & Martin-Cannici, 1985; Walker & Greene, 1991). Shapiro and Rosenfeld (1987) proposed revised criteria for somatization disorder in childhood, emphasizing symptoms of at least 1 year's duration, at least five separate symptoms, a family history of somatization, and the presence of other psychiatric symptoms, such as anxiety and depression. The International Classification of Diseases (ICD-10) includes a less restrictive category for chronic and persistent somatization called *multiple somatization disorder*, without a specific age of onset or required symptom counts (World Health Organization, 1988).

When all age groups are grouped together, somatization is more common in girls, although the sex distribution appears to be equal in earlier childhood, with female symptom reporting predominating during adolescence (Campo & Fritsch, in press; Garber, Walker, & Zeman, 1991; Oster, 1972). Girls appear to be more consistent in their reporting of physical symptoms over time than are boys (Walker & Greene, 1991). Pseudoneurologic symptoms or conversion symptoms may show a female predominance across childhood and adolescence (Campo & Fritsch, in press). Recurrent abdominal pain may be the most common symptom in early childhood, with headaches and limb pains becoming more prominent with increasing age (Apley, 1975). Oster (1972) reported that recurrent abdominal pain peaks in prevalence at approximately 9 years of age, with headaches peaking approximately 3 years later. However, systematic and comprehensive studies with a longitudinal design have yet to be carried out in the pediatric age group in order to adequately address the contribution of age factors to somatization.

Somatization is a problem that is quite common and that is worthy of serious attention and consideration in children and adolescents for a number of reasons. Children with somatization appear to truly suffer from their physical symptoms, despite the lack of demonstrable pathology. Somatization is associated with disability and functional impairment in childhood, including difficulty in school and frequent school absences (Aro, Paronen, & Aro, 1987; Faull & Nicol, 1986; Hodges, Kline, Barbero, & Woodruff, 1985; Robinson, Alverez, & Dodge, 1990). These children are at risk for unnecessary medical investigations and treatments that may result in physical harm or needless suffering (Stickler & Murphy, 1979). Such procedures and excessive medical attention may have negative developmental consequences, as well. The costs to society of pediatric somatization cannot be minimized, as there is a suggestion that pediatric somatization may be associated with increased health care utilization (Belmaker, Espinoza, & Pogrund, 1985; Starfield, et al., 1984). Somatization disorder in adults is associated with increased health care utilization, costly medical expenditures, and marked functional impairment and decreased productivity in sufferers (Smith, Monson, & Ray, 1986). It is likely that adult somatization has its roots in childhood, with many adult somatizing patients reporting being "sickly" or in "poor health" since early in life (Kellner, 1986; Pilowsky, Bassett, Begg, & Thomas, 1982). Indeed, Briquet himself observed that the majority of his patients with "hysteria" began their sufferings prior to age 20, with one-fifth beginning prior to puberty (Mai & Merskey, 1980). Adults with a history of somatization dating to childhood appear to be especially refractory to treatment (Shorter, Abbey, Gillies, Singh, & Lipowski, 1992). Somatization may also be one of the more common ways for psychiatric disorder to present in the pediatric setting (Campo & Fritsch, in press). For all of these reasons, identifying children and adolescents who are suffering with significant somatization is relevant and may provide important information about which of these individuals will go on to develop persistent and disabling somatization later in life. While adequate research in this area is lacking, successful treatment may accomplish a decrease in individual suffering, an improvement in function at school and interpersonally, and may help prevent the development of chronic somatization.

PROTOTYPIC ASSESSMENT

Medical Assessment

The appropriate assessment of somatization in the pediatric age group is necessarily multimodal. Most importantly, in every patient presenting with presumed medically unexplained physical symptoms, undiagnosed physical disease must always be considered and the patient's medical status reevaluated. Indeed, one of the fears that immobilizes clinicians and family members in dealing with somatizing children and adolescents is the fear that physical disease will ultimately prove to be the cause of symptoms thought to be representative of somatization. There is no room for complacency in dealing with such patients, because past reports have emphasized high percentages of patients who were previously diagnosed with hysteria, and who, as follow-up,were found to have physical disease that explained the original presentation (Caplan, 1970; Rivinus, Jamison, & Graham, 1975). Early reports may have exaggerated the risk of such an occurrence, with Caplan (1970) reporting that over 40% of such patients were subsequently found to have physical disease that explained their original symptoms. Perhaps as a result of more accurate current diagnostic techniques, more recent samples suggested that the risk of faulty diagnosis is far less, occurring in less than 10% of the patients with unexplained physical symptoms (Apley, 1975; Maisami & Freeman, 1987; Spierings, Poels, Sijben, Gabreels, & Renier, 1990; Volkmar, Poll, & Lewis, 1984). Nevertheless, medical assessment in such patients is a necessity and, at the very least, should include a careful review of the available medical records and previous medical work-up, as well as a medical history and physical examination by a competent clinician or documentation that such evaluation has taken place. Close collaboration between primary care physicians and mental health workers is extremely important. A discussion of physical examination techniques that may be helpful in the assessment of patients with somatization is beyond the scope of this chapter.

Psychiatric Assessment

Comprehensive psychiatric assessment, including a review of all relevant prior psychiatric records, is a necessary aspect of any initial assessment. Somatization is frequently associated with psychiatric disorder in children and adolescents, arguing for pediatricians to consider psychiatric difficulties early in the differential diagnosis of the patient with unexplained physical symptoms (Campo & Fritsch, in press). Reports of somatic symptoms on the Children's Somatization Inventory correlate with self-report measures of anxiety, depression, and perceived competence (Garber, Walker, & Zeman, 1991). Studies utilizing semi-structured psychiatric interviews have documented the frequent occurrence of anxiety disorders in patients with recurrent abdominal pain (Garber, Zeman, & Walker, 1990; Wasserman, Whitington, & Rivera, 1988). Questionnaire-based studies have also shown an excess of anxiety in patients with recurrent abdominal pain when they were compared to normal controls (Hodges, Kline, Barbero, & Woodruff, 1985). Depression is frequently reported in children and adolescents with unexplained physical symptoms (Garber, Zeman, & Walker, 1990; Hodges, Kline, Barbero, & Flanery, 1985; Kashani, Lababidi, & Jones, 1982; Kowal & Pritchard, 1990; Larson, 1991). Disruptive behavioral difficulties and hyperactivity have also been reported in somatizing children, particularly younger children (Faull & Nicol, 1986; Stevenson, Simpson, & Bailey, 1988; Zuckerman, Stevenson, & Bailey, 1987).

Family Assessment

Family assessment is important for a number of reasons. Somatization in children and adolescents has been associated with physical illness or disability in a parent or close family member, raising the issue as to whether a model for the symptom within the family may be important in the genesis of pediatric somatization (Belmaker, 1984; Bergman & Stamm, 1967; Zuckerman et al., 1987). Family members of somatizing children may be more likely to suffer from migraine and other headaches (Apley, 1975; Mikail & von Baeyer, 1990; Robinson et al., 1990). A number of psychiatric disorders may also occur more frequently in the families of somatizing children and adolescents, with parents of such children appearing more likely to suffer from anxiety and/or depression than the parents of normal controls (Garber, Zeman, & Walker, 1990; Hodges, Kline, Barbero, & Flanery, 1985; Hodges, Kline, Barbero, & Woodruff, 1985; Walker & Greene, 1989; Zuckerman et al., 1987). Routh and Ernst (1984) reported an increased likelihood of somatization disorder in the parents of children with recurrent abdominal pain, as well as the suggestion that alcoholism and antisocial behavior occurred more frequently among the members of patients. This highlighted work suggesting that Briquet's Syndrome, roughly equivalent to somatization disorder, in women may be associated with antisocial personality or sociopathy in other family members (Cloninger, Reich, & Guze, 1975). The children of parents with somatization disorder appear to be particularly predisposed to unexplained physical symptoms, as well as to a variety of psychiatric disorders (Livingston, 1993). It is difficult to draw firm conclusions about whether the clustering of somatization within families represents environmental or genetic factors at work, although some studies suggested a role for both (Bohman, Cloninger, von Knorring, & Sigvardsson, 1984; Cloninger, Sigvardsson, von Knorring, & Bohman, 1984). Greater evidence may exist, however, for the role of genetic factors in the determination of personality traits that may predispose to somatization (Shields,1982), with traits such as negative affectivity

(Watson & Pennebaker, 1989) correlating with increased somatic symptom reporting in adults and appearing to be heritable to some degree (Pennebaker & Watson, 1991).

Life Events

Quality assessment should include an evaluation of current life circumstances, including an exploration of the presence of current or past stressors. Though plagued by the methodologic difficulties inherent in life-events research, review of available studies suggests an association between perceived adverse or negative life events and somatization in children and adolescents (Campo & Fritsch, in press). Clinical observation has suggested that somatization may be associated with the loss or the death of a close family member or relative (Aro, 1987; Aro, Hanninen, & Paronen, 1989; Greene, Walker, Hickson, & Thompson, 1985; Hodges, Kline, Barbero, & Flanery, 1984; Livingston, 1993; Maloney, 1980; Scaloubaca, Slade, & Creed, 1988). Maltreatment in childhood has been associated with somatization, with a number of reports associating childhood sexual abuse with later somatization (Klevan & DeJong, 1990; Livingston, Taylor, & Crawford, 1988; Rimza, Berg, & Locke, 1988). Pseudoneurologic symptoms, particularly pseudoseizures, have been associated with sexual abuse (Goodwin, Simms, & Bergman, 1979; Gross, 1979; LaBarbera & Dozier, 1980) In sum, maltreatment in many forms has been associated anecdotally with somatization. A history of maltreatment may be especially important in that there is increasing evidence that the inability to disclose or be expressive about traumatic childhood events may lead to adverse outcomes and physical symptoms (Pennebaker & Susman, 1988).

Psychoeducational Assessment

The school might provide important information regarding the patient's level of function. School personnel, particularly the school nurse, might be especially important in identifying both individual and family factors that may predispose to or maintain somatization. Such patients frequently suffer from school absenteeism and academic difficulties, which might be minimized by the patient and family. Understanding more about the patient's educational status and pursuing psychoeducational assessment or neuropsychological assessment when appropriate might be quite important in identifying potential skill deficits, which might drive a given patient's desire to avoid school and, thus, serve to encourage and maintain somatization (Silver, 1982).

Diagnostic Clues

A number of authors have emphasized that the diagnosis of a somatoform disorder should not simply be a diagnosis of exclusion and that a positive determination that physical symptoms are representative of somatization should be made (Dubowitz & Hersov, 1976; Friedman, 1973; Goodyer & Taylor, 1985; Maisami & Freeman, 1987). A number of clues that a particular physical symptom might be representative of somatization are offered in the literature, including the presence of a previous history of somatization, contiguity with psychosocial stressors, the presence of a model for unexplained physical symptoms within the patient's personal environment, and the history or presence of a diagnosable psychiatric disorder in the patient (Goodyer & Taylor, 1985). Other such clues include the sense that a symptom allows indirect or symbolic interpersonal communication; the impression that a symptom might result in some degree of intrapsychic or interpersonal gain; the response of the symptom to suggestion, placebo or psychological treatment; fluctuation of the symptom in relation to sleep or social factors; and the impression that the symptom violates known anatomical or physiological patterns (Friedman, 1973; Siegel & Barthel, 1986). Traditionally, *la belle indifference*, essentially a perceived sense of indifference of the patient to the physical symptom, has been described in patients with conversion disorder (Leslie, 1988; Maisami & Freeman, 1987; Volkmar, Poll, & Lewis, 1984). Unfortunately, making such a determination is quite subjective, and many authors have questioned the value of this sign (Dubowitz & Hersov, 1976; Goodyer, 1981; Siegel & Barthel, 1986; Spierings et al., 1990). Indeed, it is important to remember that, although a constellation of a number of the preceding findings might provide some greater confidence in making a positive determination that a particular patient suffers from a somatoform disorder (Friedman, 1973), patients suffering from actual physical disease can exhibit many or all of the clues previously mentioned (see Campo & Fritsch, in press).

Behavioral Assessment

There is no substitute for a careful behavioral assessment of the symptom or symptoms presented by the patient. The frequency, duration, and intensity of the symptom(s) need to be determined. Establishing a baseline for the symptom or symptom complex requires that a working definition of the target symptom be agreed upon by clinician, patient, and family. The process of behavioral assessment involves determining the form and content of the symptom or behavior; its temporal characteristics; the way it functionally impairs the patient and the extent of that impairment; its social or interpersonal context and significance; and the specific situational, cognitive, affectual, or physiological events that precede, co-occur with, or follow it (O'Brien & Haynes, 1993). The antecedents of pediatric somatization should be carefully assessed, and there should be careful examination of what the symptom allows the patient or family to avoid, as well as a search for potential rewards that may drive the symptom or maintain it. This can be accomplished by careful interview, by direct observation, by self-monitoring techniques, or by self-report inventories. However, there is currently relative lack of such instruments in the evaluation of pediatric somatization.

ACTUAL ASSESSMENT

Early Obstacles to Assessment

Practical considerations often result in the clinician facing the patient and family in situations for which the ideal assessment might not be realized. Many patients with medically unexplained physical symptoms have felt profoundly misunderstood by physicians and previous caretakers because of suggestions that nothing was wrong. Mental health professionals may have similarly missed the mark, reframing the problem as purely psychological. Patients and their families might resent any minimization of the reality of the physical symptoms. Clearly, something is wrong, even if that something is not a physical disease. The tendency of mental health workers to explain the symptom in psychological terms may also produce resentment, as it may be perceived as minimizing the subjective experience of the patient, whose suffering has primarily been experienced in physical terms. Mental health professionals might also be intimidated and frightened by the physical symptoms presented by such patients, and close collaboration with a trusted medical colleague is often difficult on the basis of geography and availability. Indeed, the setting in which a given patient presents may influence the way in which he or she describes the suffering; that is, a patient might emphasize the physical in the medical setting and the psychological in the mental health setting (Bridges & Goldberg, 1985).

Problems Associated with Medical Assessment

The presence of a physical disease does not necessarily eliminate the possibility that somatization may be present (Lipowski, 1988). In addition to undiagnosed physical disease being of concern, the presence of physical disease in a given patient may actually be a risk factor for the development of somatization, particularly for diseases that affect the central nervous system (Kellner, 1986). Pseudoseizures can be especially common in patients with confirmed epilepsy (Fenton, 1986; Williams, Spiegel, & Mostofsky, 1978). Somatization can also develop in patients with less chronic or less persistent illnesses; Creak (1938) described the "hysterical prolongation of a symptom," the development of somatization following an acute illness or accident in childhood and adolescence. Numerous reports documenting such an interesting association or prolongation of an acute physical illness have appeared subsequently (Carek & Santos, 1984; Dubowitz & Hersov, 1976; Leslie, 1988; Spierings et al., 1990). One explanation of such occurrences emphasizes an early exposure to the benefits associated with the sick role in the original illness, with such gains serving to maintain the physical symptoms beyond the time when they might be accounted for by actual physical pathology (Wooley, Blackwell, & Winget, 1978). It is also of interest to note that somatization itself may, on rare occasions, result in actual physical pathology, as in the case of physical contractures developing in some severe patients with conversion disorder (Gold, 1965).

It should be remembered that there may be no absolute end to the process of ruling out physical disease in the somatizing pediatric patient. Very often, the most important risk is that of overzealous or inappropriate use of medical investigations, treatments, or procedures, rather than a missed physical diagnosis. Inappropriate investigations might result in physical harm coming to the patient. In addition, they might strengthen the convictions of a particular patient or family that physical disease is indeed the likely cause of the symptoms under investigation and, thus, encourage continued somatization (Goodyear & Taylor, 1985; Grattan-Smith, Fairley, & Procopis, 1988). Somatization can also develop or be prolonged in the face of uncertainty of diagnosis (Walker & Greene, 1991) or inadequate medical advice (Bergman & Stamm, 1967).

It is often difficult to obtain all of the previous medical and mental health treatment records, and patients and families are often reluctant to allow contact with schools and other objective sources of information. They may refuse to sign releases of information as a consequence of anger with previous professionals or as a concern about how such information might influence the examiner. Records hand-carried by the patient or the parents should be viewed with some degree of suspicion. The hand-carried records might be chosen selectively or, worse, might contain alterations in the unusual circumstance of factitious disorder or factitious disorder by proxy.

Problems Associated with Psychiatric and Behavioral Assessments

Somatizing patients and their families are often extremely negative about psychiatric assessment, as well as quite concerned about stigma. Some clinicians have conceptualized *blame avoidance* as one of the maintaining factors in somatization (Goldberg & Bridges, 1988). Often, somatizing patients and their families are open to any exploration of physical disease, no matter how serious, while being unwilling to consider psychiatric or psychological assessments. In some instances, the family system's perspective appears to be especially relevant, with some families being more threatened by work that may explore family relationships than by potentially dangerous medical evaluations and procedures. Such conflicts are highlighted in the example of a child with conversion disorder who is being sexually maltreated within the home.

The conceptualization of somatization as a psychological defense, with such patients experiencing and expressing their distress physically, appears applicable in individual patients; they might appear quite resistant to psychological explanations of their symptoms and even to the evaluation itself because their somatization may serve to defend them against an awareness of unpleasant affect (Goldberg & Bridges, 1988; Simon, 1991). Some patients have been described as suffering from *alexithymia*, or "no words for feelings," which may make it difficult to communicate their experience of affect in relation to the physical symptom itself or in general. This typically has been conceptualized by many as a psychological defense, but it can also be viewed as reflecting a neuropsychological deficit of sorts (Nemiah, 1977). The validity of this construct remains unclear (Mullins & Olson, 1990).

In sum, resistance to adequate psychiatric assessment is frequently noted in somatizing patients and their families. Though the patient is presented for evaluation and treatment, an apparently irrational focus on the physical symptom may prevail in the clinical setting, with patients and family members actually complicating and sometimes obstructing appropriate assessment.

Careful behavioral assessment of such patients and their families is often difficult. The examiner is generally limited to historical information. Unless the patient is being seen in an inpatient setting, direct observation of the symptom, its antecedents, and its potential rewards might not be possible. Observations in the clinical setting might be less valid than those obtained naturalistically, and naturalistic observation might not be practical. Furthermore, a unidirectional model of causality for a given symptom might be overly simplistic, as causal relationships can be influenced by constitutional characteristics of the individual patient; by cognitive, affectual, or physiologic responses; by timing; and by bidirectional or reciprocal effects (O'Brien & Haynes, 1993).

Establishing a categorical psychiatric diagnosis in somatizing patients can also be quite complicated. It is often difficult to determine whether a given unexplained physical symptom is best understood as being directly caused by physical disease or whether it is best conceptualized as secondary to a psychiatric disorder, with the distinction very often appearing to be influenced by the preference of individual clinicians and their biases. It is far from simple to delineate if a symptom has "no known pathophysiologic mechanism" as is required for the diagnosis of somatoform disorder in DSM-III-R. It may be that routine medical investigation does not reveal tissue pathology or pathophysiologic changes, but more sophisticated research methodologies might do so, making classification a difficult matter (Kellner, 1991). It is also unclear in many instances how to proceed when confronted with symptoms that appear to be related to emotional arousal or excessive autonomic nervous system activity or when confronted by the physiologic consequences of behaviors such as hyperventilation (Murphy, 1990). ICD-10 includes a diagnosis termed *psychogenic autonomic dysfunction*, which addresses physical symptoms attributable to overactivity of the autonomic nervous system. Though one of the distinguishing characteristics between somatoform disorder and factitious disorder or malingering is that the symptoms do not appear to be intentionally produced in somatoform disorder, determining a patient's or family member's intent and motivation is often a matter of speculation (Campo & Fritsch, in press).

PROTOTYPIC TREATMENT

In ideal circumstances, the assessment process lays the groundwork for successful treatment. The reality of the patient's and the family's suffering should be acknowledged, and clinicians should be careful to avoid challenging the subjective reality of the physical symptom. An emphasis upon true collaboration among the patient, the family, and the clinician during the assessment process serves as the foundation for a working or therapeutic alliance with the patient and family when treatment is addressed. Formal treatment should not begin until the diagnostic and clinical impressions of the examiner or the treatment team are discussed clearly and frankly with both the patient and the family. As far as is possible, clinicians should avoid ambiguity in the presentation of the clinical impression, and they should not appear vague or embarrassed in discussing the presence of somatization. Such a demeanor establishes a counterproductive meta-communication to patient and family that somatization is indeed worthy of stigma. Instead, the patient's predicament should be treated like any other illness, and the diagnosis stated in a positive manner. Prior clinicians have frequently handled patients and their families with exaggerated and unnecessary gentleness for fear of their rejecting such diagnosis and their anger leading them to sever the treatment relationship. Physicians may sometimes be tempted to treat such patients with placebo, or by playing along with the patient's sense that the problem is caused by physical disease. Unfortunately, both of these approaches, though occasionally successful in an individual patient, hold out a real risk of reinforcing the conviction of patient and family that a real physical disease is present and, thus, might enhance and maintain somatization. In addition, such an approach might encourage the families of somatizing children and adolescents to view them as sickly or more vulnerable to physical disease than their peers. Far superior is a clearly delineated diagnosis and impression, communicating the sense that such a diagnosis may be good news, given the other differential diagnostic possibilities.

Rehabilitation

A promise of cure should be avoided (Kellner, 1991), with the focus instead being placed on treatment being a joint or collaborative venture and on helping the patient and family establish realistic goals for treatment. Many workers with children and adolescents have emphasized a rehabilitative approach, encouraging the patient to return to usual activities and discouraging behaviors associated with the sick role (Dubowitz & Hersov, 1976; Leslie, 1988; Maisami & Freeman, 1987; Schulman, 1988). Such an approach shifts the responsibility for a return to previous function to the patient, thus undermining the notion that the patient can only be expected to function when all of the symptoms have been removed by the treating clinician. Somatizing patients and their families become more difficult to treat when the clinician accepts that a return to adequate function can only take place if the condition is cured. A rehabilitative approach acknowledges the power of the symptom and makes overcoming it something of which the patient can be proud and pleased. Many patients with pseudoneurologic symptoms benefit from the use of physiotherapy, allowing a gradual return to function (Dubowitz & Hersov, 1976; Leslie, 1988; Maisami & Freeman, 1987; Thomson & Sills, 1988). Such an approach may allow escape from the symptom "with honor" (Bolton & Cohen, 1986).

Reassurance and Education

Simple reassurance and education of the patient and family regarding the nature of the problem are often effective in and of themselves in adults (Kellner, 1991) and have been advocated by many authors for younger patients as well (Goodyer & Mitchell, 1989; Grattan-Smith et al., 1988; Maisami & Freeman, 1987; Schulman, 1988; Thompson & Sills, 1988). Excessive and repetitive reassurance is often best avoided, however, particularly in patients with obsessive illness worry because excessive reassurance might actually maintain somatization (Warwick & Salkovskis, 1985). It is often useful to begin by treating the symptom presented by the patient rather than by appealing to extremes of psychologization or communicating in some way that physical symptoms are not the real problem.

Traditionally, the treatment of patients with somatization has been conceptualized as a two-step process, with the first step involving symptom removal (Shapiro & Rosenfeld, 1987) by a number of possible methods, including suggestion (Proctor, 1958; Rock, 1971), encouragement (Gold, 1965), or the use of medications such as amobarbital (Laybourne & Churchill, 1972). Actual symptom removal might be far less important than simply helping the patient and family view the physical symptom that is present as being significantly less threatening than previously thought (Kellner, 1986; Kotsopolous & Snow, 1986; Lehmkuhl, Blanz, Lehmkuhl, & Braun-Scharm, 1989; Maisami & Freeman, 1987; Schulman, 1988). The emphasis can then be shifted from the physical to the psychological at a pace that the patient and family can tolerate (Leslie, 1988).

Behavioral Treatment

Behavioral principles are important to consider in virtually every case, and, whether acknowledged overtly or not, behavioral treatment methods appear to be a central aspect of most treatment approaches. A number of approaches have been used, either singly or in conjunction with others. Rewarding healthy behavior is a mainstay of any treatment intervention, although determining the threshold for rewarding the patient may require some trial and error. Positive reinforcement in the form of rewarding healthy behavior has been endorsed by a number of writers in the child and adolescent literature (Delameter, Rosenbloom, Conners, & Hertweck, 1983; Dubowitz & Hersov, 1976; Klonoff & Moore, 1986; Lehmkuhl et al., 1989; Maisami & Freeman, 1987; Mansdorf, 1981; Mizes, 1985; Sank & Biglan, 1974). Extinction or withdrawal of reinforcement of the symptom has also been advocated (Delameter et al., 1983), and this is essentially the approach taken by many clinicians when they advocate the minimization of secondary gain. Negative reinforcement has also been utilized, with an example being the refusal to allow a hospitalized patient to return home until he shows some degree of functional improvement (Leslie, 1988). Punishment has also been used, with Miller and Kratochwill (1979) reporting on a single case design utilizing a time-out procedure in a 10-year-old girl with recurrent abdominal pain that resulted in a reduction in pain complaints over the course of treatment.

A case report by Delameter (1983) highlights the value of the thoughtful analysis of a single case. They describe the use of behavioral treatment in a 10-year-old boy with a pseudoneurologic symptom, presumed paralysis of both legs. The boy regained full mobility and returned to his previous level of function within 2 weeks of treatment and maintained the gains at 6-months follow-up, following a treatment program utilizing positive reinforcement for successive approximations of walking behavior and withdrawal of reinforcement of the physical symptom.

Self-Management Skills

Self-management skills, including training in coping and in relaxation techniques, have been advocated (Linton, 1986; Masek, Russo, & Varni, 1984). In all of the literature on the treatment of somatization in children and adolescents, the only controlled-treatment trial is that of the use of a cognitive behavioral treatment, comprised of differential reinforcement of well behavior, of cognitive coping skills training, and of self-monitoring in school-age children with recurrent abdominal pain (Sanders et al., 1989). Although the sample size was small and it is difficult to know which element of the multimodal treatment program was successful, the treatment group appeared to fare significantly better than controls. The authors emphasized that no negative side effects of the treatment program were noted (Sanders et al., 1989). Other case reports have described the use of hypnosis (Caldwell & Stewart, 1981; Elkins & Carter, 1986; Williams & Singh, 1976) and biofeedback (Klonoff & Moore, 1986; Mizes, 1985).

Psychotherapy

Individual expressive psychotherapy is widely used, and many clinicians believe that helping patients to express and identify affect may be helpful. There are no studies in the child and adolescent literature documenting its efficacy, though a review of the available adult literature supports the use of expressive techniques, including verbal expression and keeping a journal, which are particularly helpful following a traumatic event (Pennebaker & Susman, 1988).

Group psychotherapy would appear to offer several advantages in dealing with somatizing patients, though there are no reports of the use of group psychotherapy in the treatment of somatizing children and adolescents.

In virtually all cases, successful treatment of any child or adolescent generally involves some work with the family, and family therapy per se has been an area of great interest and activity in dealing with somatizing patients (Goodyer, 1981; Liebman, Honig, & Berger, 1976; Mullins & Olson, 1990). A family systems model has been championed by a number of authors, most notably Minuchin, Baker, et al., (1975), who have advocated such an approach in patients with so called psychosomatic conditions, with other authors building on this model in work with patients with more clearly defined somatization (Mullins & Olson, 1990). Such an approach views the physical symptoms experienced by the patient as potentially serving a particular function within the family system (Minuchin, Baker, et al., 1975; Mullins & Olson, 1990). The presence of a particular physical symptom can detour the family from areas of conflict and can actually serve to preserve homeostasis. Specific patterns of family interaction, including enmeshment, parental overprotection, familial rigidity, and poor conflict resolution and/or conflict avoidance (Minuchin, Baker, et al., 1975; Minuchin, Rosman, & Baker, 1978), have been associated with such circumstances. A number of authors have described difficulties in verbal communication within the families of somatizing children and adolescents (Faull & Nicol, 1986; Looff, 1970; Maloney, 1980; Wasserman et al., 1988). At times, the patient's somatization has been viewed as serving a communicative function, that is, being a form of body language or a plea for help (Goodyer & Taylor, 1985; Lask & Fosson, 1989; Maisami & Freeman, 1987). The clinical observations of some workers in the field suggest that some families of somatizing children and adolescents appear to be primarily anxious, fearful, and preoccupied with the possibility of physical disease, whereas other families of such patients may demonstrate a high degree of disorganization and appear quite chaotic (Grattan-Smith et al., 1988). Despite great interest in the use of family therapy in cases of somatization in the pediatric population, research regarding efficacy is lacking.

Medication

The rationale for the use of psychotropic medication in somatizing patients is often based upon the frequent occurrence of anxiety and/or depression in such patients and upon extrapolating from clinical experience with adults. Certainly, comorbid psychiatric disorders should be identified and treated aggressively, and, in some patients, this might involve the use of medication. There is evidence in adults that antidepressant medications reduce somatic symptoms in depressed patients and that anxiolytic medications such as benzodiazepines reduce somatic symptoms in patients with anxiety disorders (Kellner, 1991). There are no adequate studies available regarding the pharmacologic treatment of somatization in children and adolescents. Clinically, there do appear to be patients who respond well to antidepressant medications, with selective serotonin reuptake inhibitors, such as fluoxetine, and other serotonergic agents holding some promise for patients, including those with obsessional illness worry or hypochondriasis. In patients who experience somatic symptoms in association with emotional arousal and anxiety, a brief course of anxioloytic medication, such as a short course of a benzodiazepine, may prove exceedingly helpful in convincing the patient and family that their somatic symptoms are indeed the product of emotional arousal and anxiety, rather than the product of a physical disease. Concerns related to excessive use of such medications and/or the development of dependence vary with the individual patient but are not to be taken lightly. Many patients with unexplained symptoms present on numerous medications. These should be assessed early on, and unnecessary medications weaned and ultimately discontinued.

Communication

Collaboration with the primary care physician cannot be overemphasized. In a study of adults with somatization disorder, it was found that simply sending a consultation letter to primary care physicians outlining ways they might better approach their chronically somatizing patients, such as by scheduling regular office visits and avoiding unnecessary tests and procedures, was quite effective in improving the satisfaction of the treated patients with their own health care, while at the same time reducing health care expenditures (Smith, Monson, & Ray, 1986). In most instances, every attempt should be made to consolidate the medical care of such patients with a single primary physician or team leader. For some persistent somatizers, regularly scheduled office visits to their primary care physician may be helpful so that the patient need not be ill in order to visit the doctor, who in some instances is an important attachment figure to the patient and family. Close communication should take place between mental health professionals involved in the treatment of such patients and primary care medical providers.

Close communication with the school is extremely important, particularly in patients where there are frequent school absences or frank school refusal. It is often helpful to explain the patient's condition to the school, and it is sometimes necessary to communicate that absence from school without the approval of the treatment team and an appropriate medical excuse should be viewed as truancy. Collaboration with the primary care physician should make it clear that medical excuses for missed school on the basis of somatization are not in order, and this can serve as important leverage in helping such patients to return to school and to more normal functioning. A well-composed letter to the school is often of great benefit.

Inpatient Treatment

Many authors have been impressed with the potential benefits of inpatient pediatric or psychiatric treatment of somatization in children and adolescents (Goodyer, 1985; Kotsopoulos & Snow, 1986; Lehmkuhl et al., 1989; Leslie, 1988; Maisami & Freeman, 1987). An inpatient program for the treatment of somatizing adults has been reported (Shorter et al., 1992). Such an approach can be particularly helpful when there is diagnostic confusion, when there is marked functional impairment of the patient, or when previous treatment interventions have failed (Campo & Fritsch, in press). Inpatient treatment allows for 24-hour-a-day observation by skilled personnel, encourages a multidisciplinary approach, and removes the patient from the environmental matrix of the symptoms. Furthermore, inpatient treatment may help demystify the symptoms for the patient and the family, and the staff can model alternative ways of dealing with the patient for family members and other caretakers. Greater control can be effected over contingencies and reinforcement, and it is often reassuring to families when patients are able to function on the inpatient unit far better than they had managed to function prior to hospitalization (Delameter et al., 1983). Indeed, observing an improvement in the function of the patient might help persuade the family that psychosocial treatment interventions are worthy of being pursued and might decrease the anxiety associated with the symptom. Rigorous discharge planning following inpatient hospitalization is essential.

ACTUAL TREATMENT

The Power of the Sick Role

Clinical experience leads most clinicians to discover that a great many somatizing pediatric patients and their families are resistant to the notion of psychological or psychiatric treatment. Physical symptoms may be extremely powerful socially. Once a particular child or adolescent has been viewed as physically sick, the behavior of others, including professionals, can be profoundly influenced. In present society, several assumptions and expectations have been associated with the sick role (Parsons, 1964; Slavney, 1990): The sick person is judged to be powerless to overcome the sickness through an act of will and is not held responsible for the condition. The sick person is exempted from normal duties and obligations after the sick role has been legitimized by another (the physician is regarded as the final arbiter of who is granted the sick role). The sick person views his position as undesirable, with suffering being a requirement for the sick role to be granted.

Finally, the sick person is expected to seek out and cooperate with competent help, with the goal of getting well (the social sanction of the sick role is contingent on efforts made by the patient to leave it). Many of the somatizing patients seen in the clinical setting have been seen by a number of physicians and other workers previously and might have good reason to conclude that their sick role has been legitimized, essentially placing the responsibility for its resolution upon others.

It has been acknowledged that different individuals may respond to particular physical symptoms in a variety of ways, with each person perceiving, evaluating, and acting upon a given physical symptom in an individualized manner. This was conceptualized by Mechanic (1962) in the notion of *illness behavior*. Though this initially was a nonnormative concept, it was extended to that of *abnormal illness behavior* by Pilowsky (1969); he used this terminology to refer to situations in which a physician might not believe that a patient's medical assessment entitles him to a legitimized sick role, but in which the patient or family continue with that expectation despite being told that it is inappropriate by the physician. Engaging such patients and families in treatment with mental health professions is often difficult. It is no easy matter to convince an anxious parent that he should participate and support a behavioral treatment program in which it may appear that the patient is, in effect, held responsible for the physical symptom. Such parents, and even referring physicians, may be concerned that the patient will feel blamed for the physical symptom, a notion counter to the usual thinking once an individual is considered sick. Clinicians can sometimes reassure sick patients and their families by explaining that psychiatric and psychological treatment techniques can be helpful in dealing with physical diseases, such as asthma or diabetes, because physical symptoms and even laboratory findings may fluctuate in response to emotional or behavioral factors (Campo, 1993).

Diagnostic Uncertainty

The previous section addressing treatment assumes that the treating clinician is reasonably confident that somatization is present. Unfortunately, just as the dividing line between psychological health and disorder may not be clear in many instances, the dividing line between physical health and disease may be blurred as well (Kellner, 1991). Clinical circumstances sometimes occur in which significant diagnostic uncertainty exists, but practicality suggests that presumptive psychiatric treatment is indicated, with the hope that a successful treatment response might preclude the need for potentially dangerous and costly medical or surgical evaluations and treatments. Such circumstances present great dilemmas for the treating mental health professional, and frank discussion with the patient and family members in such situations is necessary to insure informed consent. Diagnostic ambiguity and the anxieties of the treating professionals lie at the heart of many treatment failures, with treatment being characterized by a progression of stops and starts, inter-rupted repeatedly by a resurgence of patient, family, or clinician anxiety. This may be especially difficult when the treating mental health professional is more concerned about possible physical disease than the referring or collaborating physician, highlighting once again the importance of interdisciplinary communication.

Need for Additional Research

The discussion on prototypic treatment also assumes the use of one treatment modality or another, although in reality, most treatment is multimodal and often begins during the assessment process. The available literature provides little in the way of systematically derived guidance as to which treatment approaches are most successful in which patients, not to mention which combination of treatment approaches might be most effective (Campo & Fritsch, in press).

Little is known about the course and prognosis of pediatric somatization because of the lack of inadequate long-term studies and the methodologies employed in the available studies. The available studies have focused primarily on the presenting physical symptom in determining outcome. One-quarter to one-half of children with recurrent abdominal pain will suffer from gastrointestinal symptoms in adulthood, according to available studies (Apley & Hale, 1973; Christensen & Mortenson, 1975; Liebman, 1978; Stickler & Murphy, 1979; Stone & Barbero, 1970). Studies of patients diagnosed with conversion disorder or pseudoneurologic symptoms suggest complete recovery in relation to the original symptom in approximately 75% of patients (see Campo & Fritsh, in press). If the focus is shifted away from the presenting symptom to the functional and psychia-tric status of the patient's being evaluated at follow-up, the outcome of pediatric somatization may be far less than positive. Such patients may be more likely to suffer from academic difficulties and depressive symptoms later in life (Lewis & Lewis, 1989). Robins and O'Neal (1953) reported that approximately 70% of patients who suffered from prominent unexplained physical symptoms early in life later exhibited significant functional disability on follow-up and that over 50% met criteria for a psychiatric diagnosis. A greater duration of somatic symptoms (Ernst, Routh, & Harper, 1984; Robins & O'Neal, 1953), the presence of multiple symptoms (Grattan-Smith et al., 1988; Robins & O'Neal, 1953), and the presence of pseudoneurologic symptoms, such as pseudoseizures (Goodyer & Mitchell, 1989; Robins & O'Neal, 1953), all may be predictive of functional disability later in life, though definitive studies are yet to be accomplished (Campo & Fritsch, in press). The role of treatment in influencing outcome remains speculative.

SUMMARY

Medically unexplained physical complaints are common in childhood and adolescence, but somatization disorder per se appears to be relatively rare. This rarity reflects the number of symptoms required to meet current diagnostic criteria, as well as the use of symptoms that may not be developmentally appropriate in younger patients, particularly those reflecting reproductive or sexual function. Nevertheless, somatization appears to be particularly common in the medical setting, with primary care physicians evaluating such patients on a regular basis. Interestingly, mental health professionals may not be as familiar with the somatizing pediatric patients, often not becoming involved until medical caretakers have been exasperated in their attempts at assessment or treatment. Somatization is an area that highlights the importance of collaboration between primary care physicians and mental health professionals. There is a need for mental health professionals to take an active role in the education of colleagues in primary care, helping to provide information regarding effective ways of incorporating psychiatric issues into the differential diagnosis early in the assessment process. The importance of being alert to the presence of undiagnosed psychiatric disorder and possible maltreatment in such patients cannot be overemphasized, and primary care physicians need to incorporate this into their work. Mental health professionals have much to offer in the development and coordination of effective treatment strategies. At present, they are limited by a relative lack of systematically obtained data regarding somatization in children and adolescents, though accumulated clinical experience suggests that such patients can and do respond to treatment interventions and that such interventions have the potential of relieving suffering, improving functional status, and perhaps even decreasing health care utilization, thus decreasing cost and the risk of unnecessary medical evaluations and treatments.

REFERENCES

Achenbach, T. M., Conners, C. K., Quay, H. C., Verhulst, F. C., & Howell, C. T. (1989). Replication of empirically derived syndromes as a basis for taxonomy of child/adolescent psychopathology. *Journal of Abnormal Child Psychology, 17*, 299–323.

American Psychiatric Association. (1987). *Diagnostic and statistical manual of mental disorders* (3rd ed., rev.) (DSM-III-R). Washington, DC: Author.

American Psychiatric Association. (1993). *DSM-IV draft criteria*. Washington, DC: Author.

Apley, J. (1958). A common denominator in the recurrent pains of childhood. *Proceedings of the Royal Society of Medicine, 51*, 1023–1024.

Apley, J. (1975). *The child with abdominal pain*. Oxford: Blackwell.

Apley, J., & Hale, B. (1973). Children with recurrent abdominal pain: How do they grow up? *British Medical Journal, 3*, 7–9.

Aro, H. (1987). Life stress and psychosomatic symptoms among 14 to 16-year-old Finnish adolescents. *Psychological Medicine, 17*, 191–201.

Aro, H., Paronen, O., & Aro, S. (1987). Psychosomatic symptoms among 14–16 year old Finnish adolescents. *Social Psychiatry, 22*, 171–176.

Aro, H., Hanninen, V., & Paronen, O. (1989). Social support, life events and psychosomatic symptoms among 14–16 year old adolescents. *Social Science and Medicine, 29*, 1051–1056.

Barsky, A. J. (1992). Amplification, somatization, and the somatoform disorders. *Psychosomatics, 13*, 28–33.

Barsky, A. J., Goodson, J. D., Lane, R. S., & Cleary, P. D. (1988). The amplification of somatic symptoms. *Psychosomatic Medicine, 50*, 510–519.

Bass, C. M., & Murphy, M. R. (1990). Somatization disorder: Critique of the concept and suggestions for future research. In C. M. Bass (Ed.), *Somatization: Physical symptoms and psychological illness* (pp. 301–332). New York: Blackwell Scientific Publications.

Beidel, D., Christ, M. A. G., & Long, P. J. (1991). Somatic complaints in anxious children. *Journal of Abnormal Child Psychology, 19*, 659–670.

Belmaker, E. (1984). Nonspecific somatic symptoms in early adolescent girls. *Journal of Adolescent Health Care, 5*, 30–33.

Belmaker, E., Espinoza, R., & Pogrund, R. (1985). Use of medical services by adolescents with nonspecific somatic symptoms. *International Journal of Adolescent Medicine and Health, 1*, 150–156.

Bergman, A. B., & Stamm, S. J. (1967). The morbidity of cardiac non-disease in school children. *New England Journal of Medicine, 276*, 1008–1013.

Bohman, M., Cloninger, C. R., von Knorring, A. L., & Sigvardsson, S. (1984). An adoption study of somatoform disorders: III. Cross-fostering analysis and genetic relationship to alcoholism and criminality. *Archives of General Psychiatry, 41*, 872–878.

Bolton, J., & Cohen, P. (1986). 'Escape with honour': The need for face-saving. *Bulletin of Anna Freud Centre, 9*, 19–33.

Bridges, K. W., & Goldberg, D. P. (1985). Somatic presentation of DSM-III psychiatric disorders in primary care. *Journal of Psychosomatic Research, 29*, 563–569.

Caldwell, T. A., & Stewart, R. S. (1981). Hysterical seizures and hypnotherapy. *American Journal of Clinical Hypnosis, 23*, 294–298.

Campo, J. V. (1993). Medical issues in the care of child and adolescent inpatients. In A. S. Bellack & M. Hersen (Eds.), *Handbook of behavior therapy in the psychiatric setting* (pp. 373–405). New York: Plenum Press.

Campo, J. V., & Fritsch, S. L. (in press). Somatization in children and adolescents. *Journal of the American Academy of Child and Adolescent Psychiatry.*

Caplan, H. L. (1970). Hysterical 'conversion' symptoms in childhood. Unpublished master's thesis. University of London: London, England.

Carek, D. J., & Santos, A. B. (1984). Atypical somatoform disorder following infection in children— A depressive equivalent? *Journal of Clinical Psychiatry, 45*, 108–111.

Carlson, G., & Kashani, J. H. (1988). Phenomenology of major depressive disorder from childhood through adulthood: An analysis of 3 studies. *American Journal of Psychiatry, 145*, 1222–1225.

Christensen, M. F., & Mortensen, O. (1975). Long-term prognosis in children with recurrent abdominal pain. *Archives of Diseases of Children, 50*, 110.

Cloninger, C. R., Reich, T., & Guze, S. B. (1975). The multifactorial model of disease transmission: III. Familial relationship between sociopathy and hysteria (Briquet's Syndrome). *British Journal of Psychiatry, 127*, 23–32.

Cloninger, C. R., Sigvardsson, S., von Knorring, A. L., & Bohman, M. (1984). An adoption study of somatoform disorders: II. Identification of two discrete somatoform disorders. *Archives of General Psychiatry, 41*, 863–871.

Creak, M. (1938). Hysteria in childhood. *British Journal of Childhood Diseases, 35*, 85–95.

Delamater, A. M., Rosenbloom, N., Conners, K., & Hertweck, L. (1983). The behavioral treatment of hysterical paralysis in a ten-year-old boy: A case study. *Journal of the American Academy of Child Psychiatry, 1*, 73–79.

Derogatis, L., Lipman, R. S., Rickels, K., Ulenhuth, E. H., & Covi, L. (1974). The Hopkins Symptom Checklist (HSCL): A self-report inventory. *Behavioral Science, 19*, 1–15.

Dubowitz, V., & Hersov, L. (1976). Management of children with non-organic (hysterical) disorders of motor function. *Developmental Medicine and Child Neurology, 18*, 358–368.

Elkins, G. R., & Carter, B. D. (1986). Hypnotherapy in the treatment of childhood psychogenic coughing: A case report. *American Journal of Clinical Hypnosis, 29*, 59–63.

Ernst, A. R., Routh, D. K., & Harper, D. C. (1984). Abdominal pain in children and symptoms of somatization disorder. *Journal of Pediatric Psychology, 9*, 77–86.

Faull, C., & Nicol, A. R. (1986). Abdominal pain in six-year-olds: An epidemiological study in a new town. *Journal of Child Psychology and Psychiatry, 27*, 251–260.

Fenton, G. W. (1986). Epilepsy and hysteria. *British Journal of Psychiatry, 149*, 28–37.

Friedman, S. B. (1973). Conversion symptoms in adolescents. *Pediatric Clinics of North America, 20*, 873–882.

Garber, J., Zeman, J., & Walker, L. S. (1990). Recurrent abdominal pain in children: Psychiatric diagnoses and parental psychopathology. *Journal of the American Academy of Child and Adolescent Psychiatry, 29*, 648–656.

Garber, J., Walker, L. S., & Zeman, J. (1991). Somatization symptoms in a community sample of children and adolescents: Further validation of the Children's Somatization Inventory. *Psychological Assessment, 3*, 588–595.

Garrick, T., Ostrov, E., & Offer, D. (1988). Physical symptoms and self-image in a group of normal adolescents. *Psychosomatics, 29*, 73–80.

Gold, S. (1965). Diagnosis and management of hysterical contracture in children. *British Medical Journal, 1*, 21–23.

Goldberg, D. P., & Bridges, K. (1988). Somatic presentations of psychiatric illness in the primary care setting. *Psychosomatic Research, 32*, 137–144.

Goodwin, J., Simms, M., & Bergman, R. (1979). Hysterical seizures in 4 adolescent girls. *American Journal of Orthopsychiatry, 49*, 698–703.

Goodyer, M. M. (1981). Hysterical conversion reations in childhood. *Journal of Child Psychology and Psychiatry, 22*, 179–188.

Goodyer, I. M. (1985). Epileptic and pseudoepileptic seizures in childhood and adolescence. *Journal of the American Academy of Child Psychiatry, 1*, 3–9.

Goodyer, I. M., & Mitchell, C. (1989). Somatic and emotional disorders in childhood and adolescence. *Journal of Psychosomatic Research, 33*, 681–688.

Goodyer, I. M., & Taylor, D. C. (1985). Hysteria. *Archives of Diseases of Children, 60*, 680–681.

Grattan-Smith, P., Fairley, M., & Procopis, P. (1988). Clinical features of conversion disorder. *Archives of Diseases of Children, 63*, 408–414.

Greene, J. W., Walker, L. S., Hickson, G., & Thompson, J. (1985). Stressful life events and somatic complaints in adolescents. *Pediatrics, 75*, 19–22.

Gross, M. (1979). Incestuous rape: A cause for hysterical seizures in 4 adolescent girls. *American Journal of Orthopsychiatry, 49*, 704–708.

Hodges, K., Kline, J. J., Barbero, G., & Flanery, R. (1984). Life events occurring in families of children with recurrent abdominal pain. *Journal of Psychosomatic Research, 28*, 185–188.

Hodges, K., Kline, J. J., Barbero, G., & Flanery, R. (1985). Depressive symptoms in children with recurrent abdominal pain and in their families. *Journal of Pediatrics, 107*, 622–626.

Hodges, K., Kline, J. J., Barbero, G., & Woodruff, C. (1985). Anxiety in children with recurrent abdominal pain and their parents. *Psychosomatics, 26*, 859–866.

Kashani, J. H., Lababidi, Z., & Jones, R. S. (1982). Depression in children and adolescents with cardiovascular symptomatology: The significance of chest pain. *Journal of the American Academy of Child Psychiatry, 21*, 187–189.

Kellner, R. (1986). *Somatization and hypochondriasis.* New York: Praeger.

Kellner, R. (1991). *Psychosomatic syndromes and somatic symptoms.* Washington, DC: American Psychiatric Press.

Klevan, J. L., & DeJong, A. R. (1990). Urinary tract symptoms and urinary tract infection following sexual abuse. *American Journal of Diseases of Children, 144*, 242–244.

Klonoff, E. A., & Moore, D. J. (1986). "Conversion reactions" in adolescents: A biofeedback-based operant approach. *Journal of Behavior Therapy and Experimental Psychiatry, 17*, 179–184.

Kotsopoulos, S., & Snow, B. (1986). Conversion disorders in children: A study of clinical outcome. *Psychiatric Journal of the University of Ottawa, 11*, 134–139.

Kowal, A., & Pritchard, D. (1990). Psychological characteristics of children who suffer from headache: A research note. *Journal of Child Psychology and Psychiatry, 31*, 637–649.

Kriechman, A. M. (1987). Siblings with somatoform disorders in childhood and adolescence. *Journal of the American Academy of Child and Adolescent Psychiatry, 26*, 226–231.

LaBarbera, J. D., & Dozier, J. E. (1980). Hysterical seizures: The role of sexual exploitation. *Psychosomatics, 21*, 897–903.

Larson, B. S. (1991). Somatic complaints and their relationship to depressive symptoms in Swedish adolescents. *Journal of Childhood Psychology and Psychiatry, 32*, 821–832.

Lask, B., & Fosson, A. (1989). *Childhood illness: The psychosomatic approach.* New York: Wiley.

Last, C. G. (1991). Somatic complaints in anxiety disordered children. *Journal of Anxiety Disorders, 5*, 125–138.

Laybourne, P. C., & Churchill, S. W. (1972). Symptom discouragement in treating hysterical reactions of childhood. *International Journal of Child Psychotherapy, 1,* 111–123.

Lehmkuhl, G., Blanz, B., Lehmkuhl, U., & Braun-Scharm, H. (1989). Conversion disorder: Symptomatology and course in childhood and adolescence. *European Archives of Psychiatry and Neurological Sciences, 238,* 155–160.

Leslie, S. A. (1988). Diagnosis and treatment of hysterical conversion reactions. *Archives of Diseases of Children, 63,* 506–511.

Lewis, C. E., & Lewis, M. A. (1989). Educational outcomes and illness behaviors in participants in a child-initiated care system: A 12-year follow-up study. *Pediatrics, 84,* 845–850.

Liebman, W. H. (1978). Recurrent abdominal pain in children: A retrospective survey of 119 patients. *Clinical Pediatrics, 17,* 149–153.

Liebman, R., Honig, P., & Berger, H. (1976). An integrated treatment program for psychogenic pain. *Family Process, 15,* 397–405.

Linton, S. J. (1986). A case study of the behavioural treatment of chronic stomach pain in a child. *Behaviour Change, 3,* 70–73.

Lipowski, Z. J. (1988). Somatization: The concept and its clinical application. *American Journal of Psychiatry, 145,* 1358–1368.

Livingston, R. (1993). Children of people with somatization disorder. *Journal of the American Academy of Child and Adolescent Psychiatry, 32,* 536–544.

Livingston, R., & Martin-Cannici, C. M. (1985). Multiple somatic complaints and possible somatization disorder in prepubertal children. *Journal of the American Academy of Child Psychiatry, 24,* 603–607.

Livingston, R., Taylor, J. L., & Crawford, S. L. (1988). A study of somatic complaints and psychiatric diagnosis in children. *Journal of the American Academy of Child and Adolescent Psychiatry, 27,* 185–187.

Looff, D. H. (1970). Psychophysiologic and conversion reactions in children. *Journal of the American Academy of Child Psychiatry, 9,* 318–331.

Mai, F. M., & Merskey, H. (1980). Briquet's treatise on hysteria. *Archives of General Psychiatry, 37,* 1401–1405.

Maisami, M., & Freeman, J. M. (1987). Conversion reactions in children as body language: A combined child psychiatry/neurology team approach to the management of functional neurologic disorders in children. *Pediatrics, 80,* 46–52.

Maloney, M. J. (1980). Diagnosing hysterical conversion reactions in children. *Journal of Pediatrics, 97,* 1016–1020.

Mansdorf, I. J. (1981). Eliminating somatic complaints in separation anxiety through contingency management. *Journal of Behavior Therapy and Experimental Psychiatry, 12,* 73–75.

Masek, B., Russo, D. C., & Varni, J. W. (1984). Behavioral approaches to the management of chronic pain in children. *Pediatric Clinics of North America, 31,* 1113–1131.

McCauley, E., Carlson, G. A., & Calderon, R. (1991). The role of somatic complaints in the diagnosis of depression in children and adolescents. *Journal of the American Academy of Child and Adolescent Psychiatry, 30,* 631–635.

Mechanic, D. (1962). The concept of illness behavior. *Journal of Chronic Diseases, 15,* 189–194.

Mikail, S. F., & von Baeyer, C. L. (1990). Pain, somatic focus, and emotional adjustment in children of chronic headache sufferers and controls. *Social Sciences and Medicine, 31,* 51–59.

Miller, A. J., & Kratochwill, R. T. (1979). Reduction of frequent stomachache complaints by time out. *Behaviour Therapy, 10,* 211–218.

Minuchin, S., Baker, L., Rosman, B. L., Liebman, R., Milman, L., & Todd, T. C. (1975). A conceptual model of psychosomatic illness in children. *Archives of General Psychiatry, 32,* 1031–1038.

Minuchin, S., Rosman, B. L., & Baker, L. (1978). *Psychosomatic families: Anorexia nervosa in context.* Cambridge, MA: Harvard University Press.

Mizes, J. S. (1985). The use of contingent reinforcement in the treatment of a conversion disorder: A multiple baseline study. *Journal of Behavior Therapy and Experimental Psychiatry, 16,* 341–345.

Mullins, L. L., & Olson, R. A. (1990). Familial factors in the etiology, maintenance, and treatment of somatoform disorders in children. *Family Systems and Medicine, 8,* 159–175.

Murphy, M. R. (1990). Classification of the somatoform disorders. In M. Bass (Ed.), *Somatization: Physical symptoms and psychological illness* (pp. 10–39). New York: Blackwell Scientific Publications.

Nemiah, J. C. (1977). Alexithymia: Theoretical considerations. *Psychotherapy and Psychosomatics, 28,* 199–206.

O'Brien, W. H., & Haynes, S. N. (1993). Behavioral assessment in the psychiatric setting. In A. S. Bellack & M. Hersen (Eds.), *Handbook of behavior therapy in the psychiatric setting* (pp. 39–71). New York: Plenum Press.

Offord, D. R., Boyle, M. H., Szatmari, P., Rae-Grant, N. I., Links, P. S., Cadman, D. T., Byles, J. A., Crawford, J. W., Blum, H. M., Byrne, C., Thomas, H., & Woodward, C. A. (1987). Ontario child health study: II. Six-month prevalence of disorder and rates of service utilization. *Archives of General Psychiatry, 44,* 832–836.

Oster, J. (1972). Recurrent abdominal pain, headache and limb pains in children and adolescents. *Pediatrics, 50,* 429–436.

Parsons, T. (1964). *Social structure and personality.* New York: Free Press.

Pennebaker, J. W., & Susman, J. R. (1988). Disclosure of traumas and psychosomatic processes. *Social Sciences and Medicine, 26,* 327–332.

Pennebaker, J. W., & Watson, D. (1991). The psychology of physical symptoms. In L. J. Kirmayer & J. M. Robbins (Eds.), *Current concepts of somatization: Research and clinical perspectives,* Washington, DC: American Psychiatric Press.

Pilowsky, I. (1969). Abnormal illness behaviour. *British Journal of Medicine and Psychiatry, 42,* 347–351.

Pilowsky, I. Bassett, D. L., Begg, M. W., & Thomas, P. G. (1982). Childhood hospitalization and chronic intractable pain in adults: A controlled retrospective study. *International Psychiatry in Medicine, 12,* 75–84.

Proctor, J. T. (1958). Hysteria in childhood. *American Journal of Orthopsychiatry, 28,* 394–407.

Rimsza, M. E. Berg, R. A., & Locke, C. (1988). Sexual abuse: Somatic and emotional reactions. *Child Abuse and Neglect, 12,* 201–208.

Rivinus, T. M., Jamison, D. L., & Graham, P. J. (1975). Childhood organic neurological disease presenting as psychiatric disorder. *Archives of Diseases of Children, 40,* 115–119.

Robins, E., & O'Neal, P. (1953). Clinical features of hysteria in children—with a note on prognosis: A two to seventeen year follow-up study of 41 patients. *Nervous Child, 10,* 246–271.

Robinson, J. O., Alverez, J. H., & Dodge, J. A. (1990). Life events and family history in children with recurrent abdominal pain. *Journal of Psychosomatic Research, 34,* 171–181.

Rock, N. (1971). Conversion reactions in childhood: A clinical study on childhood neuroses. *Journal of the American Academy of Child Psychiatry, 10,* 65–93.

Routh, D. K., & Ernst, A. R. (1984). Somatization disorder in relatives of children and adolescents with functional abdominal pain. *Journal of Pediatric Psychology, 9,* 427–437.

Rutter, M., Tizard, J., & Whitmore, K. (1970). *Education, health and behavior.* London: Longman.

Ryan, N. D., Puig-Antich, J., Ambrosini, P., Nelson, B., & Krawiec, V. (1987). The clinical picture of major depression in children and adolescents. *Archives of General Psychiatry, 44,* 854–861.

Sanders, M. R., Rebgetz, M., Morrison, M., Bor, W., Gordon, A., Dadds, M., & Shepherd, R. (1989). Cognitive-behavioral treatment of recurrent nonspecific abdominal pain in children: An analysis of generalization, maintenance, and side effects. *Journal of Consulting and Clinical Psychology, 57*, 294–300.

Sank, L. I., & Biglan, A. (1974). Operant treatment of a case of recurrent abdominal pain in a 10-year-old boy. *Behaviour Therapy, 5*, 677–681.

Scaloubaca, D., Slade, P., & Creed, F. (1988). Life events and somatization among students. *Journal of Psychosomatic Research, 32*, 221–229.

Schulman, J. L. (1988). Use of a coping approach in the management of children with conversion reactions. *Journal of the American Academy of Child and Adolescent Psychiatry*, 785–788.

Shapiro, E. G., & Rosenfeld, A. A. (1987). *The somatizing child.* New York: Springer-Verlag.

Shields, J. (1982). Genetical studies of hysterical disorders. In A. Roy (Ed.), *Hysteria* (pp. 41–56). New York: Wiley.

Shorter, E., Abbey, S. E., Gillies, L. A., Singh, M., & Lipowski, Z. J. (1992). Inpatient treatment of persistent somatization. *Psychosomatics, 33*, 295–301.

Siegel, M., & Barthel, R. P. (1986). Conversion disorders on a child psychiatry consultation service. *Psychosomatics, 27*, 201–204.

Silver, L. B. (1982). Conversion disorder with pseudoseizures in adolescence: A stress reaction to unrecognized and untreated learning disabilities. *Journal of the American Academy of Child Psychiatry, 5*, 508–512.

Simon, G. E. (1991). Somatization and psychiatric disorder. In L. J. Kirmayer & J. M. Robbins (Eds.), *Current concepts of somatization: Research and clinical perspectives* (pp. 37–62). Washington, DC: American Psychiatric Press.

Slavney, P. R. (1990). *Perspectives on "hysteria."* Baltimore, MD: The Johns Hopkins University Press.

Smith, G. R., Monson, R. A., & Ray, D. C. (1986). Psychiatric consultation in somatization disorder. *New England Journal of Medicine, 314*, 1407–1413.

Spierings, C., Poels, P. J. E., Sijben, N., Gabreels, F. J. M., & Renier, W. O. (1990). Conversion disorders in childhood: A retrospective follow-up study of 84 patients. *Developmental Medicine and Child Neurology, 32*, 865–871.

Starfield, B., Katz, H., Gabriel, A., Livingston, G., Benson, P., Hankin, J., Horn, S., & Steinwachs, D. (1984). Morbidity in childhood—A longitudinal view. *New England Journal of Medicine, 310*, 824–829.

Stefansson, J. G., Messina, J. S., & Meyerowitz, S. (1976). Hysterical neurosis, conversion type: Clinical and epidemiological considerations. *Acta Psychiatric Scandinavic, 53*, 119–138.

Stevenson, J., Simpson, J., & Bailey, V. (1988). Research note: Recurrent headaches and stomachaches in preschool children. *Journal Child Psychology and Psychiatry, 29*, 897–900.

Stickler, G. B., & Murphy, D. B. (1979). Recurrent abdominal pain. *American Journal of Diseases of Children, 133*, 486–489.

Stone, R., & Barbero, G. (1970). Recurrent abdominal pain in childhood. *Pediatrics, 45*, 732–738.

Thomson, A. P. J., & Sills, J. A. (1988). Diagnosis of functional illness presenting with gait disorder. *Archives of Diseases of Children, 63*, 148–153.

Turgay, A. (1980). Conversion reactions in children. *Psychiatric Journal of the University of Ottawa, 5*, 287–294.

Volkmar, R. R., Poll, J., & Lewis, M. (1984). Conversion reactions in children and adolescents. *Journal of the American Academy of Child and Adolescent Psychiatry, 23*, 242–430.

Walker, L. S., Garber, J., & Greene, J. W. (1991). Somatization symptoms in pediatric abdominal pain patients: Relation to chronicity of abdominal pain and parent somatization. *Journal of Abnormal Child Psychology, 19*, 379–394.

Walker, L. S., & Greene, J. W. (1989). Children with recurrent abdominal pain and their parents: More somatic complaints, anxiety, and depression than other patient families? *Journal of Pediatric Psychology, 14*, 231–243.

Walker, L. S., & Greene, J. W. (1991). Negative life events and symptom resolution in pediatric abdominal pain patients. *Journal of Pediatric Psychology, 16*, 341–360.

Warwick, H. M., & Salkovskis, P. M. (1985). Reassurance. *British Medical Journal, 290*, 1028.

Wasserman, A. L., Whitington, P. F., & Rivera, F. P. (1988). Psychogenic basis for abdominal pain in children and adolescents. *Journal of the American Academy of Child and Adolescent Psychiatry, 27*, 179–184.

Watson, D., & Pennebaker, J. W. (1989). Health complaints, stress, and distress: Exploring the central role of negative affectivity. *Psychology Review, 96*, 234–254.

Williams, D. T., & Singh, M. (1976). Hypnosis as a facilitating therapeutic adjunct in child psychiatry. *Journal of the American Academy of Child Psychiatry, 15*, 326–342.

Williams, D. T., Spiegel, H., & Mostofsky, D. I. (1978). Neurogenic and hysterical seizures in children and adolescents: Differential diagnostic and therapeutic considerations. *American Journal of Psychiatry, 135*, 82–86.

Wooley, S. C., Blackwell, B., & Winget, C. (1978). A learning theory model of chronic illness behavior: Theory, treatment, and research. *Psychosomatic Medicine, 40*, 379–401.

World Health Organization. (1988). *International classification of diseases* (10th revision). Geneva, Switzerland: Author.

Zuckerman, B., Stevenson, J., & Bailey, V. (1987). Stomachaches and headaches in a community sample of preschool children. *Pediatrics, 79*, 677–682.

CHAPTER 22

Pediatric Pain

KENNETH J. TARNOWSKI AND RONALD T. BROWN

DESCRIPTION OF THE PROBLEM

Since 1970, there has been a marked growth in the field of pain theory and the assessment and treatment of pain. Currently, there exists a considerable data base on the application of behavioral assessment and treatment strategies to the multiple problems of the adult pain patient (Holzman & Turk, 1986). Unfortunately, a parallel data base for children has been slow to develop (Tarnowski & Kaufman, 1988). Between 1970 and 1975, for example, over 1,000 articles on pain were identified, of which less than 3% referred to children (Eland & Anderson, 1977). Of the pediatric articles, 32 were focused on physical pathology. Since 1975, increased attention has been devoted to the psychological study of pediatric pain. This expanded data base is reflected, in part, in the recent publication of two comprehensive texts on the topic (Bush & Harkins, 1991; McGrath, 1990).

Defining Pain

Although everyone has experienced pain and can describe pain experiences in detail, it has been difficult to arrive at an acceptable definition of the term. Initially conceptualized in terms of an emotion, with the development of sensory physiology, pain was redefined in terms of sensory input. Controversy still remains concerning how to best conceptualize the contribution of emotional, cognitive, and sensory stimulation factors to the experience of pain. It has been established that a unidimensional focus (e.g., sensory input) is of little utility in defining pain. Current conceptualizations of pain acknowledge that it is a complex multidimensional psychophysiological phenomenon that involves sensory, affective, emotional, neurochemical, and motivational factors that function synergistically to produce varying degrees of distress (Beecher, 1959; Melzack 1973; Varni, 1981). Thus, pain involves much more than simple tissue damage. Psychological variables including suggestion, attention, anxiety, learning history, culture, attributed meaning of pain, and the ability to understand causes and consequences each have been deemed important.

Beecher (1959) noted two basic components of pain: sensory and reactive. Sternbach (1968) described pain as a private and personal sense of hurt, signal of danger, and pattern of responses that function to protect the individual from harm. Melzack (1973) discussed interacting sensory, affective, and motivational factors in pain. Merskey (1980) described pain as an experience of hurt associated with tissue damage. Fordyce (1976) provided a behavioral conceptualization that described pain in terms of a pattern of responses to both nocioceptive stimuli and environmental contingencies. More recently, Jay (1985) conceptualized pain as the interaction of overt, covert, and physiological responses that can be stimulated by tissue damage but can also be produced by other antecedent and consequent conditions. Finally, because younger children are less able to use language to describe the complexities of their subjective experiences and because pain in younger children appears inextricably intertwined with other types of negative affect, some investigators have suggested that the terms *behavioral distress* and *pain* be used interchangeably (Katz, Kellerman, & Siegel, 1980). In sum, although there is a lack of consensus on how to best define pain, there is considerable agreement that pain comprises both physical and psychological responses. The defining characteristics proposed by Jay (1985) guide current thinking in the area. Variants include comprehensive models that attempt to contextualize and individualize the pain experience and that emphasize an array of motivational, developmental, social, and cognitive factors (Karoly, 1991).

In the remainder of the chapter, types of pediatric pain, developmental factors, tripartite pediatric pain assessment methods, and pharmacological and behavioral intervention strategies are reviewed. An attempt is made to highlight some of the constraints of the socioenvironmental contexts in which assessments and interventions occur.

Types of Pediatric Pain

Pain is typically differentiated into two types, based on duration: acute and chronic. Varni, Katz, and Dash (1982) noted that attempts to distinguish between acute and chronic pain for some pediatric conditions may have little applied significance. There are, however, a number of pertinent distinctions between acute and chronic pain in terms of etiology, neurophysiology, function, assessment, and response to intervention (Bonica, 1979).

Acute pain serves an adaptive function signaling the presence of some noxious stimulus. Acute pain is often self-limiting, and the individual typically is able to localize the distress and take appropriate action (e.g., rest, obtain medical care). While acute pain is frequently of sudden onset, the intensity might not correspond with the amount of tissue damage that has occurred (e.g., excruciating pain with minor tissue insult). Varni (1981) suggested that the severe intensity and anxiety associated with acute pain may be the factors that distinguish it from chronic pain.

Chronic pain refers to pain of long duration (i.e., greater than 6 months) often caused by severe injury or progressive disease. Chronic pain might commence with an episode of acute pain or might be of insidious onset. In chronic pain, the fear component may be lacking or markedly diminished (Varni, Katz, & Dash, 1982). Pain can be continuous or intermittent and can persist after the original injury has healed; it can involve adjacent areas not originally subjected to injury or disease; and it is characterized by a set of pain behaviors (e.g. grimacing, compensatory posturing) that can be reinforced and become entirely independent of the original organic etiology (Fordyce, 1976).

In addition to the acute-chronic distinction, Varni (1983) has proposed four categories of pediatric pain: disease-related pain (e.g., sickle cell anemia), trauma-related pain (e.g., burns), procedure-related pain (e.g., bone marrow aspiration), and pain not associated with an identifiable injury or specific disease state.

Cognitive-Developmental Factors

One preliminary issue that needs only brief discussion is the question of whether young children and infants do, in fact, experience pain. Since the 1930s, conventional wisdom held that infants did not experience pain (or experienced a muted version of childhood pain) due to immature cortical functions. Peiper (1936) relied on infant motor reaction time and onset of vocalization following noxious stimulation to assess infant pain responses. McGraw (1941) was perhaps the first to employ motion picture film in the study of infant pain. Results of these early studies concluded that infant pain responses were decorticate in nature. Although it is known that infants have incomplete myelinization at birth, there is considerable individual variability in the rate at which myelinization is completed as well as in the functional integrity of infant cortical pathway (Swafford & Allen, 1968). More recent evidence (see summary by Craig & Grunau, 1991) has rendered the conclusions of Peiper (1936) and McGraw (1941) invalid.

Among others, Abu-Saad (1981) has noted that the available evidence on this issue no longer permits one to view children's pain as a muted version of what adults experience. Although child and adult behavioral responses to noxious stimuli may differ qualitatively, this by no means implies that children experience less subjective distress. Certainly, there are several variables that complicate the task of pain assessment and treatment with children. Factors such as physical, emotional, and cognitive development have a direct influence on what will be assessed as well as the manner in which the assessment is conducted.

This leads to a consideration of developmental issues in pediatric pain. Although beyond the scope of the present chapter, it is imperative that clinicians become well acquainted with the growing body of empirical research on developmental aspects of pediatric pain assessment and intervention (Bush & Harkins, 1991). Specifically, one needs to be familiar with the range of reactions and competencies that children exhibit with respect to pain expression and control at different developmental levels. Infant behavioral expressions of pain may include, for example, crying, gaze patterns, postural change, characteristic autonomic responses, and facial expressions, as well as specific neurological and endocrinological events. Other early developmental changes include modifications in nonverbal pain-responding during the first 2 years. Toddlers exposed to painful stimuli often respond with limb withdrawal in addition to the more generalized behavior response typical of infants. Teeth-clenching, body rocking, clenched fists, physical aggression, and crying are common responses. Preschool children display similar reactions but also might begin to attach special meaning to the pain experience. In addition, preschool children begin developing causal and self-implicating hypotheses about the origins of pain. Observations of older children suggest increased variability in response to noxious stimulation. The increased intersubject response variability observed in older children is likely attributable to specific cultural and family variables, which, by and large, are learned phenomena. Variables such as anxiety, expectation, cognitive preparation, pain history, and family-peer models become salient factors influencing the behavioral expression of physical distress in older children.

Thompson and Varni (1986) proposed that the child's cognitive-developmental level might markedly influence the perception and report of discomfort. One central factor that has made pain assessment difficult with younger children is the limited communicaion skill of toddlers and prelingual children. Many words that are used to describe pain, even the word *pain* itself, might be absent from a child's vocabulary. Thus, information about a child's cognitive-developmental status is needed in order to use language and explanations appropriate to the child's level of understanding.

Several researchers have described stages of health and illness conceptualizations that are similar to the cognitive-developmental stages described by Piaget (Bibace & Walsh, 1980). Bibace and Walsh classified children's conceptualizations of health and illness into six categories. These categories progress from conceptualizations of phenomonism and contagion at ages 2 to 6, to contamination and internalization at ages 7 to 10, and then to physiological and psychophysiological at age 11 and beyond. Thompson and Varni (1986) noted that empirical evidence is lacking concerning the effects of cognitive-developmental level on the assessment of pediatric pain. However, there is general agreement that cognitive factors require increased attention if clinicians are to generate strategies for pediatric pain assessment that are developmentally appropriate.

PROTOTYPIC ASSESSMENT

This review of specific methods used to assess pediatric pain begins with a brief discussion of the tripartite assessment model that has guided much of the work in the area.

Historically, behavioral assessment has focused on the measurement of motor responses. Current assessment strategies are not restricted to the observation of motor responding and include a variety of methods for the assessment of responses from three response systems: cognitive-verbal, physiological, and behavioral-motoric. This focus has been referred to as triple response mode assessment, or *tripartite assessment*. Although responses from the three systems may covary systematically, this need not always be the case because there can be low to moderate correspondence among response systems. It is important to obtain assessment data for each response system because different controlling variables (environmental and/or organismic) can be identified for each system. The relative importance of data gleaned from each response system will vary as a function of client characteristics and of the nature of the patient's presenting problem(s). The following presentation is based, in part, on a recent review of the pediatric pain behavioral assessment literature by Tarnowski and Kaufman (1988). As in any clinical evaluation, results of pain-specific assessments should be integrated with data from clinical interviews (i.e., unstructured, semistructured, structured), detailed cross-informant (e.g., child, parent, staff) and cross-situational analyses (e.g., ward, clinic, home, school), and basic developmental and socioecological assessments. Multidisciplinary inpatient and outpatient staffings are an integral component of any assessment protocol (Hurt & Tarnowski, 1990).

Cognitive-Verbal Response Measures

Self-report measures used to assess client cognitive-verbal functioning include the rating-scale approach, the graphic assessment approach, and the descriptive approach. Although the accuracy of patient self-reports can be difficult to ascertain, it is essential to assess the private and unobservable aspects of pain phenomenon.

Rating Scales

Rating scales can be divided into three categories: (a) simple descriptive scales (SDS), (b) visual analogue scales (VAS), and (c) graphic rating scales (GRS).

SDS comprises the most basic approach to the assessment of pediatric pain. Scales may be as simple as a segmented line accompanied by a few anchor points or as complex as a 0 to 100 numeric scale that incorporates adjective anchors. VAS differ in that only the end points of the continuum have adjective descriptors (e.g., *no pain at all* and *the worst pain possible*). For GRS, additional adjectives are listed on the continuum without marking their exact point on the line. For VAS and GRS, the line is often set to a standard length (e.g., 5 cm).

The advantages of the SDS include simple administration and purported comprehensibility. Limitations include that (a) assessment is restricted to one dimension (intensity) or a multidimensional phenomenon; (b) adjective anchors can have different meanings for clients; and (c) the actual distances between anchor points are not usually known, despite the fact that they are frequently treated statistically as if they were equal.

The VAS represent an improvement over both the SDS and the GRS by avoiding the subjectiveness of numbers and adjectives as descriptors and by meeting the assumption of equal intervals. In general, the VAS and GRS are both considered more sensitive than the SDS. However, subjects might not take advantage of the sensitivity of GRS and might choose to endorse only points on the continuum that correspond with an adjective anchor. Finally, some clients encounter difficulty in understanding the VAS and GRS.

Scaling approaches have been used extensively to assess pediatric pain. SDS have been used, for example, with children and adolescents undergoing painful procedures related to cancer treatment (Hilgard & LeBaron, 1982), and suffering arthritic pain associated with hemophilia (Varni, 1981), and burn-related pain (Tarnowski, McGrath, Calhoun, & Drabman, 1987), and to study pain in hemophilic children with Factor VIII inhibitor (Varni, Gilbert, & Dietrich, 1981). Paired graduated drawings of a pain thermometer with a 0 to 100 numerical scale (*no hurt* to *the worst possible hurt*) have been used to assess procedural pain. A modified SDS technique has also been used in which a series of faces were presented to patients that displayed increasing amounts of distress and were associated with the numbers one to five. Poker chips have also been used to represent pain intensity (Hester, 1979).

Graphic Assessment Approaches

To mitigate methodological concerns associated with young children's limited cognitive abilities, simple graphic representations of pain have been used. Graphic assessment approaches include pain mannequins, drawings, and color models.

PAIN MANNEQUINS.   The simplest form of mannequin assessment is an outline of a human figure. The respondent is instructed to place an X on the drawing to designate pain location. Savedra and associates (Savedra, Gibbons, Tesler, Ward, & Wegner, 1982; Savedra, Tesler, Ward, Wegner, & Gibbons, 1981) have used this approach in a series of studies examining children's descriptions of pain. O'Donnell and Curley (1985) reported that the technique has good predictive validity in locating pain that is later identified in the context of a medical examination. Varni, Thompson, and Hanson (1987) incorporated this approach as part of a multidimensional scale to assess pediatric musculoskeletal pain in rheumatoid arthritis patients. Lang (1980) developed a series of mannequins that each represent a degree of pain on a pictorial rating scale—more graphically distorted mannequins reflect greater distress.

DRAWINGS.   Unruh, McGrath, Cunningham, and Humphreys (1983) examined the usefulness of children's drawings in assessing pain. Children with a principal pain complaint related to either recurrent migraine headaches or chronic musculoskeletal difficulties were asked to draw a picture of their pain and of themselves when they were in pain. Pictures were reliably and meaningfully categorized by content. A study of drawings by healthy children offered support for the notion that drawings may represent a useful assessment modality (Jeans, 1983).

COLOR MODELS.   Color selection methods have been used to assess pain intensity. Scott (1978) reported that nonhospitalized children (4 to 6 years old) chose the color red more often than other colors to describe cartoon sequences of a child injury. Other investigators also reported that pediatric respondents exhibited a preference for the color red for describing pain (Savedra, Tesler, et al., 1981; Varni, Thompson, & Hanson 1987).

Descriptive Approaches

Several nonverbal descriptive approaches have been developed in response to concerns about the subjective nature of pain and children's lack of verbal ability. However, some authors (Abu-Saad & Holzemer, 1981; Beales, 1982) have argued for the inclusion of children's verbal self-reports, in conjunction with so-called nonverbal measures, to improve the accuracy and thoroughness of pediatric pain evaluation.

Much of the existing literature on children's verbal reports of pain is based on the work of Melzack and Torgerson (1971) with adults. Words commonly used to describe pain were categorized into subclasses within the three major categories of sensory, affective, and evaluative distress. Savedra, Gibbons, et al. (1982) concluded that verbal descriptors were justified for the assessment of pediatric pain. Ross and Ross (1984) concurred and reported that 70% of the 994 children they surveyed (5 to 12 years of age) provided excellent single (one-word) pain descriptors. They noted that most children's pain definitions (81%) were unidimensional and that only 2% mentioned the process of pain. Karoly (1991) noted that children can be trained to use a self-monitoring assessment package comprised of a combination of verbal ratings and numeric/visual analogue scales that are completed on a predetermined schedule.

PAIN DIARIES.   Hoelscher and Lichstein (1984) noted that a pain diary is the most frequently employed technique for obtaining data from adult headache patients. Diaries possess several features not shared by other self-report methods. First, the diary may be more reliable and objective than global measures. Second, it is sensitive to patterns of pain that may fluctuate by setting, time of day, day of the week, or situational factors. Third, diaries attempt to expand assessment foci beyond simple ratings of intensity to include affective reactions and cognitive features. Finally, a diary is sensitive to variations based upon treatment effects, and its simplicity offers a natural advantage with pediatric populations. A diary may be most appropriate for children who have reached the concrete-operational stage of development. In general, this means use with children greater than 8 years of age.

PAIN QUESTIONNAIRES.   In an effort to capitalize on the strengths of adult multidimensional assessment instruments, Thompson and Varni (1986) developed the Pediatric Pain Questionnaire (PPQ) with a format similar to that of the McGill Pain Questionnaire. The PPQ was intended as a comprehensive, multidimensional assessment instrument for use in the study of acute and chronic pain in children. Child forms and parent forms include measures of intensity; sensory, affective, and evaluative components; and pain location. A comprehensive family history is also included in the parent form. Similar measures include the Pediatric Pain Questionnaire (Tesler, Ward, Savedra, Wegner, & Gibbons, 1983) and the Children's Comprehensive Pain Questionnaire (McGrath, 1987).

ADULT RATINGS.   Parent, staff, and teacher ratings are often used as behavioral indexes of distress. There is, however, considerable variability in the complexity of such measures. Most often, staff rate patient distress on a simple multipoint scale. Such ratings have been found to correlate well with distress (Jay & Elliott, 1984) and patient cooperation during medical procedures (Kelley, Jarvey, Middlebrook, McNeer, & Drabman, 1984). Parent and teacher ratings, in particular, offer a vantage point on the adult perception of the child's adaption in the extrahospital or clinic environment. Of course, other commonly used indexes of child behavioral functioning (e.g., Child Behavior Checklist) and family functioning (e.g., Family Environment Scale) can be administered.

Physiological Response Measures

Relatively few studies of pediatric pain have employed physiological measures. The dearth of such physiological data in the literature might be related to a number of unresolved methodological problems. First, variability in both the individual's response to pain and the type of stimuli eliciting the pain have deterred adequate description of the relationship between physiological responses and the pain experience (Sternbach, 1974). Second, study findings have not demonstrated the concurrent validity of self-report, behavioral observation, and physiological measurements (Epstein, 1976). Finally, physiological approaches present practical demands that, under certain circumstances, can complicate clinical care.

Sternbach (1974) suggested the use of several physiological measures assumed to be related to the pain experience. These include measures of respiration, muscular tension, blood pressure, pulse rate, and skin resistance. As with other pain indexes, physiological measures might lack discriminatory utility (Peterson & Shigetomi, 1981).

A promising physiological assessment technique involves the measurement of beta-endorphines. *Beta-endorphines* refer to endogenous, morphine-like materials. It is noteworthy that Szyfrelbein, Osgood, and Carr (1985) identified a significant relationship between beta-endorphine levels and multiple self-reports of pain for pediatric burn patients undergoing debridement and burn dressing changes. The authors concluded that plasma beta-endorphine levels may have particular utility in assessing pain with young preverbal children. Finally, recent technological advances have made telemetric monitoring devices more readily available. Currently, such devices have not been widely used for the physiological assessment of pediatric pain but would appear to hold considerable potential in this regard.

Behavioral-Motoric Response Measures

The assessment of behavioral-motoric responding typically involves reliance upon observers who use operational definitions to observe and record the responses of one or more subjects. Operational definitions recast general descriptions of behavior (e.g., pain) into clearly defined and observable aspects (e.g., crying). Typically, the response of interest is quantified according to one or more of the following dimensions: frequency, time, duration, distance, occurrence per opportunity, or percentage of response components completed. Interobserver reliability is established under conditions whereby two or more observers code the same behavioral sequence and quantify the extent of agreement.

Several coding systems are available to observe the behavioral-motoric aspects of children's pain. The Procedure Behavioral Rating Scale (PBRS) (Katz et al., 1980) is the prototypic code for most pediatric pain observation codes in current use. The PBRS is basically a frequency recording system. Observers record the occurrence of 13 specific responses during each of the discrete phases of the medical procedure. The frequency of responses collapsed across all phases comprises the total score. There is empirical support for the sensitivity of the PBRS. Katz et al. (1980) found that the scores for the four phases of the Bone Marrow Aspiration (BMA) differed as expected (i.e., lowest rates of distress responding during preparation, highest rates during the procedure). The code also differentiated age groups examined. Concurrent validity was reflected by a significant moderate correlation between PBRS total score and nurse's rating of patient distress (5-point Likert ratings of anxiety). Stability of the PBRS was demonstrated via reevaluation of a subsample of children who were required a second procedure. Finally, the PBRS coding system appears to be sensitive to both quantitative (frequency) and qualitative (response-type) changes in children's responding; for example, older children were noted to emit fewer types of anxious responses in comparison with younger children.

Several modifications and variants of the PBRS have been reported. The Procedure Behavior Check List was developed by LeBaron and Zeltzer (1984) as an observational tool to assess acute pain and anxiety. The Observation Scale of Behavioral Distress (OSBD) (Jay, Ozolins, Elliott, & Caldwell, 1983) represents a revised version of the Katz et al. (1980) PBRS. The OSBD is comprised of 11 operationally defined behaviors that reflect pain or anxiety in children and includes pain intensity weightings for each behavioral category. The PBRS (or its variants) has also been modified to fit the assessment needs of various clinical populations, including cancer and burn patients (Elliott & Olsen, 1983; Tarnowski, McGrath, et al., 1987). A second development has involved attempts to modify the original code (e.g., more or fewer categories, weighted intensity ratings) in the interest of improving its reliability and validity. The results of these modifications have been mixed.

Some have produced improved interobserver reliability (Tarnowski, McGrath, et al., 1987), whereas others increased the complexity and time-intensiveness of the code without improving upon the psychometric integrity and clinical utility of the basic code (Jay & Elliott, 1984).

A behavioral observation scheme designed for infant use is the Infant Pain Behavior Rating Scale (IPBRS) (Craig, McMahon, Morison, & Zaskow, 1984). The code is composed of 13 discrete behaviors within four categories (i.e., vocal actions, nonvocal-face, nonvocal-torso, and nonvocal-limbs), and was intended for observing infants' reactions to immunizations.

An early example of a dyadic-interaction coding scheme that focuses not only on patient responses but also on staff reactions to patient behavior is that developed by Klein and Charlton (1980). The code, a modification of one developed by Lewinsohn (1976), includes categories for somatic complaints, somatic well-being, psychological complaints, psychological well-being, criticism, praise, other people's problems, and requests for information. An advantage of this coding scheme is that it includes categories for positive and negative staff reactions to patient responding and, thus, permits one to examine if specific staff responses are implicated in the maintenance of specific patient pain behaviors.

Other interaction codes include the Child-Adult Medical Procedure Interaction Scale (CAMPIS) (Blount et al., 1989). This coding scheme includes a variety of verbal and behavior codes (adult and child) that reflect distress, coping, and affective responding and specifically emphasizes parent-child/staff-child interactions.

It is clear that the development of this first generation of behavioral pain codes has focused largely on the assessment of procedural distress in young children and adolescents. Although there has been increased attention devoted to the design of coding schemes for infants and toddlers, developments in this area as well as those related to the assessment of chronic/recurrent pain have been slow to emerge.

ACTUAL ASSESSMENT

As previously described, under optimal conditions, one seeks to conduct a broad-spectrum multimodal assessment of pain that includes use of multidimensional self-report ratings (e.g., intensity, coping, cognitive processes, physiological correlates of well-being and distress, and direct behavioral observation of the target behavior(s) of interest (e.g., pain, affective distress, coping, positive adjustment) in a variety of critical life contexts (e.g., family, school, hospital).

Those experienced in conducting such assessments with children understand well that routine assessment data almost invariably fall short of the ideal assessment approach previously outlined. This occurs for a variety of reasons, including those related to sociopolitical realities of the service-delivery environment (e.g., patient "turfing," the requesting of psychology consult only after all else has failed), economic/staff constraints (e.g., understaffed hospital settings, minimal resource to conduct cost- and labor-intensive behavioral observations, staff moral problems, lack of support staff), antibehavioral/ psychology biases, doctor shopping by families of pediatric pain patients, institutional/ staff/family pressure for instant assessment/treatment results, and limitations associated with multidisciplinary staff model (e.g., unclear role boundaries, diffusion of responsibility). Consultants should be well acquainted with the socioenvironmental realities of conducting pediatric pain consults in their own settings. Those new to consultation are referred to Gillman and Mullins (1991) for an excellent overview of some of the major problems and prospects concerning this aspect of the consultation enterprise.

Although considerable homage has been paid to the need and usefulness of tripartite assessment in the evaluation of pediatric pain, to date, there have been few attempts to obtain this type of comprehensive assessment data. Most often, assessment data consist of staff, parent, and child interviews coupled with some form of self-report and informal behavioral observation. The breadth of existing self-report approaches allows instruments to be matched with most clinical and research populations and settings. However, the development of multidimensional pain questionnaires, such as the PPQ, represents movement away from the historical overreliance on intensity ratings toward the acquisition of information regarding physical location, temporal, perceptional, and topographic factors. Pain questionnaires may be improved further with the addition of diary and scatter-plot components (Tarnowski & Kaufman, 1988) that permit investigation of the relationship between pain patterns and specific environmental antecedents and consequences. However, the psychometric characteristics of self-report measures are not well documented, and, for the most part, their use has been aimed toward the assessment of procedural/acute distress with little emphasis on the evaluation of chronic or recurrent pain. Although time- and cost-effective, the exigencies of day-to-day clinical work typically result in an overreliance on such measures.

Data on physiological approaches to the assessment of pediatric pain may be considered sparse at best. Further, existing studies have yet to demonstrate the superiority of such approaches over simpler, less invasive techniques. However, it is also clear that clinicians could better integrate available simple physiological data (e.g., chart data on heart rate) with behavioral assessment data.

Although observation has formed the cornerstone of behavioral approaches to pain assessment, quite often it is simply impractical for practitioners to employ systematic and time-intensive behavioral-observation coding schemes in their routine assessment of patient functioning. The staff resources and time needed to conduct sophisticated behavioral observations often render their use beyond the practical reach of many clinicians. Other more cost-efficient behavioral indexes of patient well-being are often quite readily available. These indexes include a number of positive and negative patient responses, for example, amount of up time (out of bed), play time, ambulation (e.g., number of steps taken), frequency of medication requests, analgesics ordered, coping statements, number of hospital readmissions, school days attended, type and dosage of medication, frequency of peer interactions, food consumed, repetitions in physical therapy (e.g., arm extensions for burn patients), days of hospitalization, school grades, number of outpatient visits, school nurse records, and patient sleep records (nursing or parent) may be used effectively to index children's adjustment to acute and/or chronic physical distress. These indices vary widely on how directly or indirectly they assess patient well-being. The appropriateness of these indices for a given case depends, in part, upon the child's developmental level, type and degree of physical distress (e.g., burn versus cancer-related pain), medical and psychological treatments in effect, topography of the child's pain response, and the staff's evaluation needs. The authors have found in their clinical efforts that many of these indexes possess a high degree of social validity from the perspective of children, parents, and physicians; for example, an increase in the number of days of school attended by a child with chronic pain is often viewed as a success by most individuals involved in a child's care. At a minimum, the use of some of these indexes should be encouraged in that they may provide additional criteria against which to evaluate the adequacy of other measures (e.g., predictive validity of observational data).

Given the expenses involved in direct observational recording, one must question whether useful data can be obtained without large time expenditures. The answer to this question is dependent upon the purpose of the assessment, setting determinants, population characteristics, and sensitivity requirements. It certainly is possible to obtain meaningful patient data via the use of self-report measures. However, the global nature of most of these measures and inappropriateness for specific settings, populations, and/or procedures can render these measures of limited utility. For hospital and clinic-based practitioners, the use of some combination of child/parent staff rating, simple staff-implemented behavioral observation method, and some easily obtained physiological measure (e.g., heart rate) may be both practical and useful.

PROTOTYPIC TREATMENT

Many treatment modalities are available for alleviating pain in children. These techniques range from pharmacological therapies, the most pervasive form of treatment, to behavior therapies. These treatment methods, as well as their associated effectiveness, are reviewed here.

Pharmacological Treatment

Antipyretics

Antipyretic agents have been the drugs of choice for controlling low-intensity pain, fever, and inflammation. Aspirin compounds and acetaminophen are the most frequently prescribed antipyretic agents for pediatric populations. Aspirin has been the drug of choice for relieving mild- and moderate-intensity pain associated with inflammation. Administered orally, aspirin is absorbed rapidly, and peak blood levels typically occur approximately 2 hours after ingestion. The most common side effects are gastrointestinal upset and bleeding, although when administered with food or milk, gastrointestinal upset is minimized. Because aspirin inhibits the production of prostaglandin (Roth & Majerus, 1975), it is also contraindicated for children with liver disease, hemophilia, and Vitamin K deficiency. Moreover, because aspirin has been implicated as a factor in the development of Reye's syndrome when administered to children with influenza (American Academy of Pediatrics, Committee on Infectious Diseases, 1982), caution is also advised.

Acetaminophen is frequently administered to children for alleviation of symptoms associated with colds and influenza. It does not have the gastrointestinal or hematologic side effects associated with aspirin or the connection with Reye's syndrome and is often administered for moderate pain in children. Acetaminophen does not have antiinflammatory properties.

Opioid Analgesics

Opioid analgesics, or narcotics, constitute the class of analgesic drugs that produce a drowsy stupor along with pain relief. Morphine is the standard analgesic drug typically used for relief of severe acute and chronic pain. Despite the efficacy of morphine, there are serveral adverse effects associated with its administration. It may cause respiratory depression in acute administration, light headedness, dizziness, sedation, nausea, vomiting, and sweating. Moreover, because it can produce mental and physical dependency, its potential for abuse is quite high (McGrath, 1991). Codeine is a weaker opioid analgesic that has a fairly low addictive potential. Its effectiveness in comparison to morphine depends upon mode of administration, with oral administration being the most potent. Its side effects are similar to those of morphine and include nausea, constipation, dizziness, and sedation.

Synthetic derivatives of morphine and codeine are classified according to their structural similarity to morphine or codeine, their analgesic potency relative to morphine or codeine, their agonist (facilitating) or antagonist (blocking) relationship to morphine, their potential for abuse, or their adverse side effects (McGrath, 1991). The most commonly prescribed synthetic agents include meperidine (Demerol), hydromorphone (Dilaudid), fentanyl citrate (Sublimaze), oxycodone (Percocet, Percodan), and pentazocine (Talwin). These drugs are prescribed according to the specific needs of the child and the nature of the pain; for example, fentanyl (Sublimaze) is frequently used for relatively short invasive procedures such as cardiac catheterizations, because it alleviates pain for a very short period of time.

Adjunctive and Combination Drugs

To potentiate the effects of morphine and to diminish anxiety, oral opioids are sometimes combined with other medications, including phenothiazines (major tranquilizers), and are particularly useful for children scheduled for invasive procedures in outpatient clinics. This mixture tends to work well for children who prefer to swallow pain medications (McGrath, 1991).

Other adjunctive drugs that traditionally have been used to treat psychiatric disorders in children and adolescents are frequently administered to diminish the anxiety that sometimes accompanies pain in children. These include major tranquilizers (i.e., phenothiazine and butyrophenones). Moreover, these agents have antiemetic properties that control the vomiting associated with narcotic medications. The minor tranquilizers, or anxiolytics (i.e., benzodiazepines), have also been used successfully as an adjunct to other pain medications to reduce anxiety and tension that often tend to exacerbate pain. Antidepressants are the drugs used to treat vegetative symptoms of depression. They have been used successfully with morphine in alleviating symptoms of pain. McGrath (1990) observed that tricyclics, in combination with a cognitive-behavioral program, were effective in reducing the frequency and intensity of recurrent headaches associated with depression in adolescents.

Central Issues in Drug Treatment

Physical Drug Dependency

There is a great deal of clinical folklore that dictates practice regarding the insufficient dosing of children with narcotic analgesics for severe pain. There are no published studies documenting physical or psychological dependence on narcotic analgesics in pediatric populations, and there is little evidence to suggest that addiction is a valid concern in pediatrics (Porter & Jick, 1980). Nonetheless, as McGrath (1990, 1991) has pointed out, the fear of drug dependence is one of the most common reasons why children might receive inadequate doses of narcotic analgesics for controlling severe pain.

Children can develop tolerance to a particular drug such that they require progressively higher doses of the drug to achieve the same effects. This is not the same as drug addiction, which is fairly rare for patients hospitalized for pain control (McGrath, 1990, 1991). Additionally, as McGrath (1991) has pointed out, the majority of such patients are adults with severe chronic pain due to malignancies, not children. There is, in fact, little empirical evidence to support the notion that children should be denied narcotic analgesics because of drug dependence or addiction.

Drug dependence occurs when children become accustomed to the physiological or psychological effects of a drug such that they require the drug on an ongoing basis. Physical dependence may become a problem after a child has been receiving narcotic analgesics for several weeks and then abruptly ceases taking the medication. Mild symptoms, including restlessness or sleeplessness, may occur 8 to 12 hours after the last dose of narcotics. Major withdrawal symptoms, including irritability, nausea, tremors, and muscle pains, may develop 48 to 72 hours after cessation of the medication. Dependence may be controlled by gradually tapering the dosage of the medication.

Administration Guidelines

The physician should carefully weigh the severity and etiology of the child's pain simultaneously with the properties of the particular drug. Typically, antipyretics are designated as appropriate for mild pain, whereas narcotic analgesics may be necessary to relieve severe pain (for a review of various analgesics, dosages, and side effects, see Goodman & Gilman, 1985). For children, the route of drug administration is particularly important, and they prefer oral medications over injections. Fear of injections can influence children to refrain from requesting medication, to minimize their pain, or even to deny pain. Portacatheters and continuous intravenous infusion pumps that allow drugs to be injected into an external tube are frequently useful for children with severe pain where oral medications are not possible due to vomiting. Spinal administration of opioid drugs and anesthetics for children's postsurgical pain that is refractory to conventionally administered drugs has also demonstrated potential promise (Krane, Tyler & Jacobson, 1989; McIlvanie, 1990).

Regardless of the route of administration, it is important that pain medication be administered regularly and prophylactically on an ongoing basis. Eliminating any kind of constant pain is important. Even mild pain may intensify behavioral problems as well as anxiety, which may in turn intensify existing pain. Recently, the use of patient-controlled analgesia (PCA) has been found to be effective in relief of pain. This technique allows the patient to press a button to administer medication through an intravenous catheter. Children use less analgesia postoperatively with PCA as compared to conventional dosing regimens (McGrath, 1990, 1991).

Other Medical Treatments

Surgical Techniques

Because children do not experience chronic intractable pain to the same degree as adults, few surgical procedures have been used to alleviate chronic pain in children (McGrath, 1990). Typically surgical techniques are used with adults whose pain has been refractory to numerous pharmacological and nonpharmacological interventions (McGrath, 1990). It is frequently difficult to identify and ablate a single section of the nervous system to eliminate pain selectively (Melzack & Wall, 1982), and neurosurgical procedures have only provided temporary relief of pain.

Anesthetic Blocks

Local anesthetics are frequently used to manage children's pain during invasive medical treatments, minor surgery, and restorative dental surgery (Mather & Cousins, 1986; McGrath, 1990). Local anesthetics include lidocaine and bupivacaine, which are injected into a nerve or infiltrated into a general area (McGrath, 1990). There has been a burgeoning interest in the efficacy and safety of various blocks for children undergoing surgical procedures, including circumcisions, hypospadia repair, and hernia repair (Brown, 1985; Mather & Cousins, 1986; Schulte-Steinberg, 1980). Abajian, Mellish, Browne, Lambert, and Mazuzan (1984) have recommended the use of spinal analgesia for infants with congenital anomalies, a history of prematurity, or a history of neonatal respiratory disease who are at significant risk for general anesthesia. McGrath (1990) has reviewed the potential benefits of nerve blocks for children in reducing pain during and after surgery. Nerve blocks provide localized analgesia without the risks of general anesthesia or the side effects of narcotic analgesics. For this reason, the use of regional anesthesia will likely increase in pediatrics.

Electrical Nerve Stimulation

For the alleviation of many painful conditions in adults, electrical stimulation is applied to the surface of the skin or by surgically implanted electrodes. The most widely used form of cutaneous stimulation is transcutaneous electrical nerve stimulation (TENS). For infants and children who have serious medical conditions that may contraindicate the use of narcotic analgesics, pain may be more safely controlled by the use of a TENS unit (McGrath, 1990). One clinical study successfully employed TENS therapy to reduce children's postoperative pain (Epstein & Harris, 1978). Additional research is needed to further validate the efficacy and safety of TENS for children.

Pressure and Massage

Pressure applied to specific body regions can often induce analgesia (McGrath, 1990). Moreover, children in pain appear to be comforted by massage, strokes, or other types of touch, such as hugs. No clinician would dispute that children fare better when they are physically reassured during medical procedures. Nonetheless, no empirical studies can be located that have examined the efficacy of therapeutic touch in pediatric pain.

The use of acupuncture is related to the use of pressure to alleviate pain. Acupuncture involves the insertion of thin needles into various body points. Only one published study was located that has examined the efficacy of acupuncture therapy in children, specifically in alleviating sore throat pain (Gunsburger, 1973). Although the findings were encouraging, much more research will be needed to assess the efficacy of this technique.

Behavioral and Cognitive Methods

Relaxation

Many interventions have been used in an attempt to minimize pain by physically and mentally relaxing patients. These interventions have included progressive muscle relaxation, yoga, meditation, and biofeedback. The underlying physiologic mechanism of these procedures is the relaxation response, which involves decreased sympathetic nervous system activity and results in decreased oxygen consumption and respiratory rate, increased skin resistance, and production of alpha waves (Benson, Pomeranz, & Kutz, 1984). Relaxation techniques have been demonstrated to alleviate children's pain associated with cancer treatments (Jay, Elliott, Ozolins, Olson, & Pruitt, 1985), burns (Wakeman & Kaplan, 1978), sickle cell disease (Zeltzer, Dash, & Holland, 1979), and headaches (McGrath, 1983). Deep breathing exercises, progressive muscle relaxation, and biofeedback have been frequently used to help children relax (McGrath, 1991). During progressive muscle relaxation, children are trained to tighten and relax various muscle groups from the observable (e.g., leg or fist) to more specialized areas. The success and appropriate implementation of such procedures is contingent on the child's cognitive level, with younger children requiring more concrete examples, such as imagining that they are floppy relaxed dolls (McGrath, 1990, 1991).

Biofeedback is a procedure whereby an unobserved activity of the body is amplified and translated into auditory or visual signals. This technique has been demonstrated to be very effective for managing pain in children (Attanasio et al., 1985, Jessup, 1984; Turk, Meichenbaum, & Berman, 1979). Biofeedback allows children to receive immediate feedback regarding specific physiological parameters and assists children to discriminate between relaxed and tense body states. Its use with children has primarily been for headaches in which electromyogram activity in the frontalis muscle is monitored (McGrath, 1991). Potential disadvantages include children's short attention span and limited cognitive understanding of the task and very young children's fear of electrical equipment (Attanasio et al., 1985).

Imagery

Imagery is the process in which a child concentrates intensely on the mental image of an experience or situation. This technique is a powerful means by which children at all developmental levels may alleviate pain (Hilgard & Le Baron, 1984; McGrath, 1990,

1991). Imagery typically involves the use of auditory, visual, and kinesthetic senses for producing physiologic changes that result in relaxation. McGrath (1991) has suggested that images be developed by the children themselves; for example, McGrath described a young girl with cancer who invented "magic sparkles," an invisible air to breathe in deeply just prior to invasive medical procedures.

Modeling

Modeling is a procedure whereby a child learns vicariously by observing another child's behavior in a particular situation and eventually acquires that behavior. Modeling has long been employed in behavioral research (Bandura, 1976) and has been particularly effective for children in reducing fears and avoidance behaviors (Melamed & Siegel, 1980). This technique has been demonstrated to be effective in reducing pain for young children undergoing invasive medical and dental procedures and may reduce the anxiety and pain associated with injections, dressing changes, bone marrow aspirations, and lumbar punctures (McGrath, 1991). The efficacy of any modeling procedure is contingent upon an appropriate match between the model and the patient, taking into account age, previous experience with medical procedures, and type of pain (McGrath, 1990).

Contingency Management

Fordyce (1976) described how traditional pain therapies (e.g., rest, medication) can facilitate the continuation of pain beyond the usual time needed for healing. Masek, Russo, and Varni (1984) have extended this interpretation for children. They have suggested that it is first necessary to identify verbal and nonverbal pain behaviors and then to evaluate the response of significant others (i.e., parents, teachers, peers, physicians, and nurses) to the child's pain. The rationale for operant conditioning is rooted in the belief that children's pain behaviors are frequently, albeit inadvertently, reinforced by significant others. Such reinforcement occurs when children perceive that the special attention they receive is contingent on their need for pain relief and comfort (McGrath, 1991). Thus, behaviors that facilitate increased interaction with the child might continue even at the cost of prolonged disability and increased dependence on caretakers or medication.

In employing operant conditioning, a thorough evaluation is conducted concerning the child's pain, including relevant behavioral, emotional, situational, and family factors (McGrath, 1991). Subsequently, the most pain-maintaining behaviors are targeted for change, and a reward system is developed to motivate the child. Typically, medical staff and caretakers are involved in the program, and rewards are contingent on the child's completing a designated behavior criteria.

Desensitization

In the development of a desensitization program, specific anxiety-producing components of the treatment are identified. A program is subsequently established that exposes children gradually to the less anxiety-inducing components, while teaching them coping strategies to relax and gain control of the situation (Wolpe, 1982). The anxiety elicited from each situation is paired with a response, such as relaxation, that is incompatible with anxiety (Wolpe, 1982). Systematic desensitization has been demonstrated to be particularly beneficial for children who have undergone repeated invasive treatments resulting in conditioned fears and anxiety (McGrath, 1990, 1991; McGrath & deVeber, 1986).

Distraction

Distraction is a procedure commonly employed by parents and hospital staff to alleviate children's pain. The child's perception of pain is altered by diverting their attention away from the pain stimuli and focusing them on another stimulus. Commonly employed distraction strategies include singing, describing a favorite cartoon, playing a video game, describing a novel object, deep breathing, and hand squeezing (McGrath, 1990). It has been hypothesized that the child's concentration may directly weaken the neuronal impulses evoked by noxious stimuli (McGrath, 1991). Support for this hypothesis has been demonstrated in animal studies in which neuronal activity, evoked by a constant noxious activity, varies depending on the animal's attention (Dubner, Hoffman, & Hayes, 1981; Price, 1988). The child's capacity to deploy attention to something other than the pain is critical in this technique.

Stress Inoculation

The stress inoculation model (Turk, 1978) is a combination of cognitive-behavioral treatments that has been successfully employed with pediatric populations. Such multi-component packages might include many of the behavioral and cognitive procedures previously described. In an early study with pediatric cancer patients, researchers successfully used relaxation, imagery, and contingency management to decrease observed and self-reported distress for the patients (Dahlquist, Gil, Armstrong, Ginsberg, & Jones, 1985). In a similar type of intervention for children undergoing lumbar punctures, McGrath and DeVeber (1986) found a decrease in pain and anxiety, with reductions remaining at 3- and 6-month follow-ups. In a study of children undergoing dental treatment, significantly fewer body movements were observed in children receiving stress inoculation than in control groups (Nocella & Kaplan, 1982).

Other Psychological Treatments

Family-Focused Behavioral Interventions

Recent research in pediatric psychology, particularly in pediatric cancer (Kazak & Nachman, 1991), has demonstrated the impact of chronic illness on overall family adaptation as related to children's adjustment to a chronic illness. Family members can assist the pain patient in coping with and managing pain during stressful procedures. In a recent study of children undergoing cancer treatment, Kazak (1993) used a combined pharmacologic-phychologic protocol, the Analgesia Protocol for Procedures in Oncology (APPO). The interventions are individualized and include distraction, relaxation, and hypnosis. Parents participate in the intervention and assume increased responsibility for the intervention program over time. Data from the study support the integration of behaviorally focused techniques with family involvement in assisting children to adjust and cope with the stress of painful procedures. Similarly, Tarnowski and Brown (in press) reviewed a case study of an adolescent with sickle cell syndrome. Family therapy included basic education about the disease, pain management techniques (deep breathing, relaxation, and imagery, with family members as coaches), and setting attainable short- and long-term goals.

School-based Interventions

Although returning to school is often a formidable task for a youngster suffering from pain, few studies have investigated the efficacy of school-based interventions. Ross and Ross

(1988) discussed an educational program designed to teach elementary school children about the various aspects of pain. The program targeted primary and secondary prevention of chronic pain in order to prevent the subsequent development of chronic pain behaviors. Children were provided with information on the etiology and treatment of pain and on coping skills for managing pain. The data from this program have yielded encouraging results in educating children and altering their behaviors accordingly (Ross & Ross, 1988).

Implications of Assessment Data for Design of Intervention Programs

There is an array of pharmacologic and nonpharmacologic interventions available for controlling children's pain. McGrath (1990, 1991) has lamented that the choice of a method for the management of pain is frequently based on the biases of health professionals, rather than on the specific criteria of the child. In a recent study of children with sickle cell syndrome, for example, researchers found that nurses provided lower dosages of narcotic analgesics to children with histories of frequent hospitalization for pain, than for those with only occasional hospitalization (Armstrong, Pegelow, Gonzalez, & Martinez, 1992). However, the nurses did not differ in their pain ratings of children with these histories.

Pain must be considered in relationship to the child's developmental level, the context in which the child is experiencing the pain, and the type of pain (acute, recurrent, or chronic) experienced. McGrath (1990) has indicated that when pain is not a symptom of an underlying disease, the causative factors for the pain must be identified and managed to assure lasting control of pain. This requires meticulous evaluation of both the sensory attributes of the pain (quality, intensity, location, duration, and frequency) and the psychological and situational factors that may contribute to the pain (McGrath, 1990). In a recent review of cognitive factors that have been hypothesized to be associated with persistent pain in adults, Turk and Rudy (1992) have stressed the central importance of *catastrophizing* in patients with persistent pain. This underscores the role of psychological factors, particularly coping, in mediating persistent pain. Careful attention must be paid to the child experiencing the pain and the context in which the pain is being experienced. This requires careful pain assessment and the development of a multistrategy program that can be specifically tailored to an individual child's coping abilities, his or her family and school environment, and contingencies that may be reinforcing the pain experience.

ACTUAL TREATMENT

Typically, pediatric psychologists are consulted for pain management as a last line of defense when other efforts have failed (Gillman & Mullins, 1991). Thus, the psychologists are faced with the referral source, the child, and the family, each of whom often may have a rather pessimistic outlook in response to inadequate pain control. Moreover, very frequently, ethical dilemmas arise in the process of referring a child for pain management. It is not uncommon to have children referred not specifically because of pain problems, but because they are causing the staff difficulties by means of irritating or externalizing behavioral problems. In this case, it is sometimes necessary for the pediatric psychologist to advocate for the child and to negotiate issues between the child's family and the health care professionals or to recommend another type of intervention, such as behavior management. Thus, as a consultant, the pediatric psychologist must be sensitive to issues affecting the patient, and the family, as well as to issues relevant to other health care providers.

The optimal pain management program incorporates a multidisciplinary team approach (Berde, Sethna, Masek, Tosburg, & Rocklin, 1989; Hurt & Tarnowski, 1990) whereby the pediatric psychologist manages and organizes other team members. The pediatric psychologist in a major medical center is meeting the service needs of various departments simultaneously. Most psychologists are likely to be involved in many training and research endeavors; thus, coordinating the services of many professionals to develop a pediatric pain program is apt to pose a formidable task. The best possible situation is one in which a program in pediatric psychology has had a long history of involvement in pain management at a particular medical center and in which long-standing relationships are established with clear boundaries and lines of communication between the psychologist and other health care professionals (Gillman & Mullins, 1991). This scenario is more ideal than typical, and the pediatric psychologist usually must begin the consultation process with the establishment of professional relationships and an interdisciplinary team, specifying those services that can be realistically provided. Very frequently, complex professional boundaries and territories already exist, requiring significant sensitivity and social skills on the part of the pediatric psychologist. At this point, education of ancillary staff (e.g., nurses, physicians' assistants, physical and occupational therapists) must begin, and their support needs to be solidified. As Gillman and Mullins (1991) suggest, without the support of these other team members by means of direct communication, even the best treatment plan could fail. Maintaining relationships with individuals who hold prominent roles on the interdisciplinary team is also necessary to assure successful treatment of the child and to ensure that the team does not become dysfunctional and exhibit behavior (e.g., apathy, anger, depression) that is inconsistent with patient care. Thus, each of the individuals participating in the care of the child must understand and be in agreement with all of the details of the plan so that the plan may be successfully implemented in a consistent manner.

Gillman and Mullins (1991) have recommended that the parents, medical staff, and psychologist participate in an initial care conference. Input can be obtained from all team members, with each member understanding their role and responsibilities in the program. This should be followed up by regularly scheduled conferences to measure progress and to determine if revisions in the program are needed. In this process, it will be important to carefully delineate behaviors to be modified and appropriate interventions. Finally, it has been recommended that, after shared consent has been obtained, a copy of the program be distributed among team members and placed in the child's medical chart and at bedside (Gillman & Mullins, 1991). Very frequently, health professionals fail to consult and seek the support of parents, and, as a result, the child and the parents may not understand the reason for pain management. This is fairly typical, particularly in major medical centers and hospitals where parents may be very deferential to authority. At this point, it is essential to engage the parents' support in the pain management process because the success of the pain program rests on parents' compliance to the various regimens involved in a comprehensive pain management program. Finally, engaging the child's family in various aspects of pain management is critical because family stress may further exacerbate pain in children. A very common example is recurrent abdominal pain, the origins of which are the result of internal distress over familial dysfunction (e.g., alcoholism, marital conflict).

Ethical Issues

There is an abundance of empirical research indicating that children are undermedicated for pain (Anand & Aynsley-Green, 1988; Schechter, Allen, & Hanson, 1986). Hypotheses accounting for this situation include the notion that children's central nervous systems are immature such that they are unable to experience the same pain intensity as adults, that children are at greater risk for addiction and respiratory depression from narcotic analgesics, and that children are unable to communicate their pain to medical staff (Eland & Anderson, 1977; Mather & Mackie, 1983). In recent years, however, each of these hypotheses has been refuted (McGrath, 1991). Additionally, nurses are frequently reluctant to administer painful injections for the purpose of relieving children's pain (Eland & Anderson, 1977). These findings are particularly alarming in view of the fact that research indicates that children experience pain to the same degree as adults (Eland & Anderson, 1977). McGrath (1990) suggested that physicians receive far too little education and training pertaining to pain management. As an example, McGrath noted that the majority of pediatric departments and children's hospitals do not subscribe to any major journals devoted to pain management.

As Gillman and Mullins (1991) suggested, many pediatric psychologists have a strong bias against the use of medication. This is largely due to their graduate training, which tends to deemphasize the medical model. Although the pediatric psychologist might come to the pain unit with an impressive armamentarium of strategies to decrease pain, such strategies might reduce severe pain by only 5% to 10% at best (Gillman & Mullins, 1991), which is of little comfort to a small child. Further, for some children, a trained coach is necessary to ensure compliance with interventions taught in treatment sessions (Elliott & Olson, 1983), and the financial burden of having a coach for many families is likely to be prohibitive. Nonetheless, the literature does suggest that psychological strategies do reduce the emotional and behavioral distress of some children suffering from certain types of pain (Gillman & Mullins, 1991). Thus, the pediatric psychologist must weigh carefully the selected strategy, the cost of the intervention, and the ultimate yield in managing a child's pain. Gillman and Mullins (1991) also have stressed that it is necessary for the psychologist to inform physicians of the limitations regarding the efficacy of psychologically based treatment interventions and to inform the physician when traditionally effective treatment strategies are not working. Additionally, they pointed out that it is the psychologists' responsibility to inform physicians of the empirical literature demonstrating that children do have significant pain experiences and that this literature does not support the lore that children become easily addicted to pain medication.

SUMMARY

A vast array of pharmacological approaches is available to physicians for relieving pain in children. The agent of choice should be determined only after a thorough assessment, considering the properties of particular medications, dosing intervals, and routes of administration. Much more education and research are needed to dispel some of the common myths held by physicians, particularly those that suggest that children become addicted to pain medication. Although several nonsomatic techniques show considerable promise with adults, their demonstrated efficacy with pediatric populations awaits long-needed research. Behavioral and cognitive interventions have been demonstrated to relieve pain by increasing physical activity, reducing postural restrictions, decreasing muscular tensions, and helping children control noxious stimuli. The programs that have demonstrated the most promise with children have been multicomponent packages, fashioned after the stress inoculation model (Turk, 1978). Family- and school-based interventions that have only recently been employed also show considerable promise and await further clinical trials. Multicomponent types of approaches whereby pharmacological approaches have been combined with behavioral and cognitive techniques have demonstrated the most success with children.

The ideal and the real assessment and treatment of pain in children are frequently quite different. Appropriate pain assessment and management of children at most major medical centers are frequently contingent on a multidisciplinary team approach whereby health care professionals work together. This often requires the skill of an experienced, patient, empathic, and diplomatic pediatric psychologist who works well in a team setting. Further, in the management of pain, the pediatric psychologist is likely to encounter a number of ethical dilemmas that must be resolved if appropriate treatment is to ensue. Finally, in view of the many misconceptions concerning pain in children, the psychologist is likely to be charged with important teaching responsibilities, research endeavors, and decisions regarding the most appropriate and effective intervention techniques for managing pain in children.

REFERENCES

Abajian, J. C., Mellish, R. W. P., Browne, A. F., Lambert, D. H., & Mazuzan, J. E. (1984). Spinal anesthesia for surgery in the high-risk infant. *Anesthesia and Analgesia, 63*, 359–362.

Abu-Saad, H. (1981). The assessment of pain in children. *Issues in Comprehensive Nursing, 5*, 327–335.

Abu-Saad, H., & Holzemer, W. (1981). Measuring children's self-assessment of their pain. *Issues in Comprehensive Nursing, 5*, 337–349.

American Academy of Pediatrics, Committee on Infectious Diseases. (1982). Special report: Aspirin and Reye's syndrome. *Pediatrics, 69*, 810–812.

Anand, K. J. S., & Aynsley-Green, A. (1988). Does the newborn infant require potent anesthesia during surgery? Answers from a randomized trial of halothane anesthesia. In R. Dubner, G. F. Gebhart, & M. R. Bond (Eds.) *Pain research and clinical management* (Vol. 3, pp. 329–335). Amsterdam, The Netherlands: Elsevier.

Armstrong, F. D., Pegelow, C. H., Gonzalez, J., & Martinez, A. (1992). Impact of children's sickle cell history on nurse and physician ratings of pain and medication decisions. *Journal of Pediatric Psychology, 17*, 651–664.

Attanasio, V., Andrasik, F., Burke, E. J., Blake, D. D., Kabela, E., & McCarran, M. S. (1985). Clinical issues in utilizing biofeedback with children. *Clinical Biofeedback and Health, 8*, 134–141.

Bandura, A., (1976). Effecting change through participant modeling. In J. D. Krumboltz & C. E. Thoresen (Eds.), *Counseling methods* (pp. 248–265). New York: Holt, Rinehart, & Winston.

Beales, J. (1982). The assessment and management of pain in children. In P. Karoly, J. Steffen, & D. O'Grady (Eds.), *Child health psychology: Concepts and issues* (pp. 154–179). Toronto: Pergamon Press.

Beecher, H. K. (1959). *Measurement of subjective responses: Qualitative effects of drugs*. New York: Oxford.

Benson, H., Pomeranz, B., & Kutz, I. (1984). The relaxation response and pain. In P. D. Wall & R. Melzack (Eds.), *Textbook of pain* (1st ed. pp. 817–822). Edinburgh, Scotland: Churchill Livingstone.

Berde, C., Sethna, N. F., Masek, B., Tosburg, M., & Rocklin, S. (1989). Pediatric pain clinics: Recommendations for their development. *Pediatrician, 16*, 94–102.

Bibace, R., & Walsh, M. E. (1980). Development of children's concepts of their illness. *Pediatrics, 66*, 912–917.

Blount, R. L., Corbin, S. M., Sturges, J. W., Wolfe, V. V., Prater, J. M., & James, L. D. (1989). The relationship between adults' behavior and child coping and distress during BMA/LP procedures: A sequential analysis. *Behavior Therapy, 20*, 585–601.

Bonica, J. J. (1979). The need of a taxonomy. *Pain, 6*, 247–252.

Brown, T. C. K. (1985). Local and regional anesthesia in children. *Anesthesia, 40*, 407–409.

Bush, J. P., & Harkins, S. W. (1991). *Children in pain: Clinical and research issues from a developmental perspective*. New York: Springer-Verlag.

Craig, K. D., & Grunau, R. V. E. (1991). Developmental issues: Preschool and school-age children. In J. P. Bush & S. W. Harkins (Eds.), *Children in pain: Clinical and research issues from a developmental perspective* (pp. 171–193). New York: Springer-Verlag.

Craig, K., McMahon, R., Morison, J., & Zaskow, C. (1984). Developmental changes in infant pain expression during immunization injections. *Social Science Medicine, 19*, 1331–1337.

Dahlquist, L. M., Gil, K. M., Armstrong, F. D., Ginsberg, A., & Jones, B. (1985). Behavior management of children's distress during chemotherapy. *Journal of Behavior Therapy and Experimental Psychiatry, 16*, 325–329.

Dubner, R., Hoffman, D. S., & Hayes, R. L. (1981). Neuronal activity in medullary dorsal horn of awake monkeys trained in a thermal discrimination task: III. Task-related responses and their functional role. *Journal of Neurophysiology, 46*, 444–464.

Eland, J. M., & Anderson, J. E. (1977). The experience of pain in children. In A. K. Jacox (Ed.), *Pain: A source book for nurses and other health professionals* (pp. 453–471). Boston: Little, Brown.

Elliott, C. H., & Olson, R. A. (1983). The management of children's distress in response to painful medical treatment for burn injuries. *Behaviour Research and Therapy, 21*, 675–683.

Epstein, L. (1976). Psychophysiological measurement in assessment. In M. Hersen & A. Bellack (Eds.), *Behavioral assessment: A practical handbook* (pp. 221–235). Oxford, England: Pergamon Press.

Epstein, M. H., & Harris, J., Jr. (1978) Children with chronic pain: Can they be helped? *Pediatric Nursing, 4*, 42–44.

Fordyce, W. E. (1976) *Behavioral methods for chronic pain and illness*. St. Louis, MO: Mosby.

Gillman, J. B., & Mullins, L. L. (1991). Pediatric pain management: Professional and pragmatic issues. In J. P. Bush & S. W. Harkins (Eds.), *Children in pain: Clinical and research issues from a developmental perspective* (pp. 117–148). New York: Springer-Verlag.

Goodman, L. S., & Gilman, A. G. (Eds.). (1985). *The pharmacological basis of therapeutics* (7th ed.). New York: Macmillan.

Gunsburger, M. (1973). Acupuncture in the treatment of sore throat symptomatology. *American Journal of Chinese Medicine, 1*, 337–340.

Hester, N. (1979). The preoperational child's reaction to immunization. *Nursing Research, 20*, 250–255.

Hilgard, J. R., & LeBaron, S., (1982). Relief of anxiety and pain in children and adolescents with cancer: Qualitative measures and clinical observations. *International Journal of Clinical and Experimental Hypnosis, 30*, 417–442.

Hilgard, J. R., & LeBaron, S. (1984). *Hypnotherapy of pain in children with cancer*. Los Altos, CA: William Kaufmann.

Hoelscher, T., & Lichstein, K. (1984). Behavioral assessment and treatment of child migraine. *Headache, 24,* 94–103.

Holzman, A. D., & Turk, D. C. (1986). *Pain management: A handbook of psychological treatment approaches*. New York: Pergamon Press.

Hurt, F. J., & Tarnowski, K. J. (1990). Behavioral consultation in the management of pediatric burns. *Medical Psychotherapy, 3,* 117–124.

Jay, S. M. (1985). Pain in children: An overview of psychological assessment and intervention. In A. R. Zeiner, D. Bendell, & C. E. Walker (Eds.), *Health psychology: Treatment and research issues* (pp. 167–196). New York: Plenum Press.

Jay, S. M., & Elliott, C. M. (1984). Behavioral observation scales for measuring children's distress: Effects of increased methodological rigor. *Journal of Consulting and Clinical Psychology, 52,* 1106–1107.

Jay, S. M., Elliott, C. H., Ozolins, M., Olson, R. A., & Pruitt, S. D. (1985). Behavioural management of children's distress during painful medical procedures. *Behaviour Research and Therapy, 23,* 513–552.

Jay, S. M., Ozolins, M., Elliott, C. H., & Caldwell, S. (1983). Assessment of children's distress during painful medical procedures. *Health Psychology, 2,* 133–147.

Jeans, M. (1983). Pain in children. In R. Melzack (Ed.), *Pain measurement and assessment* (pp. 23–37). New York: Raven Press.

Jessup, B. A. (1984). Biofeedback. In P. D. Wall & R. Melzack (Eds.), *Textbook of pain* (pp. 776–786). Edinburgh, Scotland: Churchill Livingstone.

Karoly, P. (1991). Assessment of pediatric pain. In J. P. Bush & S. W. Harkins (Eds.), *Children in pain: Clinical and research issues from a developmental perspective* (pp. 59–82). New York: Springer-Verlag.

Katz, E. R., Kellerman, J., & Siegel, S. E. (1980). Distress behavior in children with cancer undergoing medical procedures: Developmental considerations. *Journal of Consulting and Clinical Psychology, 48,* 356–365.

Kazak, A. (1993, August). *Family adaptation related to procedural distress in childhood leukemia*. Paper presented at the annual meeting of the American Psychological Association, Toronto.

Kazak, A. E., & Nachman, G. S. (1991). Family research on childhood chronic illness: Pediatric oncology as an example. *Journal of Family Psychology, 4,* 462–483.

Kelley, M., Jarvie, G., Middlebrook, J., McNeer, M., & Drabman, R. S. (1984). Decreasing burned children's pain behavior: Impacting the trauma of hydrotherapy. *Journal of Applied Behavior Analysis, 17,* 147–158.

Klein, R. M., & Charlton, J. E., (1980). Behavior observation and analysis of pain behavior in critically burned patients. *Pain, 9,* 27–40.

Krane, E. J., Tyler, D. C., & Jacobson, L. J. (1989). The dose response of caudal morphine in children. *Anesthesiology, 71,* 48–52.

Lang, P. (1980). Behavioral treatment and bio-behavioral assessment: Computer applications. In J. Sidowski, J. Johnson, & T. Williams (Eds.), *Technology in mental healthcare delivery systems* (pp. 199–132). Norwood, NJ: Ablex.

LeBaron, S., & Zeltzer, L. (1984). Assessment of acute pain and anxiety in children and adolescents by self-reports, observer reports, and a behavior checklist. *Journal of Consulting and Clinical Psychology, 52,* 729–738.

Lewinsohn, P. (1976). Manual of instructions used for the observation of interpersonal behavior. In E. Mash & L. Terdal (Eds.), *Behavior therapy assessment: Diagnosis, design, and evaluation* (pp. 335–343). New York: Springer.

Masek, B. J., Russo, D. C., & Varni, J. W. (1984). Behavioral approaches to the management of chronic pain in children. *Pediatric Clinics of North America*, *31*, 1113–1131.

Mather, L. E., & Cousins, M. J. (1986). Local anesthetics: Principles of use. In M. J. Cousins & G. D. Phillips (Eds.), *Acute pain management* (pp. 105–131). New York: Churchill Livingstone.

Mather, L. E., & Mackie, J. (1983). The incidence of postoperative pain in children. *Pain*, *15*, 271–282.

McGrath, P. A. (1987). The multidimensional assessment and management of recurrent pain syndromes in children. *Behavior Research and Therapy*, *25*, 251–262.

McGrath, P. A., & deVeber, L. L. (1986). The management of acute pain evoked by medical procedures in children with cancer. *Journal of Pain and Symptom Management*, *1*, 145–150.

McGrath, P. J. (1983). Migraine headaches in children and adolescents. In P. Firestone, P. J. McGrath, & W. Fedman (Eds.), *Advances in behavioral medicine for children and adolescents* (pp. 39–57). Hillsdale, NJ: Erlbaum.

McGrath, P. J. (1990). *Pain in children: Nature, assessment and treatment*. New York: Guilford Press.

McGrath, P. J. (1991). Intervention and management. In J. P. Bush & S. W. Harkins (Eds.), *Children in pain: Clinical and research issues from a developmental perspective* (pp. 83–115). New York: Springer-Verlag.

McGraw, M. B. (1941). Neural maturation exemplified in the changing reactions in the infant to the pin prick. *Child Development*, *12*, 31–41.

McIlvanie, W. B. (1990). Spinal opioids for the pediatric patient. *Journal of Pain and Symptom Management*, *5*, 183–190.

Melamed, B. G., & Siegel, L. J. (Eds.). (1980). *Behavioral medicine: Practical applications in health care*. New York: Springer.

Melzack, R. (1973). *The puzzle of pain*. Harmondsworth, England: Penguin.

Melzack, R., & Torgenson, W. (1971). On the language of pain. *Anesthesiology*, *34*, 50–59.

Melzack, R., & Wall, P. D. (1982). *The challenge of pain*. New York: Penguin Books.

Merskey, H. (1980). Some features of the history of pain. *Anesthesiology, 34*, 50–59.

Nocella, J. & Kaplan, R. M. (1982). Training children to cope with dental treatment. *Journal of Pediatric Psychology, 7*, 175–178.

O'Donnell, P., & Curley,H. (1985). Validation of a nonverbal instrument for pain location descriptions in children. *Perceptual and Motor Skills, 60*, 1010.

Peiper, A. (1936). Hautschutzereflexe. *Jarlbuch Kinderheilkundle 146*, 233.

Peterson, L., & Shigetomi, C. (1981). The use of coping techniques to minimize anxiety in hospitalized children. *Behavior Therapy, 12*, 1–14.

Porter, J., & Jick, H. (1980). Addiction rate in patients treated with narcotics. *New England Journal of Medicine, 302*, 123.

Price, D. D. (1988). *Psychological and neural mechanisms of pain*. New York: Raven Press.

Ross D., & Ross, S. (1984). Childhood pain: The school-aged child's viewpoint. *Pain, 20*, 179–191.

Ross, D. M., & Ross, S. A. (1988). *Childhood pain: Current issues, research, and management*. Baltimore: Urban & Schwarzenberg.

Roth, G. J., & Majerus, P. W. (1975). The mechanism of the effect of aspirin on human platelets: I. Acetylation of a particulate fraction protein. *Journal of Clinical Investigation, 56*, 624–632.

Savedra, M., Gibbons, P., Tesler, M., Ward, J., & Wegner, C. (1982). How do children describe pain? A tentative assessment. *Pain, 14*, 95–104.

Savedra, M., Tesler, M., Ward, J., Wegner, C., & Gibbons, P. (1981). Description of the pain experience: A study of school-age children. *Issues in Comprehensive Pediatric Nursing, 5*, 373–380.

Schechter, N. L., Allen, D. A., & Hanson, K. (1986). Status of pediatric pain control: A comparison of hospital analgesic usage in children and adults. *Pediatrics, 77,* 11–15.

Schulte-Steinberg, O. (1980). Neural blockade of pediatric surgery. In M. J. Cousins & P. O. Bridenbaugh (Eds.), *Neural blockade in clinical anesthesia and management of pain* (pp. 503–523). Philadelphia: Lippincott.

Scott, R. (1978). "It hurts red": A preliminary study of children's perception of pain. *Perceptual and Motor Skills, 47,* 787–791.

Sternbach, R. (1968). *Pain: A psychophysiological analysis.* New York: Academic Press.

Sternbach, R. (1974). *Pain patients: Traits and treatments.* New York: Academic Press.

Swafford, L. E., & Allen, D. (1968). Pain relief in the pediatric patient. *Medical Clinics of North America, 52,* 131–136.

Szyfrelbein, S., Osgood, P., & Carr, D. (1985). The assessment of pain and plasma B-endorphin immunoactivity in burned children. *Pain, 22,* 173–182.

Tarnowski, K. J., & Brown, R. T. (in press). Psychological aspects of pediatric disorders. In M. Hersen & R. T. Ammerman (Eds.), *Advanced abnormal child psychology.* Hillsdale, NJ: Erlbaum.

Tarnowski, K. J., McGrath, M., Calhoun, B., & Drabman, R. S. (1987). Self- versus therapist-mediated debridement in pediatric burn injury. *Journal of Pediatric Psychology, 12,* 567–579.

Tarnowski, K. J., & Kaufman, K. L. (1988). Behavioral assessment of pediatric pain. In R. J. Prinz (Ed.), *Advances in behavioral assessment of children and families* (Vol. 4, pp. 119–158). New York: JAI Press.

Tesler, M., Ward, J., Savedra, M., Wegner, C., & Gibbons, P. (1983). Developing an instrument for eliciting children's descriptions of pain. *Perceptual and Motor Skills, 56,* 315–321.

Thompson, K. L., & Varni, J. W. (1986). A developmental cognitive-behavioral approach to pediatric pain assessment. *Pain, 25,* 283–296.

Turk, D. C. (1978). Cognitive behavioral techniques in the management of pain. In J. P. Foreyt & D. P. Rathjen (Eds.), *Cognitive behavior therapy* (pp. 199–232). New York: Plenum Press.

Turk, D. C., Meichenbaum, D., & Berman, W. H. (1979). Application of biofeedback for the regulation of pain: A critical review. *Psychological Bulletin, 86,* 1322–1338.

Turk, D. C., & Rudy, T. E. (1992). Cognitive factors and persistent pain: A glimpse into Pandora's box. *Cognitive Therapy and Research, 16,* 99–122.

Unruh, A., McGrath, P., Cunningham, S., & Humphrey, P. (1983). Children's drawings of their pain. *Pain, 17,* 385–392.

Varni, J. W. (1981). Behavioral medicine in hemophilia arthritic pain management: Two case studies. *Archives of Physical Medicine and Rehabilitation, 62,* 183–187.

Varni, J. W. (1983). *Clinical behavioral pediatrics: An interdisciplinary biobehavioral approach.* New York: Pergamon Press.

Varni, J. W., Gilbert, A., & Dietrich, S. (1981). Behavioral medicine in pain and analgesia management for the hemophiliac child with factor VII inhibitor. *Pain, 11,* 121–126.

Varni, J. W., Katz, E. R., & Dash, J. (1982). Behavioral and neurochemical aspects of pediatric pain. In D. C. Russo & J. W. Varni (Eds.), *Behavioral pediatrics: Research and practice* (pp. 177–224.) New York: Plenum Press.

Varni, J. W., Thompson, K. L., & Hanson, V. (1987). The Varni-Thompson Pediatric Pain Questionnaire: I. Chronic-musculo-skeletal pain in juvenile rheumatoid arthritis. *Pain, 28,* 27–38.

Wakeman, R. J., & Kaplan, J. Z. (1978). An experimental study of hypnosis in painful burns. *American Journal of Clinical Hypnosis, 21,* 3–12.

Wolpe, J. (1982). *The practice of behavior therapy.* Elmsford, NY: Pergamon Press.

Zeltzer, L., Dash, J., & Holland, J. P. (1979). Hypnotically induced pain in sickle cell anemia. *Pediatrics, 64,* 533–536.

Afterword

Child behavior therapy has progressed dramatically since 1960. For some disorders, such as mental retardation and autism, behavior therapy is the clear treatment of choice. For other conditions, some of which have only recently been recognized as prevalent in childhood (e.g., obsessive-compulsive disorder), behavior therapy has emerged as an indispensable option for successful treatment. Moreover, in the small but growing empirical literature on treatment of childhood psychiatric disorders, behavioral interventions are prominently represented. The chapters in this book examined behavior therapy as it is practiced in the psychiatric setting. Both inpatient wards and outpatient clinics were considered. The unique advantages and limitations of carrying out treatment in such settings were examined. Finally, impediments to assessment and treatment were identified by contrasting prototypic versus actual clinical practices.

Newcomb and Drabman opened the book with a comprehensive examination of child behavioral assessment in Chapter 1. The authors endorsed a broad assessment focus that addresses biological, behavioral, and emotional systems. However, they clearly differentiated the features of behavioral assessment and more traditional approaches in the psychiatric setting. The foremost characteristics of behavioral strategies are their emphases on (a) contemporary influences in behavior, (b) direct observation of behavior, and (c) the situational contexts in which psychopathology is expressed. In addition, unlike other forms of evaluation in which treatment sequentially follows assessment, behavioral assessment and treatment are both ongoing and intricately linked. With its strong empirical base and rich resource of strategies and options, behavioral assessment is a critical tool in the psychiatric setting.

In Chapter 2, Petti, Laite, and Blix provided a comprehensive overview of psychiatric assessment and diagnosis, particularly as they interface with behavior therapy. Diagnostic nosologies (such as DSM-III-R and DSM-IV), which arise from the medical model, have typically been viewed with skepticism by many behavior therapists. Traditional behavioral assessment eschews classification schemes in favor of direct observation of behaviors that are subsequently targeted for intervention. More recently, however, common ground between these two approaches has emerged, and diagnosticians and behavior therapists alike have acknowledged the heuristic value of combining both approaches when conducting a thorough evaluation. Indeed, the authors present guidelines that go beyond the restrictions of any given theoretical approach to arrive at a detailed and informative clinical picture of the child. Diagnosis, behavioral classification, mental status, school performance, and establishing a good rapport are but a few of the areas touched upon by the authors. The chapter concluded with consideration of future developments in psychiatric assessment, with emphasis placed on the integration of multiple strategies and disciplines.

In Chapter 3, Martini discussed medical issues and complications in the psychiatric setting. Physical illness and psychopathology are often enmeshed in the clinical presentation, and assessment must address the possible contributions of medical problems to psychiatric disorder. In some cases (e.g., hypothyroidism), psychopathology emanates from physical illness, and complete relief may occur if the medical problem is treated. In other instances (e.g., head injury), the relationship is more complex, and physical injury or illness may not be the sole contributor to the psychiatric presentation. The author reviewed the most frequently encountered medical problems that contribute to or coexist with psychiatric disturbance. Included are head trauma, endocrine problems, and genetic disorders, among others. It is evident that, to the extent that medical problems may at least partially account for or exacerbate many psychiatric disorders, clinicians should carry out a careful medical as well as behavioral/psychiatric assessment.

Kaufman and Mannarino discussed child maltreatment in Chapter 4. Psychiatrically disordered children frequently present with concurrent abuse and/or neglect by family members (or others). Maltreatment has been linked to a variety of psychopathologies, including anxiety, depression, and aggression. Victims of severe trauma may develop posttraumatic stress disorder. Moreover, to the extent that abuse and neglect compromise the family system and negatively impact on the child's development, treatment is likely to have limited success. The authors pointed out that treating children who are abused and neglected requires a close working relationship with a variety of legal and social service agencies. Effective interventions must also take into account the possible community contributors (e.g., inadequate neighborhood resources) and societal contributors (e.g., poverty) to maltreatment.

Ferrari provided a lucid discussion of developmental issues in child behavior therapy in Chapter 5. Although it is widely acknowledged that assessment and treatment must consider the developmental contexts in which they are administered, the behavioral literature is almost devoid of studies that consider normal development. One reason for this is the emphasis in behavior therapy on quantitative aspects of behavior, which has, until recently, excluded qualitative aspects of children's social, emotional, and cognitive development. The author recommended that behavior therapy be carried out with an understanding and appreciation of the fact that behavior is embedded in complex developmental processes.

In Chapter 6, Handen addressed the combined application of pharmacotherapy and behavioral interventions. As he pointed out, despite the widely accepted notion that combined treatments are superior to any one applied alone, very little research has been conducted on this topic. Indeed, with the exception of child disorders (like attention-deficit/hyperactivity disorder (ADHD), there is a dearth of empirical work on pharmacotherapy with children in general. That having been said, it is still true that pharmacological agents are important components of treatment in the psychiatric setting. Most experts agree that pharmacotherapy should rarely be used in isolation, but rather it should augment psychosocial interventions. The author reviewed the various drug classes and offered a review of the extant literature on combined treatments. The strongest support for synergistic treatments is for ADHD, where intensive contingency management and psychostimulants are especially efficacious in combination. Clearly, future research must focus on the heuristic value of combining behavioral and pharmacological treatments.

The behavioral management of child psychiatric inpatient wards was discussed by Johnson in Chapter 7. Behavioral approaches (such as token economy) to unit management provide a system for day-to-day operations, we well as a therapeutic milieu within which treatment can be implemented. From the perspective of the behavior therapist, a behaviorally structured inpatient unit permits control of environmental consequences and offers frequent opportunities for observational assessment. Perhaps the most serious drawback of inpatient wards, in general, is the difficulty encountered in generalizing treatment gains to the child's home and school environments. The author described features of inpatient settings that are run using behavioral principles, pointing out that full implementation of behavioral systems greatly facilitates assessment and treatment.

Kobe and Mulick discussed mental retardation in Chapter 8. Child behavior therapy perhaps has its longest history with mental retardation. The limited success of and diminished interest in psychodynamic therapies with children with mental retardation led to a dramatic increase in research and clinical activity on the part of behavior therapists. Accordingly, there is an extensive literature on this topic. The authors pointed out that children with mental retardation require considerable support from the community, school, and home. Psychiatric assessment and treatment must be conducted in conjunction with the many and diverse services that are often in place for the child and family. Treatment that fails to take into account discharge planning and the resources available to the child outside of the clinic or hospital will, in all likelihood, fail. The authors also considered the importance of assessing for comorbid psychiatric disorders (e.g., depression) in children with mental retardation.

Hoza, Vallano, and Pelham discussed attention-deficit/hyperactivity disorder (ADHD) in Chapter 9. ADHD is frequently seen in the psychiatric setting, and it is characterized by impulsiveness, inattention, and motoric overactivity. Comorbidity is common, and children with ADHD frequently exhibit problems in socialization and academic achievement. Assessment is comprehensive, addressing multiple areas of potential deficit. Numerous questionnaires, checklists, and observational approaches are available for this purpose. Behavioral interventions are essential to treatment of ADHD and typically involve contingency management programs implemented by parents and teachers. Also, psychostimulants are used as adjunctive treatments in resistant cases.

Conduct disorders were reviewed by Frick and O'Brien in Chapter 10. In the psychiatric setting, conduct disordered children represent a sizable proportion of patients. Comorbidity is high, with attention-deficit/hyperactivity disorder being the most frequently observed additional diagnosis. Prognosis is often poor, especially if there are coexisting disorders. Moreover, poor academic achievement and family dysfunction frequently accompany conduct disorder. Assessment must involve multiple sources of information, given the considerable risk of bias from any one reporter. Behavioral treatment can be quite effective under certain circumstances. Intensive parent training and cognitive-behavioral interventions for the patient have a strong empirical literature behind them. Unfortunately, maintenance of gains and generalization of improvements across settings are difficult to achieve. Given this less than optimistic state of affairs, the authors advocate that increased efforts be directed towards the development and evaluation of prevention programs.

Separation anxiety disorder (SAD) was reviewed by Bell-Dolan in Chapter 11. SAD is one of the most frequently encountered anxiety disorders in children, with an estimated prevalence of 2% to 4%. It is diagnostically challenging because children with SAD will often refuse to go to school, thereby necessitating a careful assessment to differentiate SAD from school refusal secondary to conduct disorder. Assessment should focus on behavioral symptoms (avoidance), cognitions (fear), and affective characteristics (anxiety). Several behavioral treatments have been proposed, although few have been subjected to empirical scrutiny. Some form of exposure-based treatment is necessary; gradual exposure in vivo shows considerable promise. An adjunctive cognitive approach may be helpful if the child is at an appropriate developmental level to benefit from such an intervention.

Phobia was addressed by Kennedy in Chapter 12. Irrational fears are relatively common in childhood, although prolonged fear of an object or situation that severely compromised the child's functioning requires treatment. The behavioral treatment of childhood phobias has a long history, stretching back to the classic studies of Watson and Jones. Phobias lend themselves well to direct observation because avoidance of the feared stimulus is a core feature of phobias. Behavioral treatment consists primarily of gradual in vivo exposure. Unfortunately, such interventions typically require that treatment be carried out in the natural environment, rather than in the clinic or hospital. The author noted that limited or inflexible resources can, therefore, interfere with effective treatment.

Francis, in Chapter 13, reviewed the behavioral treatment of obsessive-compulsive disorder (OCD). It was once thought that OCD was relatively rare in children, but it is now recognized that OCD often emerges in childhood and early adolescence. Behavioral assessment consists of monitoring occurrence of and antecedents to rituals and obsessions. Various questionnaires are available to gauge the severity of OCD, which are administered to children, parents, and teachers. In contrast to adults, the literature on treatment of children and adolescents with OCD is sparse. However, preliminary research supports exposure and response prevention as primary components of effective interventions. In addition, the drug clomipramine shows promise in reducing obsessions and compulsions. Potential impediments to treatment include the presence of comorbid psychiatric disorders, nonadherence to behavioral regimens by the child and family, and uncomfortable side effects from medications.

Depressive disorders were reviewed in Chapter 14 by Stark, Swearer, Delaune, Knox, and Winter. Despite the prevalence of depressive disorders in child and adolescent patients, the research literature on treatment of depression is in its infancy. At this stage, therefore, both assessment and treatment are broad in focus. Assessment, for example, emphasizes the use of multiple measurement techniques from several sources. Areas that are measured include affect, social skill and competence, academic achievement, and family functioning. Behavioral treatment is comprehensive, involving a problem-solving and skills-enhancing approach to the aforementioned areas of functioning. The authors underscored the importance of an integrated team approach in which the child or adolescent and the family are actively engaged in treatment.

The eating disorders anorexia and bulimia nervosa were covered by Shafer and Garner in Chapter 15. Both of these conditions are characterized by profound emotional disturbance and potentially life-threatening medical complications. Eating disorders occur predominantly in adolescent girls and are often long-term in course with occasional relapses following remediation. Physical deterioration and/or severe depression often necessitate hospitalization. Cognitive-behavior therapy is the treatment of choice, focusing on restoring and maintaining adequate weight and altering irrational cognitions regarding food, self-image, and self-esteem. Adjunctive pharmacotherapy may also be beneficial. In many cases, family therapy is desirable to address systems influences that may partially play a role in or exacerbate the eating disorder. The authors presented a detailed case example that elucidates the roadblocks and pitfalls of treatment, with particular emphasis placed on the importance of establishing a good rapport with the patient and family to facilitate a positive outcome.

In Chapter 16, Mansdorf examined the behavioral treatment of tic disorders in children. Tic disorders encompass a variety of conditions, ranging from transient, discrete motor tics to the more involved symptoms of Tourette's disorder. The overt, observable nature of tics makes them especially well suited to behavior therapy. Assessment consists of measurement of tic frequency, in addition to possible functional relationships between occurrence of tics and environmental stimuli. Various interventions have been shown to be effective with tic disorders, including massed practice, environmental manipulation, habit reversal, and self-control training. Treatment of indirect contributors to tics (e.g., relaxation training to reduce stress) may also be needed. For difficult cases, in particular Tourette's disorder, pharmacotherapy is an important adjunct to treatment.

Elimination disorders (functional enuresis and encopresis) were covered by Mellon and Houts in Chapter 17. The authors strongly endorsed a biobehavioral model when treating these disorders. Accordingly, a thorough medial assessment is warranted to identify organic causes and contributions to enuresis and encopresis. In addition to measurement of elimination behaviors, assessment should encompass other areas of child and family functioning, given that stress and emotional dysfunction can contribute to or exacerbate elimination disorders. The research literature on enuresis is larger and more highly developed than that for encopresis. For enuresis, the authors recommend Full Spectrum Treatment, a comprehensive behavioral protocol involving urine alarm treatment, cleanliness training, retention control training, and overlearning. Treatment of encopresis, which is typically adjunctive to medial interventions, should incorporate reinforcement for appropriate defecation and for clean underwear.

Adolescent substance use and abuse were reviewed by Wagner and Kassel in Chapter 18. Although substance use and abuse are widely recognized as major public health problems, little systematic research has been carried out on this problem. The authors pointed out that there are difficulties inherent in defining the problem partly because substance use among adolescents is widespread and the transition to the relatively less frequent problem of abuse is poorly understood. Assessment measures of use patterns abound, although few approaches (with the exception of behavioral assessment) directly link assessment to treatment. The authors advocated a functional approach to treatment selection, in which problem areas are identified and treatments (e.g., stress reduction) match needs. Significant impediments to both assessment and treatment are the multiple problems often exhibited by adolescents and their families, ranging from psychiatric comorbidity to family violence.

In Chapter 19, Koverola examined behavioral interventions for children suffering from posttraumatic stress disorder (PTSD). PTSD emerges in response to a traumatic event, most often sexual abuse, witnessing violence, or natural disasters. Symptoms include anxiety, hyperarousal, and avoidance. Unfortunately, the literature on PTSD in children is sparse, and guidelines for assessment and treatment are only now being developed. Few standardized assessment instruments are available; a behavioral interview represents current state of the art. Difficulties in gathering accurate information may arise if parents, too, are traumatized by the event or if they deny the occurrence of or downplay the traumatic event (such as in some cases of sexual abuse). As in adult PTSD, treatment includes exposure to trauma cues in a safe environment. Anecdotal reports suggest that PTSD is often chronic and resistant to treatment, thereby requiring long-term, multicomponent interventions.

Obesity was covered in Chapter 20 by Foreyt and Goodrick. Up to one-quarter of adolescents are obese, and incident rates have risen dramatically in recent decades. While the causes of obesity are multidetermined, incorporating genetic, psychophysiological, and environmental factors, behavioral interventions focus almost exclusively on environmental manipulations of cues for eating and enhancing exercise behavior. Obesity lends itself relatively easily to behavioral assessment, given that the indexes of interest (e.g., weight, body fat composition, activity level) are readily observable. Self-monitoring of food intake, however, is prone to inaccuracy, particularly in children. Treatment, which must necessarily include active parental involvement, focuses on decreasing food intake and increasing activity level. Nonadherence to treatment, particularly over the long term, interferes with successfully obtaining and maintaining significant weight loss.

Somatization disorder was reviewed by Campo in Chapter 21. The author did not restrict his discussion to somatization disorder per se, but rather considered the assessment and treatment of somatising symptoms in general, which are often encountered in psychiatric and pediatric settings at levels less than that found in the full-blown disorder. Somatization has only recently been subject to empirical scrutiny, and the assessment and treatment literatures are limited. It is acknowledged that a comprehensive assessment is required, including a medical exam, diagnostic evaluation, and review of family, social, emotional, and academic functioning. A significant roadblock to treatment is the reluctance of most children and their families to view somatic symptoms from a psychological perspective. Good rapport and a downplaying of the stigma of conceptualizing physical complaints as symptomatic of psychosocial difficulties are critical to a positive outcome. Treatment emphasizes increasing functional activities (thereby diminishing the perceived impact of symptoms) and engaging the family to not reinforce the child's sick role. Concurrent interventions, such as family or group therapy, may also be useful.

Finally, in Chapter 22, Tarnowski and Brown reviewed the emergent literature on pediatric pain. Formulations of pain in general, and pediatric pain in particular, have become more complex over the past two decades. Prior to that, pain was viewed solely as a physiologic response to an organic insult; it was even widely questioned whether infants and toddlers were capable of experiencing pain in the same manner as adults. Current models of pain acknowledge the contribution of physiological, neurological, emotional, and cognitive factors to the experience and perception of pain. Moreover, developmental influences may alter perception and reporting of pain. Ideally, a tripartite assessment of pediatric pain is conducted whereby behavioral, cognitive, and physiological domains are measured. Unfortunately, limited resources typically impinge on the coordinate administration of all three assessment strategies. Pharmacological treatments are primary in the amelioration of pain, although a variety of behavioral interventions show promise as adjunctives. The authors underscored the importance of an integrated, multidisciplinary approach to treatment in order to achieve an optimal outcome.

Taken together, the chapters in this volume highlight the overall clinical utility of behavior therapy in the psychiatric setting. This is most evident in areas where child behavior therapy is relatively highly developed, as in mental retardation. For some disorders, the transfer of treatments from adults to children has been uncharacteristically smooth. Illustrative is the treatment of phobia and obsessive-compulsive disorder, where exposure is the *sine qua non* of behavioral treatment of both children and adults. In other disorders or conditions, such as adolescent substance abuse and somatization in children, behavior therapy is in its infancy. Still, it can now be said with confidence that behavior therapy is an important and efficacious option in the treatment of the majority of psychiatric disorders in children.

Robert T. Ammerman
Michel Hersen

Author Index

483

Subject Index